The *Autodesk® Fusion 360™ Introduction to Parametric Modeling* student guide includes a series of supporting Video Lessons. Access to these Video Lessons is available at no additional cost to purchasers of this book.

Simply forward your valid Shipping Confirmation as proof of purchase to:

courseware@ASCENTed.com

You will receive login information for complimentary 1-year access to the latest digital content, including 118 Video Lessons.

© 2016, ASCENT - Center for Technical Knowledge®

Autodesk® Fusion 360™
Introduction to Parametric Modeling

Student Guide
2nd Edition
Software Version: 2.0.2377

CADLearning
Enhanced with CADLearning Video

Authorized Publisher

ASCENT - Center for Technical Knowledge®
Autodesk® Fusion 360™
Introduction to Parametric Modeling

2nd Edition - Software Version 2.0.2377

Prepared and produced by:

ASCENT Center for Technical Knowledge
630 Peter Jefferson Parkway, Suite 175
Charlottesville, VA 22911

866-527-2368
www.ASCENTed.com

Lead Contributors: Jennifer MacMillan and Paul Burden

ASCENT - Center for Technical Knowledge is a division of Rand Worldwide, Inc., providing custom developed knowledge products and services for leading engineering software applications. ASCENT is focused on specializing in the creation of education programs that incorporate the best of classroom learning and technology-based training offerings.

The CADLearning® video content linked in this student guide is the property of and is developed by 4D Technologies, LLC.

We welcome any comments you may have regarding this student guide, or any of our products. To contact us please email: feedback@ASCENTed.com.

© ASCENT - Center for Technical Knowledge, 2016

All rights reserved. No part of this guide may be reproduced in any form by any photographic, electronic, mechanical or other means or used in any information storage and retrieval system without the written permission of ASCENT, a division of Rand Worldwide, Inc.

The following are registered trademarks or trademarks of Autodesk, Inc., and/or its subsidiaries and/or affiliates in the USA and other countries: 123D, 3ds Max, Alias, ATC, AutoCAD LT, AutoCAD, Autodesk, the Autodesk logo, Autodesk 123D, Autodesk Homestyler, Autodesk Inventor, Autodesk MapGuide, Autodesk Streamline, AutoLISP, AutoSketch, AutoSnap, AutoTrack, Backburner, Backdraft, Beast, BIM 360, Burn, Buzzsaw, CADmep, CAiCE, CAMduct, Civil 3D, Combustion, Communication Specification, Configurator 360, Constructware, Content Explorer, Creative Bridge, Dancing Baby (image), DesignCenter, DesignKids, DesignStudio, Discreet, DWF, DWG, DWG (design/logo), DWG Extreme, DWG TrueConvert, DWG TrueView, DWGX, DXF, Ecotect, Ember, ESTmep, FABmep, Face Robot, FBX, Fempro, Fire, Flame, Flare, Flint, ForceEffect, FormIt 360, Freewheel, Fusion 360, Glue, Green Building Studio, Heidi, Homestyler, HumanIK, i-drop, ImageModeler, Incinerator, Inferno, InfraWorks, Instructables, Instructables (stylized robot design/logo), Inventor, Inventor HSM, Inventor LT, Lustre, Maya, Maya LT, MIMI, Mockup 360, Moldflow Plastics Advisers, Moldflow Plastics Insight, Moldflow, Moondust, MotionBuilder, Movimento, MPA (design/logo), MPA, MPI (design/logo), MPX (design/logo), MPX, Mudbox, Navisworks, ObjectARX, ObjectDBX, Opticore, P9, Pier 9, Pixlr, Pixlr-o-matic, Productstream, Publisher 360, RasterDWG, RealDWG, ReCap, ReCap 360, Remote, Revit LT, Revit, RiverCAD, Robot, Scaleform, Showcase, Showcase 360, SketchBook, Smoke, Socialcam, Softimage, Spark & Design, Spark Logo, Sparks, SteeringWheels, Stitcher, Stone, StormNET, TinkerBox, Tinkercad, Tinkerplay, ToolClip, Topobase, Toxik, TrustedDWG, T-Splines, ViewCube, Visual LISP, Visual, VRED, Wire, Wiretap, WiretapCentral, XSI.

NASTRAN is a registered trademark of the National Aeronautics Space Administration.

All other brand names, product names, or trademarks belong to their respective holders.

General Disclaimer:

Notwithstanding any language to the contrary, nothing contained herein constitutes nor is intended to constitute an offer, inducement, promise, or contract of any kind. The data contained herein is for informational purposes only and is not represented to be error free. ASCENT, its agents and employees, expressly disclaim any liability for any damages, losses or other expenses arising in connection with the use of its materials or in connection with any failure of performance, error, omission even if ASCENT, or its representatives, are advised of the possibility of such damages, losses or other expenses. No consequential damages can be sought against ASCENT or Rand Worldwide, Inc. for the use of these materials by any third parties or for any direct or indirect result of that use.

The information contained herein is intended to be of general interest to you and is provided "as is", and it does not address the circumstances of any particular individual or entity. Nothing herein constitutes professional advice, nor does it constitute a comprehensive or complete statement of the issues discussed thereto. ASCENT does not warrant that the document or information will be error free or will meet any particular criteria of performance or quality. In particular (but without limitation) information may be rendered inaccurate by changes made to the subject of the materials (i.e. applicable software). Rand Worldwide, Inc. specifically disclaims any warranty, either expressed or implied, including the warranty of fitness for a particular purpose.

AS-FUS1701-IPM2MU-AMZ // IS-FUS1701-IPM2MU-AMZ

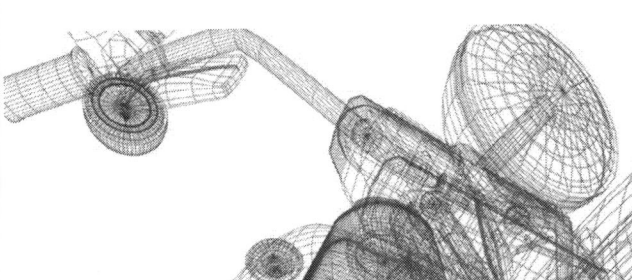

Contents

Preface xi

In this Guide xv

Practice Files xix

Certification xxi

Chapter 1: Introduction to Autodesk Fusion 360 1-1

   1.1 **Autodesk Fusion 360 Fundamentals** 1-2
       Feature-Based Modeling 1-3
       Parametric Features 1-5
       Direct Modeling 1-6
       Managing Assembled Designs 1-7
       Design Documentation 1-8
       Associativity 1-8

   1.2 **Getting Started** 1-9
       Understanding Workspaces 1-9
       Understanding Projects 1-9

   1.3 **The Autodesk Fusion 360 Interface** 1-11
       Ribbon 1-12
       BROWSER 1-12
       Accessing Commands 1-13
       Accessing Help 1-13
       Preferences 1-13

   1.4 **Design Navigation & Display** 1-14
       Design Navigation 1-14
       ViewCube 1-14
       Named Views 1-15
       Design Display 1-16
       Geometry Selection 1-17
       Environment and Effects 1-17

    Practice 1a Getting Started 1-18
    Chapter Review Questions 1-29
    Command Summary 1-31

Chapter 2: Creating the First Feature with Quick Shapes 2-1

    2.1 Design Units and Origin 2-2
          Units 2-2
          Origin 2-3

    2.2 Quick Shape Creation 2-4

    Practice 2a Creating Shapes I 2-6

    Practice 2b Creating Shapes II 2-12

    Chapter Review Questions 2-15

    Command Summary 2-17

Chapter 3: Creating Sketched Geometry 3-1

    3.1 Introduction to the Sketching Workflow 3-2

    3.2 Sketch Entities 3-4
          Line 3-4
          Spline 3-4
          Points 3-5
          Rectangles 3-5
          Circle 3-7
          Arcs 3-9

    3.3 Dimensioning 3-11
          Dynamic Input 3-11
          Adding Sketch Dimensions 3-11
          Modifying Sketch Dimensions 3-13
          Deleting Sketch Dimensions 3-13

    3.4 Sketch Constraints 3-14

    3.5 Extruding a Sketch 3-16

    3.6 Revolving a Sketch 3-17

    Practice 3a Extruded Solid Features 3-18

    Practice 3b Revolved Solid Features 3-26

    Practice 3c Additional Designs 3-32

    Chapter Review Questions 3-33

    Command Summary 3-36

Chapter 4: Additional Sketching Tools 4-1

4.1 Additional Entity Types 4-2
Polygons 4-2
Ellipse 4-4
Slot 4-4
Tangent Arc Using a Line 4-6
Tangent Line Between Two Circles or Arcs 4-6
Fillets 4-7
Construction Entities 4-8

4.2 Editing Tools 4-9
Trim 4-9
Extend 4-9
Mirror 4-10
Sketch Scale 4-11

4.3 Additional Dimension Tools 4-12
Center Dimensions 4-12
Radius or Diameter Dimensions 4-13
Angular Dimensions 4-13
Over- Constrained Sketches 4-14

4.4 Moving and Copying 4-15
Move 4-15
Copy and Paste 4-16

4.5 Rectangular Sketch Patterns 4-17

4.6 Circular Sketch Patterns 4-19

Practice 4a Applying Constraints 4-21
Practice 4b Creating Sketched Geometry I 4-27
Practice 4c Creating Sketched Geometry II 4-34
Practice 4d Manipulating Entities 4-40
Practice 4e Copy and Paste Sketches 4-41
Practice 4f Patterning Sketched Entities 4-45
Chapter Review Questions 4-49
Command Summary 4-52

Chapter 5: Sketched Secondary Features 5-1

5.1 Sketched Secondary Features 5-2

5.2 Using Existing Geometry 5-6
Projected Geometry 5-6
Offset 5-7
Reusing Sketches 5-8
Features from Planar Faces 5-8

Practice 5a Creating Sketched Extrusions I 5-9
Practice 5b Creating Sketched Extrusions II 5-16
Practice 5c Reusing Sketches 5-23
Chapter Review Questions 5-27
Command Summary 5-29

Chapter 6: Pick and Place Features 6-1

6.1 Fillets 6-2
Constant Radius Fillet 6-2
Variable Radius Fillet 6-4
Chordal Fillet 6-6
Rule Fillets 6-7

6.2 Chamfers 6-9

6.3 Holes 6-10

6.4 Editing Pick and Place Features 6-12

Practice 6a Constant Radius Fillets 6-13
Practice 6b Creating Rule Fillets 6-18
Practice 6c Fillets and Chamfers 6-22
Practice 6d Fillet Shapes 6-30
Practice 6e Holes 6-33
Chapter Review Questions 6-42
Command Summary 6-44

Chapter 7: Construction Features 7-1

7.1 Construction Planes 7-2
Default Origin Planes 7-2
Create Construction Planes 7-3

7.2 Construction Axes 7-6
Default Origin Axes 7-6
Creating Construction Axes 7-6

7.3 Construction Points 7-9
Default Origin Point 7-9
Creating Construction Points 7-9
Editing Construction Features 7-11

Practice 7a Using Construction Features to Create Geometry I 7-12
Practice 7b Using Construction Features to Create Geometry II 7-18
Chapter Review Questions 7-29
Command Summary 7-31

Chapter 8: Equations and Parameters 8-1
   8.1 Equations 8-2
   8.2 Parameters 8-6
   Practice 8a Adding Equations 8-7
   Practice 8b Add Parameters 8-13
   Chapter Review Questions 8-18
   Command Summary 8-21

Chapter 9: Additional Features and Operations 9-1
   9.1 Draft 9-2
   9.2 Shell 9-3
   9.3 Rib 9-4
   9.4 Split Face 9-5
   9.5 Scale 9-6
   9.6 Thread 9-7
   9.7 Press Pull 9-9
   Practice 9a Creating Shells and Ribs 9-11
   Practice 9b Using Advanced Design Tools 9-15
   Chapter Review Questions 9-23
   Command Summary 9-24

Chapter 10: Design and Display Manipulation 10-1
   10.1 Reordering Features 10-2
   10.2 Inserting Features 10-3
   10.3 Suppressing Features 10-5
   10.4 Measure and Section Analysis 10-6
      Measure 10-6
      Section Analysis 10-7
   10.5 Direct Modeling 10-8
      Direct Edit Tools 10-9
   Practice 10a Section Analysis 10-13
   Practice 10b Feature Order 10-19
   Practice 10c Direct Edit 10-26
   Chapter Review Questions 10-32
   Command Summary 10-34

Chapter 11: Single Path Sweeps 11-1

11.1 Sweeps 11-2
Practice 11a Creating Swept Geometry I 11-4
Practice 11b Creating Swept Geometry II 11-10
Practice 11c Additional Swept Geometry (Optional) 11-14
Chapter Review Questions 11-15
Command Summary 11-18

Chapter 12: Loft Features 12-1

12.1 Lofts 12-2
Practice 12a Creating Rail Lofts 12-5
Practice 12b Creating Centerline Lofts I 12-9
Practice 12c Creating Centerline Lofts II 12-11
Chapter Review Questions 12-17
Command Summary 12-19

Chapter 13: Feature Duplication Tools 13-1

13.1 Mirroring Geometry 13-2
13.2 Patterning Features 13-3
   Rectangular Patterns 13-3
   Circular Patterns 13-4
   Pattern on Path 13-5
Practice 13a Mirroring Geometry 13-6
Practice 13b Patterning Geometry 13-10
Chapter Review Questions 13-18
Command Summary 13-20

Chapter 14: Distributed Design 14-1

14.1 Assembly Design Methods 14-2
14.2 Distributed Design 14-3
   Inserting Components 14-3
   MOVE Palette 14-5
   Grounding Components 14-6
14.3 Joint Origins 14-7
   Selecting Joint Origins 14-7
   Creating Joint Origins 14-9
14.4 Assigning Joints 14-12
   Joint Types 14-13

Practice 14a Creating a Distributed Design 14-20
Chapter Review Questions 14-40
Command Summary 14-42

Chapter 15: Component Design Tools 15-1

15.1 Rigid Groups 15-2

15.2 Interference Detection 15-4

15.3 Miscellaneous Joint Tools 15-5
Joint Limits 15-5
Drive Joints 15-6
Contact Sets 15-7
Motion Linking 15-7
Motion Studies 15-8

Practice 15a Incorporating Motion Between Components in a Design 15-9
Chapter Review Questions 15-35
Command Summary 15-37

Chapter 16: Multi-Body Design 16-1

16.1 Multi-Body Design 16-2

16.2 Multi-Body Design Tools 16-4

16.3 Components 16-6
Creating Components 16-6
Using the BROWSER 16-7
Reusing Components 16-8
Positioning Components 16-9

16.4 As-Built Joints 16-10

Practice 16a Multi-Body Design 16-12
Practice 16b Working with Multi-Bodies to Create an Assembled Design 16-25
Chapter Review Questions 16-38
Command Summary 16-41

Chapter 17: Sculpting Geometry 17-1

17.1 Introduction to the Sculpt Environment 17-2
Control Mesh 17-3
Display Modes 17-4
Performance Options 17-5

17.2 Surface Quick Shapes 17-6
Exiting the Sculpt Environment 17-8

17.3 Creating Sketched T-Spline Surfaces 17-9
17.4 Creating Faces & Filling Holes 17-11
    Creating a Face 17-11
    Filling a Hole 17-12
Practice 17a T-Spline Surface Modeling I 17-14
Practice 17b T-Spline Surface Modeling II 17-25
Chapter Review Questions 17-30
Command Summary 17-33

Chapter 18: Editing Sculpted Geometry 18-1

18.1 Editing Form Geometry 18-2
18.2 Deleting Entities 18-7
18.3 Working with Edges 18-8
18.4 Working with Faces 18-13
18.5 Working with Points 18-15
18.6 Controlling Symmetry 18-17
18.7 Thickening Geometry 18-20
Practice 18a Box T-Spline Modeling 18-22
Practice 18b Cylinder T-Spline Modeling 18-32
Practice 18c Working with Multiple T-Spline Bodies 18-41
Practice 18d Bridging T-Spline Geometry 18-49
Chapter Review Questions 18-53
Command Summary 18-55

Chapter 19: Drawing Basics 19-1

19.1 Creating a New Drawing 19-2
    Base Views 19-3
    Projected Views 19-4
19.2 Additional Drawing Views 19-6
    Section Views 19-6
    Detail Views 19-9
19.3 Exploded Views 19-10
19.4 Manipulating Drawings 19-14
    Delete Views 19-14
    Move Views 19-14
    View Alignment 19-14
    View Orientation 19-15

Change View Scale	19-15
Editing View Labels	19-16
Add Component or Exploded Views to an Assembly Drawing	19-16
Modifying the Title Block and Border	19-18
Drawing Templates	19-20
Sheets	19-20
Practice 19a Creating a Drawing I	**19-21**
Practice 19b Creating a Drawing II	**19-27**
Practice 19c Creating a Drawing III	**19-34**
Chapter Review Questions	**19-41**
Command Summary	**19-44**

Chapter 20: Detailing Drawings ... 20-1

20.1 Dimensions	**20-2**
20.2 Other Annotations	**20-4**
Text Notes	20-4
Centerlines and Center Marks	20-5
Symbols	20-6
20.3 Parts List and Balloons	**20-7**
20.4 Annotation and Dimension Settings	**20-9**
20.5 Drawing Output	**20-11**
Practice 20a Annotations and Dimensions	**20-12**
Practice 20b Parts List and Balloons	**20-22**
Chapter Review Questions	**20-25**
Command Summary	**20-27**

Chapter 21: Static Analysis Using the Simulation Environment ... 21-1

21.1 Introduction to the Simulation Environment	**21-2**
Creating a Design Study	21-3
Typical FEA Workflow	21-5
21.2 Setting up a Structural Static Analysis	**21-6**
Assigning Study Materials	21-6
Assigning Constraints	21-8
Assigning Loads	21-9
Assigning Contacts	21-12
Reviewing the Setup in the BROWSER	21-13
21.3 Setting up the Mesh	**21-15**
21.4 Solving a Design Study	**21-17**
21.5 Visualizing the Results	**21-19**

Practice 21a Cantilever Beam Analysis 21-21
Practice 21b Plant Hanger Analysis 21-32
Chapter Review Questions 21-41
Command Summary 21-44

Appendix A: Outputting for 3D Printing A-1
A.1 Generating a .STL File A-2

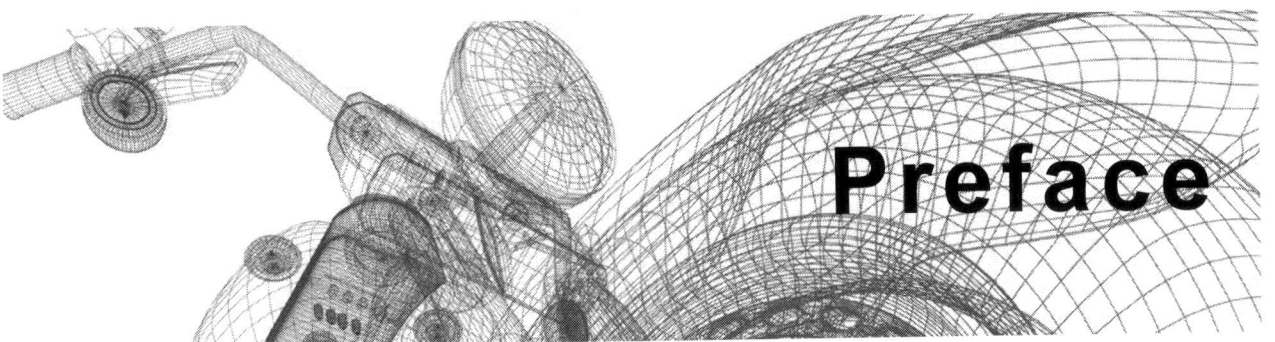

Preface

The *Autodesk® Fusion 360™ Introduction to Parametric Modeling* student guide provides you with an understanding of the parametric design philosophy using the Autodesk® Fusion 360™ software. Through a hands-on, practice-intensive curriculum, you will learn the key skills and knowledge required to design models using the Autodesk Fusion 360 software. Enhanced with CADLearning videos from 4D Technologies, LLC., this student guide will also assist you in preparing for the Autodesk Fusion 360 Certified User exam.

Software Version

As a cloud-based platform, updates are frequently available for the Autodesk Fusion 360 software. This student guide has been developed using software version: 2.0.2377. If you are using a version of the software later then version 2.0.2377, you might notice some variances between images and workflows in this student guide and the software that you are using.

Topics Covered

- Understanding the Autodesk Fusion 360 interface
- Creating, constraining, and dimensioning 2D sketches
- Creating and editing solid 3D features
- Creating and using construction features
- Creating equations and working with parameters
- Manipulating the feature history of a design
- Duplicating geometry in a design
- Placing and constraining/connecting components in a single design file
- Defining motion in a multi-component design
- Creating components and features in a multi-component design
- Creating and editing T-spline geometry
- Documenting a design in drawings
- Defining structural constraints and loads for static analysis

This student guide has been enhanced with CADLearning® video. You can watch and listen as the subject-matter expert explains features and functions related to a particular student guide topic.

Note on Software Setup

This student guide assumes a standard installation of the software using the default preferences during installation. Chapters and practices use the standard software preferences unless they are specifically changed as prescribed in practice steps.

Students and Educators can Access Free Autodesk Software and Resources

Autodesk challenges you to get started with free educational licenses for professional software and creativity apps used by millions of architects, engineers, designers, and hobbyists today. Bring Autodesk software into your classroom, studio, or workshop to learn, teach, and explore real-world design challenges the way professionals do.

Get started today - register at the Autodesk Education Community and download one of the many Autodesk software applications available.

Visit www.autodesk.com/joinedu/

Note: Free products are subject to the terms and conditions of the end-user license and services agreement that accompanies the software. The software is for personal use for education purposes and is not intended for classroom or lab use.

Co-Lead Contributor: Jennifer MacMillan

With a dedication for engineering and education, Jennifer has spent over 20 years at ASCENT managing courseware development for various CAD products. Trained in Instructional Design, Jennifer uses her skills to develop instructor-led and web-based training products as well as knowledge profiling tools.

Jennifer has achieved the Autodesk Certified Professional certification for Inventor and is also recognized as an Autodesk Certified Instructor (ACI). She enjoys teaching the training courses that she authors and is also very skilled in providing technical support to end-users.

Jennifer holds a Bachelor of Engineering Degree as well as a Bachelor of Science in Mathematics from Dalhousie University, Nova Scotia, Canada.

Jennifer MacMillan is the Co-Lead Contributor for this second edition of the *Autodesk® Fusion 360™ Introduction to Parametric Modeling* student guide.

Co-Lead Contributor: Paul Burden

Paul Burden is the Director of Product Development for ASCENT – Center for Technical Knowledge. He has been in the business of technical training and support for CAD systems since 1995. During that time, he has led courseware projects for CAD and PDM software from most of the major developers of this type of software.

Paul holds a Bachelor of Engineering degree from Memorial University in Newfoundland Canada, and is a licensed Professional Engineer in Ontario Canada. Paul's latest projects include implementation of digital formats for student guides, including eBooks and online learning portals.

Paul Burden is the Co-Lead Contributor for this second edition of the *Autodesk® Fusion 360™ Introduction to Parametric Modeling* student guide.

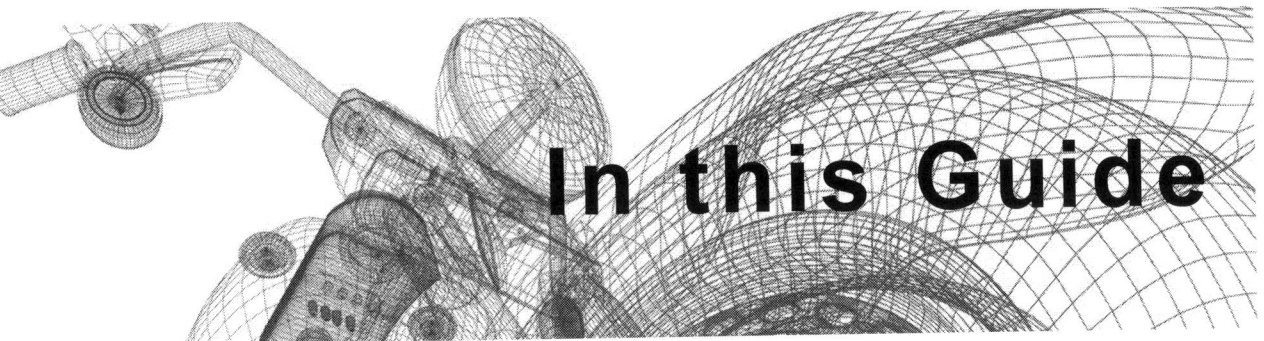

In this Guide

The following images highlight some of the features that can be found in this Student Guide.

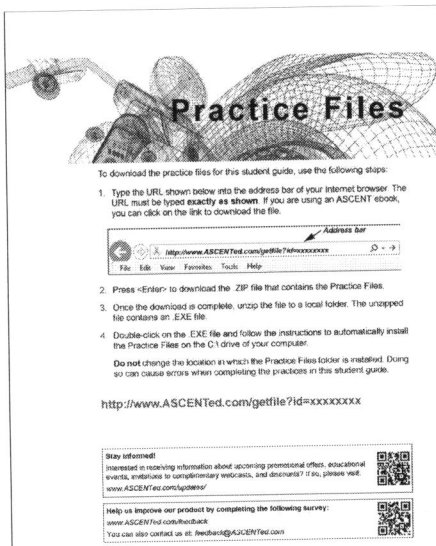

Practice Files

The Practice Files page tells you how to download and install the practice files that are provided with this student guide.

FTP link for practice files

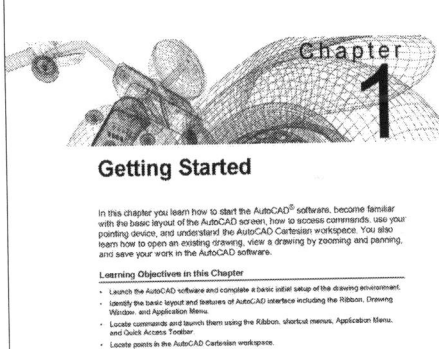

Chapters

Each chapter begins with a brief introduction and a list of the chapter's Learning Objectives.

Learning Objectives for the chapter

© 2016, ASCENT - Center for Technical Knowledge®

xv

Side notes

Side notes are hints or additional information for the current topic.

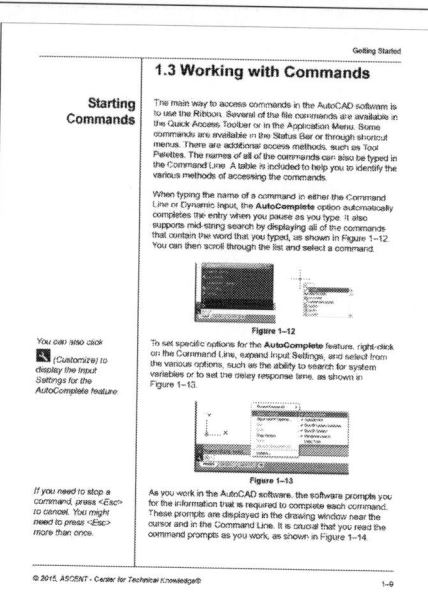

Instructional Content

Each chapter is split into a series of sections of instructional content on specific topics. These lectures include the descriptions, step-by-step procedures, figures, hints, and information you need to achieve the chapter's Learning Objectives.

Practice Objectives

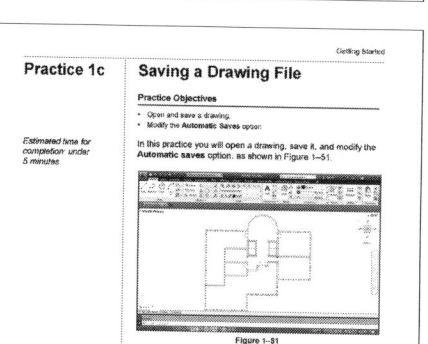

Practices

Practices enable you to use the software to perform a hands-on review of a topic.

Some practices require you to use prepared practice files, which can be downloaded from the link found on the Practice Files page.

Chapter Review Questions

Chapter review questions, located at the end of each chapter, enable you to review the key concepts and learning objectives of the chapter.

xvi © 2016, ASCENT - Center for Technical Knowledge®

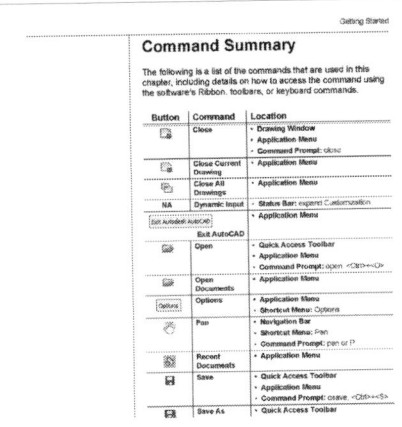

Command Summary

The Command Summary is located at the end of each chapter. It contains a list of the software commands that are used throughout the chapter, and provides information on where the command is found in the software.

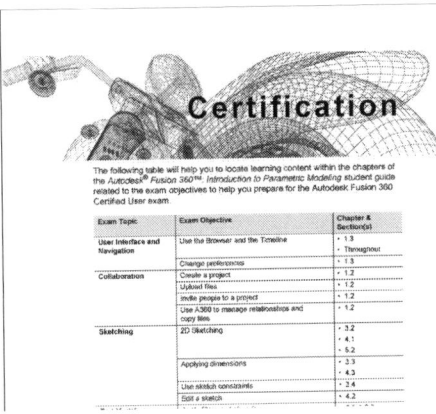

Autodesk Certification Exam Guide

This guide includes a list of the topics and objectives for the Autodesk Certification exams, and the chapter and section in which the relevant content can be found.

Video Lessons

This student guide includes links to video lessons provided by CADLearning®. An example of a link to a video lesson is shown below.

Video Lesson Available

Introducing Autodesk Fusion 360

Video Length: 3:29

Access to these video lessons is available at no additional cost to purchasers of this book. Simply forward your valid Shipping Confirmation as proof of purchase to: **courseware@ASCENTed.com**

You will receive login information for complimentary 1-year access to the latest digital content.

© 2016, ASCENT - Center for Technical Knowledge®

Practice Files

To download the practice files for this student guide, use the following steps:

1. Type the URL shown below into the address bar of your Internet browser. The URL must be typed **exactly as shown**. If you are using an ASCENT ebook, you can click on the link to download the file.

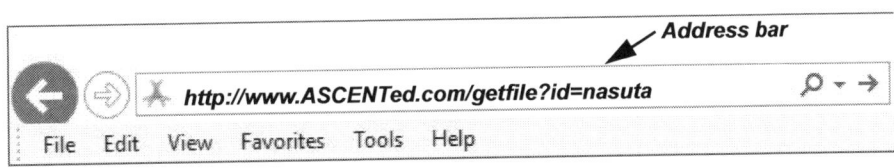

2. Press <Enter> to download the .ZIP file that contains the Practice Files.

3. Once the download is complete, unzip the file to a local folder.

4. The unzipped file contains a **README.txt** document that provides instruction on where to install the Practice Files on your computer.

http://www.ASCENTed.com/getfile?id=nasuta

Stay Informed!
Interested in receiving information about upcoming promotional offers, educational events, invitations to complimentary webcasts, and discounts? If so, please visit:
www.ASCENTed.com/updates/

Help us improve our product by completing the following survey:
www.ASCENTed.com/feedback
You can also contact us at: *feedback@ASCENTed.com*

Certification

The following table will help you to locate learning content within the chapters of the *Autodesk® Fusion 360™: Introduction to Parametric Modeling* student guide related to the exam objectives to help you prepare for the Autodesk Fusion 360 Certified User exam.

Exam Topic	Exam Objective	Chapter & Section(s)
User Interface and Navigation	Use the Browser and the Timeline	• 1.3 • Throughout
	Change preferences	• 1.3
Collaboration	Create a project	• 1.2
	Upload files	• 1.2
	Invite people to a project	• 1.2
	Use A360 to manage relationships and copy files	• 1.2
Sketching	2D Sketching	• 3.2 • 4.1 • 5.2
	Applying dimensions	• 3.3 • 4.3
	Use sketch constraints	• 3.4
	Edit a sketch	• 4.2
Part Modeling	Apply fillets and chamfers	• 6.1 & 6.2
	Create a pattern of features	• 13.2
	Create a 3D thread feature	• 9.6
	Create a shell feature	• 9.2
	Create extrude features	• 3.5 • 5.1
	Create revolve features	• 3.6 • 5.1
	Create construction planes and axes	• 7.1 & 7.2
	Edit existing geometry using Direct Edit tools	• 10.5
	Inspect command; measure, and section analysis	• 10.4

© 2016, ASCENT - Center for Technical Knowledge®

Exam Topic	Exam Objective	Chapter & Section(s)
Assembly Modeling	Create and manage top level assembly and subassemblies	• 14.1 & 14.2 • 16.1 & 16.2
	Create a component from a body	• 16.1 to 16.3
	Align and assembly joints	• 14.3 & 14.4 • 15.1 & 15.3 • 16.4
	Interference	• 15.2
Drawing	Create drawing views (base, projected, section, detail)	• 19.1 & 19.2
	Add annotations	• Chapter 20 (All)
	Edit views	• 19.4
	Edit border and title block	• 19.4
Advanced Modeling	Sweep	• Chapter 11 (All)
	Loft	• Chapter 12 (All)
	Split and combine bodies	• 16.2
Sculpt	Create form	• Chapter 17 (All)
	Edit form	• 18.1
	Thicken	• 18.7
3D Printing - Additive MFG	Create a .STL (3D print) file	• Appendix A (All)
Simulation	Structural constraints and loads	• Chapter 21 (All)

© 2016, ASCENT - Center for Technical Knowledge®

Introduction to Autodesk Fusion 360

The Autodesk® Fusion 360™ software is a hybrid application that combines locally installed software and cloud-based tools. It enables users to use parametric modeling and direct manipulation modeling techniques to create 3D designs. To successfully begin creating geometry using the Autodesk Fusion 360 software, you must install the software, access your A360 account, create a project in the cloud, and become familiar with the interface and navigation tools.

Learning Objectives in this Chapter

- Identify the key areas of the Autodesk Fusion 360 interface.
- Create a new project for use in the Autodesk Fusion 360 software.
- Load files into an Autodesk Fusion 360 project.
- Open files in the Autodesk Fusion 360 software.
- Use the design orientation commands to pan, zoom, rotate, and view a design.
- Change the Visual Style, Environment, and Effects settings to customize the display of a design.

1.1 Autodesk Fusion 360 Fundamentals

The Autodesk Fusion 360 software is a flexible design tool that enables you to incorporate a variety of 3D modeling techniques and strategies. Its characteristics and capabilities include:

- Feature-based modeling
- Parametric features
- Direct manipulation modeling
- Managing assembled designs
- Design documentation
- Associativity

Video Lesson Available

Introducing Autodesk Fusion 360

Video Length: 3:39

Video Lesson Available

Introducing 3D Modeling

Video Length: 1:32

Feature-Based Modeling

In feature-based modeling, a design can evolve by creating features one by one, while keeping the feature history. Each feature is individually recognized by the software. A design that consists of several individual features is shown in Figure 1–1.

Extruded features can either join or cut material from the design.

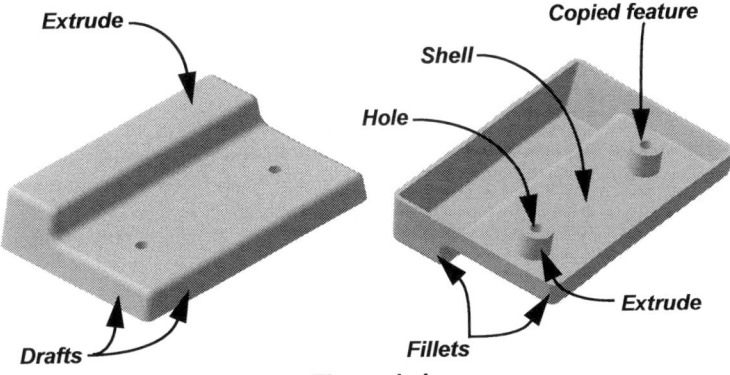

Figure 1–1

To start a design, create a simple extruded feature that approximates the shape of the design. Continue adding features until the design is complete, as shown in Figure 1–2.

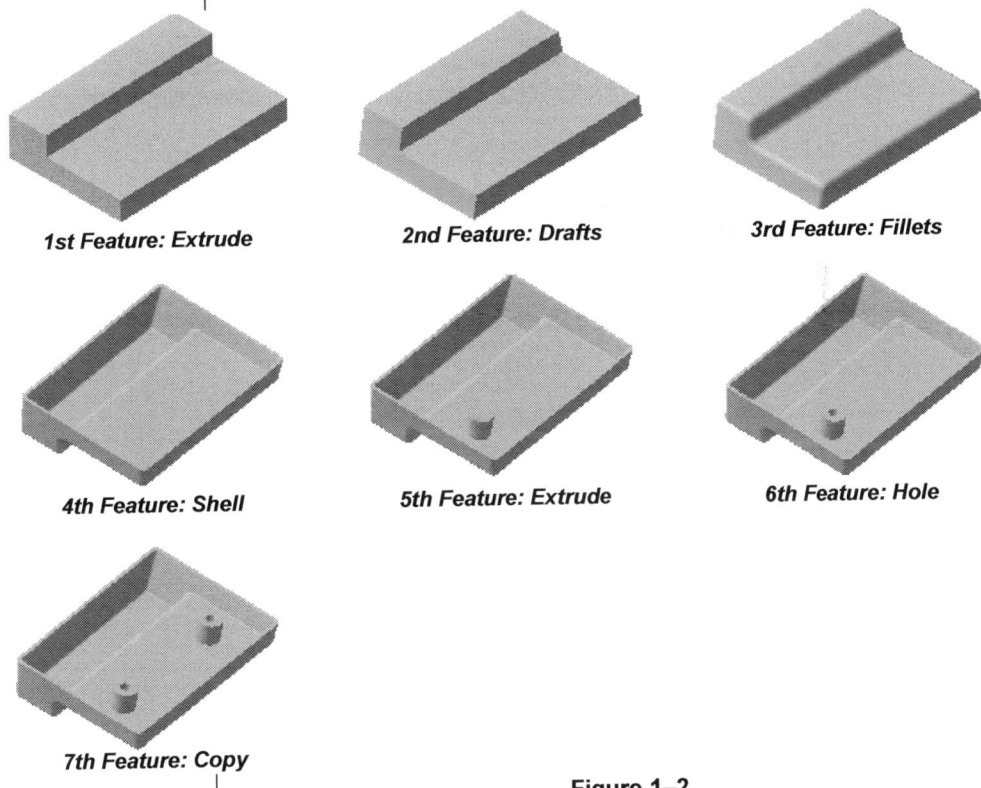

Figure 1–2

Features from Profiles

Features can be created from 2D profiles that can be extruded (as shown in Figure 1–3), swept, lofted, etc. Features created from profiles can add or remove material.

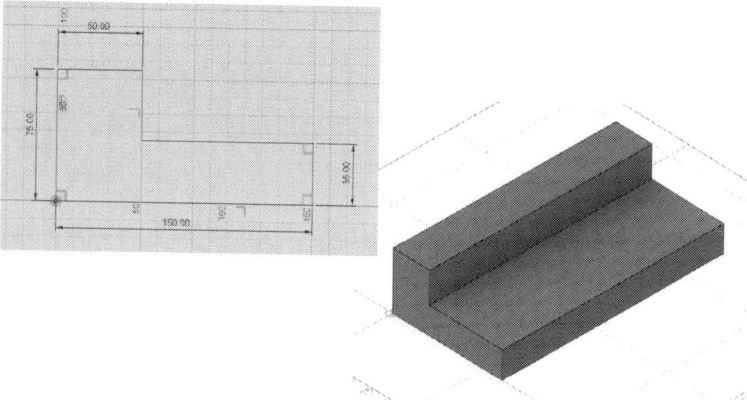

Figure 1–3

Pick and Place Features

Pick and place features (e.g., fillets, chamfers, etc.) perform operations on existing geometry. These types of features usually require you to select references to locate them on the existing geometry, such as edges or surfaces. Figure 1–4 shows an example of a design where chamfers and fillets have been added.

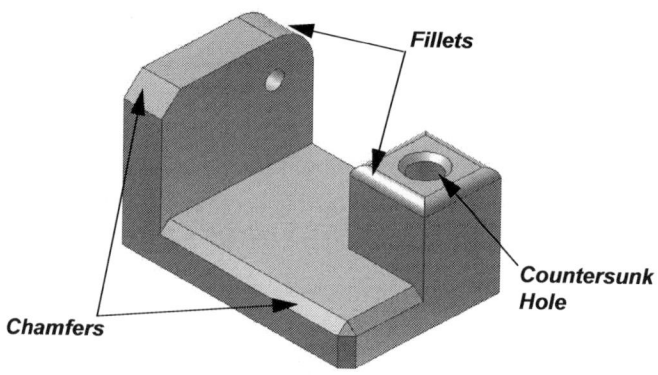

Figure 1–4

Feature Relationships

Relationships between features are formed as a design is created.

In feature-based modeling, features are added one after another. The complete history of the features and the relationships between them is retained. Relationships are created as new features reference existing ones.

For example, the countersunk hole shown in Figure 1–4 references the top surface of the rectangular extrude. If the extruded feature is deleted, the hole becomes undefined because at least one of the references that defines its location no longer exists.

Video Lesson Available

Introducing Solid Modeling

Video Length: 1:47

Parametric Features

Fully constrained features created through parametric modeling have dimensions (also known as parameters) that define their shape, size, and position. You can change the values of the dimensions or parameters at any time, and the features update accordingly. Figure 1–5 shows how the geometry of a design changes when the dimensional value that positions an extruded cut feature changes.

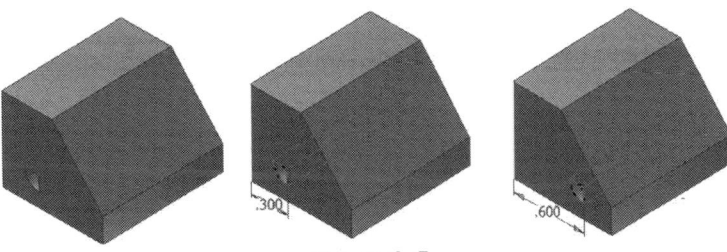

Figure 1–5

*Names are assigned automatically to dimension parameters. You can change the name of a parameter to be more descriptive (e.g., change **d127** to **Width**).*

Dimensioning is an important step in parametric modeling. When you are creating dimensions, consider the following:

- **Changes:** How might the design need to change? Do the dimensions help or hinder these changes?

- **"What if" scenarios:** Periodically modify dimension values to ensure that the design behaves as expected. This is known as flexing the design.

Equations are user-defined mathematical relations.

Parameters and dimensions can be used in equations to capture and control design intent. For example, you can use an equation to force the width of a rectangular block to be equal to half of its height. Using equations in a design can help you to make a robust design that captures your design intent.

Video Lesson Available

Exploring Parametric Modeling

Video Length: 2:41

Direct Modeling

Direct modeling enables you to create and edit designs very quickly, without needing dimensional constraints. Instead, you make manipulations with operations on faces, such as Move and Offset. The design shown in Figure 1–6 is manipulated in Figure 1–7 in a non-parametric fashion by moving (rotating) a face.

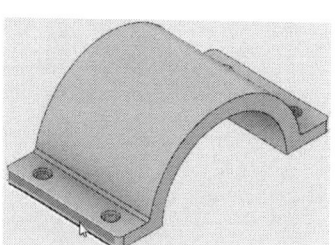
Figure 1–6

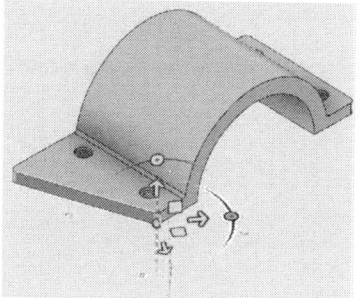
Figure 1–7

Video Lesson Available

Understanding Direct Manipulation Modeling

Video Length: 1:05

Managing Assembled Designs

A design can consist of multiple components that communicate how an assembled product is designed. There are two methods that can be used in the Autodesk Fusion 360 software to design a product with multiple components:

- Components can be inserted into a single design, or
- Components can be created within the context of a single design.

In either scenario, joints are added to create relationships between components to define their degrees of freedom and enabling you to build an intelligent, multi-component design. The design shown in Figure 1–8 is comprised of over 40 individual components.

This barbecue *design is shown in multi-colors to help identify all of the components. You can use this color assignment tool in the INSPECT panel by clicking* **Component Color Cycling Toggle**.

Figure 1–8

Design Documentation

The tools available in the drawing environment enable you to quickly create production-ready drawings for manufacturing, such as the example shown in Figure 1–9. Drawings can be created from designs that represent single or multi-components. Adding details to your drawings enables you to communicate additional information about the design.

There is a link between the drawing and the source design that can always be refreshed to get the latest design. If a change is made to the source design, you can update all of the drawing views that reference with the latest information.

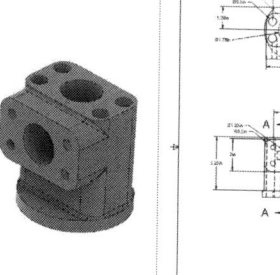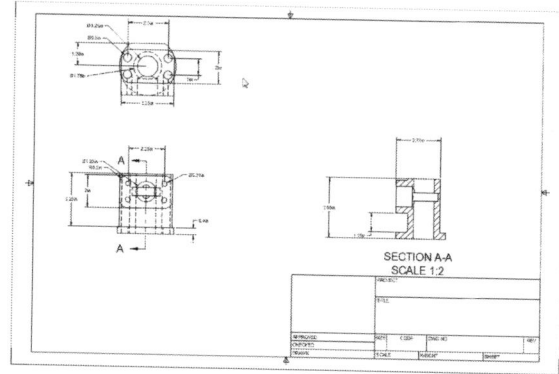

Figure 1–9

Associativity

The Autodesk Fusion 360 software is fully associative, which means that it operates in a concurrent engineering environment. You can work with the same design in different contexts (e.g., a stand-alone component, a component within a multi-component design, and a drawing of the component), and all modes are fully associative. Any changes made to a design in any of these contexts propagate to all of the other contexts.

1.2 Getting Started

Understanding Workspaces

The Autodesk Fusion 360 software combines related tools and functions into groups called workspaces. When a workspace is activated, you are only able to pick tools from that workspace until another workspace is activated. The two most frequently used workspaces are Model and Sculpt.

Video Lesson Available

Understanding Workspaces

Video Length: 1:45

Understanding Projects

The Autodesk Fusion 360 software uses projects to manage and organize data. Similar to folders, each project only contains data that is specific to that particular project. If you create a project, you are designated as the owner, administrator, and moderator.

- Projects include permissions that restrict who has access to the data and what they can do with it.

- Projects can be used for communication and collaboration. Within your project, you can post comments, use a shared calendar, publish documents to a project-specific wiki, and generate polls to gather input from project members.

- You can open your project in Autodesk 360 to further manage the project files and members, as shown in Figure 1–10.

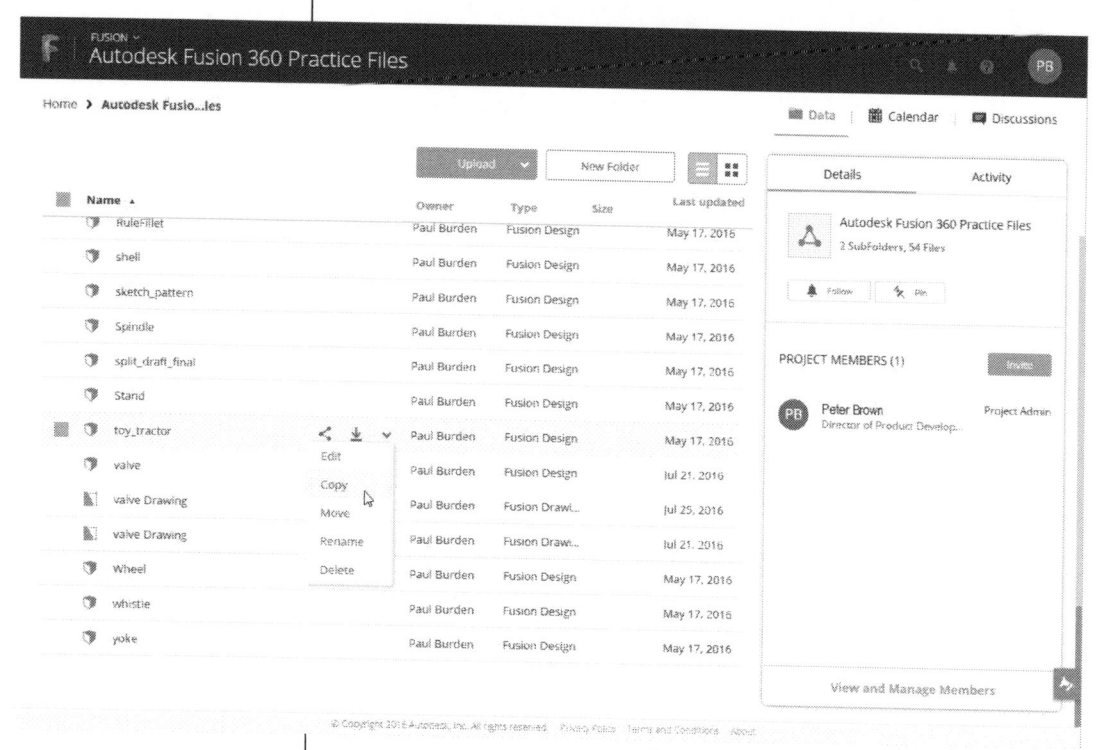

Figure 1–10

Video Lesson Available

Understanding Projects

Video Length: 2:17

1.3 The Autodesk Fusion 360 Interface

When you launch the Autodesk Fusion 360 software, one of the first things you might note is that the interface has a minimalistic layout that presents only the information needed, when it is required. Figure 1–11 shows an example of the interface once a design is opened, including the ribbon, panels, BROWSER, and other interface elements. Multiple designs can be open at once.

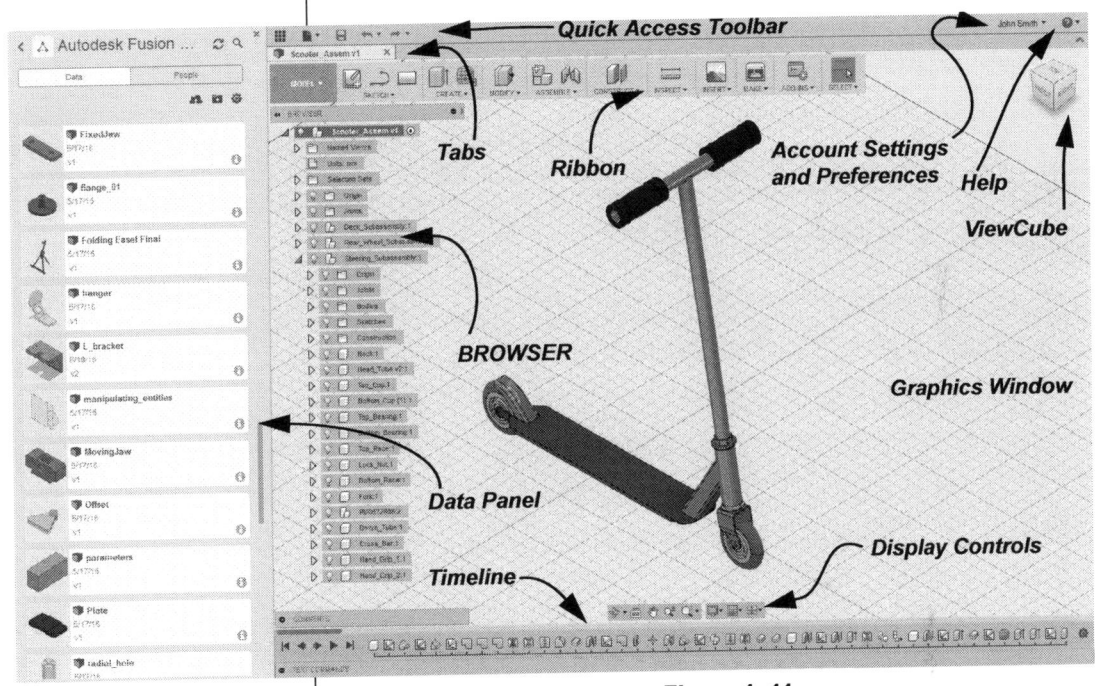

Figure 1–11

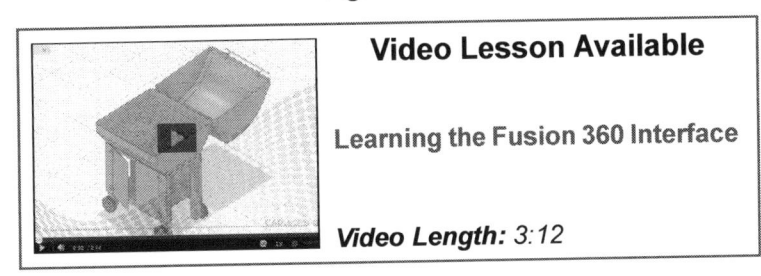

Video Lesson Available

Learning the Fusion 360 Interface

Video Length: 3:12

Ribbon | The ribbon interface (shown in Figure 1–12) is a dynamic interface that provides access to many of the tools and options available in the Autodesk Fusion 360 software.

Figure 1–12

Video Lesson Available

Using the Ribbon

Video Length: 1:23

BROWSER | The BROWSER is where all of the design data is organized in a tree-like structure, as shown in Figure 1–13. The BROWSER can contain design information, features, work features, folders and more.

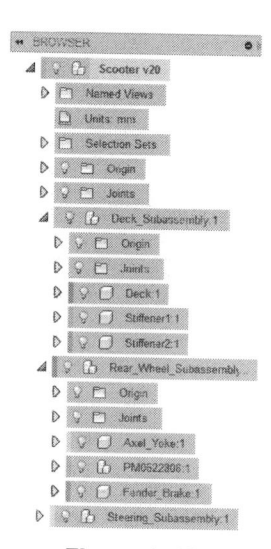

Figure 1–13

Video Lesson Available

Introducing the Browser

Video Length: 5:16

Accessing Commands

The majority of commands are located within panels opened from the ribbon interface. Additional tools are also available in context menus or contextual ribbons.

Video Lesson Available

Locating Commands in the User Interface

Video Length: 4:43

Accessing Help

The Help tool enables you to access resources, such as online help, tutorials, and forums.

Video Lesson Available

Accessing the Help and Communication Center

Video Length: 3:51

Preferences

There are a number of preferences you can set to configure the Autodesk Fusion 360 environment.

Video Lesson Available

Setting Your Preferences

Video Length: 3:02

1.4 Design Navigation & Display

Design Navigation

There are many ways that you can navigate around the Autodesk Fusion 360 interface, which can make working with your designs easier. This includes techniques for zooming, panning, and orienting the design using the mouse or the on-screen tools.

Video Lesson Available

Navigating the Model

Video Length: 4:49

ViewCube

One of the quickest and most convenient ways to change the orientation of a design is using the ViewCube, shown in Figure 1-14. It enables you to quickly snap to standard orthographic views, such as Front, Top, Side, and Bottom.

Figure 1-14

Video Lesson Available

Navigating with the ViewCube

Video Length: 3:00

Named Views

Named views (as shown in Figure 1–15) can also be used to quickly orient your design to specific views that are predefined in the software, or to views that you have created and saved.

▲ 📁 Named Views
      📄 TOP
      📄 FRONT
      📄 RIGHT
      📄 HOME

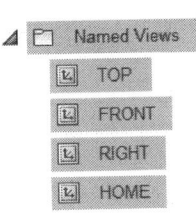

Figure 1–15

Video Lesson Available

Creating and Applying Named Views

Video Length: 2:16

Design Display

To make a design easier to work with, its display can be customized by changing its visual style. These options are located in the **Display Settings** menu at the bottom of the interface. The **Visual Style** settings are an application setting and are not saved with the design file. Figure 1–16 shows examples of the display styles that can be used.

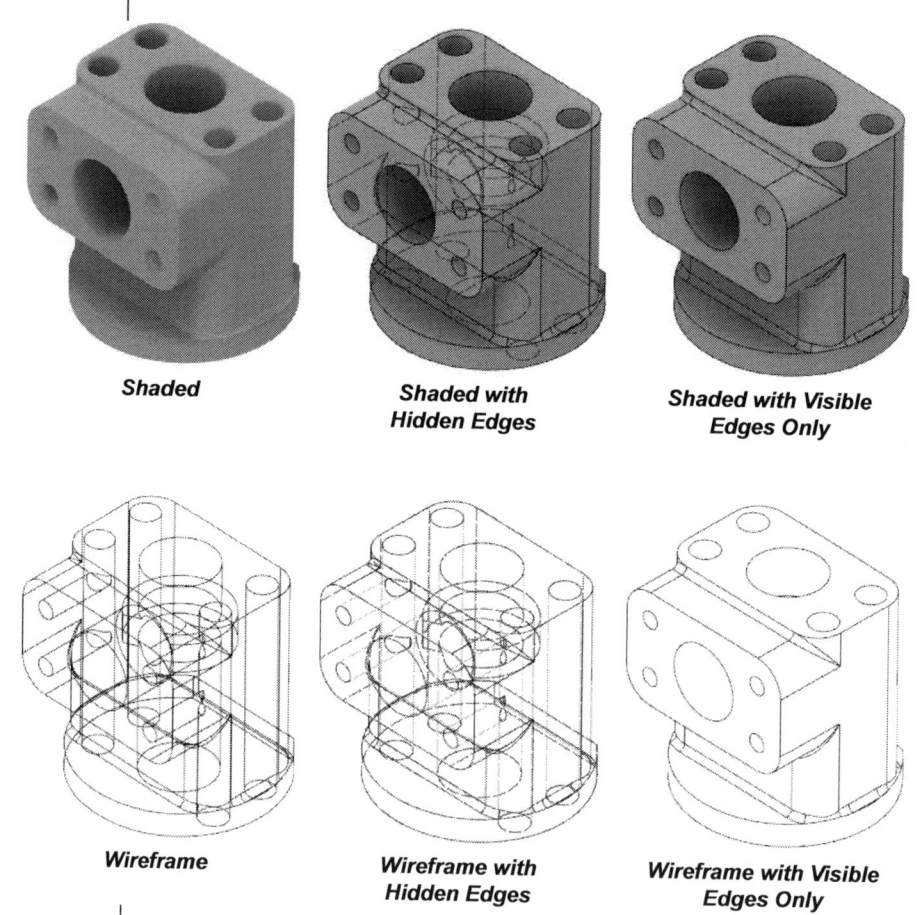

Shaded   *Shaded with Hidden Edges*   *Shaded with Visible Edges Only*

Wireframe   *Wireframe with Hidden Edges*   *Wireframe with Visible Edges Only*

Figure 1–16

Video Lesson Available

Adjusting the Visual Styles

Video Length: 1:50

Geometry Selection

When working in a design, you work with faces, features, bodies, components, work features, etc. To make this process easier, you can use selection filters to enable control over which items are selectable. The selection filter tools are available in the SELECT panel. Selection techniques include the following:

- Items in the graphics window highlight as you move the cursor over them. By default, faces and edges are selectable.

- To select an entire body, you can click on the body or component in the BROWSER.

- You can use the **Selection Filter** options to customize exactly what can or cannot be selected. The options that are available change depending on the design and items that being used.

Video Lesson Available

Using the Selection Filters and Tools

Video Length: 2:22

Environment and Effects

The Autodesk Fusion 360 software has a variety of environments and effects that can be used to improve the display of your model. These options are located in the **Display Settings** menu at the bottom of the interface. Similar to the visual style options, environments and effects are application settings and are not saved with the design file.

Video Lesson Available

Adjusting the Environment and Effects

Video Length: 3:53

Practice 1a

Getting Started

Practice Objectives

- Create a new Autodesk Fusion 360 project and upload files to the project.
- Open a file from an Autodesk Fusion 360 project.
- Use the BROWSER to control the visibility of components in the design.
- Practice orienting the design using several different methods.
- Change the visual style of a design.
- Create a new Autodesk Fusion 360 design.

In this practice, you will begin by setting up an Autodesk Fusion 360 project that will be used with this student guide, and you will then upload files to the project. To become familiar with the software's interface and navigation controls, you will then open one of the provided designs and practice using all of the navigation tools that are available in the software. To complete the practice, you will create a new file that will be used when you begin learning how to create geometry in the Autodesk Fusion 360 software.

Task 1 - Setting up the practice files.

1. Launch the Autodesk Fusion 360 software.

2. Log into your A360 account, if not already logged in. If you do not have an A360 account, create one using the **Create an Account** option.

3. Verify that the *C:\Autodesk Fusion 360 Practice Files* folder exists and contains the files that are required for this student guide. If it does not, return to the Practice Files page at the beginning of the student guide to download and extract the files to your local computer to prepare the files for upload.

4. At the top of the interface, in the Application Bar, click ▦ (Show Data Panel).

5. At the top of the Data Panel, click **New Project**.

If the software has not been updated recently, you might be prompted to update it to the latest version of the software.

6. Create a new project called **Autodesk Fusion 360 Practice Files**. This project should now be included in your list of projects, as shown in Figure 1–17.

Autodesk Fusion 360 Practice Files

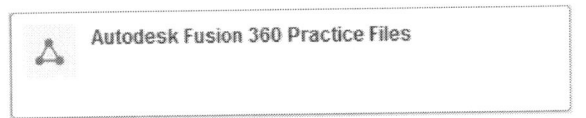

Figure 1–17

7. Double-click on the new project.

8. Ensure that the *Data* tab is selected at the top of the project page.

There are a number of methods that can be used to upload and open files in the Autodesk Fusion 360 software. The following method involves uploading files directly to the project file. In a upcoming chapter you will learn how to open files directly in the software and then save them to the project file.

9. Click (Upload) and select **Select Files**.

10. Using the Open dialog box, navigate to the *C:\Autodesk Fusion 360 Practice Files* folder. Select **BBQ.f3d** and then click **Open**.

11. In the Select files to upload window, click **Upload**. The barbecue design will upload to your project in A360.

12. Once the files have been uploaded, in the Upload progress window, click **Close**. The new project and its files should display as shown in Figure 1–18.

Files can be displayed in the data panel in either List ( ) or Grid ( ) view.

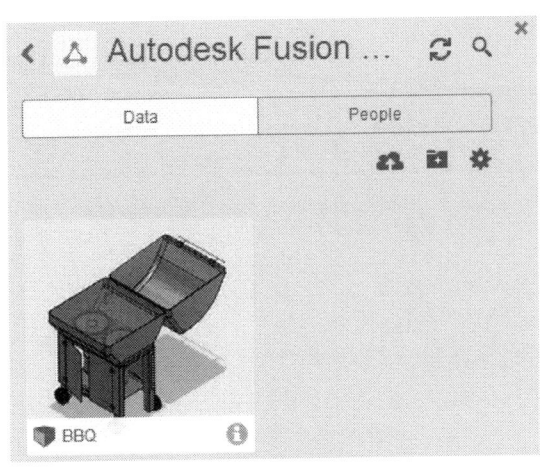

Figure 1–18

Task 2 - Opening a file in the Autodesk Fusion 360 software.

1. In the Data Panel, ensure that the *Autodesk Fusion 360 Practice Files* project is active and displayed. In the list of files, double-click on **BBQ** to open the file.

2. Close the Data Panel by clicking [icon] (Hide Data Panel). The design displays as shown in Figure 1–19

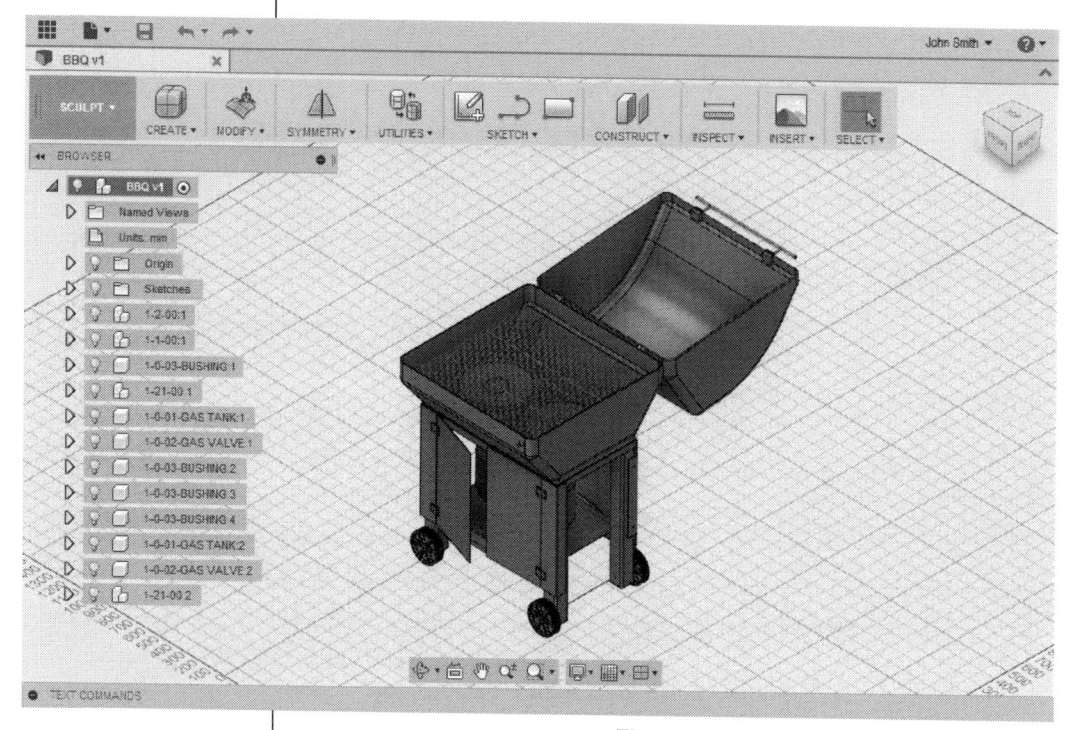

Figure 1–19

3. In the interface, note the following:
   - The SCULPT workspace is currently active. This is the default workspace for direct model designs that do not have a design history.
   - The BROWSER contains the default folders (i.e., *Named Views*, *Origin*) and the *Sketches* folder.
   - Multiple components ([icon]) and sub-assemblies ([icon]) are listed in the BROWSER, defining the BBQ design.

Task 3 - Use the BROWSER to select and hide components.

1. In the BROWSER, adjacent to the *Named Views* folder, click ▷ to expand the folder. Select the **TOP**, **FRONT**, **RIGHT**, and **HOME** views to reorient the design to the preset views.

2. In the BROWSER, hover the cursor over the component names to highlight them in the design.

3. Select the 1-0-01-GAS TANK:1 component. The tank highlights in the graphics window.

4. Hold <Ctrl> and select the 1-0-01-GAS TANK:2 component. Both tank components are highlighted in the design.

5. Click in the graphics window to clear the selection.

6. Click 💡 (Show/Hide) adjacent to one of the tank components. The component is hidden from the display.

   💡 (Show/Hide) displays, indicating that the component is not visible.

7. Repeat Step 6 to hide the display of the other tank component.

8. In the BROWSER, expand the 1-1-00:1 component (📁) by clicking ▷ adjacent to its name. This node contains the components that form the top of the BBQ.

9. In the BROWSER, click 💡 (Show/Hide) adjacent to the 1-1-00:1 component. Note how the top of the BBQ is entirely hidden in the display, as shown in Figure 1–20.

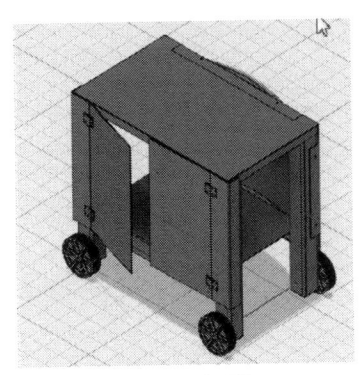

Figure 1–20

10. Click again to return the 1-1-00:1 component to the display.

11. Practice hiding components by hiding the COVER and HANDLE components, as shown in Figure 1–21.

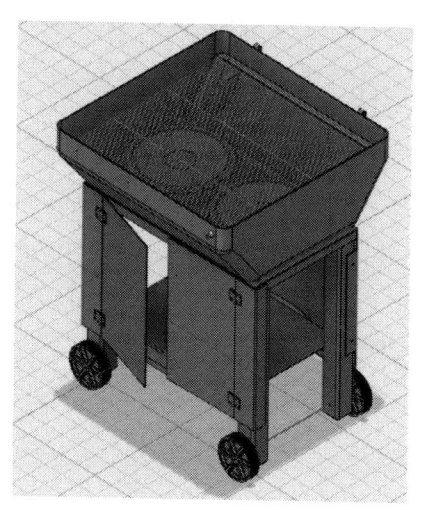

Figure 1–21

12. On the right of the BROWSER bar, click ![] to collapse the BROWSER. Click ![] to expand the BROWSER.

13. On the left of the BROWSER bar, click ![] to compress the BROWSER. The collapse and compress options can be used individually or together to provide additional space for manipulating and viewing a design.

Task 4 - Navigate the design using the mouse scroll wheel.

1. To zoom in and out, scroll the mouse scroll wheel forward and backward. Note that the view zooms based on the position of the cursor in the design.

2. To pan, hold the mouse scroll wheel down as you move the cursor around the design.

3. Reposition and zoom the design as required.

Task 5 - Navigate the design using the ViewCube.

1. In the top right corner of the graphics window, hover the cursor over the ViewCube. Click (Home) to return the design to its default view.

2. Select the top face of the ViewCube (**TOP**) to reorient the design to the top view.

3. Hover the cursor over the ViewCube until the rotational arrows display in the top right corner, as shown in Figure 1–22. Select the left arrow to rotate the view.

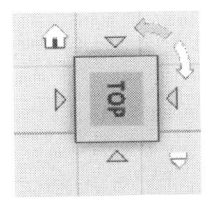

Figure 1–22

4. Hover the cursor over the ViewCube until the triangles pointing to the four edges display. Click the bottom to switch to the **FRONT** view.

5. Click (Home) to return to the **Home** view.

6. Use the ViewCube to orient the design as shown in the two views in Figure 1–23. In addition to selecting faces on the ViewCube, you can also select edges and corners to orient the design, as required.

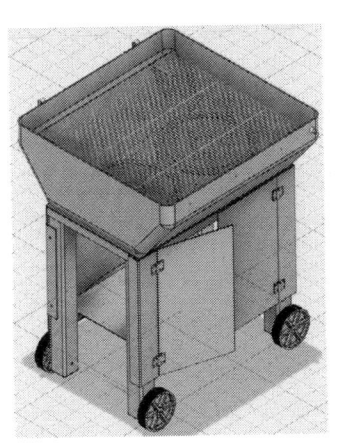

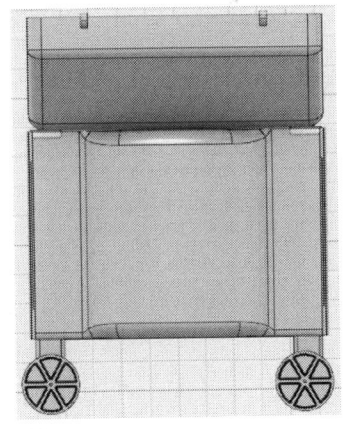

Figure 1–23

7. Once the **Back** view is oriented, click ▶▶ to expand the BROWSER, if required.

8. Expand the *Named Views* folder.

9. Right-click on the *Named Views* folder and select **New Named View**. Click once on the **NamedView** folder to edit its name. Enter **BACK** as the new name for the view.

10. In the *Named Views* folder, select **Home**.

11. In the BROWSER, make the COVER and HANDLE components visible again.

12. In the *Named Views* folder, select **BACK**. Note that the design orientation is changed to the saved orientation, but that the component visibility was not saved with the view.

13. Return to the **Home** view.

14. Enable the display of the two gas tanks.

15. Hover the cursor over the ViewCube. Select ▽ to expand the ViewCube options, as shown in Figure 1–24.

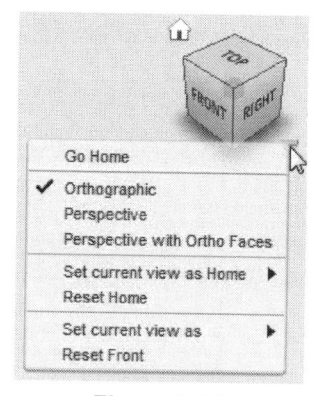

Figure 1–24

16. Note that **Orthographic** is currently selected. Click **Perspective** to compare the design display.

17. Return the design to the **Orthographic** setting.

Task 6 - Navigate the design using the Navigation Bar.

1. In the Navigation Bar at the bottom of the graphics window, activate the Look At tool by clicking ▣. Select a planar face on the design to reorient that face parallel to the screen.

2. Using the Look At tool, reorient the design as shown in Figure 1–25.

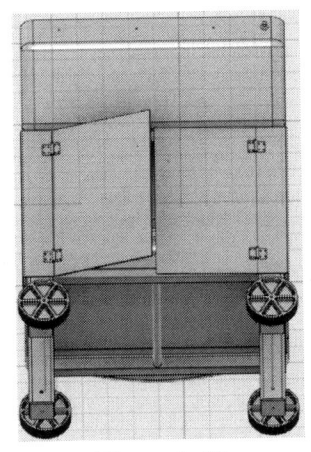

Figure 1–25

3. Return to the **Home** view.

4. On the Navigation Bar, click ✋ (Pan). Hold the left mouse button, and then move the cursor to move the design. The design pans in the same way as pressing the middle mouse button did.

5. On the Navigation Bar, click 🔍 (Zoom). Hold the left mouse button, and then move the cursor to zoom in on the design.

6. On the Navigation Bar, click ✥ (Orbit). A circular outline displays around the design and the cursor displays as ✥.

You can also start the Orbit command by holding <Shift> and holding the middle mouse button or scroll wheel as you move the cursor.

7. Hold the left mouse button and move the cursor to spin the design in any direction.

8. Hover the cursor over one of the lines that extends horizontally or vertically from the circular outline. The cursor displays as ⬒ (vertical) or ⬓ (horizontal). Click and drag on these lines to spin the design horizontally or vertically in the current plane.

9. With ⊕ (Orbit) still active, select a point anywhere on the design. Once selected, that point is centered in the circular outline.

10. Practice spinning, panning, and zooming the design using the Navigation Bar.

11. If required, orbit the design until at least one of the barbeque's wheels is visible. Click 🔍 (Zoom Window) and draw a box around one of the wheels to zoom into that area.

12. Click ▼ adjacent to 🔍 and then click 🔍 (Fit). Once selected, the design resizes to fit in the graphics window while staying in the same orientation.

13. Return to the **Home** view.

Task 7 - Manipulating the design display.

1. In the Navigation Bar, click 🖥️▼ (Display Settings). Expand **Visual Style**, as shown in Figure 1–26.

*The **Camera** options on the Display Settings menu enables you to choose between an Orthographic and Perspective display, as an alternative to using the ViewCube.*

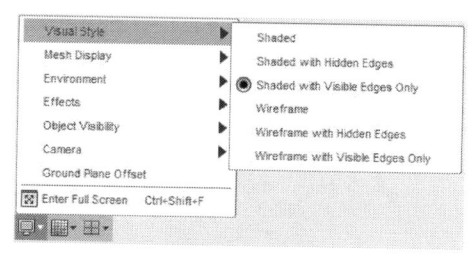

Figure 1–26

2. Click on each of the display settings to review how they change the design's appearance.

3. Return the design to the **Shaded with Visible Edges Only** option.

4. In the Navigation Bar, click ▣▾ (Display Settings). Expand **Environment**, as shown in Figure 1–27.

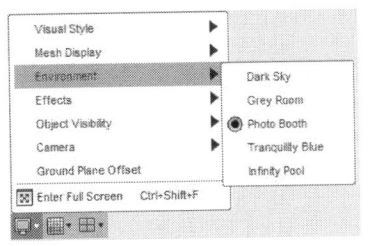

Figure 1–27

5. Click on each of the Environment settings to review how they change the appearance of the design.

6. Return the design to the **Photo Booth** option.

7. In the Navigation Bar, click ▣▾ (Display Settings). Expand **Effects**. Toggle the various effect settings to customize the view as required.

8. Clear the **Ground Shadow** option before continuing. The shadow is removed from the ground plane.

The display settings are set for the current Autodesk Fusion 360 session and are not saved with the design.

Task 8 - Create a new design in the Autodesk Fusion 360 software.

1. In the Application Bar, click ▮▾ (File) to access the commands in the File drop-down menu.

2. Click **New Design**.

3. In the Autodesk Fusion 360 interface, note the following:
   - A new document tab called *Untitled* is added at the top of the window.
   - The MODEL Workspace is active.
   - The BROWSER has the *Named Views* and *Origin* folders created by default.
   - A **Units** folder lists the unit of measure for the new design

4. In the Application Bar, click ![save icon] (Save). Enter **New Design** for the filename and then click **Save**. This design will be used in the next chapter of this student guide when you begin learning about the modeling tools in the Autodesk Fusion 360 software.

5. Click ✖ in the **BBQ v1** document tab to close it. When prompted to save changes to the design, click **Don't Save**.

Chapter Review Questions

1. Match the numbers shown in Figure 1–28 with the interface components listed below.

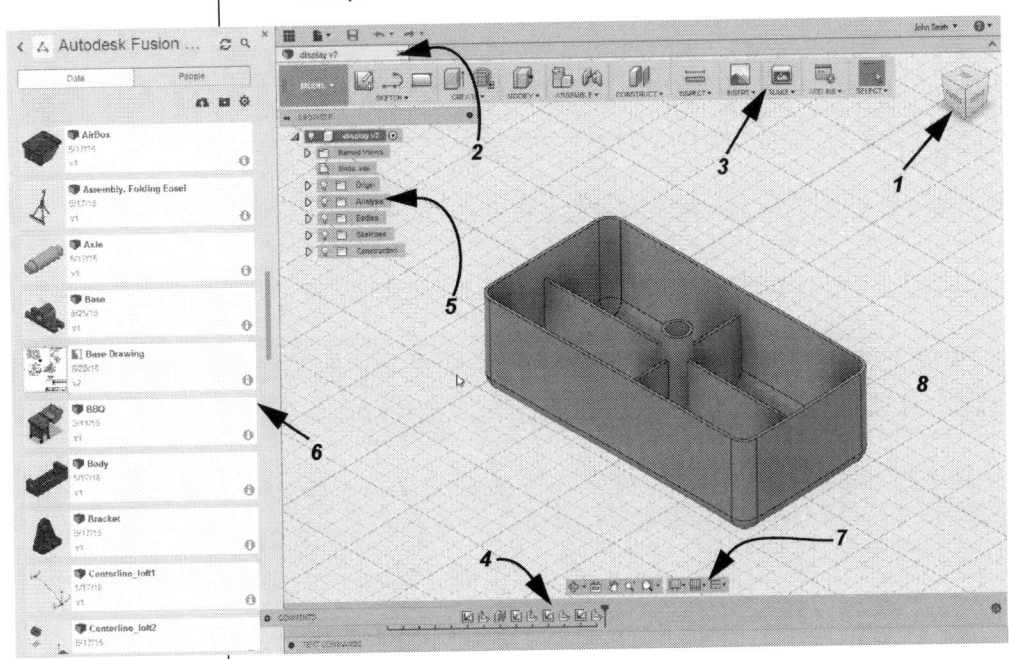

Figure 1–28

Interface Element	Answer
a) Data Panel	
b) BROWSER	
c) Timeline	
d) Display Controls	
e) Ribbon	
f) Graphics Window	
g) ViewCube	

2. Clicking ![icon] enables you to automatically reorient the display of the design to the **TOP** view.

    a. True

    b. False

3. Which mouse button do you use to pan the design in the graphics window?

    a. Left

    b. Middle

    c. Right

4. Which combination of items do you select to quickly orient a design face parallel to the screen without spinning? (Select all that apply.)

    a. A surface and ![icon].

    b. A planar surface and ![icon].

    c. A surface and ![icon].

    d. A planar surface and ![icon].

    e. A face on the ViewCube.

5. You can have multiple designs open in the Autodesk Fusion 360 software at the same time.

    a. True

    b. False

Answers: 1. (a=6, b=5, c=4, d=7, e=3, f=8, g=1), 2. b, 3. b, 4. (d,e), 5. a

Command Summary

Button	Command	Location
	Display Settings	• Display Controls
	File	• Quick Access Toolbar
	Fit	• Display Controls
	Help	• Quick Access Toolbar
	Home View	• ViewCube
	Look At	• Display Controls
	Orbit (rotate)	• Display Controls
	Pan	• Display Controls
	Projects	• Quick Access Toolbar
	Save	• Quick Access Toolbar
	Zoom	• Display Controls
	Zoom Window	• Display Controls

Chapter 2

Creating the First Feature with Quick Shapes

In the Autodesk® Fusion 360™ software, the first solid feature that you create in your design can form the foundation on which other features and geometry are built. One way to create this first solid feature is to use one of the available quick shapes.

Learning Objectives in this Chapter

- Identify and change the units for the design.
- Identify and locate the origin features of a new design.
- Create geometry using the Box, Cylinder, Sphere, Torus, and Coil quick shape modeling tools.

2.1 Design Units and Origin

In addition to the default named views, the BROWSER of a new design also includes the **Units** node and the **Origin** folder.

Units

The default unit for a new design is millimeters (mm), as indicated in the **Units** node of the BROWSER, shown in Figure 2–1.

You can change the default units for a new design in the Preferences dialog box.

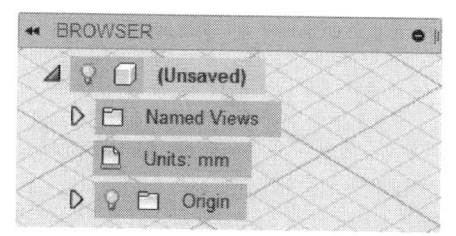

Figure 2–1

To change the active units, in the BROWSER, hover the cursor over the **Units** node and click (Change Active Units). In the CHANGE ACTIVE UNITS palette, you can select one of the unit types shown in Figure 2–2.

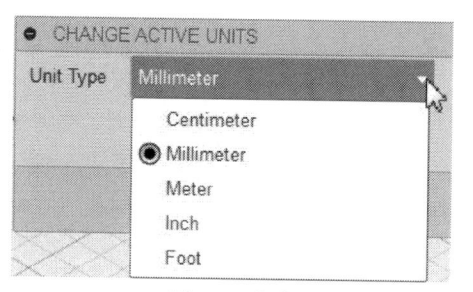

Figure 2–2

Origin

The *Origin* folder in the BROWSER (shown in Figure 2–3) contains the following items:

- Three orthogonal planes: XY plane, XZ plane, and YZ plane
- Three axes: X-axis, Y-axis, and Z-axis
- A center point O at the default (0,0,0) location

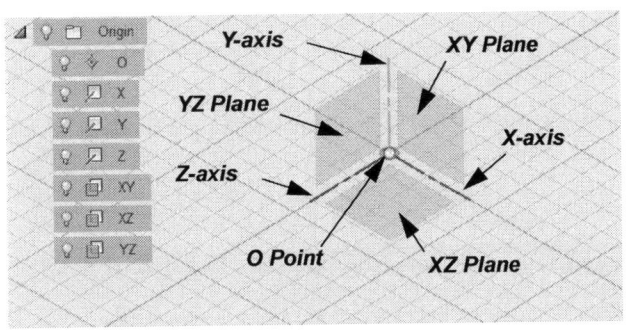

Figure 2–3

By default, when you create a new design, the origin features are not displayed because visibility is turned off for the *Origin* folder.

Click ![bulb] to display the origin features.

2.2 Quick Shape Creation

The Autodesk Fusion 360 software includes quick shape creation tools that enable you to create the first solid feature as one of five quick shapes. Using these tools, you can draw the sketch and the 3D shape in at the same time.

The five quick shapes are **Box**, **Cylinder**, **Sphere**, **Torus**, and **Coil**, and are shown in Figure 2–4.

Box Timeline icon:

Sphere Timeline icon:

Cylinder Timeline icon:

Torus Timeline icon:

Coil Timeline icon:

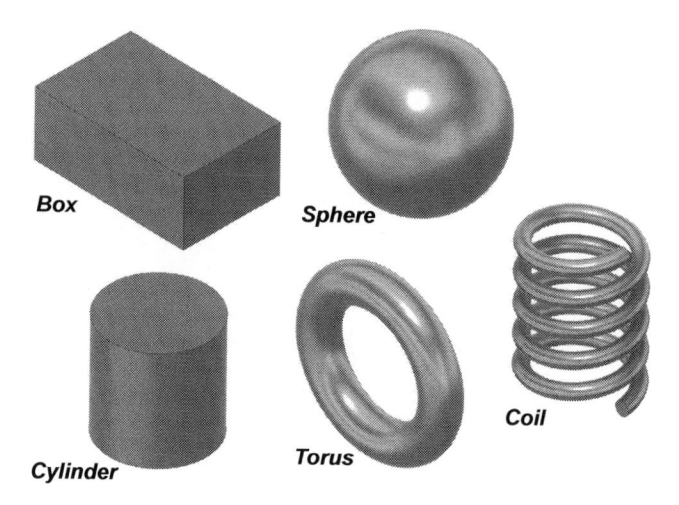

Figure 2–4

The quick shape creation options are located in the ribbon in the CREATE panel, as shown in Figure 2–5.

The options in this portion of the CREATE panel are quick shape creation options.

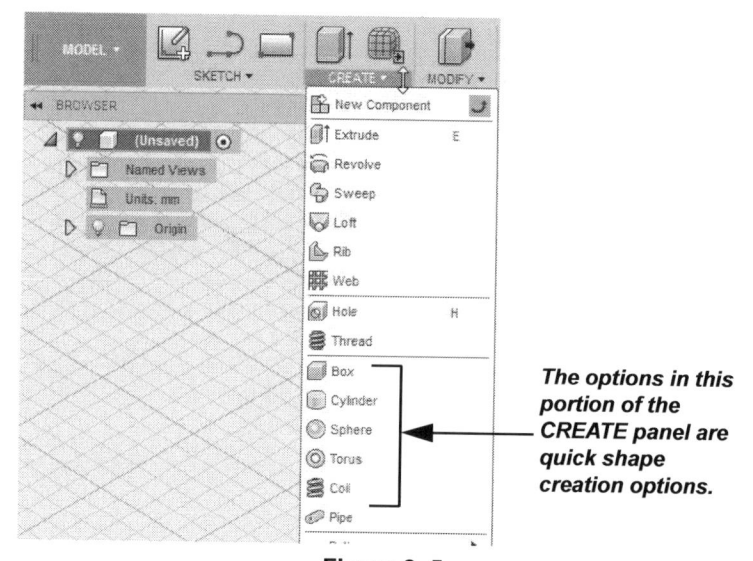

Figure 2–5

Video Lesson Available

Creating a Box Using Quick Shape Creation

Video Length: 3:36

Video Lesson Available

Creating a Cylinder Using Quick Shape Creation

Video Length: 3:19

Video Lesson Available

Creating a Sphere Using Quick Shape Creation

Video Length: 3:02

Video Lesson Available

Creating a Torus Using Quick Shape Creation

Video Length: 4:06

Video Lesson Available

Creating a Coil Using Quick Shape Creation

Video Length: 3:29

Practice 2a

Creating Shapes I

Practice Objective

- Create geometry using the Box, Cylinder, and Sphere modeling tools.

In this practice, you will learn the general workflow for creating some of the basic shapes that are available in the CREATE panel. You will start by following detailed steps to create a box using both free-form sizing and data entry. You will then create cylinder and sphere geometry to practice these steps and use more flexibility in how you choose to define the size of the geometry.

Task 1 - Create a Box design.

1. Ensure that the *New Design* document tab is active. This is the new design that was created in the previous practice. If you did not finish the previous practice, complete the following:
    1. In the Application Bar, click (File) to access the commands in the File drop-down menu.
    2. Click **New Design**.
    3. Click (Save) in the Application Bar.
    4. Enter **New Design** as the filename and then click **Save**.

2. In the CREATE panel, click (Box).

The ground plane lies on the XZ plane.

3. When prompted to choose a plane, select the XZ plane. To ensure that the correct plane is selected, you can expand the *Origin* folder in the BROWSER and select **XZ**, or you can select the plane in the graphics window.

4. Select any location on the grid to set the first corner of the rectangular shape.

Now that the start point is set, a tooltip prompts you to specify the size of the rectangle. There are two ways that you can do this. The following steps will show you the method that you can use if you do not need precise dimension values.

5. To create the box, drag the cursor to form the shape until you reach the required size and orientation of the rectangle sketch.

6. Click to create the box sketch. The shape is automatically given a third dimension, similar to that shown in Figure 2–6. Five manipulator arrows display surrounding the shape of the box, and the BOX palette opens.

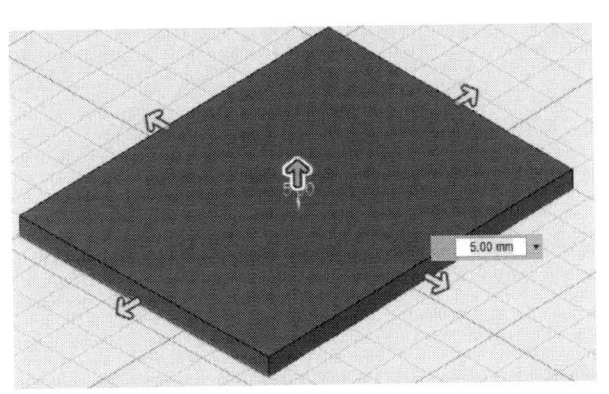

Figure 2–6

7. Select and drag any of the manipulator arrows to free-form adjust the length, width, or height of the box.

8. In the BOX palette, click **OK** to create the box. Since this box was free-formed by dragging, the exact dimensions of the box are unknown.

9. In the lower left corner of the Autodesk Fusion 360 window, in the Timeline, hover the cursor over [icon], as shown in Figure 2–7. The icon is identified as **BoxPrimitive1** in the pop-up note and the box geometry highlights in the main window.

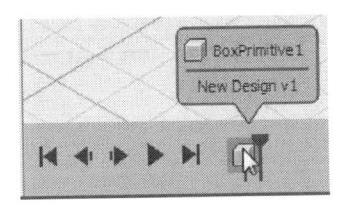

Figure 2–7

10. In the Timeline, right-click on ▢ (BoxPrimitive1) and select **Delete** to delete the feature, as shown in Figure 2–8.

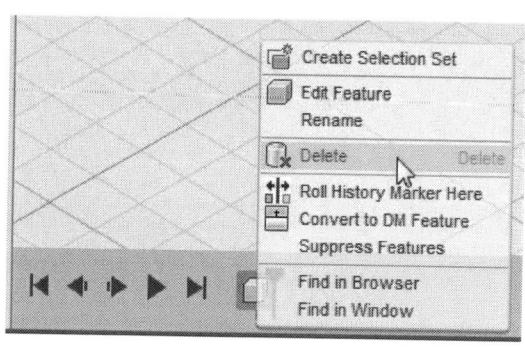

Figure 2–8

11. In the CREATE panel, click ▢ (Box).

12. When prompted to choose a plane, select the XZ plane.

13. Select any location to set the first corner of the rectangular shape. To locate the first corner at 0,0,0, hover the cursor near ✥ on the sketch plane. Once the cross-hairs on the cursor snap to this point, select it by clicking on it.

The following steps will show you the method that you can use if precise dimension values are required.

14. Begin to drag the box to define the shape and display the input boxes. Do not click to set the size of the shape.

15. In the active input box, enter **150**. The active input box is highlighted in blue.

16. To assign the entry and activate the next input box, press <Tab>.

    - As soon as you press <Tab>, a lock icon displays next to the entered value. This locks that dimension.

17. In the next input box, for the length, enter **300**. Press <Tab>. A lock icon displays next to both dimensions.

18. To finalize the sketch, you must select another point to lock the orientation of the box. Drag the cursor to the four quadrants relative to the start point of the sketch. Click inside quadrant one to create the box.

19. The shape is automatically given a third dimension. Five manipulator arrows display surrounding the shape of the box, and the BOX palette opens, as shown in Figure 2–9.

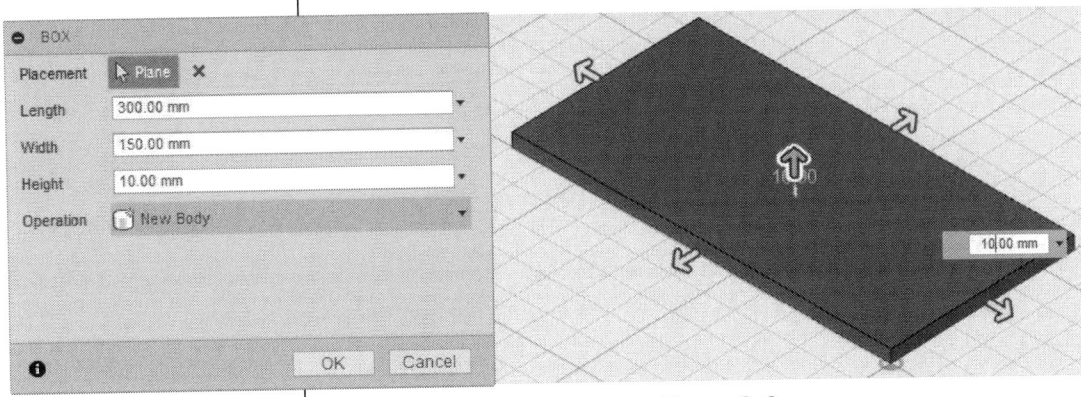

Figure 2–9

20. In the input box that displays on the geometry, enter a height of **100**. Alternatively, you can enter a *Length*, *Width*, and *Height* value in the fields in the BOX palette.

21. In the *Height* field, enter **150** to further change the shape.

22. Click **OK** to create the box.

23. In the Timeline, right-click on and select **Edit Feature**. The five manipulator arrows display surrounding the box and you can use them to modify the size of the box. To enter precise values, either:
    - Enter values into the input boxes that display when you select a manipulator arrow, or
    - Use the EDIT FEATURE palette to enter values in the *Length*, *Width*, and *Height* fields.

24. Click **Cancel**.

25. In the Timeline, right-click on and select **Delete**.

Task 2 - Create additional shapes.

In this task you will create the cylinder and sphere shapes. The creation workflow for these shapes is similar to the one that you used to create the box in the previous task. You will create the shapes using a combination of free-form manipulation and manual entry to define their size.

1. In the CREATE panel, select ☐ (Cylinder).

2. Select the XZ plane.

3. Select any location to set the center of the cylinder.

4. Drag the cursor to expand the diameter until you reach the required size and then enter **150** in the input box. Press <tab> to lock the dimension value.

5. Click in the XZ plane to confirm the sketch. The cylinder is automatically given a third dimension, similar to that shown in Figure 2–10. Two manipulator arrows display surrounding the shape and the CYLINDER palette opens.

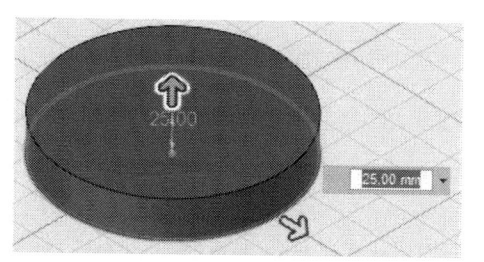

Figure 2–10

6. Drag any of the arrows to free-form adjust the diameter or height of the cylinder.

7. Assign a height of **100** for the cylinder using one of the sizing options.

8. Click **OK** to create the cylinder.

9. In the Timeline, right-click on ☐ and select **Delete**.

10. In the CREATE panel, select ◯ (Sphere).

11. Select the XZ plane.

12. Select any location to set the center of the sphere.

13. Unlike the **Box** and **Cylinder** tools, the **Sphere** tool does not start with a sketch. Instead, as soon as you select the center point, a 3D sphere is immediately added, similar to that shown in Figure 2–11. One arrow displays surrounding the shape and the SPHERE palette opens.

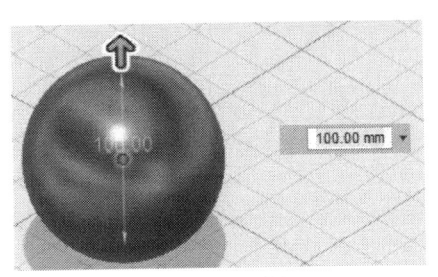

Figure 2–11

14. Drag the arrow to free-form adjust the diameter, which is the only value that can be defined for a sphere.

15. Click **OK** to create the sphere.

16. In the ViewCube, select **FRONT**. Note that the center of the sphere is aligned on the XZ plane and that the geometry is created on both sides of the plane. Return to the **Home** view.

17. Save the file. Click ✖ in the *New Design* document tab to close the file.

Practice 2b

Creating Shapes II

Practice Objective

- Create geometry using the Torus and Coil modeling tools.

In this practice, you will continue to create shape geometry, similar to that in the previous practice. You will use the **Torus** and **Coil** modeling. When creating the coil geometry, only a final image is provided. You are expected to create similar geometry using your knowledge of the creation tools, palettes, and manipulator tools.

Task 1 - Create a Torus design.

In this task you will crate a torus design. Shaped like a ring, a torus is a revolved circle with a hollow center. The steps for creating a torus are similar to that of the other shapes that have been previously discussed, but require additional selections that enable you to customize the size and how the internal hole is measured.

1. In the Application Bar, expand ![] (File menu) and click **New Design**.
2. In the CREATE panel, select ![] (Torus).
3. When prompted to choose a plane, select the YZ plane.
4. Select any location to set the center of the torus.
5. Similar to creating the other shapes, you can enter the diameter of the initial sketched circle or drag and click to define its size. Define the circle's diameter as **200**.

The ground plane lies on the XZ plane.

6. Click on the plane to create the torus. The shape is automatically given a third dimension, similar to that shown in Figure 2–12.

Figure 2–12

In the TORUS palette that opens, there are two different diameter values. The *Inner Diameter* is the diameter of the original circle that you created. The *Torus Diameter* is the thickness of the revolved circle around the original circle sketch. The *Torus Diameter*, by default, measures one-quarter of the size of the *Inner Diameter*.

7. Drag any of the arrows to free-form adjust the size of the torus.

8. In the TORUS palette, expand the Position drop-down list, as shown in Figure 2–13. The Position determines where the *Torus Diameter* is in relation to the *Inner Diameter*.

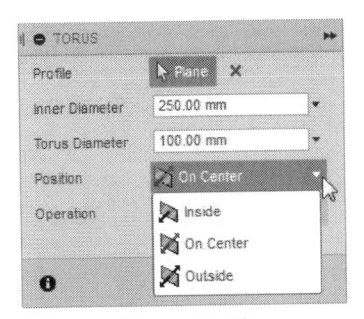

Figure 2–13

9. In the Position drop-down list, select the various options to review how the geometry reacts.

10. Select the **On Center** option and then click **OK** to create the torus.

11. Close the file without saving.

Task 2 - (Optional) Create a Coil design.

If time permits, use your knowledge of the shape tools, free-form editing options, and feature palette to create a coil.

1. Create a coil shape similar to that shown in Figure 2–14. Explore the options in the COIL palette to achieve this shape.

Figure 2–14

Chapter Review Questions

1. Identify the Timeline Icons in the table below.
    a. Box
    b. Cylinder
    c. Sphere
    d. Torus
    e. Coil

Icon	Answer
(sphere icon)	
(torus icon)	
(coil icon)	
(box icon)	
(cylinder icon)	

2. When using the **Cylinder** tool, after you have chosen your plane, what does your first click do?
    a. Selects the diameter
    b. Locks in a dimension
    c. Selects the center point
    d. Specifies the height

3. How does the **Sphere** tool differ from the **Box** or **Cylinder** tools?
    a. No sketch is required.
    b. You cannot input a specific dimension.
    c. You do not select the sketch plane.
    d. You cannot define the center point.

4. When using the **Torus** tool, what two types of diameter values can you define?
    a. *Inner Diameter* and *Outer Diameter*
    b. *Outer Diameter* and *Torus Diameter*
    c. *Original Diameter* and *Thickness Diameter*
    d. *Inner Diameter* and *Torus Diameter*

5. In the COIL palette (shown in Figure 2–15), what does the *Section* value control?

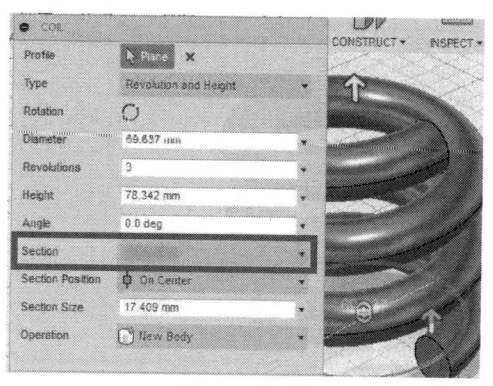

Figure 2–15

a. The height of the coil.

b. The shape of the coil's profile.

c. The cut profile.

d. The diameter of the coil.

Answers: 1.(c,d,e,a,b), 2.c, 3.a, 4.d, 5.b

Command Summary

Button	Command	Location
	Box	• **Ribbon:** *Model* Workspace>CREATE panel
	Coil	• **Ribbon:** *Model* Workspace>CREATE panel
	Cylinder	• **Ribbon:** *Model* Workspace>CREATE panel
	Sphere	• **Ribbon:** *Model* Workspace>CREATE panel
	Torus	• **Ribbon:** *Model* Workspace>CREATE panel

Chapter 3

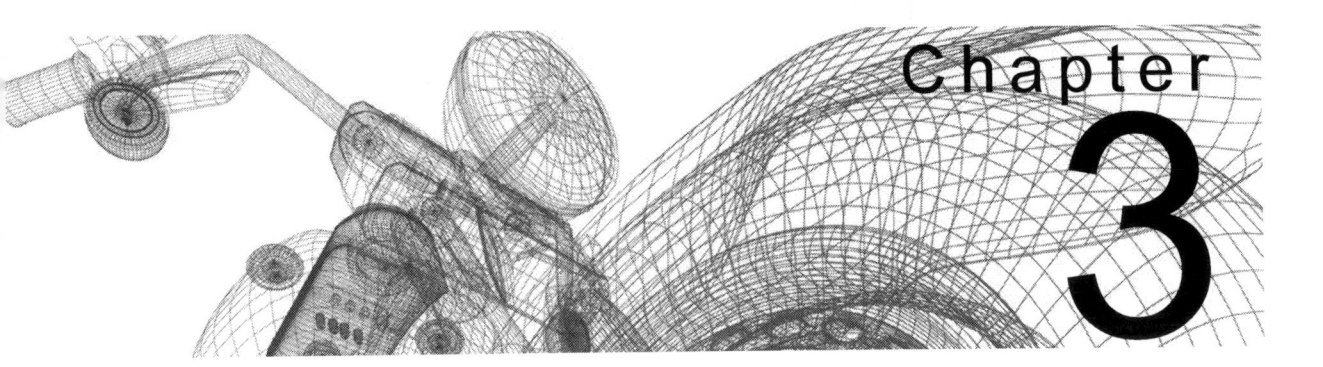

Creating Sketched Geometry

In addition to using the quick shape tools in the CREATE panel, you can also create solid geometry by referencing a sketch and using it to create 3D geometry. To efficiently create sketches in the Autodesk® Fusion 360™ software, an understanding of the sketch workflow, entity creation workflows, and editing tools are required. This chapter focuses on the sketching tools.

Learning Objectives in this Chapter

- Describe the general workflow to create a new sketch in an Autodesk Fusion 360 design.
- Use the sketch entity types to create lines, splines, points, rectangles, circles, and arcs.
- Sketch entities so that the required dimensions and constraints are assigned as entities are sketched.
- Add dimensions to sketch entities.
- Assign constraints to a sketch to control the required relationships between sketch entities.
- Use a sketch to create extruded or revolved geometry in a design.

3.1 Introduction to the Sketching Workflow

Even though the Autodesk Fusion 360 software is a 3D modeling application, many designs can be started with a 2D sketch. To start a 2D sketch, in the ribbon, on the SKETCH panel, select (Create Sketch). Sketch tools are located in the SKETCH panel drop-down list, or accessed by right-clicking in the graphics window to open the marking menu, as shown in Figure 3–1.

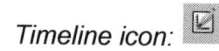

Timeline icon:

*Once a feature is created you can make changes to a sketch by right-clicking on the Timeline icon and selecting **Edit Sketch**.*

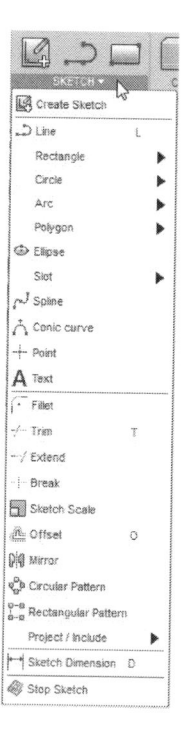

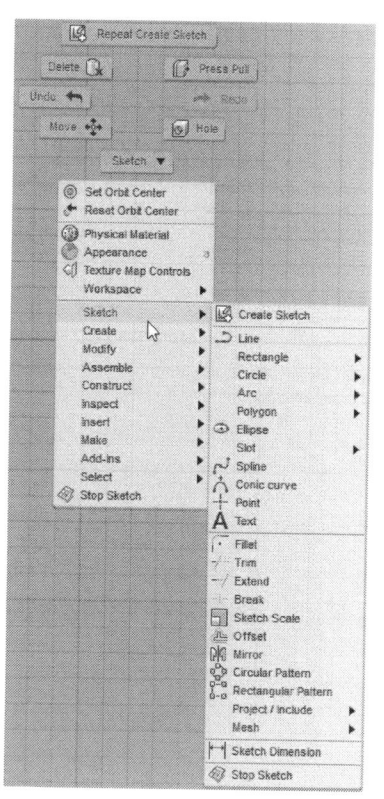

Figure 3–1

The following describes the general workflow for creating a sketch in a design. Although the steps to create each sketch entity type varies slightly, the overall workflow for creating a sketch is the same. Each entity type is discussed in more detail later in this chapter.

1. Initiate the creation of a new sketch.
2. Select a construction plane or planar face on which you want the sketch to be created.
3. Use the available entity creation options to define the shape of the sketch.
4. Assign constraints and dimensions to fully define the sketch.
5. Complete the creation of the sketch.

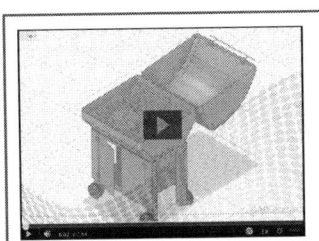

Sketches can also be created by selecting the sketch plane first, and then initiating the start of a new sketch.

Video Lesson Available

Creating a New Sketch

Video Length: 3:48

3.2 Sketch Entities

Line

Use the **Line** tool to create a single line or a continuous series of connected lines, similar to that shown in Figure 3–2.

Timeline icon: ☑

A closed loop sketch is highlighted to indicate that it is a closed profile.

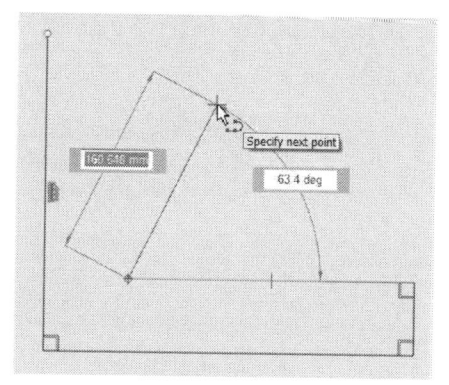

Figure 3–2

Use any of the following methods to start the **Line** tool:

- In the SKETCH panel, click (Line).

- Right-click in the graphics window and select **Sketch>Line** from the context menu.

- Press <L>.

Spline

Use the **Spline** tool to sketch a free-form 2D curve, as shown in Figure 3–3.

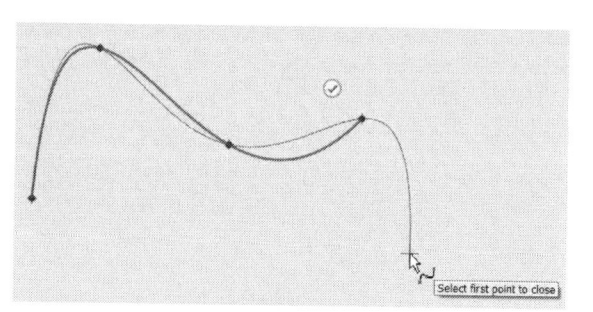

Figure 3–3

Use either of the following methods to start the **Spline** tool:

- In the SKETCH panel, click (Spline).

- Right-click in the graphics window and select **Sketch>Spline** from the context menu.

Points

Points will snap to grid points if snapping is enabled.

Use the **Point** tool to sketch individual points.

Use either of the following methods to start the **Point** tool:

- In the SKETCH panel, click ⊕ (Point).
- Right-click in the graphics window and select **Sketch>Point** from the context menu.

Video Lesson Available

Learning to Sketch with Lines, Splines, and Points

Video Length: 3:33

Rectangles

Use the **Rectangle** tool to create a predefined rectangular shape, as shown in Figure 3–4, Figure 3–5, and Figure 3–6.

Use either of the following methods to start the **Rectangle** tool:

- In the SKETCH panel, click **Rectangle** and select the appropriate creation type.
- Right-click in the graphics window and select **Sketch> Rectangle** from the context menu.

There are three Rectangle creation types:

- ▱ (2-Point Rectangle)

Press <R> to sketch a 2-point rectangle.

Horizontal and vertical constraints are automatically added to the sides of a 2-point rectangle.

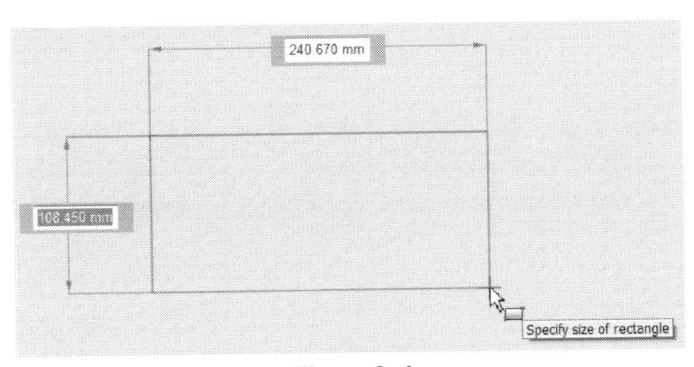

Figure 3–4

© 2016, ASCENT - Center for Technical Knowledge®

- ◊ (3-Point Rectangle)

Parallel constraints are automatically added to the sides of a 3-point rectangle.

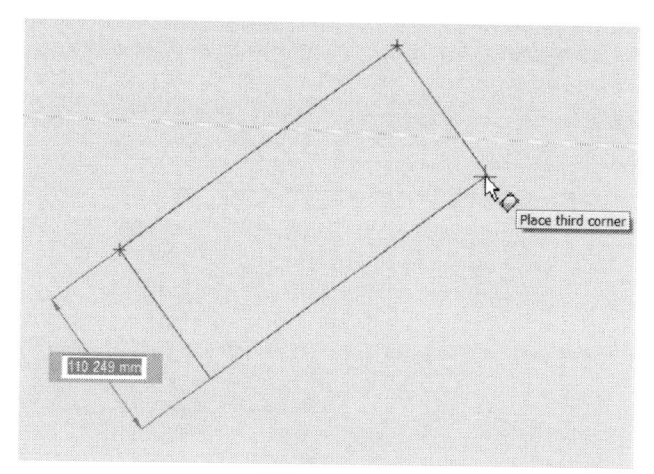

Figure 3–5

- ▫ (Center Rectangle)

A point and construction lines are automatically created to locate the center of the rectangle.

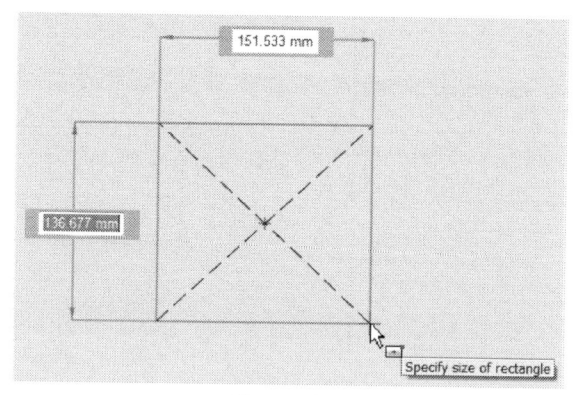

Figure 3–6

Video Lesson Available

Sketching Rectangles

Video Length: 2:50

Circle

Use the **Circle** tool to create a predefined circular shapes, as shown in Figure 3–7 to Figure 3–11.

Use either of the following methods to start the **Circle** tool:

- In the SKETCH panel, click **Circle** and select the appropriate creation type.
- Right-click in the graphics window and select **Sketch>Circle** from the context menu.

There are five Circle creation types:

- ⊕ (Center Diameter Circle)

Press <C> to sketch a center diameter circle.

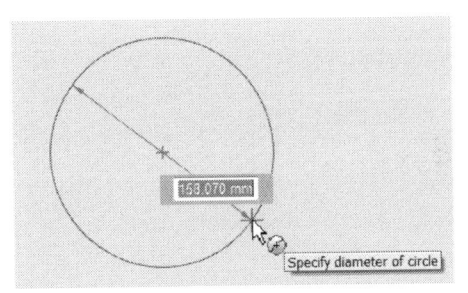

Figure 3–7

- ○ (2-Point Circle)

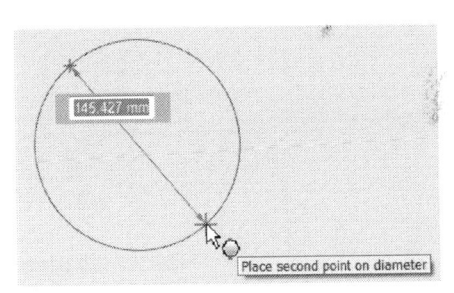

Figure 3–8

- (3-Point Circle)

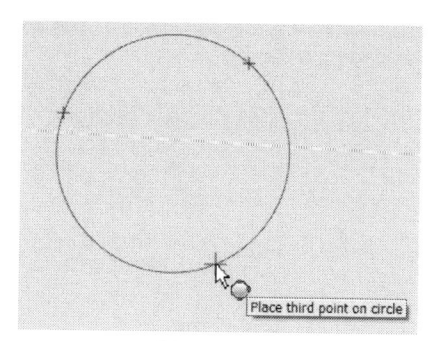

Figure 3–9

- (2-Tangent Circle)

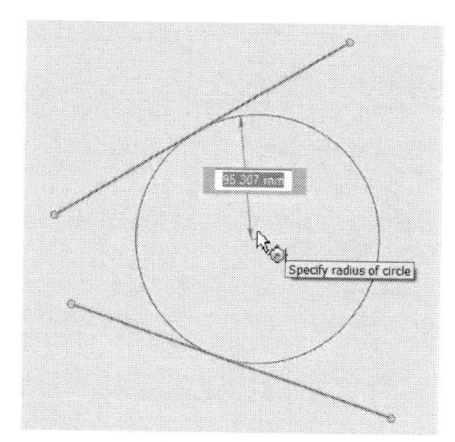

Figure 3–10

- (3-Tangent Circle)

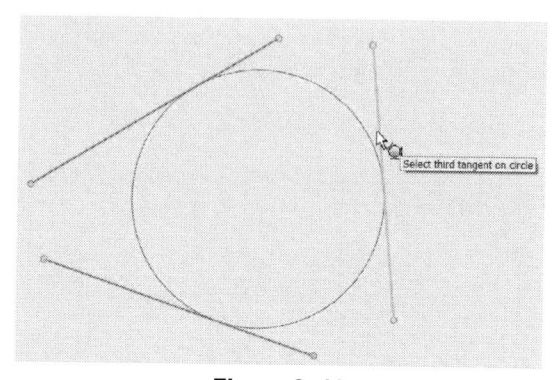

Figure 3–11

Video Lesson Available

Creating Circles

Video Length: 2:22

Arcs

Use the **Arc** tool to create predefined arc shapes, as shown in Figure 3–12 to Figure 3–14.

Use either of the following methods to start the **Arc** tool:

- In the SKETCH panel, click **Arc** and select the appropriate creation type.

- Right-click in the graphics window and select **Sketch>Arc** from the context menu.

There are three Arc creation types:

- (3-Point Arc)

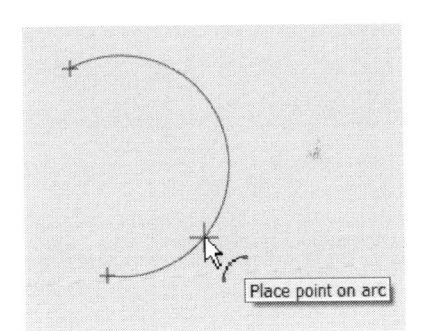

Figure 3–12

- ⌒ (Center Point Arc)

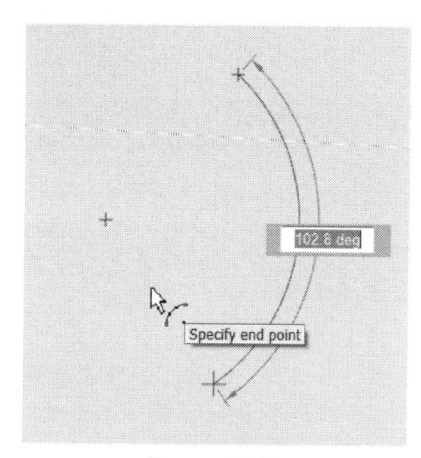

Figure 3–13

- ⌒ (Tangent Arc)

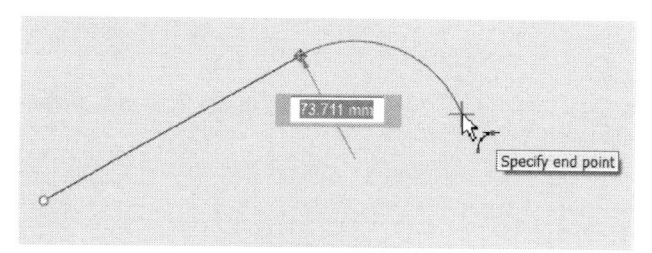

Figure 3–14

Video Lesson Available

Creating Arcs

Video Length: 3:14

3.3 Dimensioning

Dimensions define the size and location of objects in the sketch.

Dynamic Input

When creating entities, a dynamic input line displays when you move the cursor in the graphics window. This line provides you with a heads-up display for the input fields. These fields enable you to enter explicit values for the start location of an entity, values to extend the entity, and angular values to position the entity, as shown in Figure 3–15. The field highlighted in blue is the active value, indicating that you can enter a value in the field.

To place an entity without creating the dimension, simply click to place the entity. You can assign dimensions after the entity has been created.

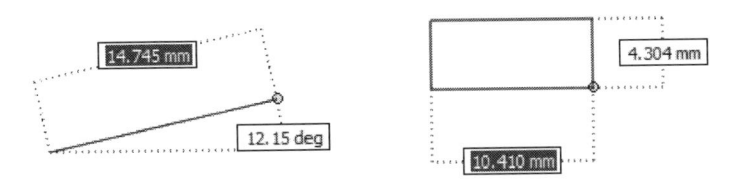

Figure 3–15

After entering a value in a dynamic input field, press <Tab> to toggle to the next field to enter its value. After all of the values have been entered, finalize the entity by pressing <Enter>. A dimension is automatically created when a dynamic input field is used to define a value.

Adding Sketch Dimensions

Use the following steps to create a dimension:

1. In the SKETCH panel, click (Sketch Dimension). Alternatively, you can right-click in the graphics window and select **Sketch>Sketch Dimension**.
2. Select the entity or entities.
3. Move the cursor to the dimension's placement location and click to place the dimension.

To sketch a center diameter circle, press <C>.

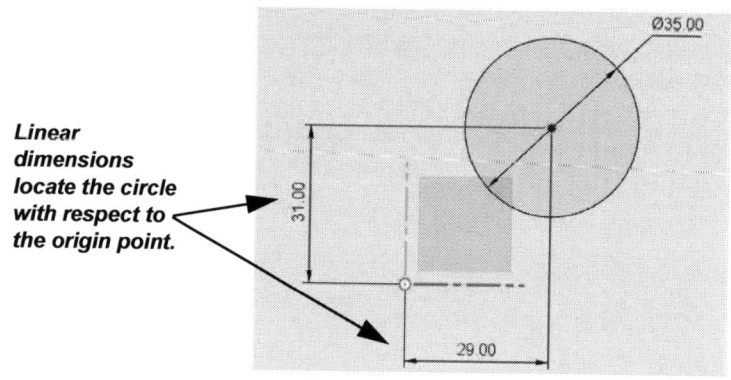

A fully dimensioned sketch is shown in Figure 3–16.

Linear dimensions locate the circle with respect to the origin point.

Figure 3–16

- The dimension type that is created depends on whether you select an entity or its endpoints. For example, selecting two non-parallel lines creates an angular dimension, while selecting two end points creates a linear dimension.

- Where you place the dimension can also impact the dimension type. Consider the inclined line shown in Figure 3–17. The dimension type will default to horizontal or vertical, depending on where the dimension is placed.

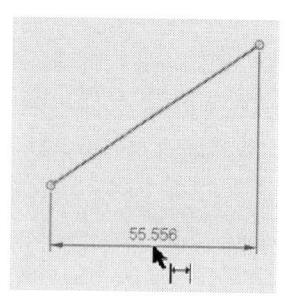

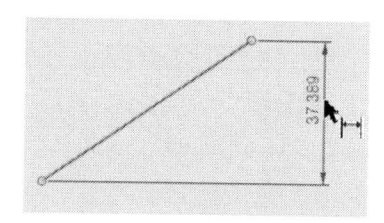

Figure 3–17

- To control the dimension type, right-click in the graphics window to access the marking and context menus. In the context menu (bottom), you can access options to lock the dimension type to **Horizontal**, **Vertical**, or **Aligned**, as shown in Figure 3–18.

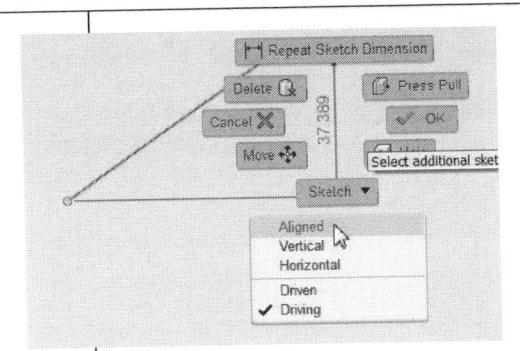

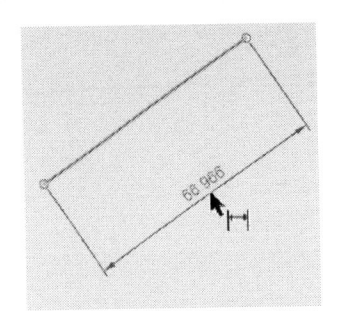

Figure 3–18

- When dimensioning a sketch to be used to create a revolved feature, you can create a diameter dimension. To dimension, select the centerline for the revolved cross-section, select the geometry, and then right-click and select **Diameter Dimension**. Place the dimension, as shown in Figure 3–19.

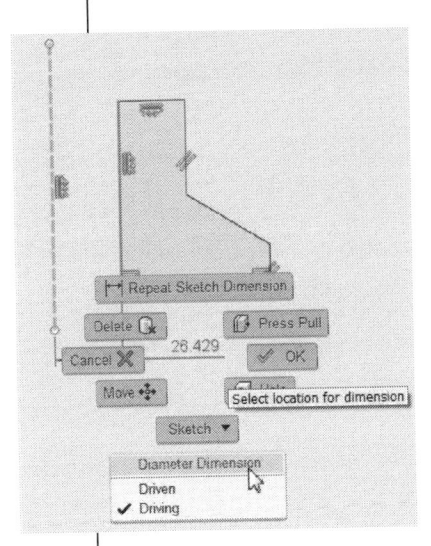

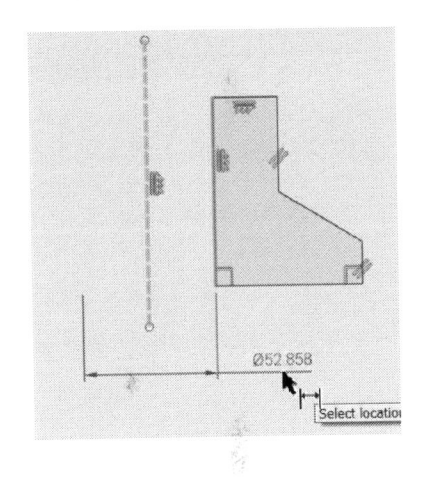

Figure 3–19

Modifying Sketch Dimensions

As soon as a dimension is placed, the entry field activates, enabling you to enter a value for the dimension. Press <Enter> to complete the placement. To edit a placed dimension, double-click on a dimension to change its value. The sketched geometry updates to reflect the new value.

Deleting Sketch Dimensions

To delete a dimension, select the dimension, right-click, and then select (Delete). You can also select the dimension and press <Delete>.

3.4 Sketch Constraints

Sketch constraints force a positional relationship between two or more entities. For example, you can force two sketched lines to be parallel by applying a Parallel constraint, which is then indicated by a symbol adjacent to both lines, as shown in Figure 3–20.

In this example, the lower line was selected first, so its orientation is applied to the upper line to make them parallel.

Parallel constraint symbols

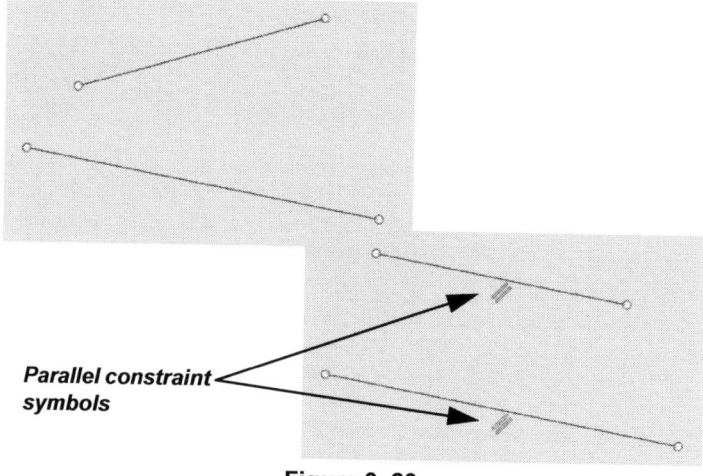

Figure 3–20

When sketching entities, constraints are automatically applied as you place entities in the sketch. Constraints govern how multiple entities interact with one another and dictate what changes can be made to the sketch. For example, if two lines are constrained to be perpendicular, then the only way you could change the lines to be anything other than perpendicular is to remove the constraint.

Constraint Types

You can select and assign constraints in the SKETCH PALETTE. The icons beside the constraint names are the same symbols that display on the geometry when the constraint is applied.

Constraint	Icon	Description
Coincident		Connects a point or vertex with other sketch geometry. Can also be used to constrain linear entities.
Colinear		Forces two lines to be colinear. The lines do not need to be in contact to have this constraint applied.

Concentric	⊚	Forces two arcs, two circles, or an arc and a circle to share the same center point.
Equal	=	Forces two entities (such as two lines or two circles) to have the same size.
Fix/UnFix	🔒	Grounds the geometry, fixing it in place regardless of the constraints or dimensions applied to the geometry.
Horizontal/ Vertical		Forces lines to be horizontal or vertical in the 2D plane of the sketch. It can also force two points or vertices to remain horizontally or vertically aligned to each other.
Midpoint	△	Snaps a point or vertex to the midpoint of another entity.
Parallel	//	Forces two lines to be parallel.
Perpendicular	⊥	Forces two lines to remain at a 90° angle to each other. The lines do not need to be in contact to have this constraint applied.
Smooth		Creates a curvature continuous condition between a spline and another entity.
Symmetry	[:]	Creates a symmetrical relationship about a selected line, commonly referred to as a mirrored relationship.
Tangent	⌒	Forces an arc or circle to be tangent to another entity.

Deleting Constraints

To delete a constraint (whether it was created during sketching or explicitly assigned), select the constraint in the graphics window and press <Delete>.

Video Lesson Available

Understanding Sketch Constraints

Video Length: 4:00

3.5 Extruding a Sketch

Use the **Extrude** tool to create a solid by adding linear depth to a closed-profile sketch, as shown in Figure 3–21.

- In the CREATE panel, click (Extrude).

- Right-click in the graphics window and select **Create> Extrude** from the context menu.

Timeline icon:

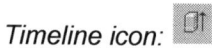

*Once the feature is created, you can right-click on in the Timeline and select **Edit Feature** to make changes to the feature creation options. You must select **Edit Profile Sketch** to change the profile sketch.*

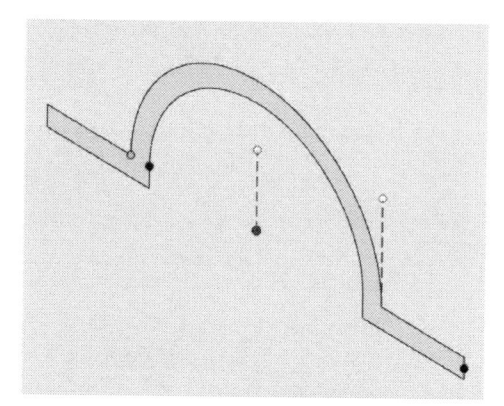

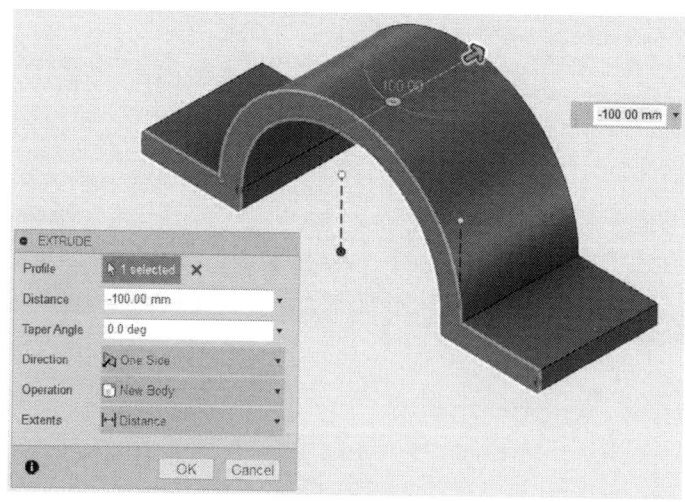

Figure 3–21

Video Lesson Available

Creating a Solid Using Extrude

Video Length: *3:30*

3.6 Revolving a Sketch

Use the **Revolve** tool to create a solid by adding angular depth to a closed-profile sketch, as shown in Figure 3–22.

- In the CREATE panel, click (Revolve).

- Right-click in the graphics window and select **Create>Revolve** from the context menu.

Timeline icon:

*Once the feature is created, you can right-click on in the Timeline and select **Edit Feature** to make changes to the feature. You must select **Edit Profile Sketch** to change the profile sketch.*

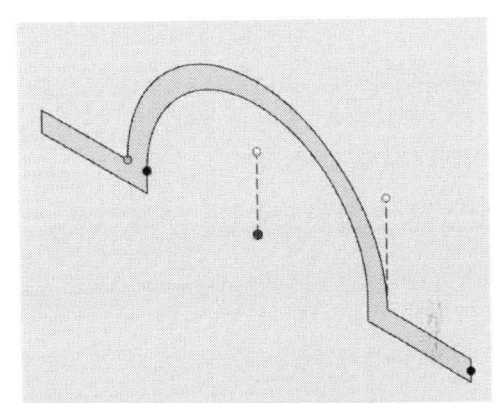

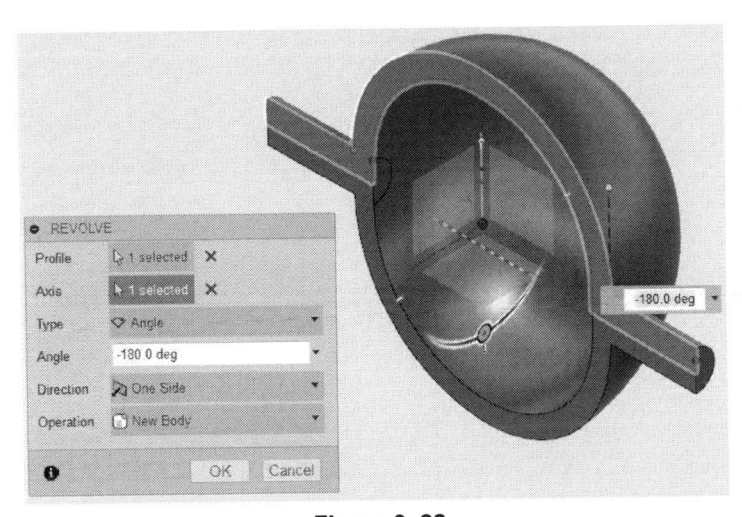

Figure 3–22

Video Lesson Available

Creating a Solid Using Revolve

Video Length: 3:10

Practice 3a

Extruded Solid Features

Practice Objectives

- Create a new design.
- Create an extruded solid feature on an origin plane using a provided dimension and constraint scheme.
- Modify the extruded solid feature to incorporate dimensional and feature direction changes.

In this practice, you will create a new design consisting of an extruded solid feature, as shown in Figure 3–23.

Figure 3–23

Task 1 - Create a new design and sketch its geometry.

1. Click (File) and select **New Design** to create a new component. The **Units** node in the BROWSER indicates **mm** as the units.

2. In the BROWSER, adjacent to the *Origin* folder, select (Show/Hide) to make the origin features visible.

3. Expand the *Origin* folder and select the XY plane.

4. In the SKETCH panel, click (Create Sketch). Alternatively, you can initiate the command first, and then select the XY Plane as the sketching plane.

Task 2 - Sketch a profile.

1. Click ↻ (Line) on the SKETCH panel in the ribbon, or press <L> to access the Line command.

2. Hover the cursor over the Origin Point at the center of the sketch. The cursor should snap to this reference. Start the sketch by clicking on the Origin Point, as shown in Figure 3–24.

The SKETCH PALETTE has checkbox options that enable you to toggle the sketch grid and the ability to snap to the grid.

Figure 3–24

3. Sketch the six lines shown in Figure 3–25. Click to start and end each line segment. When you are drawing the last line segment (which returns to the Origin Point), ensure that the cursor snaps to this reference before clicking.

*If the Line command is deactivated, you can restart it as you did in Step 1, or right-click to access the marking menu and select **Repeat Line**.*

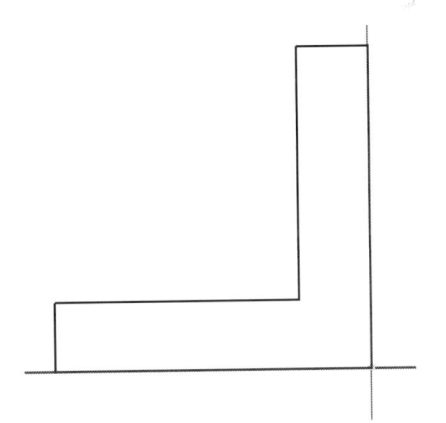

Figure 3–25

4. Depending on how you sketched your shape, your sketch should look similar to Figure 3–26. Your constraints might be different then the ones shown in the figure.

5. To apply the Equal constraint, in the SKETCH PALETTE, select =. Select the two lines indicated in Figure 3–26.

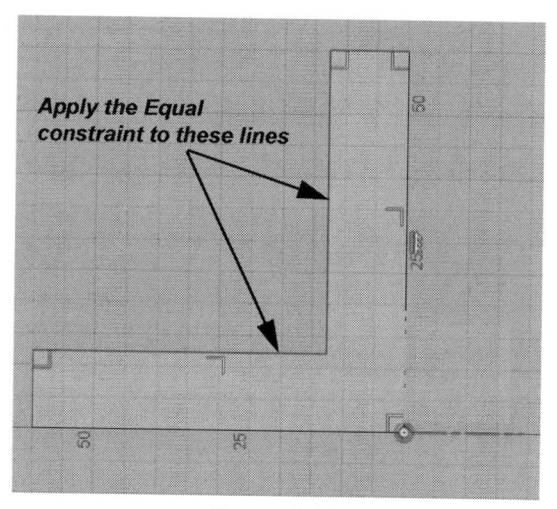

Figure 3–26

6. Apply the Equal constraint to the pair of lines indicated in Figure 3–27.

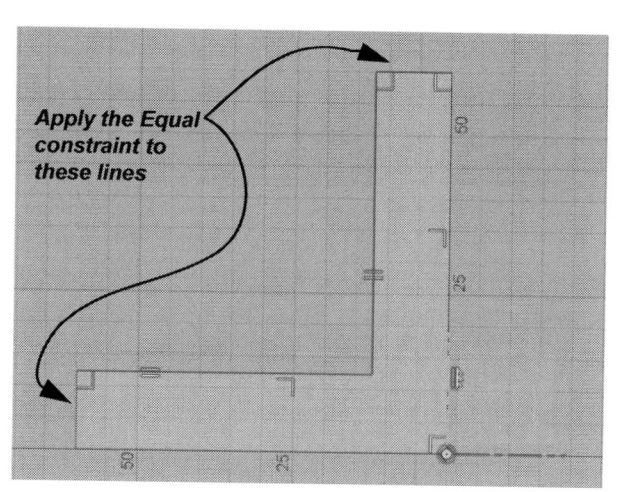

Figure 3–27

7. Right-click and select **OK**, or press <Esc> to end the Equal constraint command.

8. Select a vertex anywhere on the sketch and drag it. The vertex aligned to the Origin Point should remain fixed. The two pairs of lines that were made equal should change size, but remain equal in size to their partners.

9. Drag your sketch back to the same general shape as in Figure 3–27. If your lines did not remain vertical or horizontal, apply the horizontal ( ), vertical ( ), perpendicular ( ), or parallel ( ) constraints, as required.

10. In the SKETCH panel, click (Sketch Dimension) or press <D>.

11. Select the right-most vertical line and click to place the dimension. The dimension displays similar to that shown in Figure 3–28.

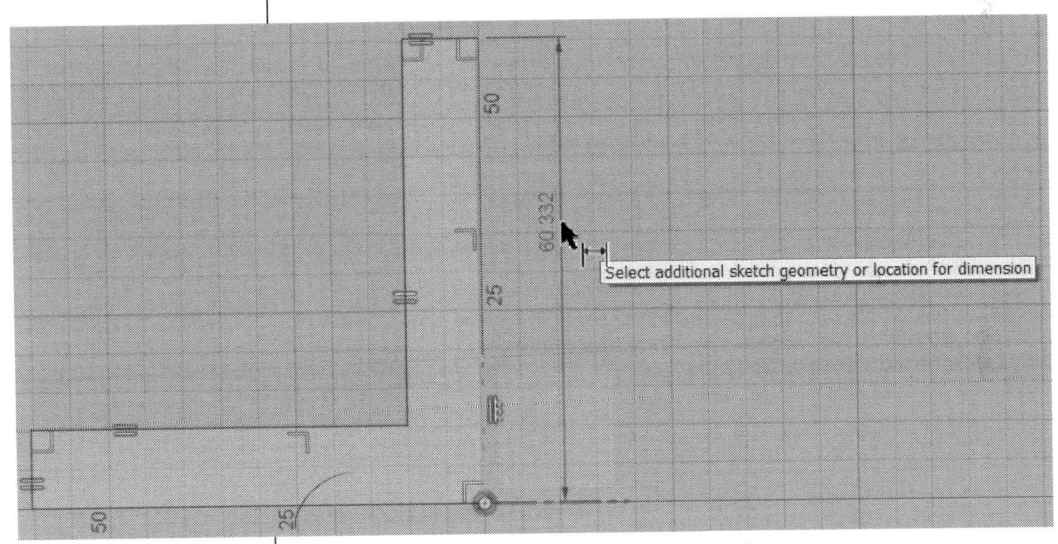

Figure 3–28

12. For the dimension's value, enter **50** and press <Enter>.

You do not have to fully dimension or constrain a sketch to create 3D geometry in the Autodesk Fusion 360 software. Using dimensions and constraints is recommended to ensure that your design intent is captured.

13. Select the top-most horizontal line and place the dimension as shown in Figure 3–29.

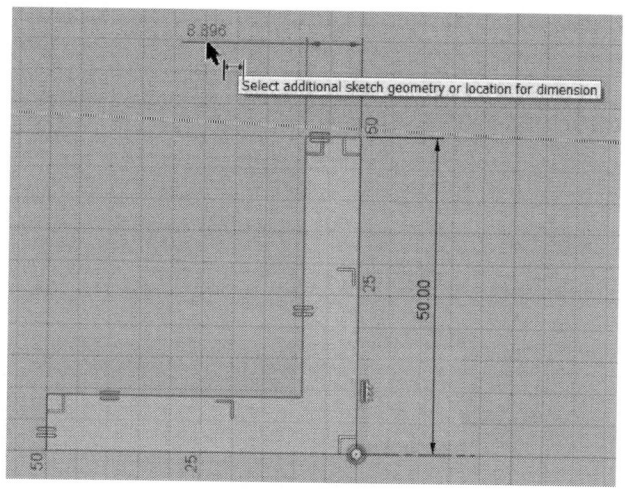

Figure 3–29

14. Change the value to **10** and press <Enter>.

15. Right-click and select **OK** or press <Esc> to finish dimensioning.

16. Select any vertex and attempt to drag the sketch. There should now be sufficient dimensions and constraints to fully define the size and location of the sketch. If the sketch can still be dragged, add additional constraints to it. The final sketch should be similar to that shown in Figure 3–30.

*The Autodesk Fusion 360 software is currently previewing a feature that will provide a visual distinction between sketch entities that are fully constrained, and those that have remaining degrees of freedom. To activate this feature, click your display name in the top-right corner and select **Preferences**. This option is found on the Preview page.*

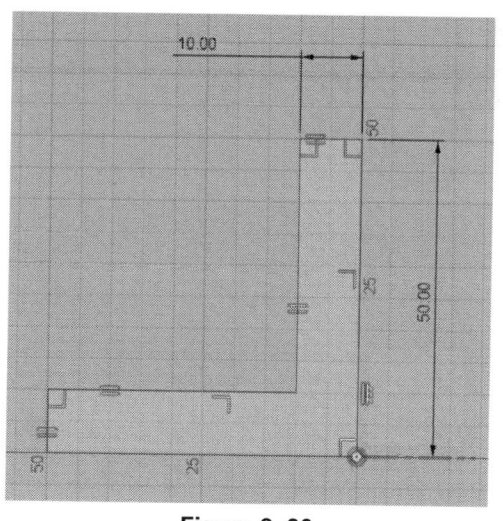

Figure 3–30

17. In the ribbon, click (STOP SKETCH).

18. If the design does not automatically return to its default orientation, hover the cursor over the ViewCube and click (Home).

Task 3 - Select the feature type and define the depth.

1. In the CREATE panel, select (Extrude). Alternatively, in the graphics window, right-click and select **Create>Extrude** on the context menu. The EXTRUDE palette displays with the **Select** action highlighted for the profile.

2. Select anywhere inside the highlighted area of the profile you just sketched. The area highlights blue, and an input field for the depth of the extrusion and a manipulator arrow displays.

3. Select and drag the manipulator arrow. Note that the value in the input field updates dynamically as a positive or negative value, depending on the direction you drag the manipulator arrow.

If you are unsure of what action is required for a command, leave the cursor inactive for a moment. A tip will display next to the cursor with the required action.

4. In the input field, enter **30**. In the EXTRUDE palette, click **OK**. The figure displays as shown in Figure 3–31

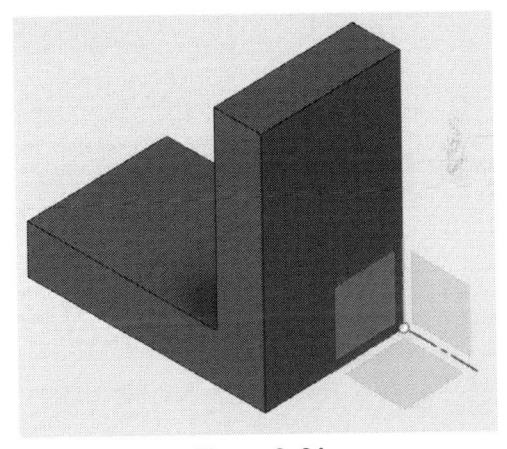

Figure 3–31

5. Note that the sketched profile is no longer displayed. In the BROWSER, expand the **Sketches** folder. All of the sketches that you create in the design are be listed here. Click adjacent to the one sketch listed to make it visible.

*In the BROWSER, you can toggle the visibility of the origin features by clicking adjacent to the **Origin** folder.*

Task 4 - Modify dimension of the extrusion and the sketched profile.

1. The feature Timeline is located in the bottom-left corner of the main window. The sketch and the extrude feature are both represented by icons. In the Timeline, right-click on ![icon] and select **Edit Feature**, as shown in Figure 3–32. The EDIT FEATURE palette displays, enabling you to modify the Extrude1 feature.

*You can also double-click on the icon for the **Extrude1** feature in the Timeline. The EDIT PALETTE panel opens, enabling you to modify the extrusion details.*

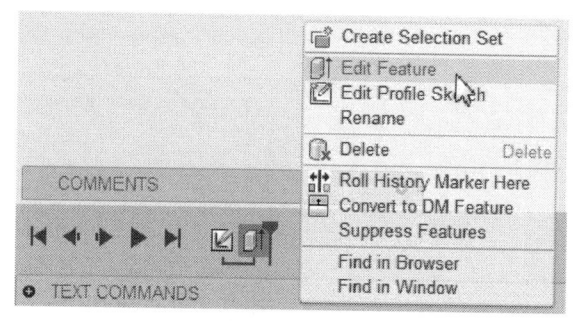

Figure 3–32

2. The input field and the blue manipulator arrow controlling the depth of the extrusion are displayed. Change the depth value to **[-30]** and click **OK**. The extrusion direction should now be in the other direction relative to the XY plane, and the sketch should display on the front face of the design.

3. The dimensions of the sketch did not display when you edited the Extrude1 feature because they belong to the sketch, which is considered a separate feature on the Timeline. In the BROWSER, in the **Sketches** folder, right-click **on Sketch1** and select **Show Dimension**.

4. Double-click on the dimension that currently has a value of **10**. Enter **25** as the new dimension value and press <Enter>. The design updates as shown in Figure 3–33.

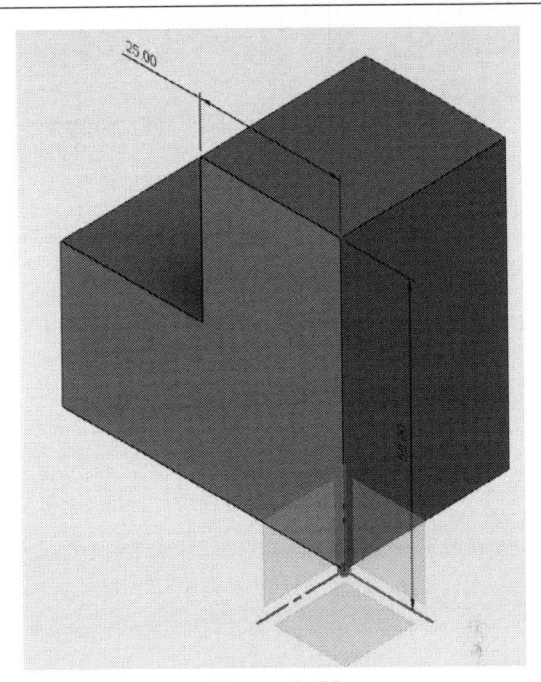

Figure 3–33

5. In the BROWSER, in the **Sketches** folder, right-click on **Sketch1** and select **Hide Dimension**.

Task 5 - Save the design and close the file.

1. In the Application Bar, click ![save icon] to save the design. The Save dialog box opens.

2. In the *Name* field, enter **L_shape**. The *Save to a project in the cloud* field should indicate that it is being saved to the **Autodesk Fusion 360 Practice Files** project, as shown in Figure 3–34.

3. Click **Save** and close the design.

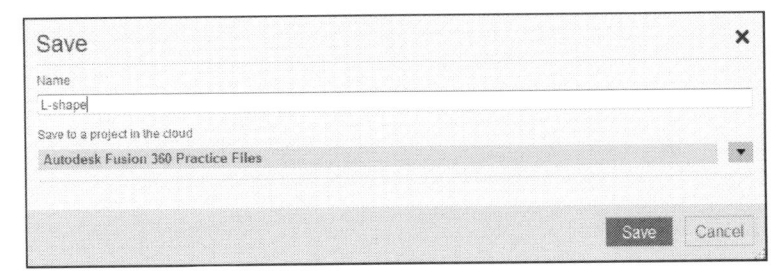

Figure 3–34

Practice 3b

Revolved Solid Features

Practice Objectives

- Create a new design.
- Create a revolved solid feature on an origin plane using a provided dimension and constraint scheme.

In this practice, you will create a new design consisting of a revolved solid feature, as shown in Figure 3–35.

Figure 3–35

Task 1 - Create a new design and set its units to inches.

1. Click ![ ] > **New Design** to create a new design.

2. Hover the cursor over the **Units** node in the BROWSER and click ![ ] (Change Active Units).

3. In the CHANGE ACTIVE UNITS palette, in the *Unit Type* drop-down list, select **Inch**. Click **OK**.

4. In the BROWSER, adjacent to the *Origin* folder, click ![ ] to make the origin features display.

5. Expand the *Origin* folder and select the **XZ** plane.

6. In the SKETCH panel, click ![ ] (Create Sketch).

Task 2 - Sketch a construction line.

1. Sketch a vertical line that starts on and is snapped to the Origin Point.

2. Click a location for the endpoint of the line. Right-click and click **OK** to complete the line.

3. Select the line and click ◁ (Normal/Construction) from the *Contextual Options* section of the SKETCH PALETTE. The line style changes to a dashed style to indicate that this line is now a construction entity. It will be used later as the axis of revolution for the revolved feature.

Press <L> or click (Line) on the SKETCH panel.

Construction entities in a sketch are not considered edges or boundaries of the profile. They are used as reference elements and can be useful in creating the required dimensions and constraints.

Task 3 - Sketch the section.

1. Use the **Line** command to sketch the closed profile shown in Figure 3–36. Begin at the bottom right vertex and sketch the five lines.

You can toggle the display of constraints in the SKETCH PALETTE.

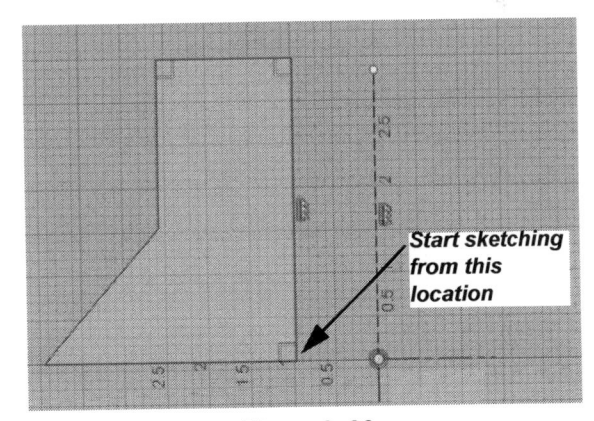

Figure 3–36

2. To complete the command, you can select a new option, right-click and click **OK**, or press <Esc>.

3. Select each of the constraint symbols that were applied automatically and delete them.

4. In the SKETCH PALETTE, click (Coincident constraint).

To delete a constraint, select it and press <Delete>.

You do not always need to delete constraints. Consider if the constraints applied automatically capture your design intent.

5. Select the Origin Point and the bottom line to apply the constraint. This ensures that the bottom line would pass through the Origin Point if it were extended, even if the line is not yet horizontal.

6. Apply additional constraints, as shown in Figure 3–37.

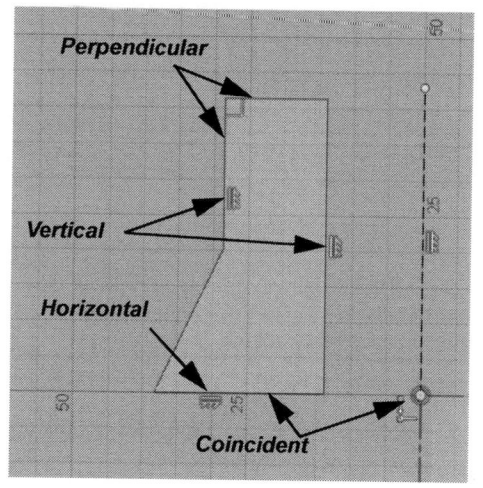

Figure 3–37

7. Click ⊢⊣ (Sketch Dimension) on the SKETCH panel or press <D>.

8. Create the four dimensions shown in Figure 3–38. The angular dimension is created by selecting the two angled lines and placing the dimension between them.

To delete a dimension, select it and press <Delete>.

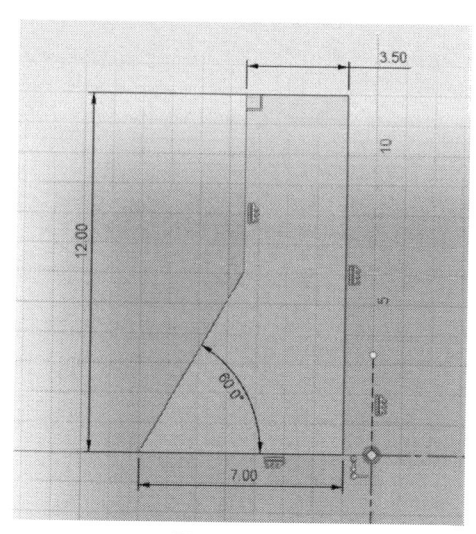

Figure 3–38

When creating this type of diameter dimension, select the entity that represents the axis of revolution first.

If you activate the **Sketch - Color sketch geometry based on constraint status**, all of the sketch entities are black to indicate that they are fully constrained. This option is located in the preferences on the Preview page.

9. The profile needs to be located relative to the construction line created earlier. You will do this with a diameter dimension because this profile will be revolved. Activate the dimension command, if not already active.

10. Click the vertical construction line.

11. Click the vertical line on the right of the closed profile.

12. Before you click to place the dimension, right-click and select **Diameter Dimension**.

13. Select a location to place the dimension and change its value to **3.5**. The sketch should look similar to Figure 3–39.

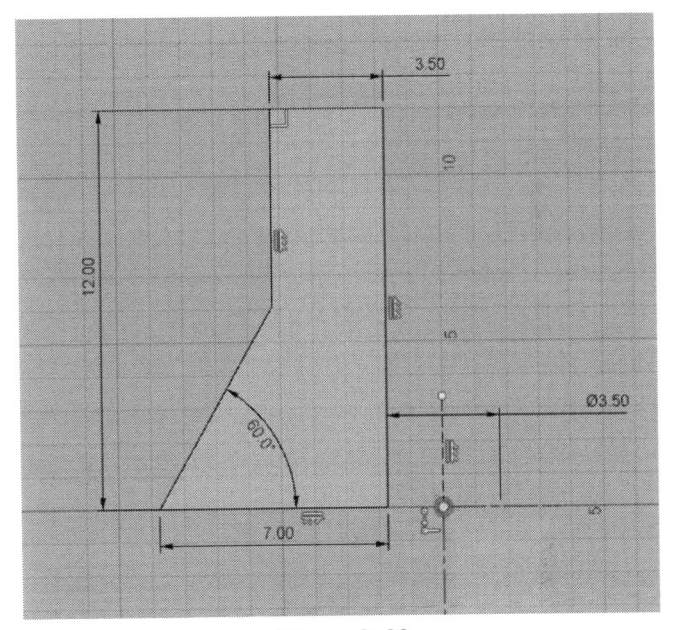

Figure 3–39

14. In the ribbon, click (STOP SKETCH).

15. If the design does not automatically return to its default orientation, move the cursor over the ViewCube and click (Home).

Task 4 - Create a Revolve feature.

1. In the CREATE panel, click (Revolve). Alternatively, right-click in the graphics window and select **Create>Revolve** on the context menu. The REVOLVE palette displays with the **Select** action highlighted for the profile.

2. Select anywhere inside the highlighted area of the profile you just sketched. The area highlights in blue.

3. Next, select the axis of revolution for the profile. In the REVOLVE palette, click inside the *Axis* field to activate it.

4. Select the construction line that was previously sketched as the *Axis* reference for the revolve, as shown in Figure 3–40.

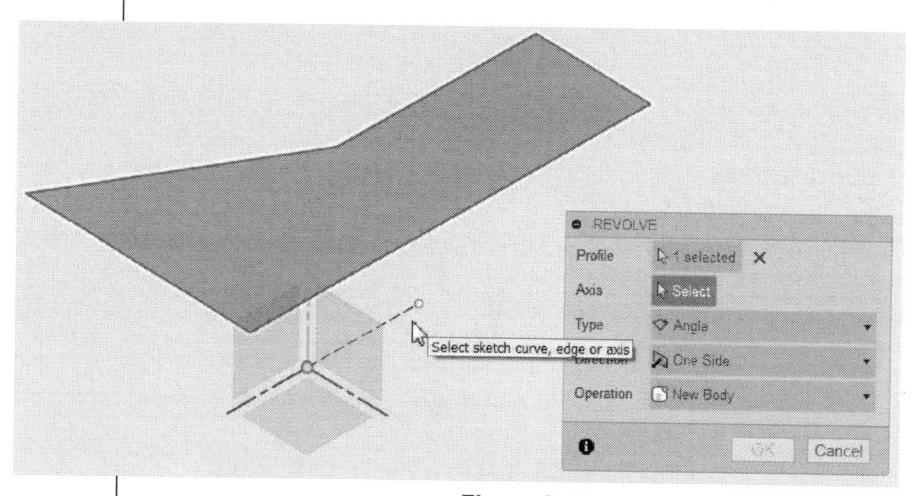

Figure 3–40

5. The revolved geometry is previewed and a blue manipulator handle displays. Select the manipulator handle and drag it. Note that the angular value in the input field updates dynamically as a positive or negative value, depending on the direction you drag the handle.

6. Enter **360** in the input field and click **OK** in the REVOLVE palette. The figure displays as shown in Figure 3–41.

In the BROWSER, you can hide the origin features by clicking 💡 adjacent to the Origin folder.

Figure 3–41

Task 5 - Save the design and close the file.

1. In the Application Bar, click 💾 to save the design.

2. In the Save dialog box, in the *Name* field, Enter **revolve**. The *Save to a project in the cloud* field should indicate that it is being saved to the **Autodesk Fusion 360 Practice Files** project, as shown in Figure 3–42.

3. Click **Save** and close the design.

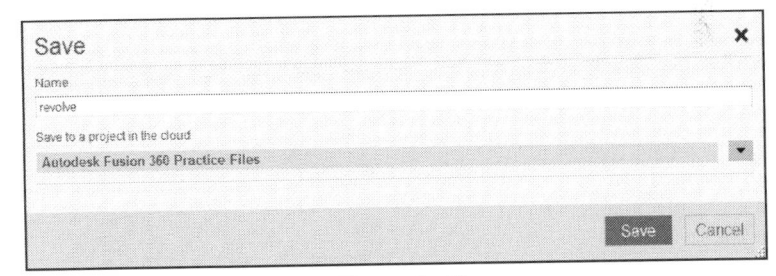

Figure 3–42

Practice 3c

Additional Designs

Practice Objectives

- Create designs with a single solid feature.
- Decide on the best sketching plane.
- Decide the best solid feature type.

In this practice, you will create designs with a single solid feature.

Task 1 - Create a new design and set its units to inches.

1. Create each of the designs shown in Figure 3–43 using either a single solid **Extrude** or **Revolve** feature. As you begin each design, consider which Origin plane to use as the sketch plane in order to obtain the same **Home** view as shown. As you create each sketch, practice assigning an appropriate dimension and constraint scheme.

One of the designs can be created as either an Extrude or a Revolve feature.

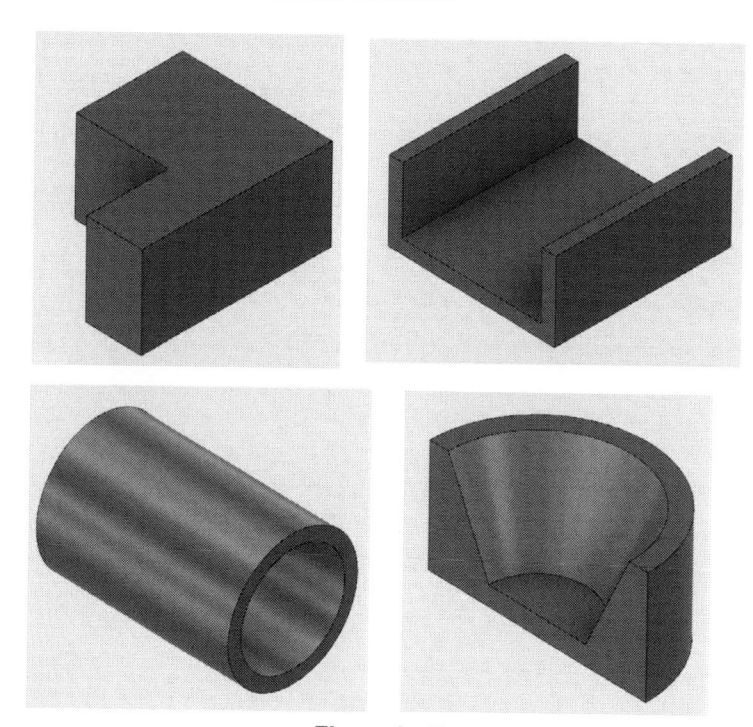

Figure 3–43

Chapter Review Questions

1. Which of the following is required to begin the creation of a new sketch?

    a. Sketch Plane

    b. Sketch References

    c. Constraints

    d. Dimensions

2. An Origin Plane cannot be selected as a sketch plane.

    a. True

    b. False

3. Identify the interface icons in the table below.

    a. Dimension
    b. Line
    c. Extrude
    d. Create Sketch
    e. Change Active Units

Icon	Answer
↶	
⬆	
🗒	
↔	
🗒	

4. Which of the following options opens the EDIT FEATURE palette, which enables you to make a change to an existing feature (such as, flipping the extrusion direction)?

    a. **Edit Sketch**

    b. **Show Dimensions**

    c. **Edit Feature**

    d. **Properties**

5. What options enable you to make changes to the sketch used in creating an Extrude? (Select all that apply.)
   a. **Show Dimension**
   b. **Edit Sketch**
   c. **Edit Feature**
   d. **Edit Profile Sketch**

6. Which of the following can be made equal using the (Equal) constraint? (Select all that apply.)
   a. Angles between lines
   b. Line Lengths
   c. Arc Radii
   d. Circle Diameters

7. Which constraints enable you to create two circles with the same center? (Select all that apply.)
   a. Concentric
   b. Colinear
   c. Coincident
   d. Tangent

8. What is the purpose of using the (Fix) constraint?
   a. To position one point exactly on another.
   b. To edit an existing constraint.
   c. To resolve conflicts among other constraints.
   d. To fix a point relative to the default coordinate system of the sketch.

9. Based on the constraint symbols shown in Figure 3–44, which constraint types are applied to the bottom horizontal entity? (Select all that apply.)

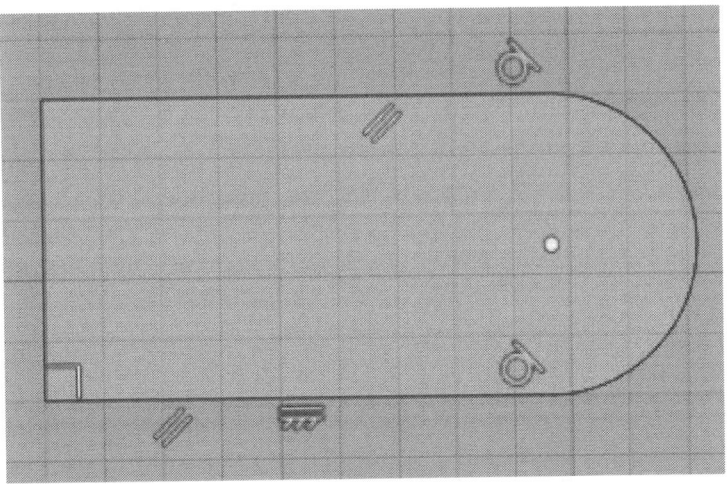

Figure 3–44

    a. Symmetric
    b. Parallel
    c. Perpendicular
    d. Tangent
    e. Collinear
    f. Coincident
    g. Horizontal
    h. Vertical

Answers: 1.a, 2.b, 3.(b,c,e,a,d), 4.c, 5.(b,d), 6.(b,c,d), 7.(a,c), 8.d, 9.(b,c,d,g)

Command Summary

Button	Command	Location
○	2-Point Circle	• **Ribbon:** *Model* Workspace>SKETCH panel • **Context Menu:** Right-click in the graphics window and select **Sketch>Circle**.
▭	2-Point Rectangle	• **Ribbon:** *Model* Workspace>SKETCH panel • **Context Menu:** Right-click in the graphics window and select **Sketch>Rectangle**.
◎	2-Tangent Circle	• **Ribbon:** *Model* Workspace>SKETCH panel • **Context Menu:** Right-click in the graphics window and select **Sketch>Circle**.
⌒	3-Point Arc	• **Ribbon:** *Model* Workspace>SKETCH panel • **Context Menu:** Right-click in the graphics window and select **Sketch>Arc**.
○	3-Point Circle	• **Ribbon:** *Model* Workspace>SKETCH panel • **Context Menu:** Right-click in the graphics window and select **Sketch>Circle**.
◇	3-Point Rectangle	• **Ribbon:** *Model* Workspace>SKETCH panel • **Context Menu:** Right-click in the graphics window and select **Sketch>Rectangle**.
◉	3-Tangent Circle	• **Ribbon:** *Model* Workspace>SKETCH panel • **Context Menu:** Right-click in the graphics window and select **Sketch>Circle**.
⊕	Center Diameter Circle	• **Ribbon:** *Model* Workspace>SKETCH panel • **Context Menu:** Right-click in the graphics window and select **Sketch>Circle**.
⌒	Center Point Arc	• **Ribbon:** *Model* Workspace>SKETCH panel • **Context Menu:** Right-click in the graphics window and select **Sketch>Arc**.
⊡	Center Rectangle	• **Ribbon:** *Model* Workspace>SKETCH panel • **Context Menu:** Right-click in the graphics window and select **Sketch>Rectangle**.
⊥	Coincident Constraint	• SKETCH PALETTE

	Colinear Constraint	• SKETCH PALETTE
	Concentric Constraint	• SKETCH PALETTE
	Create Sketch	• **Ribbon:** *Model* Workspace>SKETCH panel
	Delete	• **Context Menu**: Right-click in the graphics window with the entity or constraint selected. • Press <Delete>
	Equal Constraint	• SKETCH PALETTE
	Extrude	• **Ribbon:** *Model* Workspace>CREATE panel • **Context Menu**: Right-click in the graphics window and select **Create**.
	Fix/UnFix Constraint	• SKETCH PALETTE
	Horizontal/ Vertical Constraint	• SKETCH PALETTE
	Line	• **Ribbon:** *Model* Workspace>SKETCH panel • **Context Menu**: Right-click in the graphics window and select **Sketch**.
	Midpoint Constraint	• SKETCH PALETTE
	Parallel Constraint	• SKETCH PALETTE
	Perpendicular Constraint	• SKETCH PALETTE
	Point	• **Ribbon:** *Model* Workspace>SKETCH panel • **Context Menu**: Right-click in the graphics window and select **Sketch**.
	Revolve	• **Ribbon:** *Model* Workspace>CREATE panel • **Context Menu**: Right-click in the graphics window and select **Create**.
	Sketch Dimension	• **Ribbon:** *Model* Workspace>SKETCH panel • **Context Menu**: Right-click in the graphics window and select **Sketch**.
	Smooth Constraint	• SKETCH PALETTE

	~	Spline	• **Ribbon:** *Model* Workspace>SKETCH panel • **Context Menu:** Right-click in the graphics window and select **Sketch**.
	[¦]	Symmetry Constraint	• SKETCH PALETTE
	⌒	Tangent Arc	• **Ribbon:** *Model* Workspace>SKETCH panel • **Context Menu:** Right-click in the graphics window and select **Sketch>Arc**.
	ᓂ	Tangent Constraint	• SKETCH PALETTE

Chapter 4

Additional Sketching Tools

When creating a sketch, an understanding of all of the available sketched entity types, editing tools, and dimensioning and constraining techniques enables you to create sketches that can be used to create the required solid geometry.

Learning Objectives in this Chapter

- Create 2D sketch entities so that they capture design intent.
- Dimension 2D sketch entities so that they capture design intent.
- Edit existing 2D sketches.
- Move and copy sketch geometry.
- Pattern sketch geometry.

4.1 Additional Entity Types

Beyond lines, rectangles, circles, and arcs, there are additional entity types that you can use in the creation of a sketch.

Polygons

A polygon is defined as a closed shape with at least three straight sides.

Use either of the following methods to start the **Polygon** tool:

- In the SKETCH panel, click **Polygon** and select the appropriate creation type.

- In the graphics window, right-click and select **Sketch>Polygon** from the context menu.

There are three Polygon creation types, shown in Figure 4–1, Figure 4–2, and Figure 4–3:

- (Circumscribed Polygon)

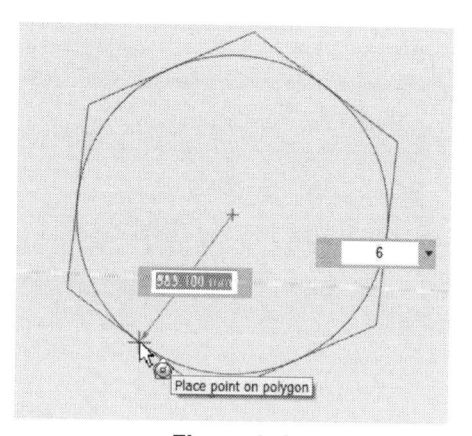

Figure 4–1

- ⊕ (Inscribed Polygon)

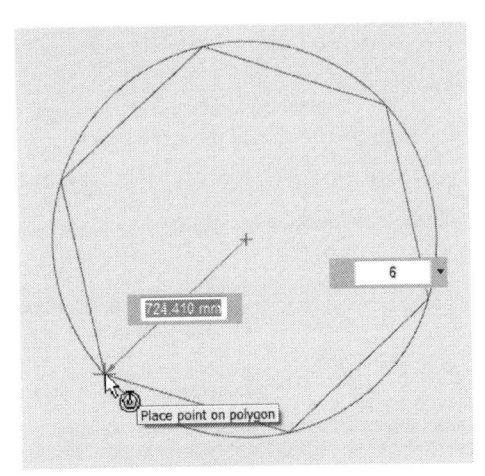

Figure 4–2

- ⌂ (Edge Polygon)

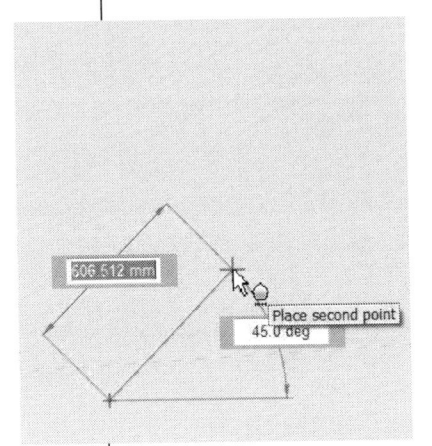

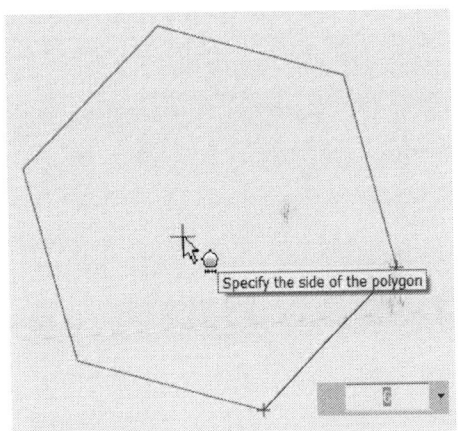

Figure 4–3

Video Lesson Available

Sketching Polygons

Video Length: 3:41

Ellipse

Use the **Ellipse** tool to create a predefined shape, as shown in Figure 4–4.

Construction lines are automatically created along the major and minor axes of the ellipse.

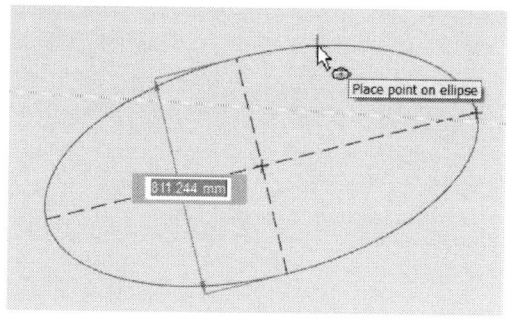

Figure 4–4

Use either of the following methods to start the **Ellipse** tool:

- In the SKETCH panel, click (Ellipse).

- In the graphics window, right-click and select **Sketch>Ellipse** from the context menu.

Video Lesson Available

Sketching an Ellipse

Video Length: 0:57

Slot

Use the **Slot** tool to create a a closed symmetrical shape with two parallel lines enclosed by two arcs of equal radius.

Use either of the following methods to start the **Slot** tool:

- In the SKETCH panel, click **Slot** and select the appropriate creation type.

- In the graphics window, right-click and select **Sketch>Slot** from the context menu.

There are three Slot creation types, shown in Figure 4–5, Figure 4–6, and Figure 4–7:

- ⌬ (Center to Center Slot)

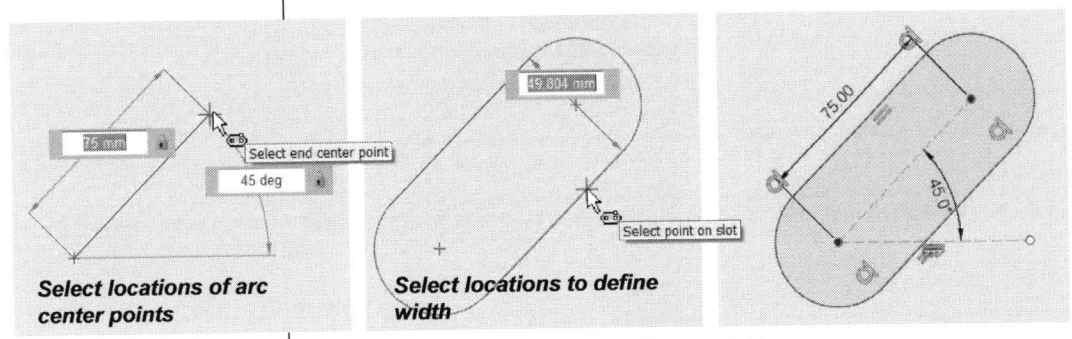

Figure 4–5

- ⌬ (Overall Slot)

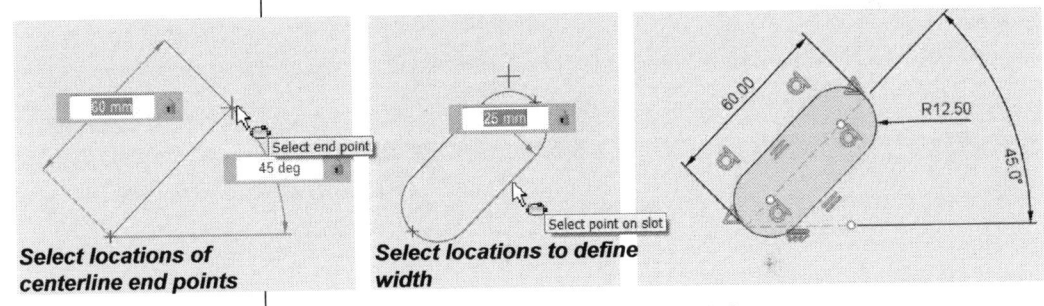

Figure 4–6

- ⌬ (Center Point Slot)

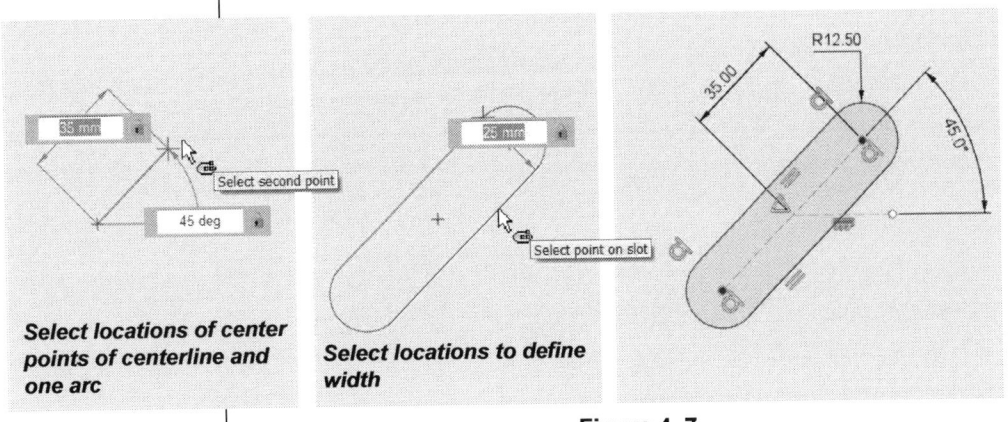

Figure 4–7

Video Lesson Available

Sketching Slots

Video Length: 2:27

Tangent Arc Using a Line

The (Line) tool also enables you to sketch tangent arcs, as shown in Figure 4–8. When locating the endpoint of a line, press and hold the left mouse button and drag the cursor. A tangent arc will extend from the end of the line. After you locate the endpoint of the tangent arc, the next entity reverts back to a line unless you hold the left mouse button down again.

A Tangency constraint is automatically created at the intersection of the line and the arc.

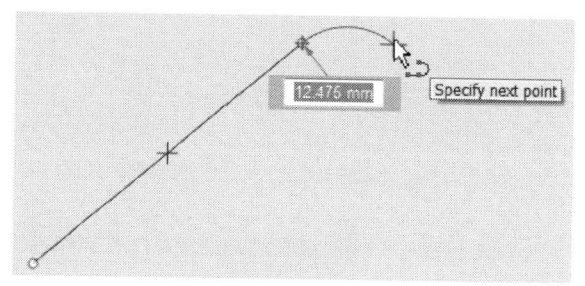

Figure 4–8

Tangent Line Between Two Circles or Arcs

To sketch a line that is tangent to two circles or arcs:

1. Start the (Line) tool.
2. Click and hold the cursor over one of the circles or arcs.
3. While holding the left mouse button, drag the cursor to the next circle until the Tangent constraint displays.
4. Release the mouse button to locate the tangent line, as shown in Figure 4–9.

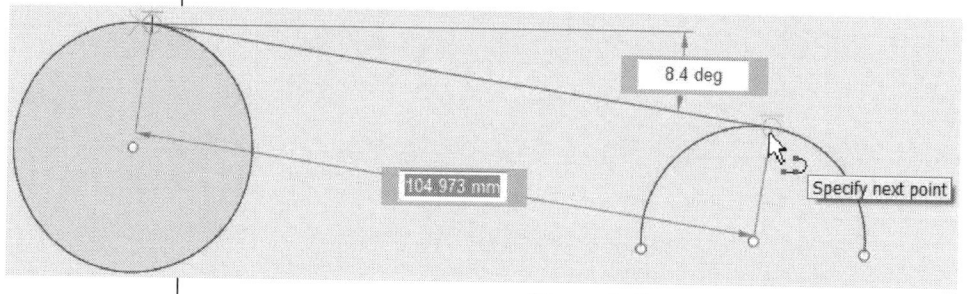

Figure 4–9

Fillets

The (Fillet) command enables you to modify the intersection of two lines in a 2D sketch, as shown in Figure 4–10. The fillet rounds corners in a sketch by placing an arc at the intersection of two lines. The fillet arc is always tangent to the intersecting entities.

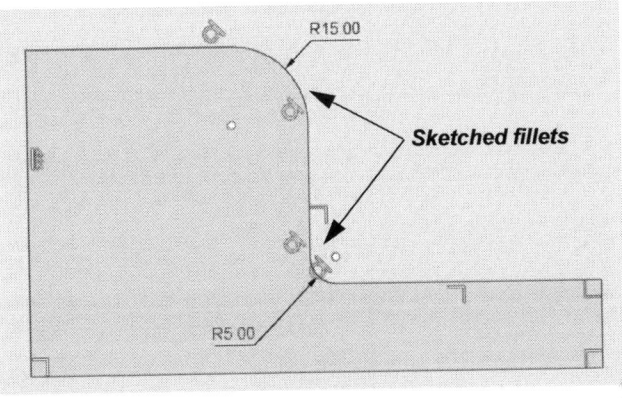

Figure 4–10

Use the following steps, to create a fillet:

1. In the SKETCH panel, click (Fillet). Alternatively, in the graphics window, right-click and select **Fillet**.
2. Select the lines or arcs between which the fillet will be created or click directly on the intersection point to create the fillet. The dimension is added to the fillet arc and Tangency constraints are applied.

To create multiple fillets that are driven with the same dimension value, continue to select vertices prior to entering the value for the fillet.

Features versus 2D Sketched Entities

When modeling a design, you can include fillets in your 2D sketches or create them as separate fillet features. Consider the following:

- Separate fillet features can be deleted, modified, and suppressed without needing to access the original sketch.

- If you need to change the edges selected for fillets or chamfers, you can easily edit the feature and select the edges you want to add or remove from the feature.

- A design is more robust and easier to modify if fillets are created as separate features, rather then as part of the sketch.

Construction Entities

Construction entities are used as references and aid in sketching. They do not create solid geometry as they are not considered to be a boundary of the resulting profile. It is common to use construction lines when sketching to indicate that arcs or circles lie along the same line or to indicate the midpoint of a line.

To create a construction entity:

1. Select a entity in the sketch.

2. In the SKETCH PALETTE, click (Normal/Construction) to convert it to a construction entity. Alternatively, in the graphics window, right-click and select **Normal/Construction**, or press <X>.

Construction entities are dashed and you can add dimensions and constraints to them. An example of construction entities used as dimension and constraint references is shown in Figure 4–11.

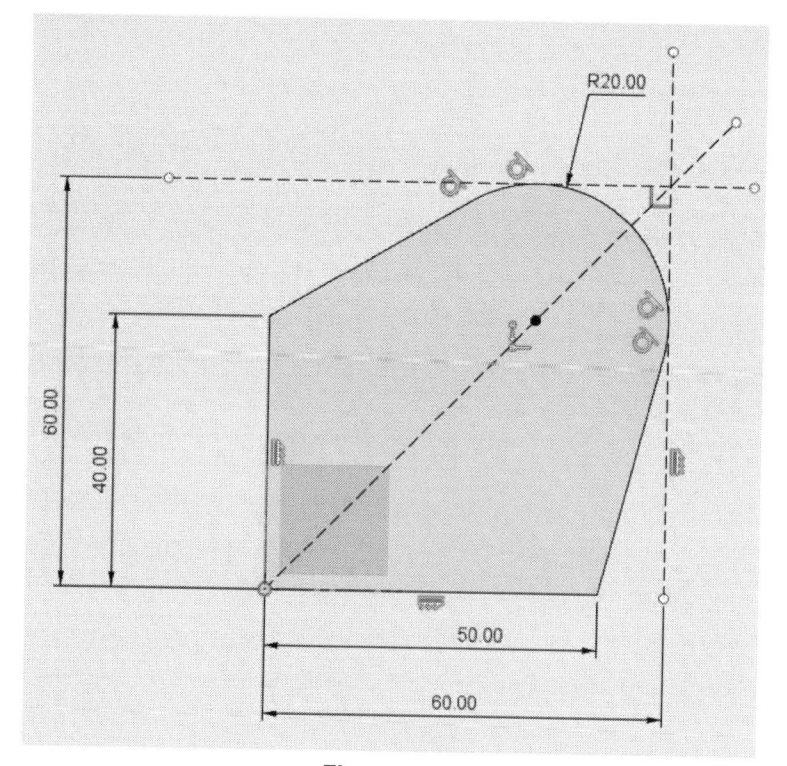

Figure 4–11

4.2 Editing Tools

Available on the SKETCH panel, the **Trim**, **Extend**, and **Mirror** editing tools provide basic editing commands that you can use to modify sketch entities.

Trim

Trim removes a segment of an entity to the nearest intersection in each direction from the selected point. The selected portion of an object (e.g., lines or arcs) is removed, as shown in Figure 4–12. Selecting an object without an intersection deletes the object.

Use any of the following methods to start the **Trim** command:

- In the SKETCH panel, click (Trim).
- In the graphics window, right-click and select **Sketch>Trim** from the context menu.
- Press <T>.

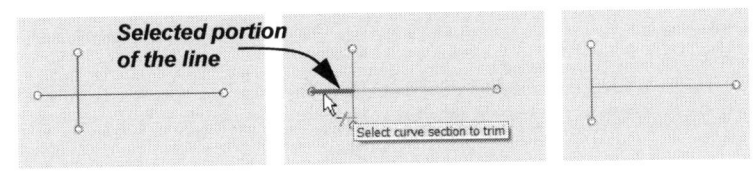

Figure 4–12

Extend

Extend continues an entity to meet the next entity in its path or to close an open sketch, as shown in Figure 4–13.

Use either of the following methods to start the **Extend** command:

- In the SKETCH panel, click (Extend).
- In the graphics window, right-click and select **Sketch>Trim** from the context menu.

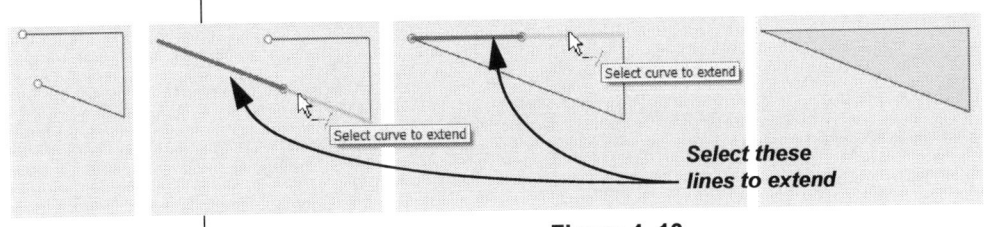

Figure 4–13

Mirror

Mirroring enables you to quickly create a mirror image of a selected image using a mirror line. The mirror line can be a:

- Part of the geometry that is selected to mirror
- Projected Origin feature
- Projected edge from other geometry
- Straight sketched or construction line

The sketch shown in Figure 4–14 is created using the (Mirror) sketch tool and a construction line as the mirror line.

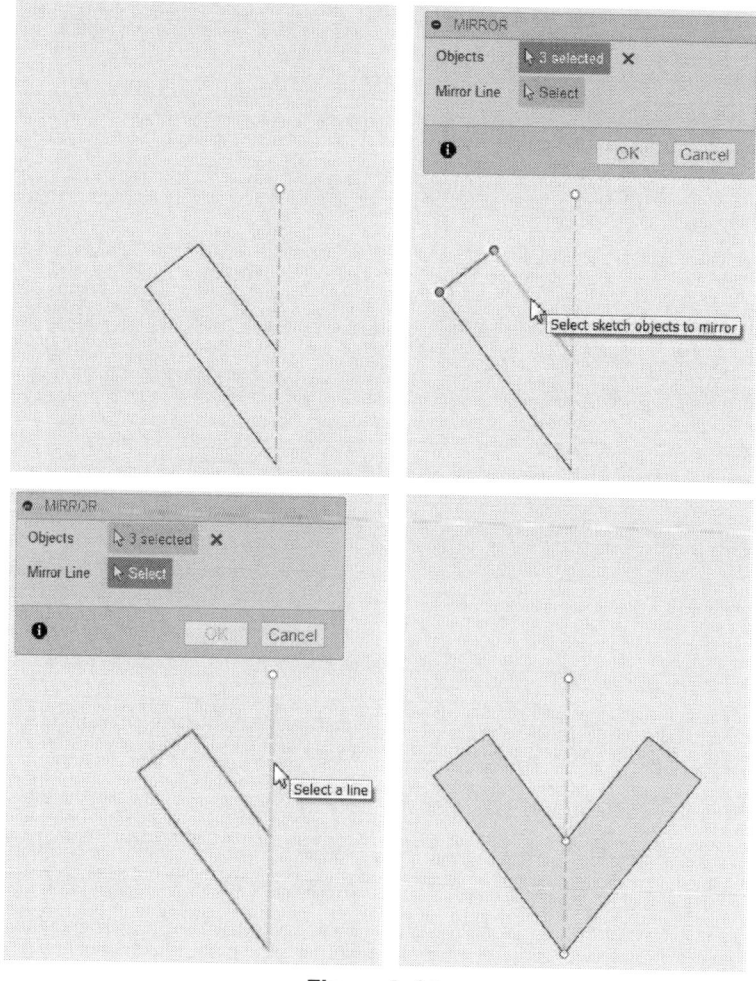

Figure 4–14

To mirror entities:

1. In the SKETCH panel, click (Mirror). Alternatively, in the graphics window, right-click and select **Sketch>Mirror**.
2. Select the sketch entities that you want to mirror.
3. Activate the *Mirror Line* field and select a mirror line reference to mirror about.
4. Click **OK** to mirror the selected entities.

Video Lesson Available

Editing Sketch Geometry

Video Length: 6:51

Sketch Scale

You can scale the size of sketch entities up or down. To do this, select one or more sketch entities and then in the SKETCH panel, click (Sketch Scale). Alternatively, select one or more sketch entities, right-click in the graphics window, and then select **Sketch > Sketch Scale**.

In the sketch shown in Figure 4–15, the circle has been selected to scale and the center of the circle was selected as the scaling point. The circle has been scaled to 1.25 times its original size.

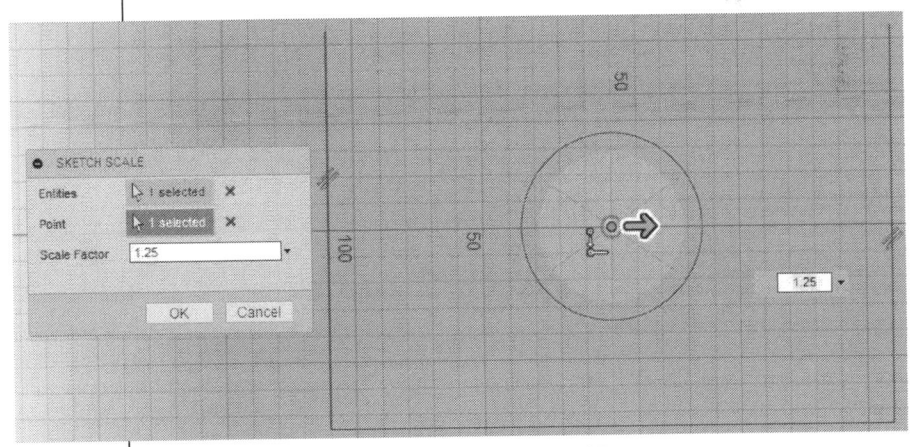

Figure 4–15

© 2016, ASCENT - Center for Technical Knowledge®

4.3 Additional Dimension Tools

You can also press <D> to start dimensioning.

Linear dimensions can be placed using the ⊢⊣ (Sketch Dimension) tool and clicking to select entities and place the dimensions. The type of dimension created depends on whether you select an entity or the points related to the entity. The following are additional types of dimensions that can be placed on a sketch once the dimensioning command is active.

Center Dimensions

To create center dimensions, select two entities to dimension the distance between circles and arcs. Move the cursor to the required location, right-click to select the dimension type, and then click to place the dimension. The different methods for dimensioning the linear entities shown in Figure 4–16 are as follows:

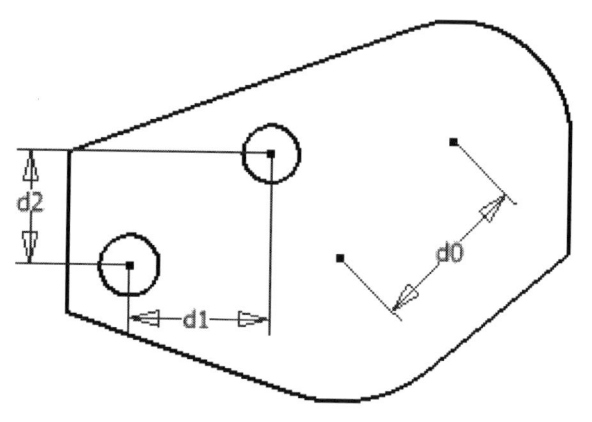

Figure 4–16

To place dimension d0	Select the centers of the arcs. Position the cursor in the location in which you want to place the dimension, right-click, and select **Aligned**. Alternatively, place the dimension at a location between the two centers.
To place dimensions d1 and d2	Select the centers of the circles or circular entities. Position the cursor in the location at which you want to place the dimension and click the left mouse button.

Radius or Diameter Dimensions

To create radius or diameter dimensions, select an arc or circle, position the cursor at the location in which you want to place the dimension and click the left mouse button. By default, the dimension type created for arcs is radius, and the dimension type for circles is diameter, as shown in Figure 4–17.

To delete a dimension, right-click on the dimension and select (Delete).

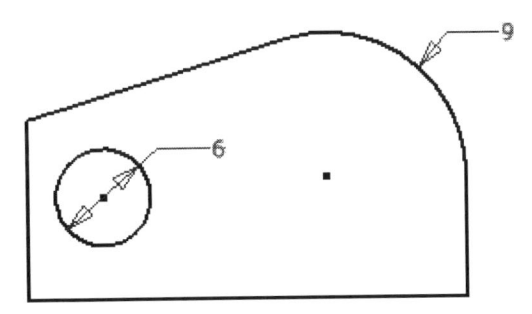

Figure 4–17

To change the type of dimensions, right-click and select **Radius** or **Diameter** before placing the dimension. Position the cursor at the location at which you want to place the dimension and click the left mouse button.

Angular Dimensions

To create angular dimensions, select lines A and B and place the angular dimension by clicking the left mouse button. The resulting angle is dependent on the placement location of the dimension, as shown in Figure 4–18. Alternatively, you can create an angular dimension by selecting three points.

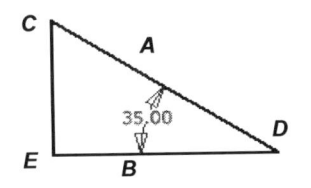

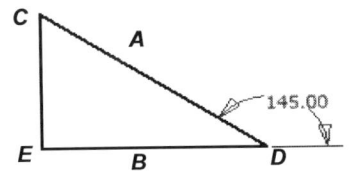

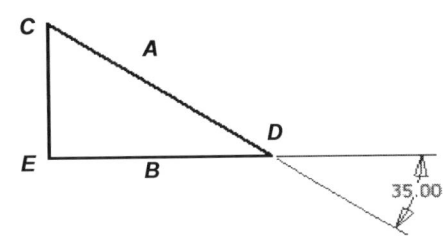

Figure 4–18

Over-Constrained Sketches

If you try to apply a dimension that is going to over-constrain the sketch, the dialog box shown in Figure 4–19 displays. You can cancel the command or place the dimension as a driven dimension. Driven dimensions are displayed in parentheses, as shown in Figure 4–19. You cannot modify a driven dimension, but they update automatically if other dimensions are changed.

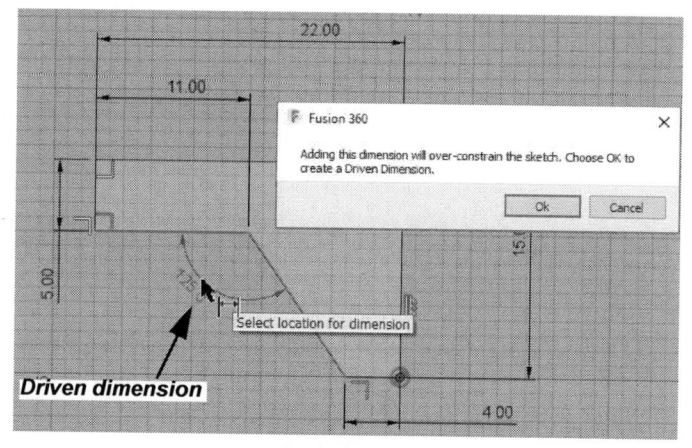

Figure 4–19

If you encounter an over-dimensioned sketch, keep the dimension that best suits the design intent.

4.4 Moving and Copying

Move

You can move one or more entities in a sketch by selecting them and dragging them with the cursor. If you need more precision, you can use the **Move** command. There are several ways to start the MOVE command:

- In the MODIFY panel, click (Move).

- In the graphics window, right-click and select **Modify>Move** from the context menu.

- Press <M>.

You can also select the entities first and then select .

After you select one or more entities, the MOVE palette opens and manipulators display on the sketch, as shown in Figure 4–20.

*The location of the manipulators defaults to the center or mid point of the first entity selected. You can change this in the MOVE palette using the **Set Point** option.*

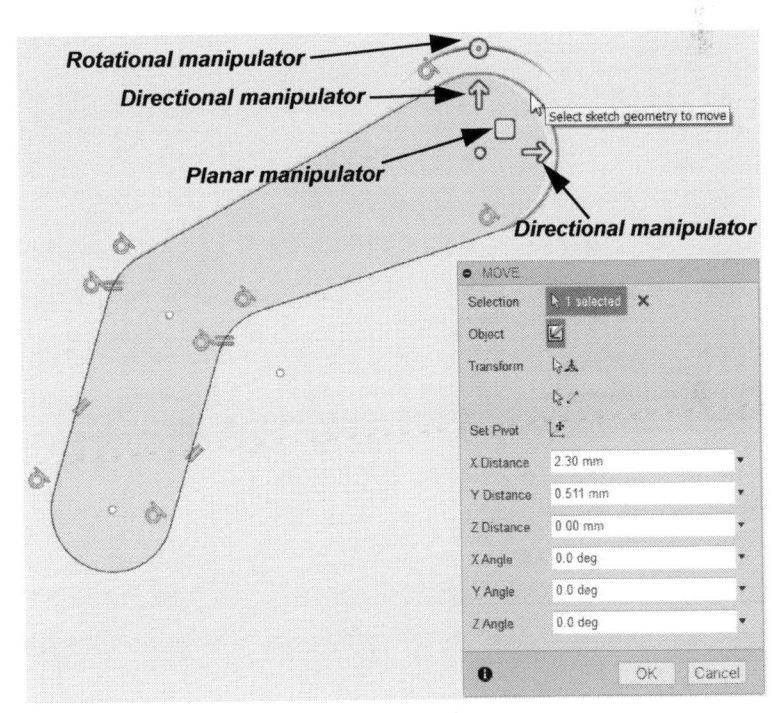

Figure 4–20

- Selecting a directional manipulator enables you to drag the selected entities in that direction. As you drag, the conditions of the current constraints and dimensions are maintained. A dynamic input field displays enabling you to enter a precise translational value.

- Selecting the planar manipulator enables you to drag the selected entities in any direction within the sketch plane. Dynamic input fields display enabling you to enter precise translational values.

- Selecting the rotational manipulator enables you to drag the selected entities through an angle. As you drag, some constraints might be removed. A dynamic input field displays enabling you to enter a precise angular value.

Copy and Paste

The standard keyboard driven **Copy** and **Paste** commands can be used to copy sketch entities within the same sketch, to a different sketch in the same design, or to a sketch in a different design.

- **Copy:** Right-click and select **Copy**, or press <Ctrl>+<C>.
- **Paste:** Right-click and select **Paste**, or press <Ctrl>+<P>.

To copy, select the source entities and initiate the **Copy** command. Within the same sketch or a sketch in the same design, initiate the **Paste** command. The entities will be pasted with the same controls as the **Move** tool, enabling you to position them in the current sketch.

If you are pasting into the sketch of a different design, you must first pick a reference in the target sketch (i.e., a point, a vertex, or the Origin Point), and then paste the entities.

4.5 Rectangular Sketch Patterns

Patterning enables you to quickly create identical entities in your sketch. The array of circles shown in Figure 4–21 is patterned horizontally and vertically using a rectangular sketch pattern.

Sketched patterns should only be used when absolutely necessary. Where possible, it is better to create a feature pattern. Sketched patterns are less robust and harder to modify. They can also make sketches very large and difficult to work with.

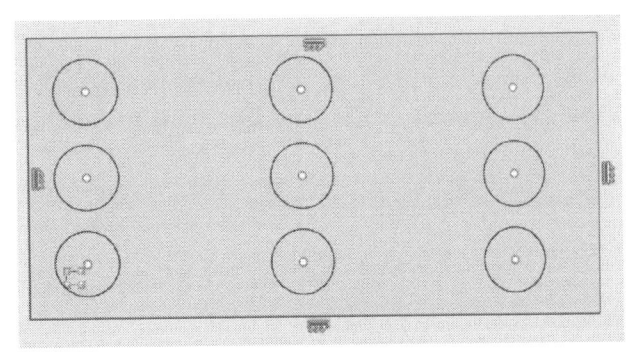

Figure 4–21

Use the following steps to create a rectangular sketch pattern:

1. In the SKETCH panel, click (Rectangular Pattern). Alternatively, in the graphics window, right-click and select **Sketch>Rectangular Pattern**.
2. Select the entities to pattern.
3. The default directions for the pattern will be horizontal and vertical, relative to the current sketch orientation. If you want to pattern in a different direction, activate the *Direction/s* field and select a line to define the rectangular directions. The pattern is created normal and parallel to the reference you select.
4. Use the manipulator arrows and the RECTANGULAR PATTERN palette to control the quantity and spacing of the pattern instances.

   - You can set the *Distance Type* to (Extent) or (Spacing). With **Extent**, you specify the total distance for the pattern in a direction, and the quantity of instances are spaced equally over that distance. With **Spacing**, you specify the equal distance between each instance a that direction.
   - The **Suppress** checkbox controls whether individual instances in the pattern can be removed.

- *Quantity* and *Distance* are defined for each direction, as shown in Figure 4–22. If the pattern should only go in one direction, enter **0** for the other direction.

- The *Direction Type* can be set to (One Direction) or (Symmetric), as shown in Figure 4–22. With **One Direction**, the number of instances of the pattern are generated in one direction from the original. With **Symmetric**, the quantity of instances of the pattern are generated symmetrically on both sides of the original.

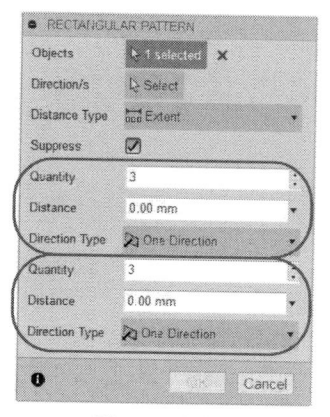

Figure 4–22

The geometry shown in Figure 4–23 is patterned in two directions.

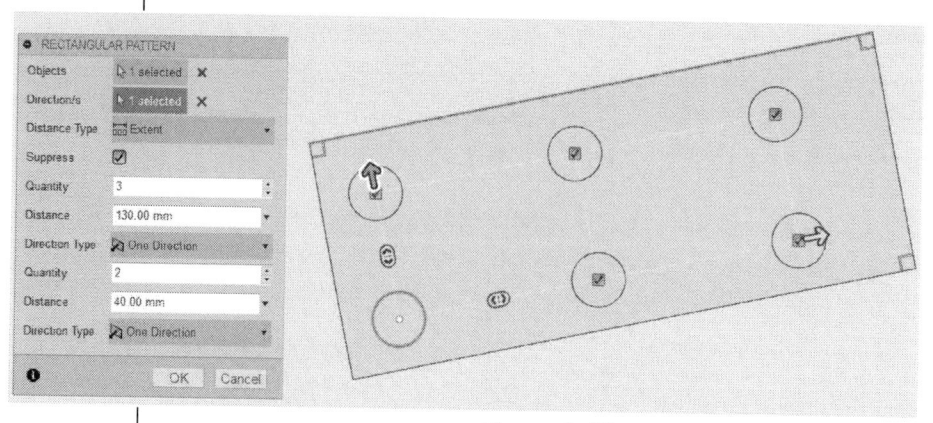

Figure 4–23

To edit the pattern and change the number of instances or the spacing, double-click on adjacent to the pattern entities. The RECTANGULAR PATTERN palette displays, enabling you to edit the values.

4.6 Circular Sketch Patterns

A circular pattern is created similarly to a rectangular pattern, except the pattern direction is axial rather than linear, as shown in Figure 4–24.

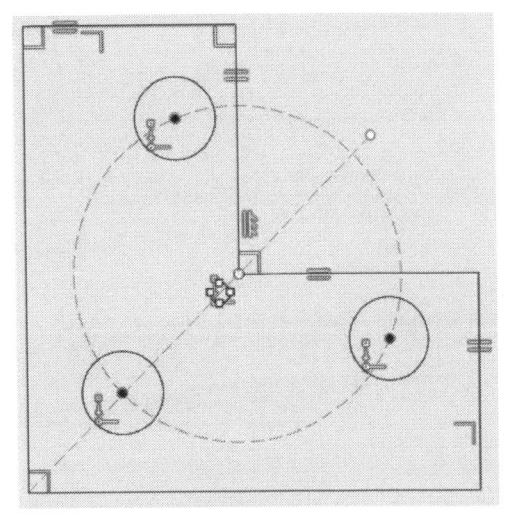

Figure 4–24

Use the following steps to create a rectangular sketch pattern:

1. In the SKETCH panel, click (Circular Pattern). Alternatively, in the graphics window, right-click and select **Sketch>Rectangular Pattern**.
2. Select the entities to pattern.
3. In the CIRCULAR PATTERN palette, click in the *Center Point* field to activate it. Select a point, a vertex, or the Origin Point as the axis for the circular pattern.
4. Use the manipulator handle and the CIRCULAR PATTERN palette to control the quantity and spacing of the pattern instances.

- The *Type* can be set to (Full), (Angle), or (Symmetric):
  - **Full:** The number of instances of the pattern are generated along a full circle, equally spaced.
  - **Angle:** Specify an arc angle through which the number of instances of the pattern are generated, equally spaced.
  - **Symmetric:** The number of instances of the pattern are generated symmetrically on both sides of the original entity through the total angle specified.

The geometry shown in Figure 4–25 is patterned using the values shown in the CIRCULAR PATTERN palette.

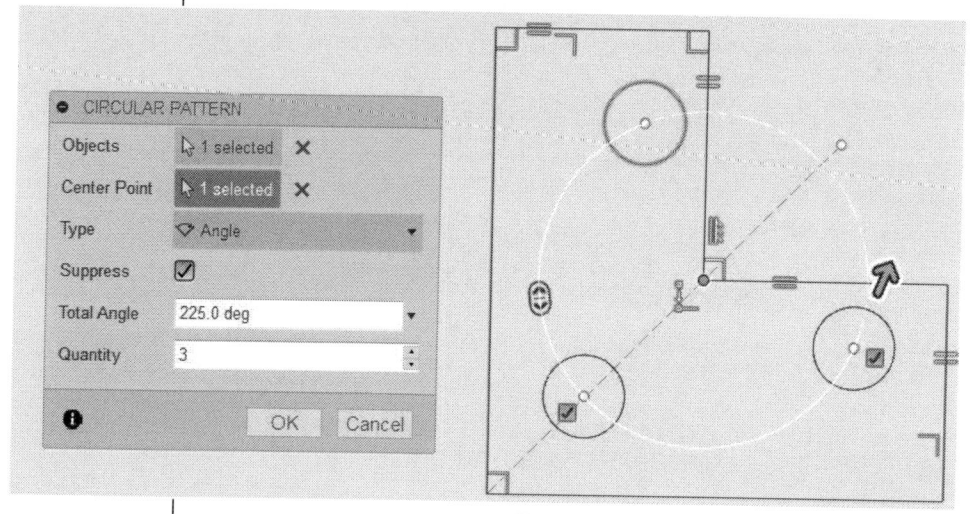

Figure 4–25

To edit the pattern and change the number of instances or spacing, double-click on ✥ adjacent to the pattern entities. The CIRCULAR PATTERN palette displays, enabling you to edit the values.

Video Lesson Available

Creating Sketch Patterns

Video Length: 7:49

Practice 4a

Applying Constraints

Practice Objectives

- Open an existing design and edit its sketch.
- Add constraints to the sketch.
- Add dimensions to ensure that the sketch is fully constrained.
- Create an extrude from the sketch.

In this practice, you will apply constraints to define the shape of the sketched geometry shown in Figure 4–26. You will also use dimensions to fully constrain the geometry.

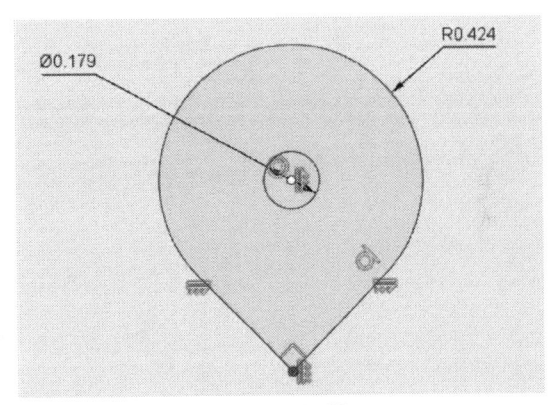

Figure 4–26

Task 1 - Create a new design from a file.

1. Click (File) > **New Design from File**.
2. In the Open dialog box, navigate to the *C:\Autodesk Fusion 360 Practice Files* folder, select **constraints_1.f3d**, and click **Open**. The design displays as shown in Figure 4–27.

*To toggle off the display of the grid, in the Navigation Bar, expand (Grid and Snaps) and clear the **Layout Grid** option.*

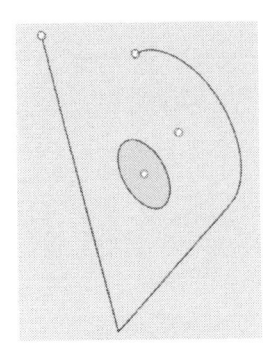

Figure 4–27

3. In the BROWSER, expand the *Sketches* folder.

4. Right-click on **Sketch1** and click **Edit Sketch**. Note that there are no dimensions or constraints applied to the sketch.

Task 2 - Apply constraints.

1. In the BROWSER, adjacent to the *Origin* folder, click 💡 to toggle on the visibility of the origin features.

2. In the SKETCH PALETTE, click (Coincident Constraint). Select the Origin Point and the bottom vertex on the sketched geometry, as shown in Figure 4–28. The sketch displays as shown in Figure 4–29.

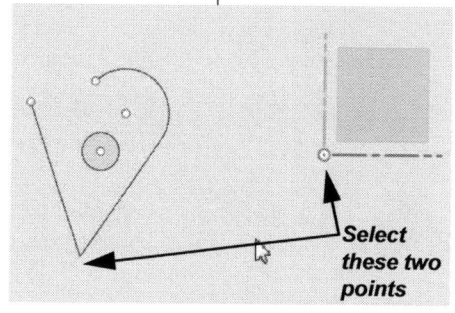

Figure 4–28

Figure 4–29

3. Click 💡 again to toggle off the visibility of the origin features.

4. In the SKETCH PALETTE, click (Horizontal/Vertical Constraint). Select the center point of the arc and the bottom vertex on the sketched geometry, as shown in Figure 4–30. The sketch displays as shown in Figure 4–31.

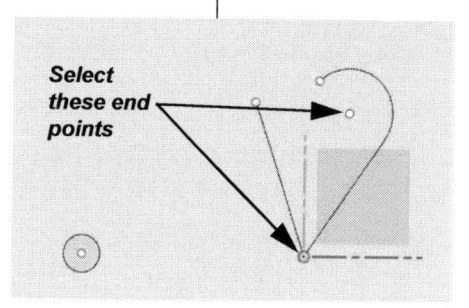

Figure 4–30

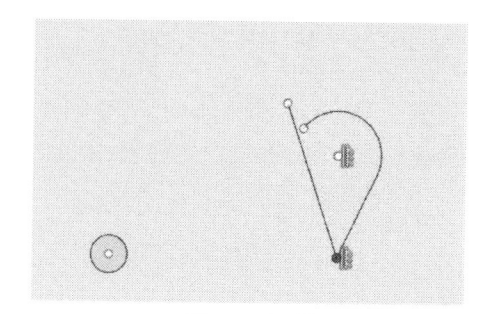

Figure 4–31

5. In the SKETCH PALETTE, click ⌐ (Coincident Constraint) and select the end points of the arc and line, as shown in Figure 4–32. The sketch displays as shown in Figure 4–33.

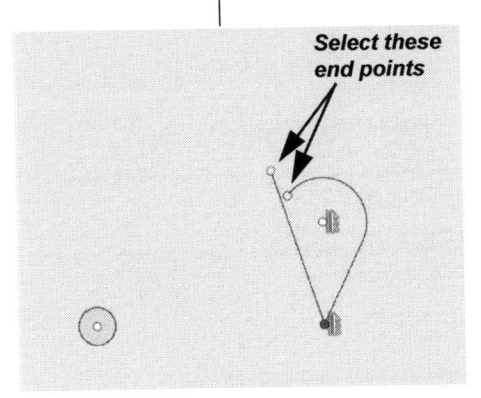

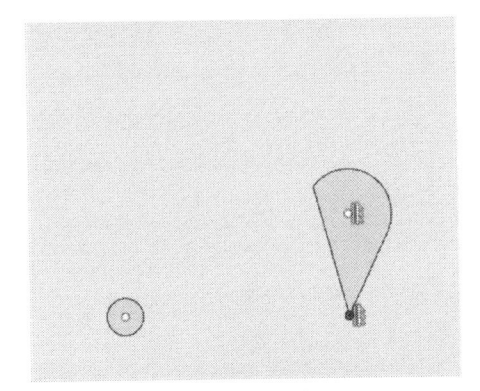

Select these end points

Figure 4–32   Figure 4–33

6. Apply a (Horizontal/Vertical) constraint to the two end points of the arc. The result should display as shown in Figure 4–34.

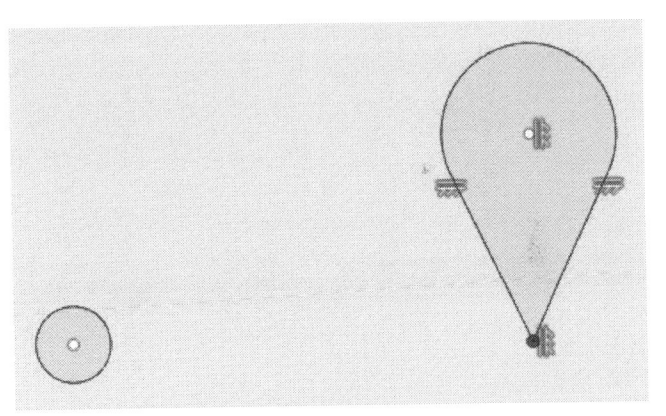

Figure 4–34

7. Click (Tangent Constraint) and select the arc and line on the right side of the sketch.

8. Click ✓ (Perpendicular Constraint) and select the two lines. The sketch displays as shown in Figure 4–35.

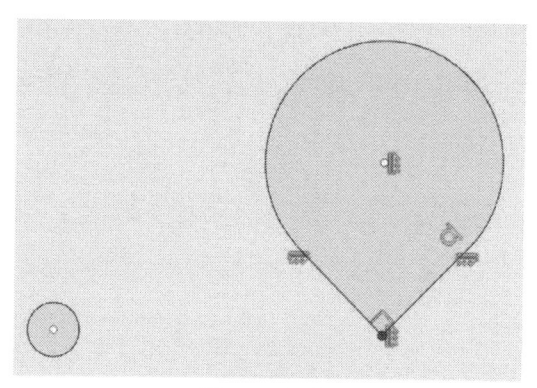

Figure 4–35

9. Click ◎ (Concentric Constraint) and select the center points of the circle and arc. The sketch displays as shown in Figure 4–36.

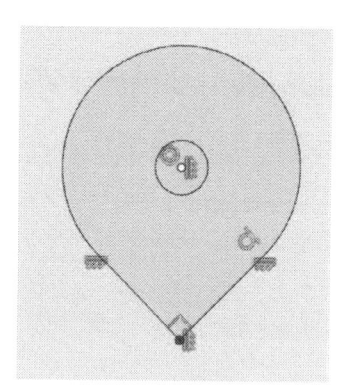

Figure 4–36

Task 3 - Dimension the sketch.

The shape of the sketched geometry is defined, but some of the geometry is not fully constrained.

1. Click ⊢⊣ (Dimension), or press <D>.

2. Select the circle and place a diameter dimension by clicking the left mouse button. Change its value to **0.179**.

3. Select the arc and place a radius dimension. Change its value to **0.424**.

4. Select each dimension and drag them to the locations shown in Figure 4–37.

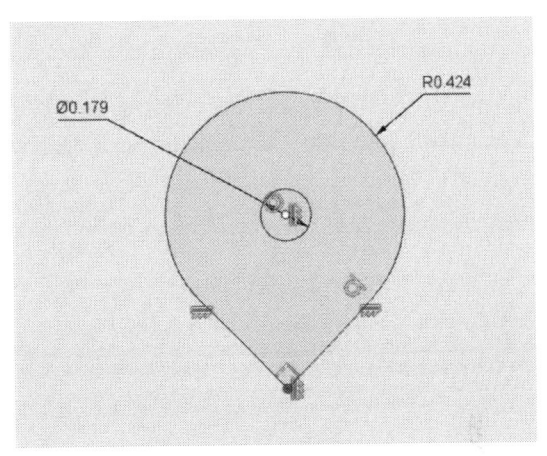

Figure 4–37

5. In the ribbon, click (Stop Sketch).

Task 4 - Set the workspace to Model.

1. Move the cursor over the ViewCube and click (Home) to return to the design to its default 3D orientation.

2. The current workspace is set to SCULPT, as that is the default. In the ribbon, select **SCULPT** to access the workspace menu and select **MODEL**.

3. To change the default workspace, click on your display name in the top right corner of the software and select **Preferences**.

4. In the left panel, select the **Design** page.

5. In the *Default Workspace* drop-down menu, select **Model**.

6. Click **OK** to apply the changes.

Task 5 - Create a solid extrude.

1. In the CREATE panel, click (Extrude).
2. Click on the profile between the arc and the circle so that the selection displays as shown in Figure 4–38.

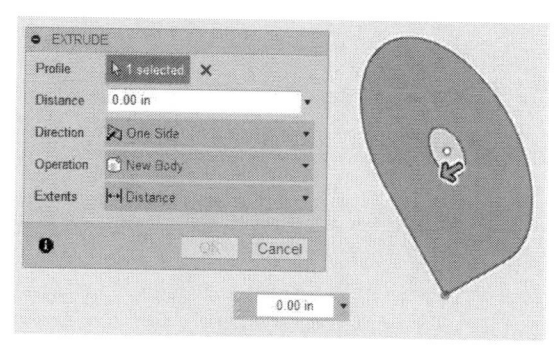

Figure 4–38

3. Drag the manipulator handle to a distance of **0.5 in**.
4. Click **OK**. The design should display as shown in Figure 4–39.

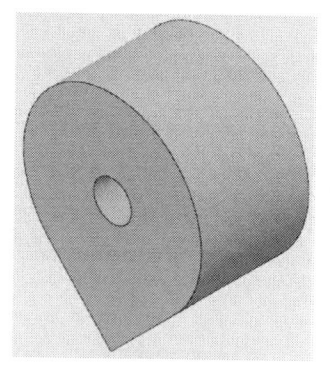

Figure 4–39

5. In the Application Bar, click to save the design.
6. Enter **constraints_1** as the name and ensure that the selected project to save to is **Autodesk Fusion 360 Practice Files**.
7. Click **Save**.
8. Close the file.

Multiple profiles can be selected when creating an extrude. For example, the small hole could also be selected to create a solid extrusion.

Practice 4b

Creating Sketched Geometry I

Practice Objectives

- Sketch, dimension, and constrain entities to fully constrain a sketch.
- Toggle between Driven and Driving dimension settings.

In this practice, you will create sketch geometry in a new design. The sketched geometry that you will create is shown in Figure 4–40.

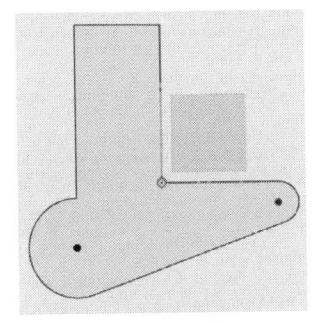

Figure 4–40

Task 1 - Create a new design and create a sketch.

1. Click ▬▾ > **New Design** to create a new design.
2. Toggle on the display of the origin features.
3. In the BROWSER, expand the *Origin* folder. Right-click on plane **XY** and select (Create Sketch).

Task 2 - Sketch the section.

1. Start the **Line** command by pressing <L>.

2. Sketch the five linear entities as shown in Figure 4–41. Begin at the Origin Point so that the beginning of the vertical line is coincident with the projected Center Point. Sketch the first vertical line (shown in Figure 4–41) so that it is approximately **40 mm** to determine the overall scale of the sketch.

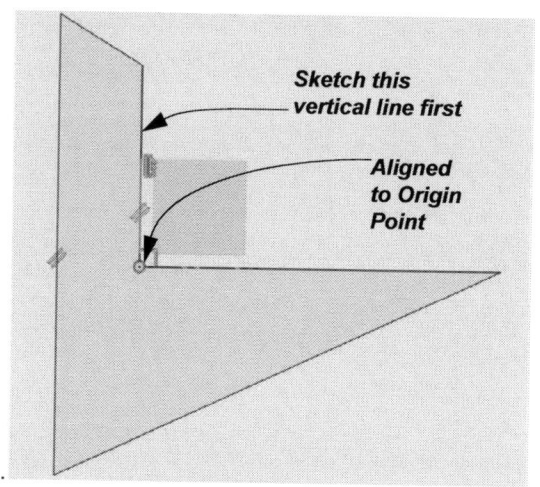

Sketch this vertical line first
Aligned to Origin Point

Figure 4–41

3. In the SKETCH panel, click (Fillet).

4. Select the two lines shown in Figure 4–42. Drag the blue manipulator handle toward the intersection of the two lines until **5.00 mm** displays in the dynamic input field. Press <Enter>. A fillet arc is created and the two lines are automatically trimmed.

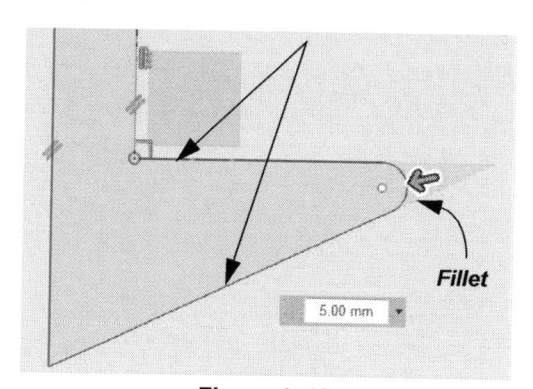

Fillet

Figure 4–42

5. In the SKETCH panel, click **Arc >** (3-Point Arc).

6. Select the vertex and edge shown in Figure 4–43 to locate the arc. Drag the edge of the arc to the location shown to define the size of the arc. Drag the arc to a size that does not apply a tangency constraint at either end point of the arc.

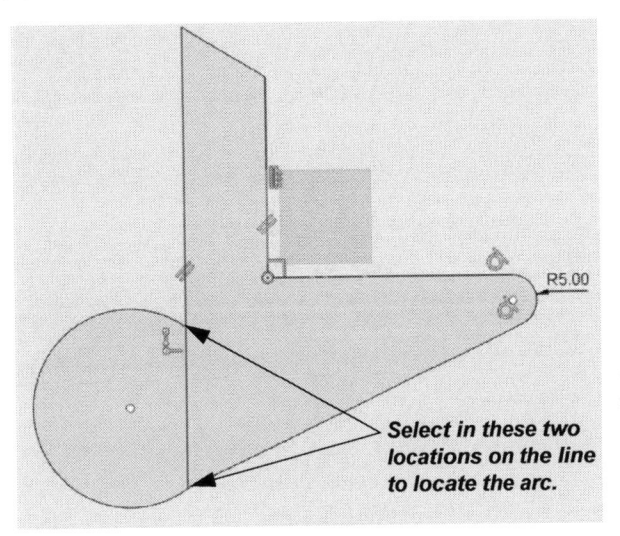

Figure 4–43

7. In the SKETCH PALETTE, click to apply a Coincident constraint to the center of the arc and the left vertical line, as shown in Figure 4–44.

When sketching the arc, if tangency is assumed with the vertex, assigning the Coincident constraint changes the shape of the geometry to maintain both constraint requirements. Display the constraint, delete the Tangent constraint, and then assign the Coincident constraint.

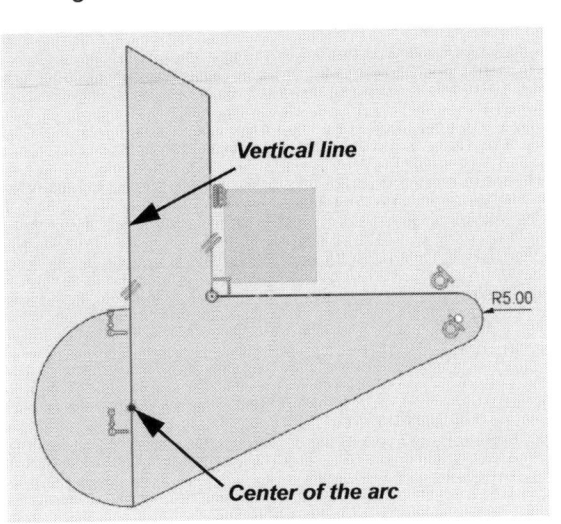

Figure 4–44

8. In the SKETCH panel, click (Trim). Alternatively, press <T> to start the **Trim** command.

9. Trim the inner intersection of the arc with the left vertical line by selecting it. The sketch displays as shown in Figure 4–45.

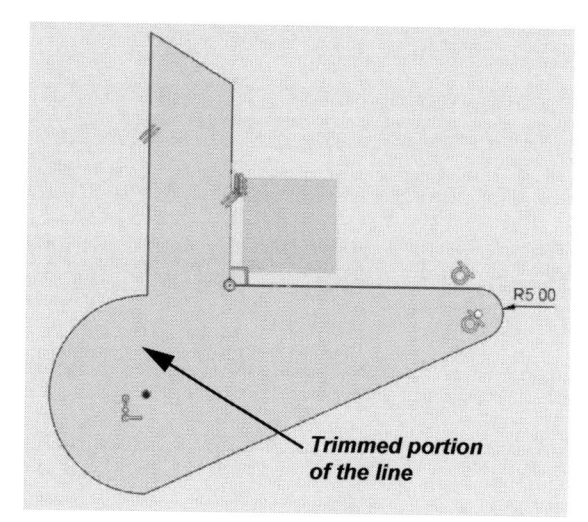

Trimmed portion of the line

Figure 4–45

10. In the SKETCH PALETTE, click (Tangent Constraint) and select the arc and line shown in Figure 4–46.

Select these two entities

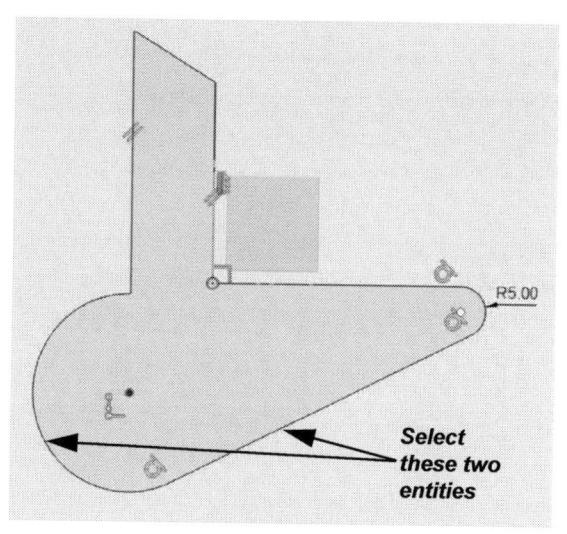

Figure 4–46

*To apply the 25 unit dimension, select the entity. Before placement, right-click and select **Aligned**. Place the dimension by clicking at that point.*

11. In the SKETCH panel, click (Dimension) or press <D>.

12. Add and modify the dimensions as shown in Figure 4–47.

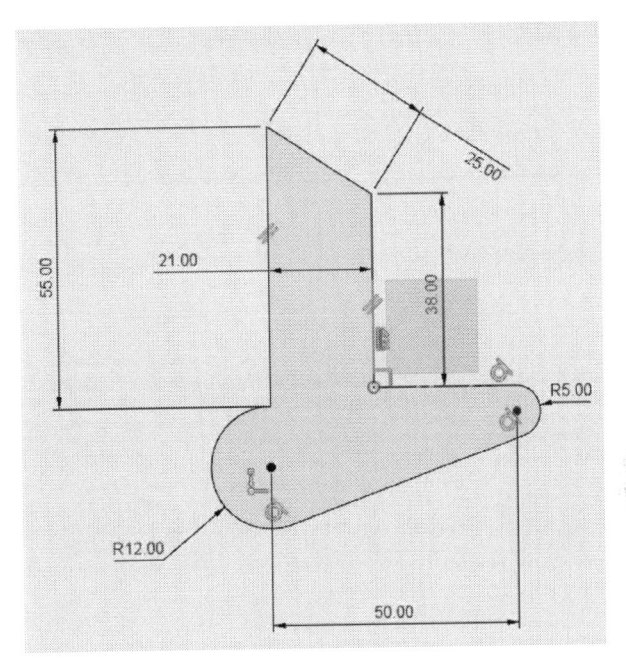

Figure 4–47

13. Press <Esc> to end the Dimension command.

14. Select any entity and vertex on the sketch and try to drag or reposition them. Note that this is not possible because the sketch is fully defined with dimensions and constraints.

15. Select the 25.00 aligned dimension, right-click and select **Toggle Driven**. The dimension is now enclosed in parentheses to indicate that it is a driven dimension.

16. Select the 55.00 vertical dimension, right-click and select **Toggle Driven**.

17. Select the vertex shown in Figure 4–48 and drag it downwards so that the top line becomes approximately horizontal. Note that the driven dimensions update dynamically as you drag the vertex.

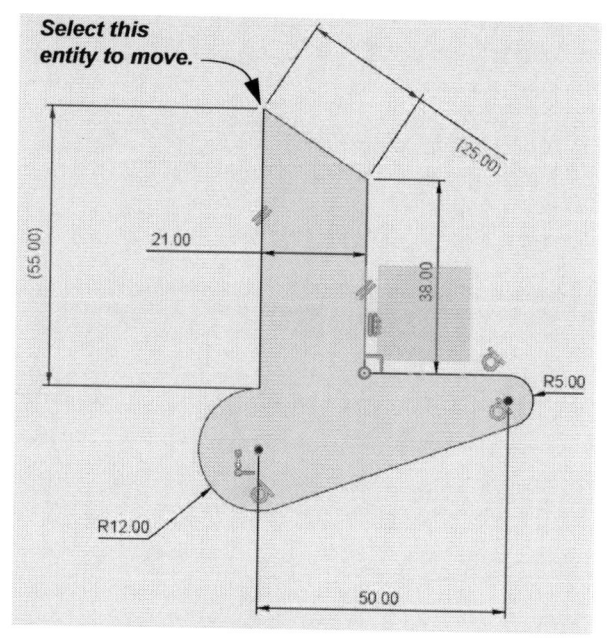

Figure 4–48

18. Hold <Ctrl> and select both driven dimensions on the sketch. Right-click on the **25.00** aligned dimension and select **Toggle Driving**. Both dimensions once again display without parentheses and have locked the sketch.

19. In the ribbon, click (Stop Sketch). The **Front** view of the design is shown in Figure 4–49.

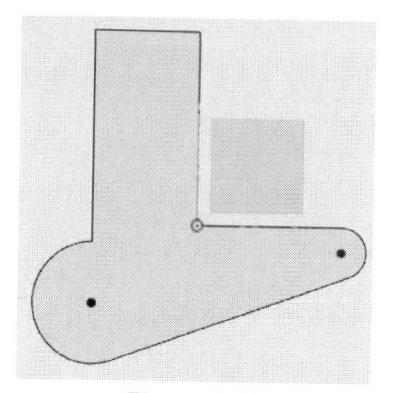

Figure 4–49

20. Create a Revolve using one of the sketched lines as the axis so that the resulting design displays in its Home view as shown in Figure 4–50.

Figure 4–50

21. Click ![save icon] to save the design. Save it in the *Autodesk Fusion 360 Practice Files* project with the name **sketch_revolve**.

22. Close the file.

Practice 4c

Creating Sketched Geometry II

Practice Objectives

- Create a new sketch on an origin plane.
- Sketch and mirror entities to create the required shape.
- Apply dimensions and constraints so that the sketch captures the design intent and is fully constrained.

In this practice, you will create extruded geometry in a new design, as shown in Figure 4–51.

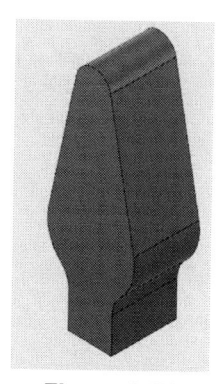

Figure 4–51

Task 1 - Create a new design and create a sketch.

1. Click ▬▾ > **New Design** to create a new design.
2. Toggle on the display of the origin features.
3. In the BROWSER, expand the *Origin* folder.
4. In the BROWSER, right-click on plane **XY** and select (Create Sketch).

Task 2 - Add construction lines.

1. Press <L> to initiate the Line command.

One line can be made horizontal or vertical while the other is constrained to be perpendicular.

2. Sketch a horizontal line and a vertical line as shown in Figure 4–52. Add constraints to make the lines horizontal and vertical. The size and position of the lines is not important yet.

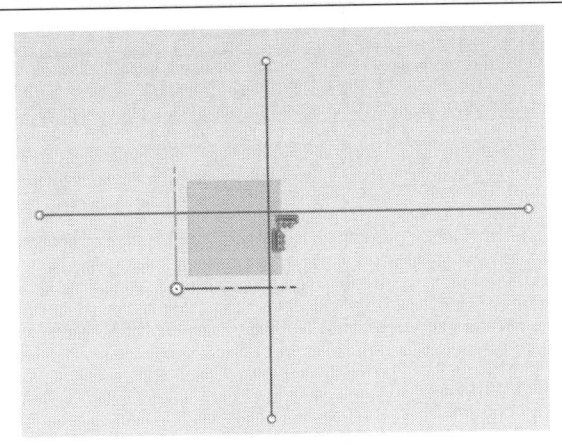

Figure 4–52

3. Press <Esc> to cancel any active commands.

4. Hold <Ctrl> and select both lines.

5. Right-click and select ![icon] (Normal/Construction). Both lines should now display in a dashed style to indicate that they are construction geometry.

6. Apply a Coincident constraint between each line and the Origin Point to locate them.

7. Toggle off the display of the Origin features. The sketch should display similar to that shown in Figure 4–53.

To toggle between normal and construction geometry, you can also press <X> or use the SKETCH PALETTE.

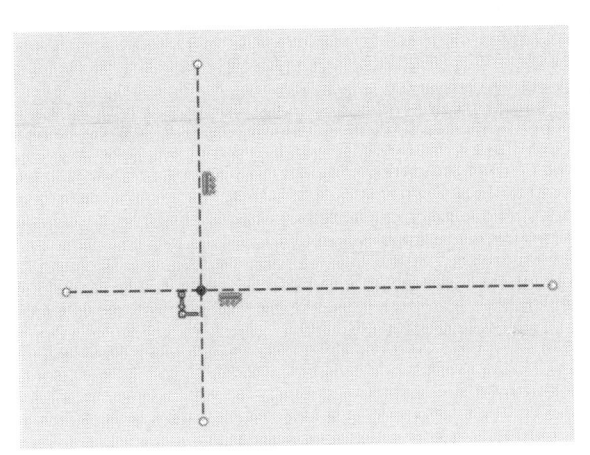

Figure 4–53

Task 3 - Sketch the geometry.

To sketch a line that is tangent to two circles, start the ⤴ (Line) command. Click on one of the two circles and hold the left mouse button. While continuing to hold, drag the cursor to the next circle and position it so that the Tangent constraint is displayed. Release the mouse button to locate the tangent line. You can use the same procedure for tangent lines between arcs.

1. Start the sketch by sketching two circles, two tangent lines, and a vertical attached line, as shown in Figure 4–54. Position the circles relative to the reference entities. Note that after you sketch the entities, you might need to manually add the Tangent constraint between the lines and circles.

Tangent geometry lines

Vertical geometry line

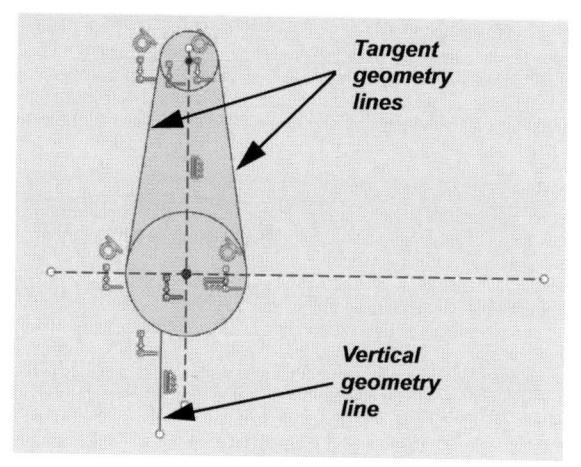

Figure 4–54

2. In the SKETCH panel, click ▷|◁ (Mirror) to mirror the vertical geometry line about the vertical construction line. The MIRROR palette opens as shown in Figure 4–55.

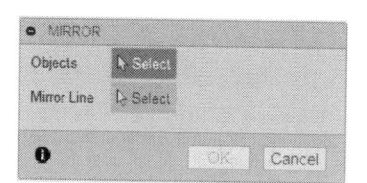

Figure 4–55

3. Select the vertical geometry line as the object to mirror.

4. In the MIRROR palette, click in the *Mirror Line* field to activate it. Select the vertical construction line, as shown in Figure 4–56. Click **OK**.

    - Symmetry constraint symbols are applied to the endpoints of the two vertical geometry lines to indicate that they are symmetric about the vertical centerline as a result of the mirror action.

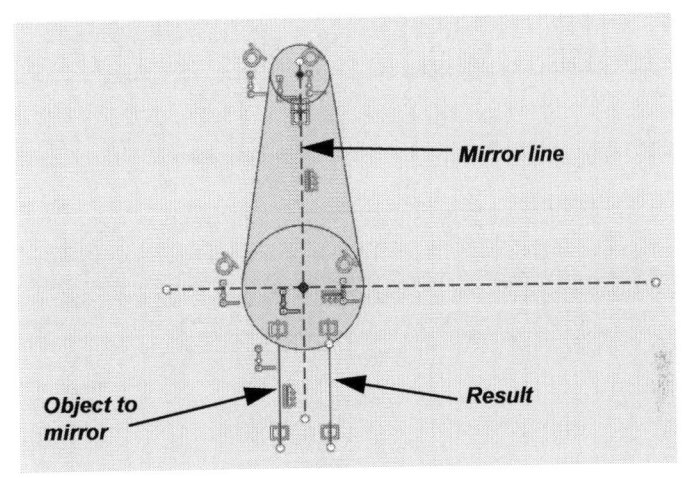

Figure 4–56

5. Press <T> to activate the Trim command. Trim the unwanted segments of the circles so that the sketch displays as shown in Figure 4–57.

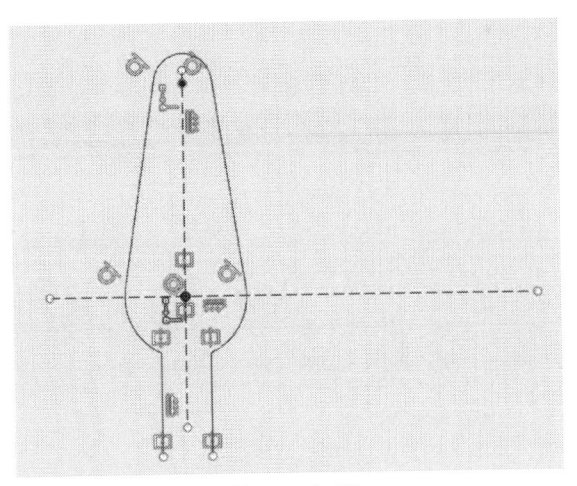

Figure 4–57

6. In the SKETCH panel, click (Fillet).

7. Place fillets with a radius of **6.00** at the two locations shown in Figure 4–58. Before you accept or change the radius for the first fillet, select the vertex to place the second radius. Enter **6.00** in the dynamic input field. Both fillets should now be controlled by one dimension and the Equal constraint symbol is displayed adjacent to each of them.

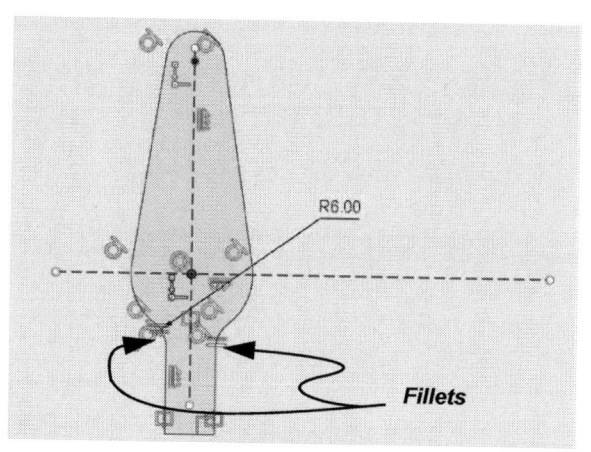

Figure 4–58

8. Sketch a horizontal line at the bottom to close the profile.

9. Add and modify the dimensions, as shown in Figure 4–59. Add additional constraints, if needed.

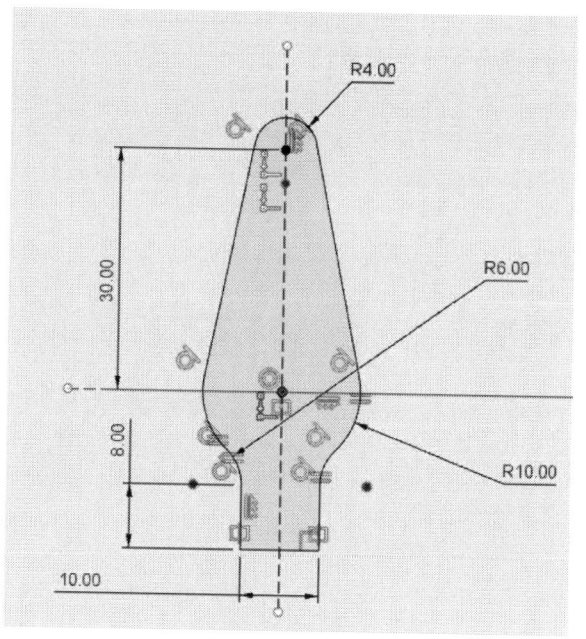

Figure 4–59

10. In the ribbon, click ▦ (Stop Sketch).

11. Move the cursor over the ViewCube and click ⌂ (Home) to return the design to its default orthographic **Home** view.

12. Create an Extrude feature with a distance of **15 mm**, as shown in Figure 4–60.

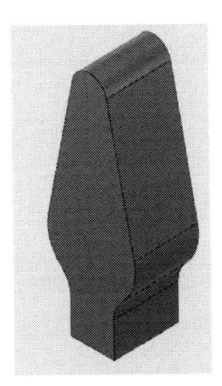

Figure 4–60

13. Save the design with the name **mirror_sketch** to your *Autodesk Fusion 360 Practice Files* project.

14. Close the file.

Practice 4d Manipulating Entities

Practice Objectives

- Open an existing design.
- Modify the existing entities into a alternate sketch.

In this practice, you will open a design and use the editing tools to obtain the required final geometry. You can use the **Trim**, **Extend**, and **Mirror** tools, but you cannot create any new entities.

Task 1 - Open a design and edit a sketch.

1. Click (File) > **New Design from File**.

2. Using the Open dialog box, navigate to the *C:\Autodesk Fusion 360 Practice Files* folder. Select **manipulating_entities.f3d**, and click **Open**. The design contains one sketch.

3. In the BROWSER, right-click on **Sketch1** and select **Edit Sketch**.

4. Using only the (Trim), (Extend), and (Mirror) tools, edit the sketch so that it displays as shown on the right in Figure 4–61. No new entities need to be sketched.

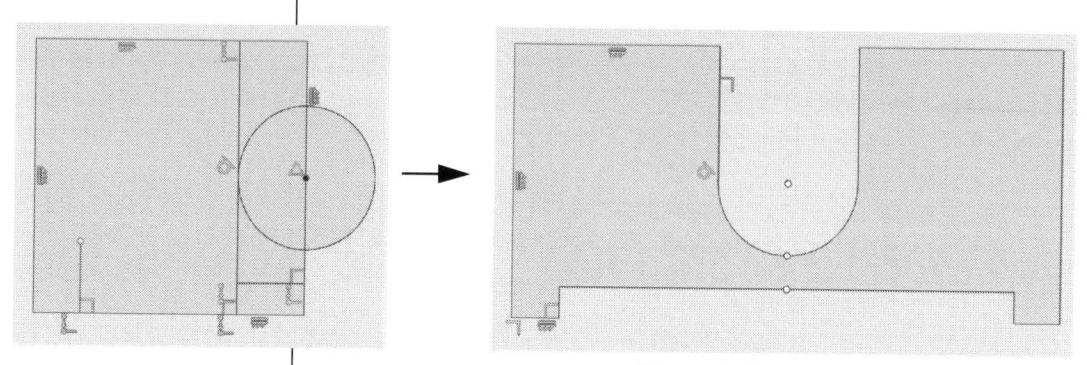

Figure 4–61

5. Save the design and close the file.

Practice 4e

Copy and Paste Sketches

Practice Objectives

- Use the **Copy** and **Paste** keyboard shortcuts to duplicate entities between different sketches.
- Move entities in a sketch.
- Apply dimensions and constraints to fully constrain a sketch.

In this practice, you will create the sketch shown on the left of Figure 4–62 by copying and pasting existing sketch geometry from another design. Using this method, you can reuse a sketch in multiple designs. This sketch geometry can be used to create the revolved feature shown on the right in Figure 4–62.

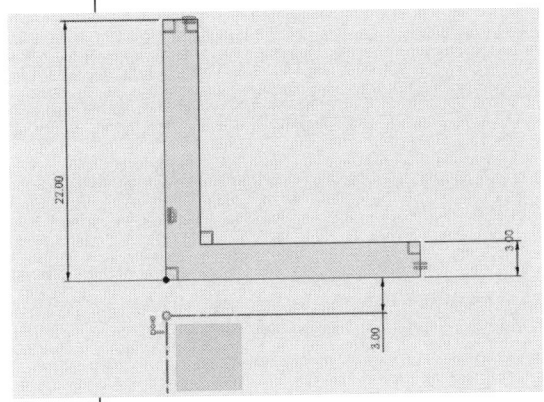

Figure 4–62

Task 1 - Create a new design from a file and copy a sketch.

1. Click (File) > **New Design from File**.

2. Using the Open dialog box, navigate to the *C:\Autodesk Fusion 360 Practice Files* folder. Select **copy_sketch_extrude.f3d**, and click **Open**. The design displays as shown in Figure 4–63.

Figure 4–63

3. Expand the **Sketches** folder in the BROWSER.
4. Toggle on the visibility of **Sketch1**.
5. Right-click on **Sketch1** and select **Edit Sketch**.
6. Drag a selection window over the entire sketch, including the dimensions.
7. Right-click and select **Copy**, or press <Ctrl>+<C> to copy the sketch entities, constraints, and dimensions.

Task 2 - Create a new design and paste the sketch.

1. Create a new design using the standard metric (mm) units.
2. Toggle on the display of the origin features.
3. In the BROWSER, expand the *Origin* folder. Right-click on the plane **XZ** and select ![] (Create Sketch).
4. Select the Origin Point in the sketch.
5. Right-click in the graphics window and select **Paste**, press <Ctrl>+<V> to paste the sketch entities, constraints, and dimensions, as shown in Figure 4–64. The MOVE palette displays with the sketch.

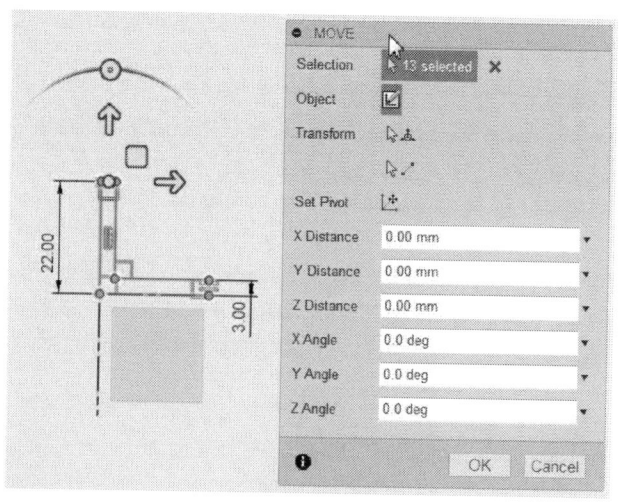

Figure 4–64

6. Drag the vertical manipulator arrow up 3 mm, or enter **3** in the *Y Distance* field in the palette.
7. Click **OK**.

If the manipulator arrow is moving in increments greater than 3mm, zoom in on the sketch.

8. Create a Coincident constraint between the Origin Point and the left vertical line.

9. Create a dimension between the Origin Point and the bottom horizontal line, as shown in Figure 4–65.

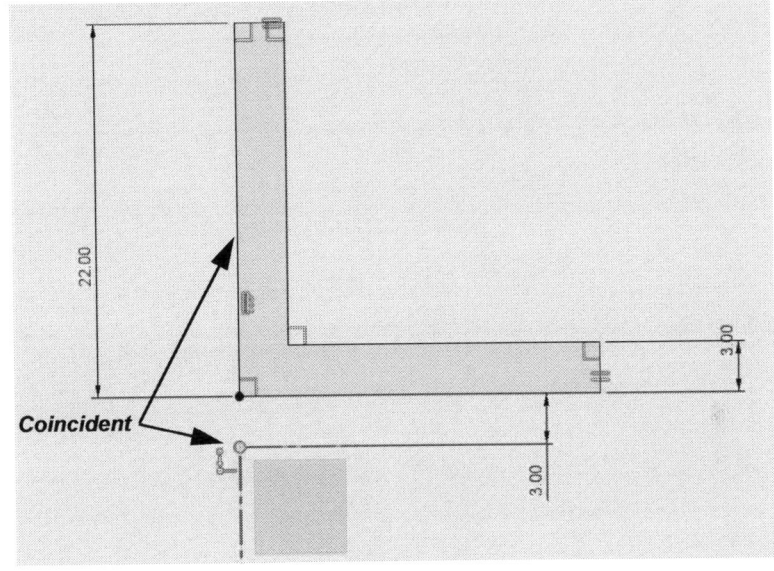

Figure 4–65

10. In the ribbon, click (Stop Sketch).

11. Move the cursor over the ViewCube and click (Home) to return the design to its default orthographic **Home** view.

12. Create a Revolve feature, as shown in Figure 4–66.

An origin axis can be selected as the axis for a revolved feature.

Figure 4–66

13. Save the design with the name **copy_sketch_revolve** to your *Autodesk Fusion 360 Practice Files* project.

14. Close the file.

15. Close the original design file without saving.

Practice 4f

Patterning Sketched Entities

Practice Objectives

- Create a circular pattern of sketched entities that rotate about a selected point in a sketch.
- Create a rectangular pattern of sketched entities that translate along a first and second direction in a sketch.

In this practice, you will pattern the circular and rectangular sketched entities shown in Figure 4–67.

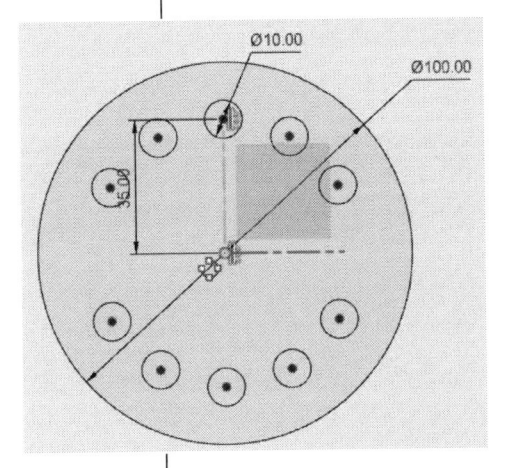

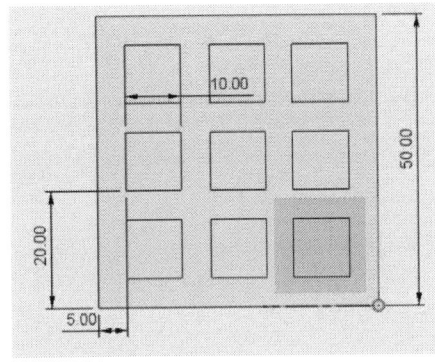

Figure 4–67

Task 1 - Create a new design from a file and copy a sketch.

1. Click ▼ > **New Design from File**.

2. In the Open dialog box, navigate to the *C:\Autodesk Fusion 360 Practice Files* folder, select **sketch_pattern.f3d**, and click **Open**.

3. Only the Origin features are displayed. Toggle on the display of sketches. The design currently contains two sketches.

4. In the BROWSER, expand the *Sketches* folder and toggle off the visibility of **Sketch2**.

Task 2 - Create a circular pattern of entities.

1. In the BROWSER, right-click on **Sketch1** and select **Edit Sketch**.

2. In the SKETCH panel, click (Circular Pattern). The CIRCULAR PATTERN palette opens.

3. Select the small interior circle as the object to pattern, as shown in Figure 4–68.

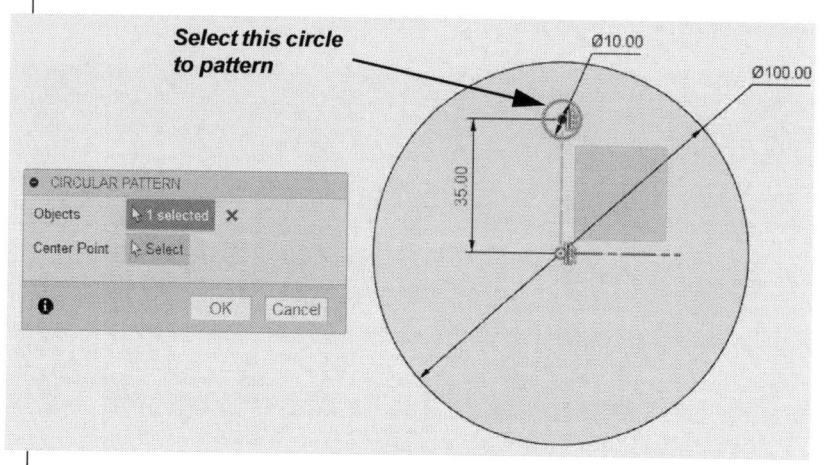

Figure 4–68

4. In the CIRCULAR PATTERN palette, click in the *Center Point* field to activate it. Select the center point of the sketch as the reference.

5. The *Type* field is currently set to (Full), which means that the pattern occurs through 360°. Enter **8** in the *Quantity* field.

6. The **Suppress** option is selected, which means that individual pattern instances can be suppressed. Clear the checkboxes on the pattern instances in the 3 o'clock and 9 o'clock positions.

7. Click **OK** to complete the pattern. The sketch displays as shown in Figure 4–69.

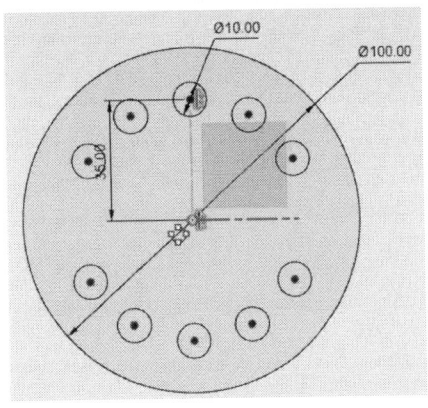

Figure 4–69

8. In the ribbon, click (Stop Sketch).

Task 3 - Create a rectangular pattern of entities.

1. Toggle off the visibility of **Sketch1** and toggle on **Sketch2**.

2. Edit **Sketch2**.

3. In the SKETCH PALETTE, clear the **Show Constraints** option to hide the display of the constraint symbols to simplify the display.

4. In the SKETCH panel, select (Rectangular Pattern). The RECTANGULAR PATTERN palette opens.

5. Select the four lines that form the interior square as the objects to pattern. The pattern directions default to the horizontal and vertical directions of the current sketch orientation.

6. In the *Distance Type* drop-down list, select (Spacing). This enables you to enter the distance between pattern instances, rather than the overall distance extent for the pattern.

7. In the first *Quantity* field, enter **3**, and in the first *Distance* field, enter **15 mm** to define the instances in the first direction. The *Direction Type* remains as (One Direction).

8. In the second *Quantity* field, enter **3** and in the second *Distance* field, enter **15 mm** to define the instances in the second direction.

9. Change the second *Direction Type* to ![] (Symmetric) so that the pattern in the second direction is created symmetrically on both sides of the original objects. The selections should display as shown in Figure 4–70.

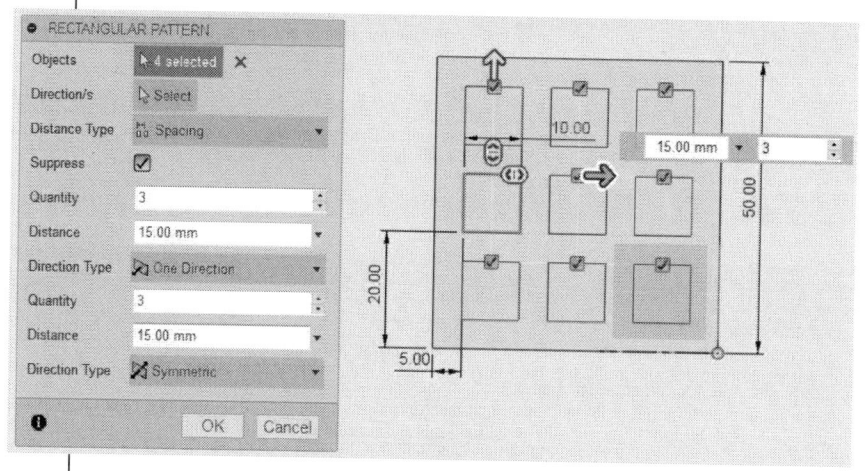

Figure 4–70

10. Click **OK** to complete the pattern. The sketch displays as shown in Figure 4–71.

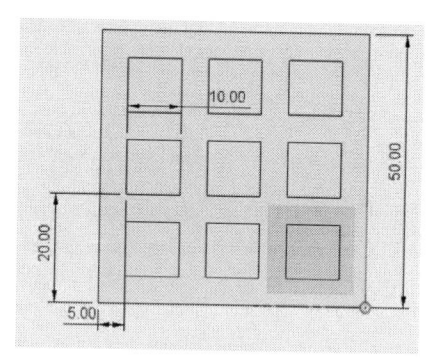

Figure 4–71

11. Double-click on the 20 dimension and enter **17**. The entire pattern updates to reflect the change because the occurrences are located with respect to the initial entities.

12. In the ribbon, click ![] (Stop Sketch).

13. Save the design with the name **sketch_pattern** to your *Autodesk Fusion 360 Practice Files* project.

14. Close the file.

Chapter Review Questions

1. Construction entities can be used directly to create solid geometry.
   a. True
   b. False

2. How does the **Trim** tool manipulate sketch entities?
   a. Continues an entity to meet the next entity in its path or to close an open sketch.
   b. Removes the segment of the entity to the nearest intersection in each direction from the point selected.
   c. Duplicates a source entity to one or more locations in the sketch or to another sketch.
   d. Provides a specific tool for stretching sketched entities versus simply selecting and dragging them in the sketch.

3. How does the **Extend** tool manipulate sketch entities?
   a. Continues an entity to meet the next entity in its path or to close an open sketch.
   b. Enables you to relocate original 2D sketch geometry.
   c. Duplicates a source entity to one or more locations in the sketch or to another sketch.
   d. Provides a specific tool for stretching sketched entities versus simply selecting and dragging them in the sketch.

4. How was the profile shown in Figure 4–72 created in sketch mode?

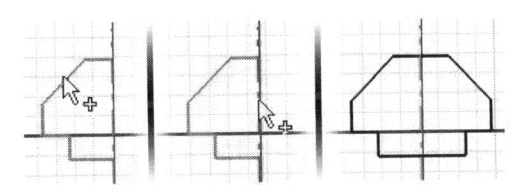

   Figure 4–72

   a. **Mirror**
   b. **Revolve**
   c. **Extend**
   d. **Trim**

5. Once a sketch has been completed, fillets that are added in the sketch become separate Fillet features in the BROWSER. These features can be selected and deleted independent of the sketch.

    a. True
    b. False

6. What types of sketch entities can you use as a mirror line when mirroring geometry? (Select all that apply.)

    a. Construction line
    b. Sketched line
    c. Projected edge from other geometry
    d. Projected origin plane

7. How does the **Move** tool manipulate sketch entities?

    a. Continues an entity to meet the next entity in its path or to close an open sketch.
    b. Enables you to relocate original 2D sketch geometry.
    c. Removes the segment of the entity to the nearest intersection in each direction from the point selected.
    d. Provides a specific tool for stretching sketched entities versus simply selecting and dragging them in the sketch.

8. You can copy a sketch from one design into another design.

    a. True
    b. False

9. Which of the following are required when creating a rectangular pattern in two directions that are horizontal and vertical.

    a. Objects to pattern
    b. Pattern Direction/s
    c. Angle between occurrences
    d. Pattern axis
    e. Quantity and Distance in the first direction
    f. Quantity and Distance in the second direction

10. The sketched entities shown on the left in Figure 4–73 are fully constrained. Which of the following statements best describes the **(113.91)** dimension value, as shown on the right in Figure 4–73?

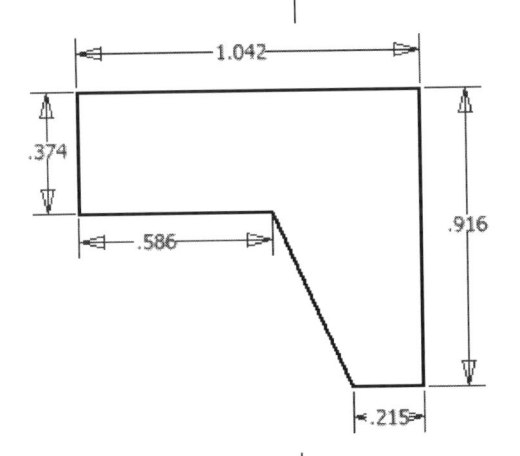

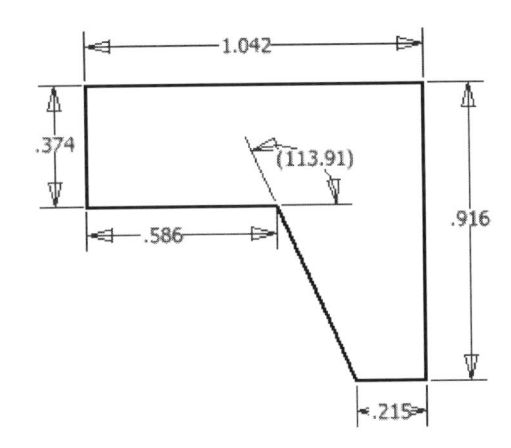

Figure 4–73

a. The (113.91) dimension is a Driven Angular Dimension and cannot be modified to change the size of the sketch.

b. The (113.91) dimension is a General Angular Dimension and cannot be modified to change the size of the sketch.

c. The (113.91) dimension is a Driven Angular Dimension and can be modified to change the size of the sketch.

d. The (113.91) dimension is a General Angular Dimension and can be modified to change the size of the sketch.

Answers: 1.b, 2.b, 3.a, 4.a, 5.b, 6.(a,b,c,d), 7.b, 8.a, 9.(a,e,f), 10.a

Command Summary

Button	Command	Location
	Center Point Slot	• **Ribbon:** *Model* Workspace>SKETCH panel • **Context Menu:** Right-click in the graphics window and select **Sketch>Slot**.
	Center to Center Slot	• **Ribbon:** *Model* Workspace>SKETCH panel • **Context Menu:** Right-click in the graphics window and select **Sketch>Slot**.
	Circular Pattern	• **Ribbon:** *Model* Workspace>SKETCH panel • **Context Menu:** Right-click in the graphics window and select **Sketch**.
	Circumscribed Polygon	• **Ribbon:** *Model* Workspace>SKETCH panel • **Context Menu:** Right-click in the graphics window and select **Sketch>Polygon**.
	Edge Polygon	• **Ribbon:** *Model* Workspace>SKETCH panel • **Context Menu:** Right-click in the graphics window and select **Sketch>Polygon**.
	Ellipse	• **Ribbon:** *Model* Workspace>SKETCH panel • **Context Menu:** Right-click in the graphics window and select **Sketch**.
	Extend	• **Ribbon:** *Model* Workspace>SKETCH panel • **Context Menu:** Right-click in the graphics window and select **Sketch**.
	Fillet	• **Ribbon:** *Model* Workspace>SKETCH panel • **Context Menu:** Right-click in the graphics window and select **Sketch**.
	Inscribed Polygon	• **Ribbon:** *Model* Workspace>SKETCH panel • **Context Menu:** Right-click in the graphics window and select **Sketch>Polygon**.
	Mirror	• **Ribbon:** *Model* Workspace>SKETCH panel • **Context Menu:** Right-click in the graphics window and select **Sketch**.

	Move	• **Ribbon:** *Model* Workspace>SKETCH panel • **Context Menu:** Right-click in the graphics window and select **Sketch**.
	Normal/ Construction	• SKETCH PALETTE • Keyboard: <X>
	Overall Slot	• **Ribbon:** *Model* Workspace>SKETCH panel • **Context Menu:** Right-click in the graphics window and select **Sketch>Slot**.
	Rectangular Pattern	• **Ribbon:** *Model* Workspace>SKETCH panel • **Context Menu:** Right-click in the graphics window and select **Sketch**.
	Trim	• **Ribbon:** *Model* Workspace>SKETCH panel • **Context Menu:** Right-click in the graphics window and select **Sketch**.

Chapter 5

Sketched Secondary Features

Sketched secondary features (such as extrudes) can add or remove material from a design. As features and design intent become more complex, additional options are available to help you create more advanced secondary features.

Learning Objectives in this Chapter

- Create an extruded and revolved secondary feature.
- Create offset entities that reference existing features.
- Project geometry to create references between sketched entities and existing features.
- Create a shared version of an existing sketch so that it can be used again to create design geometry.

5.1 Sketched Secondary Features

Solid geometry features that are created after the first solid feature are often referred to as secondary features. They can be created from sketches as extruded and revolved features, or as features with implied shapes (e.g., holes and fillets).

The workflow for creating a sketched secondary feature is similar to that of the first solid feature, but, the following differences and available tools should be noted:

- As an alternative to selecting an Origin Plane as the sketching plane, you can also select planar faces of existing features.

- Existing geometry can used as constraint and dimension references. Additionally, as you reference design edges while sketching (i.e., dimensioning or offsetting), these edges or vertices are automatically projected into the current sketch.

- When the sketch plane is located in or behind other geometry, you can temporarily remove the portion of the design that is in front of the sketch plane using the SKETCH PALETTE's **Slice** option, as shown in Figure 5–1.

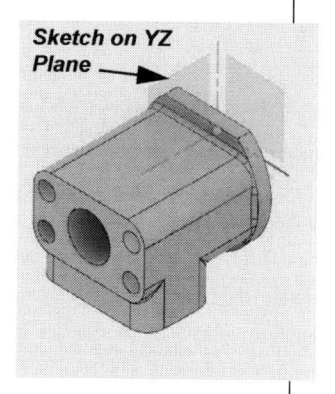

The first solid feature in the design defaults to a new body.

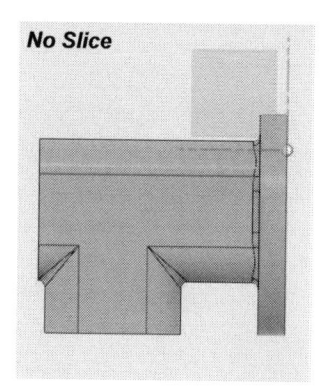

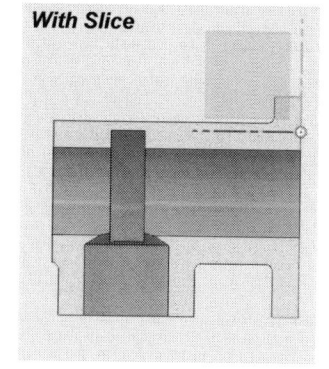

Figure 5–1

- The (New Body) option creates the sketched secondary feature as a new body in the design. Individual bodies can be manipulated independently in the design and combined with other bodies to create a single solid. Bodies are listed in the BROWSER in the *Bodies* folder.

*When creating a base feature, only the **Join** option is available.*

- When creating secondary extrude or revolve features, the ⌂ (Join), ⌂ (Cut), and ⌂ (Intersect) options all become available. These options enable you to specify whether the feature will add material (Join), remove material (Cut), or create the feature as an intersection (Intersect).
    - The **Intersect** option creates geometry from the shared volume of the new and existing features and removes material outside of the shared volume.
    - Examples with material added, removed, and intersected for a revolved and extruded secondary feature are shown in Figure 5–2.

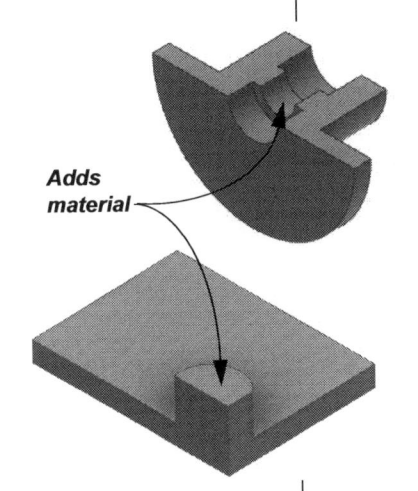

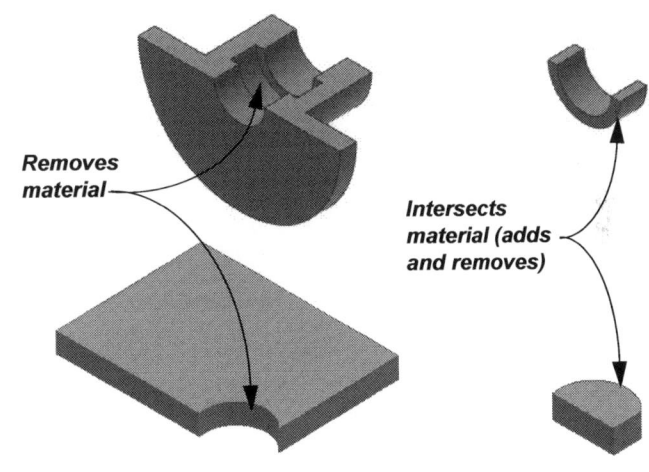

Adds material

Removes material

Intersects material (adds and removes)

Figure 5–2

Hover the cursor over the icon to display its tooltip information.

- When creating the first solid feature as an Extrude, you typically define the *Extents* with ↔ (Distance). For a Revolve, the *Type* is usually ↻ (Full) or ∡ (Angle).
    - When creating these features on existing geometry, you can also use the ⇥ (To) and ⇥ (All) options for Extrudes and the ⇥ (To) option for Revolves, as shown in Figure 5–3.

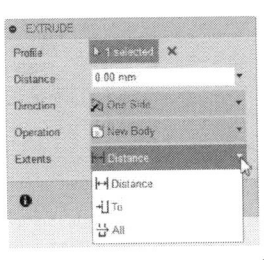

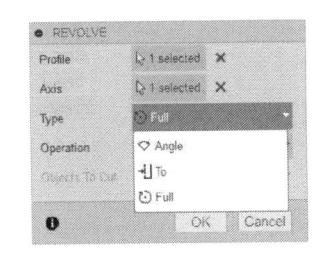

Figure 5–3

To	Creates an extruded or revolved feature so that it extends to the face or plane that you select.
All	Creates an extruded or revolved feature through all of the geometry in a defined direction.

- You can specify a *Taper Angle* for an extruded feature, as shown in Figure 5–4. This is available for all of the *Extent* options. A positive taper angle increases the cross-section in the direction of the extrude, while a negative taper angle decreases the cross-section in the direction of the extrude.

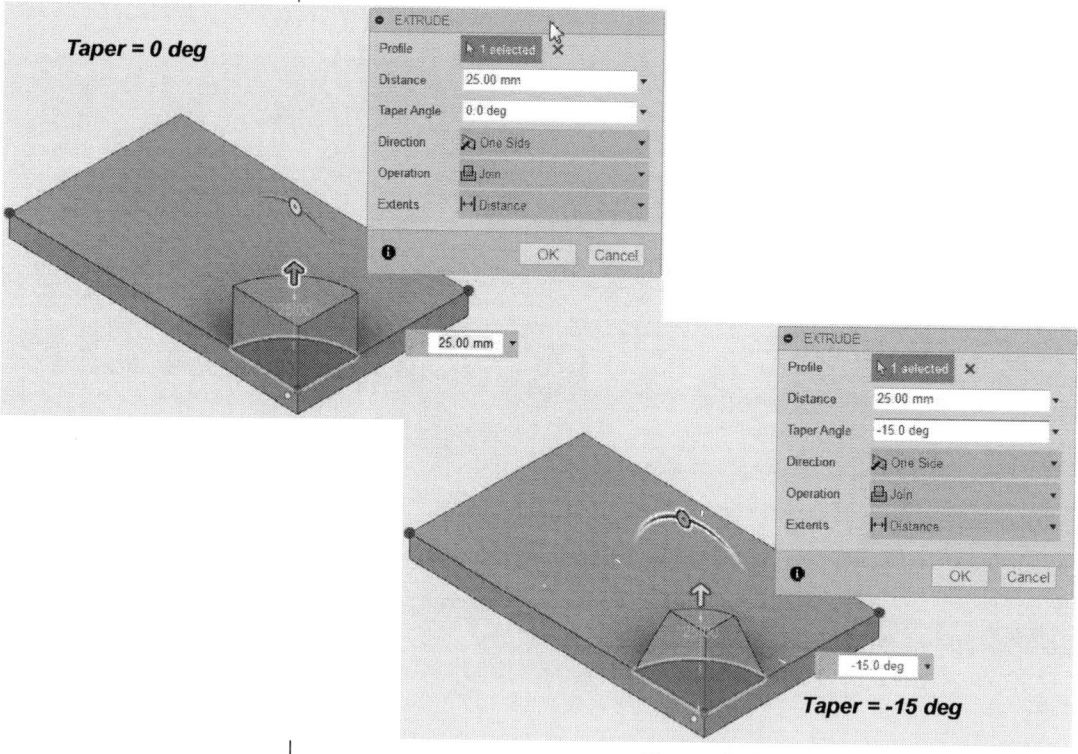

Figure 5–4

Video Lesson Available

Creating Extruded Secondary Features

Video Length: 2:20

Video Lesson Available

Creating Revolved Secondary Features

Video Length: 2:40

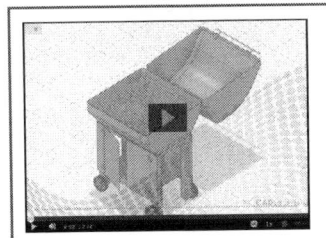

Video Lesson Available

Understanding the Operation Drop-Down

Video Length: 3:01

5.2 Using Existing Geometry

Once a base feature exists in a design, additional geometry is created by referencing it. The following sketching tools enable you to create new entities based on existing geometry.

Projected Geometry

Incorporating the use of projected geometry into a sketch enables you to build relationships between features. In Figure 5–5 the edges of the hole were projected onto a sketch on the front face. The sketch was completed by adding lines between the points and the sketch was extruded as shown on the right. The projected edges create a relationship between the hole and the extrusion so that if the diameter of the hole changes, the height of the extrusion changes accordingly.

*The **Project** option with the **Specified Entities** filter selected will only project entities such as lines, arcs, and points. It does not project silhouette edges.*

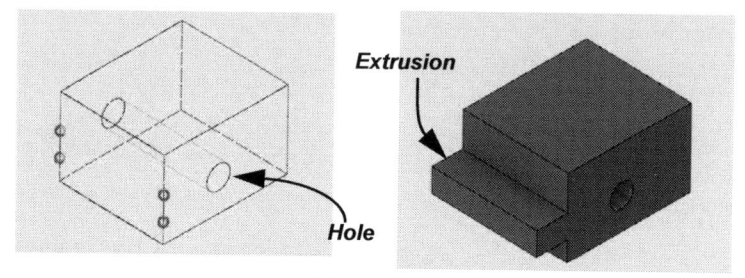

Figure 5–5

Use either of the following methods to start the **Project** tool:

- In the SKETCH panel, click **Project/Include >** (Project).

- In the graphics window, right-click and select **Sketch > Project/Include >** (Project).

Video Lesson Available

Projecting Geometry

Video Length: 3:18

Offset

The **Offset** tool enables you to create new entities by offsetting existing feature edges. Rather than sketching each set of entities separately, offsetting enables you to create a copy of edges or sketch geometry and position it at a set distance from the original, creating and maintaining a relationship between the entities.

An example of a sketch created by offsetting feature edges is shown in Figure 5–6. The edges of the face on which the sketch is being created are projected into the sketch. A dimension is created to show the offset distance and the offset constraint symbol ( ) displays adjacent to the projected and offset entities. The constraint symbol can be deleted to remove the relationship between the original and offset entities.

Projected geometry and sketch geometry can be offset.

Projected entities

Offset entities

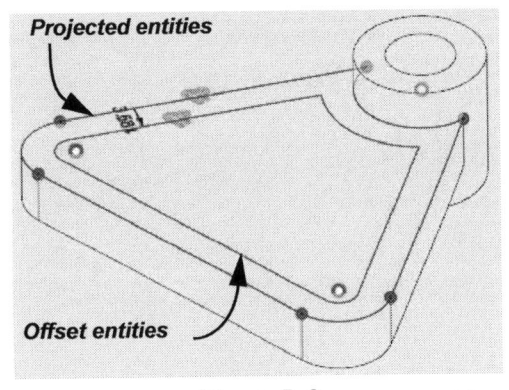

Figure 5–6

- Offset geometry only needs one offset dimension to fully locate it relative to its parent entities. If you delete the offset dimension, right-click on   and select **Add Offset Dimension**.

Use the following steps to offset individual entities:

1. Sketch or project the geometry that is to be offset.
2. In the SKETCH panel, click   (Offset), or press <O>.
3. To select an entire chain of connected entities, in the OFFSET palette, select the **Loop Select** checkbox. To select individual entities, clear this option.
4. Select the entities or projected geometry to offset.
5. Drag the entities to the offset location and click to place them.

Reusing Sketches

You can reuse a single sketch to create multiple features. The sketch shown on the left in Figure 5–7 contains two closed profiles. Both profiles were selected to create the extrude shown in the middle. Then the semi-circular profile from the sketch was used to create the revolve feature. The visibility of a sketch is automatically toggled off after it has been used once, but you can make it visible again in the BROWSER.

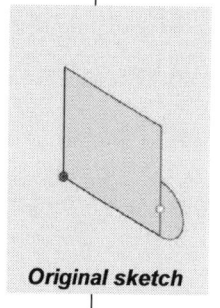

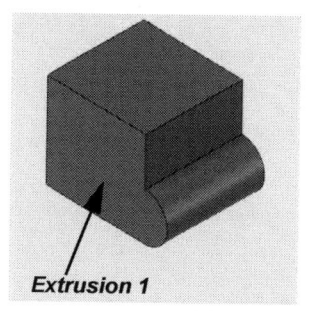

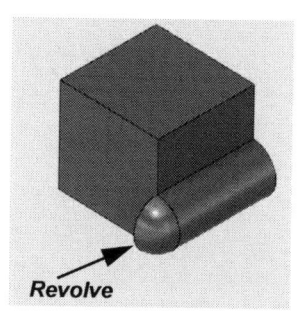

Original sketch *Extrusion 1* *Revolve*

Figure 5–7

Features from Planar Faces

When creating features (such as extrudes or revolves), in addition to using a sketch as a profile, you can also select a planar face as the profile.

The front face of the extrusion shown on the left in Figure 5–8 has been selected as the profile for the revolve created on the right.

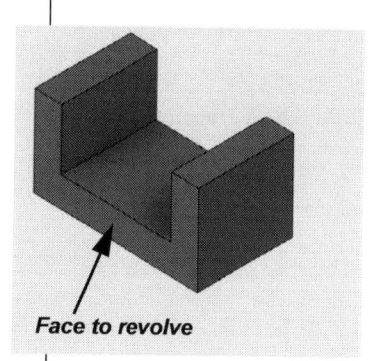

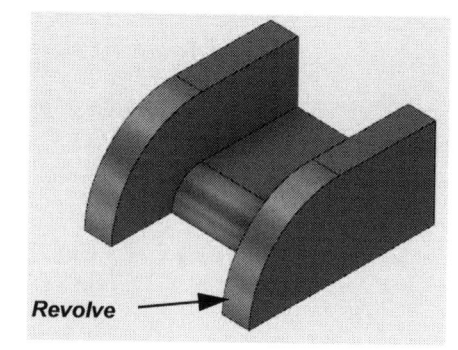

Face to revolve *Revolve*

Figure 5–8

Practice 5a

Creating Sketched Extrusions I

Practice Objective

- Create a secondary extruded feature that references a face and entities in the geometry to fully constrain it.

In this practice, you will create a revolved base feature from an existing sketch and create an extruded cut on a face of the base feature, as shown in Figure 5–9.

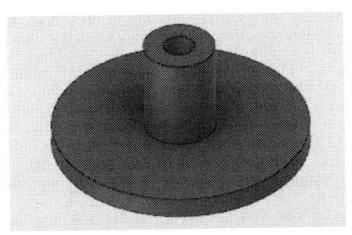

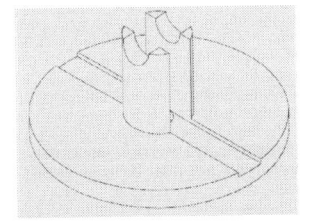

Figure 5–9

Task 1 - Create a new design from file.

1. Click ![icon] > **New Design from File**.

2. In the Open dialog box, navigate to the *C:\Autodesk Fusion 360 Practice Files* folder, select **flange_01.f3d**, and click **Open**.

Task 2 - Create an extruded cut by sketching the section.

1. Select the top circular face of the design (shown in Figure 5–10) and create a new sketch on the selected plane. The design is reoriented so that the selected sketch plane is facing you, as shown in Figure 5–11.

Sketch on this face

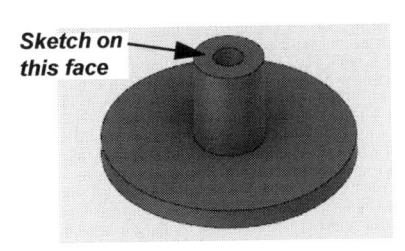

Figure 5–10

Alternatively, you can right-click on the top circular face of the design and click

![icon] *(Create Sketch) to create a new sketch on the plane.*

2. Activate the **Line** command.

3. As you move the cursor over the existing geometry, note that the cursor snaps to the edges (including those that are not on the sketch plane).

4. Sketch a horizontal line with both ends snapped to the largest diameter circular edge, as shown in Figure 5–11. Apply a **Horizontal** constraint, if one is not automatically applied.

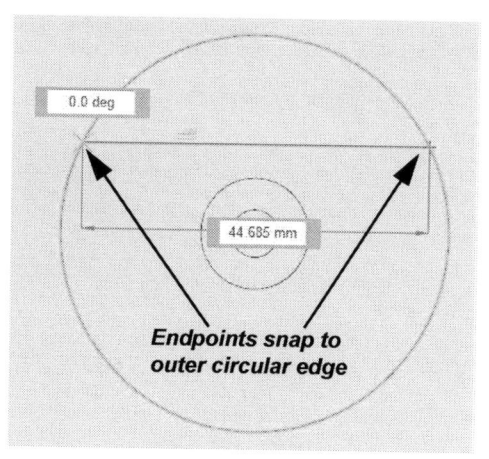

Figure 5–11

To change the display to shaded or wireframe, use the options on the (Display Settings) > Visibility Style menu.

5. Move the cursor over the ViewCube and click (Home) to return the design to its default orthographic **Home** view. The edge that you snapped the line to has automatically been projected onto the sketch plane, as shown in Figure 5–12.

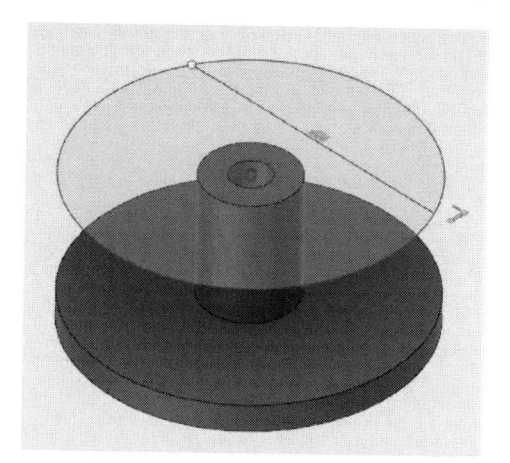

Figure 5–12

6. In the SKETCH PALETTE, click ▫ (Look At) to orient the sketch plane to face you.

7. A **Coincident** constraint was automatically applied to the start point of the line. Apply a second **Coincident** constraint to the endpoint and the outer circular edge.

8. Apply a **Tangent** constraint to the horizontal line and the inner circular edge. The sketch should display as shown in Figure 5–13.

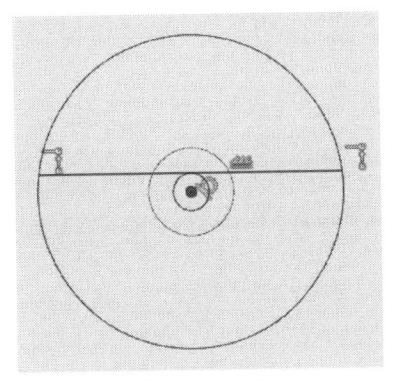

Figure 5–13

9. Using the same process, sketch a second horizontal line to match the one shown in Figure 5–14.

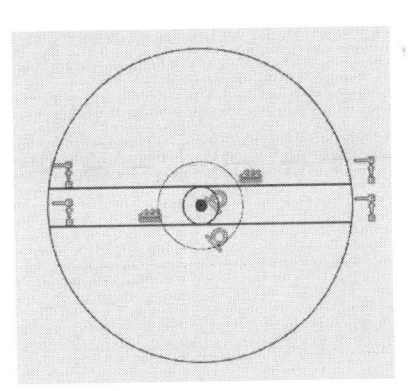

Figure 5–14

10. The two lines are fully constrained. Stop the sketch.

11. Reorient the design to its default orthographic **Home** view.

12. Move the cursor over the sketch you just created. Note how each closed profile highlights as the cursor moves over them. There are now nine closed profiles on that plane. You can select any profile or any combination of profiles to create a feature (such as an extrude).

13. Hold <Ctrl> and select the four profiles shown in Figure 5–15.

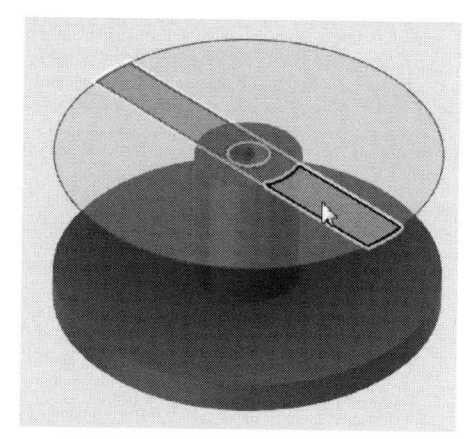

Figure 5–15

In the CREATE panel, select (Extrude), or press <E>.

14. Start the creation of an extrude.

15. In the EXTRUDE palette, note that *Operation* defaults to (New Body).

16. Drag the manipulator arrow down into the part. As the profile intersects existing solid geometry, the *Operation* automatically changes to (Cut), as shown in Figure 5–16.

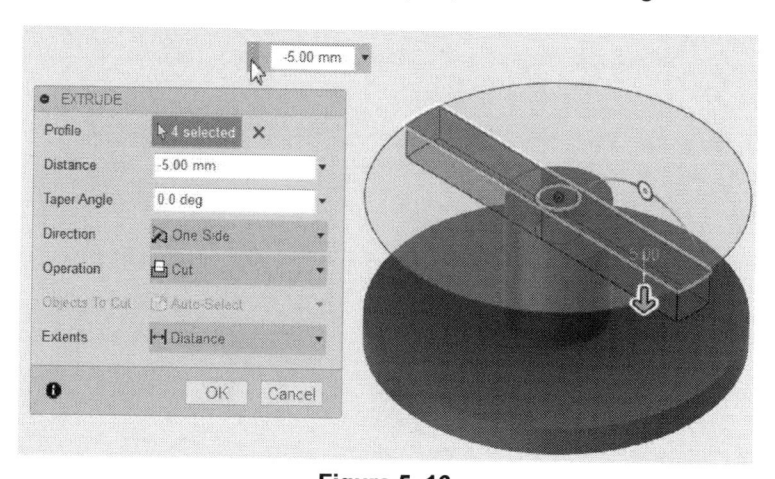

Figure 5–16

17. For the extrude distance, enter **-19** and click **OK**. The design should display as shown in Figure 5–17.

Figure 5–17

Task 3 - Create an extruded symmetric cut.

1. Create a sketch on XY plane. This plane passes through the center of the design.

2. In the SKETCH PALETTE, select the **Slice** checkbox to slice the design back to the sketch plane.

3. The YZ plane is perpendicular to the sketch plane and will be used as a reference. In the SKETCH panel, select **Project/Include >** (Project). In the BROWSER, select the YZ plane. Click **OK**. You can also select the YZ plane in the graphics window, if it is displayed.

4. A projected entity is created in your sketch. Select it and convert it to a construction entity. It should now display as a dashed line.

5. Sketch a 3-point arc with both endpoints snapped to the top horizontal edge, as shown in Figure 5–18.

To convert a selected solid entity to construction (or vise-versa), press <X>.

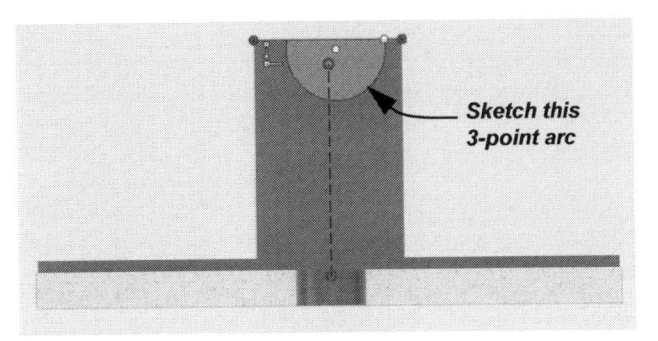

Sketch this 3-point arc

Figure 5–18

6. Ensure that **Coincident** constraints are applied to both endpoints of the arc and the top horizontal edge.

7. Apply a **Coincident** constraint to the center point of the arc and the top horizontal edge.

8. Apply a **Coincident** constraint to the center point of the arc and the vertical centerline.

9. Dimension the radius of the arc, giving it a value of **3.5 mm**. The sketch is now fully constrained and should display as shown in Figure 5–19.

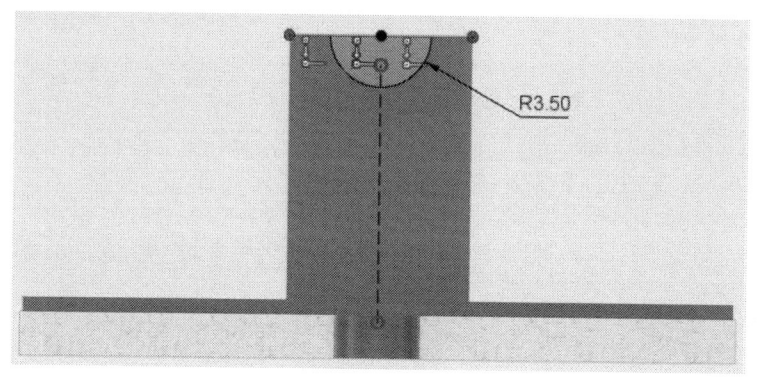

Figure 5–19

10. Stop the sketch and reorient it to its default orthographic **Home** view.

11. Select the semi-circular profile.
    - Because of the small size of the profile, you might have difficulty selecting it. Hover the cursor over the profile and hold the left mouse button. A menu displays listing everything currently under the cursor. Select **Profile**, as shown in Figure 5–20.

You can filter the selectable items using the SELECT panel> ***Selection Filters*** *option.*

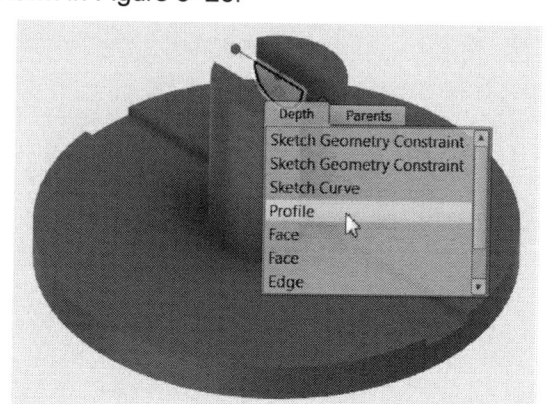

Figure 5–20

In the CREATE panel, select ◫ (Extrude), or press <E>.

12. Start the creation of an extrude.

13. Without moving the manipulator handle, change *Operation* to ⊟ (Cut).

14. Change *Extents* to ⊔ (All).

15. Change *Direction* to ⋈ (Two Sides). The preview of the cut should show the extrude cutting through all of the geometry it intersects in both directions, as shown in Figure 5–21.

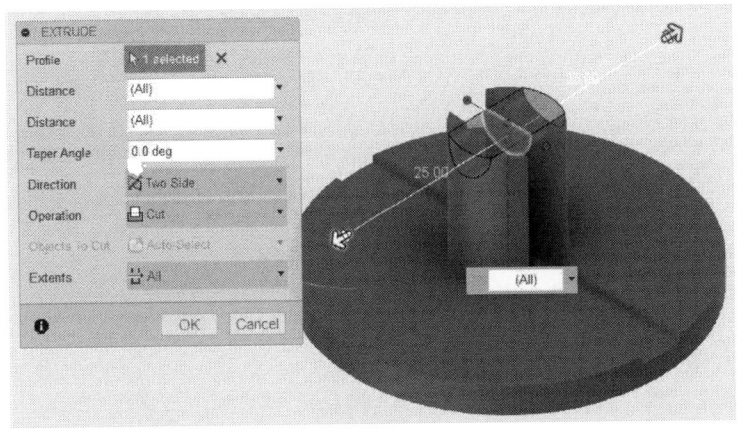

Figure 5–21

16. Complete the feature. The design should display as shown in Figure 5–22.

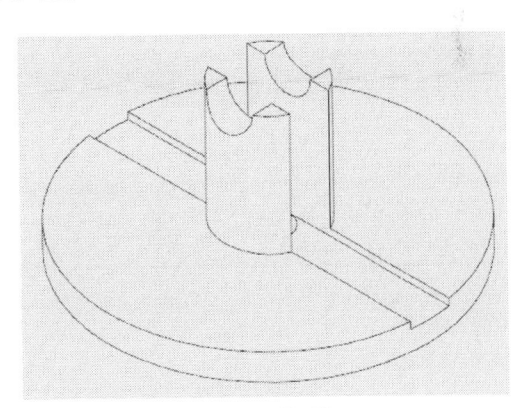

Figure 5–22

17. Save the design with the name **flange_01** to your *Autodesk Fusion 360 Practice Files* project.

18. Close the file.

Practice 5b

Creating Sketched Extrusions II

Practice Objectives

- Create features that add and remove material in a design.
- Use the **Offset** command to create entities that reference other features so that the design intent is built into the design.
- Modify features in the design to ensure that the new features update based on the references that were established.

In this practice, you will create two extruded features using geometry that exists in a design. The new geometry will be created using the **Offset** command. The initial and final designs are shown in Figure 5–23.

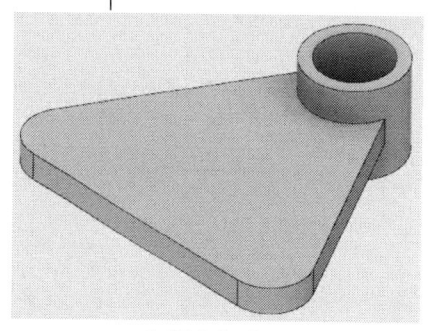

Initial design   *Final design*

Figure 5–23

Task 1 - Create a new design from file.

1. Click ▾ > **New Design from File**.

2. In the Open dialog box, navigate to the *C:\Autodesk Fusion 360 Practice Files* folder, select **Offset.f3d**, and click **Open**.

Task 2 - Offset geometry.

1. Create a new sketch on the face shown in Figure 5–24.

Sketch plane

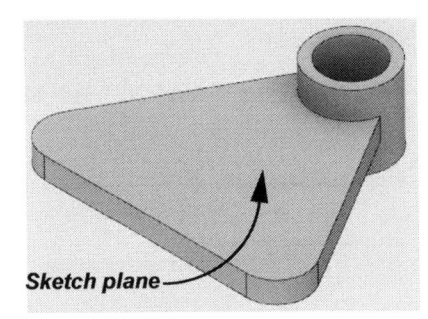

Figure 5–24

2. In the SKETCH panel, click (Offset), or press <O>.

3. Select any edge on the face that was selected as the sketch plane. Note that the entire loop of edges from that face are automatically selected and offset by a distance of -1.00 mm. The **Loop Select** checkbox in the OFFSET palette causes all connected edges on the face to be selected.

4. Enter a *Offset position* value of **-3.15 mm**, as shown in Figure 5–25.

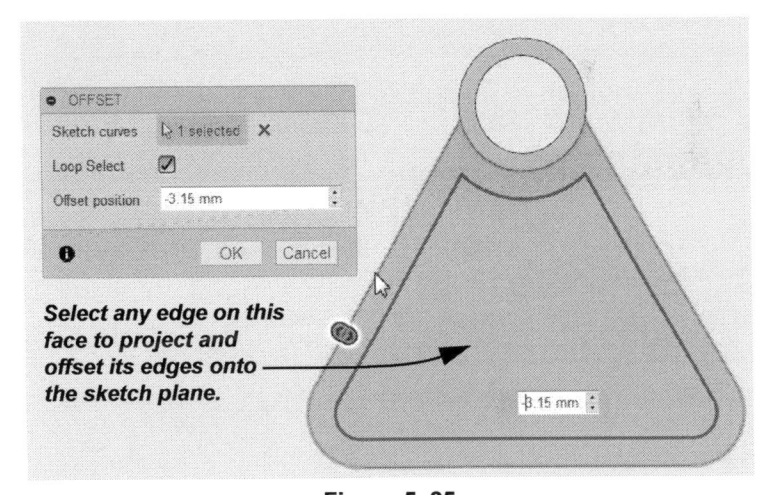

Select any edge on this face to project and offset its edges onto the sketch plane.

Figure 5–25

5. In the OFFSET panel, click **OK**. The Offset constraint symbols and the dimension are added to the sketch.

6. End the sketch.

Note that the edges you selected to offset in the previous task have also been projected into that sketch.

Task 3 - Extrude the sketch.

1. Create an Extrude. Select the inner profile so that the extrusion displays similar to that shown in Figure 5–26.

2. Set a *Distance* value of **7 mm** and accept the defaults to complete the extrusion. This extrusion is created to add material.

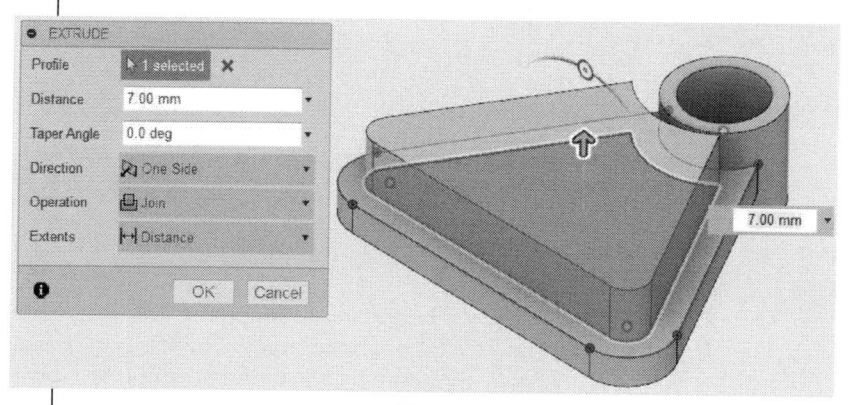

Figure 5–26

Task 4 - Offset projected edges.

1. Select the top face that you created and create a new sketch.

2. In the SKETCH panel, click (Offset).

3. Clear the **Loop Select** checkbox so that individual edges can be selected.

4. Select the first edge to offset, as shown in Figure 5–27. For the *Offset position* value, enter **-1**.

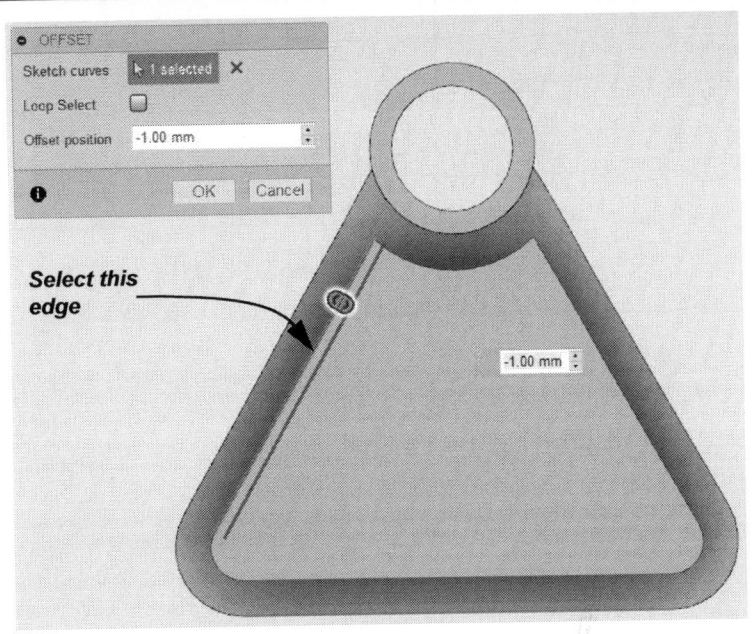

Figure 5–27

5. Select the four additional edges shown in Figure 5–28. In the OFFSET palette, click **OK**.

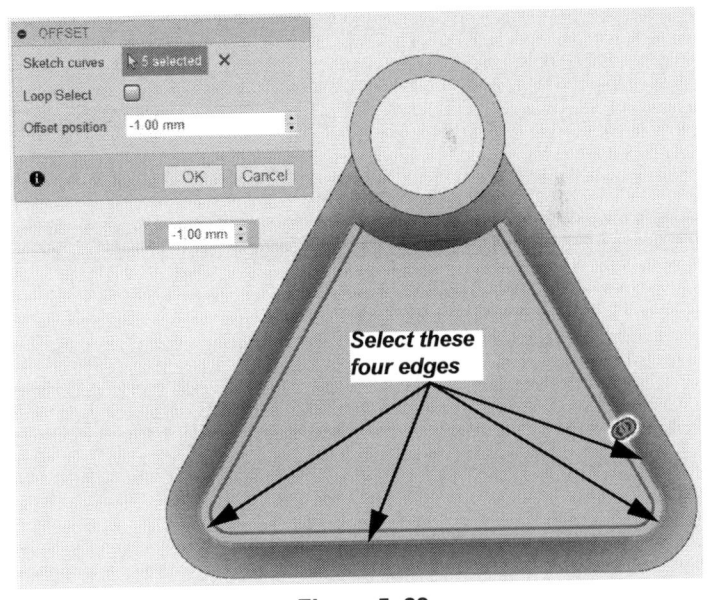

Figure 5–28

If you modify the offset entities (e.g., by trimming), the offset relationship is lost.

6. Stop the sketch. The completed sketch should display as shown in Figure 5–29.

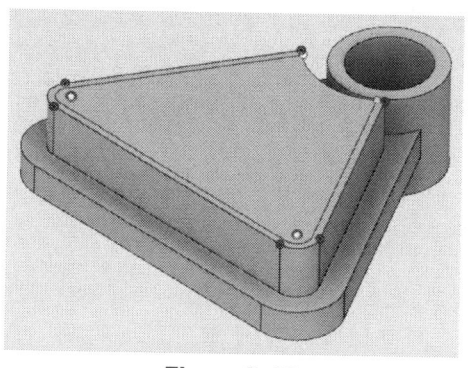

Figure 5–29

7. Create an extrude to remove material using the sketch you created and select the inner profile.

8. Drag the manipulator arrow down into the part to remove material. In the EXTRUDE palette, the Operation drop-down list automatically changes to ▢ (Cut). Note that even though the sketch did not contain a closed loop, its intersection with existing edges results in a closed profile that can be selected for the extrude.

9. In the Extents drop-down list, select ⇅ (All) to make the cut go through the entire design.

10. Complete the feature. The design should display as shown in Figure 5–30.

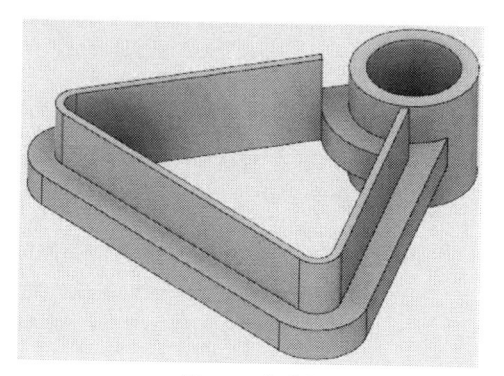

Figure 5–30

Task 5 - Edit the design.

1. Hover the cursor over the last item on the right in the Timeline. It identifies the feature as an Extrude.

2. In the Timeline, double-click on the Extrude icon, or right-click and select **Edit Feature**. The EDIT FEATURE palette displays with the same options that were available when the feature was created.

3. In the Extents drop-down list, select (To). Select the face indicated in Figure 5–31 to have the extrude terminate there.

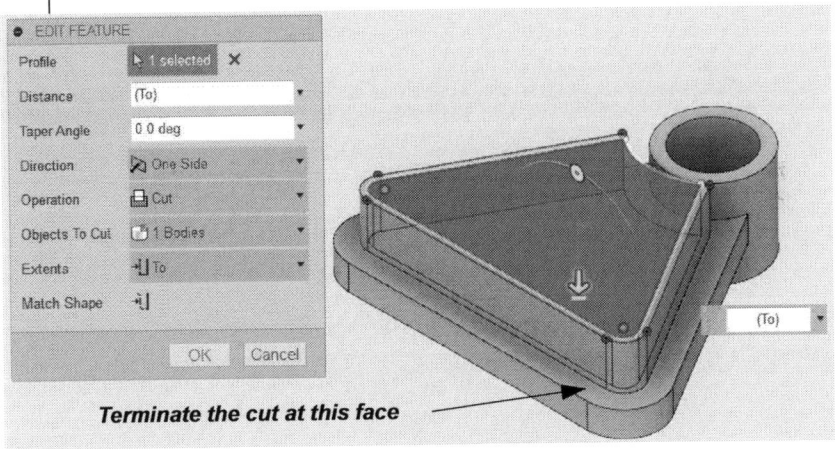

Figure 5–31

4. Click **OK**. The cut no longer goes all of the way through the design.

5. In the BROWSER, expand the *Sketches* folder and toggle on the display of **Sketch3**. This was used to create the original geometry of the design.

6. In the BROWSER, right-click on **Sketch3** and select **Show Dimension**. The dimensions for the design display, as shown in Figure 5–32.

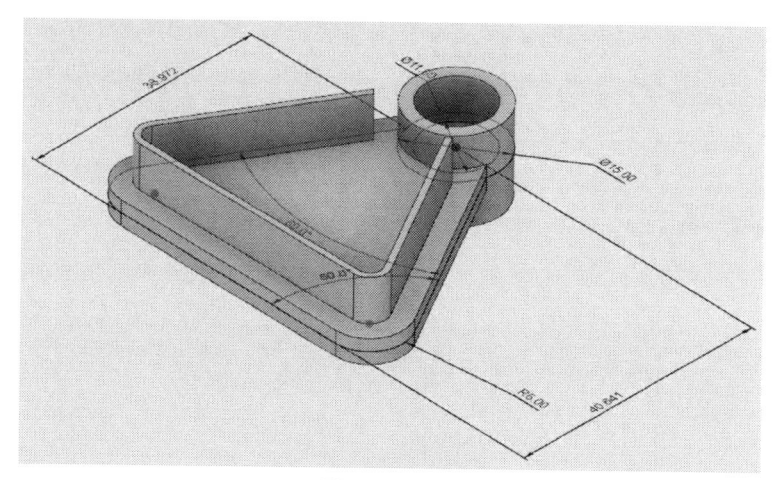

Figure 5–32

7. Double-click on the **R6.00** dimension. An input field displays enabling you to change the value of the radius dimension.

8. Change the radius dimension to **8** and press <Enter>. The parametric relationship created through the use of the **Offset** tool causes the two extrude features to update accordingly, as shown in Figure 5–33.

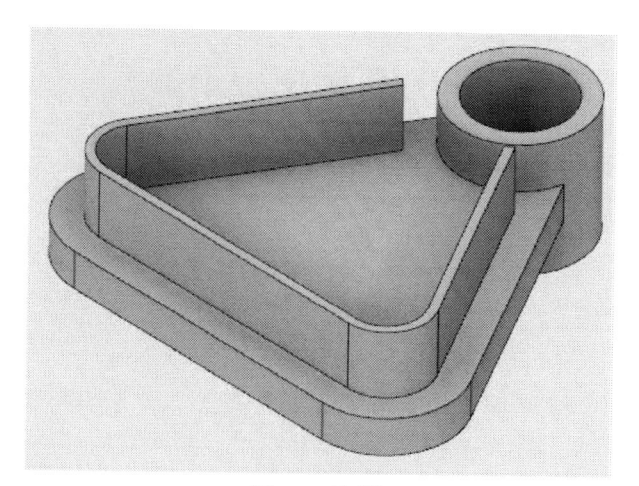

Figure 5–33

9. Save the design with the name **offset** to your *Autodesk Fusion 360 Practice Files* project.

10. Close the file.

Practice 5c

Reusing Sketches

Practice Objectives

- Reuse a sketch to create required geometry in a design.
- Control the visibility of sketched entities and dimensions.

In this practice, you will reuse a single sketch to create multiple extrusions in order to create the geometry shown in Figure 5–34. To reuse the same sketch for multiple features, you will use various closed profiles within the sketch.

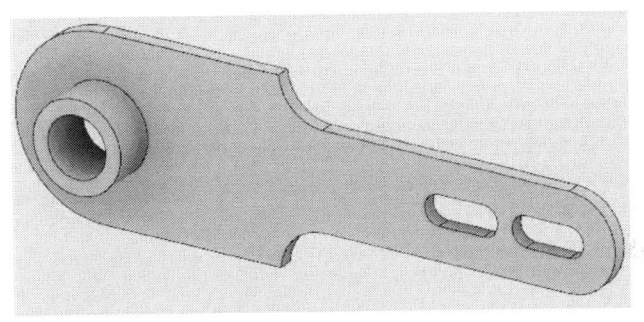

Figure 5–34

Task 1 - Create a new design from file.

1. Click > **New Design from File**.

2. In the Open dialog box, navigate to the *C:\Autodesk Fusion 360 Practice Files* folder, select **reuse_sketch.f3d**, and click **Open**. The design displays as shown in Figure 5–35.

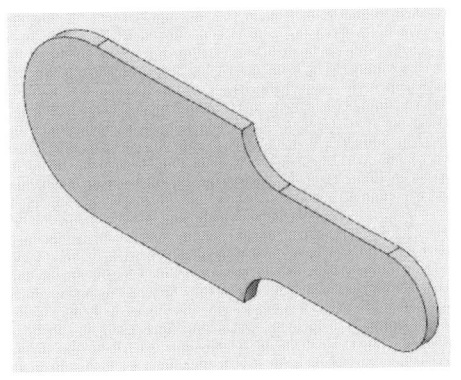

Figure 5–35

Task 2 - Toggle on the visibility of the existing sketch.

1. In the BROWSER, expand the **Sketches** folder.

2. Toggle on the display of **Sketch1**. Note that the sketch includes multiple closed profiles, including the profile used to create the existing solid geometry.

*A sketch is not consumed by the extruded features which are created from it. The sketch can always be found in the BROWSER in the **Sketches** folder.*

Task 3 - Create additional features.

1. Create the extrusion shown in Figure 5–36 using the existing sketch. Both of the cuts are created as a single extruded feature and they remove all material through the entire design.

*The profiles might be behind the solid geometry. Reorient the design to select them, or use the select menu for hidden geometry. Hover the cursor over the hidden profile, click and hold the left mouse button until the pop-up menu displays, and then select **Profile**.*

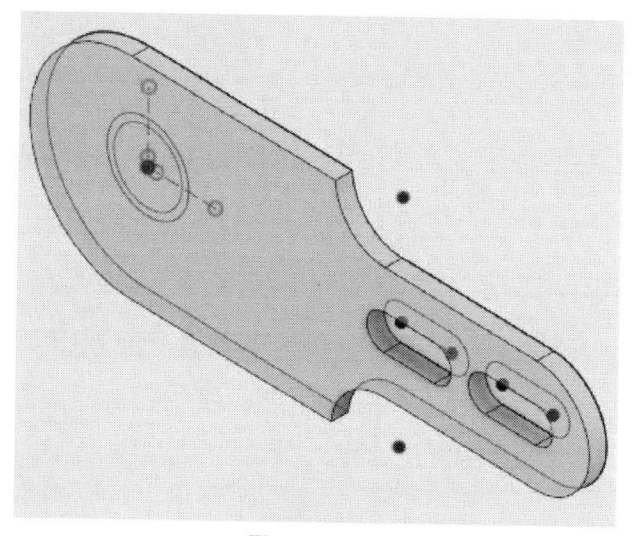

Figure 5–36

2. Create the extrusion shown in Figure 5–37. Set the depth of the extrusion to be **20**. Note that the feature initially tries to cut material because it is extruding through the existing solid geometry. The extrusion cannot cut through the base feature and add material at the same time, so expand the Operation drop-down list and select (Join) to add new material to the existing solid body.

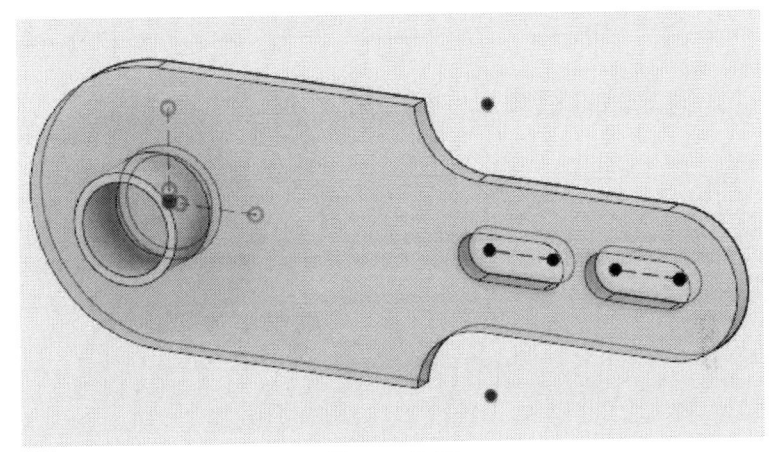

Figure 5–37

3. Create another extrusion that removes the material shown in Figure 5–38.

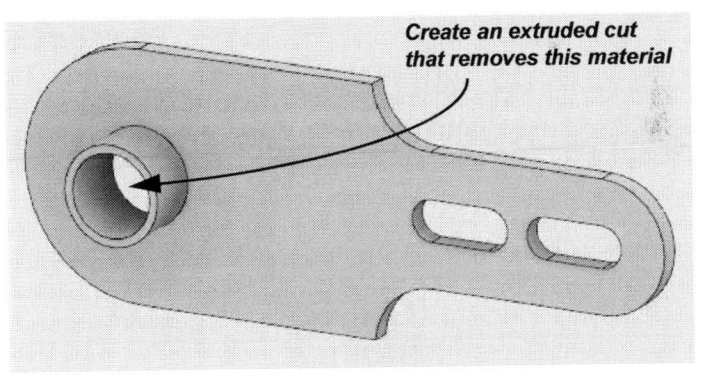

Create an extruded cut that removes this material

Figure 5–38

4. Toggle off the display of **Sketch1**.

Task 4 - Modify the sketch.

1. Toggle on the display of **Sketch1** again.

2. In the BROWSER, right-click on **Sketch1** and select **Show Dimension**.

3. Double-click on the 120 dimension and enter **160**.

4. Double-click on the 24 diameter dimension and enter **30**. Note how all of the features that referenced the sketch update automatically.

5. Hide the display of **Sketch1**. The model should display as shown in Figure 5–39.

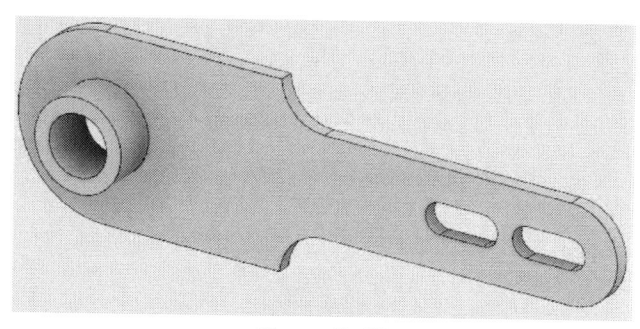

Figure 5–39

6. Save the design with the name **reuse_sketch** to your *Autodesk Fusion 360 Practice Files* project.

7. Close the file.

Chapter Review Questions

1. The **Offset** tool is commonly used to create sketched entities offset from projected geometry. In the sketch shown in Figure 5–40, how many dimensions are required to fully constrain the sketch? (Note: Assume that **Loop Select** is turned on.)

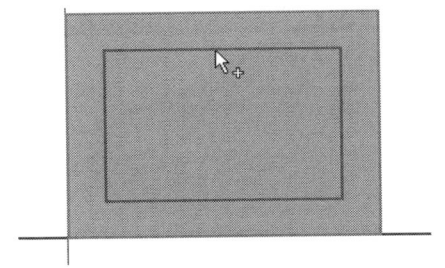

   Figure 5–40

   a. 1
   b. 2
   c. 3
   d. 4
   e. More than 4

2. You cannot reuse an sketch that has already been used to create a feature (such as an extrude).

   a. True
   b. False

3. When using Projected Geometry in a sketch, which of the following is true?

   a. You can only project edges into a sketch that lie in the same plane as the sketching plane.
   b. When selecting an origin plane as a sketching plane, the edges that lie in the plane are automatically projected into the sketch.
   c. When selecting an existing edge as a constraint or dimension reference, the edge is automatically projected into the sketch.
   d. When you use a projected edge as a dimension reference, no relationship between the sketch and the projected edge's parent feature is established.

4. Which *Operation* option is used to create an extrusion that adds material to existing solid body?

   a. (Join)

   b. (Intersect)

   c. (Cut)

   d. (New Body)

5. Which *Extent* option would you use to have an Extrude feature terminate at a specific face?

   a. (Distance)

   b. (To)

   c. (One Side)

   d. (All)

6. Which tool temporarily hides the portion of a design that is above the sketch plane so that the plane displays more clearly for sketching, as shown in Figure 5–41?

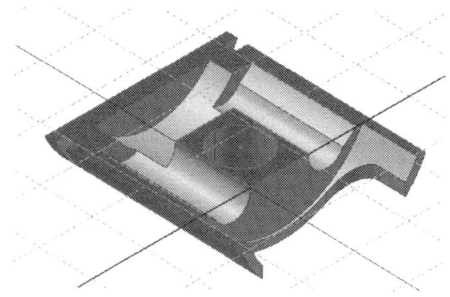

Figure 5–41

   a. **Slice**
   b. **Snap**
   c. **Look At**
   d. **Shaded with Hidden Edges**

Answers: 1.a, 2.b, 3.c, 4.a, 5.b, 6.a

Command Summary

Button	Command	Location
	Offset	- **Ribbon:** *Model* Workspace>SKETCH panel - **Context Menu:** Right-click in the graphics window and select **Sketch**.
	Project	- **Ribbon:** *Model* Workspace>SKETCH panel - **Context Menu:** Right-click in the graphics window and select **Sketch**.

Chapter 6

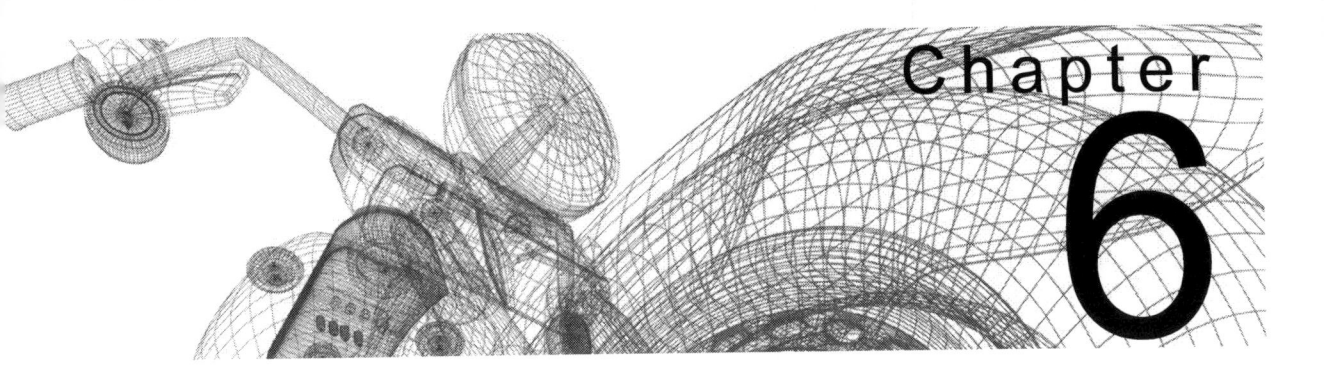

Pick and Place Features

Fillets, chamfers, and holes are sometimes known as Pick and Place features. The shape of the feature is implied, so you are not required to sketch the section. Pick and place features can be added once the design's first solid feature has been created to help add detail to your design.

Learning Objectives in this Chapter

- Create constant, variable, chordal, and rule-based fillets in a design.
- Create chamfers in a design
- Create simple, counterbore, and countersink holes in a design.

6.1 Fillets

Fillets can add or remove material, as shown in Figure 6–1. You can create constant radius, variable radius, and chord length fillet types.

Constant radius fillet (material added)

Variable radius fillet

Constant radius fillet (material removed)

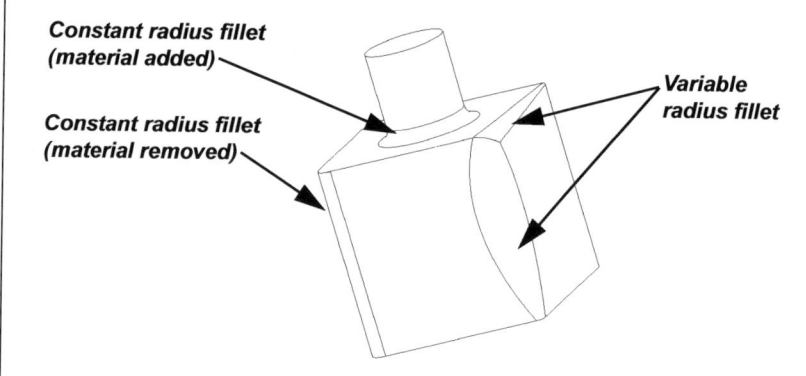

Figure 6–1

Timeline icon:

Use any of the following methods to start the **Arc** tool:

- In the MODIFY panel, click (Fillet).
- In the graphics window, right-click and select **Modify>Fillet**.
- Press <F>.

Constant Radius Fillet

A (Constant Radius) fillet has a constant radius along the entire reference edge. To create a constant radius fillet, you must select the edge or edges on which the fillet is to be placed. Figure 6–2 shows an example of a constant edge fillet feature.

Multiple edges can be selected by holding <Ctrl> while selecting the references.

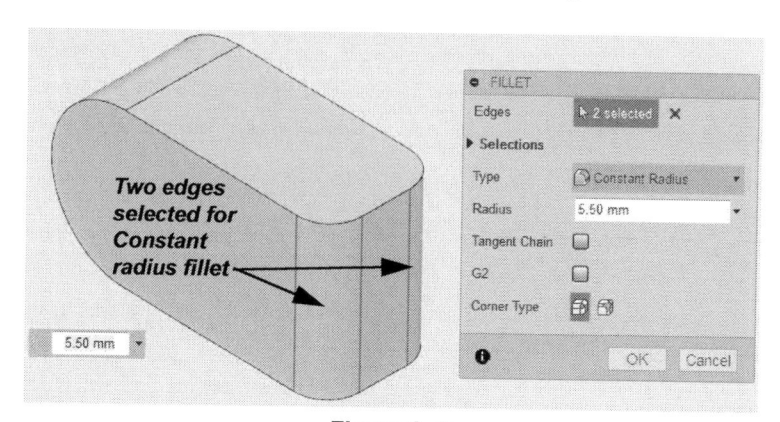

Two edges selected for Constant radius fillet

5.50 mm

FILLET
Edges — 2 selected
Selections
Type — Constant Radius
Radius — 5.50 mm
Tangent Chain
G2
Corner Type

Figure 6–2

- In the FILLET palette, the **Tangent Chain** option (shown in Figure 6–3) enables you to create a fillet on multiple tangent edges with one selection.

- In the FILLET palette, the **G2** option (shown in Figure 6–3) can be used to apply curvature continuity between the fillet and the adjacent surfaces, as well as tangency (G1).

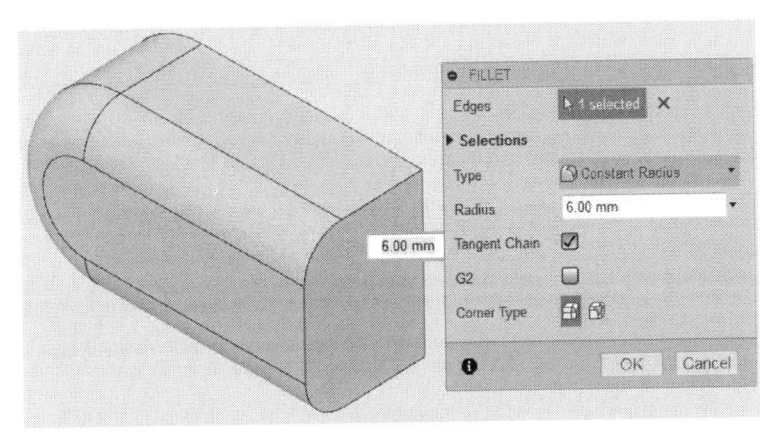

Figure 6–3

- The Corner Type drop-down list provides options that change the fillet shape that is created on intersecting edges, as shown in Figure 6–4.

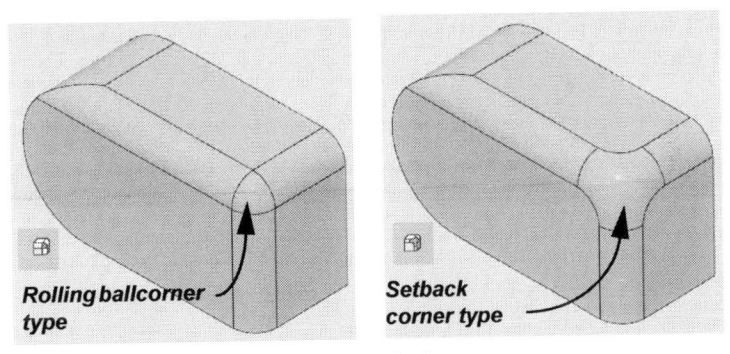

Rolling ballcorner type *Setback corner type*

Figure 6–4

Video Lesson Available

Creating Constant Radius Fillets

Video Length: 3:12

Variable Radius Fillet

A 🗔 (Variable Radius) fillet enables you to define at least two radii along the reference edge, as shown in Figure 6–5. Selecting the references for a variable edge chain fillet is the same as selecting a constant edge chain fillet, except that multiple edges can only be selected if they are tangent to one another. Manipulators display with the fillet to help you define the radius at each end of the selected edges.

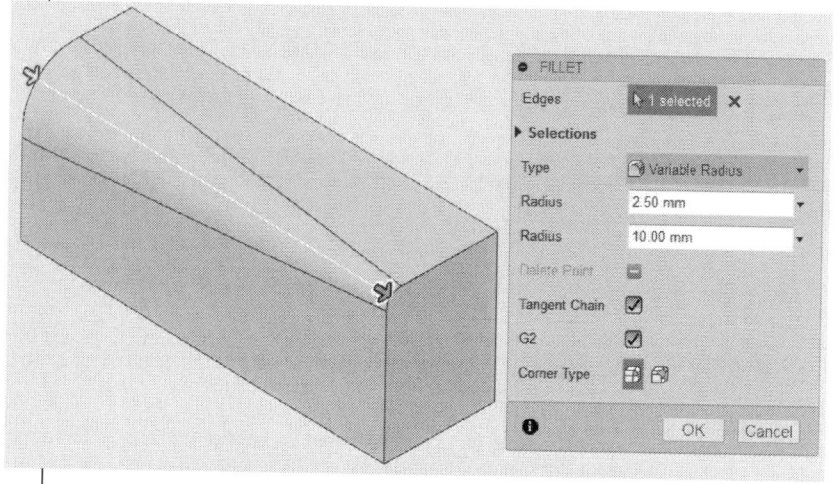

Figure 6–5

It is also possible to have intermediate points between the endpoints of a variable radius fillet with different radius values. To create an intermediate point:

1. Place the cursor along the selected edge.
   - A green dot displays if you select the midpoint between the two endpoints. Otherwise, a red dot displays indicating the relative position between the two end points, as shown in Figure 6–6. You can enter a precise value for the relative position along the edge after the intermediate location has been selected.

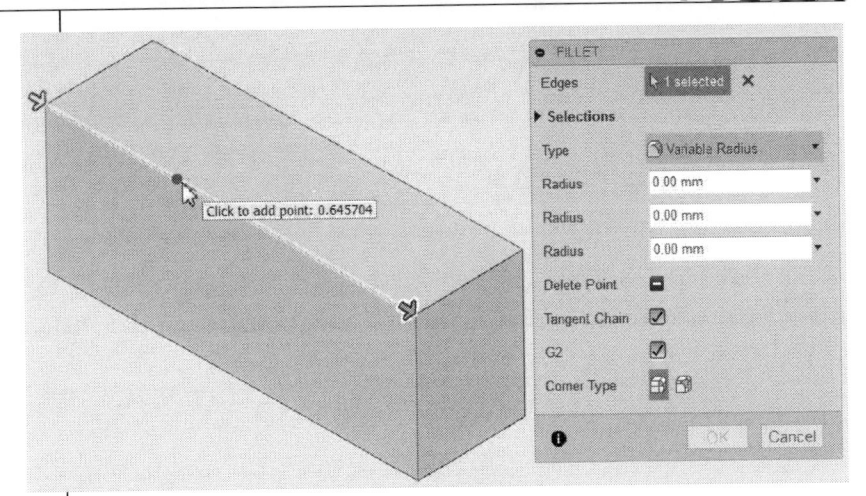

Figure 6–6

2. Assign the intermediate point's value in the FILLET palette, as shown in Figure 6–7.

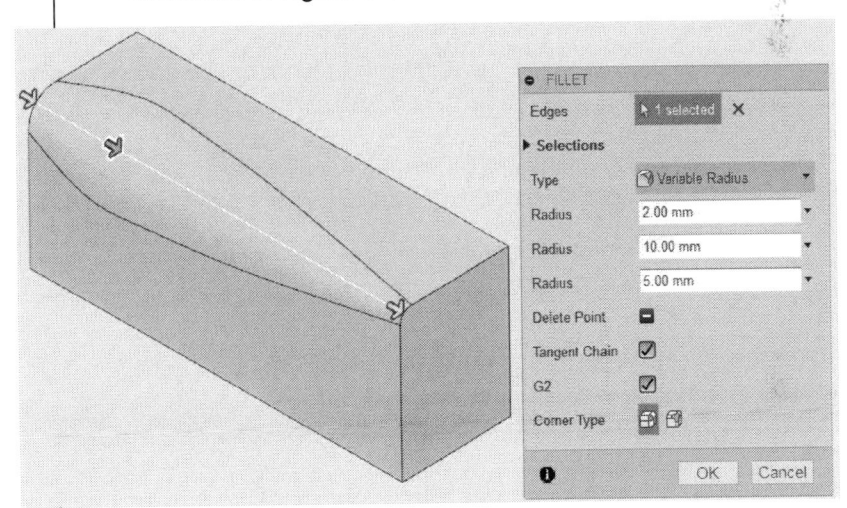

Figure 6–7

Video Lesson Available

Creating Variable Radius Fillets

Video Length: 3:37

Chordal Fillet

A ⬚ (Chord Length) fillet is a variable fillet where you specify a chord length to define the fillet, as shown in Figure 6–8. The fillet radius is determined at each location along the reference edge, ensuring that the chord length remains constant.

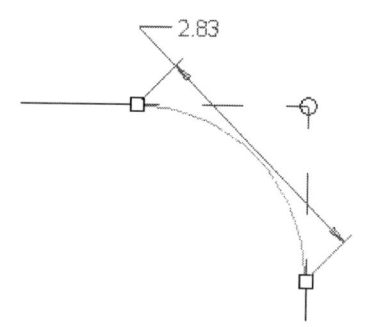

Figure 6–8

Chordal fillets are typically used when aesthetics are important. Figure 6–9 shows the difference between a chord length type and a constant radius type. Note how the edges of the fillet are parallel at all points on the chord length fillet, but not on the constant radius fillet.

Chord Length Fillet   *Constant Radius Fillet*

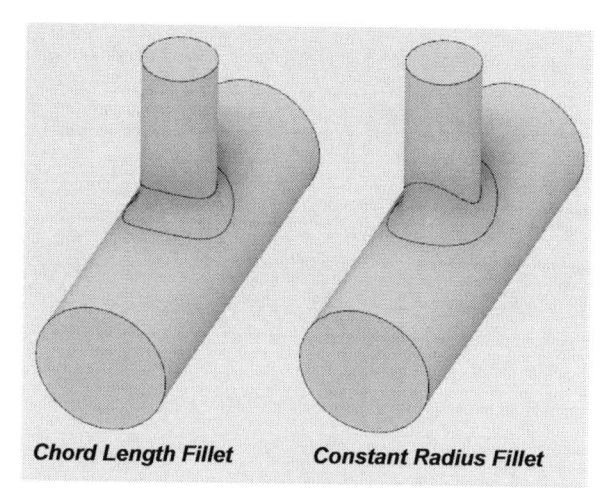

Figure 6–9

Video Lesson Available

Creating Chord Length Fillets

Video Length: 1:37

Rule Fillets

Rule fillets create a constant radius fillet feature on the edges of a selected face, rather then needing you to select individual edges or edge chains. Rule fillets are very useful with plastic parts, or when you are creating rounded corners that are cut with a particular size of tool. Using rule fillets can also be a much quicker method of applying fillets because you can select faces and bodies, rather than individual edges. Because of this, rule fillets might update more predictably than other fillets in that they do not lose edges when features change.

Timeline icon:

- The *Scope Options* drop-down list enables you to define where on the selected geometry the fillet is created.
    - **Against Features:** Creates a fillet only where the selected geometry is adjacent to other features.
    - **All Edges:** Creates a fillet on all edges of the selected geometry.

- The *Topology Options* drop-down list enables you to specify if fillets or rounds are created, as shown in Figure 6–10.
    - **Any:** The default setting, which ensures that both fillets and rounds are assigned together to the selected geometry.
    - **All Fillets:** Applies fillets only to the inside corners of the selected geometry.
    - **All Rounds:** Applies rounds only on the external edges of the selected geometry.

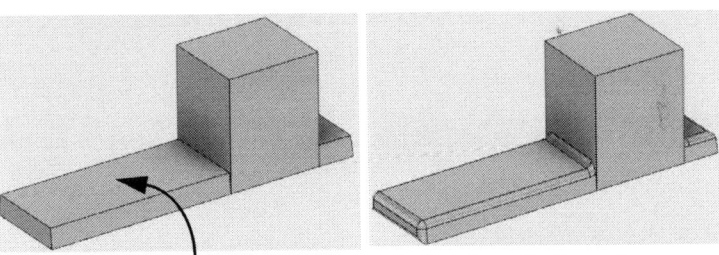

This feature was selected to be filleted.   *Topology Option = Any*

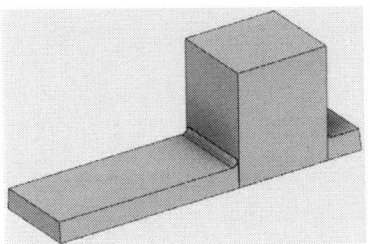

Topology Option = All Fillets   *Topology Option = All Rounds*

Figure 6–10

Use either of the following methods to start the **Rule Fillet** tool:

- In the MODIFY panel, click (Rule Fillet).
- In the graphics window, right-click and select **Modify>Rule Fillet**.

Video Lesson Available

Creating Rule Fillets

Video Length: 3:02

6.2 Chamfers

A chamfer adds a beveled edge between two adjacent surfaces, as shown in Figure 6–11. An edge chamfer can add or remove material.

Timeline icon:

Edge chamfer (material added)

Edge chamfer (material removed)

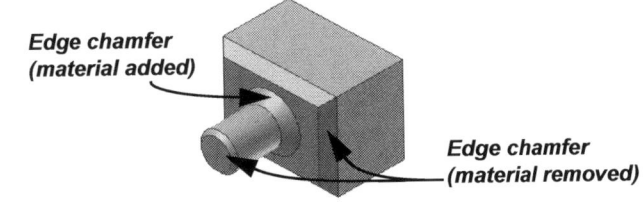

Figure 6–11

The chamfer dimension types are as follows:

(Equal distance)	The chamfer is created at the same distance from the edge on each face.	
(Two distances)	The chamfer is created at one distance from the edge of one face and a different distance from the edge of another.	
(Distance and angle)	The chamfer is created at a distance from the edge on one face and at an angle to that face.	

- To start the **Chamfer** tool, in the MODIFY panel, click (Chamfer).

Video Lesson Available

Creating Edge Chamfers

Video Length: 5:14

6.3 Holes

The Hole command enables you to create a hole on an existing solid. You can create Simple, Counterbore, and Countersink holes, as shown in Figure 6–12.

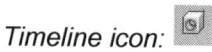

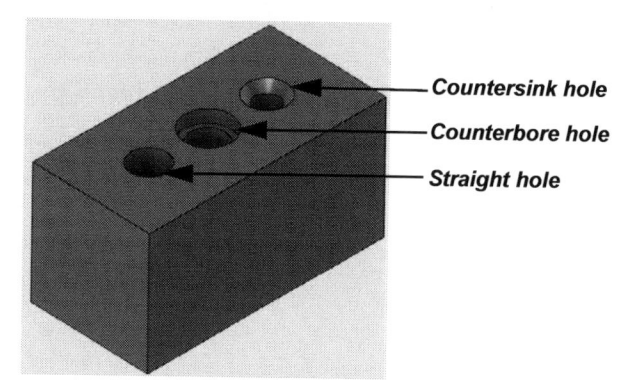

Timeline icon:

Countersink hole
Counterbore hole
Straight hole

Figure 6–12

Use any of the following methods to start the **Hole** tool:

- In the CREATE panel, click (Hole).

- In the graphics window, right-click and select **Create>Hole**.

- Press <H>.

You can create a single hole by selecting a location on a face using the (At Point (Single Hole)) option in the HOLE palette, as shown in Figure 6–13. References can be selected to locate the position of the hole on the face.

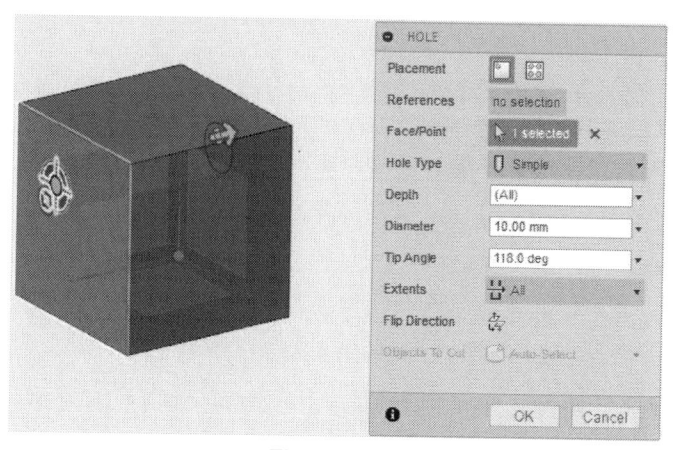

Figure 6–13

*The **Tip Angle** option controls the angle at the bottom of the hole, as if the hole were drilled using a drill bit, rather than a router or mill.*

Depending on the hole type that was selected, the required sizing options will vary. The values can be defined by activating and dragging manipulators, entering values in the input fields, or by entering a value in the HOLE palette, as shown in Figure 6–14.

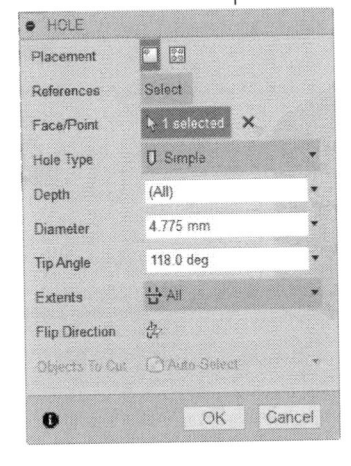

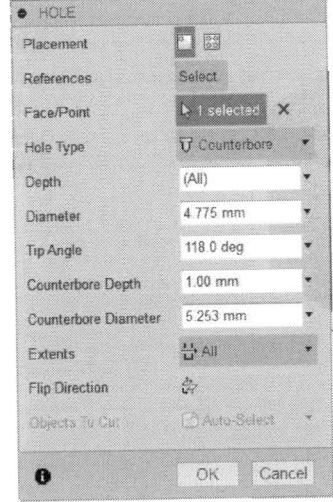

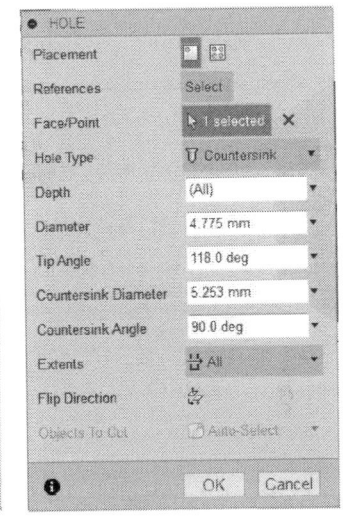

Figure 6–14

The (From Sketch (Multiple Holes)) option can be used to create multiple holes simultaneously. To use this option, a sketch must contain multiple points prior to hole creation.

Video Lesson Available

Creating a Hole

Video Length: 4:32

6.4 Editing Pick and Place Features

Once you have created a pick and place feature, you might need to modify it. Editing the feature opens the palette to redefine any of the elements used to define the feature. To clear references for fillets and chamfers, press and hold <Ctrl> or <Shift> and select the referenced edge:

To edit a fillet, chamfer, or hole, open the feature dialog box using one of the following methods:

- In the Timeline, double-click on the feature icon.

- In the Timeline, right-click on the feature icon and select **Edit Feature**.

- Select any face that is generated by the feature, right-click, and select **Edit Feature**.

Practice 6a

Constant Radius Fillets

Practice Objective

- Create constant edge fillet features along specific edges in the design.

In this practice, you will add fillets to a design. The completed part is shown in Figure 6–15.

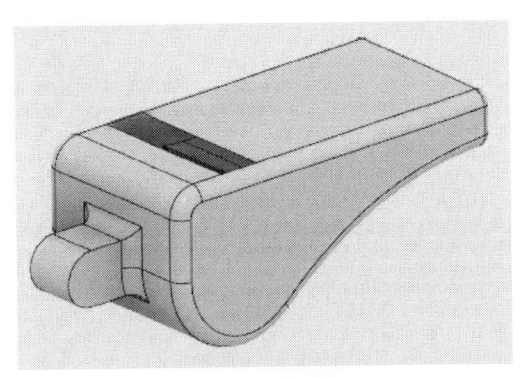

Figure 6–15

Task 1 - Create a new design from file.

1. Click ![icon] > **New Design from File**.

2. In the Open dialog box, navigate to the *C:\Autodesk Fusion 360 Practice Files* folder, select **whistle.f3d**, and then click **Open**. The design displays as shown in Figure 6–16.

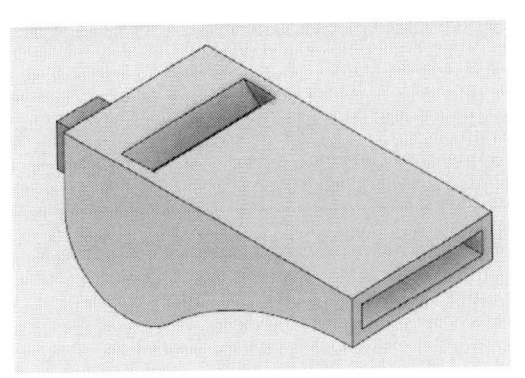

Figure 6–16

Task 2 - Create a constant radius fillet.

1. Orient the part as shown in Figure 6–17.

2. Right-click on the edge shown in Figure 6–17 and select (Fillet).

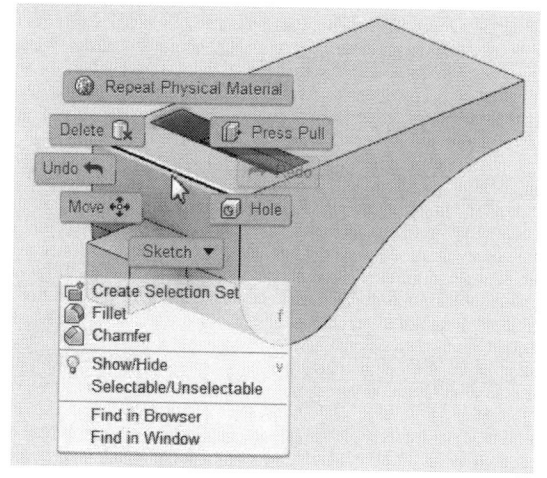

Figure 6–17

3. Using the FILLET palette settings shown in Figure 6–18, create the **0.25 in** constant radius fillet.

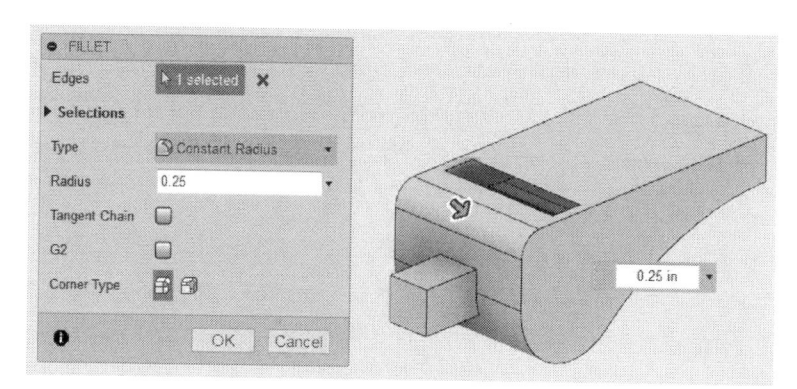

Figure 6–18

4. Click **OK**.

Task 3 - Simulate a full round fillet.

A full round fillet is typically created between two edges to replace the face between them. This can be simulated with two constant radius fillets created on parallel edges.

1. In the MODIFY panel, click (Fillet).
2. Select the two parallel edges indicated in Figure 6–19.

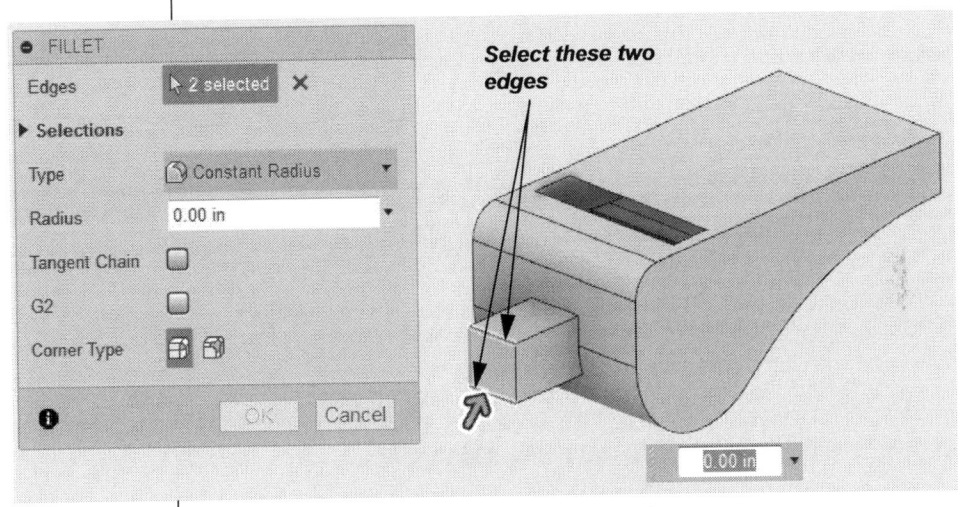

Figure 6–19

3. The distance between these two edges is 0.50 in, so set the radius to **0.25**. The completed feature should display as shown in Figure 6–20.

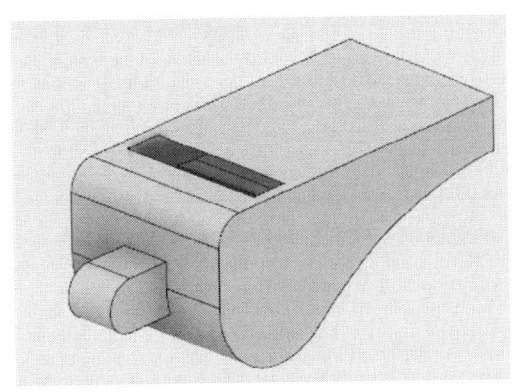

Figure 6–20

Task 4 - Create fillets along tangent edges.

1. Press <F> to create another fillet feature.

2. In the FILLET palette, select the **Tangent Chain** option, if not already selected.

3. Select the two edges indicated in Figure 6–21. Note that all of the edges that are tangent to those you selected are automatically selected as well.

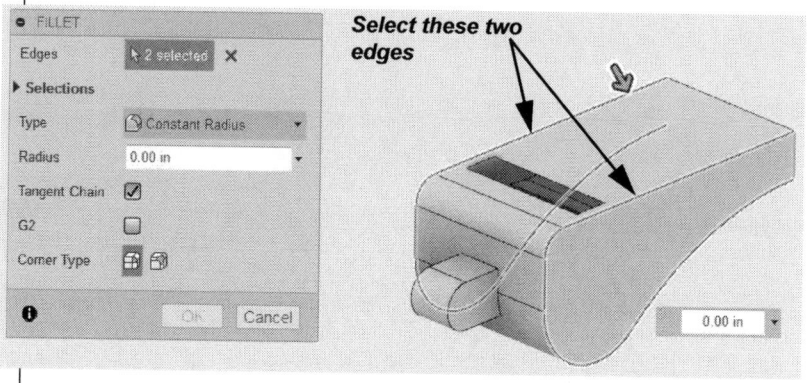

Figure 6–21

4. Complete the feature with a **0.125** radius.

5. On the tangent chain of edges indicated in Figure 6–22, create another fillet with a radius of **0.075**.

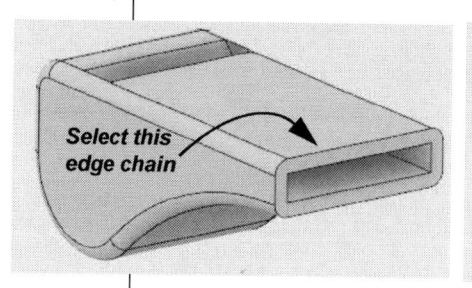

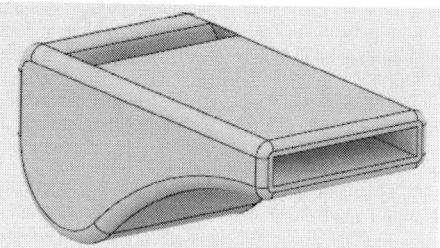

Figure 6–22

Task 5 - Create the final fillet.

1. Create the final fillet as a single feature on the four edges indicated in Figure 6–23.

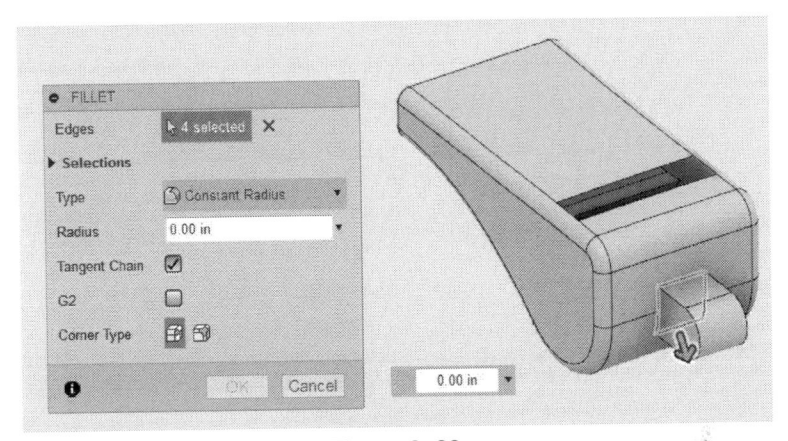

Figure 6–23

2. Set the *Radius* to **0.125**.

3. The final design should display as shown in Figure 6–24.

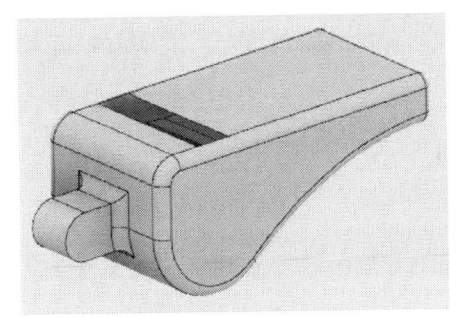

Figure 6–24

4. Save the design with the name **whistle** to your *Autodesk Fusion 360 Practice Files* project.

5. Close the file.

Practice 6b Creating Rule Fillets

Practice Objective

- Create a Rule fillet in design geometry.

In this practice, you will use the Rule Fillet command to easily create fillets and rounds in a design.

Task 1 - Create a new design from file.

1. Click ▾ > **New Design from File**.

2. In the Open dialog box, navigate to the *C:\Autodesk Fusion 360 Practice Files* folder, select **RuleFillet.f3d**, and click **Open**. The design displays as shown in Figure 6–25.

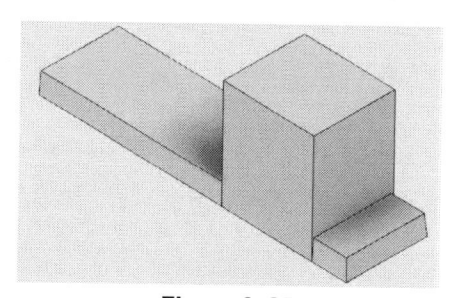

Figure 6–25

Task 2 - Create a Rule Fillet.

1. In the MODIFY panel, click (Rule Fillet). The RULE FILLET palette opens.

2. Select the face indicated in Figure 6–26.

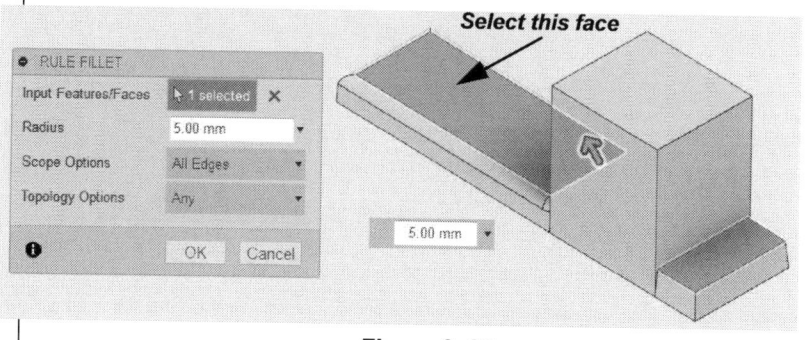

Figure 6–26

3. Use the arrow manipulator to dynamically drag the radius to a value of approximately **5mm**. Note that as soon as you drag the manipulator arrow, the top face of the other short box also highlights blue, even though it was not selected. This is because these two faces belong to the same original box primitive that was created as the first solid feature.

4. Ensure that the exact radius value is set to **5mm**.

5. Ensure that *Scope Options* is set to **All Edges**. This ensures that a fillet is created on all of the edges of the selected geometry.

6. With the *Topology Options*, you can specify that only fillets or rounds be created. Set this to **All Fillets**. The rule fillet is applied only to the inside corners.

7. Change the value to **All Rounds**. The rule fillet is created only on external edges.

8. Change the *Topology Options* value back to **Any**.

9. Click **OK** to create the fillet. The fillet is created on the top face of both of the shorter box items, as shown in Figure 6–27.

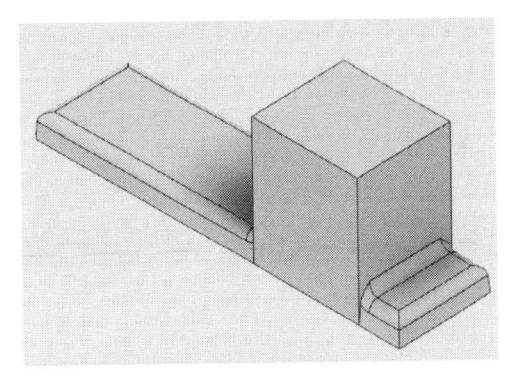

Figure 6–27

Task 3 - Repeat the Rule Fillet.

1. Rotate the view so that you can see the bottom of the design.

2. Right-click and in the Marking menu, select **Repeat Rule Fillet**.

3. Select the bottom face of the pocket (shown in Figure 6–28) as the face to be filleted.

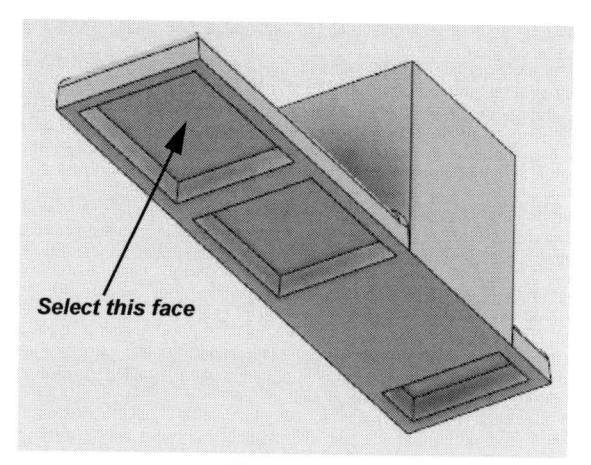

Select this face

Figure 6–28

4. Using any of the available methods, set the radius to **5 mm**.

5. Set *Topology Options* to **All Fillets**.

6. Click **OK** to create the fillet. Note that it is applied to all three pockets, as shown in Figure 6–29.

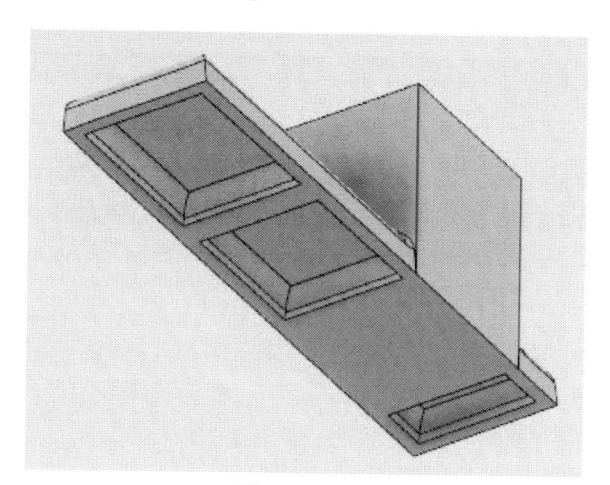

Figure 6–29

Task 4 - Edit the Rule Fillet and change its radius.

1. In the Timeline, right-click the second **Rule Fillet** feature and select **Edit Feature**.

2. Change the radius to **2.5mm** and complete the feature as shown in Figure 6–30.

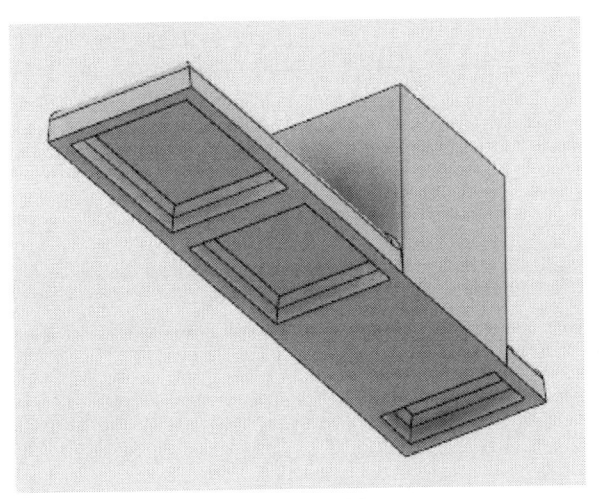

Figure 6–30

3. Save the design with the name **RuleFillet** to your *Autodesk Fusion 360 Practice Files* project.

4. Close the file.

Practice 6c

Fillets and Chamfers

Practice Objectives

- Create constant and variable radius fillets.
- Open the Parameters dialog box and manipulate the design parameters.

In this practice, you will complete the design of a toy tractor by adding a chamfer and simulating a full round to form the front of the toy. You will also create constant radius fillets to complete the cab, and a variable radius fillet to form the front hood area, as shown in Figure 6–31.

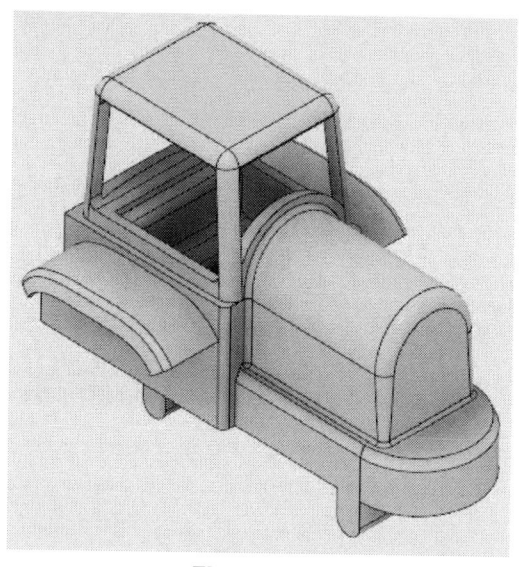

Figure 6–31

Task 1 - Create a new design from file.

1. Click > **New Design from File**.

2. In the Open dialog box, navigate to the *C:\Autodesk Fusion 360 Practice Files* folder, select **toy_tractor.f3d**, and click **Open**. The design displays as shown in Figure 6–32.

Use the ☰ (Measure) command to obtain measurements of a single entity (e.g., length of an edge, surface area of a face) and measurements between entities (e.g., distance, angle).

Measure the length of this edge

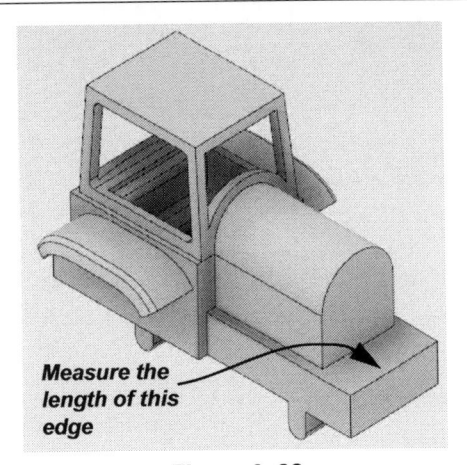

Figure 6–32

Task 2 - Simulate a full round on the front of the toy tractor.

1. In the INSPECT panel, click ☰ (Measure).

2. Select the edge indicated in Figure 6–32. The length of the edge is reported to be 5.04 in. This length will be used to create a simulated full round.

3. Close the MEASURE palette.

4. In the MODIFY panel, click ⬭ (Fillet) in the ribbon.

5. Select the two edges shown in Figure 6–33.

Select these two edges

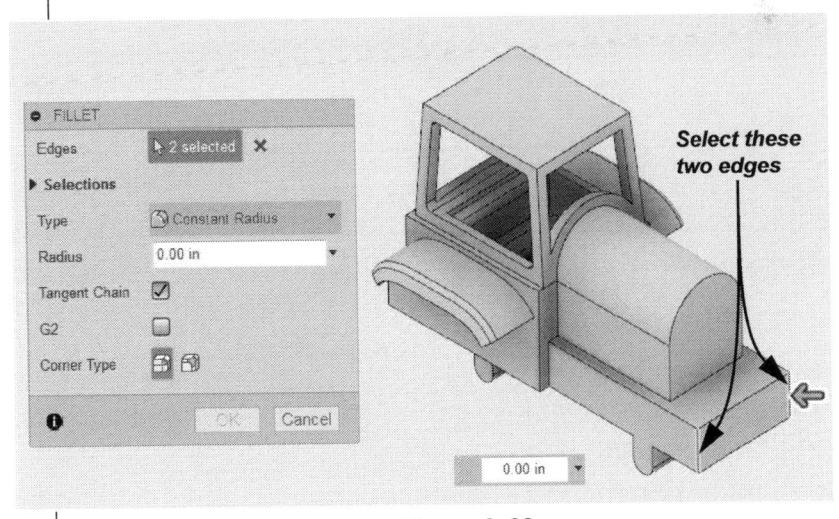

Figure 6–33

Values can be entered in the form of mathematical equations.

6. In the input field, enter **5.04/2**, as shown in Figure 6–34.

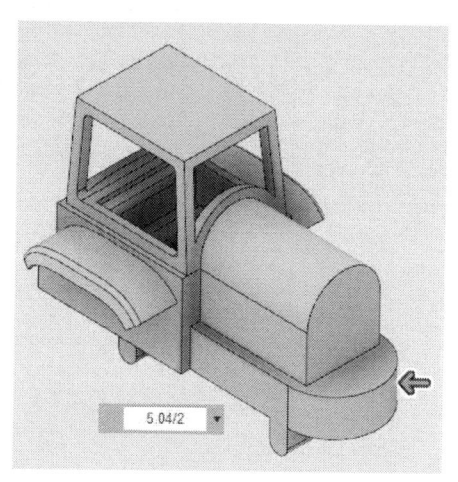

Figure 6–34

7. Click **OK** to complete the feature.

Task 3 - Create a chamfer.

1. In the MODIFY panel, click (Chamfer).
2. Select the edge indicated in Figure 6–35. Ensure that *Chamfer type is set to* (Equal distance). Set the *Distance* to **0.57**.

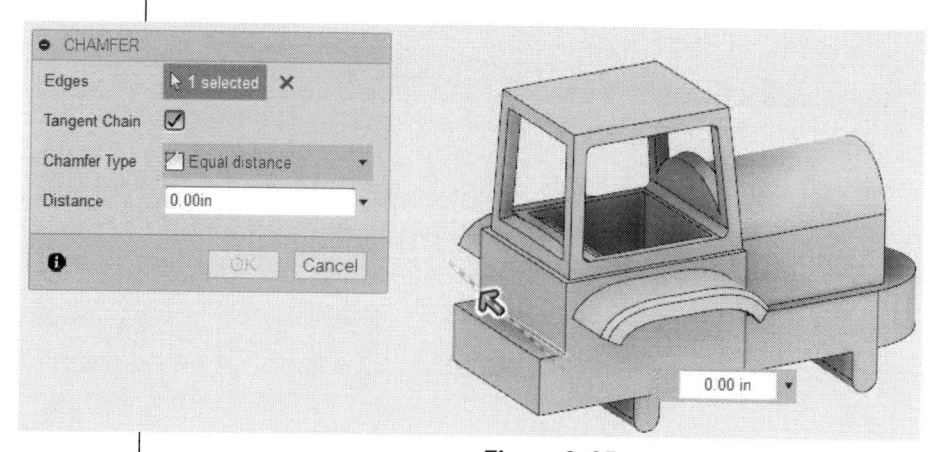

Figure 6–35

3. Click **OK** to complete the feature.

Task 4 - Create a two-distances chamfer.

1. Create a chamfer and select the edge shown in Figure 6–36. With the **Tangent Chain** option activated, all of the edges tangent to the edge you select should also be selected.

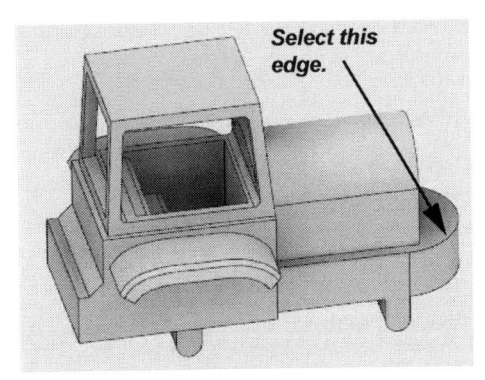

Select this edge.

Figure 6–36

2. For the *Chamfer Type,* select ▱ (Two distances).

3. Set the first *Distance* to **0.18**, and the second *Distance* to **0.375**, as shown in Figure 6–37.

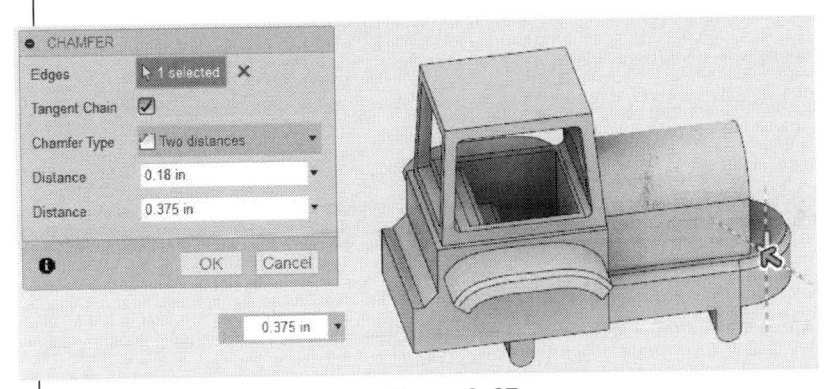

Figure 6–37

4. Complete the feature.

Task 5 - Create constant radius fillets.

1. Press <F>.

2. Create a fillet on all four outer edges of the cab with a radius of **0.50**, as shown in Figure 6–38.

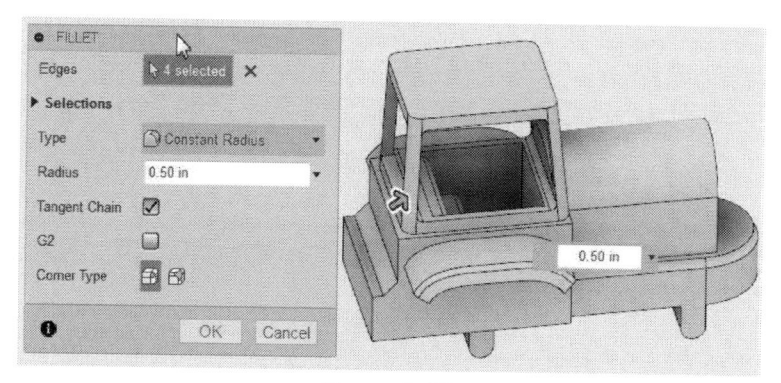

Figure 6–38

3. On the top edge of the cab, create another fillet with a value of **0.50**, as shown in Figure 6–39.

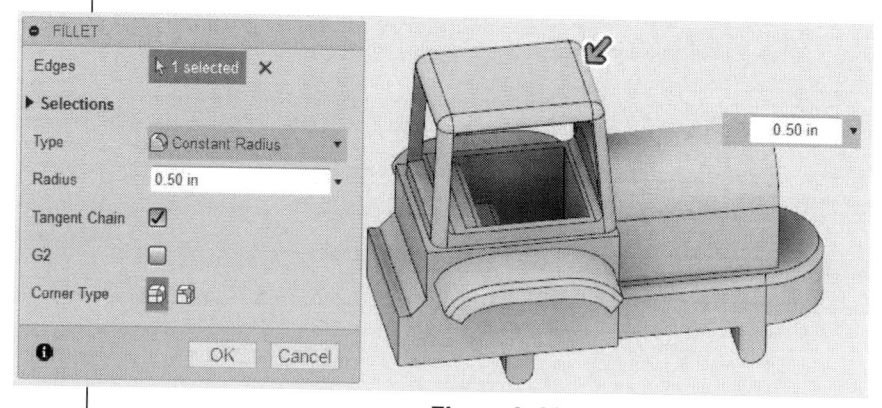

Figure 6–39

4. On the edges where the cab and the hood meet, create a fillet with a *Radius* value of **0.18**, as shown in Figure 6–40. Note that these edges are not tangent.

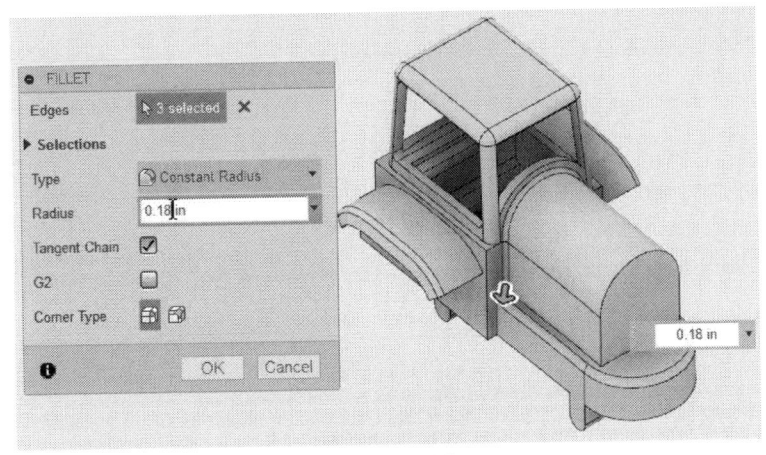

Figure 6–40

Task 6 - Create a variable radius fillet.

1. Create a fillet and select the edge shown in Figure 6–41.

2. Ensure that the **Tangent Chain** option is activated.

3. Change the *Type* to (Variable Radius).

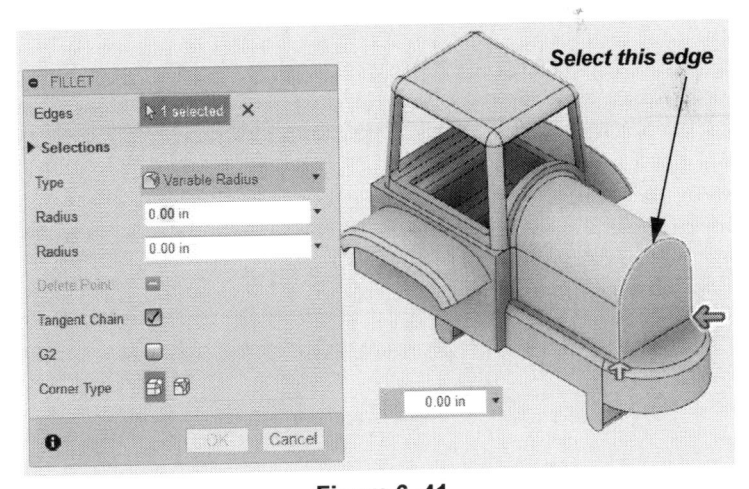

Figure 6–41

4. Hover the cursor over the selected edge at approximately the midpoint of the arc, as shown in Figure 6–42. A green dot displays to indicate the midpoint. Click that location to define an additional radius location along the selected edge.

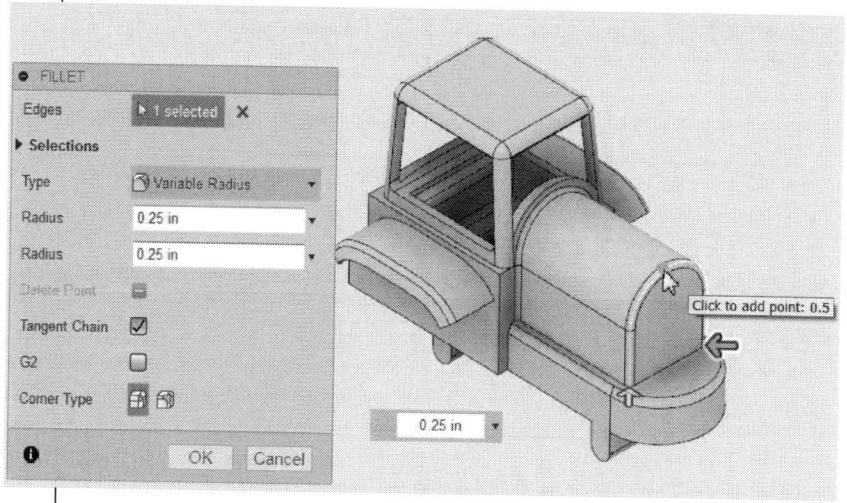

Figure 6–42

5. Enter values in the available fields so that the two ends have a **0.25 in** radius and the mid point has a **0.5 in** radius.

6. In the FILLET palette, in the third *Radius* field, enter **0.5**. Complete the variable edge fillet.

7. Create a fillet on the edge shown in Figure 6–43. For the radius, enter **0.125 in**.

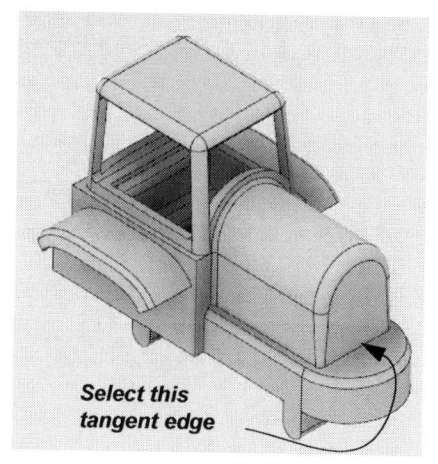

Figure 6–43

Task 7 - Create the final fillets.

1. Create fillets on the edges shown in Figure 6–44 with a radius of **0.125**.

Select these edges

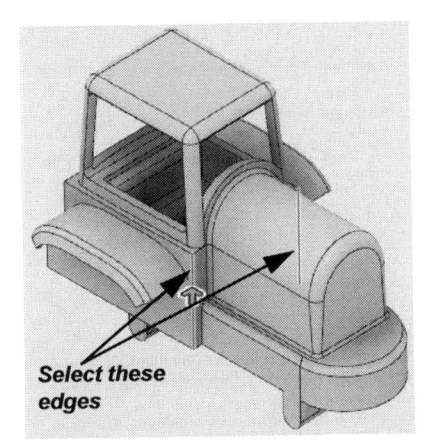

Figure 6–44

2. The completed design should display as shown in Figure 6–45.

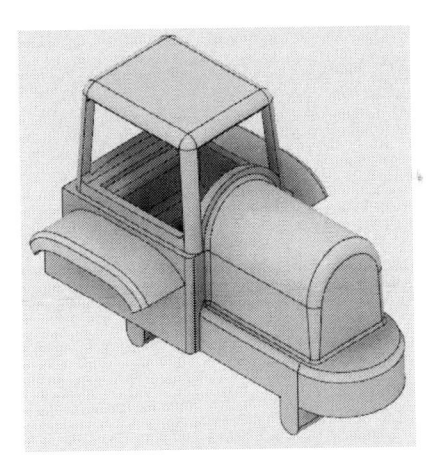

Figure 6–45

3. Save the design with the name **toy_tractor** to your *Autodesk Fusion 360 Practice Files* project.

4. Close the file.

Practice 6d

Fillet Shapes

Practice Objective

- Investigate the impact on fillet shape made by corner types and order of creation.

In this practice, you will create a number of fillets on the design shown in Figure 6–46 to investigate different fillet shapes. The final design is shown in Figure 6–47.

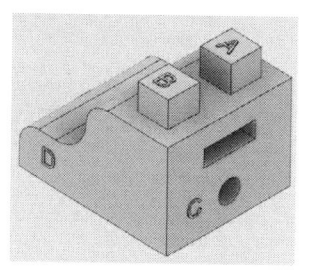

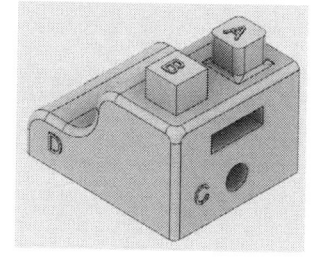

Figure 6–46

Figure 6–47

Task 1 - Create a new design from file.

1. Click ▭ ▾ > **New Design from File**.
2. In the Open dialog box, navigate to the *C:\Autodesk Fusion 360 Practice Files* folder, select **fillets.f3d**, and click **Open**.

Task 2 - Create fillets on surfaces C and D.

1. Create a fillet and select the three edges indicated on surfaces C and D in Figure 6–48. Ensure that the **Tangent Chain** option is selected.

Select these edges.

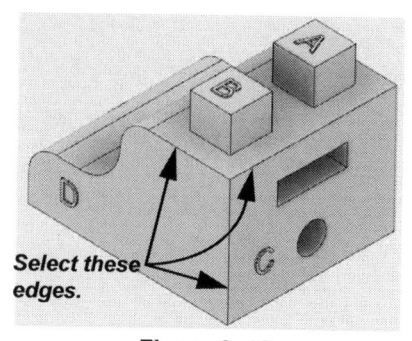

Figure 6–48

2. Set the *Radius* value to **0.50**.

3. The *Corner Type* option is currently set to ▢ (Rolling Ball). Change the option to ▢ (Setback). Note the difference in the shape on the corner, as shown in Figure 6–49.

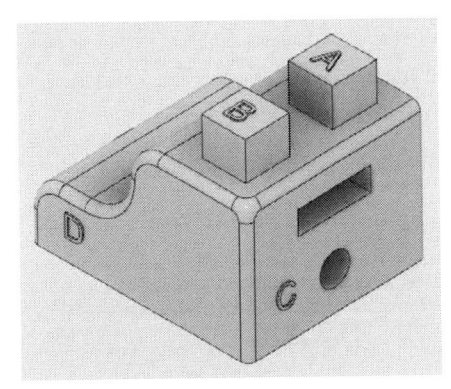

Figure 6–49

4. Click **OK** to complete the feature.

Task 3 - Create the fillets on protrusion A.

1. Where protrusion A meets the base feature, create fillets with a value of **0.3** for the four edges. Select the edges so that they are all included as one feature and are driven by one dimension. The part displays as shown in Figure 6–50.

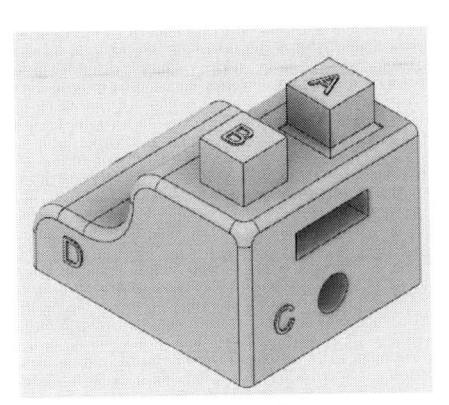

Figure 6–50

2. For the four corner edges on protrusion A, create fillets with a radius of **0.6**. The part displays as shown in Figure 6–51.

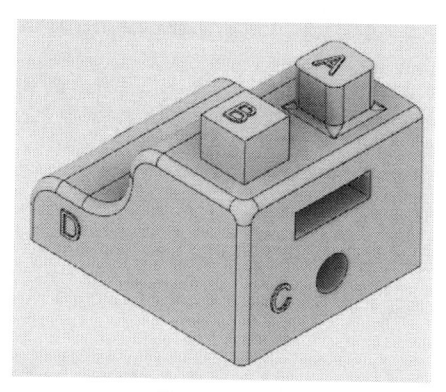

Figure 6–51

Task 4 - Create the fillets on protrusion B in the opposite order to those created on protrusion A.

1. For the four vertical corner edges of protrusion **B**, create fillets with a radius of **0.6**.

2. For the tangent edges where the protrusion meets the base feature, create fillets with a radius of **0.3**. You only need to select one edge, because the existing fillets create a tangent edge chain. The part displays as shown in Figure 6–52. Note the difference in the shape that occurs when the creation order of the two sets of fillets changed.

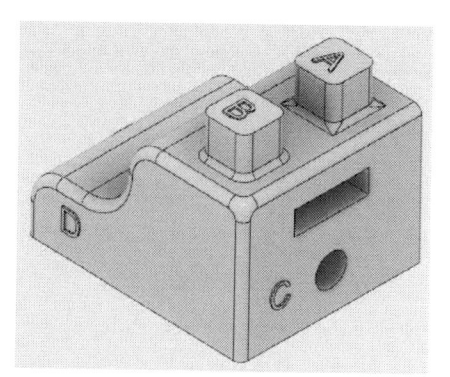

Figure 6–52

3. Save the design with the name **fillets** to your *Autodesk Fusion 360 Practice Files* project.

4. Close the file.

Practice 6e

Holes

Practice Objectives

- Create straight holes with linear placement references.
- Use sketch points to create straight holes with radial placement references.
- Create a hole with a counterbore.

In this practice, you will create simple holes using both linear and radial placement types. The completed part displays as shown in Figure 6–53.

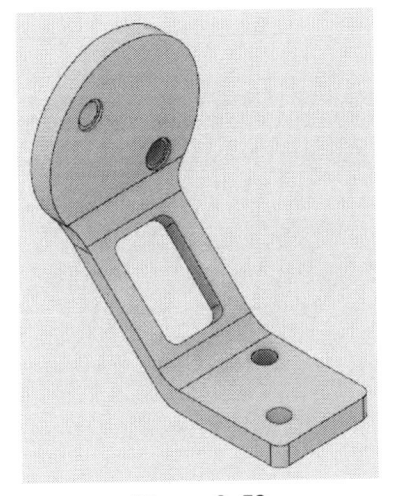

Figure 6–53

Task 1 - Create a new design from file.

1. Click ▼ > **New Design from File**.

2. In the Open dialog box, navigate to the *C:\Autodesk Fusion 360 Practice Files* folder, select **hanger.f3d**, and click **Open**.

Task 2 - Create a hole with linear dimensions.

1. In the CREATE panel, click ⌗ (Hole).

2. Specify a location for the hole by clicking anywhere on the face indicated in Figure 6–54.

Select this face to place the hole

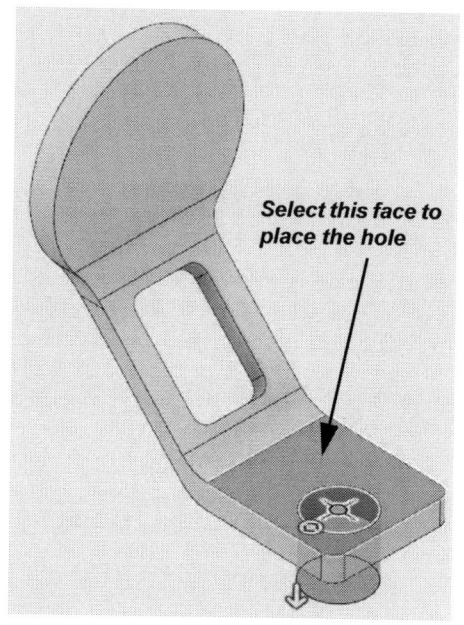

Figure 6–54

If you drag the hole completely off the face, a warning displays noting that there is no target body found to cut or intersect.

3. Move the hole around on the face by selecting the blue dot at its center and drag it with the cursor.

4. Select the edge indicated in Figure 6–55 to add a placement reference to locate the hole on the face.

5. In the active input field that displays, enter **3**.

6. Select the edge indicated in Figure 6–56 to add a second placement reference and enter **3** as the value.

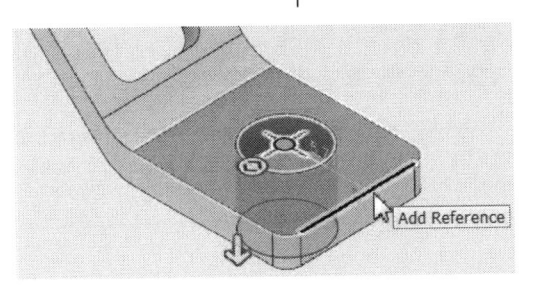

Figure 6–55

Figure 6–56

7. Click the ⊚ handle to change the diameter. Drag the handle to a diameter of **2**, or type the value.

8. Ensure that the *Hole Type* is set to ⊍ (Simple). Change E*xtents* to ⊔ (All), if required.

9. Complete the hole. The design displays as shown in Figure 6–57.

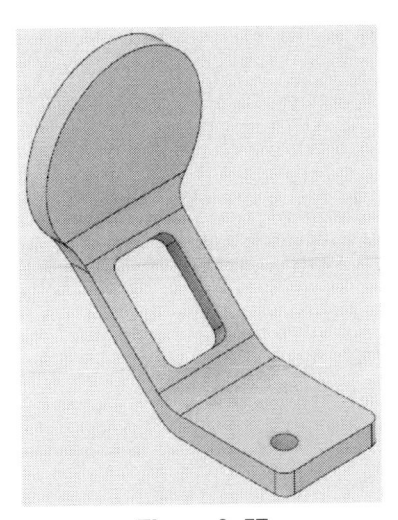

Figure 6–57

Task 3 - Create another hole using the linear placement type.

1. Create a simple hole using the references shown in Figure 6–58. Set the following options:
   - *Diameter:* **2.0**
   - *Reference* value: **9.0**
   - *Reference* value: **2.5**
   - *Extents:* **All**

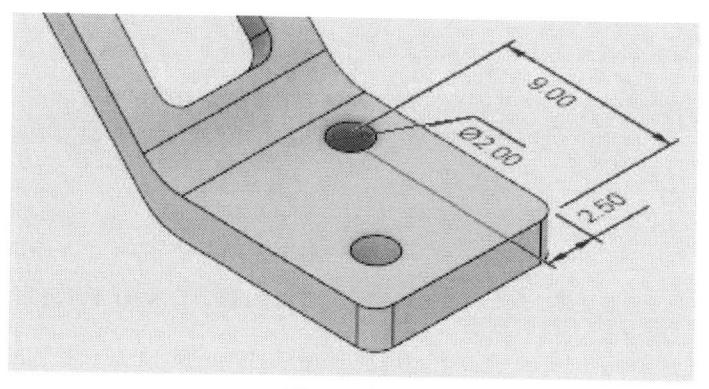

Figure 6–58

Task 4 - Create a radially placed hole.

The hole feature cannot be placed with radial dimensions. Instead, you can sketch points with radial dimensions and use those to place the holes.

1. Create a sketch on the face shown in Figure 6–59.

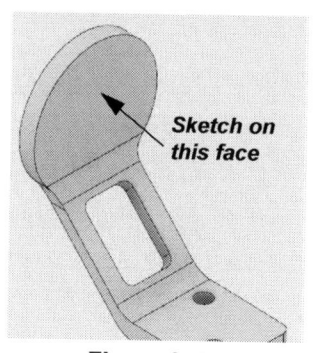

Figure 6–59

2. Toggle on the display of Origin features.

3. Starting at the Origin Point, sketch a line that is perpendicular to one of the part edges and across the circular face.

4. Convert the line construction geometry as shown in Figure 6–60.

The edge that is perpendicular to the construction line is automatically projected into the sketch.

Figure 6–60

5. Create a point and snap it to the construction line and the center of the circular edge.

6. Sketch a second construction line across the circular face, through the sketch point, and at an angle to the first construction line.

7. Apply a **Coincident** constraint between this second construction line and the sketch point.

8. Create an angular dimension between the two construction lines with a value of **60**. The sketch should display similar to that shown in Figure 6–61.

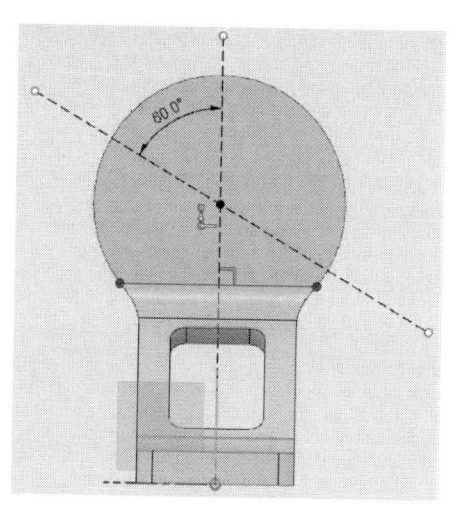

Figure 6–61

9. Sketch two points that are snapped to the second construction line, and dimensioned with respect to the first sketch point, as shown in Figure 6–62.

*To get the dimensions in the orientations shown in Figure 6–62, when you place the dimensions for the points, right-click and select **Aligned**.*

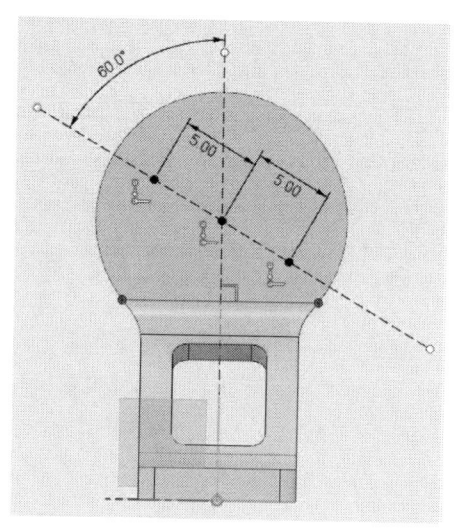

Figure 6–62

10. Stop the sketch.

11. Toggle off the display of Origin features.

12. Press <H> to create a hole feature.

13. *For the Placement* option, select ▦ (From Sketch (Multiple Holes)).

14. Select the two outer sketch points on the circular face.

15. Ensure that the *Hole Type* is set to ▯ (Simple), and the *Extents* is set to ⇊ (All).

16. Complete the feature. The design should display as shown in Figure 6–63.

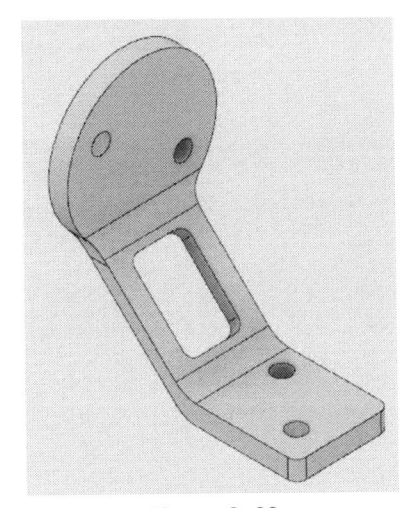

Figure 6–63

17. In the BROWSER, expand the *Sketches* folder and toggle on the display of the sketch listed there.

18. In the BROWSER, right-click on the sketch and select **Show Dimension**.

19. Double-click on the 60.0° angular dimension and change its value to **45**. Note how the position of the two holes changes accordingly.

20. Toggle off the display of the sketch.

Task 5 - Edit a hole feature to add a counterbore.

1. In the Timeline, right-click the icon for the last hole feature and select **Edit Feature**.

2. Change the *Hole Type* to ▽ (Counterbore). Note that a second ◈ handle displays so that the diameter of the counterbore can be set.

3. In the EDIT FEATURE palette, set the following options as shown in Figure 6–64:
   - Set the *Counterbore Depth* to **0.25**.
   - Set the *Counterbore Diameter* to **2.6**.

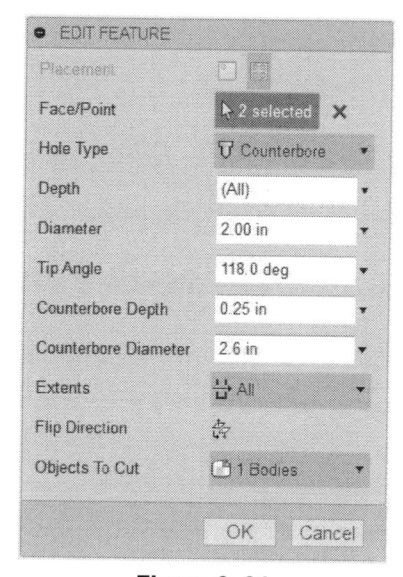

Figure 6–64

The counterbore is applied to both holes on the circular face because they both belong to the same feature. When modeling, one design consideration you should decide on is to create multiple holes as a single feature, or as independent features.

4. Complete the feature. It should display as shown in Figure 6–65.

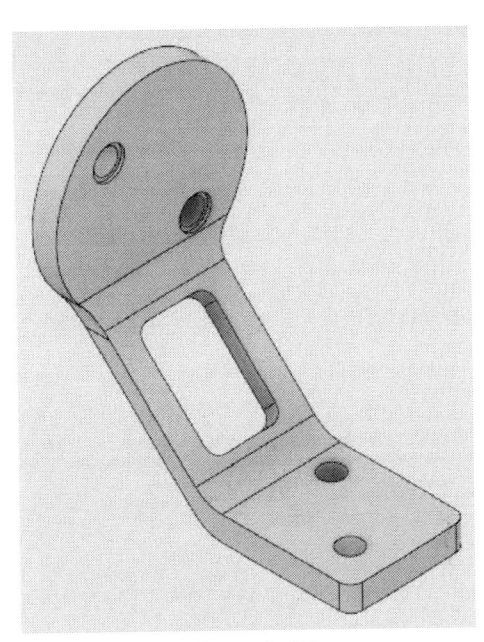

Figure 6–65

5. Save the design with the name **hanger** to your *Autodesk Fusion 360 Practice Files* project.

6. Close the file.

Chapter Review Questions

1. Which of the chamfer types require two dimension values? (Select all that apply.)
   a. Equal distance
   b. Distance and angle
   c. Two distances

2. Chamfer features always remove material.
   a. True
   b. False

3. Fillet features can add or remove material.
   a. True
   b. False

4. Fillets on multiple edges can be controlled by a single dimension.
   a. True
   b. False

5. The face indicated in Figure 6–66 was selected as the reference for a Rule Fillet. The resulting geometry is shown in Figure 6–67. Which *Topology Option* was selected to create the Rule Fillet?

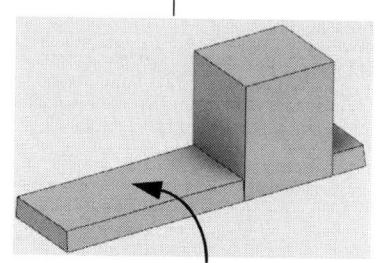

This feature was selected to be filleted

Figure 6–66

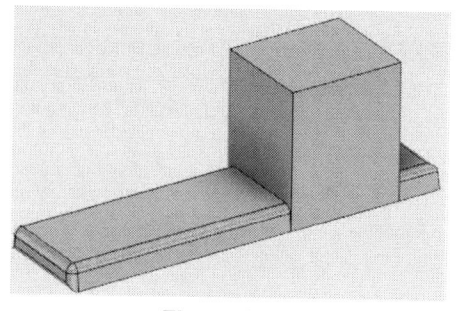

Figure 6–67

   a. **All**
   b. **All Fillets**
   c. **All Rounds**

6. How can you modify an existing placed feature, such as a fillet or chamfer?

    a. Return to the sketch mode and change the sketch profile.

    b. Double-click on the feature in either the graphics window or the BROWSER.

    c. Select the same tool that was used to create the feature.

7. What does the *Tip Angle* option control in a Hole feature?

    a. The angle of hole axis relative to the placement surface.

    b. The angle of the countersink.

    c. The angle at the bottom of the hole.

    d. The angle of the counterbore.

8. Which option do you select to change the reference edges for a chamfer?

    a. **Show Dimensions**

    b. **Edit Feature**

    c. **Edit Sketch**

    d. **Suppress Features**

9. The first reference for a Hole feature is the sketch plane.

    a. True

    b. False

Answers: 1.(b,c), 2.b, 3.a, 4.a, 5.c, 6.b, 7.c, 8.b, 9.b

Command Summary

Button	Command	Location
	Chamfer (feature)	• **Ribbon:** *Model* Workspace>MODIFY panel • **Context Menu:** Right-click in the graphics window and select **Modify**.
	Fillet (feature)	• **Ribbon:** *Model* Workspace>MODIFY panel • **Context Menu:** Right-click in the graphics window and select **Modify**.
	Hole	• **Ribbon:** *Model* Workspace>CREATE panel • **Context Menu:** Right-click in the graphics window and select **Create**.
	Measure	• **Ribbon:** *Model* Workspace>INSPECT panel • **Context Menu:** Right-click in the graphics window and select **Inspect**.
	Rule Fillet	• **Ribbon:** *Model* Workspace>MODIFY panel • **Context Menu:** Right-click in the graphics window and select **Modify**.

Chapter 7

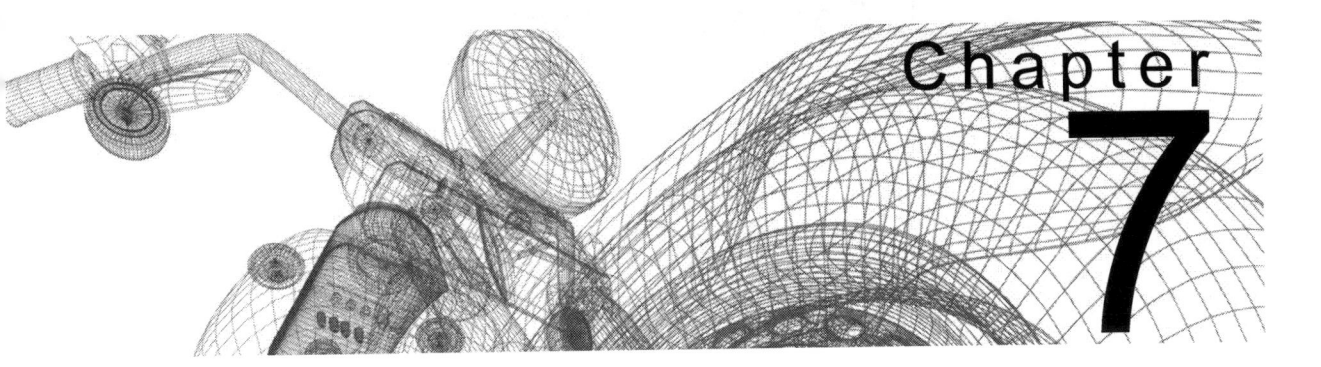

Construction Features

During the design process, the features that currently exist in a design might not provide the references required to place a new feature. In these situations, you can use construction features to create the necessary references.

Learning Objectives in this Chapter

- Create new construction planes, axes, and points in a design.
- Describe how using construction planes, axes, or points in a design can help you to create geometry that could not be created using the existing features or geometry.

7.1 Construction Planes

Construction work planes, or construction planes, are features that enable you to:

- Control how the geometry is modeled,
- Add sketches or features, and
- Create new faces on an existing solid.

Construction planes are intended for construction purposes only, and have no mass or volume. A representation of the plane is displayed in the graphics window when a Construction plane is displayed. Construction planes extend infinitely in all directions within the plane they exist. You can use them as construction geometry in the creation of other features for purposes such as sketch planes and dimensional references.

Default Origin Planes

Each new design automatically includes three orthogonal construction planes at the origin: the YZ, XZ, and XY planes. In a new design that is using the default Home orientation, the Y direction is up.

Using the default ViewCube orientation, the XZ represents the **Front**, the YZ represents the **Right** and the XY represents the **Top**, as shown in Figure 7–1. Note that since you can edit the views on the ViewCube, this default configuration might not be true for every design.

XY Plane

YZ Plane

XZ Plane

Default Construction Planes

Default ViewCube Orientation

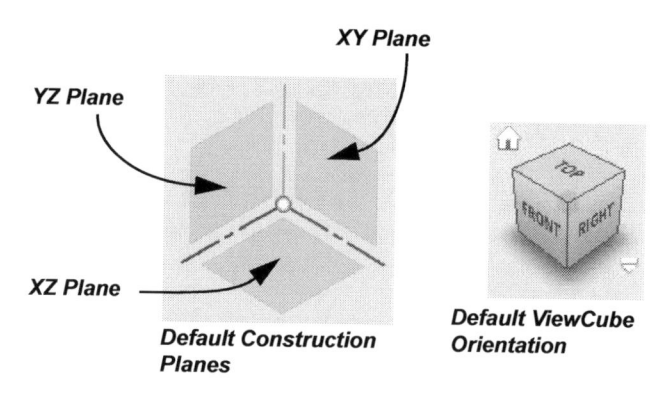

Figure 7–1

Create Construction Planes

The Construction plane options are located in the CONSTRUCT panel. Alternatively, to access the construction feature commands, you can right-click and select **Construct**.

The Construction Plane options are shown in Figure 7–2 to Figure 7–9:

- (Offset Plane)

Timeline icon:

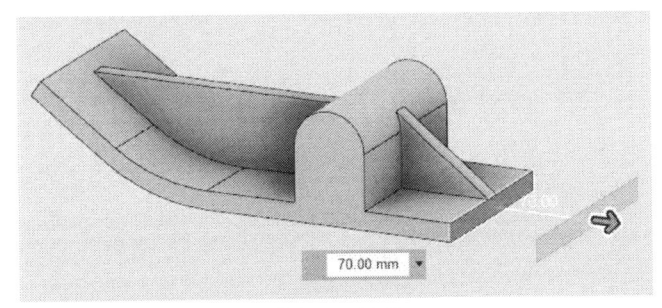

Figure 7–2

- (Plane at Angle)

Timeline icon:

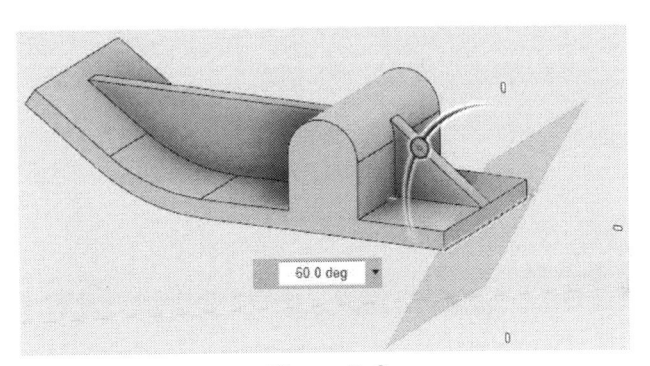

Figure 7–3

- (Tangent Plane)

Timeline icon:

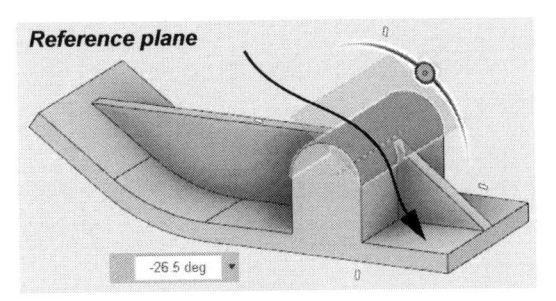

Figure 7–4

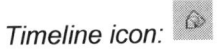

Timeline icon:

- (Midplane)

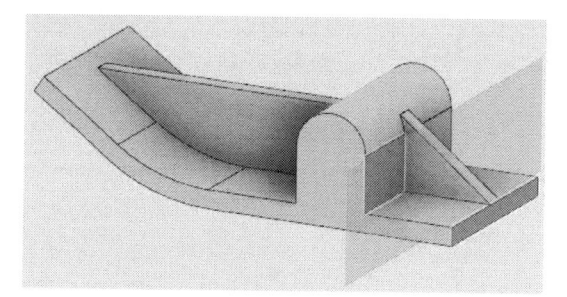

Figure 7–5

- (Plane Through Two Edges)

Timeline icon:

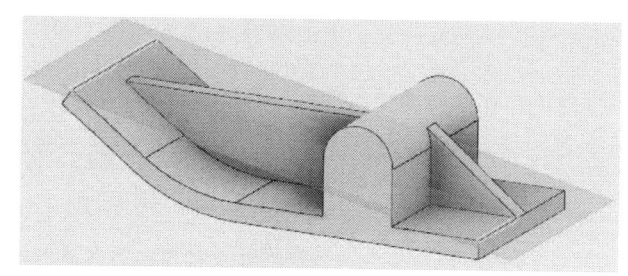

Figure 7–6

- (Plane Through Three Points)

Timeline icon:

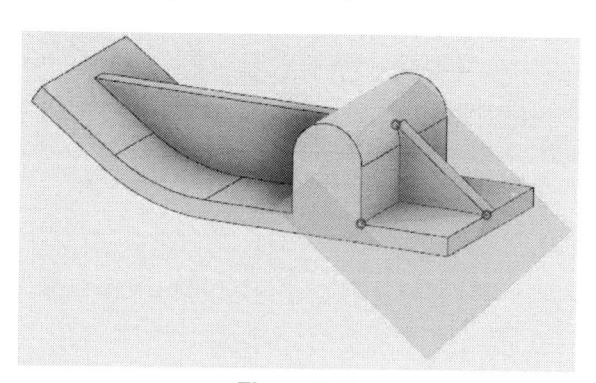

Figure 7–7

Timeline icon:

The point or vertex is used to orient the plane perpendicular to an imaginary line passing through the point and normal to the tangent surface.

Timeline icon:

The distance value is the relative position along the selected edge or curve.

- (Plane Tangent to Face At Point)

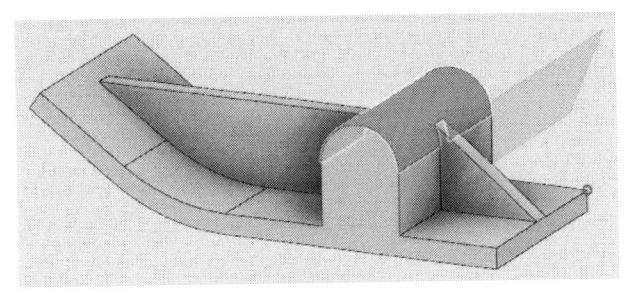

Figure 7–8

- (Plane Along Path)

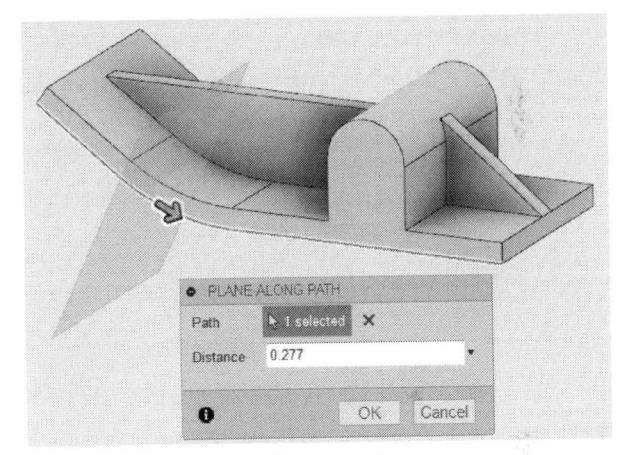

Figure 7–9

Video Lesson Available

Creating Work Planes

Video Length: *7:08*

7.2 Construction Axes

Construction work axes, or construction axes, can be used as references in creating geometry or other construction features. Construction axes have no mass or volume and extend infinitely in both directions.

Default Origin Axes

Each new design automatically includes three orthogonal construction axes at the origin: the X-, Y- and Z-axes, as shown in Figure 7–10.

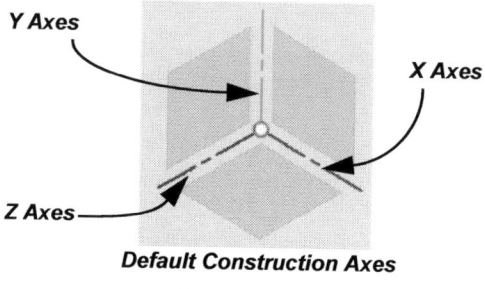

Y Axes
X Axes
Z Axes

Default Construction Axes
Figure 7–10

Creating Construction Axes

The Construction Axis options are located in the CONSTRUCT menu. Alternatively, to access the construction feature commands, you can right-click and select **Construct**.

The Construction Axis features are shown in Figure 7–11 to Figure 7–16:

- (Axis Through Cylinder/Cone/Torus)

Timeline icon:

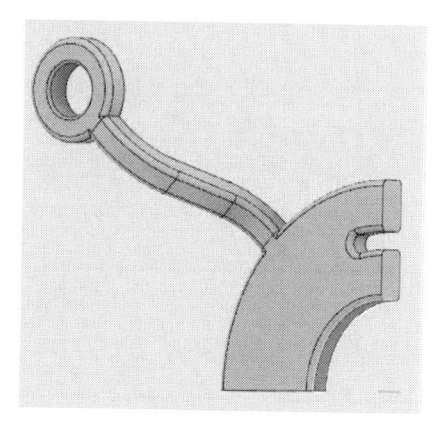

Figure 7–11

Timeline icon:

- (Axis Perpendicular at Point)

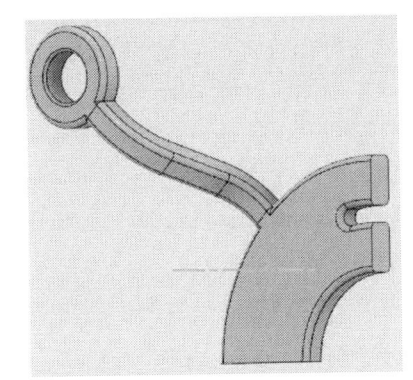

Figure 7–12

- (Axis Through Two Planes)

Timeline icon:

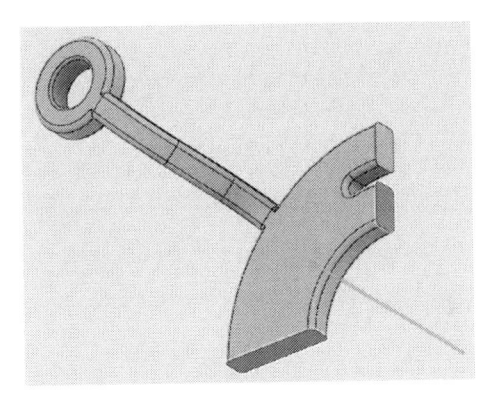

Figure 7–13

- (Axis Through Two Points)

Timeline icon:

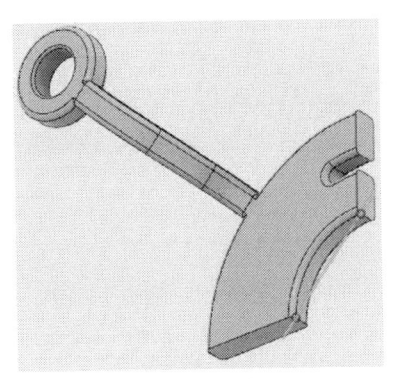

Figure 7–14

Timeline icon:

- (Axis Through Edge)

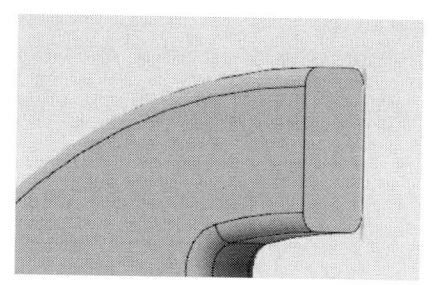

Figure 7–15

Timeline icon:

A sketched point can be used to place the axis.

- (Axis Perpendicular to Face at Point)

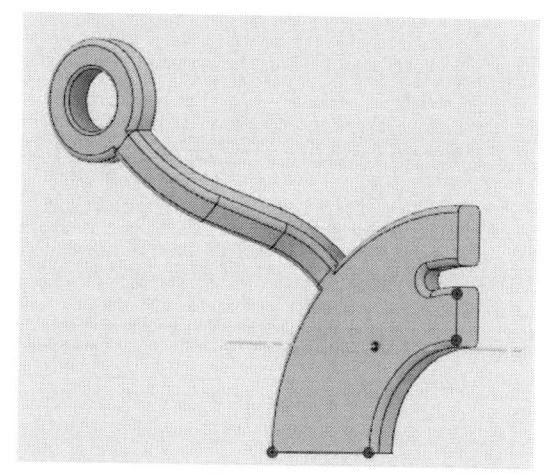

Figure 7–16

Video Lesson Available

Creating Work Axes

Video Length: 4:32

7.3 Construction Points

Construction work points, or construction points, can be used as references in creating geometry or other construction features. Construction points have no mass or volume.

Default Origin Point

Each new design automatically includes a construction point, as shown in Figure 7–17. This point represents the origin, or 0,0,0, of the 3D design. This point does not necessarily indicate the center of gravity or any other such point. It is the point at which the three Origin planes and three Origin axes intersect.

Origin Point

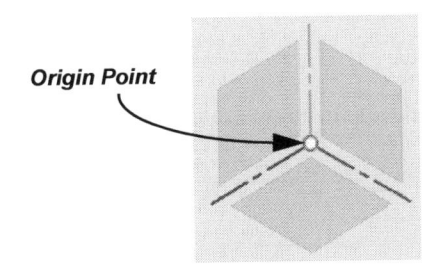

Figure 7–17

Creating Construction Points

The Construction point options are located in the CONSTRUCT menu. Alternatively, to access the construction feature commands, you can right-click and select **Construct**. The construction point features are shown in Figure 7–18 to Figure 7–22:

- (Point at Vertex)

Timeline icon:

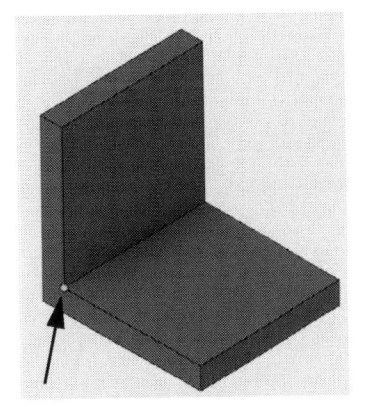

Figure 7–18

Timeline icon:

The edges do not need to physically intersect.

- (Point Through Two Edges)

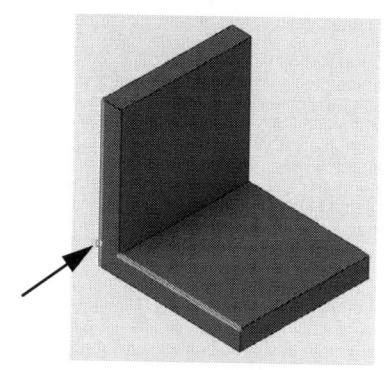

Figure 7–19

- (Point Through Three Planes)

Timeline icon:

Construction planes can be used as a planar reference.

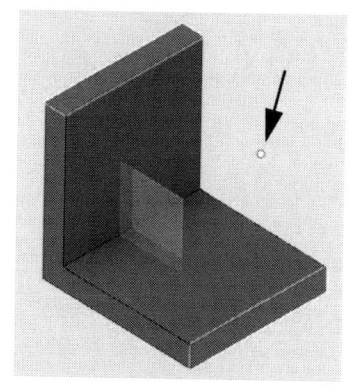

Figure 7–20

- (Point at Center of Circle/Sphere/Torus)

Timeline icon:

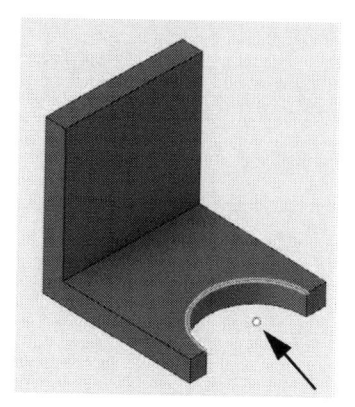

Figure 7–21

- ▯ (Point at Edge and Plane)

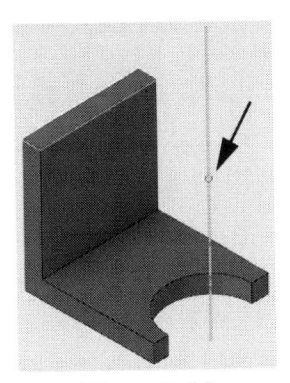

Figure 7–22

> **Video Lesson Available**
>
> **Creating Work Points**
>
> **Video Length:** *3:16*

Timeline icon: ▯

Construction axes can be used as an edge reference.

Editing Construction Features

Construction features are listed in the BROWSER in the **Construction** folder. Consider the following when working with construction planes:

- You can modify construction planes that are created with a rotational angle or distance position. To do this, right-click on the plane name in the BROWSER, Timeline, or graphics window and select **Edit Feature**. You can drag the manipulators or use the EDIT FEATURE palette to enter a new value, as required.

- To delete a construction feature, right-click on the plane, axes, or point you wish to delete and select ▯, or you can simply select it and press <Delete>. You can also use <Ctrl> or <Shift> to select multiple construction features for deletion at one time.

If you delete a construction feature that is referenced by another feature in the Timeline, you are prompted to confirm the deletion. If the construction feature is deleted, the child feature remains, and you are prompted to redefine the child feature.

Practice 7a

Using Construction Features to Create Geometry I

Practice Objective

- Create construction planes that can be used as references in the creation of a solid geometry feature.

In this practice, you will create the rod for the yoke design shown in Figure 7–23. To create the geometry for this design, you need to create two additional construction planes.

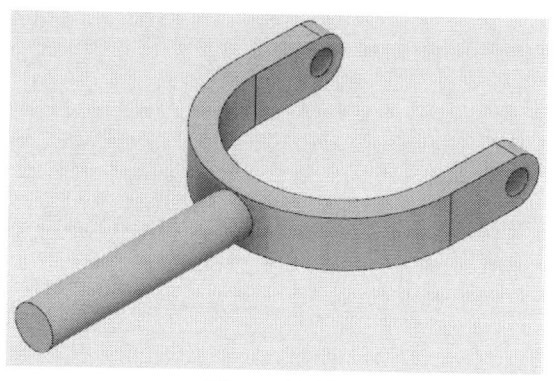

Figure 7–23

Task 1 - Create a new design from file.

1. Click ▬ > **New Design from File**.

2. In the Open dialog box, navigate to the *C:\Autodesk Fusion 360 Practice Files* folder, select **yoke.f3d**, and click **Open**. The design displays as shown in Figure 7–24.

The XY plane should be displayed.

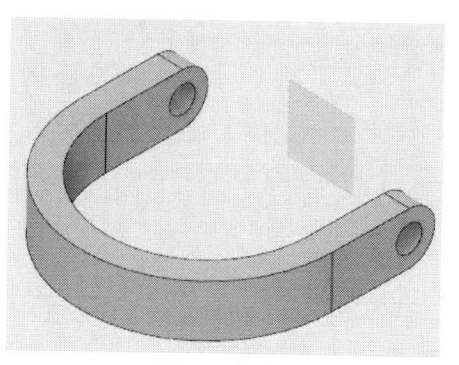

Figure 7–24

Task 2 - Create the rod for the yoke.

1. In the CONSTRUCT panel, click (Tangent Plane) to create a new construction plane.

2. Select the cylindrical face in the general location shown in Figure 7–25. The plane will be created tangent to the surface at the location you select.

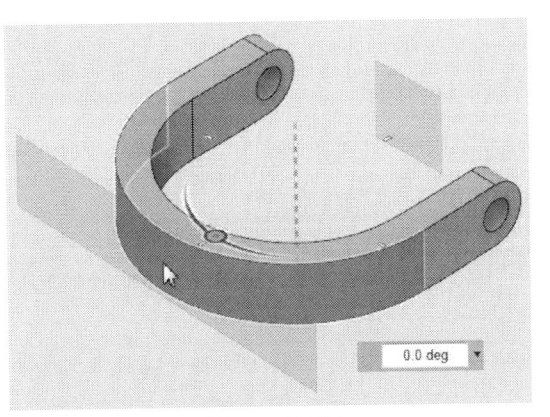

Figure 7–25

3. This plane needs to be tangent to the cylindrical face and parallel to the XY plane. Select the XY plane and specify an angle of **0.0 deg** to keep it parallel, as shown in Figure 7–26.

If the new construction plane rotates all of the way around the cylindrical face to sit on top of the XY plane, add 180 to the existing angular value in the input field to force it back to the required orientation.

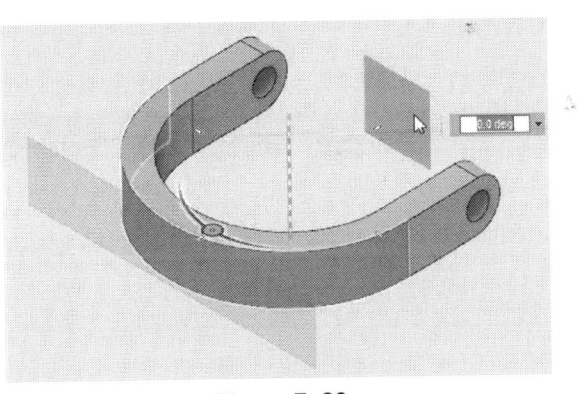

Figure 7–26

4. Click **OK**.

5. A *Construction* folder has been added to the BROWSER. Expand it and note that the new plane has been added.

6. In the BROWSER, select and then click on the name of the plane to rename it. Enter **Rod Tangent Ref** as the new name for the construction plane and press <Enter>. The model and BROWSER should display as shown in Figure 7–27.

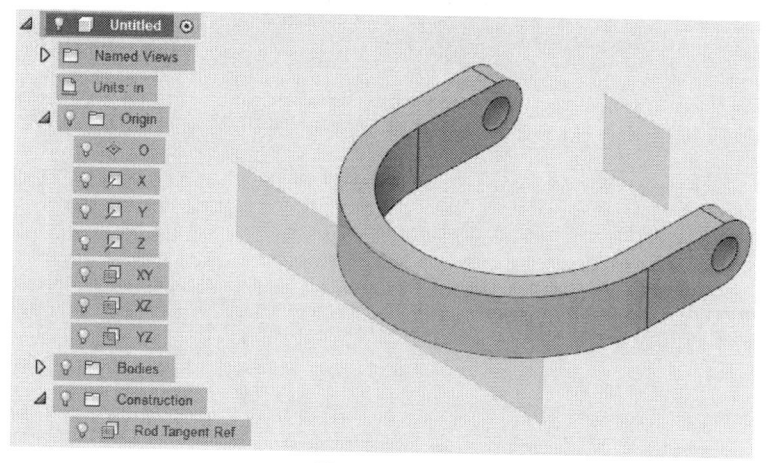

Figure 7–27

The next steps create the rod geometry. There are many different ways that this can be accomplished, but the steps below take into account that the post must be exactly 7.5 inches long. To meet this design requirement and create a robust design in case changes are needed, you will create an additional construction plane offset 7.5 inches from the construction plane that you just created. You will create a circular sketch on this construction plane and extrude it back to the fork portion of the design. Completing the design like this ensures that if dimensional changes are required, there is an easy and efficient way to make changes to the design.

7. In the CONSTRUCT panel, click (Offset Plane).
8. Select the **Rod Tangent Ref** construction plane.

9. Drag the manipulator arrow or, in the OFFSET PLANE palette, enter **7.5 in** when prompted and then click **OK**. The construction plane is created as shown in Figure 7–28.

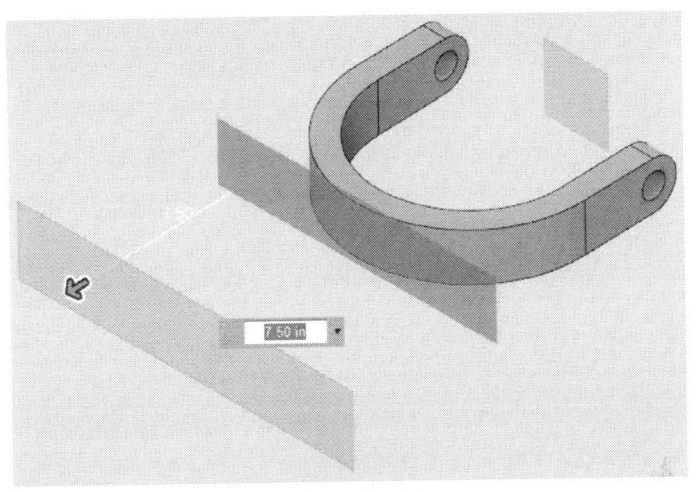

Figure 7–28

10. In the BROWSER, rename the new construction plane to **Rod Depth** and press <Enter>. The BROWSER and the design should display as shown in Figure 7–29.

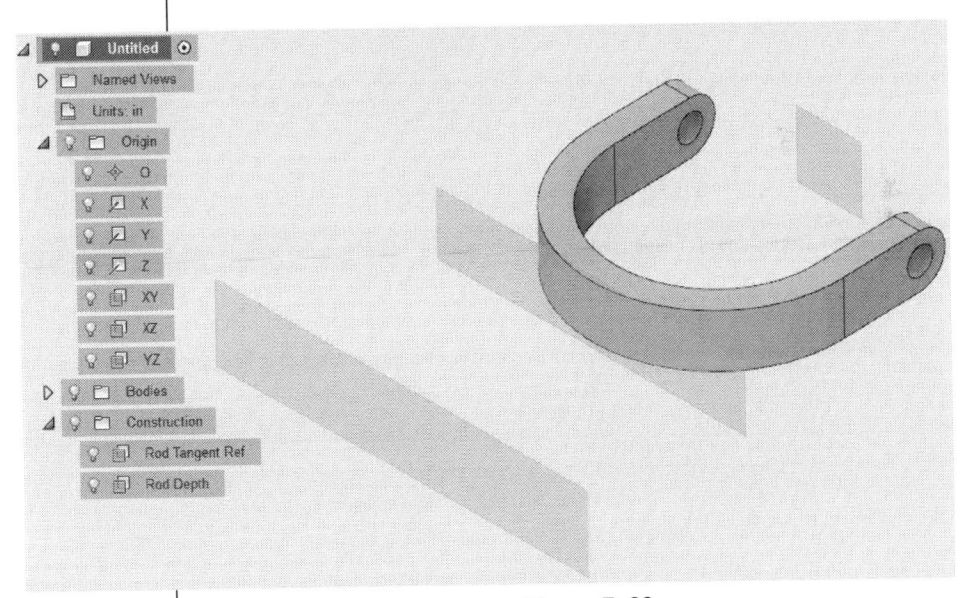

Figure 7–29

11. Create a sketch on the new **Rod Depth** construction plane.

12. In the BROWSER, toggle on the display of the Origin Point **O**.

13. Sketch a circle centered on the origin point and dimension it as shown in Figure 7–30.

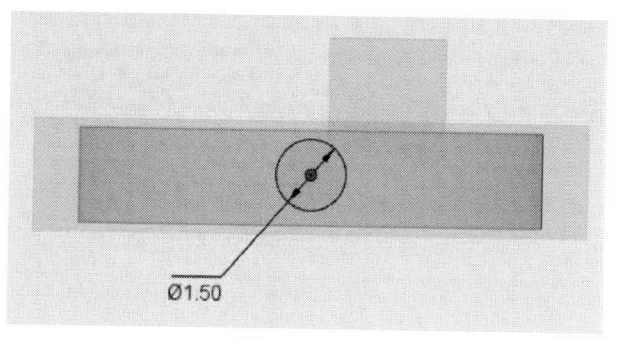

Figure 7–30

14. Stop the sketch.

The display of the Rod Depth construction plane is automatically toggled off after the creation of the sketch upon it.

15. Create an Extrude using the circular profile you just sketched.

16. In the EXTRUDE palette, set *Operation* to **Join**, and *Extents* to ↲ (To).

17. Select the outer cylindrical face on the part as the termination point of the extrude. The design displays as shown in Figure 7–31. By using the *Extent* option ↲ (To), you ensure that the rod extends as required to lie against the entire cylindrical face of the fork.

Figure 7–31

18. Click **OK**.

Task 3 - Change the size of the rod.

1. In the BROWSER, right-click on the **Rod Depth** construction plane and select **Edit Feature**.

2. In the EDIT FEATURE palette, change the *Distance* value to **9** inches and click **OK**.

3. In the BROWSER, expand the *Sketches* folder and toggle on the display of the sketch contained in it.

4. In the *Sketches* folder, right-click on the sketch and select **Show Dimension**. Change the value of the 1.5 in *Diameter* to **1.75 in**. The design displays as shown in Figure 7–32.

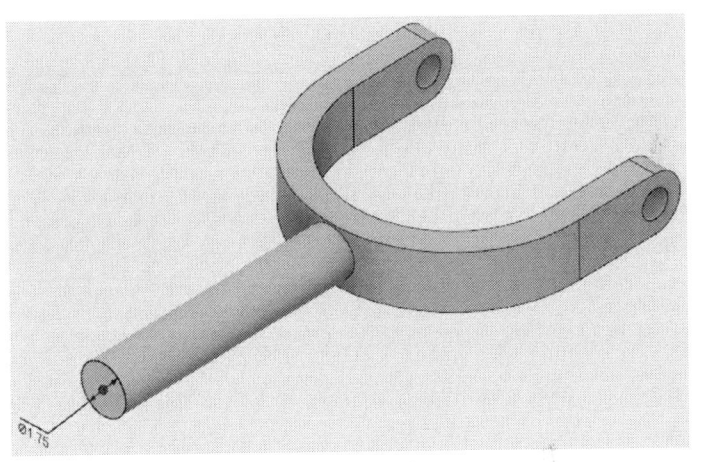

Figure 7–32

5. Save the design with the name **yoke** to your *Autodesk Fusion 360 Practice Files* project.

6. Close the file.

Practice 7b

Using Construction Features to Create Geometry II

Practice Objective

- Create a construction plane and construction axis that can be used as references in the creation of a solid geometry feature.

In this practice, you will create the design shown in Figure 7–33. To create the geometry for this design, you need to create an additional construction plane and axis.

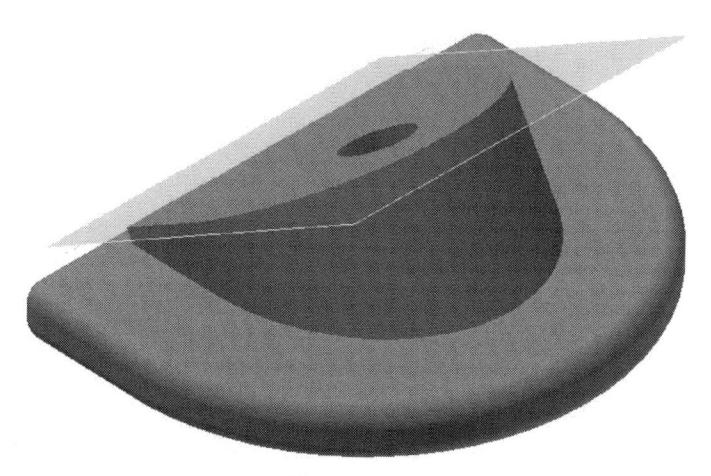

Figure 7–33

Task 1 - Create a new part and create a sketch.

1. Click ▾ > **New Design** to create a new design.
2. Create a sketch on the XZ plane.
3. Project the XY and YZ construction planes as references to locate the sketched geometry.

4. Sketch and dimension the section, as shown in Figure 7–34.

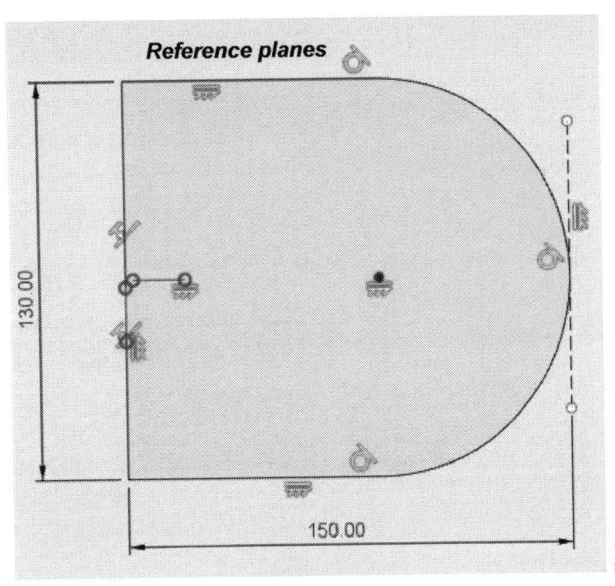

Figure 7–34

5. Stop the sketch.

6. Use the profile to create an extrude with a distance of **20 mm**, as shown in Figure 7–35.

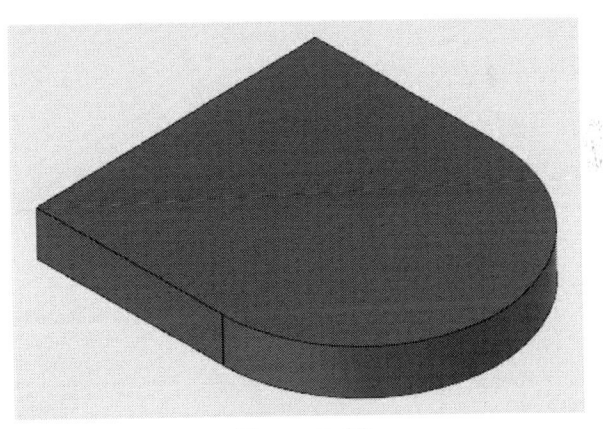

Figure 7–35

Depending on the orientation of the sketch plane, the default view of the design might vary. Spin to reorient the design as required.

Task 2 - Create fillets on all edges.

1. Press <F> to create a fillet.

2. Drag a selection box around the entire part to select all of the edges, as shown in Figure 7–36.

*If the hidden edges are not included in the selection set, review the filter settings and enable the **Select Through** option.*

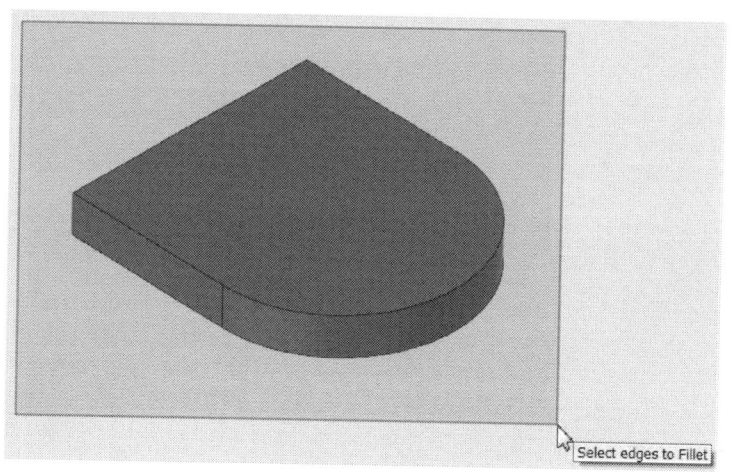

Figure 7–36

3. Set the radius to **7.00**.

4. Complete the feature. The design displays as shown in Figure 7–37.

Figure 7–37

Task 3 - Create construction features.

In the remaining tasks, you will create the extrusion shown in Figure 7–38. In this task, you will create a construction axis at the intersection of two faces on the base feature, and a construction plane referencing the axis. These construction features are required to create the geometry.

In the remaining tasks you will be creating this extrusion.

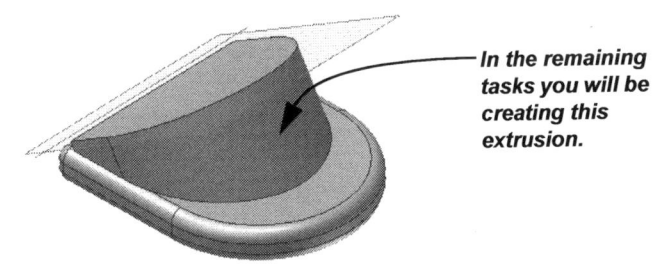

Figure 7–38

1. In the CONSTRUCT panel, click (Axis Through Two Planes) to create a construction axis.

2. Select the two faces shown in Figure 7–39 to create a construction axis at their intersection.

Select these faces

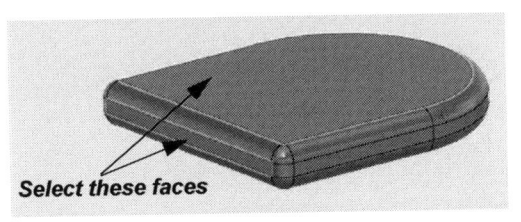

Figure 7–39

The construction axis is created at the intersection of the faces, as shown in Figure 7–40.

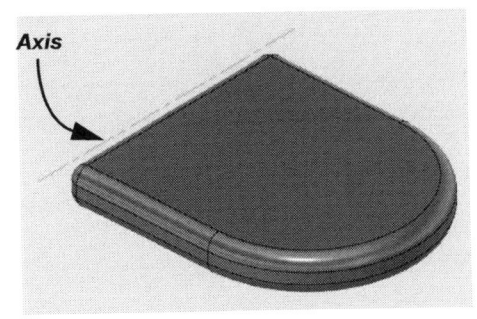

Axis

Figure 7–40

3. In the CONSTRUCT panel, click (Plane at Angle) to create a construction plane.

4. Using the BROWSER or directly in the graphics window, select the construction axis you just created.

5. Use the manipulator handle for rotation or enter a value to create the construction plane at an angle of **-30** degrees, as shown in Figure 7–41.

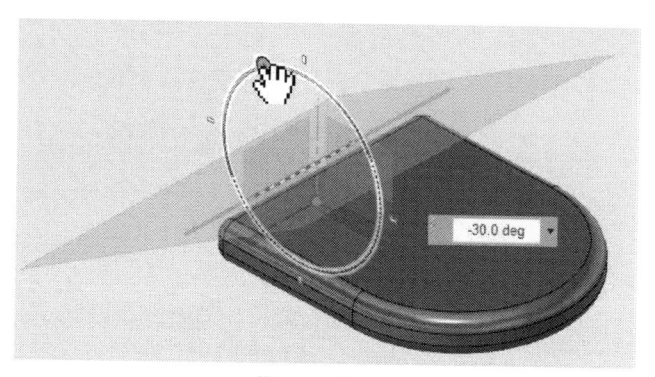

Figure 7–41

6. Complete the feature. The construction plane displays as shown in Figure 7–42.

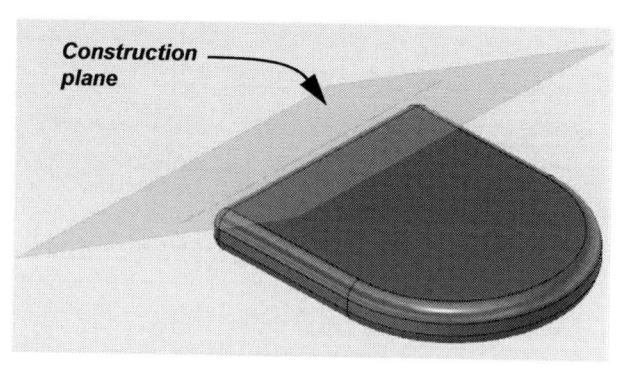

Figure 7–42

Task 4 - Create an extrusion.

1. Create a sketch on the new construction plane.
2. Project the XY Origin Plane and the construction axis onto the sketch.
3. Click **OK** to complete the operation.
4. Sketch the section with the dimensions and constraints shown in Figure 7–43.

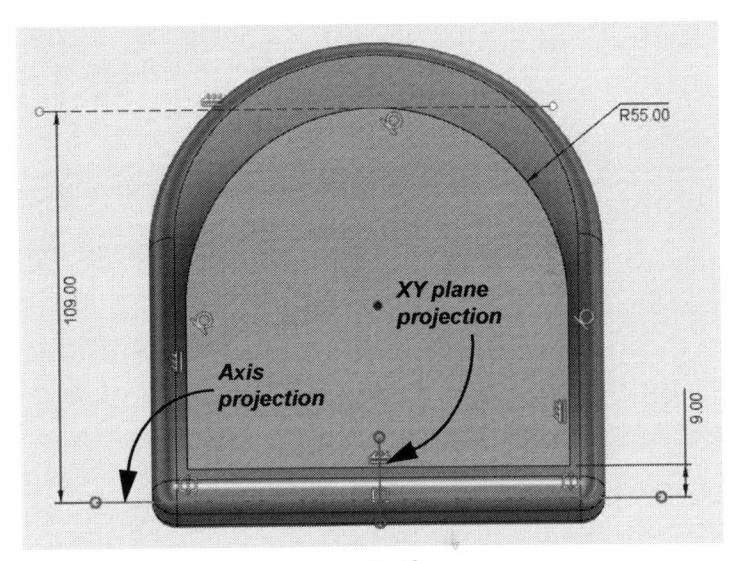

Figure 7–43

5. Stop the sketch.
6. Create an Extrude and select the profile you just sketched.
7. The sketched section is automatically selected.
8. In the EXTRUDE palette, set *Operation* to (Join) and *Distance* to (To).

9. Select the planar face of the geometry as shown in Figure 7–44. The new Extrude feature will terminate at that face.

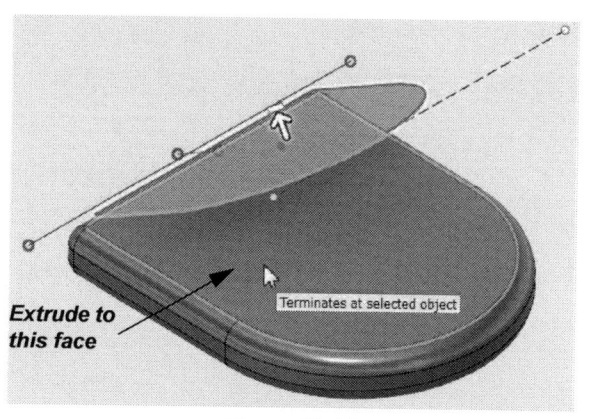

Figure 7–44

10. Complete the feature. The design displays as shown in Figure 7–45.

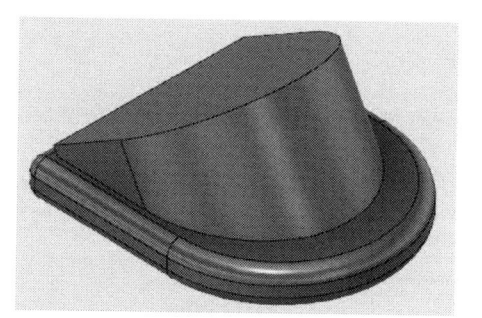

Figure 7–45

Task 5 - Create a second construction plane at an angle.

1. Create a (Plane at Angle) construction plane.
2. Select the edge indicated in Figure 7–46.

3. Select the planar face indicated in Figure 7–46 so that the angle of the plane is set so that the construction plane and the selected face are parallel.

If you cannot select the planar face, rotate the manipulator handle, activate the entry field active, and then select the face.

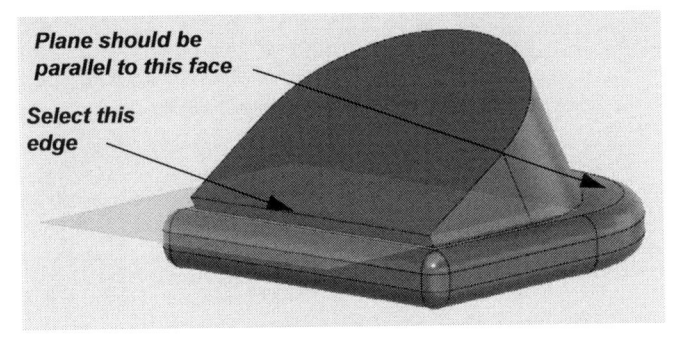

Plane should be parallel to this face

Select this edge

Figure 7–46

Task 6 - Create a sketch and extrude a cut.

1. Create a sketch on the new construction plane.

2. Project the edges of the face shown in Figure 7–47 onto the sketch.

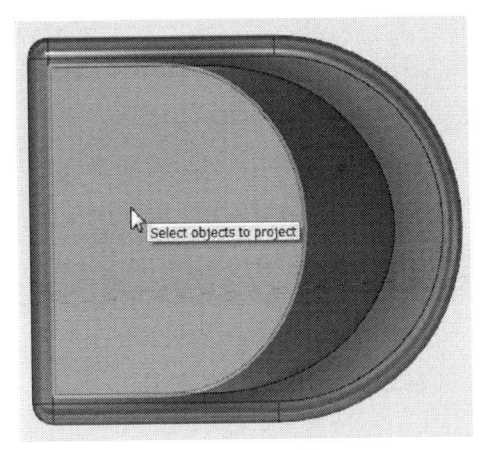

Figure 7–47

3. Offset the three projected entities shown in Figure 7–48 by a distance of **-7**.

*Clear the **Loop Select** checkbox to select the individual entities.*

Offset these three entities

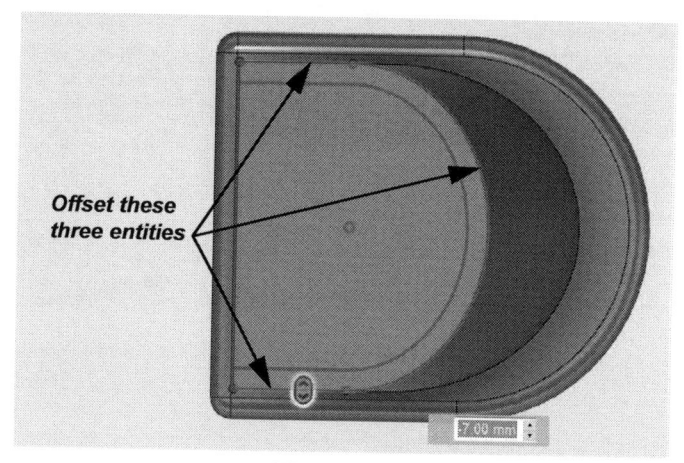

Figure 7–48

4. Stop the sketch.

5. Create an extrude and select the inner profile of the sketch you just created, as shown in Figure 7–49.

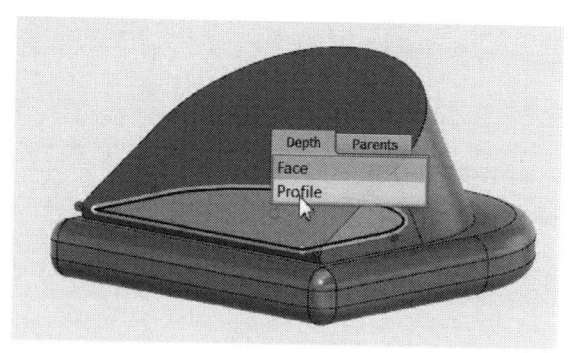

Figure 7–49

6. Drag the manipulator handle so that the extrude cuts through the part as shown in Figure 7–50.

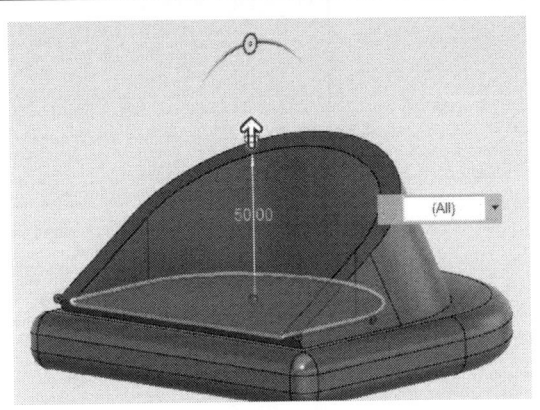

Figure 7–50

7. Set the *Extents* option to ⛿ (All) and complete the feature. The design should display as shown in Figure 7–51.

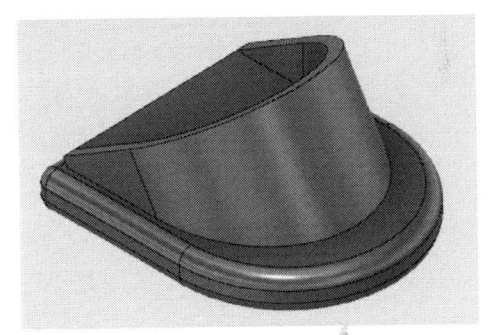

Figure 7–51

Task 7 - Modify the angle of the first construction plane.

1. In the Timeline, find the first ⧄ icon. This is the icon for the first construction plane you created at an angle.

2. In the Timeline, right-click on the ⧄ construction plane icon and select **Edit Feature**, as shown in Figure 7–52.

Right-click on this icon

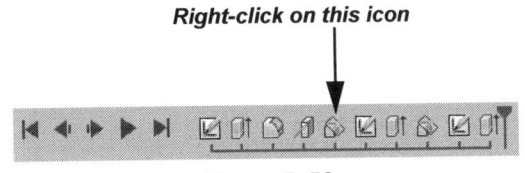

Figure 7–52

3. Change the value of the angle for the plane to **-10**, as shown in Figure 7–53.

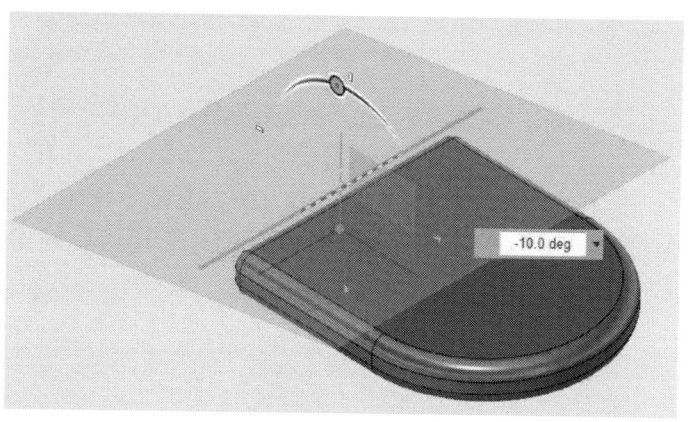

Figure 7–53

4. Click **OK** to apply the change. The subsequent features update to reflect the change in angle of the construction plane. The design should display as shown in Figure 7–54.

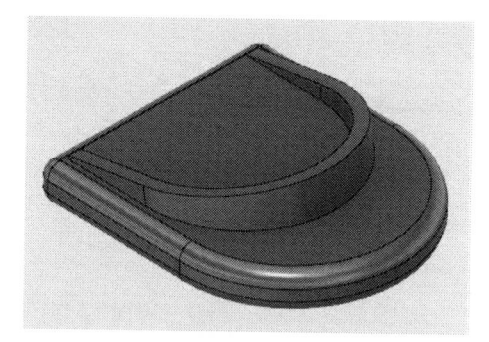

Figure 7–54

5. Save the design with the name **construction** to your *Autodesk Fusion 360 Practice Files* project.

6. Close the file.

Chapter Review Questions

1. Origin Planes are the only construction planes that can exist in a design.

    a. True
    b. False

2. Which of the following are possible uses for a construction plane, such as those shown in Figure 7–55? (Select all that apply.)

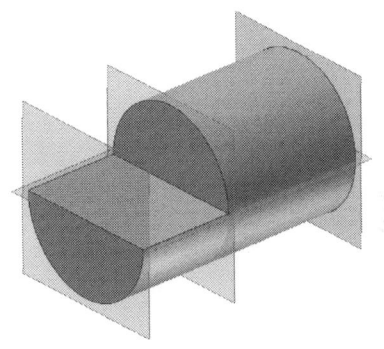

    Figure 7–55

    a. To create another construction plane.
    b. To define a sketch plane.
    c. To serve as the boundary for the depth of an extrusion.
    d. To set up a drawing sheet.

3. Which of the following are valid options to use to create a construction plane? (Select all that apply.)

    a. **Plane Through Three Edges**
    b. **Offset Plane**
    c. **Tangent Plane**
    d. **Plane Through Three Points**

4. Which option enables you to create the construction plane shown in Figure 7–56?

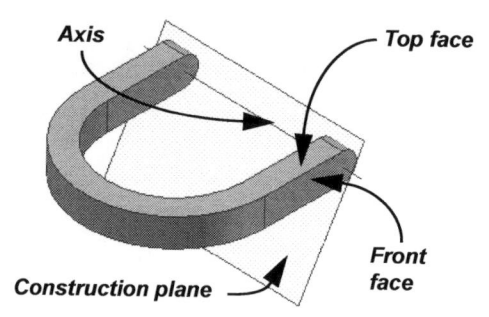

Figure 7–56

   a. **Midplane**
   b. **Plane Along Path**
   c. **Plane Through Two Edges**
   d. **Plane At Angle**

5. Which of the following are valid options for creating a construction axis? (Select all that apply.)

   a. **Axis Through Cylinder/Cone/Torus**
   b. **Axis Through Three Points**
   c. **Axis Through Edge**
   d. **Axis Perpendicular to Face At Point**

6. A construction axis can be used as a reference when creating a construction plane.

   a. True
   b. False

7. A construction point must be located on a face or a construction plane.

   a. True
   b. False

Answers: 1.b, 2.(a,b,c), 3.(b,c,d), 4.d, 5.(a,c,d), 6.a, 7.b

Command Summary

Button	Command	Location
	Axis Perpendicular at Point	• **Ribbon:** *Model* Workspace> CONSTRUCT panel • **Context Menu:** Right-click in the graphics window and select **Construct**.
	Axis Perpendicular to Face at Point	• **Ribbon:** *Model* Workspace> CONSTRUCT panel • **Context Menu:** Right-click in the graphics window and select **Construct**.
	Axis Through Cylinder/Cone/Torus	• **Ribbon:** *Model* Workspace> CONSTRUCT panel • **Context Menu:** Right-click in the graphics window and select **Construct**.
	Axis Through Edge	• **Ribbon:** *Model* Workspace> CONSTRUCT panel • **Context Menu:** Right-click in the graphics window and select **Construct**.
	Axis Through Two Planes	• **Ribbon:** *Model* Workspace> CONSTRUCT panel • **Context Menu:** Right-click in the graphics window and select **Construct**.
	Axis Through Two Points	• **Ribbon:** *Model* Workspace> CONSTRUCT panel • **Context Menu:** Right-click in the graphics window and select **Construct**.
	Midplane	• **Ribbon:** *Model* Workspace> CONSTRUCT panel • **Context Menu:** Right-click in the graphics window and select **Construct**.
	Offset Plane	• **Ribbon:** *Model* Workspace> CONSTRUCT panel • **Context Menu:** Right-click in the graphics window and select **Construct**.
	Plane Along Path	• **Ribbon:** *Model* Workspace> CONSTRUCT panel • **Context Menu:** Right-click in the graphics window and select **Construct**.
	Plane at Angle	• **Ribbon:** *Model* Workspace> CONSTRUCT panel • **Context Menu:** Right-click in the graphics window and select **Construct**.
	Plane Tangent to Face At Point	• **Ribbon:** *Model* Workspace> CONSTRUCT panel • **Context Menu:** Right-click in the graphics window and select **Construct**.

	Plane Through Three Points	• **Ribbon:** *Model* Workspace> CONSTRUCT panel • **Context Menu:** Right-click in the graphics window and select **Construct**.
	Plane Through Two Edges	• **Ribbon:** *Model* Workspace> CONSTRUCT panel • **Context Menu:** Right-click in the graphics window and select **Construct**.
	Point at Center of Circle/Sphere/ Torus	• **Ribbon:** *Model* Workspace> CONSTRUCT panel • **Context Menu:** Right-click in the graphics window and select **Construct**.
	Point at Edge and Plane	• **Ribbon:** *Model* Workspace> CONSTRUCT panel • **Context Menu:** Right-click in the graphics window and select **Construct**.
	Point at Vertex	• **Ribbon:** *Model* Workspace> CONSTRUCT panel • **Context Menu:** Right-click in the graphics window and select **Construct**.
	Point Through Three Planes	• **Ribbon:** *Model* Workspace> CONSTRUCT panel • **Context Menu:** Right-click in the graphics window and select **Construct**.
	Point Through Two Edges	• **Ribbon:** *Model* Workspace> CONSTRUCT panel • **Context Menu:** Right-click in the graphics window and select **Construct**.
	Tangent Plane	• **Ribbon:** *Model* Workspace> CONSTRUCT panel • **Context Menu:** Right-click in the graphics window and select **Construct**.

Chapter 8

Equations and Parameters

Equations help you to incorporate design intent, which ensures that the design behaves as intended when changes occur. Equations are established by creating mathematical relationships between dimensions and parameters.

Learning Objectives in this Chapter

- Create equations between dimensions to incorporate design intent into the design.
- Create user-defined parameters in a design.

8.1 Equations

Features and sketches generate dimensions in a design. Each dimension is given a unique dimension name that starts with the letter "d" followed by a unique number (e.g., d1, d2, d3, etc.).

You can define relationships between these dimensions using equations, enabling you to control a dimension's value based on a function of another dimension's value. Equations can also include user-defined parameters and mathematical expressions. When one dimension references another, the referenced dimension in the equation is considered the driving dimension. The design in Figure 8–1 shows a hole that is located based on an equation.

*When **fx:** displays as part of a dimension name, it indicates that the dimension contains an equation.*

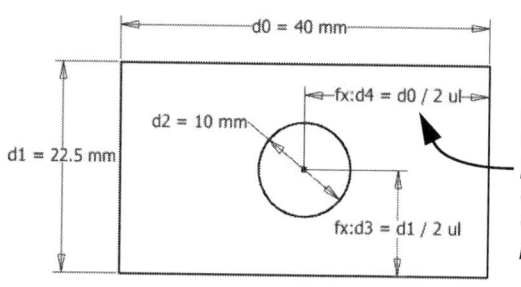

The distance from the center of the hole to the edges of the plate can be defined as half the overall dimension of the plate (i.e., d4=d0/2).

Figure 8–1

- When editing a sketch or feature dimension, you can enter an equation directly into the dimension value's input field. The equation can be a mathematical expression that does or does not include other dimensions.

- The width of the sketched rectangle shown in Figure 8–2 is set up as an equation to make the width equal to twice the height. To do this:
  1. Double-click on the width dimension to modify its value.
  2. When the input field is active, select the height dimension. Its name (in this example: d2) is added to the input field for the width dimension.
  3. Input the remainder of the equation (in this example: **d2*2**).

  The width will now automatically update whenever the value of the d2 height dimension is modified.

The width of the sketched rectangle is set to be twice the height (d2).

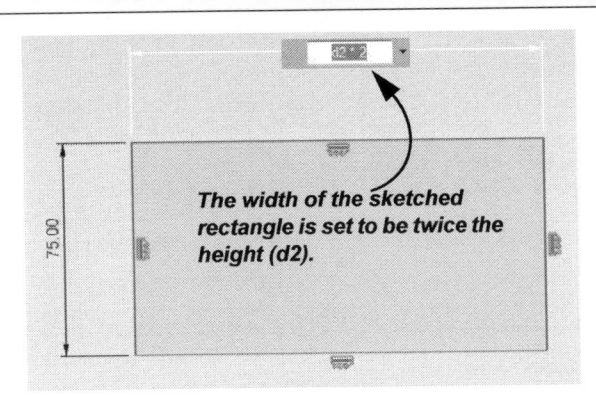

Figure 8–2

- You can enter an equation into the entry fields during feature creation, as shown for the *Height* value in Figure 8–3.

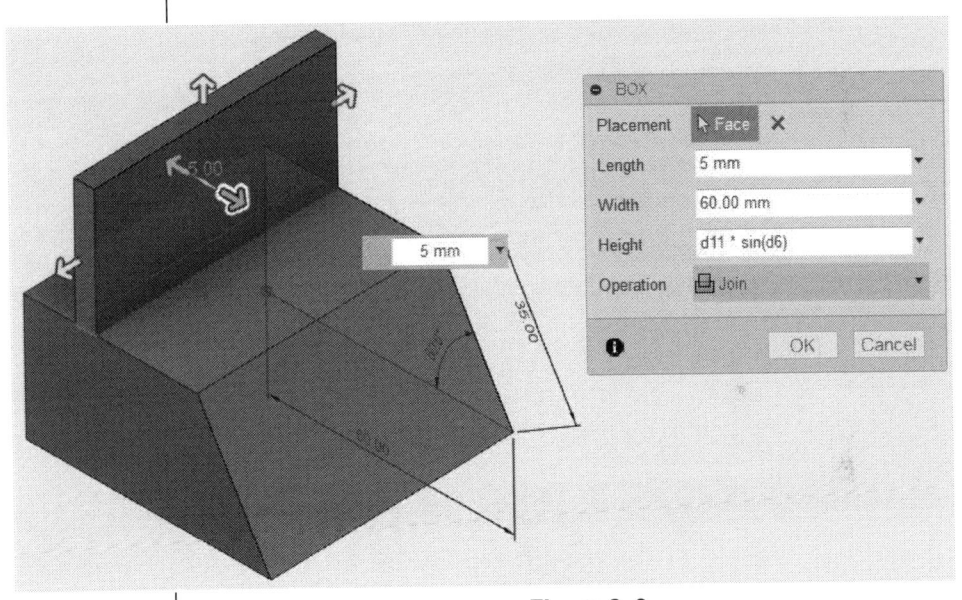

Figure 8–3

In the Parameters dialog box, you can rename model parameters to help recognize what the parameter is controlling.

- You can enter equations after sketch or feature creation using the Parameters dialog box. This dialog box enables you to review the complete list of all of the parameters (dimension names) and existing equations in the design. To open the Parameters dialog box, in the MODIFY panel, click Σ (Change Parameters). Equations are entered into the *Expression* column, as shown in Figure 8–4.

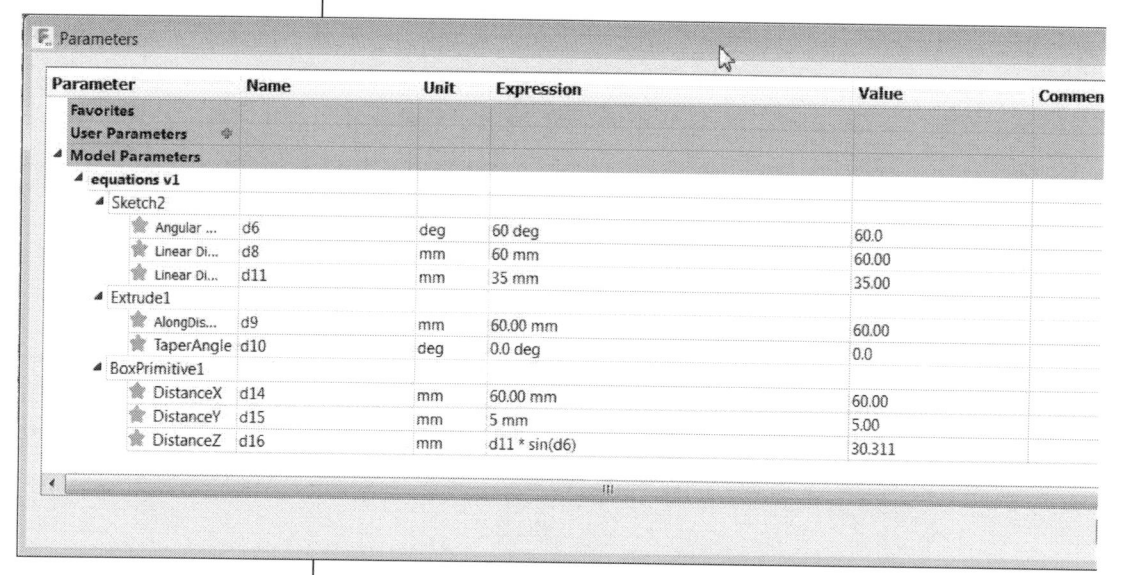

Parameter	Name	Unit	Expression	Value	Commen
Favorites					
User Parameters					
▲ Model Parameters					
▲ equations v1					
▲ Sketch2					
Angular ...	d6	deg	60 deg	60.0	
Linear Di...	d8	mm	60 mm	60.00	
Linear Di...	d11	mm	35 mm	35.00	
▲ Extrude1					
AlongDis...	d9	mm	60.00 mm	60.00	
TaperAngle	d10	deg	0.0 deg	0.0	
▲ BoxPrimitive1					
DistanceX	d14	mm	60.00 mm	60.00	
DistanceY	d15	mm	5 mm	5.00	
DistanceZ	d16	mm	d11 * sin(d6)	30.311	

Figure 8–4

Equations can be written using any of the following operators or functions to capture the intent of the equation.

Mathematical Operators

The following operators can be used in equations:

+	Addition
-	Subtraction
/	Division
*	Multiplication
()	Expression delimiter

Functions

The following functions can be used in equations.

sin( )	cos( )	tan( )
sinh( )	cosh( )	tanh( )
tan( )	log( )	ceil( ) converts arbitrary real numbers to close integers. The ceil function of a real number x, ceil(x) returns the next highest integer (e.g., ceil(3.2) = 4).
asin( )	ln( )	
acos( )	exp( )	floor( ) converts arbitrary real numbers to close integers. The floor function of a real number x, floor(x) returns the next smallest integer (e.g., floor(3.8) = 3).
atan( )	abs( )	

Once you finish adding an equation, test the design to ensure that the equation captures the required design intent. This is called flexing the design, and should involve editing the driving dimension values to verify that the design changes as expected.

8.2 Parameters

As features are created in a design, dimensions are used to define the design's shape. The name and value of the dimension are considered a Model Parameter. Model parameters are listed in the Parameters dialog box.

The Parameters dialog box also enables you to create User-Defined parameters, which can be used in equations to help you control the design. Once created, user-defined parameters are listed in the Parameters dialog box in the *User Parameters* area.

Video Lesson Available

Working with Parameters

Video Length: 5:53

Practice 8a

Adding Equations

Practice Objectives

- Add equations to dimensions in a sketch.
- Add and edit equations using the Parameters dialog box.

In this practice, you will modify dimensions in a part using dimension equations. The completed part is shown in Figure 8–5.

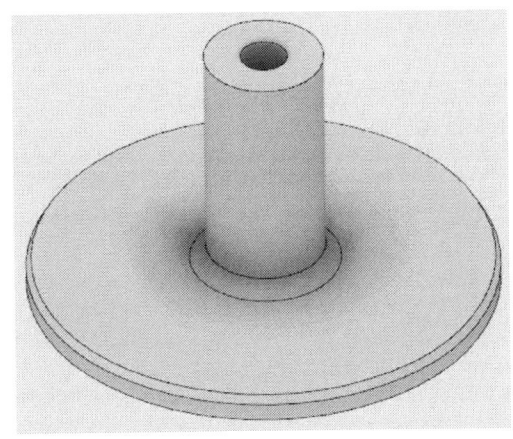

Figure 8–5

Task 1 - Create a new design from file.

1. Click ▾ > **New Design from File**.

2. In the Open dialog box, navigate to the *C:\Autodesk Fusion 360 Practice Files* folder, select **equations.f3d**, and click **Open**. The design displays as shown in Figure 8–6.

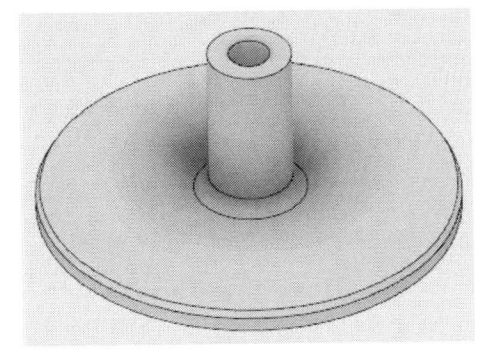

Figure 8–6

3. The Timeline consists of a sketch and a revolve. In the Timeline, right-click on the sketch and select **Edit Sketch**. The sketch displays as shown in Figure 8–7.

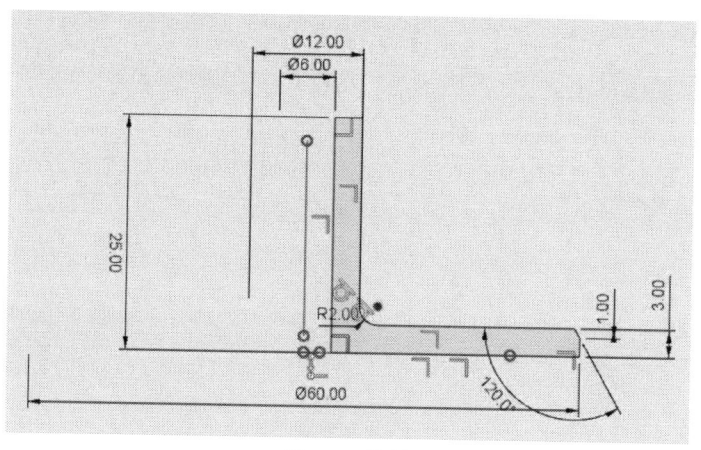

Figure 8–7

4. Change the outside diameter dimension from 60 to **50**. No other dimensions change value because no equations have been created to define relationships between the dimensions.

5. Change the outside diameter dimension back to **60**.

Task 2 - Add an equation to control the inner diameter.

In this task, you will add an equation to set the inner diameter to be 1/10th of the outer diameter.

1. Double-click on the **Ø6.00** inner diameter dimension to display the input field.

2. While the input field is active, click on the **Ø60.00** outer diameter dimension. The dimension parameter d7 is added to the input field, which is the name assigned to the outer diameter dimension.

3. In the entry field, enter **d7/10**. Press <Enter>. The inner diameter dimension now displays as **fx: Ø6.00**. The fx: prefix indicates that the dimension contains an equation.

4. Modify the outside diameter dimension from 60 to **50**. Note that the inner diameter dimension automatically changes to fx: Ø5.00 to satisfy the equation you entered. The sketch displays as shown in Figure 8–8.

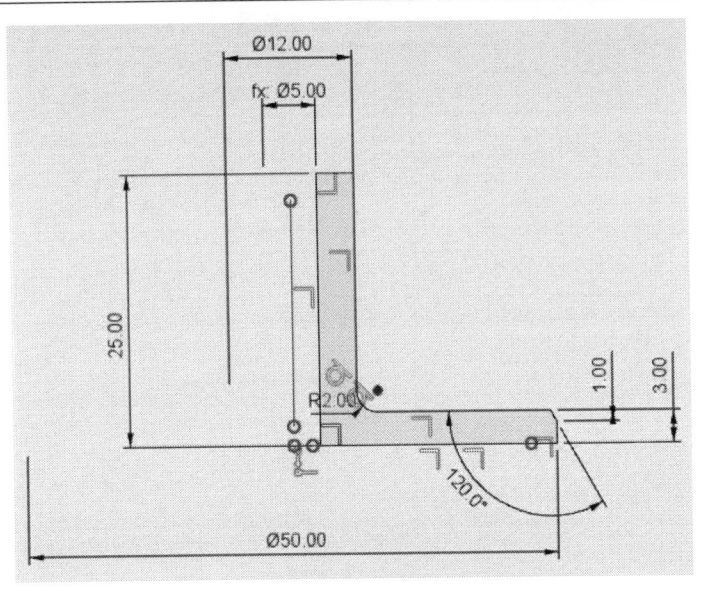

Figure 8–8

Task 3 - Add an equation to drive other dimensions.

In this task, you will add additional equations to drive the wall thickness and height.

1. Edit the **Ø12.00** diameter dimension. The difference between this outer diameter and the inner diameter should maintain a wall thickness that is equal to the thickness of the base.

2. Select the **fx: Ø5.00** dimension.

3. Enter **+ 2***.

4. Select the 3.00 dimension controlling the thickness of the base. The equation in the input field should be **d4 + 2 * d5**.

5. Press <Enter>.

6. Make the 25.00 height dimension equal to half the outer diameter plus the base thickness. The equation should display in the input field as **d7 / 2 + d5**.

7. Finally, make the 1.00 dimension equal to one third of the base height. The equation should display in the input field as **d5 / 3**.

8. Modify the outside diameter dimension from 50 to **72**.

9. Modify the base thickness from 3 to **4**. The sketch should display as shown in Figure 8–9.

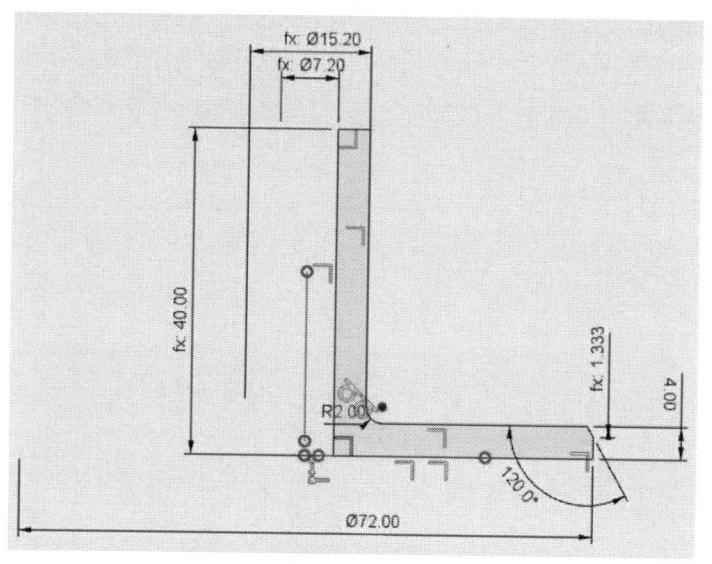

Figure 8–9

10. Stop the sketch.

11. In the BROWSER, expand the **Sketches** folder and toggle on the display of the sketch.

12. In the BROWSER, right-click on the sketch and select **Show Dimension**.

13. Double-click on the **Ø72.00** dimension and change its value to **60**. The equations you created in the sketch are still evaluated.

14. Save the design with the name **My_Equations_Design** to your *Autodesk Fusion 360 Practice Files* project.

Task 4 - Rename dimensions and add a user-defined parameter.

1. In the MODIFY panel, click Σ (Change Parameters). The Parameters dialog box opens.

2. Expand the **Model Parameters** node.

If you have not already saved the design with a new name, the section named Untitled is your design.

3. Expand the **My_Equations_Design** node. The **Sketch1** and **Revovle1** features are listed and contain all of the dimension parameters for each.

4. Expand the **Sketch1** node. Note that all of the dimension parameters that you worked with in the sketch are listed. Also note that the equations you set up are listed in the *Expression* column, as shown in Figure 8–10.

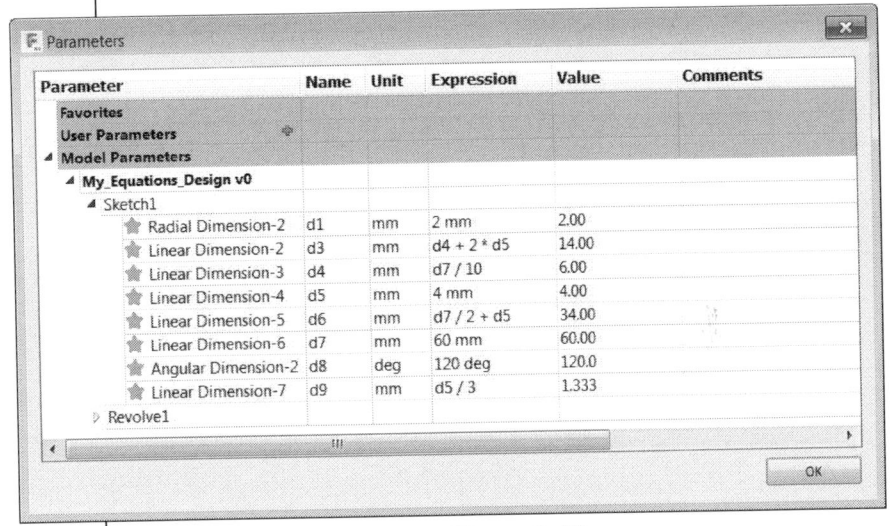

Parameter	Name	Unit	Expression	Value	Comments
Favorites					
User Parameters					
▲ Model Parameters					
▲ My_Equations_Design v0					
▲ Sketch1					
Radial Dimension-2	d1	mm	2 mm	2.00	
Linear Dimension-2	d3	mm	d4 + 2 * d5	14.00	
Linear Dimension-3	d4	mm	d7 / 10	6.00	
Linear Dimension-4	d5	mm	4 mm	4.00	
Linear Dimension-5	d6	mm	d7 / 2 + d5	34.00	
Linear Dimension-6	d7	mm	60 mm	60.00	
Angular Dimension-2	d8	deg	120 deg	120.0	
Linear Dimension-7	d9	mm	d5 / 3	1.333	
▷ Revolve1					

Figure 8–10

5. The dimension d7 controls the outer diameter in the sketch and currently has a value of 60.00. Select the cell containing d7. Enter the name **outer_diameter** and press <Enter>. Note that the expressions for the parameters that referenced d7 have updated to reflect the new name of that parameter.

6. The dimension d5 controls the base thickness in the sketch and currently has a value of 4.00. Select the cell containing d5. Enter the name **base_thickness** and press <Enter>.

7. Select the *Expression* cell for the **base_thickness** parameter which is set to 4mm.

8. Enter **outer_diameter/18** as the new expression.

9. Change the expression for the **outer_diameter** parameter from 60 mm to **72 mm**. The Parameters dialog box should display as shown in Figure 8–11.

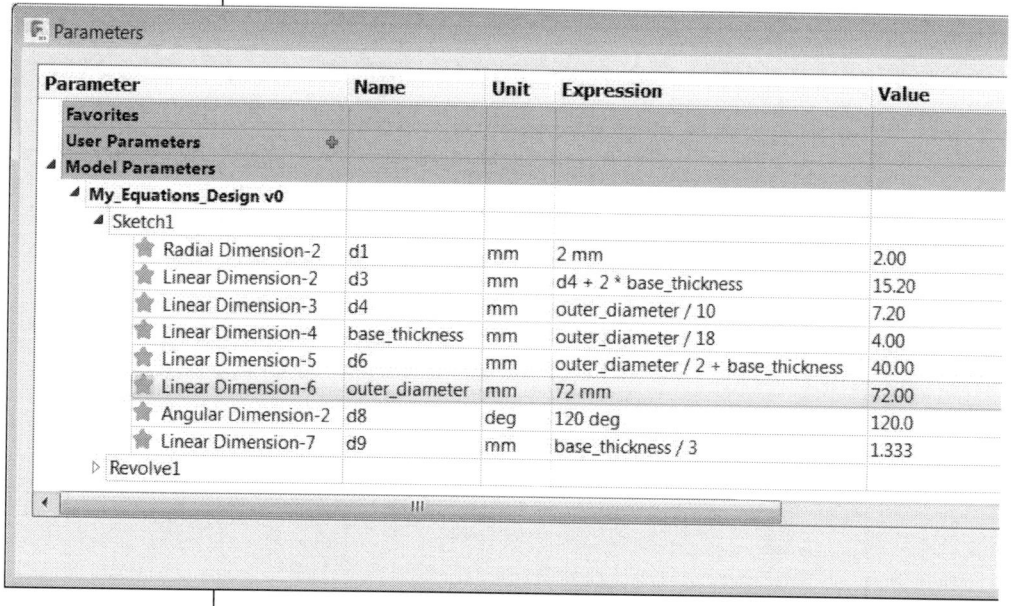

Parameter	Name	Unit	Expression	Value
Favorites				
User Parameters				
▲ Model Parameters				
▲ My_Equations_Design v0				
▲ Sketch1				
Radial Dimension-2	d1	mm	2 mm	2.00
Linear Dimension-2	d3	mm	d4 + 2 * base_thickness	15.20
Linear Dimension-3	d4	mm	outer_diameter / 10	7.20
Linear Dimension-4	base_thickness	mm	outer_diameter / 18	4.00
Linear Dimension-5	d6	mm	outer_diameter / 2 + base_thickness	40.00
Linear Dimension-6	outer_diameter	mm	72 mm	72.00
Angular Dimension-2	d8	deg	120 deg	120.0
Linear Dimension-7	d9	mm	base_thickness / 3	1.333
▷ Revolve1				

Figure 8–11

10. Click **OK** to close the Parameters dialog box. The design should display as shown in Figure 8–12.

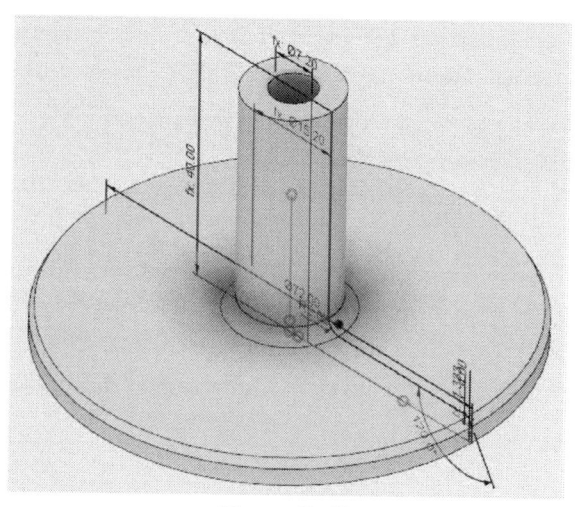

Figure 8–12

11. Save the design and close the file.

Practice 8b

Add Parameters

Practice Objectives

- Add equations to a design using the Parameters dialog box and Edit Feature dialog boxes.
- Create user-defined parameters for use in equations.

In this practice, you will modify dimensions in a part using model parameters and then add user-defined parameters. The completed design is shown in Figure 8–13.

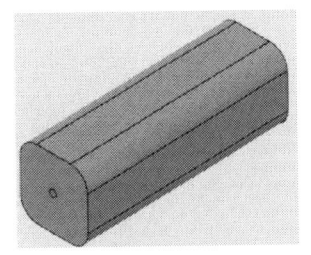

Figure 8–13

Task 1 - Create a new design from file.

1. Click ![icon] > **New Design from File**.

2. In the Open dialog box, navigate to the *C:\Autodesk Fusion 360 Practice Files* folder, select **parameters.f3d**, and click **Open**.

3. Toggle on the visibility of the sketch and its dimensions. The design displays as shown in Figure 8–14.

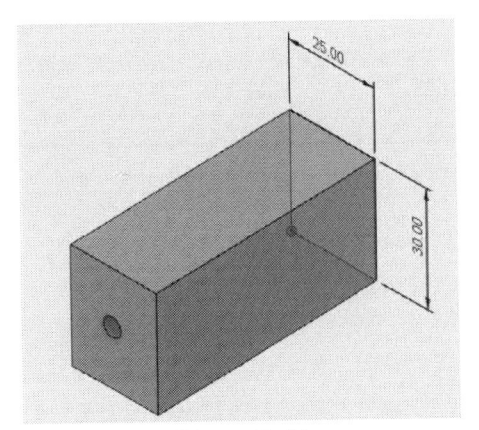

Figure 8–14

Task 2 - Change the model parameter names.

1. In the MODIFY panel, click Σ (Change Parameters).

2. In the Parameters dialog box, expand the nodes under *Model Parameters* to find the dimensions for **Sketch1**.

3. In the *Name* column, select the **d1** dimension and change the name to **width**.

4. Change the name of **d2** to **height**.

5. Expand the **Extrude1** node and change the name of **d3** to **length**.

6. Expand the **Hole1** node and change the name of **d6** to **diameter**.

7. Select the *Expression* cell for the **height** parameter and enter **width**. The height dimension is now driven by the width value.

8. Select the *Expression* cell for the **length** parameter and enter **width*3**. The Parameters dialog box displays as shown in Figure 8–15.

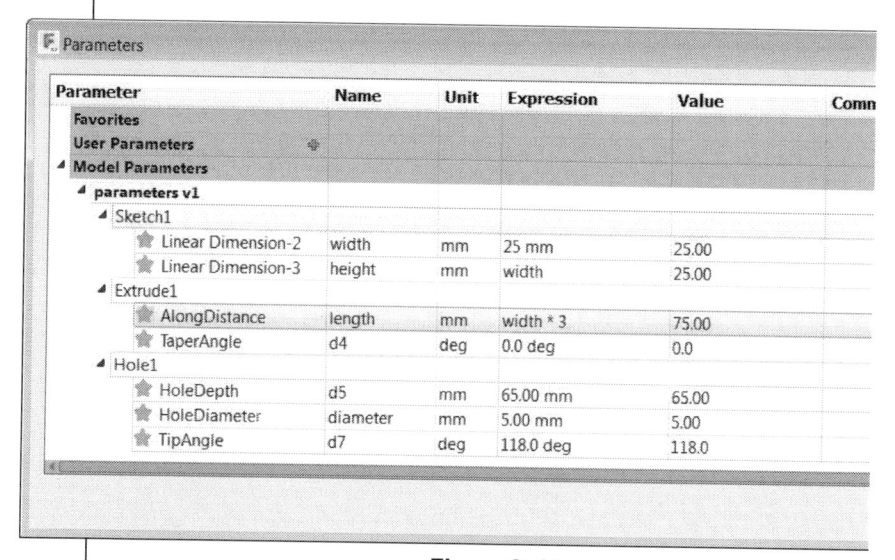

Parameter	Name	Unit	Expression	Value	Comm
Favorites					
User Parameters					
▲ Model Parameters					
▲ parameters v1					
▲ Sketch1					
Linear Dimension-2	width	mm	25 mm	25.00	
Linear Dimension-3	height	mm	width	25.00	
▲ Extrude1					
AlongDistance	length	mm	width * 3	75.00	
TaperAngle	d4	deg	0.0 deg	0.0	
▲ Hole1					
HoleDepth	d5	mm	65.00 mm	65.00	
HoleDiameter	diameter	mm	5.00 mm	5.00	
TipAngle	d7	deg	118.0 deg	118.0	

Figure 8–15

9. Click **OK** to close the Parameters dialog box.

10. In the Timeline, right-click on the Extrude1 icon and select **Edit Feature**. Note that **width * 3** displays in the *Distance* field, as shown in Figure 8–16.

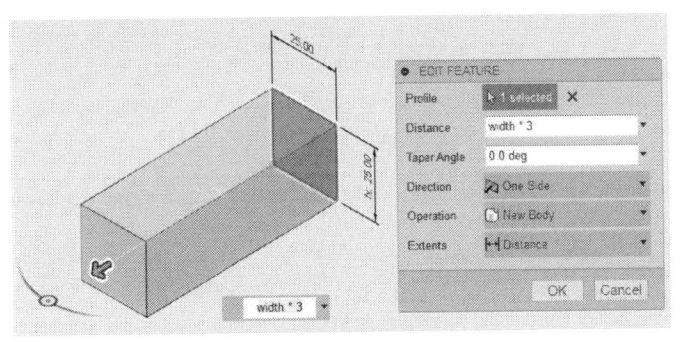

Figure 8–16

11. Click **Cancel** to close the EDIT FEATURE dialog box without making any changes.

Task 3 - Add a user-defined parameter.

1. In the MODIFY panel, click Σ (Change Parameters).

2. In the *User Parameters* row, click to add a new user-defined parameter. The Add User Parameter dialog box opens.

3. Set the following options:
   - *Name*: Enter **size**
   - *Units*: Select **No Units**
   - *Expression*: Enter **1**
   - *Comment*: Enter **determine overall size**

   The Add User Parameter dialog box should display as shown in Figure 8–17.

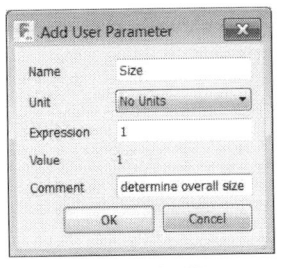

Figure 8–17

4. Click **OK**.

Task 4 - Add a second user-defined parameter.

1. In the *User Parameters* row, click ![+] to add a new user-defined parameter.

2. Set the following options:
   - *Name*: Enter **round_1**
   - *Units*: Select **mm**
   - *Expression*: Enter **3.175**
   - *Comment*: Enter **fillet radius**

3. Click **OK**.

Parameter names are case sensitive.

4. Select the *Expression* cell for the width dimension and enter **25mm*size**. The Parameters dialog box should display as shown in Figure 8–18.
   - The user-defined size parameter drives the width dimension. Since the size parameter does not have any units, you must multiply it by a distance to obtain a distance value.

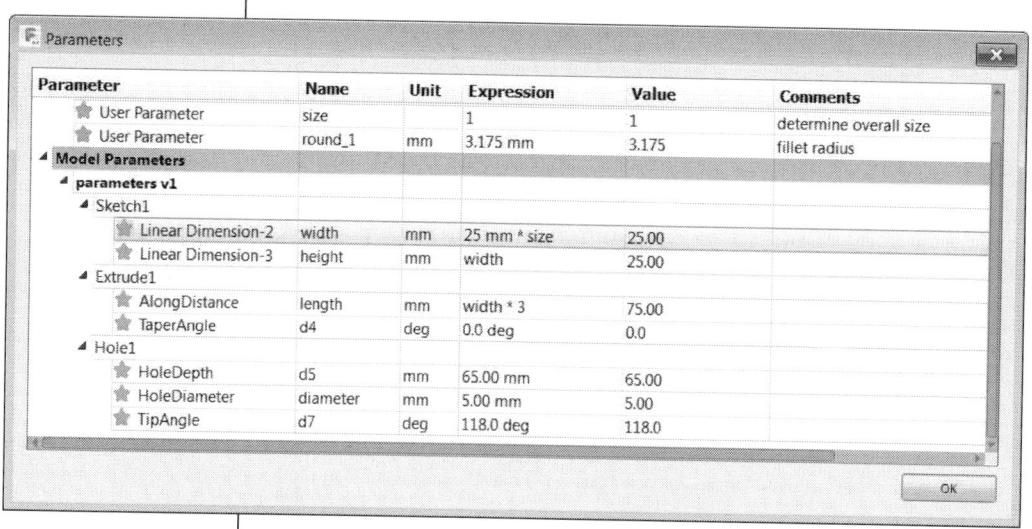

Parameter	Name	Unit	Expression	Value	Comments
⭐ User Parameter	size		1	1	determine overall size
⭐ User Parameter	round_1	mm	3.175 mm	3.175	fillet radius
▲ **Model Parameters**					
▲ parameters v1					
▲ Sketch1					
⭐ Linear Dimension-2	width	mm	25 mm * size	25.00	
⭐ Linear Dimension-3	height	mm	width	25.00	
▲ Extrude1					
⭐ AlongDistance	length	mm	width * 3	75.00	
⭐ TaperAngle	d4	deg	0.0 deg	0.0	
▲ Hole1					
⭐ HoleDepth	d5	mm	65.00 mm	65.00	
⭐ HoleDiameter	diameter	mm	5.00 mm	5.00	
⭐ TipAngle	d7	deg	118.0 deg	118.0	

Figure 8–18

5. Click **OK** to close the Parameters dialog box.

Task 5 - Add fillets.

In this task, you will add fillets to the design and use the parameters you defined to modify the fillets.

1. Start the creation of the fillet.

2. Add fillets to the four long edges of the design, as shown in Figure 8–19.

3. In the FILLET palette, in the *Radius* field, enter **round_1** as shown in Figure 8–19.

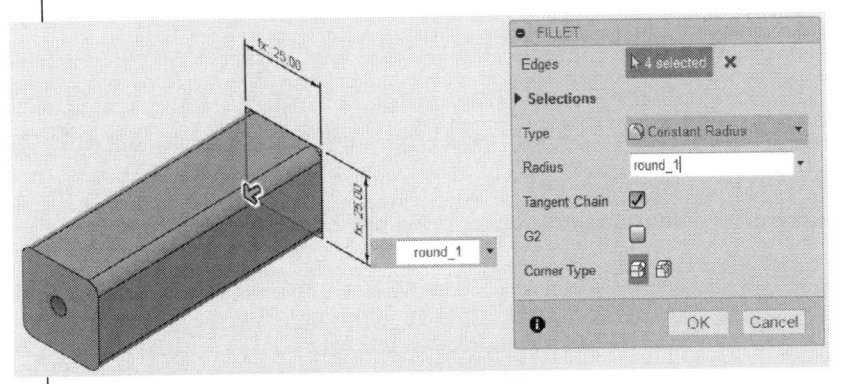

Figure 8–19

4. Complete the fillet.

5. In the Parameters dialog box, change the expression of the **round_1** parameter to **12.5**. The design displays as shown in Figure 8–20.

6. Change the equation of the size parameter to **2**. The updated design displays as shown in Figure 8–21.

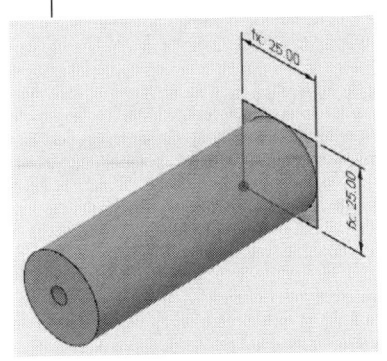

Figure 8–20

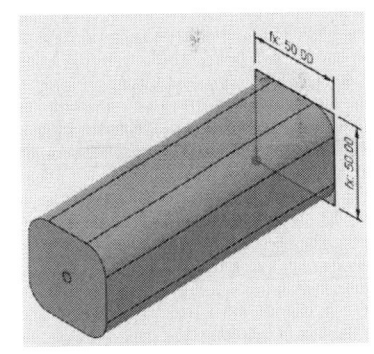

Figure 8–21

7. Close the Parameters dialog box.

8. Save the design with the name **parameters** to your *Autodesk Fusion 360 Practice Files* project.

9. Close the file.

Chapter Review Questions

1. You can only add an equation to a design using the Parameters dialog box.

    a. True
    b. False

2. Which of the following statements regarding equations are true? (Select all that apply.)

    a. Dimensions and parameters can be used in an equation to drive a value.
    b. Equations can be manually entered in the dimension value input fields.
    c. Equations can be created by selecting dimensions directly from the design.

3. Which combination of equations centers the hole, and sets the length and width as equivalent, as shown in Figure 8–22?

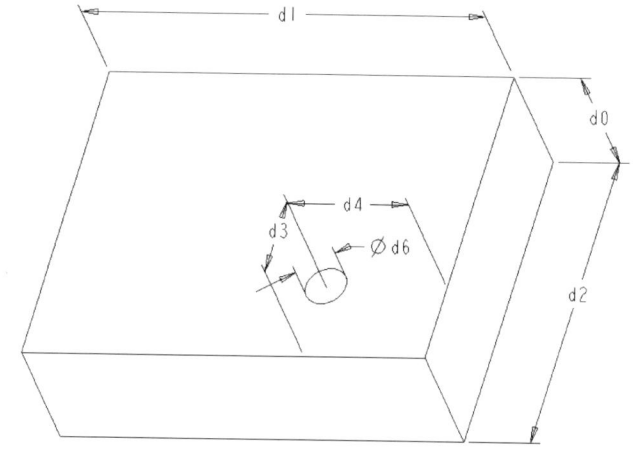

Figure 8–22

   a. d4 = d1 / 2
      d3 = d2 / 2
   b. d1 = d4 / 2
      d2 = d3 / 2
   c. d1 = d2
      d4 = d1 / 2
      d3 = d2 / 2

4. Which description best describes how the equation shown in Figure 8–23 affects the design?

*d0 = 3 * d6*
d3 = d4

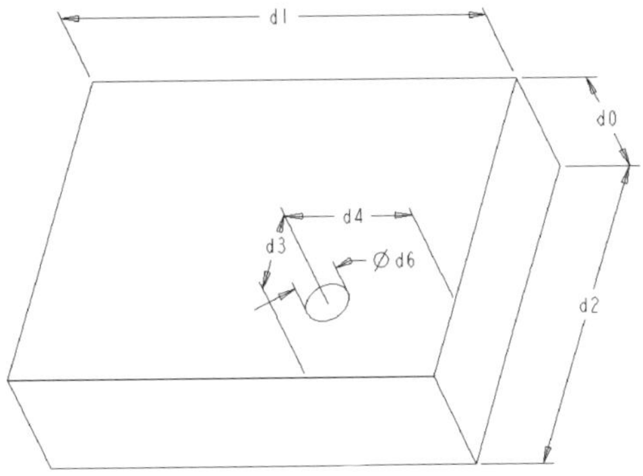

Figure 8–23

a. The depth of the base extrusion is equal to the diameter of the hole. The hole is centered on the base extrusion.

b. The depth of the base extrusion is equal to three times the diameter of the hole. The hole is centered on the base extrusion.

c. The depth of the base extrusion is equal to three times the diameter of the hole. The values of the horizontal and vertical hole dimensions are equivalent.

d. The depth of the base extrusion is equal to three times the diameter of the hole. The values of the horizontal and vertical hole dimensions are equivalent. The values of d1 and d2 are equivalent.

5. Which of the following best describe what **fx** is identifying in the sketch shown in Figure 8–24?

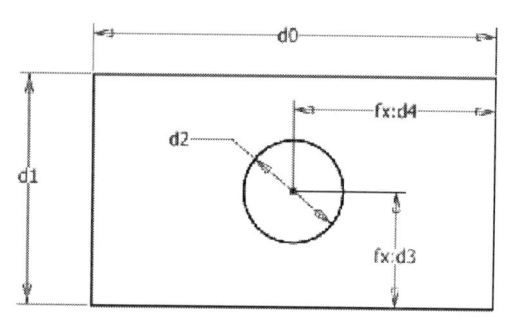

Figure 8–24

a. d3 and d4 are reference dimensions.
b. d3 and d4 are equal.
c. d3 and d4 are generated based on a user-defined equation.
d. d3 and d4 have a tolerance assigned.

Answers: 1.b, 2.(a,b,c), 3.c, 4.c, 5.c

Command Summary

Button	Command	Location
Σ	**Change Parameters**	• **Ribbon:** *Model* Workspace>MODIFY panel • **Context Menu**: Right-click in the graphics window and select **Modify**.
	Compute All	• **Ribbon:** *Model* Workspace>MODIFY panel • **Context Menu**: Right-click in the graphics window and select **Modify**.

Chapter 9

Additional Features and Operations

You can use numerous combinations of features to create a design. These can include standard sketched features and pick and place features. Drafts, splits, shells, ribs, and threads are advanced features that can be incorporated into a design to create geometry.

Learning Objectives in this Chapter

- Create a draft where the draft pull direction is normal to a selected plane or face.
- Create a shell feature that removes faces and assigns uniform wall thickness to the remaining faces in a design.
- Create a rib feature from a sketched section.
- Use the Split tool to split a face based on a split reference.
- Use the Scale tool to resize geometry in a design.
- Use the Thread tool to add threaded geometry to faces in a design.
- Use the Press Pull tool to efficiently create new features in a design.

Timeline icon:

9.1 Draft

A draft creates sloped surfaces and is often required to remove a part from a mold or casting. You can apply a draft over an entire profile, to one face, or to different faces, as shown in Figure 9–1.

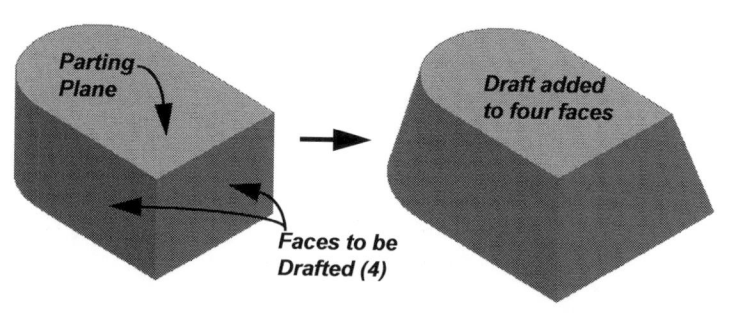

Figure 9–1

To create a split draft, you can use a parting plane, which is a construction plane that intersects the part, as shown in Figure 9–2.

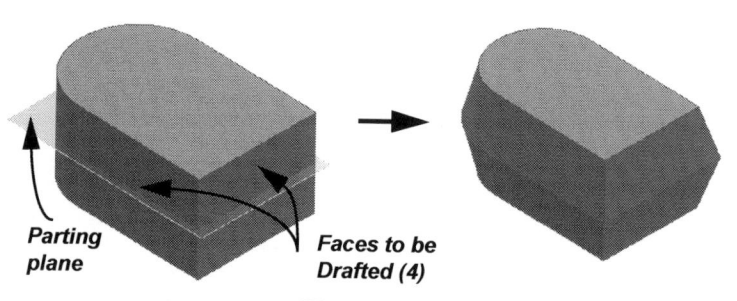

Figure 9–2

Use either of the following methods to start the **Draft** tool:

- In the MODIFY panel, click (Draft).

- In the graphics window, right-click and select **Modify>Draft**.

Video Lesson Available

Editing a Solid with Draft

Video Length: 3:59

9.2 Shell

A shell operation hollows a solid, leaving a constant wall thickness. The design shown in Figure 9–3 has a shell feature added to it that removed the front face.

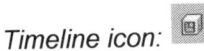

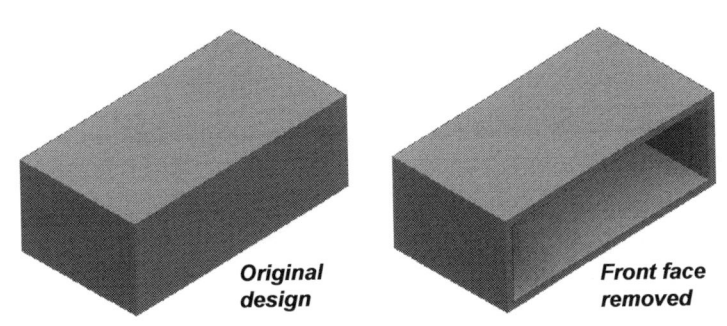

Timeline icon:

Original design

Front face removed

Figure 9–3

Use either of the following methods to start the **Shell** tool:

- In the MODIFY panel, click (Shell).
- In the graphics window, right-click and select **Modify>Shell**.

You can hollow a body without removing a face by selecting the body in the BROWSER.

Video Lesson Available

Editing a Solid with Shell

Video Length: 2:41

9.3 Rib

Timeline icon:

The **Rib** tool enables you to create solid extrusions with open geometry. The sketch in Figure 9–4 consists of a single line. In Figure 9–5, a rib feature was created so that the space up to the adjacent surfaces is filled across the thickness of the rib. In Figure 9–6, a depth is defined across the thickness of the rib so that there is a open space between it and the adjacent surfaces.

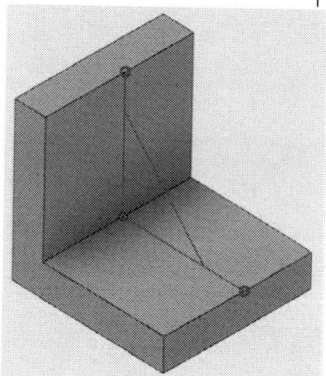

Figure 9–4

Figure 9–5

Figure 9–6

Use either of the following methods to start the **Rib** tool:

- In the CREATE panel, click (Rib).
- In the graphics window, right-click and select **Create>Rib**.

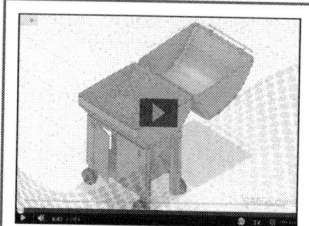

Video Lesson Available

Creating a Solid Using Rib

Video Length: 2:59

Timeline icon:

9.4 Split Face

You can split a face and manipulate each portion of the face independently. For example, a face can be split by a sketch so that a draft can be applied to one portion of it, as shown in Figure 9–7. You can use a face, construction plane, edge or sketch profile as the splitting tool.

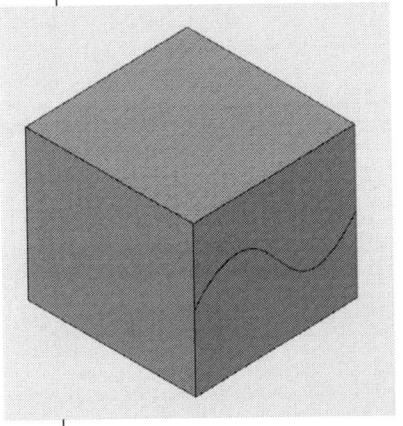

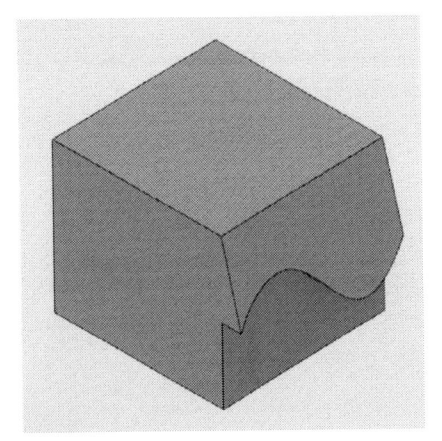

Figure 9–7

Use the following steps to split a face:

1. In the MODIFY panel, click (Split Face). Alternatively, in the graphics window, right-click and select **Modify>Split Face**. The SPLIT FACE palette opens as shown in Figure 9–8.

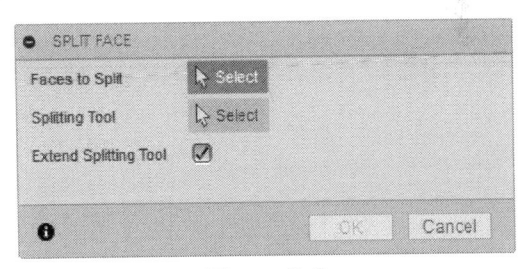

Figure 9–8

2. Select the face or faces you want to split.
3. Select the *Splitting Tool* field to activate it and select the splitting tool that will be used as the reference for splitting. Use the **Extend Splitting Tool** option to extend the tool through the design, if required.
4. Click **OK**.

9.5 Scale

You can use a scale operation to modify the size of sketch objects, bodies, or components. The scale can be done uniformly in all directions, or scaled independently in the design's X-, Y-, and Z-directions. A point is selected on the design from which the scaling will be applied.

Use either of the following methods to start the **Scale** tool:

- In the MODIFY panel, click (Scale).
- In the graphics window, right-click and select **Modify>Scale**.

Timeline icon:

Video Lesson Available

Editing a Solid with Scale

Video Length: *1:51*

9.6 Thread

You can use the Thread tool to add a thread to cylindrical faces, as shown in Figure 9–9. The thread geometry can be modeled on the design, or it can be represented by a cosmetic feature.

Timeline icon:

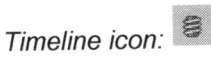

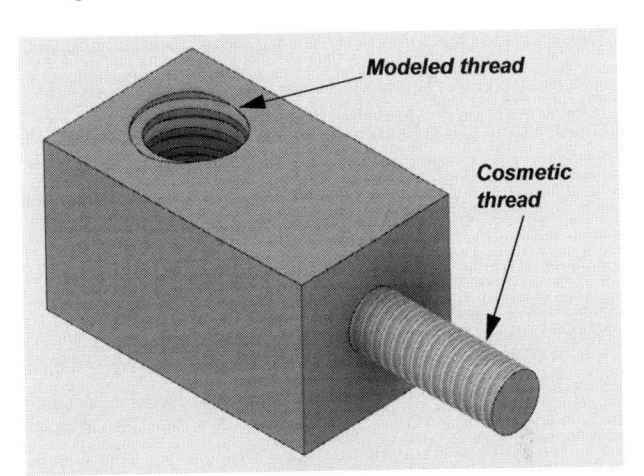

Figure 9–9

Threaded geometry cannot be added to a conical face.

Use the following steps to create a thread feature:

1. In the CREATE panel, click (Thread). The THREAD palette opens as shown in Figure 9–10.

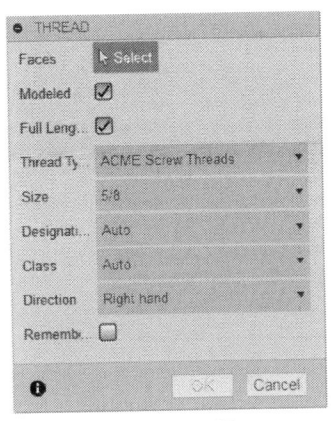

Figure 9–10

2. Select a cylindrical face on which to create the thread. Note that a thread can only be created on one face at a time.

3. Define the thread using the following options:
    - Select **Modeled** to create the thread geometry. Clear the option to create a cosmetic version.
    - Select **Full Length** to set the thread length to cover the entire length of the selected face. Clear the **Full Length** option to set the thread length. A non-full length thread starts from one end or at the required *Offset* value. Enter a value to define the *Length* of the thread.

4. Set the thread specifications. The options are as follows:

Thread Type	Sets the series of threads to apply.
Size	Sets the diameter size of the selected thread type.
Designation	Sets the number of threads based on the unit of length and bolt size.
Class	Sets the class of threads.
Direction	Sets the direction (right-hand or left-hand,) in which the threads should be applied.

5. Select **Remember** to reuse the same size for the next thread feature.

6. Click **OK** to complete the thread

Video Lesson Available

Creating Threads

Video Length: 5:33

9.7 Press Pull

Press Pull is a tool that adapts the feature type based on the reference entity you select. You can use Press Pull to offset faces, extrude sketched profiles, and create fillets on edges, as shown in Figure 9–11.

Faces do not need to be planar.

Offsets and Extrudes created with Press Pull can add or remove material.

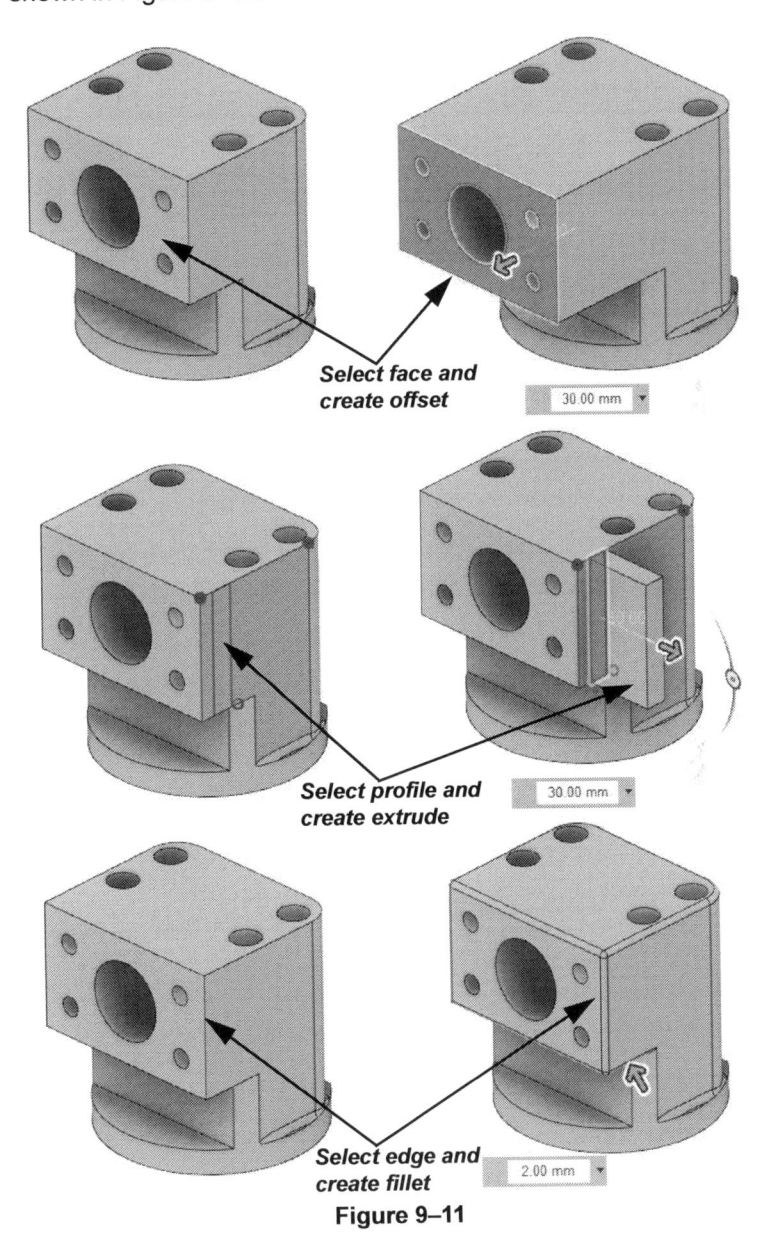

Select face and create offset

Select profile and create extrude

Select edge and create fillet

Figure 9–11

When you select faces for use with Press Pull, you can choose between creating a new offset or modifying the existing feature that the face belongs to.

Use one of the following methods to start the **Press Pull** tool:

- In the MODIFY panel, click (Press Pull).
- In the graphics window, right-click and in the marking menu, select **Press Pull**.
- In the graphics window, right-click and select **Modify>Press Pull**.
- Press <Q>.

Video Lesson Available

Creating a Solid Using Press-Pull

Video Length: 5:17

Practice 9a

Creating Shells and Ribs

Practice Objectives

- Create a Shell feature that removes required geometry from the design.
- Create a Rib feature from a sketched section.

In this practice, you will add a Shell and a Rib feature to create the geometry shown in Figure 9–12.

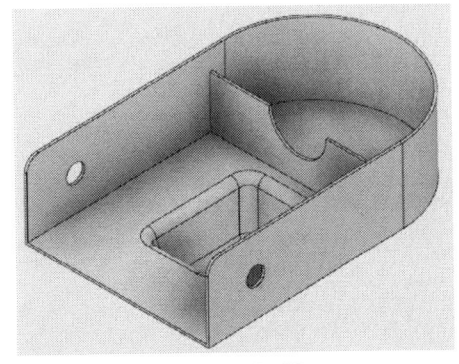

Figure 9–12

Task 1 - Create a new design from file.

1. Click ▾ > **New Design from File**.

2. In the Open dialog box, navigate to the *C:\Autodesk Fusion 360 Practice Files* folder, select **shell.f3d**, and click **Open**. The design displays as shown in Figure 9–13.

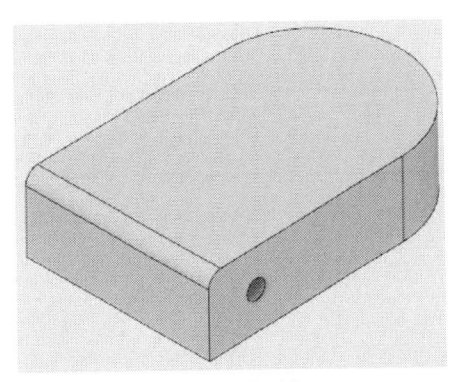

Figure 9–13

© 2016, ASCENT - Center for Technical Knowledge®

Task 2 - Shell the design.

1. In the MODIFY panel, click ▣ (Shell). The SHELL palette opens, as shown in Figure 9–14.

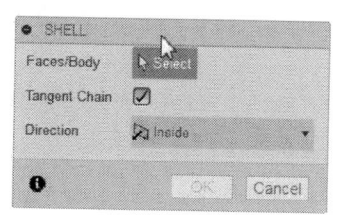

Figure 9–14

2. Select the **Tangent Chain** option, and then select the face shown in Figure 9–15 as the face to remove.

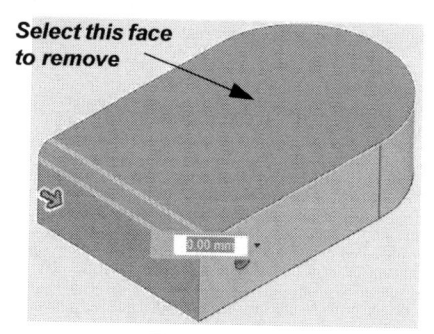

Figure 9–15

3. Ensure that the *Direction* option is set to **Inside**. Set the *Inside Thickness* value to **1**.

4. Click OK to complete the shell. The design displays as shown in Figure 9–16. The hole in the design did not shell as expected because its face was not selected for removal.

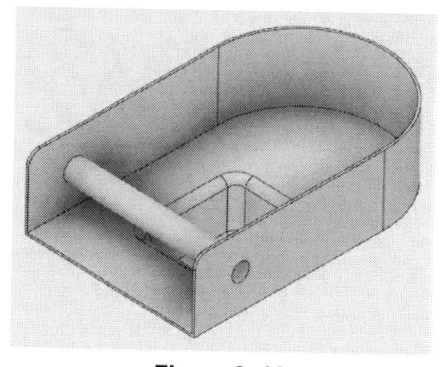

Figure 9–16

5. Edit the **Shell**. Hold <Ctrl> and select the surface of the hole to be removed, as shown in Figure 9–17.

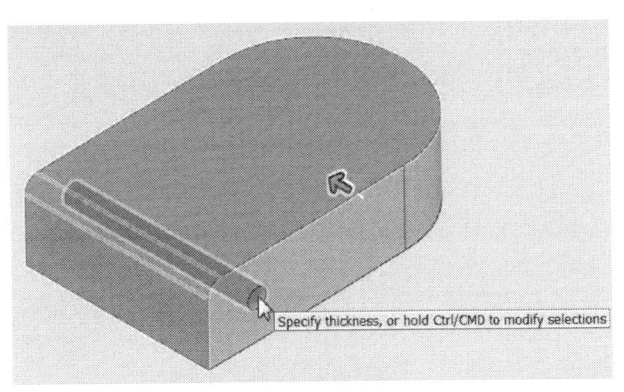

Figure 9–17

6. Complete the shell. The design displays as shown in Figure 9–18.

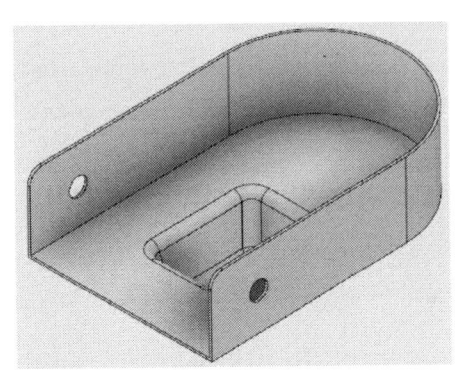

Figure 9–18

Task 3 - Create a rib.

1. In the BROWSER, expand the *Sketches* folder and toggle on the display of **Sketch1**. This sketch will be used to create a rib.

2. In the CREATE panel, click (Rib).

3. Select **Sketch1** as the curve for the rib feature.

4. For the *Thickness Option,* ensure that (Symmetric) is selected.

Ensure that the display of the Sketches folder is also on.

5. For the *Depth Option, select* ⤴ (To Next). The palette and design display as shown in Figure 9–19. If the rib is created in the wrong direction, in the RIB palette, select ⇅ to flip the direction.

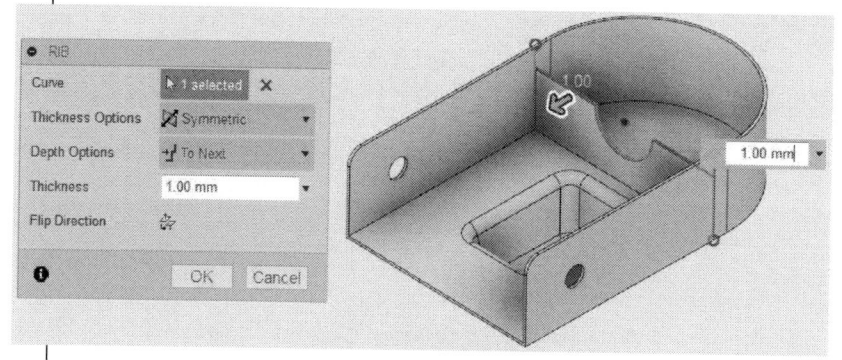

Figure 9–19

6. Change the *Thickness* to **1.00**.

7. Complete the rib. The design displays as shown in Figure 9–20.

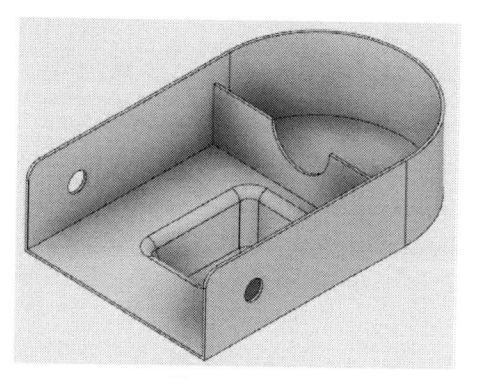

Figure 9–20

8. Save the design with the name **shell** to your *Autodesk Fusion 360 Practice Files* project.

9. Close the file.

Practice 9b

Using Advanced Design Tools

Practice Objectives

- Create a Split feature that splits a selected face based on a sketched profile.
- Create a Draft feature to add draft to a selected face in the design.
- Create an Extrude and Fillet using the Press Pull tool.
- Create a threaded hole in the design.
- Shell the design.

In this practice, you will use various tools to create the design shown in Figure 9–21, including the **Split Face**, **Draft**, **Press Pull**, **Hole**, **Thread**, and **Shell** tools.

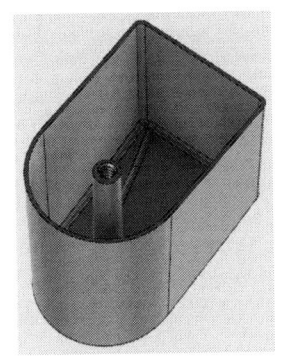

Figure 9–21

Task 1 - Create the first solid feature.

1. Start a new design with the *Unit Type* set to **Inch**.

2. On the XZ Origin plane, create the sketch shown in Figure 9–22.

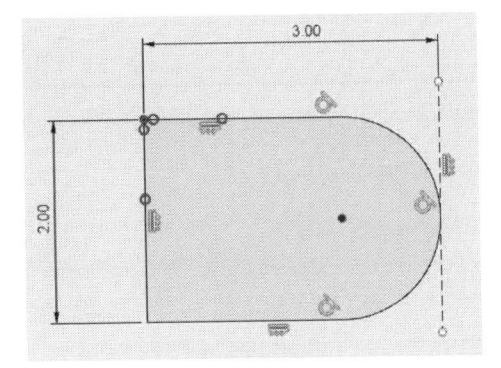

Figure 9–22

3. Stop the sketch.

4. In the MODIFY panel, click (Press Pull).

5. Select the sketched profile. Because a profile is selected, the software recognizes that an Extrude is intended, so the EXTRUDE palette replaces the PRESS PULL palette.

6. Set the extruded *Distance* value to **2.00 in**.

7. Set the *Taper Angle* to **-2.0 deg**. The taper angle can be used in place of a separate draft feature on extruded geometry.

8. Complete the feature. The part should display as shown in Figure 9–23.

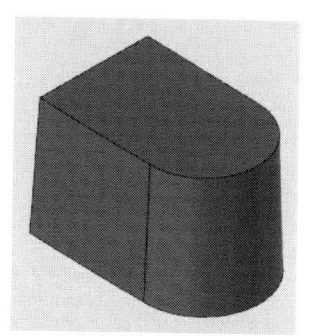

Figure 9–23

Task 2 - Create a sketch that will be used to split a face.

1. Create a new sketch on the top face of the model (the face that contains an arced edge). Sketch, constrain, and dimension the profile for the split as shown in Figure 9–24.

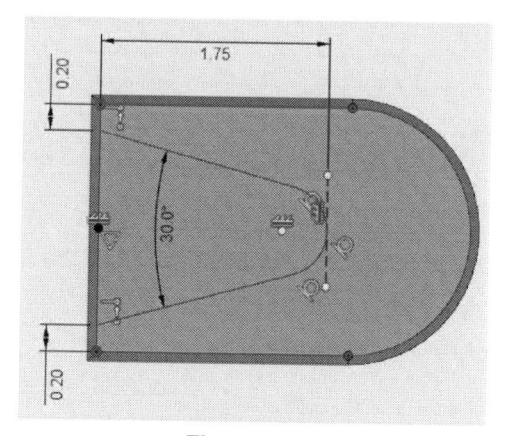

Figure 9–24

2. Stop the sketch.

Task 3 - Create the split.

1. In the MODIFY panel, click (Split Face). The SPLIT FACE palette opens as shown in Figure 9–25.

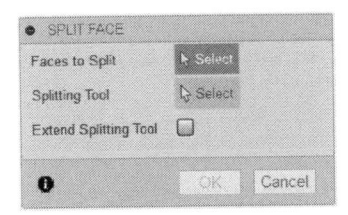

Figure 9–25

2. Select the face that you sketched on as the face to split.

3. Select the *Splitting Tool* field to activate it in the palette and select the sketch, as shown in Figure 9–26. A temporary surface is displayed to show the extension of the splitting tool and indicates how the selected face will be split.

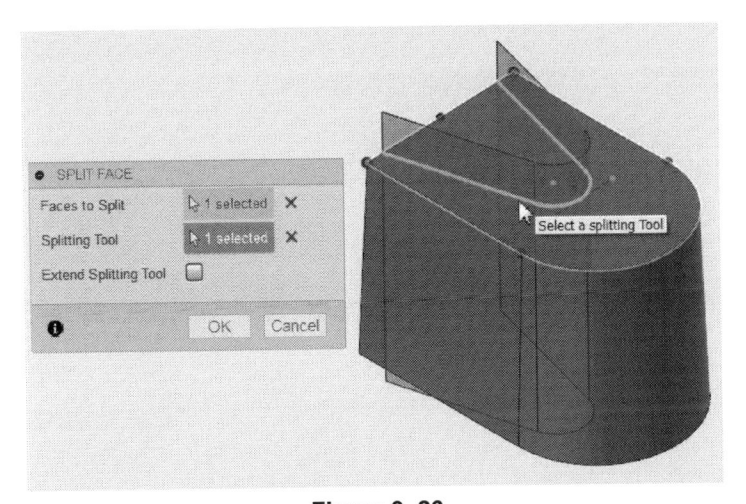

Figure 9–26

4. Click **OK** to split the face.

5. Hover the cursor over the split faces. They highlight individually (below the curve, and above the curve), as shown in Figure 9–27.

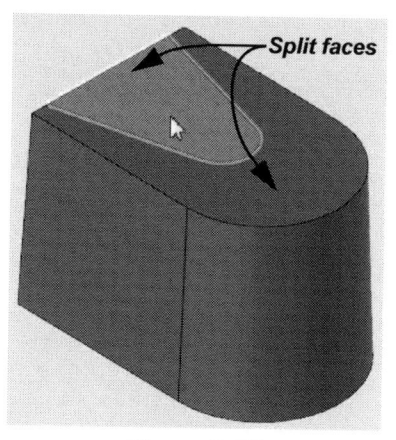

Figure 9–27

Task 4 - Create draft faces.

1. In the MODIFY panel, click (Draft). The DRAFT palette opens.

2. First you need to select the neutral plane from where the draft angle will be measured. Select the YZ Origin plane.

3. Clear the **Tangent Chain** checkbox and select the portion of the split face highlighted in Figure 9–28.

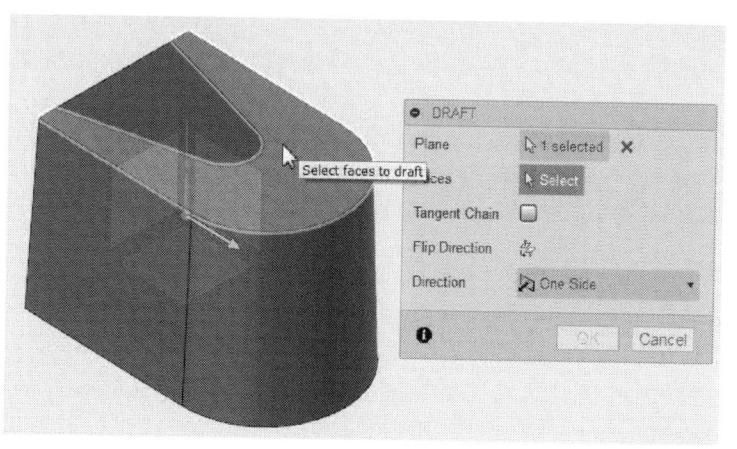

Figure 9–28

4. Set the angle to **10** degrees.

5. Click **OK** to draft the face. The design displays as shown in Figure 9–29.

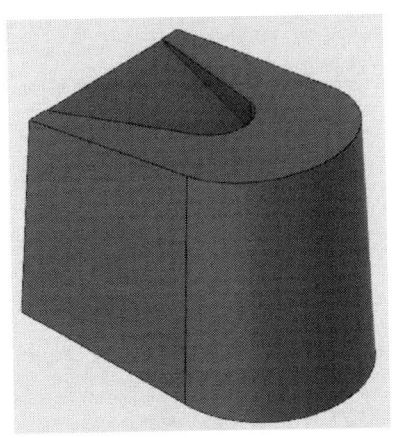

Figure 9–29

Task 5 - Create fillets using Press Pull.

1. Select the two edges highlighted in Figure 9–30 and press <Q> to activate the **Press Pull** tool. Because edges have been pre-selected, the **Press Pull** tool recognizes that the intent is to create fillets.

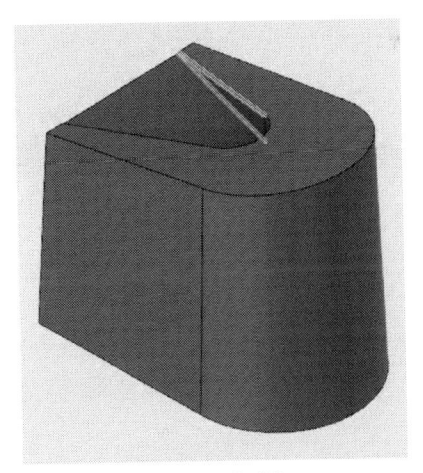

Figure 9–30

2. For the radius, enter **0.0625 in**. Ensure that the **Tangent Chain** option is selected and complete the feature.

3. Create a fillet with a radius of **0.125** in on the edge shown in Figure 9–31.

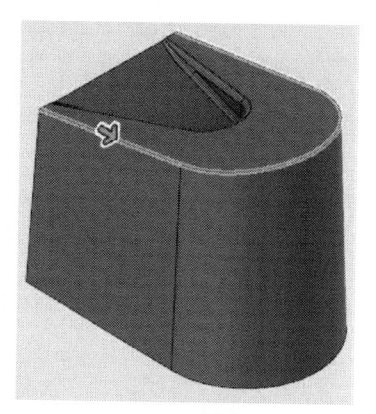

Figure 9–31

4. Create a fillet with a radius of **0.125 in** on the edge shown in Figure 9–32. The part should display as shown in Figure 9–33.

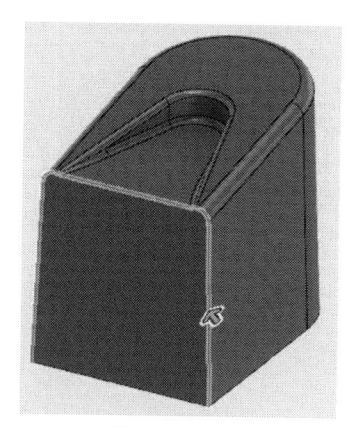

Figure 9–32

Figure 9–33

Task 6 - Create a hole, a shell, and a thread.

1. Orient the part as shown in Figure 9–34 and select the indicated face to place a hole. Position the hole on the face so that it snaps to the center of the circular edge.

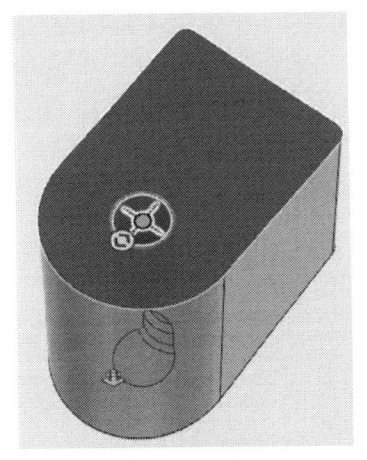

Figure 9–34

2. Set the *Diameter* value to **0.25 in** and the *Extents* option to **All**. Complete the feature. The design displays as shown in Figure 9–35.

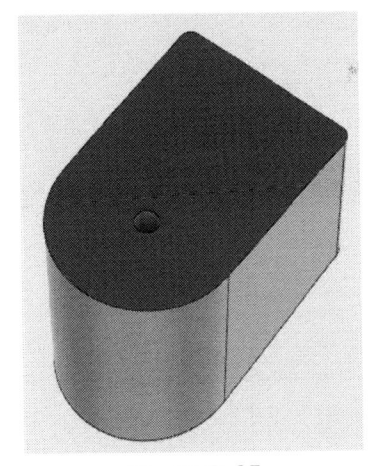

Figure 9–35

3. Create a Shell that removes the bottom face (the same face as the hole's placement face). Set the *Inside Thickness* to **0.05 in**. The design displays as shown in Figure 9–36.

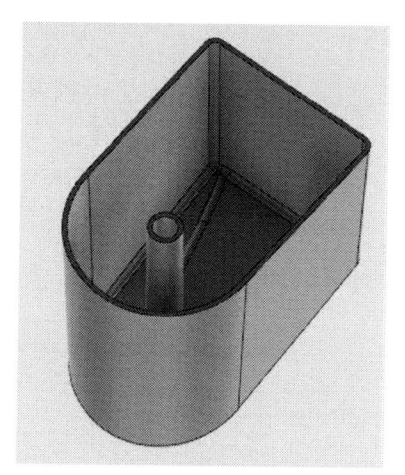

Figure 9–36

4. In the CREATE panel, click (Thread).

5. Select the inner surface of the hole.

6. In the THREAD palette, enter the parameters shown in Figure 9–37. The completed thread should display as shown in Figure 9–38.

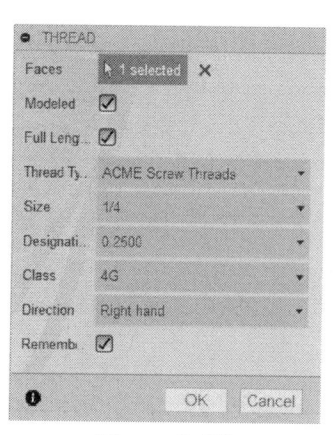

Figure 9–37 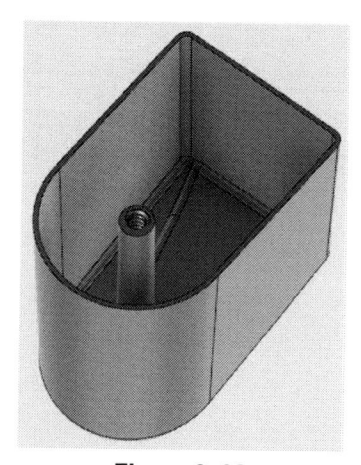   Figure 9–38

7. Save the design with the name **split_draft** to your *Autodesk Fusion 360 Practice Files* project.

8. Close the file.

Chapter Review Questions

1. Which of the following statements is true for creating a draft? (Select all that apply.)
   a. Multiple faces can be selected for drafting.
   b. Multiple faces can be selected when defining the pull direction.
   c. Only faces on the design can be selected to define the pull direction.

2. The (Split Face) tool enables you to split faces. The entire part remains as one object, but the faces can be manipulated separately.
   a. True
   b. False

3. You can shell a part without removing design faces.
   a. True
   b. False

4. Which of the following is true for shell features?
   a. To create a shell, you must select the face(s) to remove.
   b. A single face that is tangent to another face cannot be removed unless the tangent face is also removed.
   c. A shell can have walls of varying thickness.
   d. Wall thickness can be added to the inside, outside, or both sides of a design.

5. What can you do with the **Rib** tool that you cannot do with the **Extrude** tool?
   a. Create a surface object.
   b. Cut through an existing solid.
   c. Select multiple profiles for the feature.
   d. Create a solid from an open profile.

6. You can add threads to both cylindrical and conical faces.
   a. True
   b. False

Answers: 1.a, 2.a, 3.a, 4.d, 5.d, 6.b

Command Summary

Button	Command	Location
	Draft	• **Ribbon:** *Model* Workspace>MODIFY panel • **Context Menu:** Right-click in the graphics window and select **Modify**.
	Press Pull	• **Ribbon:** *Model* Workspace>MODIFY panel • **Context Menu:** Right-click in the graphics window and select **Modify**. • **Marking Menu:** Right-click in the graphics window.
	Rib	• **Ribbon:** *Model* Workspace>CREATE panel • **Context Menu:** Right-click in the graphics window and select **Create**.
	Scale	• **Ribbon:** *Model* Workspace>MODIFY panel • **Context Menu:** Right-click in the graphics window and select **Modify**.
	Shell	• **Ribbon:** *Model* Workspace>MODIFY panel • **Context Menu:** Right-click in the graphics window and select **Modify**.
	Split Face	• **Ribbon:** *Model* Workspace>MODIFY panel • **Context Menu:** Right-click in the graphics window and select **Modify**.
	Thread	• **Ribbon:** *Model* Workspace>CREATE panel • **Context Menu:** Right-click in the graphics window and select **Create**.

Chapter 10

Design and Display Manipulation

Being able to manipulate and control new and existing features in your design enables you to use flexibility when designing and helps you to more easily make changes to your design. Tools, such as the Section Analysis tool, also provide additional viewing tools to help you review the design.

Learning Objectives in this Chapter

- Change the order of features in the BROWSER.
- Use the History Marker to change the order in which new features are added to a design.
- Temporarily remove a feature from being included as part of the design geometry.
- Create half-section views in a design to help visualize the interior of a 3D design.
- Use direct modeling techniques to edit geometry.

10.1 Reordering Features

In a parametric design that has its feature history retained, the order in which features are created impacts the resulting geometry. In some cases, reordering the features in the Timeline can impact the overall geometry. To reorder a feature, select it in the Timeline and drag it left or right of its current position. Note that you cannot drag a feature before a feature that it references, or after a feature that references it.

In the example shown in Figure 10–1, shell and fillet features are added to a design. Due to the order in which the features are created, the resulting geometry after the addition of the shell is not what was wanted. Reordering the hole after the shell and adding the fillet before the shell results in the completed part.

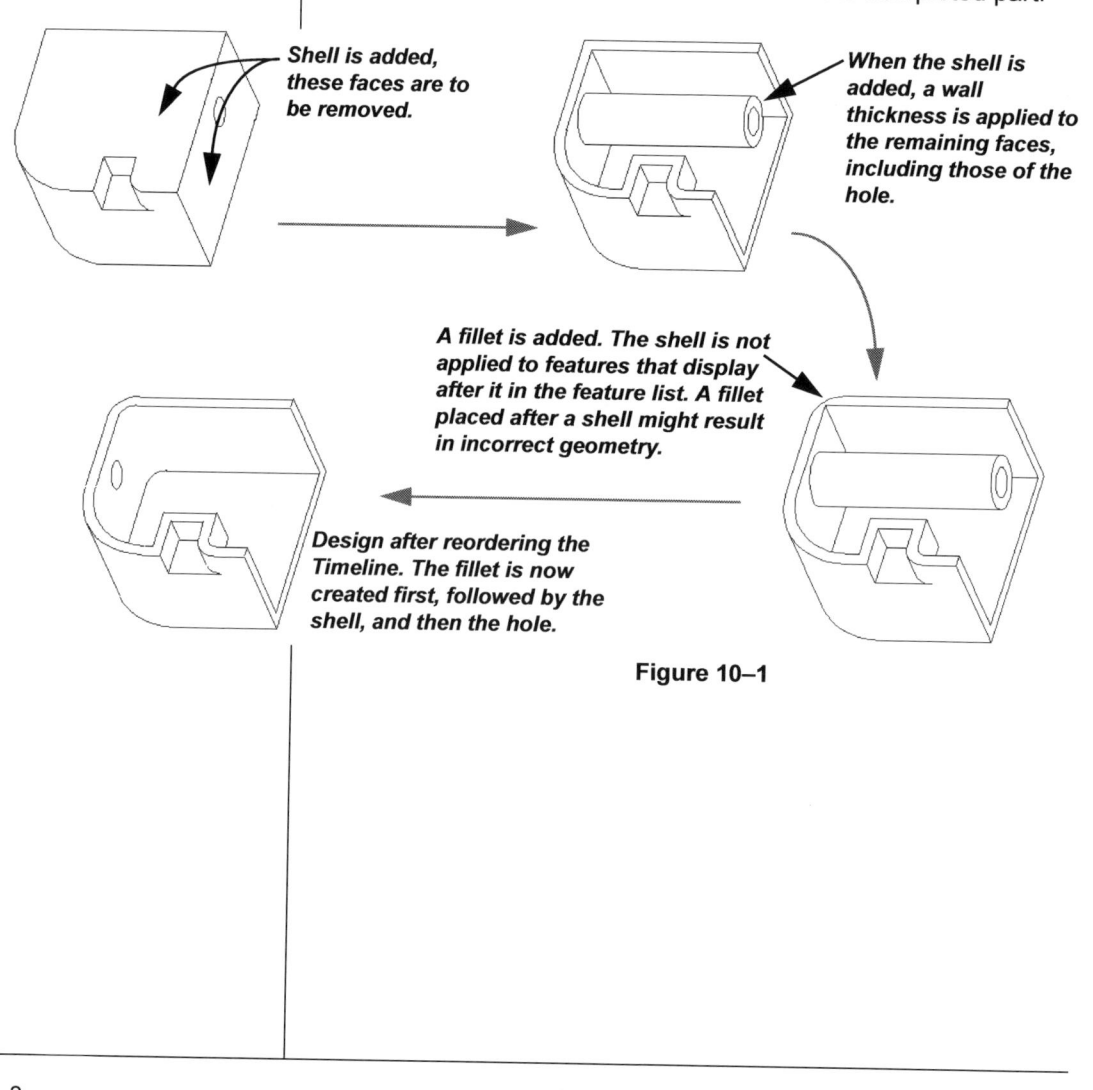

Shell is added, these faces are to be removed.

When the shell is added, a wall thickness is applied to the remaining faces, including those of the hole.

A fillet is added. The shell is not applied to features that display after it in the feature list. A fillet placed after a shell might result in incorrect geometry.

Design after reordering the Timeline. The fillet is now created first, followed by the shell, and then the hole.

Figure 10–1

10.2 Inserting Features

In a parametric design that has its feature history retained, new features are added at the end of the design list by default. To insert features at any earlier point, you must move the history marker from the far right side of the Timeline to the location at which you want to insert the feature. You can use this technique when you need to create a feature earlier in the design process.

Use any of the following techniques to move the history marker:

- In the Timeline, right-click on a feature icon and select **Roll History Marker Here**. The (History Marker) is placed after the selected feature.

- In the Timeline, select and drag the marker to the location at which you want to insert a feature.

- Use the Timeline control options (shown in Figure 10–2) to move the history marker left and right.

Figure 10–2

Figure 10–3 shows an example of a design and its Timeline before and after the ⊤ marker is moved. Once moved, all of the features after it are temporarily removed from the design. Any new feature you create will be placed at this position on the Timeline until the history marker is moved again. Move the history marker all of the way to the right to restore the suppressed features.

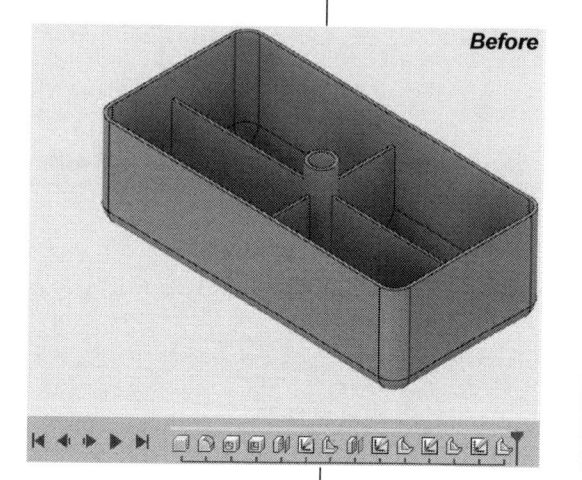

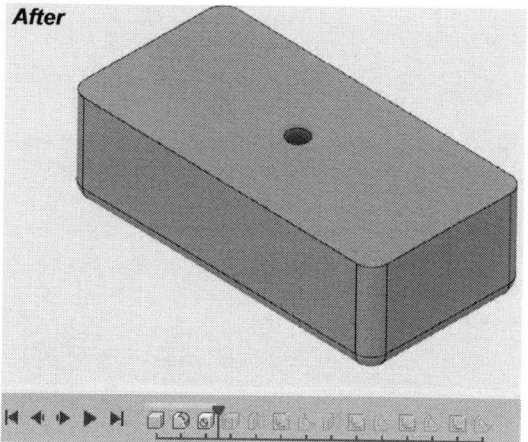

Before   After

Figure 10–3

To return the ⊤ marker to the far right of the Timeline, use one of the following techniques:

- In the Timeline, right-click on the last feature icon and select **Roll History Marker Here**. The ⊤ marker is placed after the last feature.

- In the Timeline, drag the ⊤ marker to the right.

- Use the Timeline control options to move the ⊤ marker.

10.3 Suppressing Features

As you work on complex parametric designs that have their feature history retained, you might find it difficult to identify or select features in the graphics window. You can simplify the appearance of a design by suppressing a feature to make it temporarily invisible.

- To suppress a feature, in the Timeline, right-click on the feature and select **Suppress Features**.

If you suppress a feature, all of its dependent features are also suppressed. Suppressed features and any of its dependent features are displayed in gray in the Timeline (as shown on the right in Figure 10–4) and are crossed out in the BROWSER.

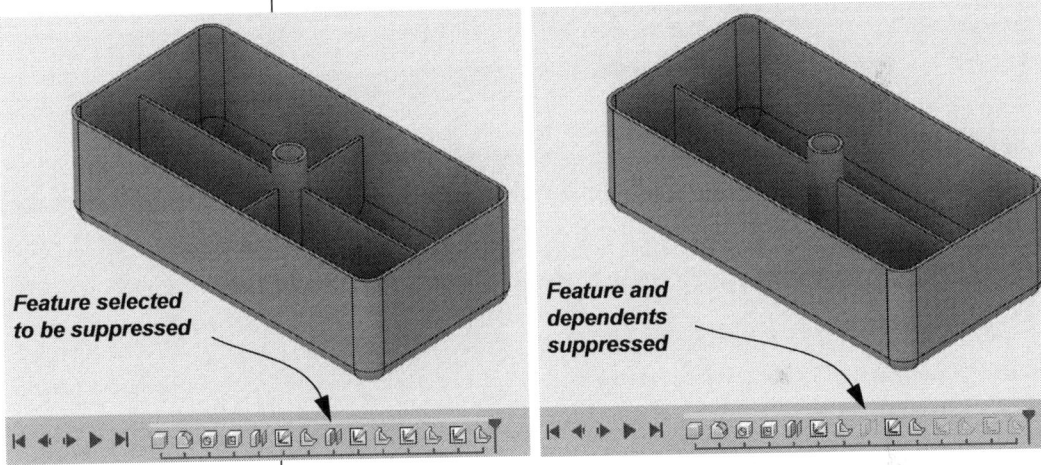

Figure 10–4

- To unsuppress a feature, in the BROWSER, right-click on the feature and select **Unsuppress Features**. Any dependent features are also unsuppressed.

10.4 Measure and Section Analysis

Measure

The INSPECT panel contains tools for interrogating a design. The Measure command can be used to measure the properties of faces, edges, vertices, bodies, and components, such as:

- Distance (i.e., the shortest distance between two selected entities)
- Area
- Loop length
- Radius or diameter
- Position

The type of measurement information that is reported depends on the entities selected. In Figure 10–5, the measurements reported are for two selected faces.

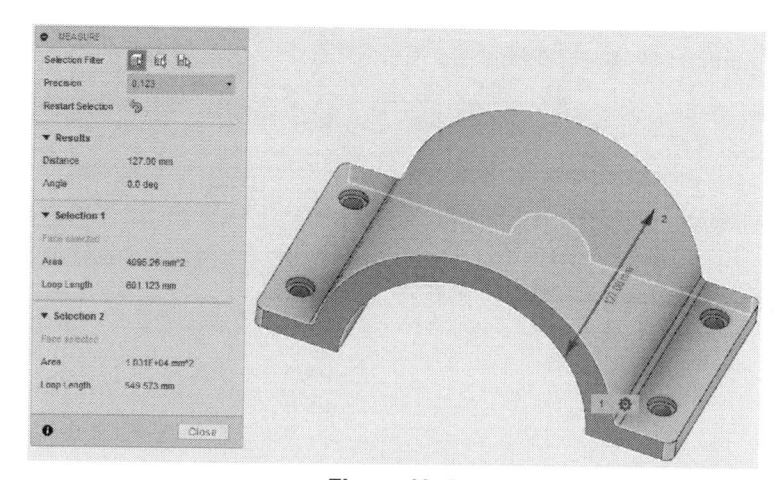

Figure 10–5

Video Lesson Available

Learning the Measure Tool

Video Length: 2:48

Section Analysis

A Section Analysis operation enables you to create a cut-away view of a design.

- In the INSPECT panel, click (Section Analysis) to create a half-section view, as shown in Figure 10–6.

Full Design View   *Half Section View*

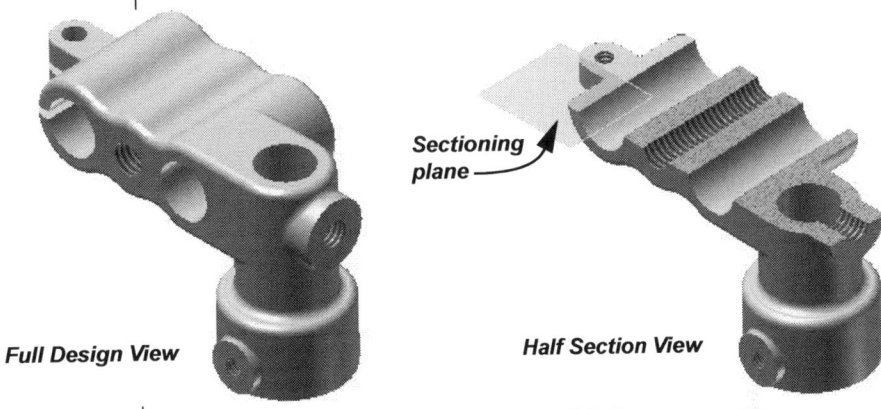

Sectioning plane

Figure 10–6

When you create a sketch, the SKETCH PALETTE>Slice option uses the sketch plane as the cutting plane. This is useful when creating sketches on the interior of a part.

You can select a planar face or construction plane to use as the cutting plane. The SECTION ANALYSIS palette enables you to offset or rotate the cutting plane to get the required section view, as shown in Figure 10–7.

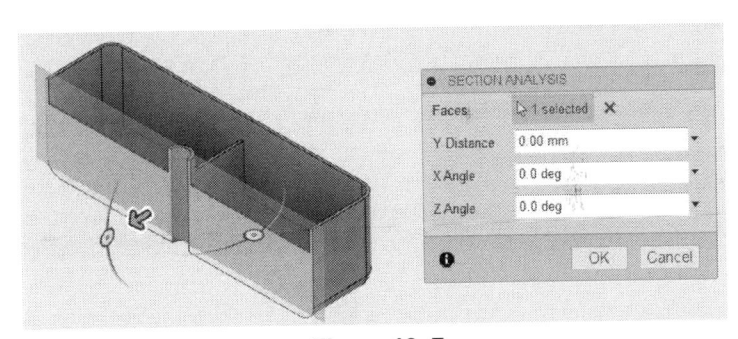

Figure 10–7

In multi-component designs, each component is assigned a different color in the cut-away for better visualization.

Sections are saved in the BROWSER in the **Analysis** folder. You can set the display of sections using the standard BROWSER controls.

Video Lesson Available

Analyzing Sections

Video Length: 1:34

© 2016, ASCENT - Center for Technical Knowledge®

10.5 Direct Modeling

While this student guide focuses on parametric modeling, direct modeling is discussed here to explain the technique as an option for designing or modifying imported or complex modeling.

The parametric modeling method of design in the Autodesk® Fusion 360™ software results in constraints and relationships that define geometry. You can make changes to existing geometry (by modifying dimension values, redefining the placement references, reordering features, etc.) because the feature history is recorded.

The direct modeling or direct edit method of design is less restrictive than parametric modeling. With direct modeling, feature history is not recorded in the Timeline and parent-child feature relationships are not enforced. Instead, geometry is simply added or removed to a single body. When changes are required, there is no feature to return to for editing, so you must use direct edit tools to make the necessary changes.

Three common scenarios for when direct modeling might be employed are:

- Creating a conceptual model: Direct modeling can be used to quickly capture a conceptual idea when dimensions and feature relationships are unimportant.

Design history for existing geometry cannot be restored after you stop capturing and begin using direct modeling techniques.

- Making changes to a complex model: As the number of features and the complexity of a model increases, changes can result in feature failures if you have not considered references and the design intent. You can stop capturing the deign history and use direct modeling techniques to make changes that would otherwise require many feature edits or a rework of the design.

- Working with imported geometry: The geometry that you import from other CAD platforms does not retain all of the parametric information that a model created directly in Autodesk Fusion 360 would have. Direct modeling techniques can be used to manipulate this imported geometry.

Video Lesson Available

Understanding Direct Manipulation Modeling

Video Length: *1:05*

You can start direct modeling using any of the following techniques:

- In the BROWSER, right-click on the design name and select **Do not capture Design History**, as shown in Figure 10–8.

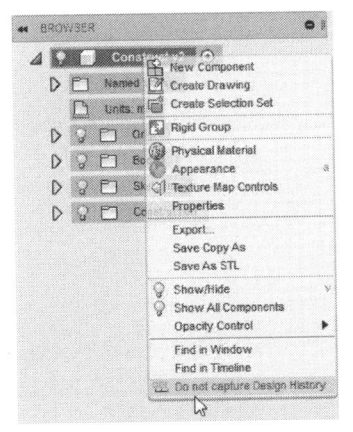

Figure 10–8

- When creating a new design, you can begin with a base feature to use direct modeling. To create the base feature, in the CREATE panel, click **Create Base Feature**. This inserts a base feature in the Timeline, and then all geometry operations are preformed on the base feature. To return to the MODEL environment, on the ribbon, click **FINISH BASE FEATURE**. You can use the direct modeling method while the base feature is active.

Direct Edit Tools

You can use the same feature types to create geometry with direct modeling as you do with parametric modeling. However, once the geometry placed or imported, you must use the direct modeling tools to edit the existing faces on the design. These commands include **Delete**, **Move**, and **Press Pull**.

Delete

To delete faces, select the faces and press <Delete>, or right-click and select **Delete**. In Figure 10–9, a face is selected and was deleted from the geometry. The geometry updates to account for the deleted face.

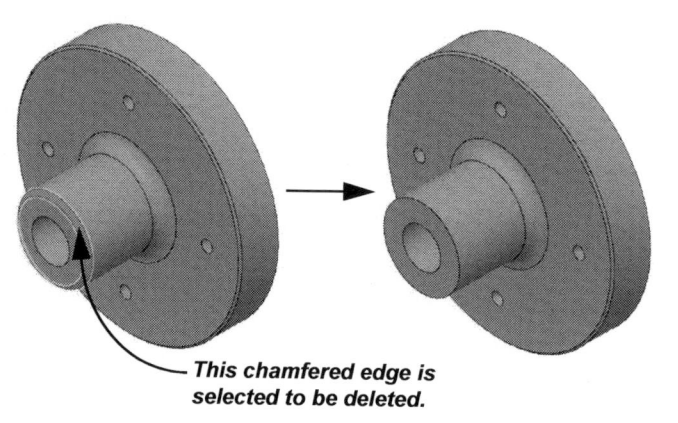

This chamfered edge is selected to be deleted.

Figure 10–9

Move

The Move command can also be used to move components, bodies, and sketch objects.

The Move command enables you to select an existing face on the geometry and move it normal to its current geometry, or rotate it. To move faces, in the MOVE palette, select ▢ (Move Faces) and then select a face to be moved. In Figure 10–10, a face on the geometry is selected and the move triad was used to move the face. Notice how the adjacent geometry updates to reflect the change.

This face is selected to be moved.

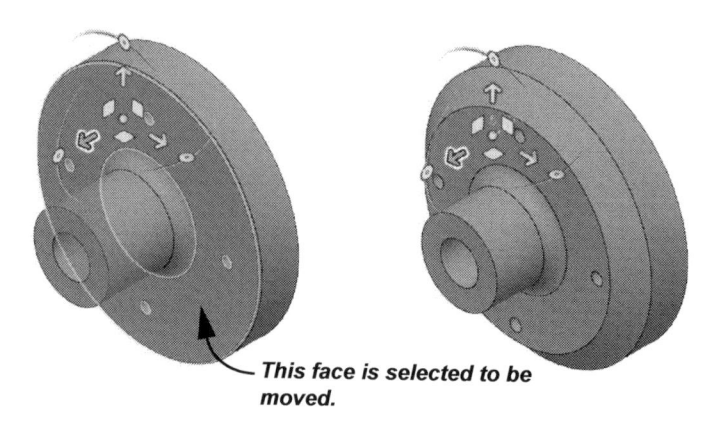

Figure 10–10

> **Video Lesson Available**
>
> Using the Manipulator
>
> *Video Length:* 2:14

Press Pull

The Press Pull command can be used as a direct editing tool to offset faces that exist in the design. Depending on the face geometry that you select, the command can do the following:

- For a planar face, the command offsets the face similar to the Move command, as shown in Figure 10–11.

- For a cylindrical or arc-shaped face, the command offsets the face to change the radius/diameter of the face, as shown in Figure 10–11.

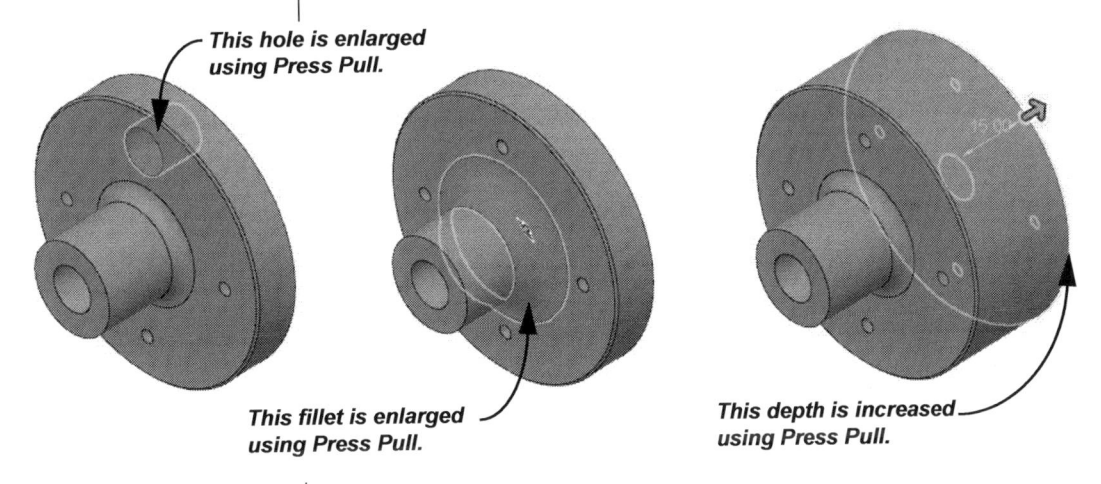

This hole is enlarged using Press Pull.

This fillet is enlarged using Press Pull.

This depth is increased using Press Pull.

Figure 10–11

Hint: Advanced Face Manipulation

The Edit Face command is an advanced direct editing tool that enables you to break up a face into smaller faces and push and pull entities (edges, vertices, or faces) to manipulate the shape of the geometry, as shown in Figure 10–12. This is similar to the Edit Form command used in the Sculpt environment and is discussed in Chapter 18 of this training guide.

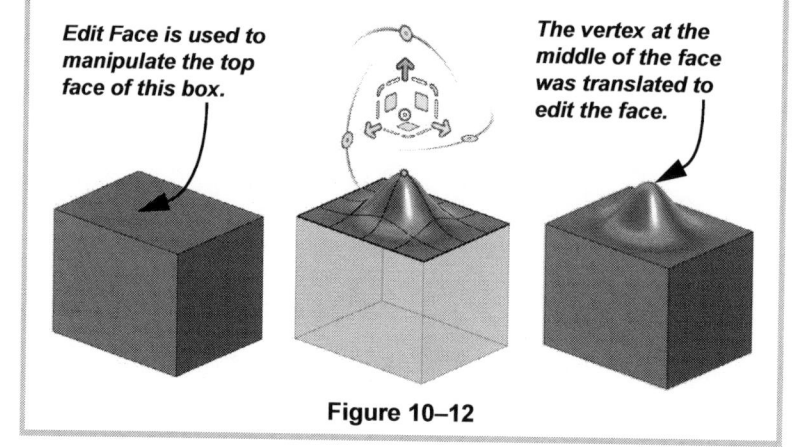

Edit Face is used to manipulate the top face of this box.

The vertex at the middle of the face was translated to edit the face.

Figure 10–12

Practice 10a

Section Analysis

Practice Objectives

- Create a section view using a construction plane as the cutting reference.
- Make changes to the design and ensure that the section view updates accordingly.

In this practice, you will open an existing design and create a section analysis. You will also use the **Slice** tool while sketching on the interior of the design. The design that will be used is shown in Figure 10–13.

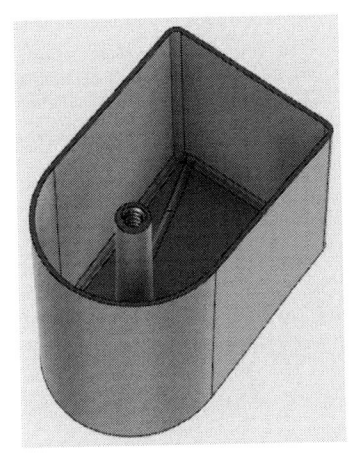

Figure 10–13

Task 1 - Open an existing design.

1. Click ▦ to open the Data Panel.

2. Ensure that you are in the *Autodesk Fusion 360 Practice Files* project.

3. Scroll down to find the design you created in the previous practice called **split_draft**. Double-click on it to open it.

*If you did not complete the previous practice, create a new design from the file **split_draft_final.f3d**.*

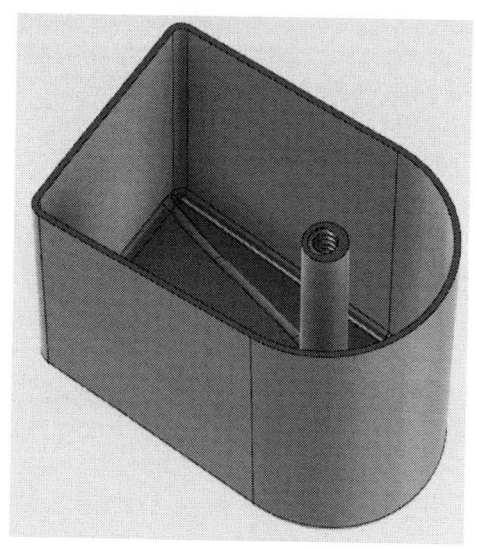

4. Orient the part similar to that shown in Figure 10–14.

Figure 10–14

5. In the BROWSER, expand the *Named Views* folder.

6. Right-click on the *Named Views* folder and select **New Named View**. *NamedView* is added to the list of views.

7. Click on *NamedView* and rename it to **UnderSide**.

Task 1 - Create a section analysis to show half the part.

1. A construction plane will be used to create the section analysis. On the CONSTRUCT panel, click (Offset Plane).

2. In the BROWSER, select the XY origin plane.

3. To define the offset distance, select the cylindrical face shown in Figure 10–15. This will set the offset distance so that the plane passes through the center of the cylinder.

Buttons shown in the ribbon are shortcuts to the most frequently used commands. You can add additional commands to the ribbon once the panel is open by clicking next to any tool.

Select this face

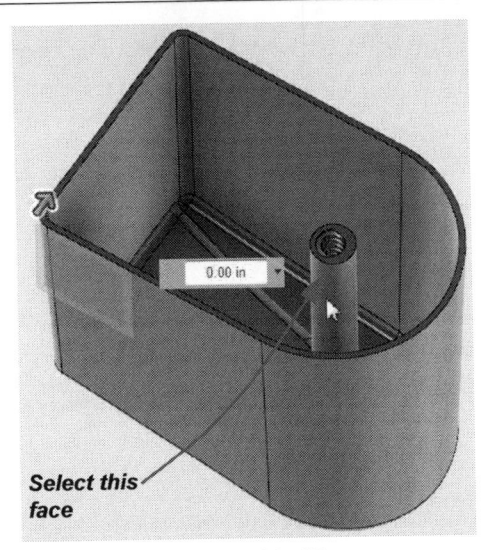

Figure 10–15

4. Click **OK** to complete the construction plane.

5. In the INSPECT panel, click (Section Analysis).

6. Select the construction plane that you just created to define the section.

7. In the SECTION ANALYSIS palette, ensure that the *Distance* and *Angle* values are **0** and complete the section. The design should display as shown in Figure 10–16 and the *Analysis* folder should be added to the BROWSER.

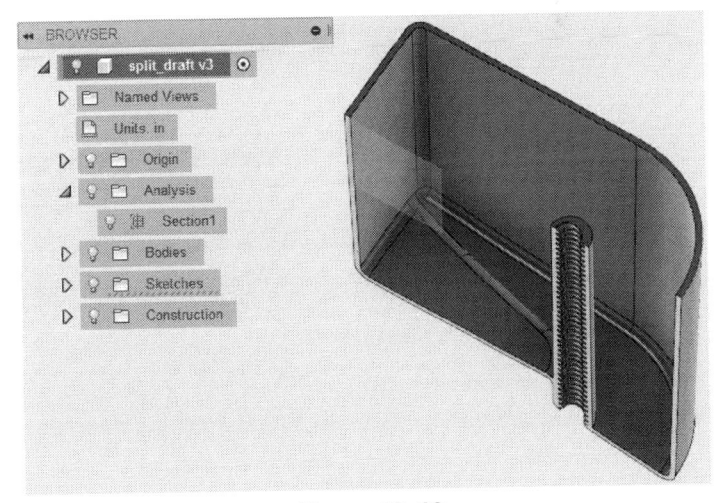

Figure 10–16

8. In the BROWSER, select next to the section name to toggle off its visibility. The entire design is displayed once again.

Task 2 - Create a rib on the interior of the design.

1. Start the creation of a new sketch on the construction plane that you created in the previous task.

2. If you are working in a shaded display setting, the design will display in the sketch orientation as shown on the left in Figure 10–17. In the SKETCH PALETTE, select the **Slice** checkbox. The design is cut back to the sketch plane, as shown on the right in Figure 10–17.

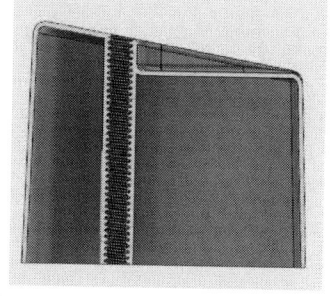

Figure 10–17

3. Sketch a line constrained to be horizontal, as shown in Figure 10–18. Create a dimension between the line and the bottom edge with a value of **0.25**. Because the line is going to be used to create a rib, the length of the line does not need to be defined, nor does its endpoints need to be constrained.

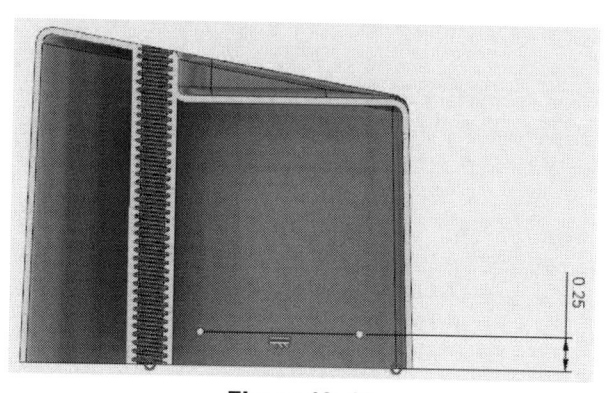

Figure 10–18

4. Stop the sketch.

5. In the BROWSER, select the **UnderSide** view to orient the part.

6. In the CREATE panel, click (Rib).

7. Select the line you just sketched as the 2D sketch curve for the rib.

8. Set the *Thickness Options* to (Symmetric).

9. Set the *Depth Options* to (To Next).

10. For the *Thickness* value, enter **0.0625**.

11. If the rib preview shows the direction of the feature extruding outside of the part (as shown on the left in Figure 10–19), flip the direction in the RIB palette by selecting . The preview should display as shown on the right in Figure 10–19.

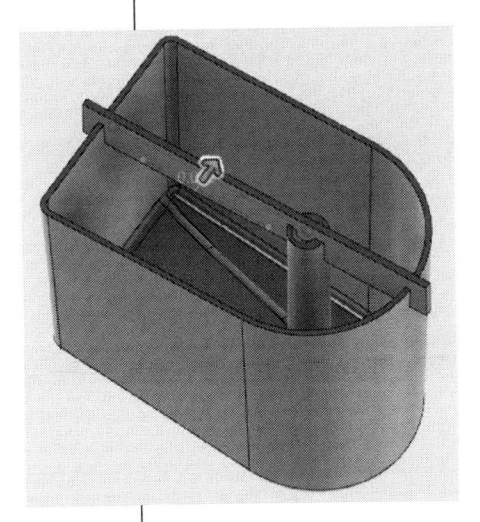

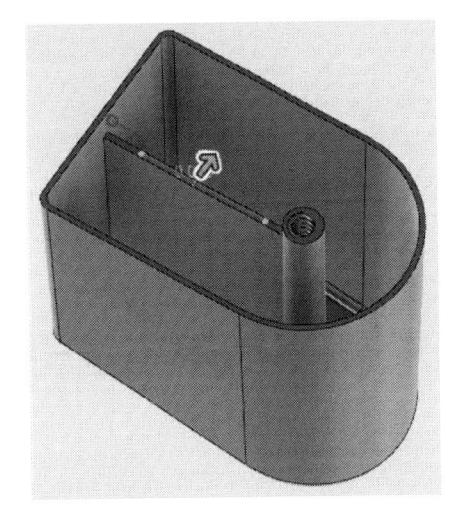

Figure 10–19

12. Click **OK** to complete the feature.

13. In the BROWSER, toggle on the display of the section. The design should display as shown in Figure 10–20. It updates to reflect the design change in the model even though it was created prior to the rib.

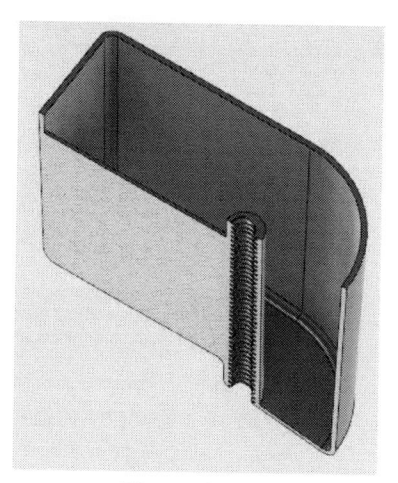

Figure 10–20

14. Save the design and close the file.

Practice 10b

Feature Order

Practice Objectives

- Change the order of features in the BROWSER to obtain required geometry.
- Use the Roll History Marker Here tool to insert a new feature at a point other than the end of the Timeline.

In this practice, you will explore the impact of feature order on a part. You will create a switch plate as shown in Figure 10–21. Once complete, you will reorder and insert features in the part and observe the results.

Figure 10–21

Task 1 - Create a new design.

1. Start a new design with the *Unit Type* set to **Inch**.

2. Create the sketch on the XY plane, as shown in Figure 10–22. Create the sketch symmetrically about the YZ and XZ origin planes.

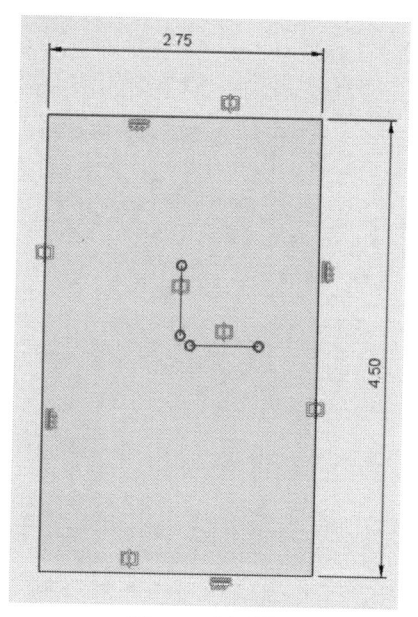

Figure 10–22

3. Extrude the sketch **0.25in** away from the sketch plane (behind the design when it is in the **Home** view). The design displays as shown in Figure 10–23.

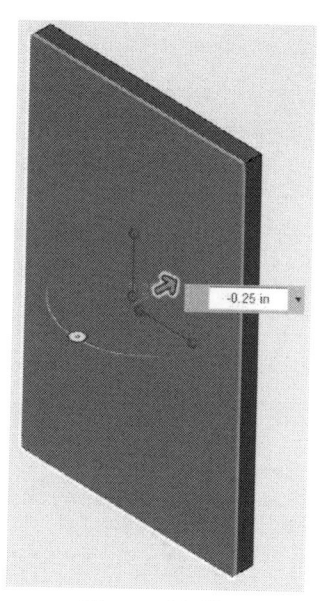

Figure 10–23

Task 2 - Create hole features.

1. Create the hole at the top of the Front View as shown in Figure 10–24. Create the hole with a diameter of **0.188 in**. It should be offset **1.1 in** from the top edge of the extrude and **1.375 in** from the left edge of the extrude, as shown in the Figure 10–24. The hole should cut though the entire part.

2. Create the second hole shown at the bottom of Figure 10–24. Create the hole with a diameter of **0.188 in**. It should be offset **1.1 in** from the bottom edge of the extrude and **1.375 in** from the left edge of the extrude. The hole should cut though the entire part.

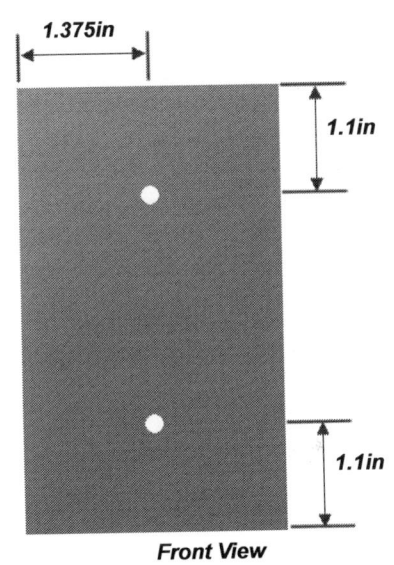

Front View
Figure 10–24

Task 3 - Create an extrude feature.

1. Create the sketch shown in Figure 10–25, using the front face of **Extrude1** as the sketching plane. Create the sketch symmetrically about the YZ and XZ origin planes.

2. Create an extruded cut feature using the new sketch, as shown in Figure 10–25.

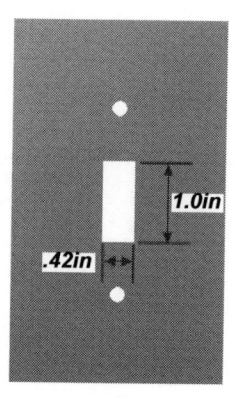

Figure 10–25

Task 4 - Shell the design.

1. Start the creation of a shell feature.

2. Reorient the view to look at the back of the design and select the back surface as the face to remove.

3. In the Shell dialog box (or in the entry field), enter an *Inside Thickness* of **0.063 in**.

4. Complete the shell. The design displays as shown in Figure 10–26.

Figure 10–26

Task 5 - Reorder features.

Extrude2 does not display as required. It should not have a wall thickness applied to it. In this task, you will use the Timeline to reorder the shell feature before Extrude2 to correct this.

1. In the Timeline, click and hold the ⬚ for Shell1. Drag it to the left so it is repositioned before ⬚ for Extrude2. The design and Timeline should display as shown in Figure 10–27.

Reordering features on the Timeline changes the order in which the features are regenerated. The shell now precedes the extruded cut, so a wall thickness is no longer applied to the faces created by the cut.

Figure 10–27

2. Return to the **Home** view.

Task 6 - Insert a feature.

You will add fillets to edges on the design, but they need to be created before the shell. The new fillet feature will be inserted by moving the history marker in the Timeline.

1. In the Timeline, right-click on [icon] for **Sketch2** and select **Roll History Marker Here**. The design and Timeline should display as shown in Figure 10–28. All of the features after the history marker have been suppressed.

Figure 10–28

2. Create a **0.175in** fillet on the four outside edges bordering the front face of the design, as shown in Figure 10–29.

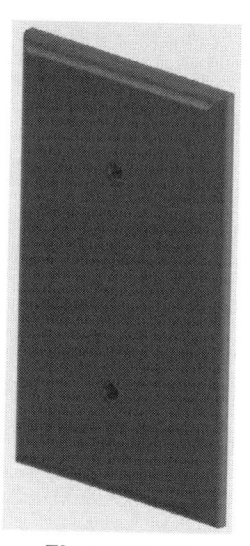

Figure 10–29

3. Reorient the design so you can see the back. Note that the fillet is not applied to the back.

4. In the Timeline, click and drag the history marker all of the way to the right so that it is positioned at the end of the Timeline, as shown in Figure 10–30.

Figure 10–30

With all of the features resumed, the shell is applied to the fillet you just inserted. The part should display as shown in Figure 10–31.

Figure 10–31

5. Save the design as **switch_plate**.

6. Close the file.

Practice 10c

Direct Edit

Practice Objectives

- Edit geometry that was created using direct modeling to delete a face, move a face, and change its size.
- Add parametric Autodesk Fusion 360 features to geometry that was created using direct modeling.

In this practice, you will open a model that was created using the direct modeling approach and you will edit it to make changes to its faces. To complete the design, you will return to the parametric modeling tools and add standard Autodesk Fusion 360 features (i.e., fillets) to the model. You will then illustrate that the fillet is parametric, although the imported geometry is not. The final model is shown in Figure 10–32.

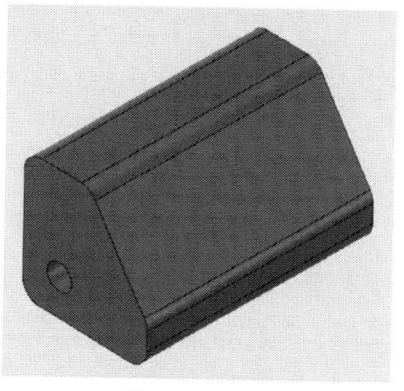

Figure 10–32

Task 1 - Open an existing design.

1. Click ▾ > **New Design from File**.

2. In the Open dialog box, navigate to the *C:\Autodesk Fusion 360 Practice Files* folder, select **Direct_Modeling.f3d**, and click **Open**. The design displays as shown in Figure 10–33.

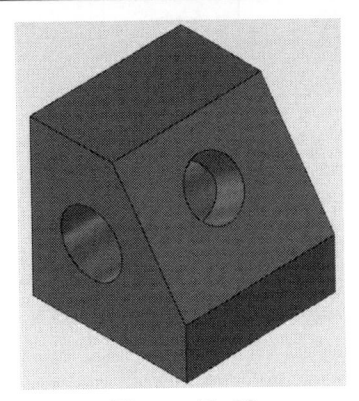

Figure 10–33

3. Note that the Timeline is not present at the bottom of the graphics window. This is because the model was created using the direct modeling method.

4. Save the model as **Direct_Modeling**.

Task 2 - Edit the model geometry.

1. Select the face of the hole shown in Figure 10–34.

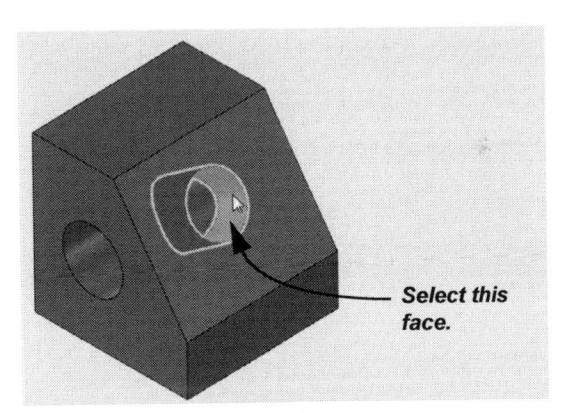

Select this face.

Figure 10–34

2. Right-click and note that the **Edit Feature** option is not present because there is no feature history stored with the design.

3. Select **Delete** to remove the hole.

4. Select the face of the other hole, as shown in Figure 10–35.

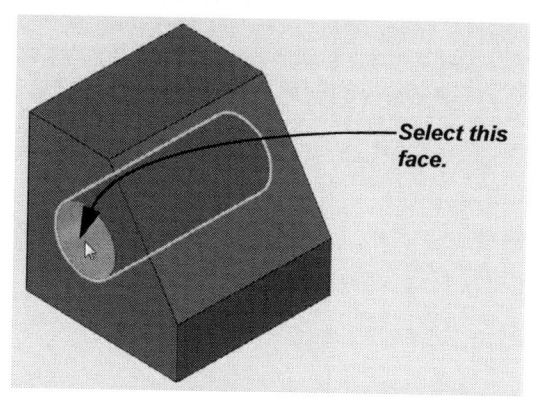

Select this face.

Figure 10–35

5. Right-click and select **Move**, or in the MODIFY panel, click **Move**. The MOVE palette displays and ▱ (Move Faces) is selected as the object type.

6. A triad manipulator displays (as shown in Figure 10–36) associated with the selected face. You can move the face of the hole anywhere as there are no dimensional constraints or parent-child feature relationships that define its location.

7. Select the handle shown in Figure 10–36 and drag it so the X Distance shown in the MOVE palette is -**10.00 mm**.

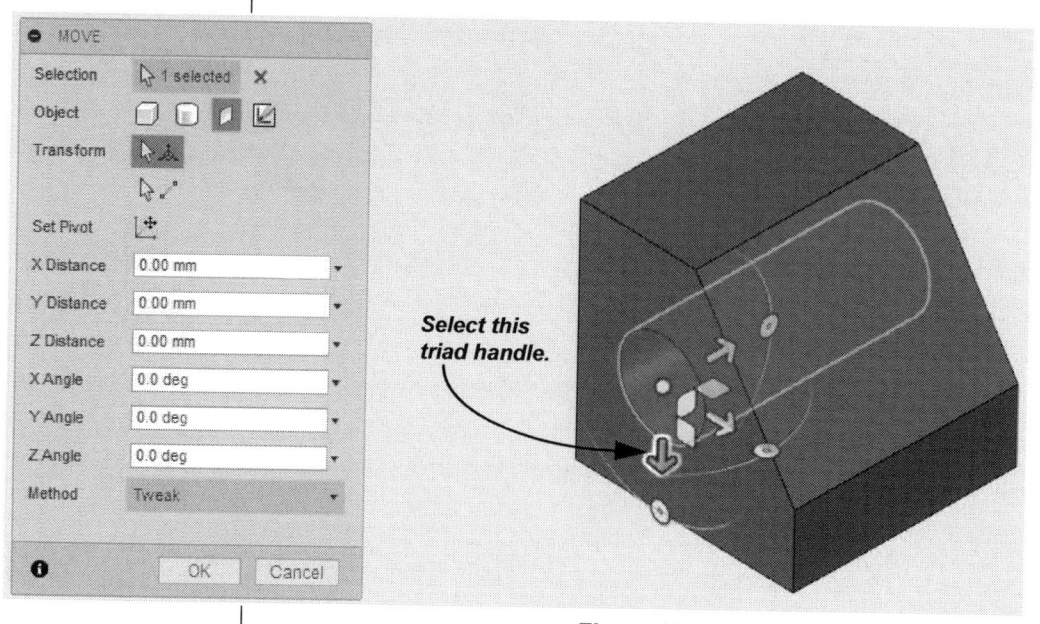

Select this triad handle.

Figure 10–36

8. Click **OK** to complete the move operation. Note that no Timeline entry is added.

9. Select the face of the hole a second time. Right-click and select (Press Pull). The Offset Faces palette displays to modify the cylindrical face. Enter a value of **5 mm**, as shown in Figure 10–37.

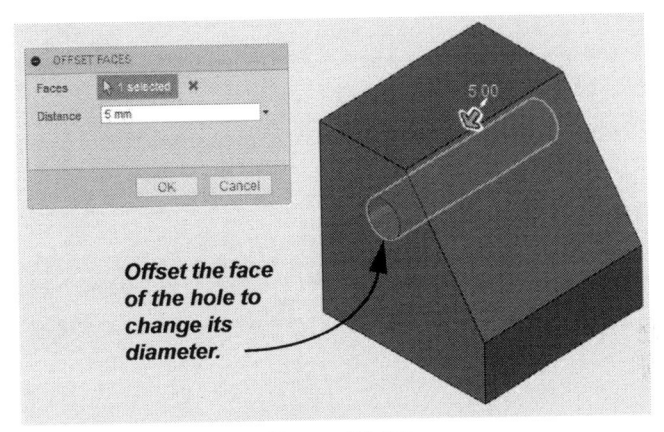

Offset the face of the hole to change its diameter.

Figure 10–37

10. Click **OK**.

11. Use the **Move** command to move the hole to the location shown in Figure 10–37.

Move the hole to this location.

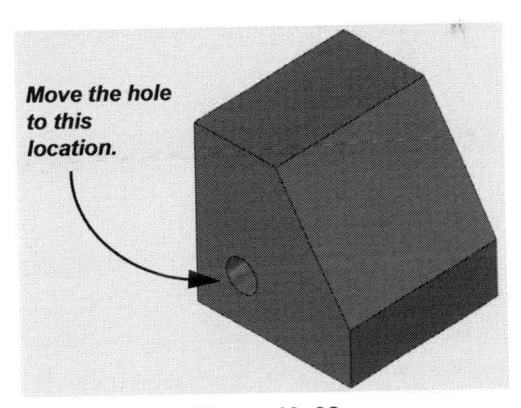

Figure 10–38

12. When a planar face is selected, the **Move** or **Press Pull** commands can provide the same result. Use either of these commands to extend the length of the geometry, as shown in Figure 10–39.

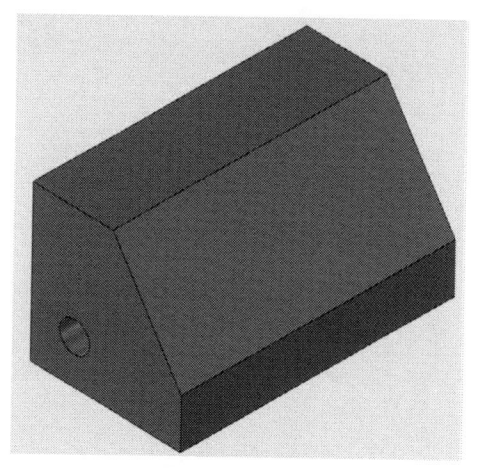

Figure 10–39

Task 3 - Switch to parametric modeling.

1. In the BROWSER, right-click on the component name and select **Capture Design History**, as shown in Figure 10–40.

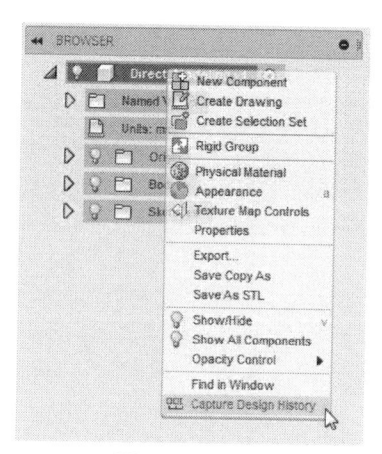

Figure 10–40

2. Note that the Timeline now displays at the bottom of the graphics window with a single feature named Base Feature1 (). The feature contains the initial geometry and the direct edits you made to it.

3. Add fillets to the horizontal edges of the model with a radius of **7.00 mm**. The parametric fillet feature displays in the Timeline (as shown in Figure 10–41) and can be edited to change the radius value.

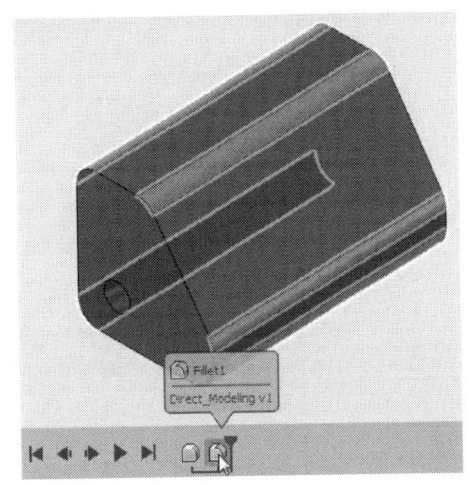

Figure 10–41

4. Save and close the design.

Hints for continuing to work with this geometry:

- To return to the base feature, in the Timeline, double-click on (Base Feature1). Once active, it only contains the initial geometry, not the fillets. You can edit it using the direct edit tools, as required.

- To incorporate the fillets into the base feature, in the BROWSER, right-click on the component name and select **Do not capture Design History**. Once in the Direct Modeling environment, the fillets are merged into the base feature and the faces can be modified, as required.

Chapter Review Questions

1. In the example shown in Figure 10–42, the *Extents* of Hole1 was set to ⊔ (All). What can you do to include the cylindrical Extrude1 in the geometry that the Hole cuts through (i.e., have the hole pass through the cylinder)?

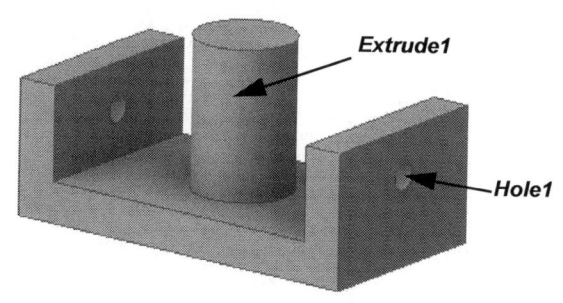

   Figure 10–42

   a. Suppress Hole1 and then recreate Extrusion1.
   b. In the BROWSER, drag the History Marker to the left of Hole1.
   c. In the BROWSER, drag Extrusion1 to the left of Hole1.
   d. Cannot be done. You must delete and recreate Extrude1.

2. Which of the following statements is true for reordering features in a design? (Select all that apply.)

   a. Reordering enables you to drag and drop features so that you can rearrange the feature creation order.
   b. When reordering, features can be moved before its parent geometry.
   c. When reordering, features can be moved after its parent geometry.
   d. Base features can be moved anywhere in the design.

3. Any features in the Timeline that are to the right of the ⊤ (History Marker) are still displayed on the design, but you cannot select them as references when creating new features.

   a. True
   b. False

4. If you suppress a feature, all dependent features are also suppressed.
   a. True
   b. False

5. Where is a section analysis saved once created in a design?
   a. A section analysis is saved with the design and is listed in the INSPECT panel.
   b. A section analysis is saved with the design and is listed in the CONSTRUCT panel.
   c. A section analysis is saved with the design and is listed in the BROWSER in the *Analysis* folder.
   d. A section analysis cannot be saved with the design.

6. Once completed, a section view can be edited.
   a. True
   b. False

7. Which of the following statements about direct modeling are true? (Select all that apply.)
   a. Parent-child feature relationships need to be redefined prior to deleting a face.
   b. Operations such as Move and Offset Face are captured in the Timeline.
   c. Direct modeling and parametric modeling techniques can be used in the same design.
   d. Feature history is not recorded.

Answers: 1.c, 2.(a,c), 3.b, 4.a, 5.c, 6.a, 7.(c,d)

Command Summary

Button	Command	Location
	Section Analysis	• **Ribbon:** *Model* Workspace>INSPECT panel • **Context Menu:** Right-click in the graphics window and select **Inspect**.

Chapter 11

Single Path Sweeps

You can use sweep features to create specific geometry that cannot be created using standard extrusions. It enables you to sketch a cross-section and sweep it along a defined path.

Learning Objectives in this Chapter

- Create swept geometry using appropriate path and profile entities.
- Edit a Sweep feature.

11.1 Sweeps

A Sweep feature creates geometry that is defined by sweeping a profile along a path. You can use it to add or remove geometry from a design. Sweeps are useful for features that have a uniform shape, but an irregular path. Figure 11–1 shows an image of a paper-clip, where a circular profile was swept along a curved path.

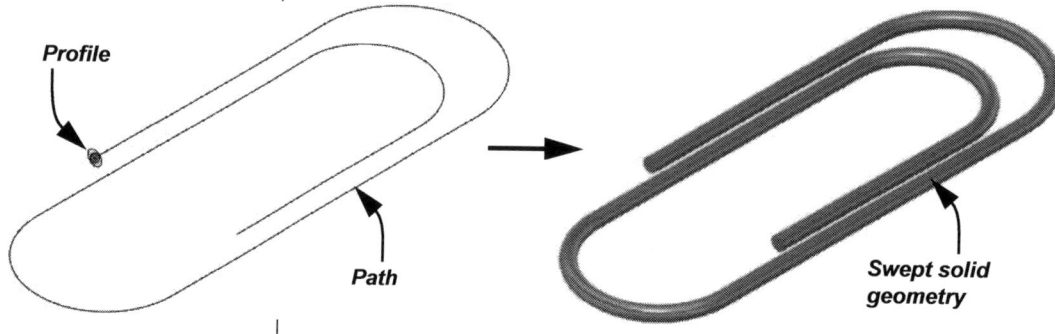

Figure 11–1

Timeline icon:

- To create a solid sweep, a sweep's profile must be a closed loop sketch.

- A sweep's path can be an open or a closed sketch and can be either 2D or 3D. The paper clip shown in Figure 11–1 is an open path, while the geometry shown in Figure 11–2 is a sweep that uses a closed path.

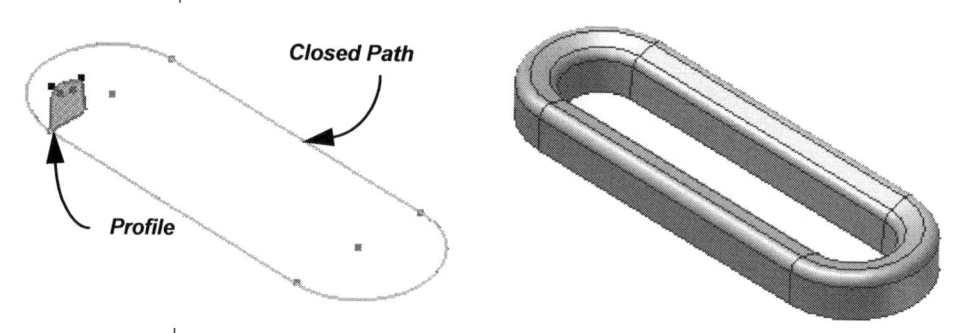

Figure 11–2

- The start point of a sweep should be located at the intersection of the profile plane and path. The profile geometry does not need to physically intersect the path.

- The profile can be swept a set distance along the path using a *Distance* value. The value is defined as a proportion of the overall path. Alternatively, you can drag the manipulator arrow to define the value, as required.

- A sweep's orientation can alter the shape of the final geometry. A **Perpendicular** orientation ensures that the profile remains perpendicular to the path, whereas a **Parallel** orientation keeps the profile parallel to the profile's sketch plane, as shown in Figure 11-3.

Path

Closed Profile

Perpendicular Orientation

Parallel Orientation

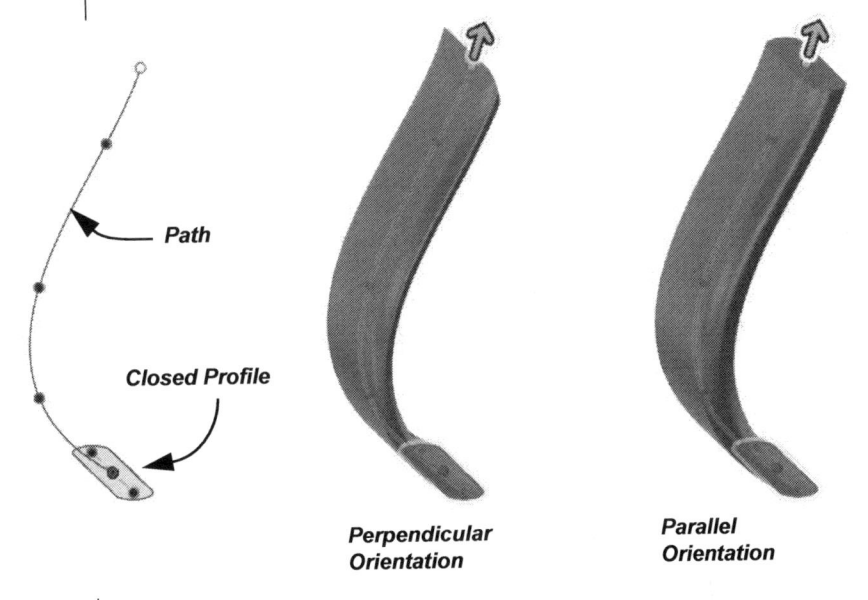

Figure 11-3

Video Lesson Available

Creating a Solid Using Sweep

Video Length: 2:14

Practice 11a Creating Swept Geometry I

Practice Objectives

- Create swept geometry using appropriate path and profile entities.
- Edit a sweep feature.

In this practice, you will create two sweep features. For both of these features, you will sketch their profile entities. However, the path for one will be sketched and the other will be selected. The model will display similar to that shown in Figure 11–4.

Figure 11–4

Task 1 - Create a new part file with a cylindrical base feature.

1. Create a new design using the **Inch** as the *Active Units*.

2. Use the **Cylinder** quick shape to create a base shape on the XZ plane. Create the geometry with a radius of **6 in** and depth of **1 in**.

Task 2 - Create the path and profile for the sweep.

1. Sketch on the flat top surface of the cylinder to create the path for the sweep. Draw and constrain the section as shown in Figure 11–5. Complete the sketch.

To sketch a line that is tangent to two circles, start the **Line** command. Hover the cursor over one of the two circles. Click and hold the left mouse button, and then drag the cursor to the next circle until the tangent constraint symbol displays. Release the left mouse button.

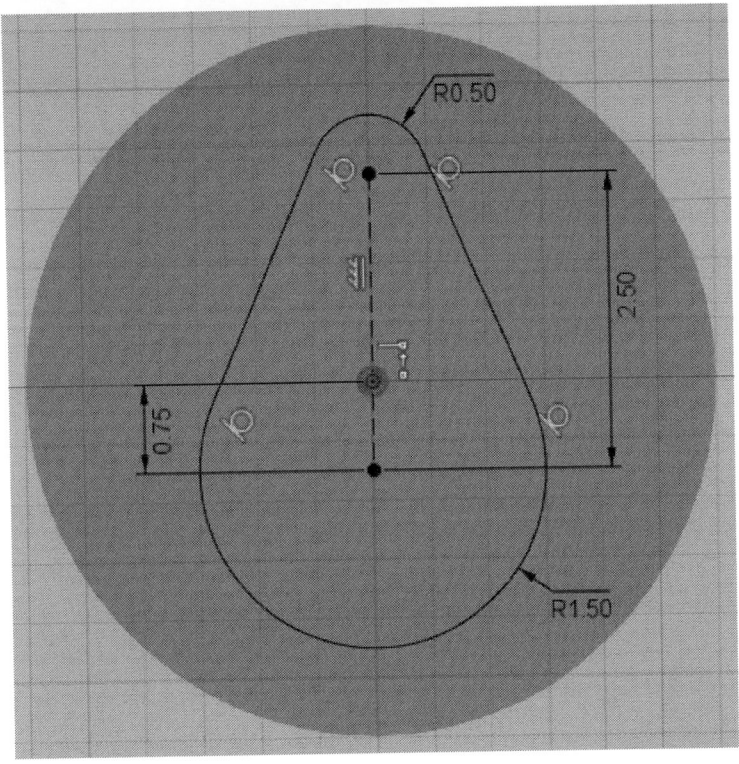

Figure 11–5

2. In the BROWSER, rename the new sketch as **Path**.

3. Sketch a circle on the YZ workplane, as shown in Figure 11–6. This will be the profile for the sweep.
   - When sketching the circle, constrain it to a point where the previously created path intersects the YZ workplane. (**Hint:** To constrain the circle, use Project Geometry to project entities in the path onto the sketch plane.)
   - Complete the sketch.

*To display a slice of the sketch plane, in the SKETCH PALETTE, click **Slice**.*

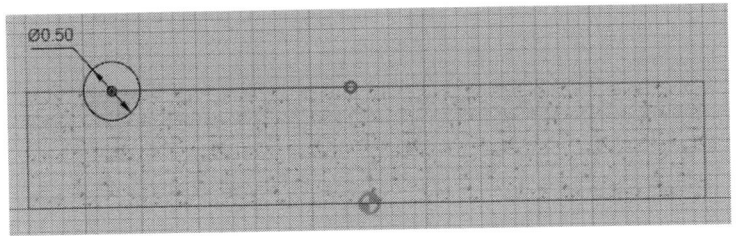

Figure 11–6

4. In the BROWSER, rename the sketch as **Profile**.

Task 3 - Create the sweep.

1. In the CREATE panel, click (Sweep). The SWEEP palette opens, as shown in Figure 11–7.

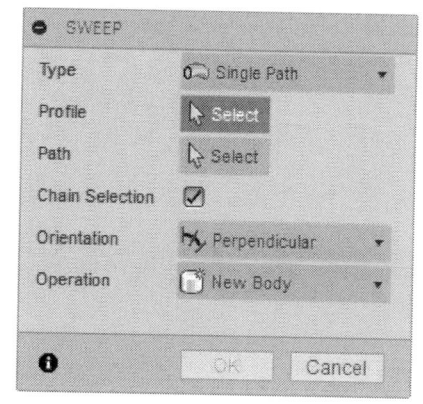

Figure 11–7

2. Ensure that the *Type* option is set to **Single Path**.

3. In the graphics window, select the **Profile** sketch as the profile for the sweep.

4. In the SWEEP palette, click inside the *Path* field to activate it. In the graphics window, select the **Profile** sketch as the path for the sweep. The geometry displays as shown in Figure 11–8.

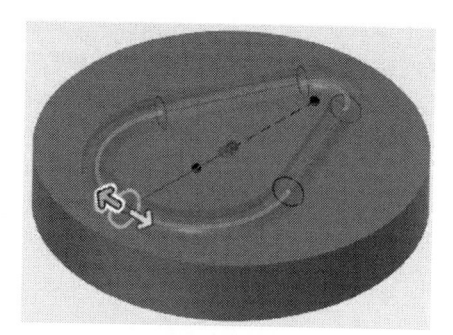

Figure 11–8

Sweeps that use open sketches as the path only have one Distance field in the SWEEP palette.

5. The two *Distance* fields define how far the profile extends along the path on both sides of the profile. In the first *Distance* field, enter **0.5**. Note how the profile extends for 50% of the entire path length. For the second *Distance* value, enter **0.25** and note how the preview displays.

6. Return the *Distance* fields to **1.0** and **0**, respectively.

© 2016, ASCENT - Center for Technical Knowledge®

7. In the *Orientation* field, ensure **Perpendicular** is selected so that the profile remains perpendicular to the path for the entire distance.

8. In the *Operation* field, select **Join** to add material to the solid model.

9. Click **OK** to create the sweep. The model displays as shown in Figure 11–9.

Figure 11–9

Task 4 - Edit the sweep.

1. Edit the sweep to open the EDIT FEATURE palette.

2. In the *Operation* field, select **Cut** to change the sweep feature from a join to a cut. By default, the *Objects to Cut* is automatically set as **1 Bodies**. This is because there is only one solid body in the model. Complete the feature. The model displays as shown in Figure 11–10.

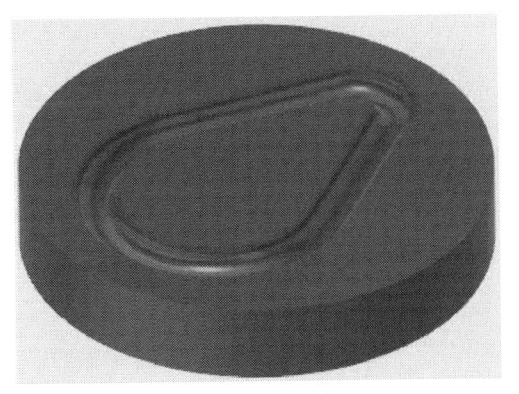

Figure 11–10

Task 5 - Create a new sweep feature that references an existing solid edge.

1. Sketch the arc shown in Figure 11–11 on the YZ workplane. This will be the profile for the sweep. When sketching the section, consider the following:
   - Use the **Intersect** projection option to project the solid body at the intersection of the sketch plane. This provides the projected references on the sides because it is a cylindrical face and does not have an edge to reference.
   - Sketch the **3-Point** arc so that no tangency is assigned and coincident constraints exist. Dimension the arc as shown in Figure 11–11. Once you select the top edge it will be projected into the sketch.
   - Finish the sketch.

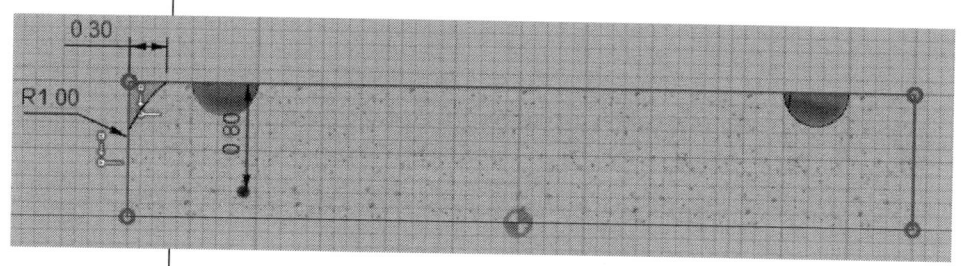

Figure 11–11

2. In the Create panel, click (Sweep).
3. Ensure that the *Type* option is set to **Single Path**.
4. In the graphics window, select the arc sketch as the profile for the sweep.
5. In the SWEEP palette, click inside the *Path* field to activate it. Select the existing outside edge of the cylinder as the path for the sweep. The geometry displays as shown in Figure 11–12.

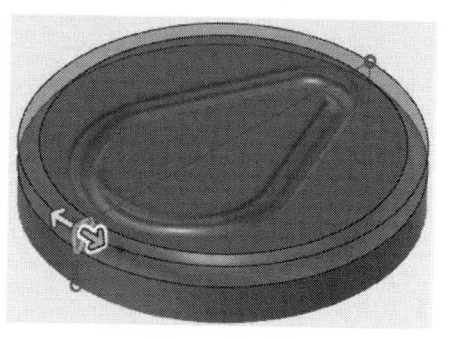

Figure 11–12

6. The sweep removes material from the entire length of the edge. Set the *Distance* fields as **1.0** and **0**, respectively.

7. In the *Orientation* field, ensure that **Perpendicular** is selected so that the profile remains perpendicular to the path for the entire distance.

8. In the *Operation* field, select **Cut** to remove material from the solid model.

9. Click **OK** to create the sweep. The model displays as shown in Figure 11–13.

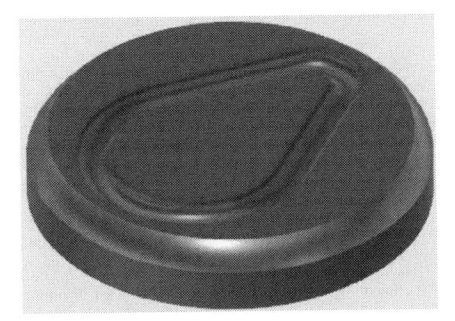

Figure 11–13

10. Save the design with the name **Sweep** to your *Autodesk Fusion 360 Practice Files* project.

11. Close the file.

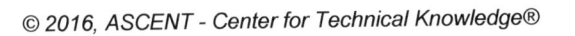

Practice 11b Creating Swept Geometry II

Practice Objective

- Create swept geometry using appropriate path and profile entities.

In this practice you will create two sweep features. The first represents the handle of the dipstick, and the second represents the metal rod on the dipstick model, as shown in Figure 11–14.

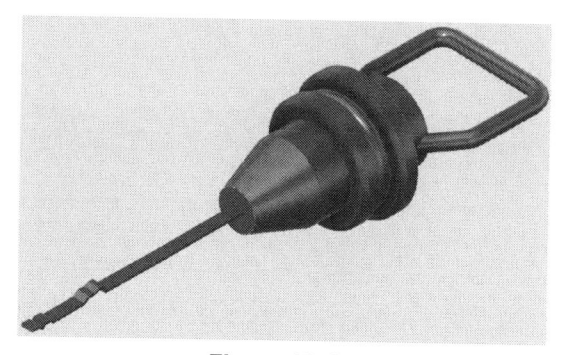

Figure 11–14

Task 1 - Open a part file.

1. Click ▯▼ > **New Design from File**.

2. In the Open dialog box, navigate to the *C:\Autodesk Fusion 360 Practice Files* folder, select **Dipstick.f3d**, and click **Open**. The model displays as shown in Figure 11–15.

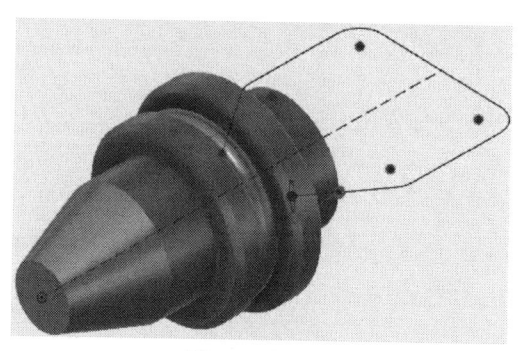

Figure 11–15

3. In the BROWSER, hover the cursor over the **Handle_Path** and **Handle_Profile** sketches to identify where they are in the model.

Task 2 - Create the sweep for the handle.

1. In the CREATE panel, click (Sweep).
2. Ensure that the *Type* option is set to **Single Path**.
3. In the graphics window, select the **Handle_Profile** sketch as the profile for the sweep.
4. In the SWEEP palette, click inside the *Path* field to activate it. In the graphics window, select the **Handle_Path** sketch as the path for the sweep. The geometry displays as shown in Figure 11–16.

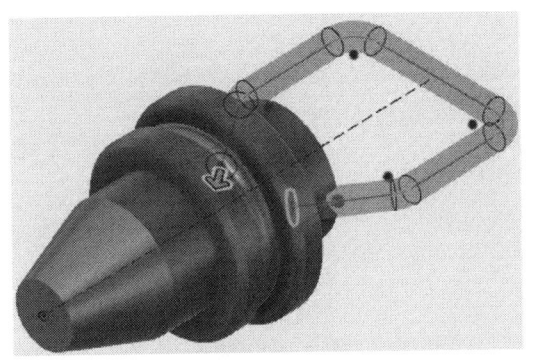

Figure 11–16

5. Note how there is only one *Distance* field because the path reference is an open profile and the profile starts at one end. Ensure that the *Distance* is set to **1.0**.
6. Set the *Orientation* option to **Perpendicular** and the *Operation* option to **Join** to add material to the solid model.
7. Click **OK** to create the sweep. The model displays as shown in Figure 11–17.

Figure 11–17

Task 3 - Create another sweep feature to represent the rod of the dipstick.

1. On the YZ workplane, sketch a sweep path similar to the one shown in Figure 11–18.
   - Project the origin centerpoint to locate the start point of the sketch.
   - When sketching, consider clearing the SKETCH PALETTE > **Sketch Grid** option to avoid snapping to the grid lines as you are sketching.
   - Do not worry about the dimensions or its exact shape.

Projected origin centerpoint

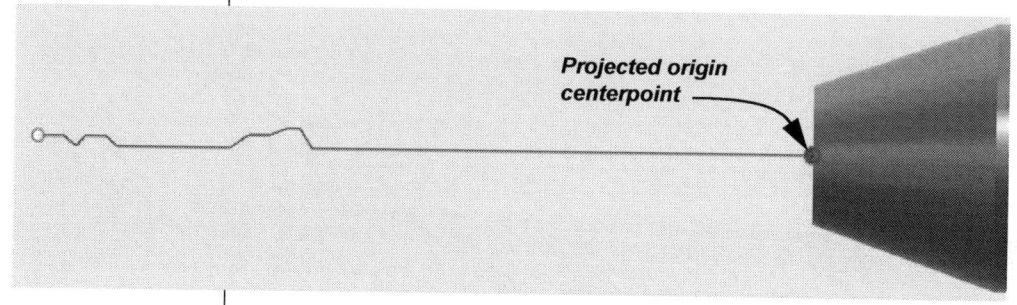

Figure 11–18

2. Sketch the sweep's rectangular profile on the bottom face of the revolved feature, similar to that shown in Figure 11–19.
   - Project the origin centerpoint and use the **Center Rectangle** sketch option to center the rectangle on the centerpoint.
   - Do not worry about the dimensions or its exact shape.

Sketch this rectangular profile

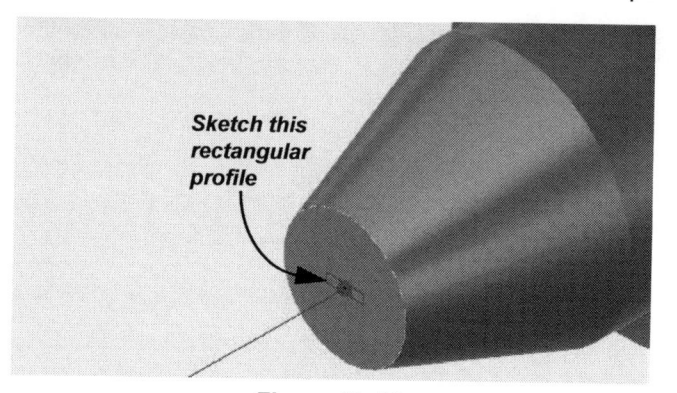

Figure 11–19

In this situation, you could have created the geometry as an extrude. However, the section to extrude would need to be a closed section. You can create the same geometry using either method. With more experience, you will establish modeling preferences.

3. The profile and path are now defined. Use the **Sweep** command to create the geometry shown in Figure 11–20.

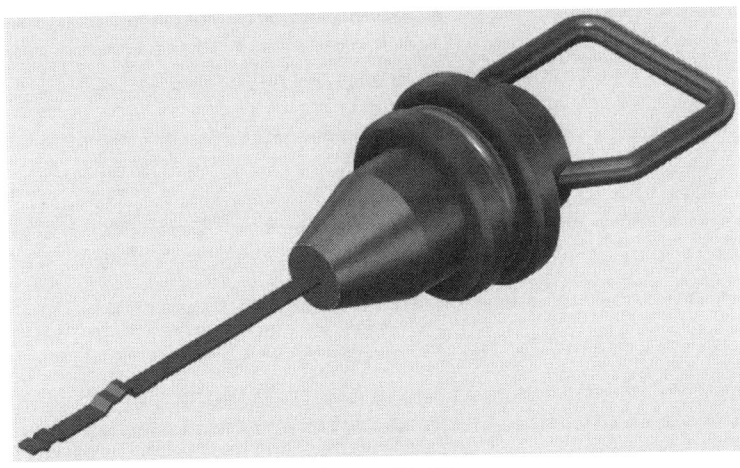

Figure 11–20

4. Save the design with the name **Dipstick** to your *Autodesk Fusion 360 Practice Files* project.

5. Close the file.

Practice 11c

Additional Swept Geometry (Optional)

Practice Objective

- Create swept geometry using appropriate path and profile entities.

In this practice you are provided some additional geometric shapes that can be created using a Sweep feature. Create each of these using appropriate path and profile geometry.

Task 1 - Create new parts using a single feature.

1. Create the parts shown in Figure 11–21 using swept features.

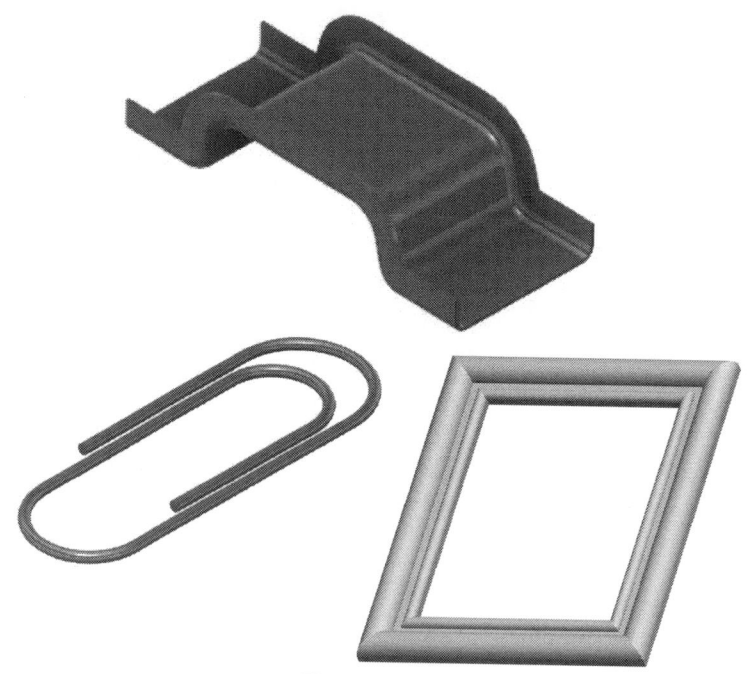

Figure 11–21

Chapter Review Questions

1. Which command would you use to create the groove shown in Figure 11–22?

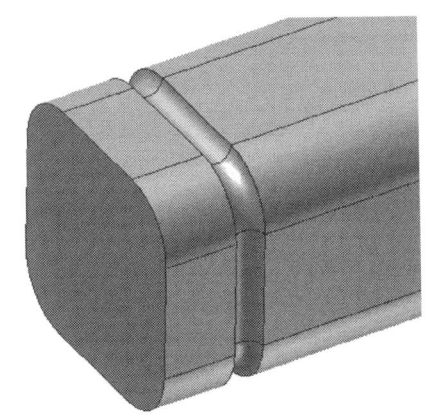

   Figure 11–22

   a. **Torus**
   b. **Revolve**
   c. **Extrude**
   d. **Sweep**

2. Which elements must exist in a design before starting the creation of a Sweep feature? (Select all that apply.)

   a. Profile
   b. Path
   c. Section
   d. Start Point

3. A Sweep feature can be used to either add or remove material.

   a. True
   b. False

4. Which of the following statements are true?
   a. A sweep creates a single feature whose geometry is blended between multiple profiles.
   b. A sweep creates a single feature whose geometry is swept along a defined path.
   c. A sweep can only be added to the model after the base extrusion has been created.
   d. A sweep path must be sketched geometry.

5. How many sketches are required to create the sweep feature shown in Figure 11–23?

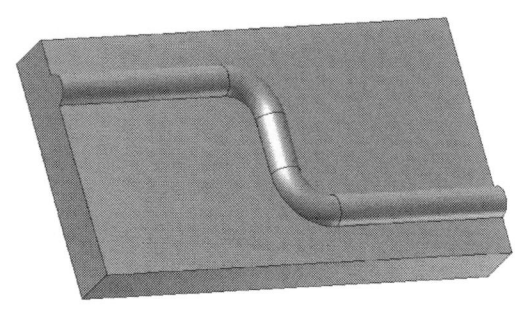

Figure 11–23

   a. 1
   b. 2
   c. 1 for 2D sweep, 2 for 3D sweep.
   d. A sweep is not based on a sketch.

6. Which *Orientation* option enables you to create the sweep shown in Figure 11–24?

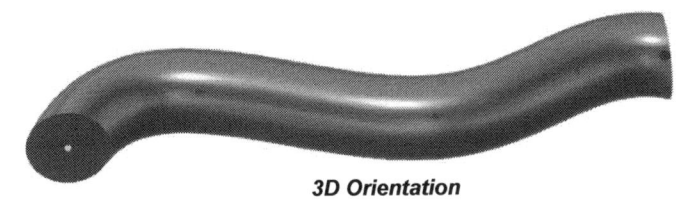

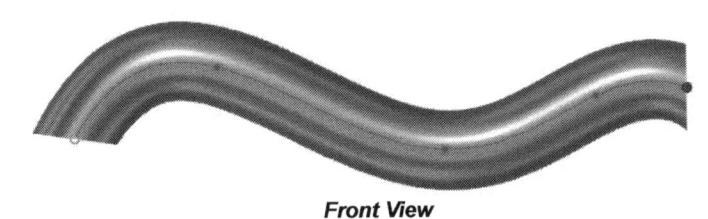

3D Orientation

Front View

Figure 11–24

   a. Perpendicular
   b. Parallel

7. The *Distance* value that the sweep extends along the path is defined in the same units as the model.

   a. True
   b. False

Answers: 1.d, 2.(a,b), 3.a, 4.b, 5.b, 6.a, 7.b

Command Summary

Button	Command	Location
	Sweep	- **Ribbon:** *Model* Workspace>CREATE panel - **Context Menu:** Right-click in the graphics window and select **Create**.

Chapter 12

Loft Features

A loft is a feature that can be used to create complex geometry that blends multiple profiles. Additional control of the resulting shape can be gained by assigning references for the geometry to follow between the profiles, defining end conditions, and manipulating the control points on each section.

Learning Objectives in this Chapter

- Create a loft feature using appropriate profile and reference entities.
- Control the shape and weight of how lofted geometry transitions from adjacent solid geometry.
- Manipulate how the control points on a section maps to the control points on adjacent sections.

12.1 Lofts

A loft feature enables you to create advanced geometry by blending multiple profiles. You can use a loft to either add or remove geometry in the design. To define how the geometry blends between profiles, you can use the following:

- End conditions at the start and end profiles.
- Reference entities (rails and centerlines).
- Control points on the sections.

Figure 12–1 shows a loft that blends a planar face, sketched profiles, and a point. End conditions are assigned to control tangency into the existing solid at the linear edge and at the end point.

Timeline icon:

Planar face profile

Linear edge

Tangent end condition

2 Sketched profiles and a point

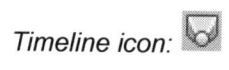

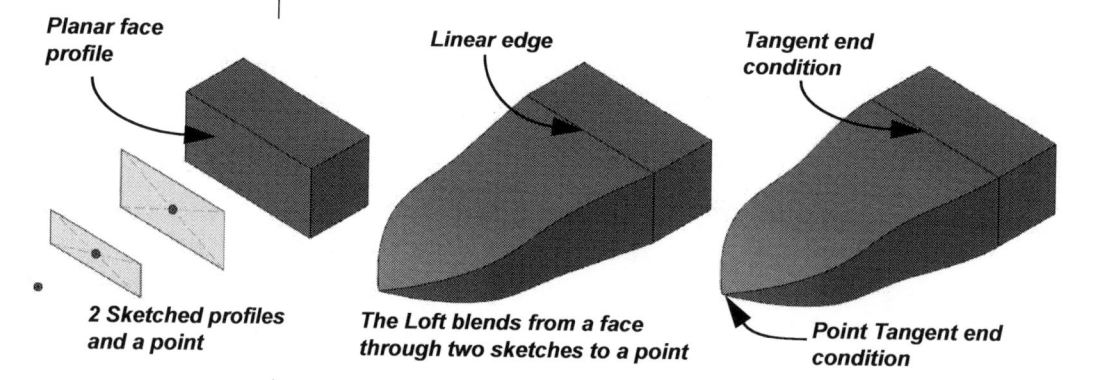

The Loft blends from a face through two sketches to a point

Point Tangent end condition

Figure 12–1

Rails or centerlines are sketched curves. They can be used to control the shape of the geometry between the profiles, but are not required.

- You can select rails to define the path that the geometry takes as it blends between the profiles.
- A centerline sets the profiles so that they remain normal to a centerline reference as it blends between the profiles.

You can select multiple rails, but only one centerline can be selected when defining a loft feature.

Figure 12–2 shows a loft that blends three sketched profiles and uses rails to control the shape of the geometry between profiles.

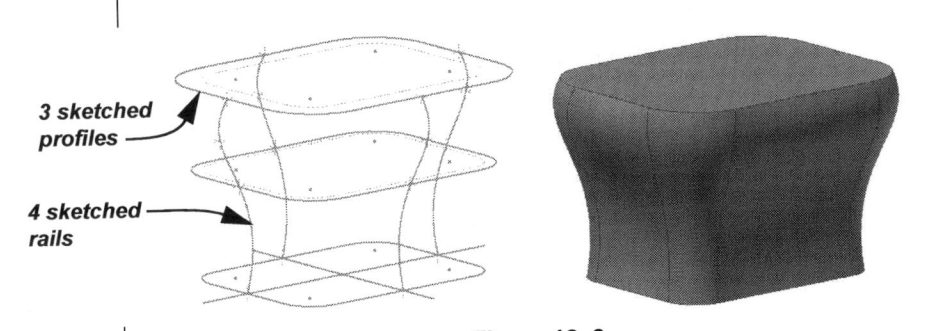

Figure 12–2

While rails must intersect each profile, a centerline is not required to intersect.

Figure 12–3 shows a loft that blends four sketched sections and uses a centerline reference to ensure that the profiles remain normal to a centerline reference as it blends.

Profiles are added in the order that they are selected. To change the order, in the graphics window, select the Profile# symbol and select a new number.

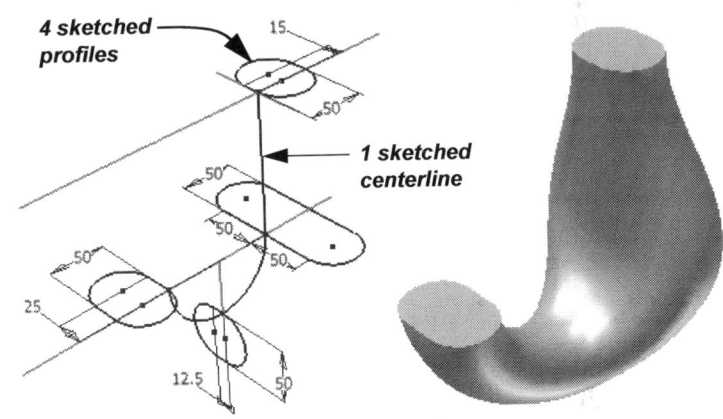

Figure 12–3

Control points (white vertices) control how sections blend. Control points can be selected and moved to change loft geometry, as shown in Figure 12–4.

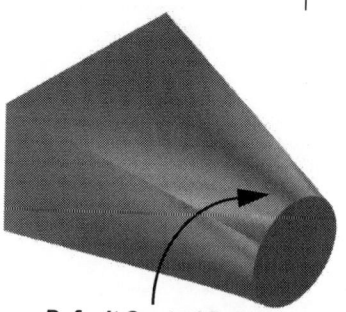

Default Control Points used to create the loft

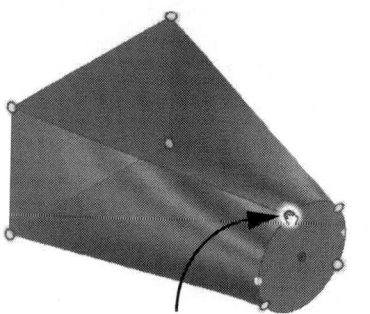

Control point

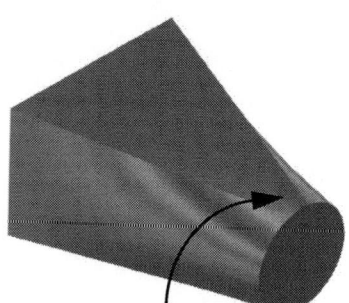

Control points moved to change loft shape

Figure 12–4

Video Lesson Available

Creating a Solid Using Loft

Video Length: 3:10

Practice 12a Creating Rail Lofts

Practice Objectives

- Create lofted geometry using appropriate profile and rail entities.
- Edit a loft feature.

In this practice, you will create the model shown in Figure 12–5 using the loft feature. You will use rails to help control the overall shape between the sections that are being blended together.

Figure 12–5

Task 1 - Open a part file and create a loft.

In this task you will open an existing model and create a solid loft feature using sections and rails that have been provided.

1. Click ▯▾ > **New Design from File**.

2. In the Open dialog box, navigate to the *C:\Autodesk Fusion 360 Practice Files* folder, select **Rail_Loft.f3d**, and click **Open**. The sections and rails required for the loft feature are provided, as shown in Figure 12–6.

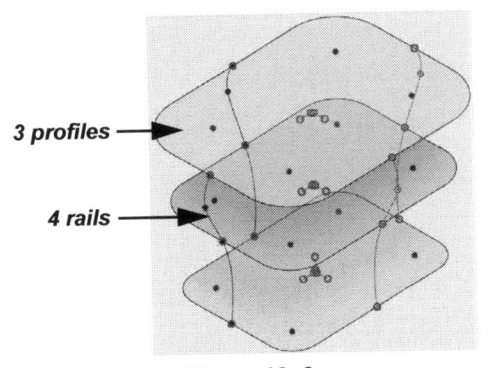

3 profiles

4 rails

Figure 12–6

3. In the CREATE panel, click (Loft). The LOFT palette opens as shown in Figure 12–7.

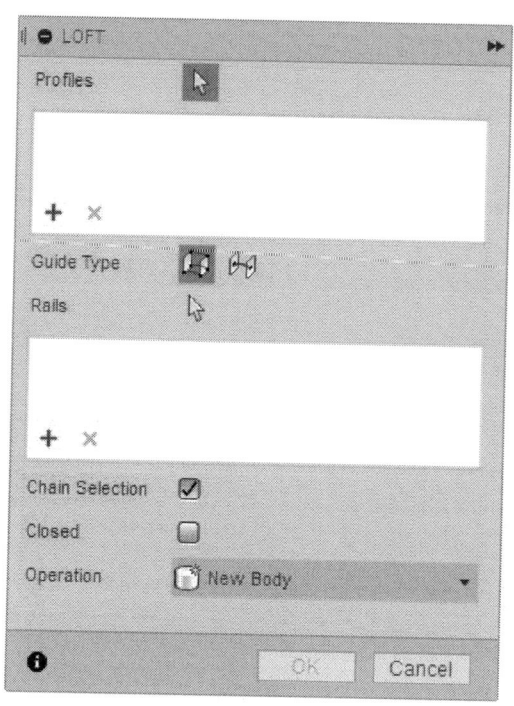

Figure 12–7

The order in which you select the profiles defines how they are lofted together.

4. By default, the *Profiles* area is active. In the graphics window, select the three profiles from bottom to top (**Profile1**, **Profile2**, and **Profile3**).

5. Note that because this is the first solid geometry in the model, the *Operation* option defaults to **New Body**.

6. Click **OK** to create the loft.

7. In the BROWSER, expand the **Sketches** folder and note that the three profile sketches are automatically toggled off once they are used. The model displays as shown in Figure 12–8.

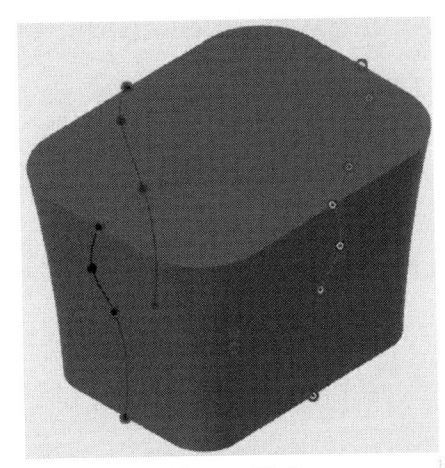

Figure 12–8

Task 2 - Add rails to the loft.

In this task, you will edit the loft feature and add rails. Rails help control the shape of a loft between sections. When creating rails, remember that they must intersect all of the sections in the loft.

1. Edit the loft feature that you just created.

2. In the Edit Feature palette, in the *Guide Type* area, click (Rails) and select the four rails, as shown in Figure 12–9. Note that the shape of the loft updates as you select the rails.

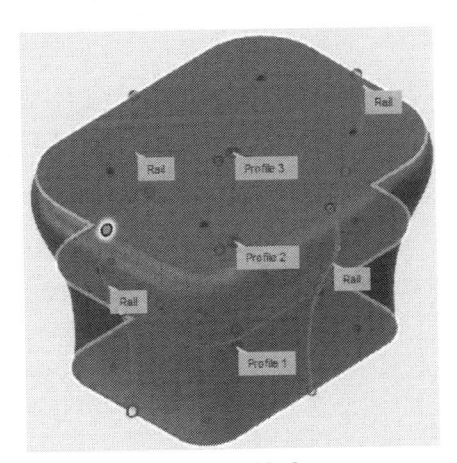

Figure 12–9

3. Click **OK** to update the loft and close the palette.

4. Note that the display of the two rail sketches are automatically turned off once they are used in the Loft feature. The model displays as shown in Figure 12–10.

Figure 12–10

5. Save the design with the name **Rail_Loft** to your *Autodesk Fusion 360 Practice Files* project.

6. Close the file.

Practice 12b

Creating Centerline Lofts I

Practice Objective

- Create a loft feature using appropriate profile and centerline entities to drive geometry based on a selected centerline.

In this practice, you will create the loft shown in Figure 12–11. The geometry is generated by selecting two profiles and a single centerline reference.

Figure 12–11

Task 1 - Open a part file and create a loft.

In this task, you will open an existing model and create a center line loft using the sketches provided.

1. Click ![icon] > **New Design from File**.

2. In the Open dialog box, navigate to the *C:\Autodesk Fusion 360 Practice Files* folder, select **CenterLine_loft1.f3d**, and click **Open**. The loft's center line and sections have been created for you.

3. In the CREATE panel, click ![icon] (Loft). The LOFT palette opens.

© 2016, ASCENT - Center for Technical Knowledge®

4. By default, the *Profiles* area is active. In the graphics window, select the two profiles (**Profile1** and **Profile2**). The loft is generated by blending between the two profile sketches, as shown in Figure 12–12.

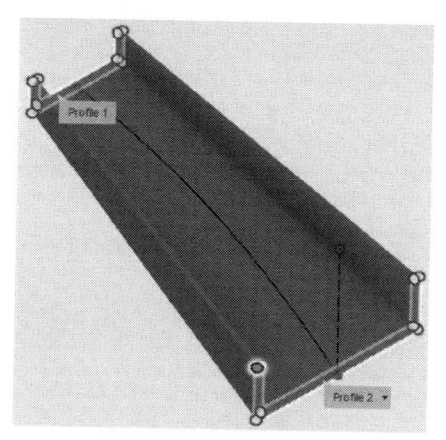

Figure 12–12

5. Click (Centerline) to create a Centerline Loft.

6. Select the **Centerline1** sketched arc.

7. This is the first solid geometry in the model, so the *Operation* option defaults to **New Body**.

8. Click **OK** to complete the loft. The model displays as shown in Figure 12–13.

Figure 12–13

9. Save the design with the name **Centerline_Loft1** to your *Autodesk Fusion 360 Practice Files* project.

10. Close the file.

Practice 12c

Creating Centerline Lofts II

Practice Objectives

- Create a loft feature using appropriate reference entities.
- Control the shape and weight of how lofted geometry transitions from adjacent solid geometry.

In this practice, you will create a loft feature between two existing solid features. You will begin by creating a Centerline Loft and then edit this to customize the transition between the existing solid and lofted geometry, as shown in Figure 12–14.

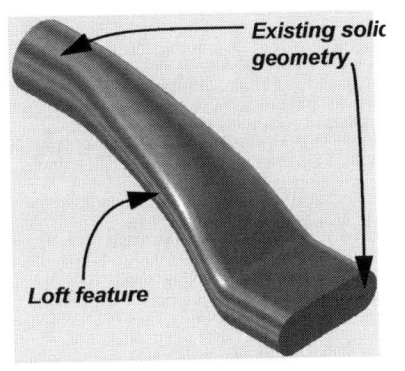

Figure 12–14

Task 1 - Open a part file and create a sketch that will be used as the centerline reference.

1. Click ▼ > **New Design from File**.

2. In the Open dialog box, navigate to the *C:\Autodesk Fusion 360 Practice Files* folder, select **Centerline_Loft2.f3d**, and click **Open**.

3. The model displays as shown in Figure 12–15. You will eventually select existing faces as the profiles for the loft, but you must first create a curve that can be used as the centerline reference.

Figure 12–15

4. Start a new sketch on the XY plane. Draw a **3-Point Arc** in the sketch that connects the centerpoints of both sections. Assign a radius of **240mm**.

5. Complete the sketch. The model should display similar to that shown in Figure 12–16.

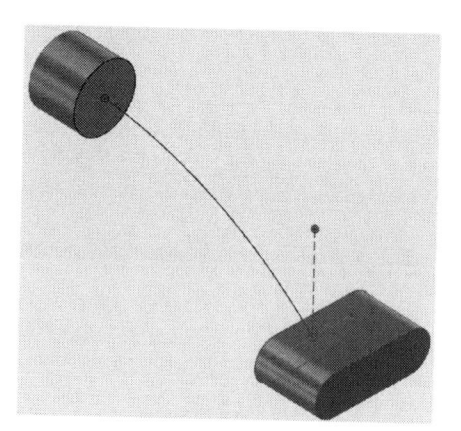

Figure 12–16

Task 2 - Create a centerline loft.

It is important that you select solid faces (as opposed to sketches), when necessary, to ensure that end conditions can be assigned to blend the new loft with existing geometry.

1. In the BROWSER, toggle off the display of **Sketch1** and **Sketch2**. These were used to create the existing solid geometry. By clearing their display, you ensure that when selecting the profiles for the loft that you will be selecting solid faces and not a sketch.

2. In the CREATE panel, click (Loft).

3. The *Profiles* area is active by default. Select the two faces shown in Figure 12–17.

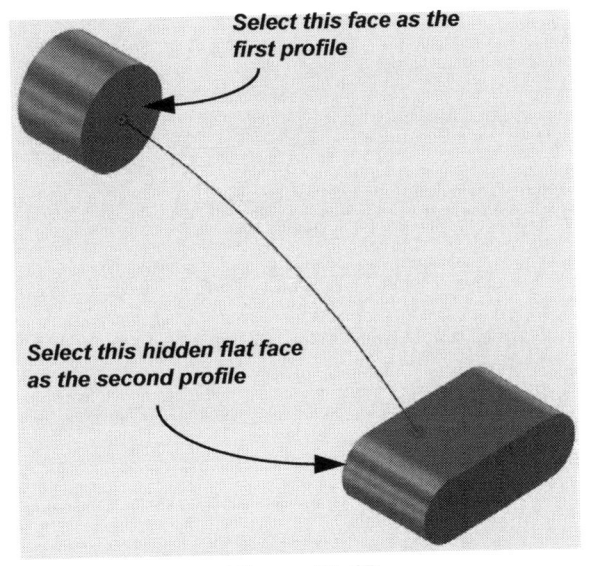

Select this face as the first profile

Select this hidden flat face as the second profile

Figure 12–17

4. The new loft geometry is previewed in the graphics window. On the ViewCube, select **FRONT** to reorient the model, as shown in Figure 12–18.

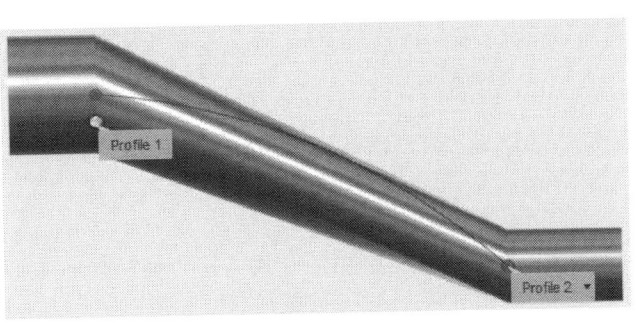

Figure 12–18

© 2016, ASCENT - Center for Technical Knowledge®

5. For the *Guide Type*, select (Centerline).

6. In the *Centerline* area, select the new sketched curve as the centerline reference. The loft geometry updates as shown in Figure 12–19. Note how the centerline controls how the geometry is shaped between the faces.

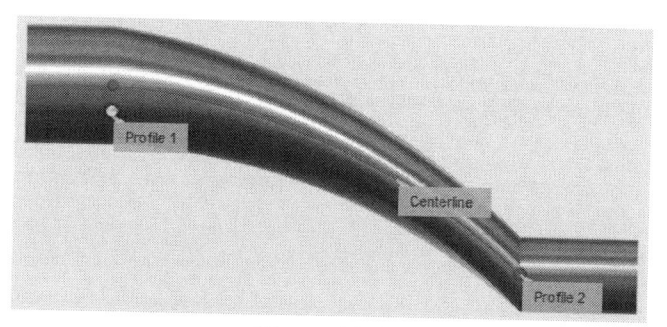

Figure 12–19

7. Click **OK**. The model displays as shown in Figure 12–20. Note how edges exist where the loft joins with the two selected faces. The Loft does not have continuity into the solid geometry.

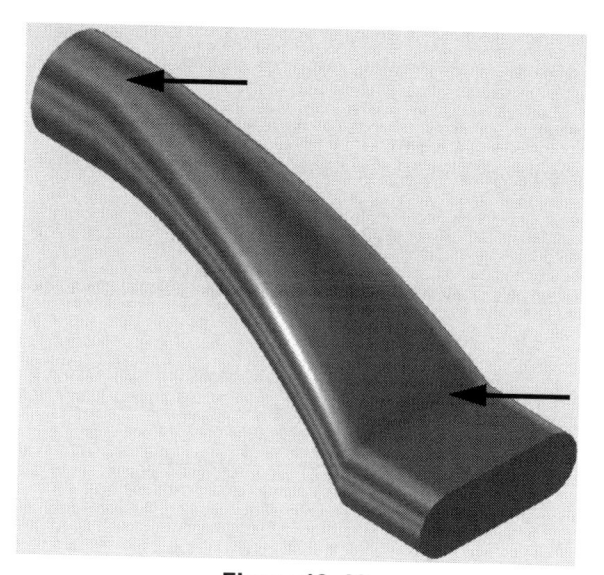

Figure 12–20

Task 3 - Customize the end conditions for the loft.

1. Edit the loft feature.

2. By default, the end condition between a new loft and selected geometry is set so that no end condition is applied (**Free**). In the *Profiles* area, expand the end condition drop-down list for *Profile1* and select **Tangent**, as shown in Figure 12–21.

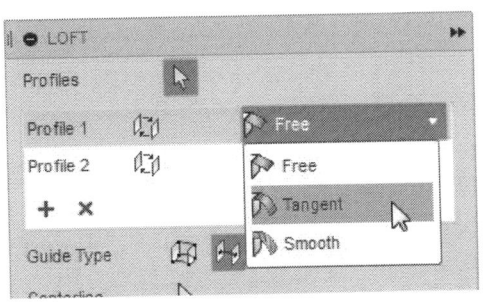

Figure 12–21

3. In the *Profiles* area, select **Profile 2**.

4. Change the end condition for *Profile 2* to **Tangent**. The loft geometry updates as shown in Figure 12–22. Note how the geometry transitions at the two selected faces to remain tangent to the existing solid geometry.

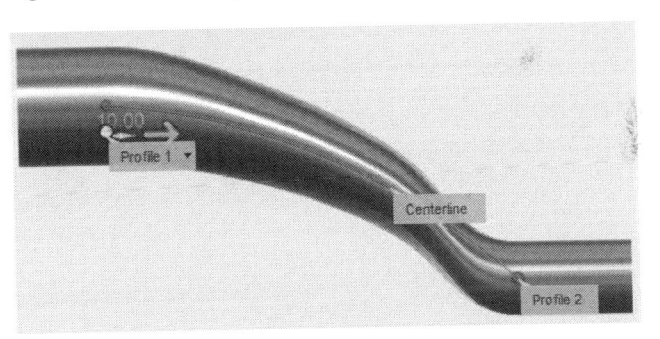

Figure 12–22

5. The *Tangency Weight* value for **Tangent** and **Smooth** end conditions can be edited to control how far the tangency/continuity is taken to establish the condition. By default, the value for a selected profile is **1**. To change the value, ensure that the profile is selected in the *Profiles* area and enter a value. Note the effect that this value has on the loft geometry when changed to **2** or **0.5** for the two profiles.

6. Return the *Tangency Weight* value for Profile 1 to **1**, and for Profile 2 to **0.5**.

7. Click **OK**. The model displays as shown in Figure 12–23.

The number of vertices in each face are equal. Control points are not available to customize the shape of the oft.

Figure 12–23

8. Save the design with the name **Centerline_Loft2** to your *Autodesk Fusion 360 Practice Files* project.

9. Close the file.

Chapter Review Questions

1. A loft can be used in a model to either add or remove material.
   a. True
   b. False

2. Which of the following best describes the type of geometry that is created using a loft feature?
   a. A loft creates multiple solid features between each of the profiles.
   b. A loft creates a feature where the geometry is blended between multiple profiles.
   c. A loft creates a feature whose geometry is swept along a defined path.
   d. A loft creates a feature that rotates a single provide around a selected centerline.

3. Which of the following statements are true? (Select all that apply.)
   a. A loft can only be added to the model after a base extrusion has been created.
   b. The profiles for lofts can only be sketched.
   c. Once you select the profiles for a loft feature, you cannot reorder them.
   d. To use an existing planar face as a section of a loft, you can select the face directly without creating a sketch.
   e. End conditions can be assigned to the second of three profiles.
   f. Control points are used to determine the twist of the loft.

4. Which *Guide Type* can be used to create a loft that passes through the three circular sections and is guided along the curve, as shown in Figure 12–24?

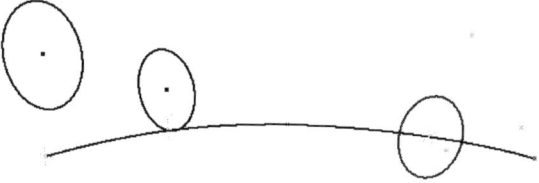

Figure 12–24

   a. Rail
   b. Centerline

5. When referencing existing geometry as the start or end section for a loft, which of the following conditions provides access to the *Weight* settings to control its shape? (Select all that apply.)

   a. Free
   b. Tangent
   c. Smooth

Answers: 1.a, 2.b, 3.(d,f), 4.b, 5.(b,c)

Command Summary

Button	Command	Location
	Loft	• **Ribbon:** *Model* Workspace>CREATE panel • **Context Menu:** Right-click in the graphics window and select **Create**.

Chapter 13

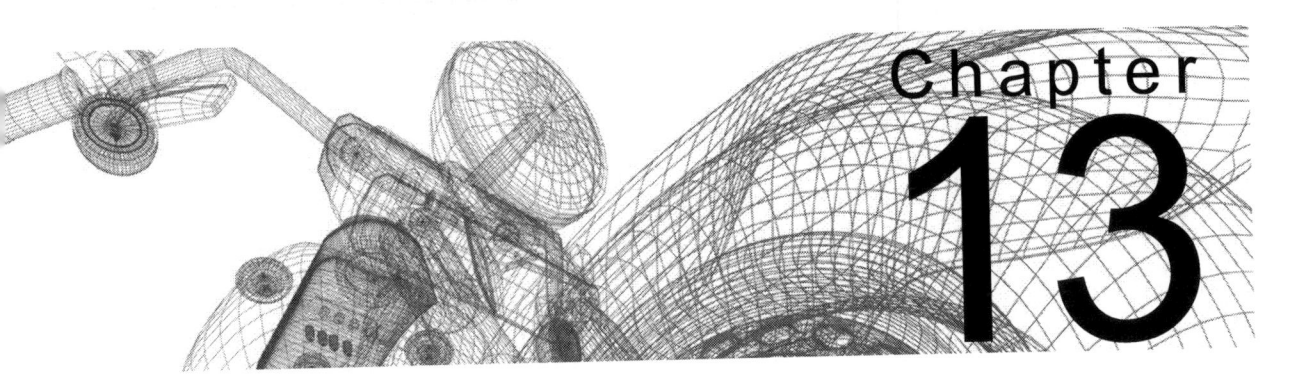

Feature Duplication Tools

When creating similar geometry, incorporating the use of duplication techniques enables you to efficiently create designs. Duplication techniques can include making mirroring copies of features or an entire body, or using patterning to make multiple copies of a feature.

Learning Objectives in this Chapter

- Mirror faces, bodies, and features in a design.
- Create a rectangular pattern of geometry.
- Create a circular pattern of geometry.
- Create a pattern of geometry that follows a sketched path or adjacent edges.

13.1 Mirroring Geometry

The Mirror tool enables you to mirror solid geometry by selecting faces, bodies, or features to be mirrored about a reference plane, as shown in Figure 13–1. If you mirror a body, a second body is created in the design.

Timeline icon:

The hole feature on the left of the work plane was mirrored to the right.

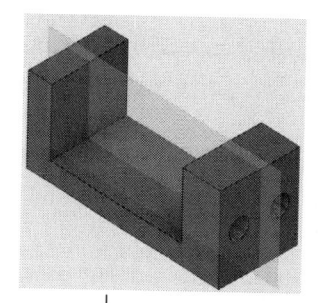

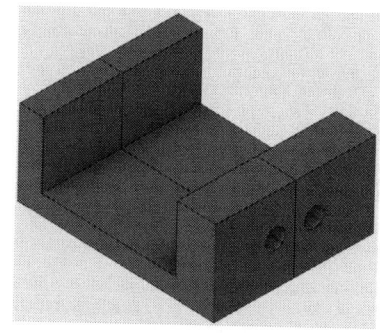

The body was mirrored to the left of the model by selecting the side face.

Figure 13–1

When features are being patterned, the object must be selected from the Timeline.

- The *Pattern Type* field used to mirror items defines whether faces (), bodies (), features (), or components () are selected for patterning. Faces are the default type.

- The mirror plane can be a construction plane or an existing face/plane on a solid feature.

- When you are mirroring features, the *Compute Option* field is added to the MIRROR palette. The options include:
    - **Adjust:** Recalculates each feature based on its mirrored location (e.g., Extent options such as To are recalculated, and mirrored geometry is updated appropriately.).
    - **Optimized:** Use this option when mirroring a large quantity of features.
    - **Identical:** Creates exact mirrored copies of the selected feature.

- In the Timeline, right-click on to access commands for editing or deleting the mirror operation.

Video Lesson Available

Duplicating a Solid Using the Mirror Operation

Video Length: 2:03

13.2 Patterning Features

There are three types of patterns that can be created for duplicating faces, bodies, features, or components: a rectangular pattern, a circular pattern, and a pattern that follows a path.

Rectangular Patterns

Timeline icon:

A rectangular pattern is used to duplicate geometry in either one or two directions. A direction reference can be a linear part edge or a construction axis. The object being patterned is duplicated at a set spacing distance along these directions and you can define the number of instances that are to be generated. Once the layout is defined, you can also individually suppress instances. Figure 13–2 shows how a hole is patterned using a **Rectangular Pattern** option.

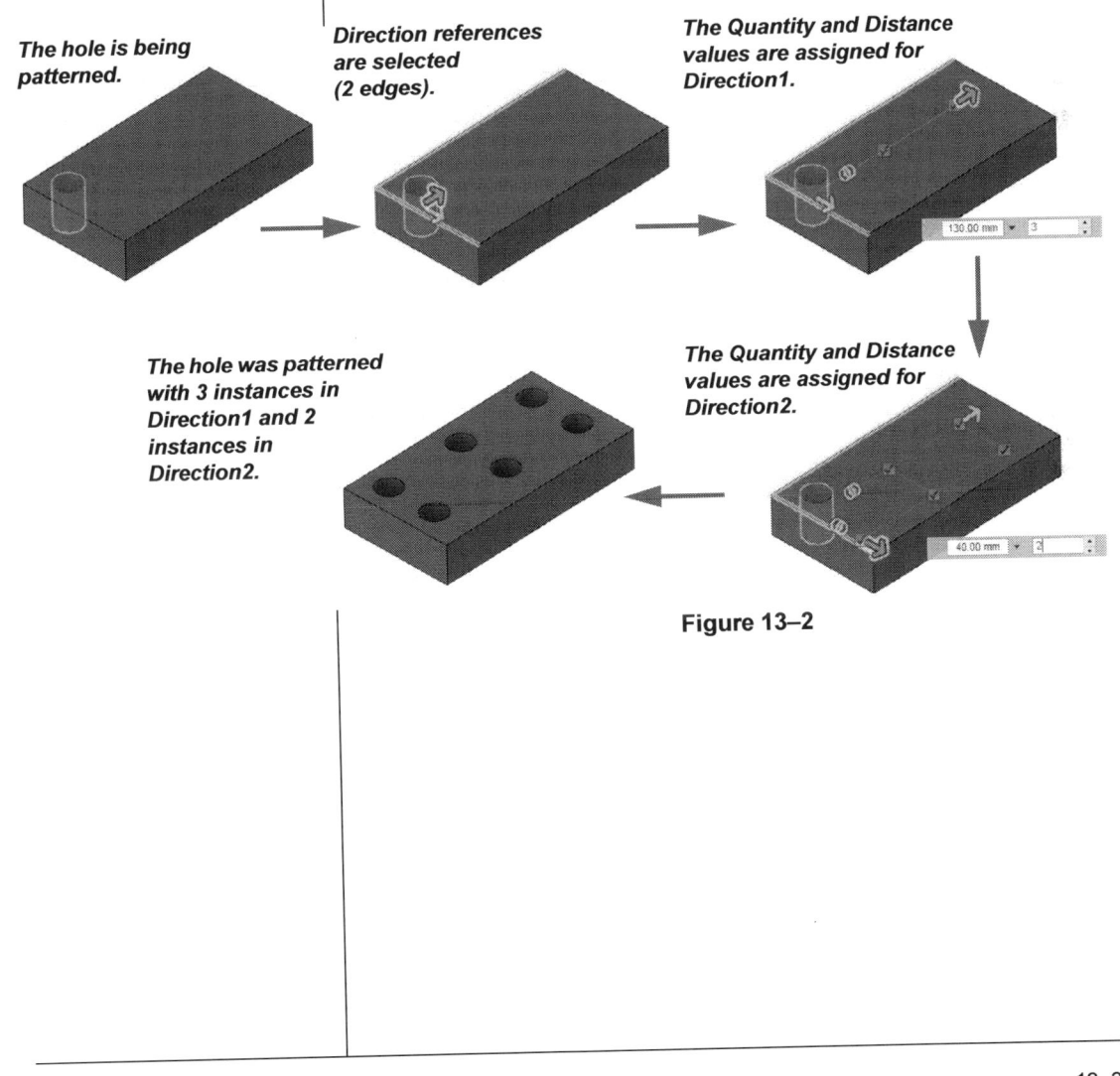

The hole is being patterned.

Direction references are selected (2 edges).

The Quantity and Distance values are assigned for Direction1.

The hole was patterned with 3 instances in Direction1 and 2 instances in Direction2.

The Quantity and Distance values are assigned for Direction2.

Figure 13–2

Circular Patterns

Timeline icon:

A circular pattern is used to create a rotating pattern of objects about a single axis of rotation. The axis of rotation can be a linear or circular edge, axis, or cylindrical face. The object is patterned based on a number of defined instances (Quantity) that are positioned evenly over the defined rotation angle. Once the pattern is defined, you can individually suppress instances as required. Figure 13–3 shows how a hole is patterned using a **Circular Pattern** option.

The hole is being patterned about the central axis.

The default pattern defaults to 3 instances about 360° (Full).

The hole was patterned to create 6 instances about 180°.

Modify the number of instances and angle of rotation, as required.

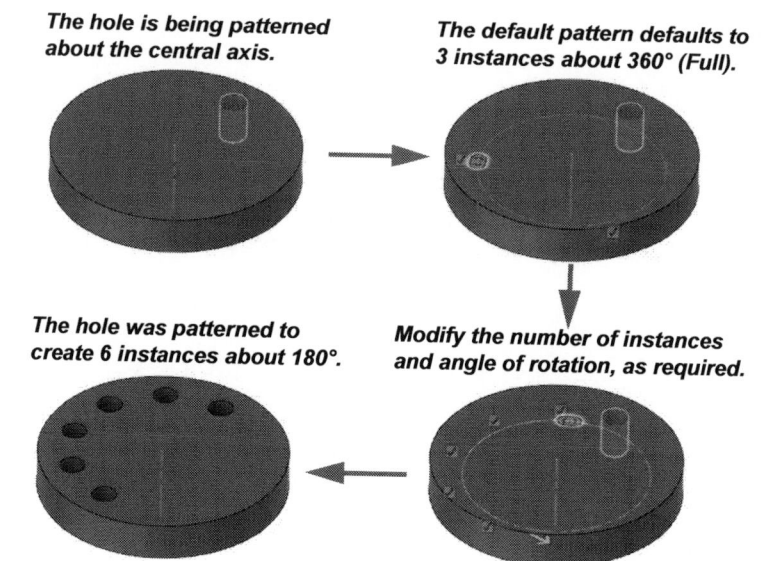

Figure 13–3

Pattern on Path

Timeline icon:

A pattern on path is used to create a pattern that follows a predefined path. The path reference can be a sketched curve or existing edges. You can customize the pattern distance, quantity, and orientation using the pattern options. Similar to rectangular and circular patterns, once the pattern is defined you can also individually suppress instances. Figure 13–4 shows how a hole is patterned using a **Pattern on Path** option.

The hole is being patterned.

A sketched line is being used as the path reference.

The hole was patterned to create 5 instances.

Modify the number of instances and the distance to extend along the path.

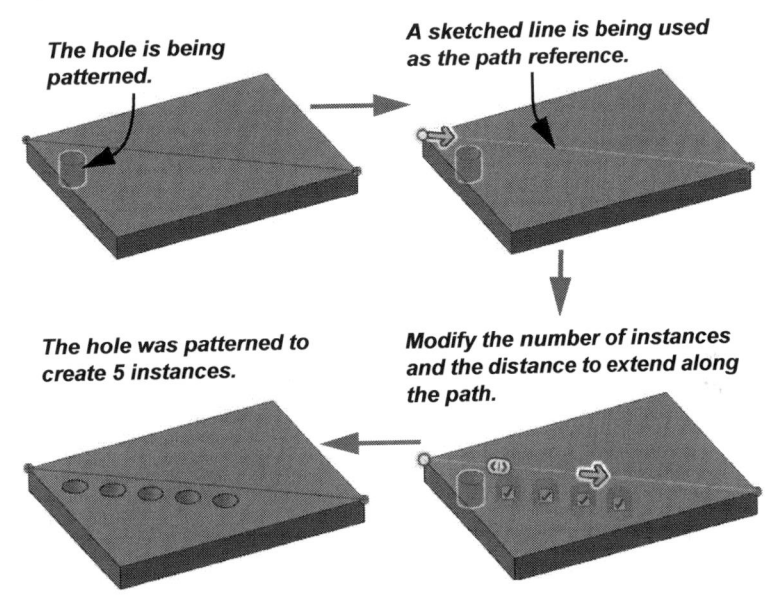

Figure 13–4

Video Lesson Available

Duplicating a Solid Using a Pattern

Video Length: 7:25

Practice 13a — Mirroring Geometry

Practice Objective

- Mirror select features and bodies to create required geometry.

In this practice, you will modify a design that has been provided for you. You will begin by creating a construction plane that will be used to mirror features in the model. You will then create several mirror operations to mirror bodies to create the final geometry. Figure 13–5 shows the initial and final models for this practice.

Initial Geometry

Final Geometry

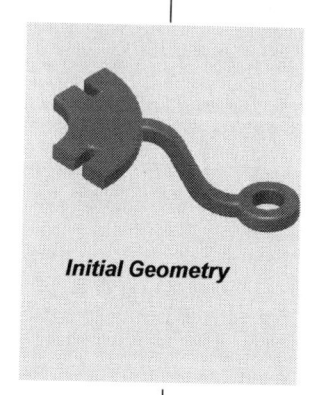

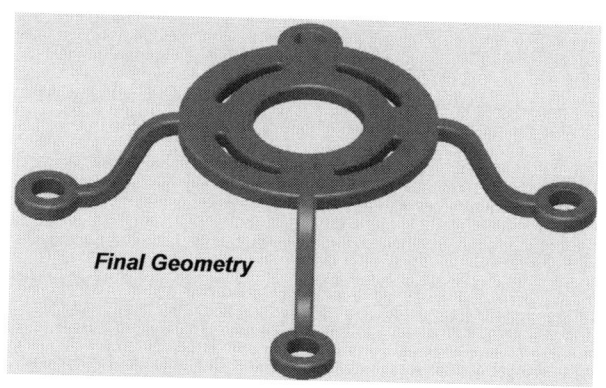

Figure 13–5

Task 1 - Open a part file and create a plane mirror features.

1. Click > **New Design from File**.

2. In the Open dialog box, navigate to the *C:\Autodesk Fusion 360 Practice Files* folder, select **Stand.f3d**, and click **Open**.

3. Create a construction plane through the middle of the existing body, as shown in Figure 13–6. Use the **Midplane** option and select the two planar faces to define its location.

*The **Midplane** option does not require that the reference faces or planes be parallel.*

Construction plane

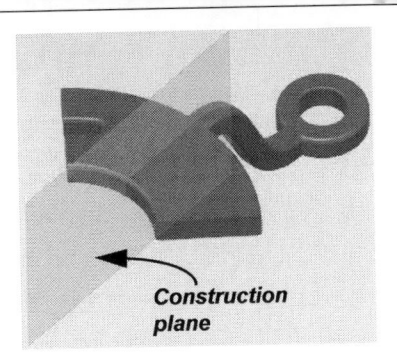

Figure 13–6

Task 2 - Mirror features in the model.

1. In the CREATE panel, click (Mirror)

2. In the MIRROR palette, click (Pattern Features) as the type of object to be mirrored.

3. In the Timeline, select the **Extrude1** and **Fillet1** features.

4. In the MIRROR palette, activate the *Mirror Plane* field by clicking in it. In the graphics window, select **Plane1** as the mirror plane reference.

5. Ensure that the *Compute Option* is set to **Adjust**. This will recalculate each mirrored feature based on its mirrored location.

6. Click **OK** to mirror the features.

7. The model displays as shown in Figure 13–7. The construction plane has been removed from the display for clarity.

When you are selecting features to be mirrored or patterned, you must select the features in the Timeline. You cannot select features in the BROWSER or graphics window.

Mirrored Features

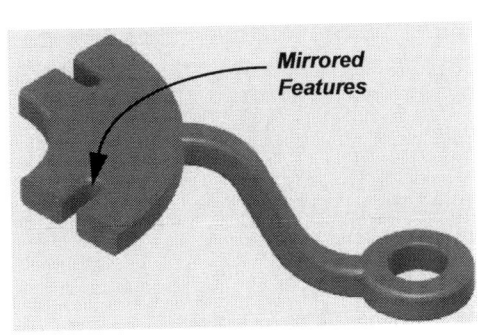

Figure 13–7

Task 3 - Mirror the part.

1. In the CREATE panel, click ▯▯ (Mirror).

2. In the MIRROR palette, click ▢ (Pattern Bodies) as the type of object to be mirrored. In the graphics window, select the model. The entire solid body is selected.

3. Activate the *Mirror Plane* field by clicking in it. Select the face shown in Figure 13–8 as the mirror plane reference.

Mirror plane

Figure 13–8

4. Click **OK** to mirror the model, as shown on the left in Figure 13–9.

5. Complete the part by creating another mirror feature, as shown on the right in Figure 13–9.
   - Note that when you are selecting the bodies to mirror you are required to select two bodies. When a body is mirrored it is created as its own body.
   - Change the *Visual Style* to **Shaded with Visible Edges Only** to display that they are all separate bodies.
   - In the next task you will learn how to combine these separate bodies into one.

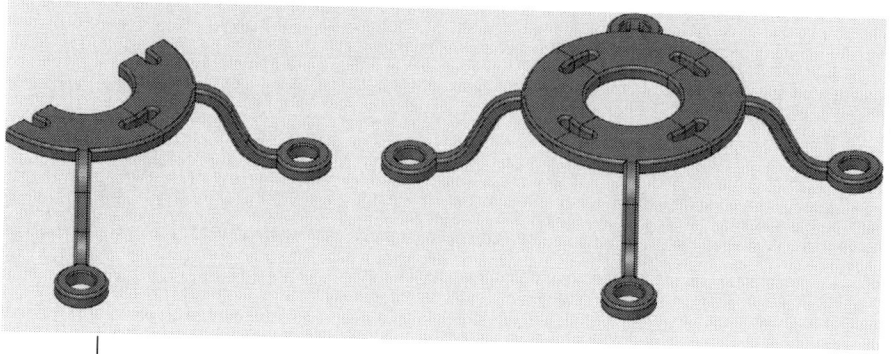

Figure 13–9

Task 4 - Combine the three mirror bodies with the initial body.

1. In the BROWSER, expand the **Bodies** folder and note that there are four bodies in the model.

2. In the MODIFY panel, click (Combine).

3. By default, the *Target Bodies* field is active. In the BROWSER, select **Body1** as the target for the combine operation.

4. Ensure that the *Tool Bodies* field is activated, and then select **Body2**, **Body3**, and **Body4**.

5. For the *Operation* value, ensure that **Join** is selected. Click **OK** to combine the four bodies into one.

Task 5 - Modify the model.

1. In the Timeline, right-click on **Extrude1** and select **Edit Profile Sketch**. The sketch that was used to create this extrusion is opened.

2. Change the 12.5° angular dimension to **25.0°**. Complete the sketch. Note how all of the mirrored features update to reflect the change, as shown in Figure 13–10.

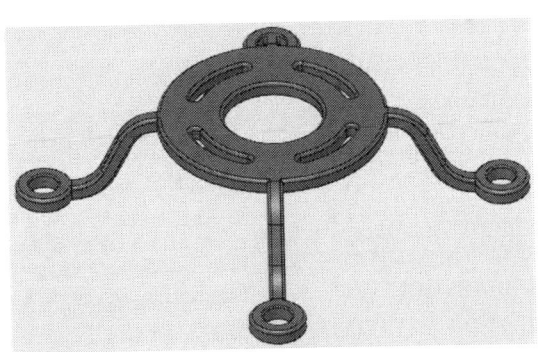

Figure 13–10

3. Save the design with the name **Stand** to your *Autodesk Fusion 360 Practice Files* project.

4. Close the file.

Practice 13b

Patterning Geometry

Practice Objective

- Pattern geometry using the Rectangular, Circular, and Pattern on Path options.

In this practice, you will open a model and create three different patterns. Each pattern will be created using one of the three patterning options.

Task 1 - Create a rectangular pattern of features in the model.

In this task you will create the rectangular pattern of features shown in Figure 13–11.

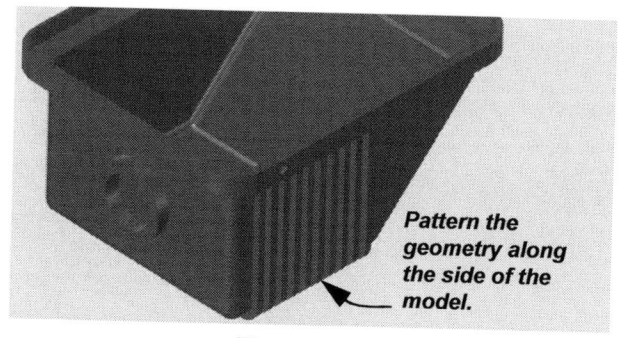

Pattern the geometry along the side of the model.

Figure 13–11

1. Click ▼ > **New Design from File**.

2. In the Open dialog box, navigate to the *C:\Autodesk Fusion 360 Practice Files* folder, select **Airbox.f3d**, and click **Open**.

3. In the ribbon, expand the CREATE panel and select **Pattern > Rectangular Pattern**. The RECTANGULAR PATTERN palette opens as shown in Figure 13–12.

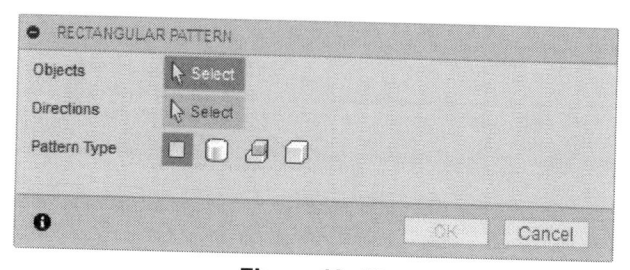

Figure 13–12

4. For the *Pattern Type,* select ▦ (Pattern Features).

5. In the Timeline, select **Extrude4** as the feature to be patterned. Once the object is selected, the *Objects* field in the palette indicates that 1 item has been selected and the object highlights in blue.

6. In the RECTANGULAR PATTERN palette, activate the *Directions* field by clicking in it. Select the edge shown in Figure 13–13 as the direction reference.

Select this edge as the Direction reference

Figure 13–13

7. For the *Distance Type* option, ensure that **Extent** is selected. This assigns the overall pattern distance value from the start of the first instance to the start of the last instance.

8. Select and drag the arrow manipulator into the model. By default, three copies of the patterned extrusion extend out in an equal distance from one another. You can adjust the number of extrudes to be patterned by either using the *Quantity* input value boxes, or by dragging the small double arrow manipulators.

9. Change the *Quantity* value to **10** using either method.

10. Change the top *Distance* value to **110 mm**. The model displays as shown in Figure 13–14.

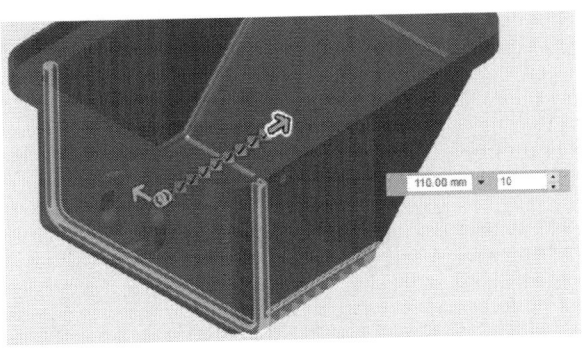

Figure 13–14

11. In the *Direction Type* drop-down list, ensure that **One Direction** is selected.

12. Click **OK** to create the pattern. The pattern is created as shown in Figure 13–15.

Figure 13–15

Task 2 - Create a circular pattern of holes.

In this task you will create a circular pattern of features shown in Figure 13–16.

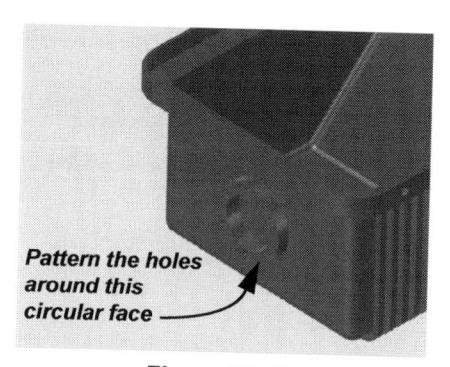

Pattern the holes around this circular face

Figure 13–16

1. In the ribbon, expand the CREATE panel and select **Pattern > Circular Pattern**.

2. For the *Pattern Type,* ensure that (Pattern Features) is selected. The CIRCULAR PATTERN palette displays as shown in Figure 13–17.

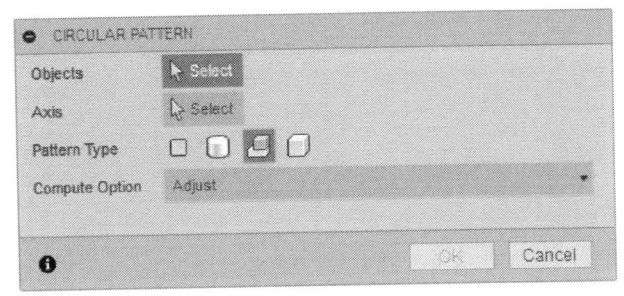

Figure 13–17

You must used the Timeline to select the features that are being patterned.

3. Select the hole shown in Figure 13–18 as the feature to be patterned. Once the object is selected, the *Objects* field in the palette indicates that 1 item has been selected, and the object highlights in blue.

Select this hole to be patterned.

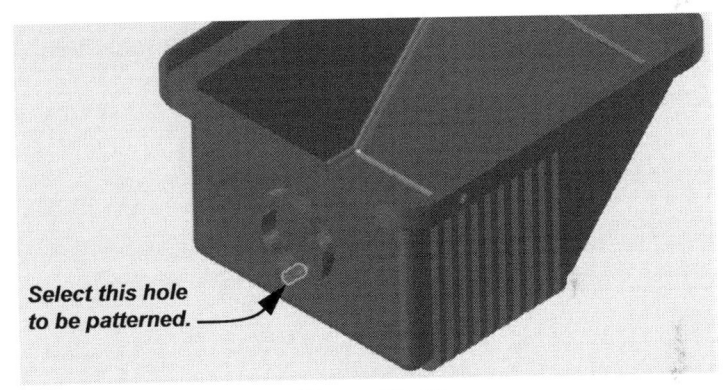

Figure 13–18

4. Click in the *Axis* field to activate it.

5. Select the outer edge of the cylinder as the rotation axis reference.

6. Increase the *Quantity* to **6** by either inputting it in the palette or dragging the manipulator until six instances of the hole display.

7. Ensure that the *Type* option is set to **Full**. This creates the pattern in a complete 360° degree circle.

8. Click **OK** to create the pattern. The model displays as shown in Figure 13–19.

Figure 13–19

Task 3 - Pattern a hole along a path.

In this task you will pattern the hole on the top lip of the model so that it follows the path of the top edge, as shown in Figure 13–20.

Pattern the holes around the lip of the model.

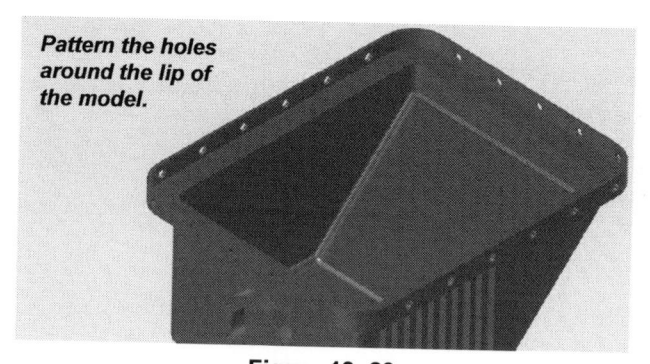

Figure 13–20

1. In the ribbon, expand the CREATE panel and select **Pattern > Pattern on Path**. The PATTERN ON PATH palette displays as shown in Figure 13–21.

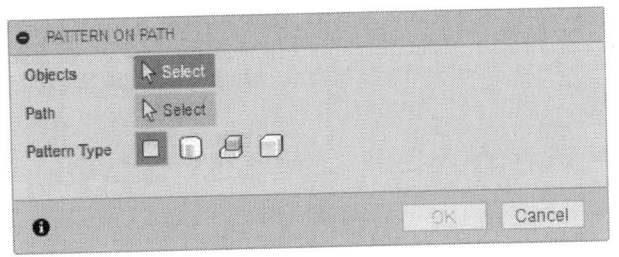

Figure 13–21

2. For the *Pattern Type*, ensure that (Pattern Features) is selected.

3. Select the hole to be patterned, as shown in Figure 13–22. Once the object is selected, the *Objects* field in the palette indicates that 1 item has been selected and the object highlights in blue.

Select the face of the hole to be patterned

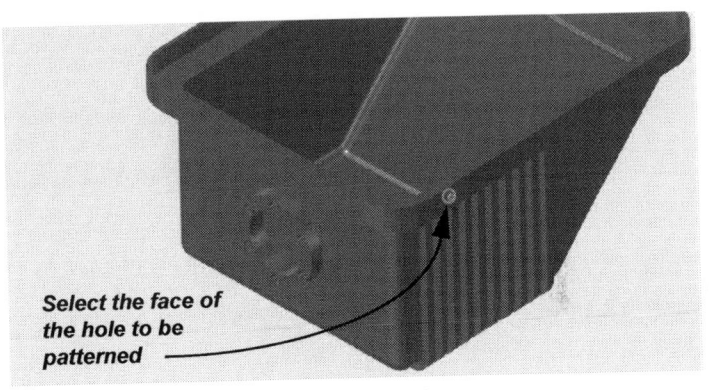

Figure 13–22

4. In the palette, activate the *Path* field by clicking in it.

5. Select the outside-top edge of the lip as the path reference.

6. Once both of these fields are defined, an arrow displays that enables you to drag additional instances of the pattern along the path. As an alternative to dragging the arrow all of the way around the edge, enter a *Distance* value of **1008 mm**. This is the length of the edge.

7. Increase the *Quantity* to **25** and keep the remaining defaults in the palette.

8. Click **OK** to create the pattern. Note how the pattern is not created correctly and the holes do not cut through the lip correctly.

9. Edit the path pattern feature and change the *Orientation* option to **Path Direction**. Click **OK**. The pattern now cuts through the lip correctly because the orientation of the hole relative to the path was kept for the entire path.

10. Note how the final hole overlaps the first hole and there are holes on each of the corners. Edit the path pattern again. In the preview of the pattern, clear the checkbox that identifies the final patterned instance. This removes the instance from the pattern.

11. Continue to remove any holes that are patterned on the corners of the lip so that the model displays similar to that shown in Figure 13–23.

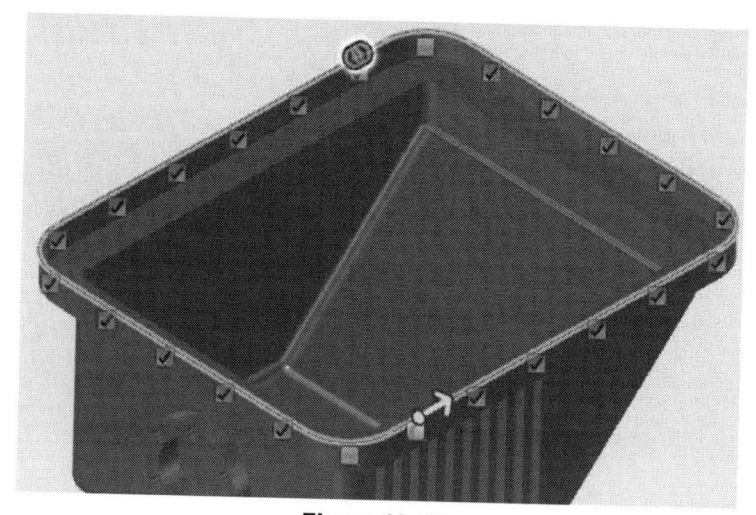

Figure 13–23

12. Complete the pattern. The model should display similar to that shown in Figure 13–24

Figure 13–24

13. Save the design with the name **Airbox** to your *Autodesk Fusion 360 Practice Files* project.

14. Close the file.

Chapter Review Questions

1. Which of the following construction features can be used as a reference for mirroring features?
   a. Construction Plane
   b. Construction Point
   c. Construction Axis

2. You can mirror an entire solid body or individual features in a model.
   a. True
   b. False

3. Only a linear part edge can be selected as a direction reference for a rectangular feature pattern.
   a. True
   b. False

4. The model shown in Figure 13–25 has a pattern of holes created in one direction. What is the number of pattern occurrences that are defined in the palette?

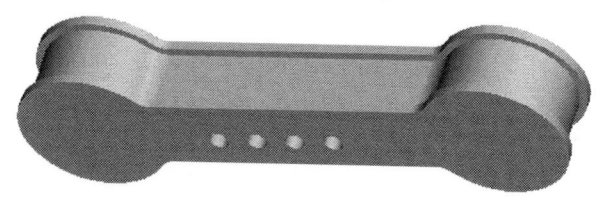

   Figure 13–25

   a. 1
   b. 2
   c. 3
   d. 4

5. Which entities can be used as the rotation axis for a circular pattern? (Select all that apply.)
   a. Construction Plane
   b. Edge
   c. Construction Axis
   d. Cylindrical face

6. What should you do if the preview of your rectangular pattern is in the wrong direction along a selected reference direction? (Select all that apply.)

    a. Select a new direction reference that is in the correct direction.
    b. Drag the direction arrow in the opposite direction.
    c. Enter a negative value as the *Distance* value.
    d. Change the *Direction Type* option.

7. The sketch that defines a pattern that follows a path must be created after the **Pattern on Path** command is initiated.

    a. True
    b. False

8. Which of the following statements are true for removing specific occurrences from a pattern?

    a. You can suppress the first occurrence of the pattern (original).
    b. You can suppress all except the first occurrence of the pattern.
    c. You can select individual occurrences in the pattern for deletion.
    d. You can use the **Delete** command to delete the first occurrence in the model.

9. Which of the following best describes the difference between the **Extent** and **Spacing** *Distance Type* options for a rectangular pattern?

    a. The **Extent** option assigns the overall pattern Distance value from the start of the first instance to the start of the last instance. The **Spacing** option assigns the overall pattern distance as a value between each instance within the pattern.
    b. The **Extent** option assigns the distance value between instances. The **Spacing** option assigns the overall pattern distance as a single value and the number of instances are equally spaced along the distance.

Answers: 1.a, 2.a, 3.b, 4.d, 5.(b,c,d), 6.(b,c), 7.b, 8.b, 9.a

Command Summary

Button	Command	Location
	Circular Pattern (feature)	• **Ribbon:** *Model* Workspace>CREATE panel • **Context Menu:** Right-click in the graphics window and select **Create**.
	Combine	• **Ribbon:** *Model* Workspace>MODIFY panel • **Context Menu:** Right-click in the graphics window and select **Modify**.
	Mirror (feature)	• **Ribbon:** *Model* Workspace>CREATE panel • **Context Menu:** Right-click in the graphics window and select **Create**.
	Pattern on Path (feature)	• **Ribbon:** *Model* Workspace>CREATE panel • **Context Menu:** Right-click in the graphics window and select **Create**.
	Rectangular Pattern (feature)	• **Ribbon:** *Model* Workspace>CREATE panel • **Context Menu:** Right-click in the graphics window and select **Create**.

Chapter 14

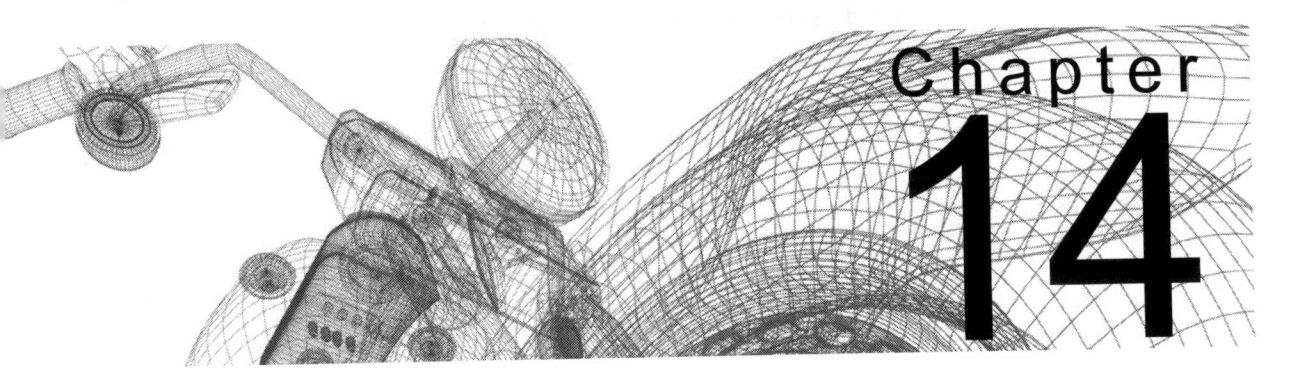

Distributed Design

A design can consist of multiple components that communicate how an assembled product is designed. In the Autodesk® Fusion 360™ software, there are two methods that can be used to design a product with multiple components: components can be combined into a single design, or all components can be created within the context of a design. This chapter discusses the Distributed design method, where components are inserted and joined with one another in a single design.

Learning Objectives in this Chapter

- Describe the methods used to create an assembly in the Autodesk Fusion 360 software.
- Insert components into a design.
- Create joint origins in a model for use in assigning joint references.
- Use the Joint command to connect components in a design while maintaining the defined degrees of freedom.
- Edit a joint connection so that the joint type, references, or its values can be changed.

14.1 Assembly Design Methods

There are two methods that can be used to create a multi-component (assembly) design in the Autodesk Fusion 360 software. These are: Distributed Design and Multi-Body Design.

- **Distributed Design:** Using this method, components are created in separate design files first, and then they are independently added into one design to create the assembled product. Each component is stored separately and is linked into the top-level design. Any changes made in the individual component can be updated in the assembled design.

- **Multi-Body Design:** Using this method, multiple individual bodies are created within the context of a design file. These bodies are then converted to components. Each component represents a separate model in the assembled product. This approach is also known as top-down design.

In either method, components represent all of the unique parts in the multi-component design. The process of creating the components varies depending on the design method used.

Components can also be imported from other CAD products or the McMaster-Carr content library.

Inserting Content from the McMaster-Carr Content Library

McMaster-Carr (www.mcmaster.com) provides many standard components that can be used in Autodesk Fusion 360 designs. These components represent purchasable components that are commonly used in a design (e.g., fasteners, screws, etc.). Models can be downloaded in multiple CAD formats for use in the Autodesk Fusion 360 software. These components can be used for either design method.

- To add a component directly into a design, expand the INSERT panel and click (Insert McMaster-Carr Component). The component is stored in the design. If the component is needed for another design, you would have to insert it again.

- To save the component as a unique file, download the file from the McMaster-Carr site to your local system. You can then upload the file to your Autodesk 360 account through the Data Panel, at which point it is available for insertion into a design.

14.2 Distributed Design

The distributed design method uses previously created components and designs which are then inserted into another design file. Once in the design, the components are constrained to one another using Joints.

Use the following steps to insert components into a design file:

1. Create a new design and save the file.
2. Open the Data Panel and locate the component to be inserted as the first component in the design.
3. Insert the first component into the design file.
4. Use the MOVE palette to locate the component in the assembly.
5. Continue to insert components to complete the design.

If the assembly model's design file was newly created, it must be saved before you can insert components.

A combination of distributed design and multi-body design can be incorporated into designing a multi-component model. This is convenient if some components are not individually created and it might be easier to create them in the context of the multi-component design to ensure fit and function.

Inserting Components

To insert a component into a design, in the Data Panel, right-click on the component's thumbnail image and select **Insert into Current Design**, as shown in Figure 14–1.

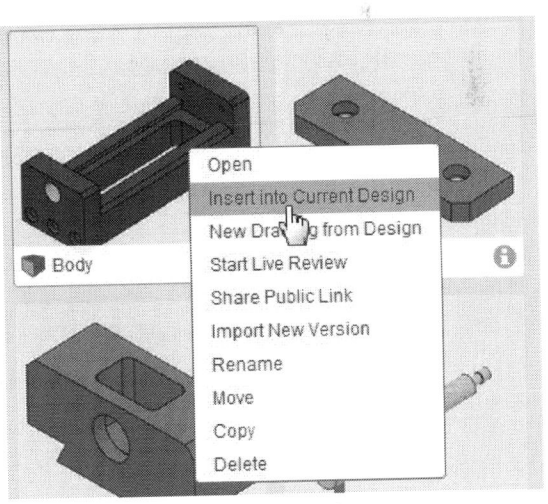

Figure 14–1

- Once inserted, you can reposition the component in the file using the MOVE palette or using the handles on the triad. Click **OK** to place the component.

Timeline icon:

© 2016, ASCENT - Center for Technical Knowledge®

To create subassembly components, insert the components together into one design file and then use that file in a top-level design.

- Inserted components are listed in the BROWSER. They are identified using 🔗 (as shown in Figure 14–2), which indicates that there is a link to the source component file.

- To break the link to a component, right-click on the component name in the BROWSER and select **Break Link**. Once broken, you can edit the component in the assembly design file, but the link cannot be restored.

- Inserted components can be either a single component design file or a subassembly where multiple components have been previously combined. In Figure 14–2, the **Body** and **FixedJaw** components are single component design files (🗋), whereas the **MovingJaw** component is a subassembly (📁).

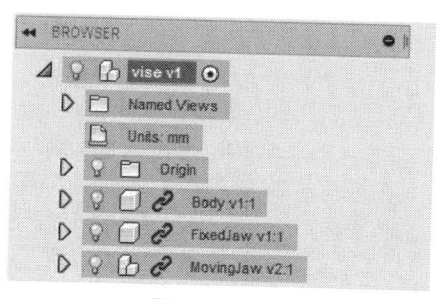

Figure 14–2

- Inserted components are read-only in the context of the top-level design. To make a change to geometry in the model, you must return to the source design file.

- If a change is made to a source component, the BROWSER icon updates to indicate that the component is out-of-date (⚠). To update an out-of-date component, right-click on the component name and select **Get Latest**. If multiple components are out-of-date, right-click on the design's name and select **Get All Latest**.

MOVE Palette

The MOVE palette displays as soon as a component is inserted into a design file. The palette and the accompanying triad (shown in Figure 14–3) can be used to position the component.

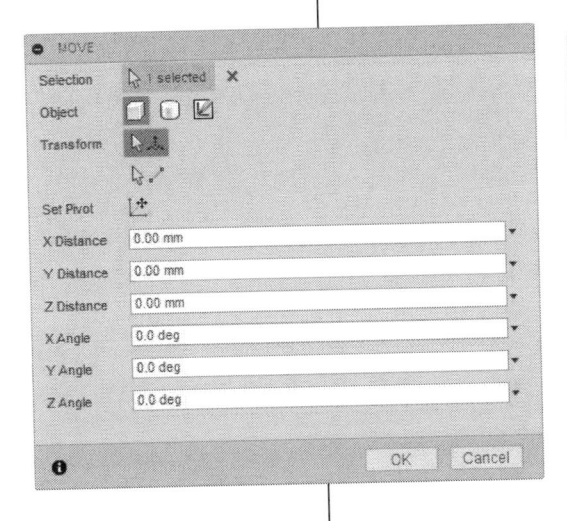

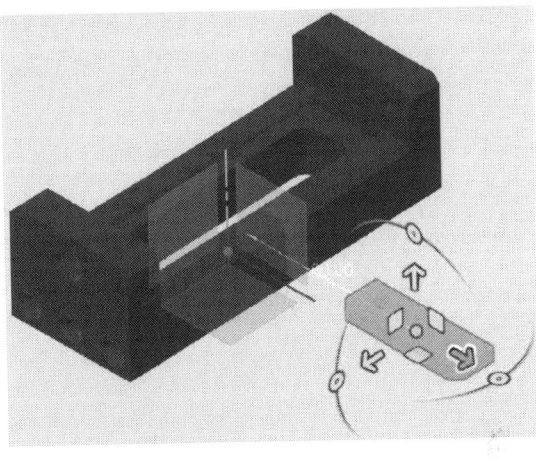

Figure 14–3

Maintain the ▭ (Move Components) option in the Object area to move the newly inserted component. If another option is select the component will be placed automatically placed at its current location.

Timeline icon: ⊕

To define the component's position, you can use any of the following methods:

- Drag the handles on the triad to locate the component.
    - Use the arrowhead icon to move linearly in the X, Y, or Z directions.
    - Use the plane icon to move in the XY, XZ, or YZ planes.
    - Use the circular icons to rotate about the X, Y, or Z axes.
- Enter translational or rotational values in the MOVE palette.
- Activate a handle on the triad and enter a value in the entry field that displays.

Once the position is defined, click **OK** in the MOVE palette to position the component in the assembly. Note that this does not define how the components are constrained relative to one another, which is done using joints.

> **Tips for Working with the MOVE Palette**
>
> Consider using the ▭ (Point to Point) transform option to align specific entities in the components. You can also use the ⊕ (Set Pivot) option to define a new location for the transform triad on the component.

Grounding Components

You can ground components in an assembly to ensure that they form a stable base for the design and do not move relative to other components. To ground a component, in the BROWSER, right-click on the component's name and select **Ground**, as shown in Figure 14–4.

Timeline icon:

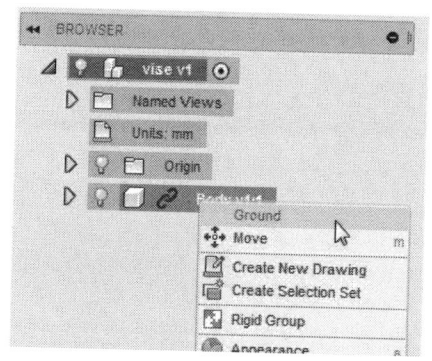

Figure 14–4

- Grounded components are identified in the BROWSER with .

- There can be a single grounded component or multiple grounded components in an assembly. Generally, the most prominent component in the design should be grounded.

Video Lesson Available

Positioning Components

Video Length: 3:10

14.3 Joint Origins

To apply a joint, you must select reference geometry on both components. The reference geometry that you select on each component is called a *Joint Origin*. A single joint origin on each component is required to fully define a joint. To join the components, the two selected joint origins are aligned to one another. Joint origins can be created directly when you are joining components, or they can be created in a component for use when joining components.

Selecting Joint Origins

Joint origins can be placed at the time of joint creation. This is done by selecting default snap-points on entities in the model. As you hover the cursor over a component face, edge, or cylindrical or spherical geometry, highlighted snap-points display with the active glyph ( ) attached to the snap-point closest to the cursor. This glyph represents the joint origin and is the point to which the joint is assigned once it is selected. The location of the cursor on the entity controls which glyph is active. If the required glyph is not active, move the cursor closer to another snap-point to activate it.

Face Snap-Points

For planar faces, the snap-points that define the joint origin can be located at one of three locations, as shown in Figure 14–5:

- Center point of the face
- Midpoint of an edge on the face
- End point of an edge on the face

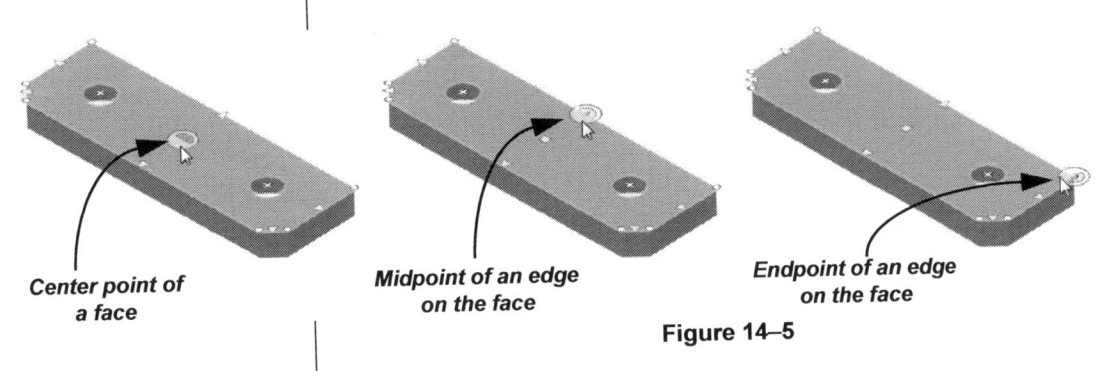

Center point of a face   *Midpoint of an edge on the face*   *Endpoint of an edge on the face*

Figure 14–5

> **Hint: Joint Origin Selection**
>
> As you move the cursor on a model the reference entity might change. To lock a reference entity, ensure that you are hovered over the required entity, press and hold <Ctrl> and continue to move the cursor to locate the required joint origin on that single entity.

Edge Snap-Points

For an edge, the snap-points that can define the joint origin can be located at one of two locations, as shown in Figure 14–6.

- Midpoint of the edge
- Ends of the edge

For a circular edge or face, the only possible snap-point is at the center.

Midpoint of a edge *Ends of an edge* *Center of a circular edge*

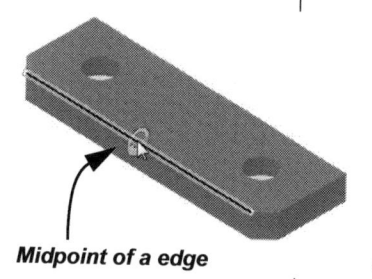

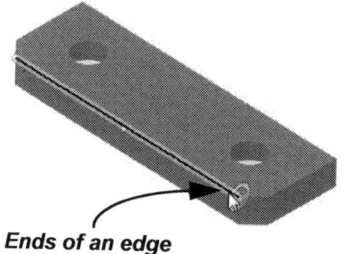

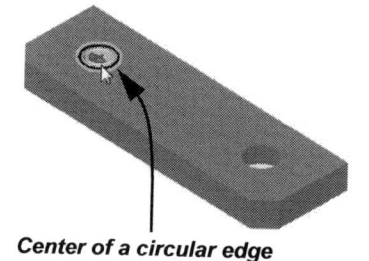

Figure 14–6

Cylindrical and Spherical Geometry Snap-Points

- For cylindrical geometry, a snap-point exists at the mid-point of the central axis and at each end.

- For spherical geometry, the only available snap-point is at the center of the geometry.

The snap-points for cylindrical and spherical geometry are shown in Figure 14–7.

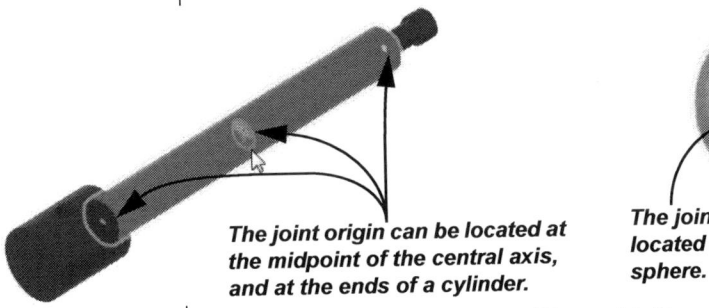

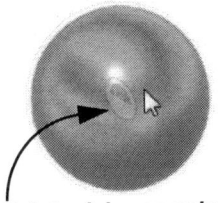

The joint origin can be located at the midpoint of the central axis, and at the ends of a cylinder.

The joint origin can only be located at the midpoint of a sphere.

Figure 14–7

Creating Joint Origins

Timeline icon:

Joint origins can be manually created in a component for later use when a joint is being assigned. To create a joint origin, expand the ASSEMBLE panel and click (Joint Origin). A joint origin can be created using the JOINT ORIGIN palette, in one of two ways: (Simple) or (Between two Faces), as shown in Figure 14–8.

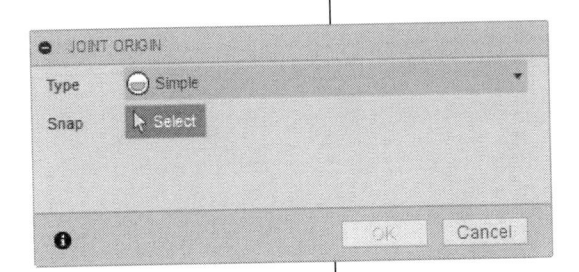

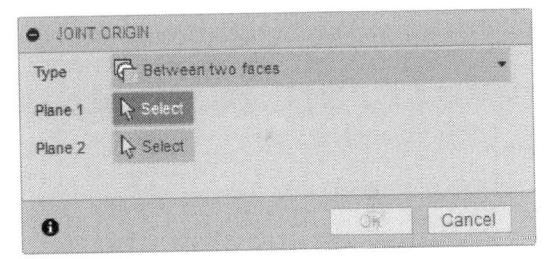

Figure 14–8

Simple

Simple joint origins reference the snap-points that are available on faces, edges, and spherical or cylindrical geometry. The benefit of creating a simple joint origin is that the Move triad is available once the snap-point is selected, enabling you to move the joint origin to a more exact location that does not lie directly on a snap-point.

- Figure 14–9 shows how a joint origin was created and then offset linearly 20mm from the midpoint of cylindrical geometry. You would not be able to create this joint origin by selecting a reference during joint assignment, so it had to be created independently

The midpoint of a cylindrical surface was selected as the placement reference for a new joint origin. The Move triad displays.

The joint origin was moved along the Z axis.

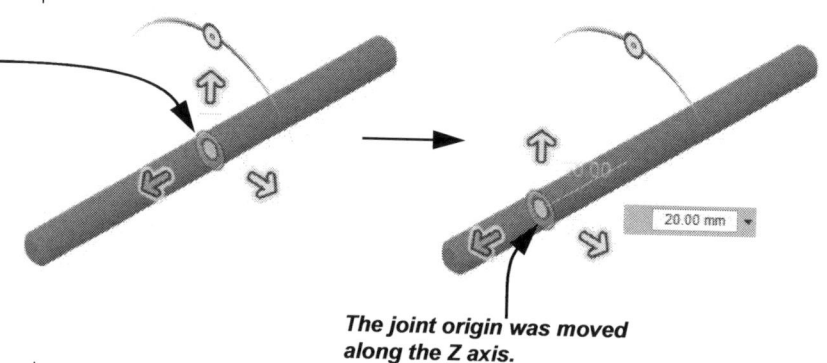

Figure 14–9

- Figure 14–10 shows how a joint origin was created on a construction point. The geometry of the model did not provide the required snap-point, so construction entities were created.

A construction axis and point were created as references for joint origin creation. A joint origin is required to line up with the hole and the center point of the surface was not appropriate.

The joint origin was created on the construction point.

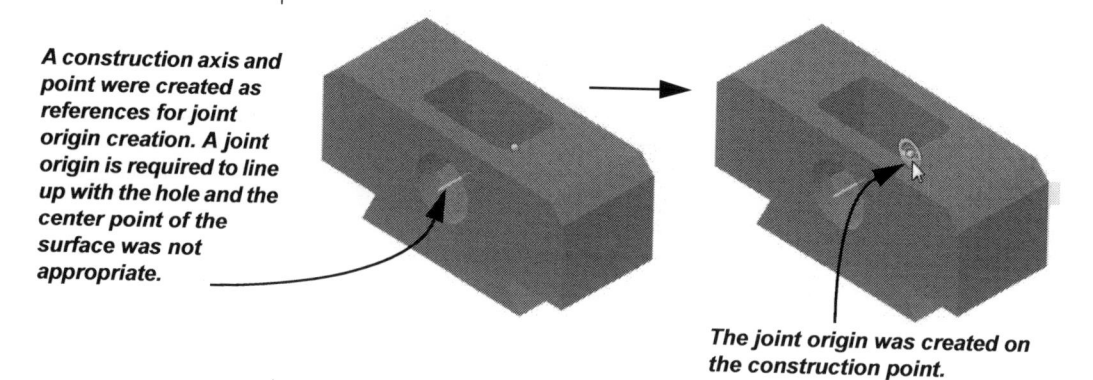

Figure 14–10

Between Two Faces

The **Between two faces** joint origin type enables you to create a joint origin so that it is placed on a mid-plane between two selected faces. The joint origin is located on the plane based on the selection of a snap reference. The snap reference can be a linear axis, edge, or snap-points on other entities. Similar to a Simple joint origin, the Move triad displays once the references are defined.

- In the assembly shown in Figure 14–11, a snap-point does not exist that permits the assembly of a pin. It needs to be constrained along the central axis at a mid-plane between the two faces. A joint origin was created between two faces and aligned to the axis of a hole.

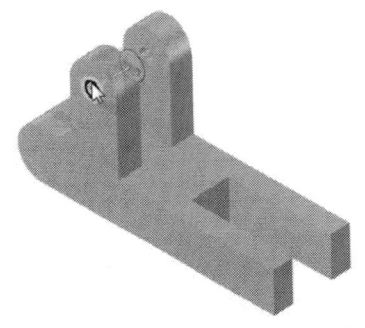

| Select the first plane. | Select a parallel plane as the second reference. | Hover over the cylindrical face of the hole to fully locate the joint origin. |

Figure 14–11

Hint: Joint Origin Creation

Joint origins are stored within the component that was referenced during placement.

- In the case of a multi-component design created using the distributed design method, the joint origin can only be created at the lowest component level where you have write access to the file.

- In the case of the multi-body design method, joint origins can be created in the top-level assembly because the components were created in the context of the top-level design and you have write access to each component. Additionally you can select references that exist on different components.

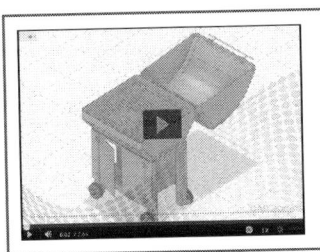

Video Lesson Available

Understanding Joint Origins

Video Length: 3:47

14.4 Assigning Joints

In the Autodesk Fusion 360 software, a joint defines the mechanical movement of a component in relation to another component. Joints are assigned between two components by selecting joint origins on the components.

There are various joint types available. Each joint type defines the degrees of freedom that remain in the model once it is assigned. For example, a rigid joint removes all degrees of freedom between components, while a cylindrical joint permits translation and rotation along and around a linear reference.

Timeline icon:

To add a joint between components, complete the following:

1. In the ASSEMBLE panel, click (Joint). The JOINT palette opens, as shown in Figure 14–12.

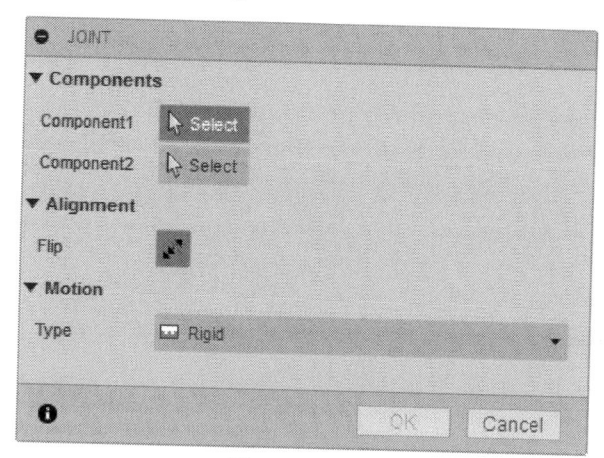

Figure 14–12

2. Select a joint origin on the first component. The first component you select should be the component to be moved into position once the joint is complete.
3. Select a joint origin on the second component.
4. If required, flip the alignment of the joint origins in the *Alignment* area by clicking (Flip). Additional options enable you to set an offset and rotational values between joint origins.
5. In the *Type* drop-down list, select the joint type. Additional options might display depending on the type of joint selected, enabling you to set additional options (e.g., to specify the permitted axis for translation or rotation, etc.).
6. To complete the joint, click **OK.**

*A Between two Faces joint origin can be created during reference selection by right-clicking in the graphics window and selecting **Between two Faces**.*

Joint Types

By default, the previously-assigned Joint Type is set in the palette. To change the type, expand the drop-list and select a new option.

Each joint type permits a specific number of degrees of freedom (DOF). The degrees of freedom that remain define the type of mechanical movement between the two components that is required in the design.

The available joint types and their degrees of freedom are as follows:.

Joint Type	Icon	Remaining DOF
Rigid		0 Translational, 0 Rotational
Revolute		0 Translational, 1 Rotational
Slider		1 Translational, 0 Rotational
Cylindrical		1 Translational, 1 Rotational
Pin-slot		1 Translational, 1 Rotational
Planar		2 Translational, 1 Rotational
Ball		0 Translational, 3 Rotational

To fully define a joint type, a joint origin reference is required on two components. Based on the selected references, the components are joined to one another and the joint type defines the permitted movement between the components. The following examples explain how components were joined using the various joint types.

Rigid

The **Rigid** joint type removes all of the degrees of freedom, preventing any relative motion between the two components.

An example of a rigid joint is shown in Figure 14–13.

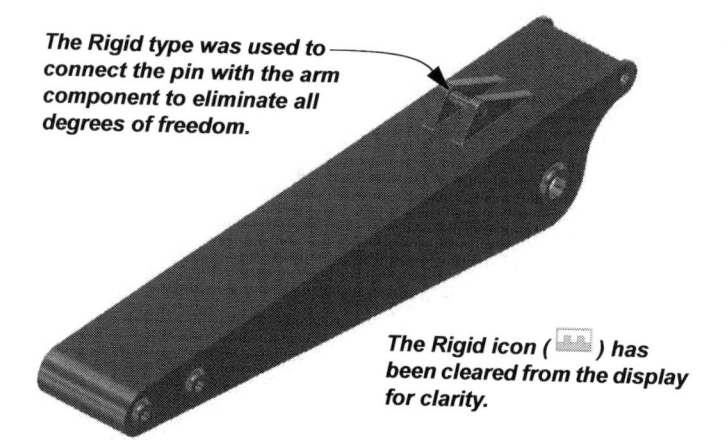

The Rigid type was used to connect the pin with the arm component to eliminate all degrees of freedom.

The Rigid icon ( ) has been cleared from the display for clarity.

Figure 14–13

Video Lesson Available

Introducing Joints - Using the Rigid Joint Type

Video Length: 7:03

Revolute

The **Revolute** joint type permits for rotation about an axis. This joint type removes five degrees of freedom. Once the component references are selected, you can select the axis of revolution in the *Motion* area (if the default selection is incorrect).

An example of a revolute joint is shown in Figure 14–14.

A custom axis can be defined if the X, Y, or Z axis do not permit the required motion.

The Revolute type was used to connect the cylinder tube and pin to permit one rotational degree of freedom.

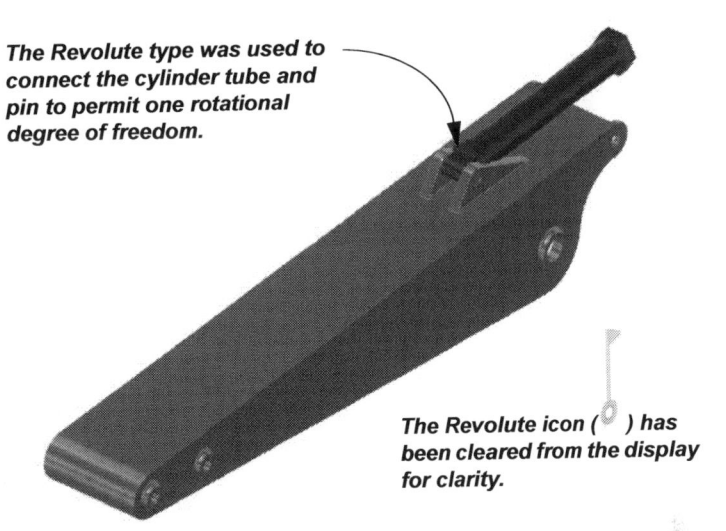

The Revolute icon ( ) has been cleared from the display for clarity.

Figure 14–14

Slider

The **Slider** joint type permits translational movement along an axis. This joint type removes five degrees of freedom. Once the component references are selected, you can select the linear axis in the *Motion* area (if the default selection is incorrect).

An example of a slider joint is shown in Figure 14–15.

A custom axis can be defined if the X, Y, or Z axis do not permit the required motion.

The Slider type was used to connect the slider and base components to permit one translational degree of freedom.

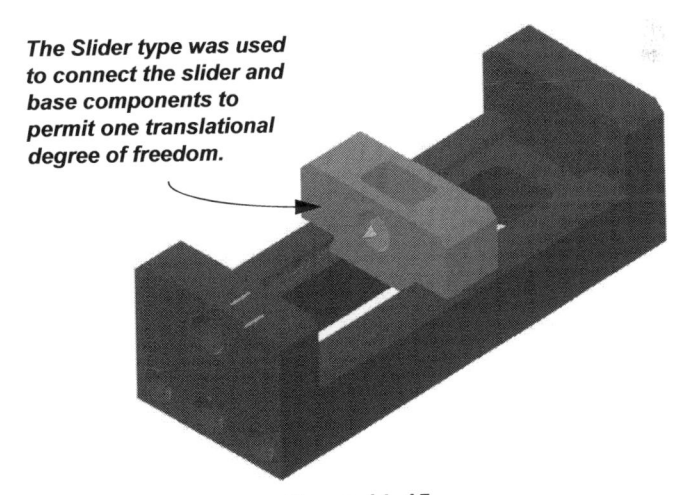

Figure 14–15

Planar

The 🖱 (Planar) joint type enables a component to move in a plane as shown in Figure 14–16. Two translational and one rotational degrees of freedom remain. Once the component references are selected, you can select the linear and normal axes in the *Motion* area (if the default selections are incorrect).

An example of a planar joint is shown in Figure 14–16.

A custom axis can be defined if the X, Y, or Z axis do not permit the required motion.

The Planar type was used to connect the peg to the base component and permit movement in the plane.

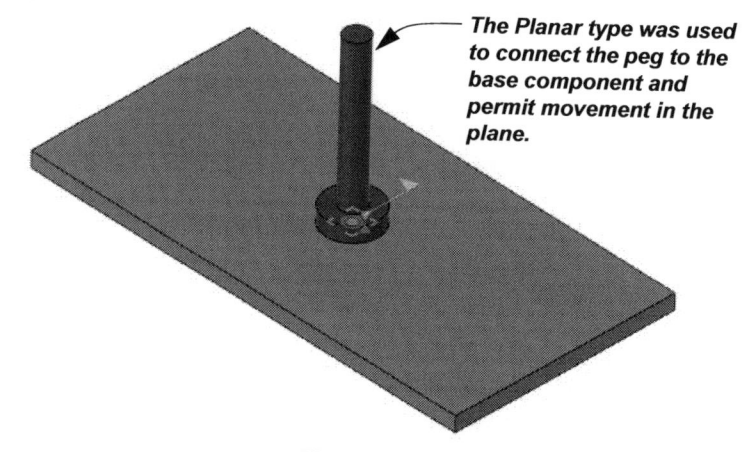

Figure 14–16

Video Lesson Available

Creating Slider and Planar Joints

Video Length: 4:31

Cylindrical

The **Cylindrical** joint type enables a component to translate and rotate about a specific axis leaving two degrees of freedom available. Once the component references are selected, you can select the axis in the *Motion* area (if the default selection is incorrect).

An example of a cylindrical joint is shown in Figure 14–17.

A custom axis can be defined if the X, Y, or Z axis do not permit the required motion.

The Cylindrical type was used to connect the cylinder to the cylinder tube leaving a translational and rotational degree of freedom.

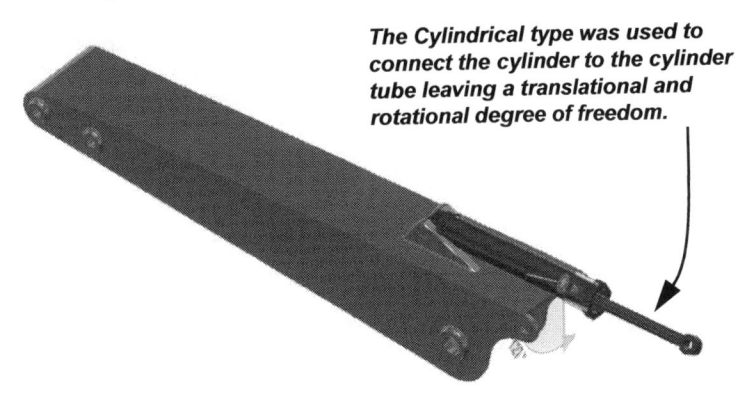

Figure 14–17

Pin-slot

The **Pin-slot** joint type enables a component to move in a slot. One translational and one rotational degree of freedom remain with the component. Once the component references are selected, you can select the linear and rotational axes in the *Motion* area to slide and rotate about (if the default selections are incorrect).

An example of a pin-slot joint is shown in Figure 14–18.

A custom axis can be defined if the X, Y, or Z axis do not permit the required motion.

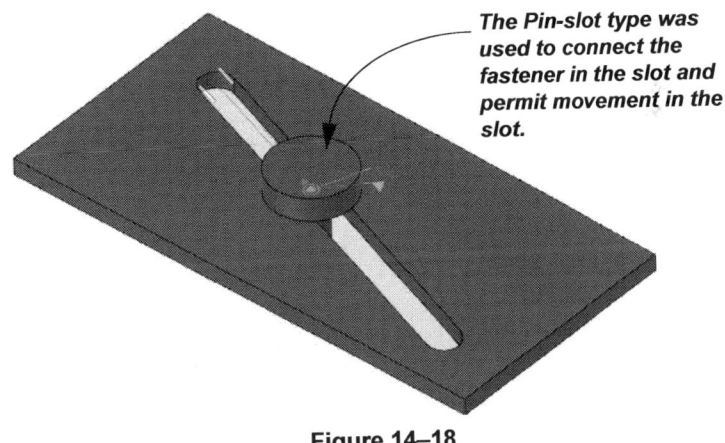

The Pin-slot type was used to connect the fastener in the slot and permit movement in the slot.

Figure 14–18

Ball

The Ball joint type enables a component to rotate in any direction about the origin joint, as shown in Figure 14–19. All translational degrees of freedom are removed. Once the component references are selected, you can select the pitch and yaw axes in the *Motion* area (if the default selections are incorrect).

An example of a ball joint is shown in Figure 14–19.

A custom axis can be defined if the X, Y, or Z axis do not permit the required motion.

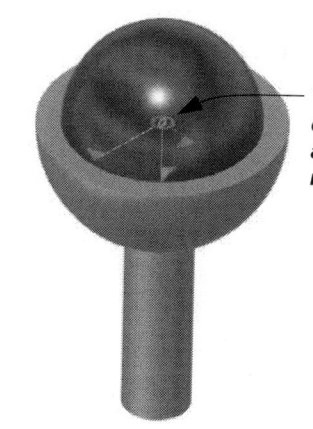

The Ball type was used to connect the components and permit only rotational movement.

Figure 14–19

Video Lesson Available

Working with the Different Types of Joints

Video Length: 9:24

Hint: Working with Joints

- The default naming structure for a joint is its type, followed by a number that indicates the number of joints that have been assigned. To rename a joint, select the joint name twice in the *Joints* folder in the BROWSER and enter a descriptive name.

- To change the joint type or its references, right-click on the joint name in the BROWSER or in the Timeline and select **Edit Joint**. The EDIT JOINT palette opens and you can change any of original settings.

- To clear the display of the Joint icon in the graphics window, locate the joint name in the *Joints* folder in the BROWSER and select ♀ (yellow lightbulb) so that it changes to white. Select it again to toggle the icon back to yellow and display the joint. To clear all Joint icons at once, toggle the ♀ adjacent to the *Joints* folder.

- If a component is able to move, you can lock the joint to temporarily disable its permitted degrees of freedom. This might help you to create additional bodies or test or add other Joints. To lock a joint, locate the joint in the BROWSER or Timeline, right-click the joint name, and select **Lock**. To unlock a joint, right-click on the joint name and select **Unlock**.

- Joints can be temporarily suppressed by right-clicking on the joint name in the BROWSER and selecting **Suppress**. Suppressed joints are displayed in dark gray in the BROWSER to easily identify them.

- Once a joint is assigned, you can animate its available motion (including any set limits) in the BROWSER by right-clicking on the joint name and selecting **Animate Joint**. To stop the animation, press <Esc>.

- To return a component to its home location, in the BROWSER, right-click on the joint's name and select **Go to Home position**. The Home position is the location where you initially placed the component when you added it to the design.

Practice 14a Creating a Distributed Design

Practice Objectives

- Use the **Joint** command to fully connect components.
- Drag components to verify the movement of the design.

In this practice, you will create a new assembly and insert the components as shown in Figure 14–20. The fasteners that are used will be inserted from the McMaster-Carr library, and the remaining components will be inserted from files that have been provided. You will also use the **Joint** tool to join components relative to one another.

Figure 14–20

Task 1 - Upload the components that will be used in the assembly design.

In this task you will begin the creation of an assembly design by loading all of the models that will be used into your Autodesk Fusion 360 project. This is an alternate method to opening the design from file and is a convenient method of uploading multiple files. The models that will be used each contain a single body and were created by importing geometry from the Autodesk® Inventor® software.

1. In the Application Bar at the top of the interface, click ▦ (Show Data Panel). Ensure that **Autodesk Fusion 360 Practice Files** is the active project.

2. At the top of the Data Panel, click (New Folder). Enter **Wheel_Assembly** as the name of the new folder.

3. Double-click on the *Wheel_Assembly* folder to open it.

4. At the top of the Data Panel, click (Upload).

5. In the Select files to upload dialog box, click **Select Files**. Navigate to the practice files folder on your local drive and select the four files in the *Wheel_Assembly* folder. Click **Open**.

6. Click **Upload** to begin the upload. The Upload progress window displays the progress of the upload.

7. Once the files have been uploaded, click **Close** in the Upload progress window. The files should display as shown in Figure 14–21.

Figure 14–21

Task 2 - Create a new design and insert the first grounded component into the design.

In this task you will insert the first component into a new design. This is one of the methods for creating a multi-component design (assembly). In a future task you will insert additional components and assign Joints to constrain the components to one another.

1. In the **File** menu, create a new design by clicking **New Design**.

2. The components cannot be inserted into the new design until it is saved. Save the new design as **Wheel_Assembly**. Ensure that the *Save to a project in the cloud* drop-down list is set to **Autodesk Fusion 360 Practice Files > Wheel_Assembly**. If not, expand the drop-down list and double-click on the project and folder to select them. Click **Save**.

3. In the Data Panel, right-click on **Plate** and select **Insert into Current Design**, as shown in Figure 14–22.

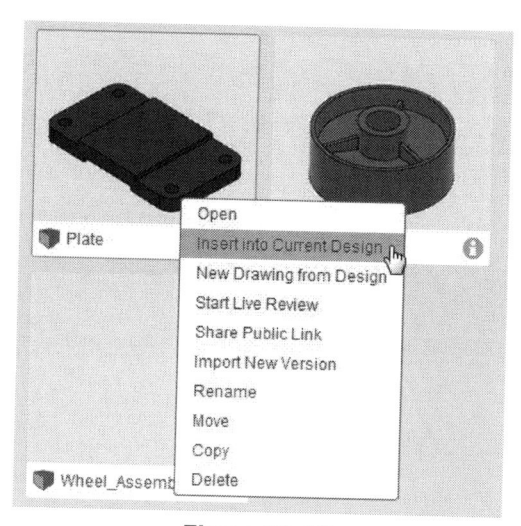

Figure 14–22

4. The component is inserted and the Move tool is immediately active. The default location for this component is satisfactory, so click **Cancel** to close the MOVE palette.

A grounded part is fixed to a location in the design and is not dependent on other parts.

5. In the BROWSER, right-click on the **Plate v1:1** component and select **Ground**, as shown in Figure 14–23. This sets the plate component as the grounded component in the assembly. The **Plate v1:1** component is used as the grounded component because it is the foundation component in the design and does not move.

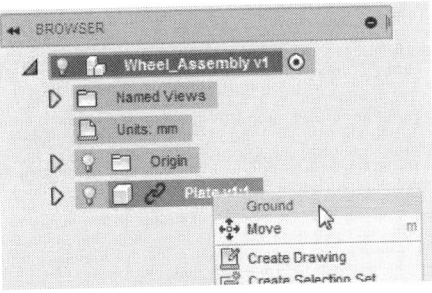

Figure 14–23

6. In the BROWSER, note that the Plate component has been added with [icon] and [icon] next to it. The [icon] indicates that the component is grounded, while the [icon] indicates that the component has been inserted from a source file and a cross-reference has been created. The model displays as shown in Figure 14–24.

*Inserted components maintain their link to the original component unless the link is explicitly broken. To break the link, right-click on the filename in the BROWSER and select **Break Link**.*

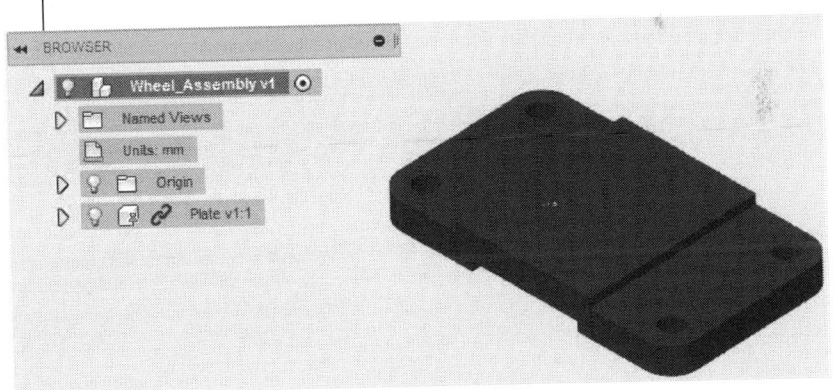

Figure 14–24

Task 3 - Add another part and add a joint to locate it in the assembly.

In this task, you will insert the **Bracket** component and assign a Rigid joint. Once inserted and placed, the assembly should display as shown in Figure 14–25.

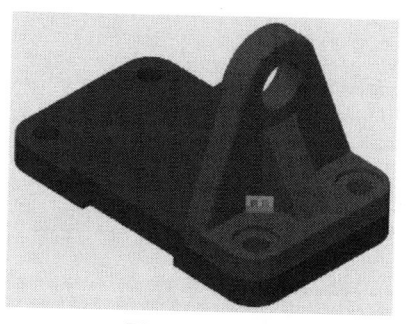

Figure 14–25

1. In the Data Panel, right-click on **Bracket** and select **Insert into Current Design**.

2. Using the Move triad that automatically displays, move the component similar to that shown in Figure 14–26 using both linear and rotational movements. This orientation makes reference selection easier when placing the joint. In the MOVE palette, click **OK** once the orientation is set.

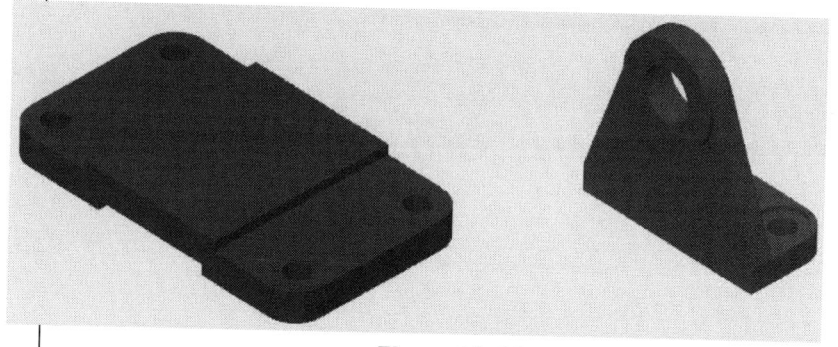

Figure 14–26

3. In the graphics window, select the bracket and drag it around the screen using the cursor. Note how the part moves freely. Now try and move the plate. This component will not move because it is grounded.

4. In the POSITION panel, click (Revert) to return the bracket component to the original location.

5. In the ASSEMBLE panel, click (Joint). The JOINT palette opens as shown in Figure 14–27.

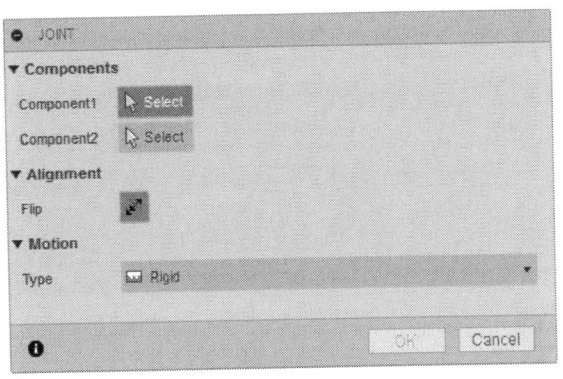

Figure 14–27

6. Note that **Rigid** is the set as the default joint type in the *Motion* area.

7. You will join the two components so that all of the degrees of freedom are removed. Keep the default **Rigid** selection and note that the **Plate** component is dimmed, indicating that it cannot be selected as the first component reference because it is grounded.

8. The *Component1* field is active by default. Hover the cursor over the bottom edge of the Bracket component, as shown in Figure 14–28. Move the cursor and note that even with slight movements, the back face can become active. Ensure that the edge is active and hold <Ctrl>. This locks reference selection to the edge, while still enabling you to move the cursor to activate other snap-points on the edge. Once the midpoint of the edge is active as the joint origin, select it using the left mouse button.

Once you have assigned a joint, that Type becomes the default until the software is restarted.

Select the midpoint of this edge as the joint origin reference for Component1.

Figure 14–28

Consider holding <Ctrl> as you are locating the snap-point for the second reference.

9. **Plate** is no longer dimmed in the assembly and the *Component2* field is active. Hover the cursor over the edge shown in Figure 14–29. Once the midpoint of the edge is active as the joint origin, click to select it.

Select the midpoint of the edge as the joint origin reference for Component2.

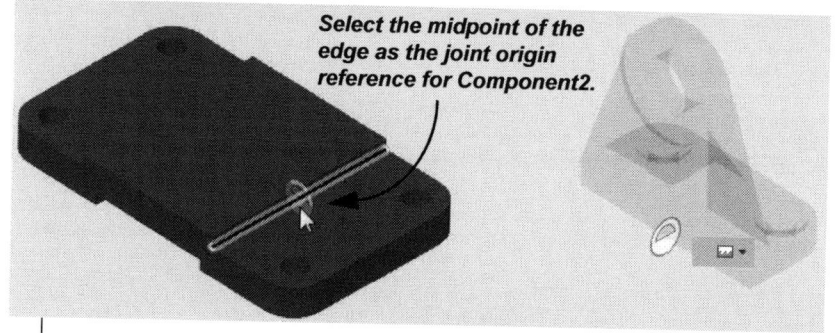

Figure 14–29

Reference Selection

While the edge on *Component2* was selected to locate the Bracket, the circular edges on each component could also be selected to ensure hole alignment.

The first component selected is the one that moves to the second component once both references are selected.

10. The **Bracket** component moves into position. A slight shaking animated motion is shown indicating the Rigid joint.
    - If the component is oriented incorrectly, review the component references to ensure that the midpoint of the edges were selected. Alternatively, click (Flip) to flip the component or enter an *Angle* value to rotate it into position. The final position should be as shown in Figure 14–30.
    - Note the linear and rotational handle that display on the model. These enable you to set an offset between the two joint origins or rotate about them. In this case, no further manipulations are required.

Angle and Offset values can be set in the JOINT palette, in the entry field in the graphics window, or by dragging the linear and rotational handles.

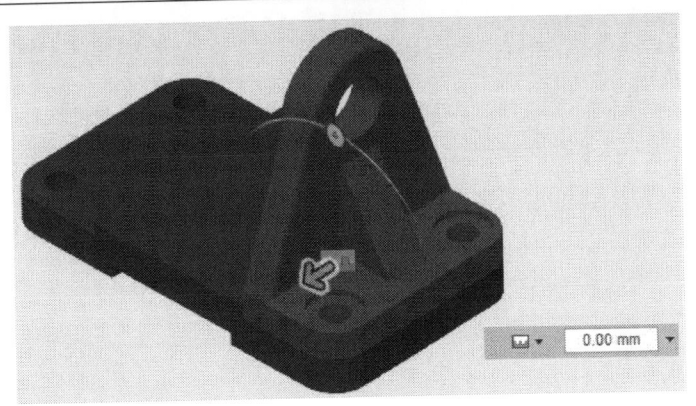

Figure 14–30

11. To replay the animation, in the *Motion* area, click ▶. Click ■ to stop the animation.

12. In the JOINT palette, click **OK** to complete the creation of the rigid joint. Figure 14–31 shows the joined components with the Rigid Joint icon ( ) displayed.

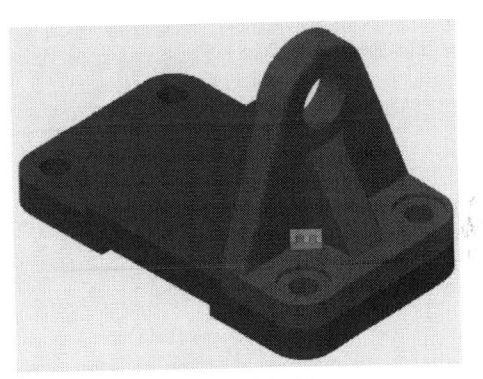

Figure 14–31

13. Select and try to drag the Bracket component. Note that you cannot drag the component.

Task 4 - Add a second instance of the Bracket component.

In this task, you will add and join another instance of the Bracket component into the assembly. The final placement of the component in the assembly is shown in Figure 14–32.

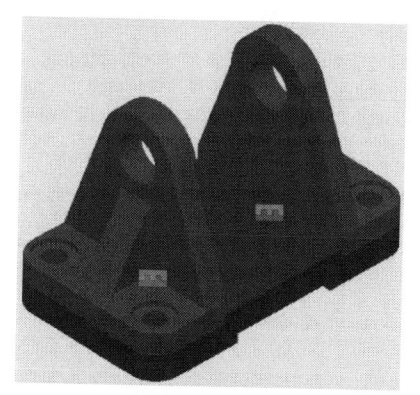

Figure 14–32

1. In the Data Panel, right-click on **Bracket** and select **Insert into Current Design**. Alternatively, you can:
   - Right-click on the existing **Bracket** component in the BROWSER and select **Copy**. Then, in the graphics window, right-click and select **Paste**.
   - Select and drag the component from the Data Panel into the graphics window.

2. Reorient the assembly and use the Move triad to arrange the components similar to that shown in Figure 14–33.

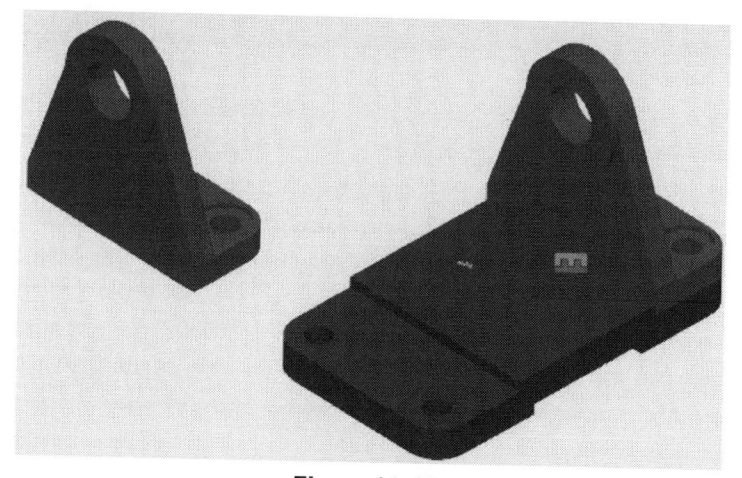

Figure 14–33

3. In the ASSEMBLE panel, click (Joint). The JOINT palette opens. Note that **Rigid** is still set as the default *Type* in the *Motion* area because that was the last joint type that was assigned.

4. The *Component1* field is active by default. Select the snap-point at the middle of the bottom edge on **Bracket v1:2**, as shown in Figure 14–34.

5. For the *Component2* reference, select the snap-point at the middle of the edge on the Plate, as shown in Figure 14–34.

Select the midpoints of the two edges as the joint origin references.

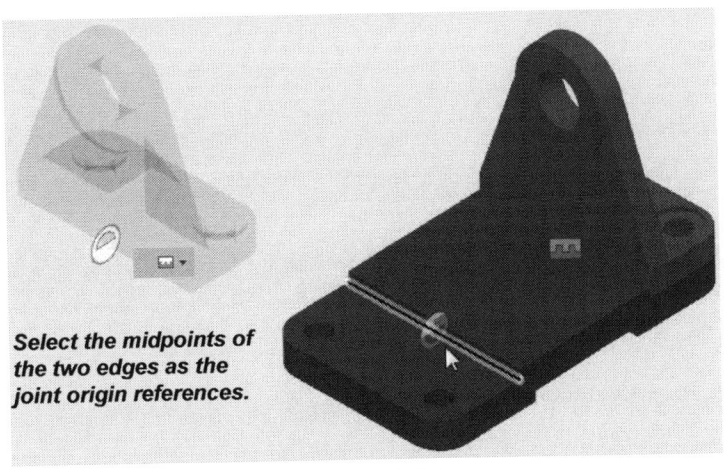

Figure 14–34

6. Based on the orientation of the joint origins, the components might not align correctly. Select (Flip) to flip the Bracket or enter a 180° rotation value to position the component correctly.

7. In the JOINT palette, click **OK** to complete the creation of the rigid joint, as shown in Figure 14–35. Note that two Rigid Joint icons display on the model, identifying how the components are joined.

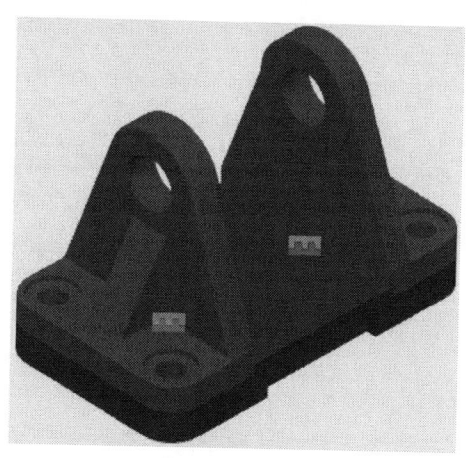

Figure 14–35

Task 5 - Insert and join the Axle component.

1. In the Data Panel, insert the **Axle** component into the assembly design using one of the techniques previously discussed.

2. Use the MOVE palette to move the component into a more convenient orientation, similar to that shown in Figure 14–36. Click **OK**.

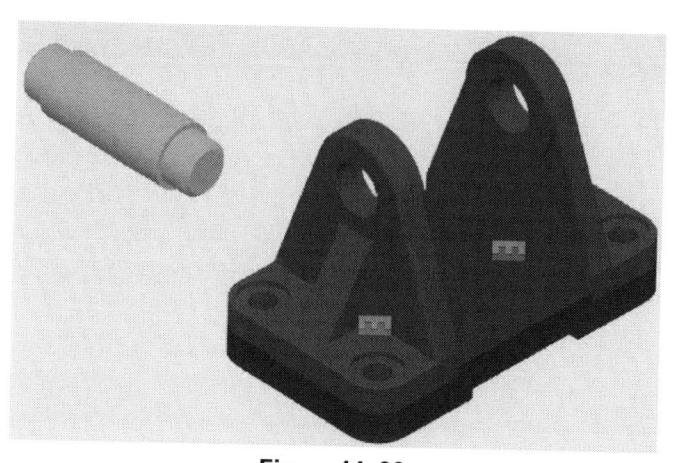

Figure 14–36

3. In the INSPECT panel, click ▭ (Measure). The MEASURE palette opens. Select the two circular faces on each of the **Bracket** components (shown in blue in Figure 14–37) to measure the distance between them. The value **57.00mm** should display in the graphics window. This value is required to join the axle.

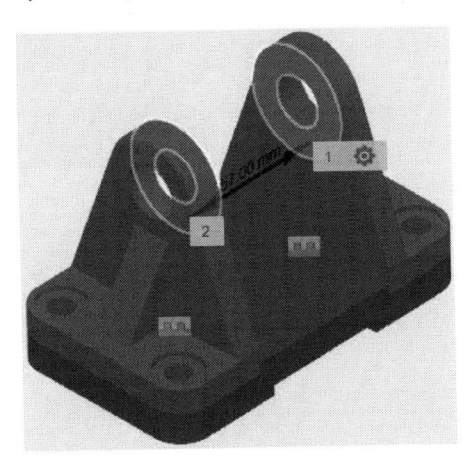

Figure 14–37

4. Initiate the creation of a new joint. In the *Type* drop-down list, ensure that the **Revolute** type is selected. The two components will be joined so that a single rotational degree of freedom remains.

5. For the *Component1* reference, select the snap-point at the middle of the central axis of the **Axle** component. The joint origin displays as shown in Figure 14–38.

6. For the *Component2* reference, select the snap-point at the end of the cylindrical face of **Bracket v1:1**, as shown in Figure 14–38.

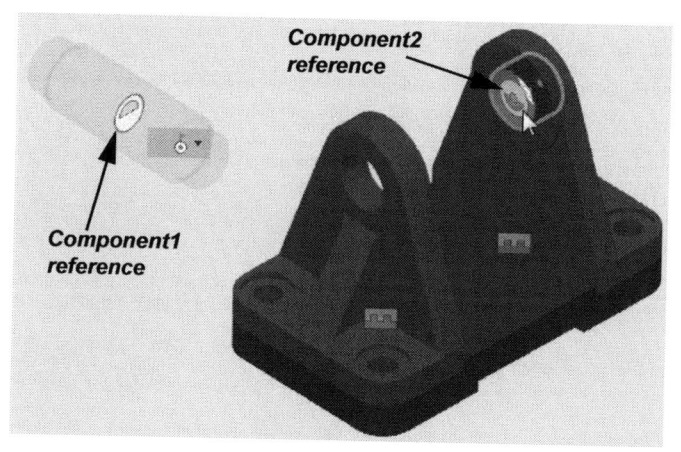

Figure 14–38

7. Once the components move into position, the **Axle** displays as shown in Figure 14–39.

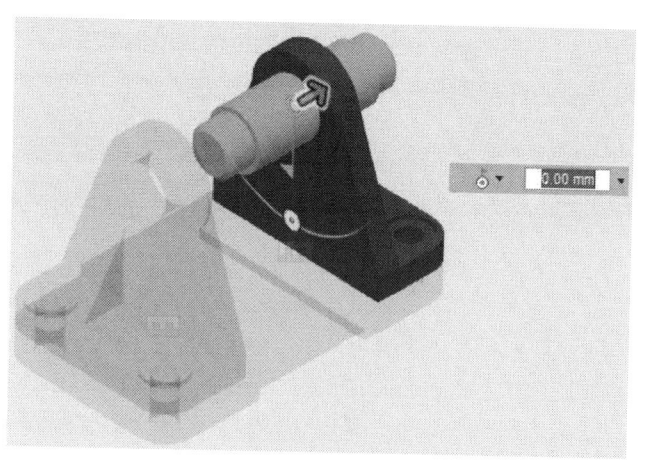

Figure 14–39

8. You must offset the two joint origins to position the **Axle** correctly. Enter **-28.5 mm** as the *Offset* value (i.e., half of the distance between the two brackets). With the arrow manipulator active (blue), you can enter the value in the entry field in the graphics window, or in the JOINT palette in the *Offset* field.

9. Note that the **Z Axis** is automatically selected as the *Rotate* reference for the joint. This is the correct motion, so selecting an alternate axis in the drop-down list is not required.

10. Click ▶ in the *Motion* area to play the motion. Note that the Axle rotates fully. Click ■ to stop the animated motion.

11. Click **OK** to create the joint. Note that the Revolute icon is displayed in the graphics window, as shown in Figure 14–40.

Figure 14–40

Task 6 - Review the joints in the design and rename them.

1. In the BROWSER, expand the *Joints* folder. Note that all three existing joints are listed.

2. The Timeline displays as shown in Figure 14–41. These icons represent the four inserted components, the three Joints, and when the ground constraint was assigned to the **Plate** component.

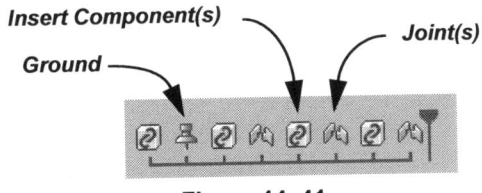

Figure 14–41

In general, selecting the constraints is easier in the Joints folder.

3. In the Timeline, you can individually identify the joints by hovering over the Joint icons to reveal their names, or by selecting them to highlight the joint the graphics window.

Renaming the joints helps identify them once multiple joints are added to the design.

4. Click twice on the **Rev3** joint in the *Joints* folder to rename it. Enter **Axle** as the new name.

5. The icons that identify the joint type can be toggled off in the graphics window, if required. In the *Joints* folder, select the 💡 (yellow lightbulb) adjacent to the two rigid joints to clear them from the display. Figure 14–42 shows the BROWSER and model after renaming the axle joint and hiding the icons from the display.

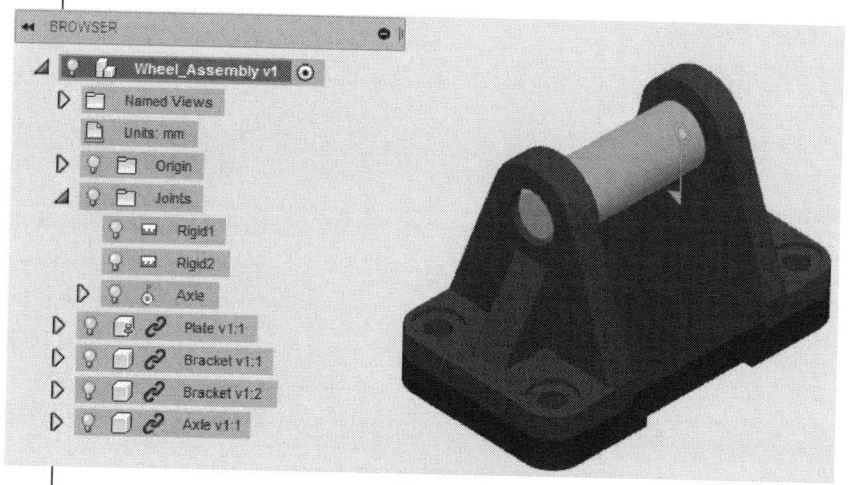

Figure 14–42

Task 7 - Modify an existing joint in the design.

As the wheel on the axle is required to rotate, and not the axle itself, edit the Axle joint to make it rigid.

1. In the BROWSER, right-click on the **Axle** joint and select **Edit Joint**.

2. In the Type drop-down menu, select **Rigid** to prevent the component from moving. Click **OK**.

3. Hide the Rigid icon from the display.

Task 8 - Insert the Wheel component.

1. Insert the Wheel component and join it as shown in Figure 14–43.
    - Assign the joint that permits rotation about the **Axle**. No translational motion is required.
    - Remember to select the **Wheel** as the first reference so that it moves onto the **Axle** once reference selection is complete.
    - When selecting the reference on the **Wheel**, consider holding <Ctrl> to ensure that the correct snap-point is selected so that the midpoint on the **Axle** and the **Wheel** are selected.
    - Ensure that the *Offset* and *Angle* values are set to **0**.

Figure 14–43

Task 9 - Insert the Screw components using a McMaster-Carr Component.

In this task you will retrieve a component from the McMaster-Carr library and use its CAD model in the design.

1. Expand the INSERT panel and select (Insert McMaster-Carr Component).

2. If you are prompted that the use of this feature will connect you to an external website, click **OK**. This website contains standard library parts that can be purchased, or you can download a SOLIDWORKS or STEP file for use in your design.

If you know the component number that is required, you can search for it. In this task you will use the 91290A526 component.

3. In the INSERT MCMASTER-CARR COMPONENT palette, a list of categories display. Select the **Fastening & Joining** category. On the right, select **Screws & Bolts**.

4. In the Screws list, select the **Socket Cap Screws** category.

5. Select **Alloy Steel Socket Head Cap Screws**, as shown in Figure 14–44.

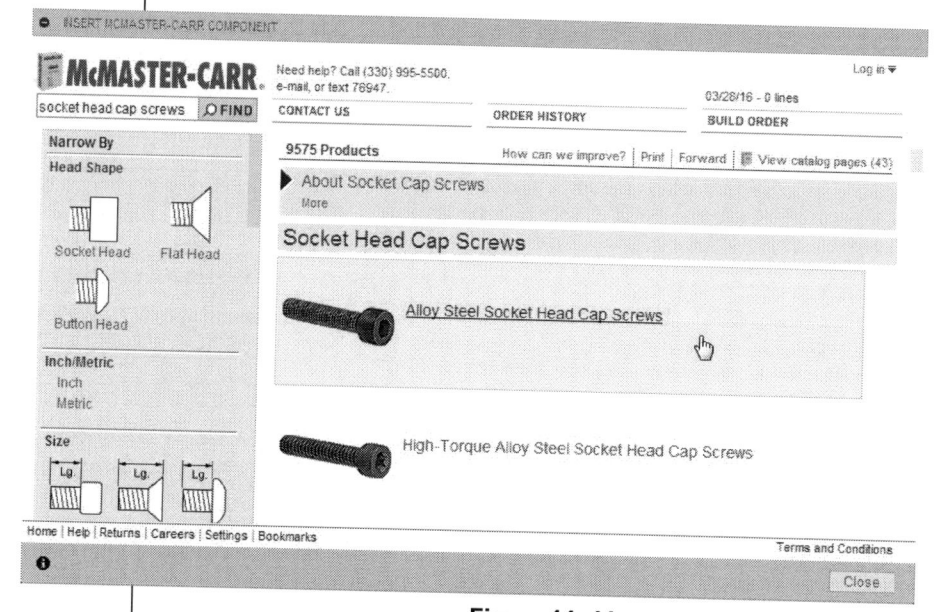

Figure 14–44

6. In the *Narrow By* area on the left side of the palette, scroll down.

7. In the *Thread Size* list, select **M10**.

8. In the *Length* list, select **35 mm**.

9. In the *Thread* area, select **Full Threads**.

10. In the list of components, scroll down and select the **91290A526** component in the list of cap screws that meet the criteria. The part number that is to be selected is highlighted in blue.

11. You can enter order details, if you are required to purchase the model. In this practice you will only be downloading a copy of the CAD data for use in your design.

12. In the expanded *Order* area, click **Product Detail**.

You can continue to select additional criteria in the Narrow By list to refine the results that are displayed, as required.

13. Scroll down. In the list of CAD formats, select **3-D STEP** and then click **SAVE**.

14. The model is inserted into the design and the MOVE palette displays. Move the component so that you can more easily select references and assign a joint. Click **OK**.

15. Begin the creation of a new joint. When prompted that some components have been moved, click **Capture Position**. This ensures that the component remains where it is for component reference selection. This is done by adding a Component Move action to the Timeline.

16. In the JOINT palette, set the *Type* to **Rigid** to permit no degree of freedom (Rigid). Define the joint origins to locate the component as it is shown in Figure 14–45.

To ensure that the cap screw is inserted correctly, conduct a Section Analysis. Hint: create a plane to conduct this analysis.

Figure 14–45

17. In the Timeline, right-click on (Capture Position) (the second to last icon) and select **Delete** to remove it. Now that the component is constrained, the icon is not needed.

18. In the BROWSER, right-click on the **91290A526:1** component and select **Copy**. In the graphics window, right-click and select **Paste**. Move the new component so that it does not overlay the source component.

19. Copy and paste two additional **91290A526** components.

20. Add Rigid joints so that the design displays as shown in Figure 14–46. All Rigid joint icons have been removed from the display.

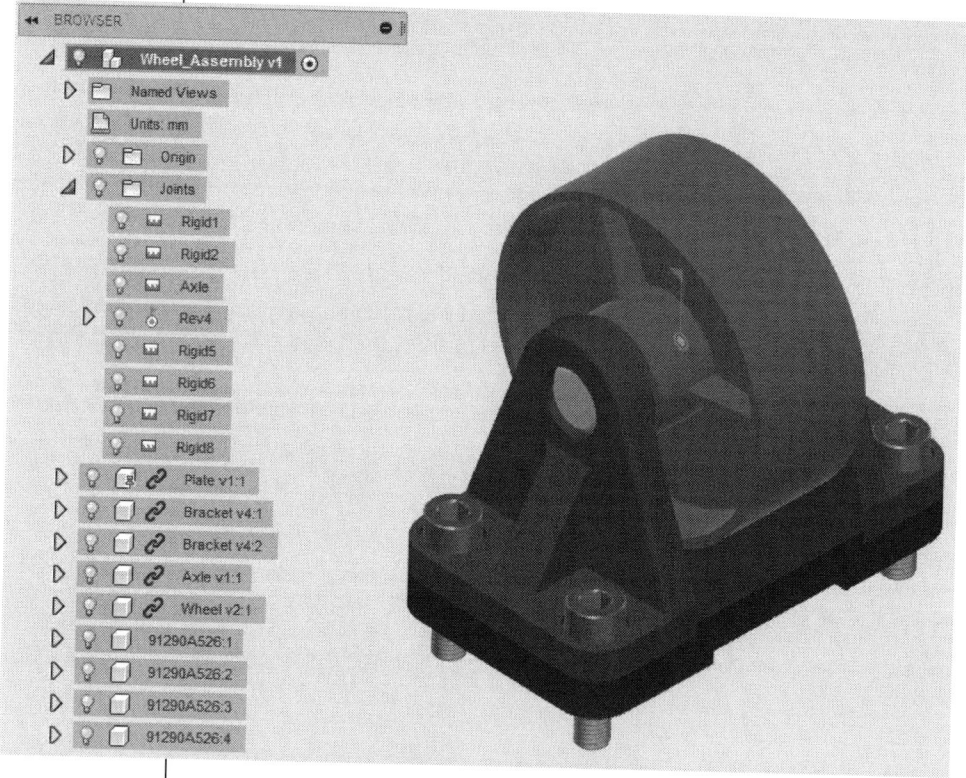

Figure 14–46

Task 10 - Make a design change and update the components.

In this task you will make a design change to the **Bracket** component and review how the change affects the assembly.

1. Right-click on one of the **Bracket** components in the BROWSER and select **Open**. The model opens in its own window.

2. Use the **Press Pull** tool to modify the height and width of the rib (3 faces) so that it is similar to that shown in Figure 14–47.

Use the Press Pull tool to modify the size of the three faces on this rib feature.

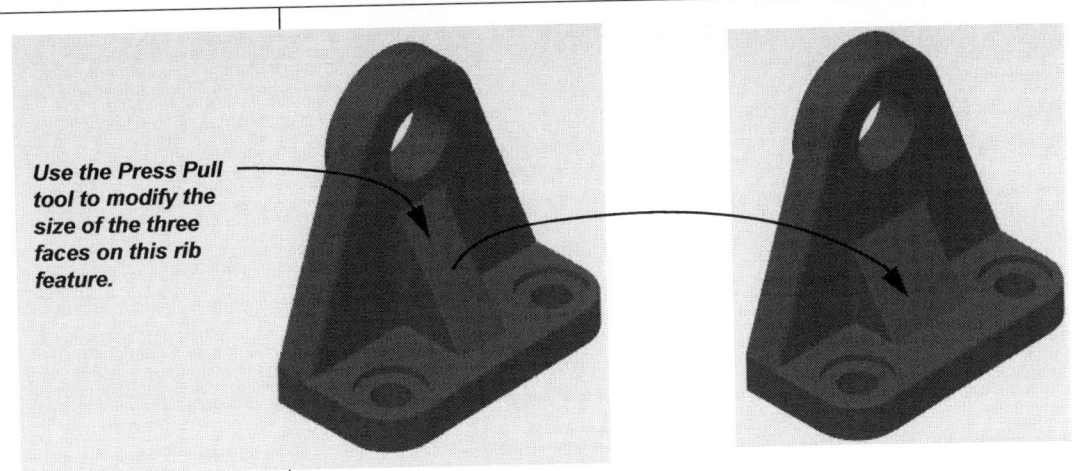

Figure 14–47

3. Save the design.

4. Return to the **Wheel_Assembly** tab. Note that the BROWSER indicates that the components and the top-level assembly are out-of-date (⚠), as shown in Figure 14–48.

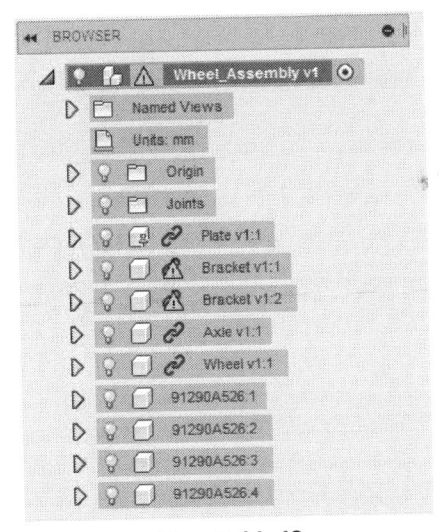

Figure 14–48

*If multiple components are displaying as out-of-date, right-click on the assembly name and select **Get All Latest** to update all of the components at once.*

5. Right-click on **Bracket v1** and select **Get Latest**. Note how the assembly updates to reflect the change to the **Bracket** component.

6. Save the design to your Autodesk Fusion 360 Practice Files project.

7. Close the file.

Chapter Review Questions

1. Which assembly design method best describes the process where components are individually inserted into a design and a reference is established between the two files?
    a. Distributed design
    b. Multi-body design

2. When selecting a joint origin during joint assignment, which button can you use to lock the selection to a single entity, making it easier to select one of the various snap-points on that entity?
    a. <Esc>
    b. <Shift>
    c. <Ctrl>
    d. <Spacebar>

3. Which of the following icons identifies a Grounded component in the BROWSER?
    a.
    b.
    c.
    d.

4. When working in an assembly where all of the components are inserted and reference a source component, you can create a joint origin that is stored at the assembly level.
    a. True
    b. False

5. To suppress a joint in an assembly design, locate the joint name in the BROWSER and select the (yellow lightbulb) so that it changes to white.
    a. True
    b. False

6. Match the joint type in the column on the left with its icon.

    a. Rigid
    b. Revolute
    c. Slider
    d. Cylindrical
    e. Planar
    f. Ball

Icon	Answer

7. Match the joint type with the degrees of freedom that remain in the component after it has been assigned.

    a. Rigid
    b. Revolute
    c. Slider
    d. Cylindrical
    e. Planar
    f. Ball

Degrees of Freedom	Answer
1 Translational, 1 Rotational	
2 Translational, 1 Rotational	
0 Translational, 0 Rotational	
0 Translational, 3 Rotational	
1 Translational, 0 Rotational	
0 Translational, 1 Rotational	

Answers: 1.a, 2.c, 3.d, 4.b, 5.b 6.(f,e,b,a,d,c), 7.(d,e,a,f,c,b)

Command Summary

Button	Command	Location
N/A	Animate Joint	• **BROWSER:** *Context Menu with a joint name selected*
N/A	Delete (Joint)	• **BROWSER:** *Context Menu with a joint name selected* • **Timeline:** *Context Menu with a joint icon selected*
N/A	Edit Joint	• **BROWSER:** *Context Menu with a joint name selected* • **Timeline:** *Context Menu with a joint icon selected*
N/A	Get All Latest	• **BROWSER:** *Context Menu with a component name selected*
N/A	Get Latest	• **BROWSER:** *Context Menu with a component name selected*
N/A	Go to Home Position	• **BROWSER:** *Context Menu with a joint name selected*
N/A	Ground	• **BROWSER:** *Context Menu with a component name selected*
N/A	Insert into Current Design	• **Data Panel:** *Context Menu with a component's thumbnail image selected*
	Joint	• **Ribbon:** *Model Workspace>ASSEMBLE panel* • **Context Menu**: Right-click in the graphics window and select **Assemble**
	Joint Origin	• **Ribbon:** *Model Workspace>ASSEMBLE panel* • **Context Menu**: Right-click in the graphics window and select **Assemble**

Chapter 15

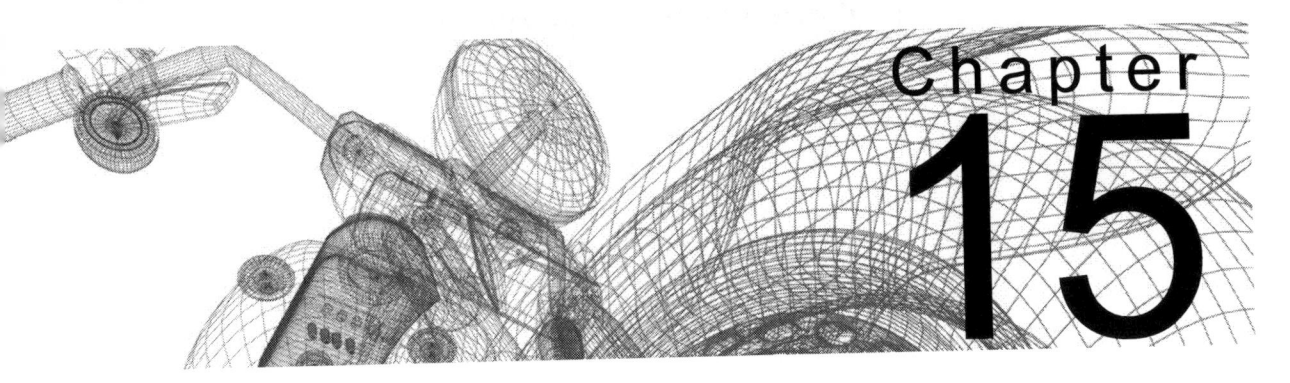

Component Design Tools

Once you have learned how to insert and join components in a design, there are additional tools that can be used to further control a component's range of motion. These tools enable you to further limit motion to that which is permitted with the joint itself. Additional tools (such as interference analysis tools, Motion Linking, and Motion Studies) can also be incorporated into a design to simulate and test its motion.

Learning Objectives in this Chapter

- Fully constrain components relative to one another using a rigid group.
- Conduct an interference analysis between components in a design.
- Assign limits to a joint to further control its range of motion.
- Define the location of a component within its range of motion.
- Incorporate Contact Analysis into a design to limit a component's range of motion.
- Establish relationships between components that move relative to one another using the Motion Linking tool.
- Conduct a motion study.

15.1 Rigid Groups

The use of rigid groups in a multi-component design enables you to fix multiple components together so that they do not move relative to one another. Rigid groups are ideal in the following situations:

- When no mechanical movement exists between components, using rigid groups avoids having to add multiple rigid joints to remove all degrees of freedom.

- When inserting imported assembly geometry from another CAD format, rigid groups can quickly constrain all of the components that do not move relative to one another.

The Spindle design shown in Figure 15–1 was imported from Autodesk® Inventor®. The four part models represent a single subassembly that moves all as one, so a rigid group was created.

Timeline icon:

A single joint can be added between a rigid group and other components in the assembly to fully define its placement and motion requirements.

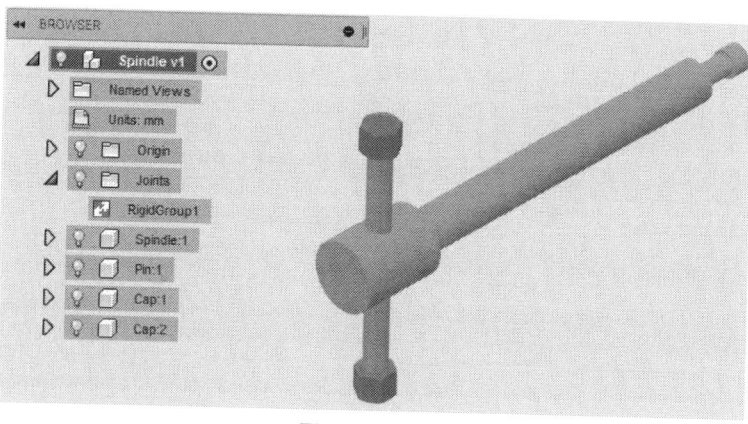

Figure 15–1

*Use the **Include Child Components** option to quickly select the children of selected components so that they do not have to be selected manually.*

- To create a rigid group, expand the ASSEMBLE panel and select ▢ (Rigid Group). Using the RIGID GROUP palette, select the components to add to the group in the BROWSER or in the graphics window, and then click **OK**.

- Rigid groups are stored in the **Joints** folder in the BROWSER and are identified with ▢ in the Timeline.

To edit a rigid group, right-click on the group you want to edit in the **Joints** folder or on the Timeline and select **Edit Rigid Group**.

Video Lesson Available

Creating Rigid Groups

Video Length: 3:46

Interference can occur when you are using either the distributed design or multi-body design approach.

15.2 Interference Detection

In a design that has multiple components, it is possible to position a component so that two components occupy the same space at the same time. To identify if components overlap, you can analyze the model for interference. To conduct an interference analysis, in the INSPECT panel, click ▣ (Interference).

Interference analyses are conducted between selected components. Components can be selected either in the graphics window or in the BROWSER. To run an interference analysis on all components, select all of them in the graphics window. Once analyzed, the results are displayed in the Interference Results dialog box and highlighted areas in the model indicate where interference is occurring, as shown in Figure 15–2.

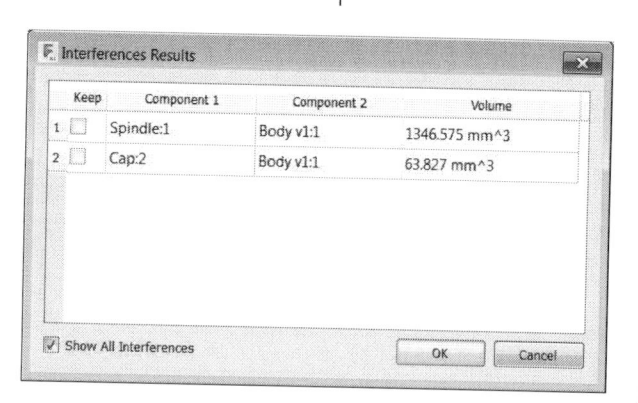

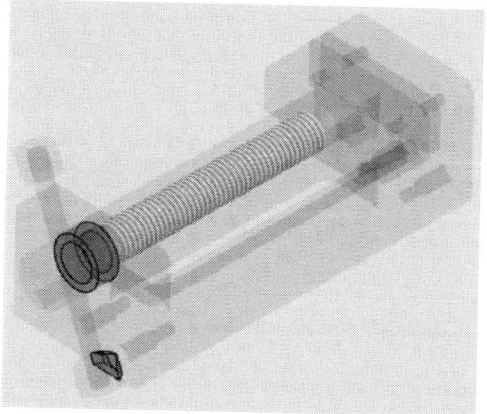

Figure 15–2

Video Lesson Available

Revealing Interferences in Your Design

Video Length: *3:16*

15.3 Miscellaneous Joint Tools

Joint Limits

To further control the motion that is permitted by a joint, you can define a specific range of motion to make the part more realistic and to limit the motion prior to when components come in contact. In the example shown in Figure 15–3, the cylinder tube was constrained to a pin using a revolute joint type, which defaults to permitting 360° of rotation. If this was permitted, interference would occur with other geometry.

Limits cannot be specified for where the degree of freedom does not exist in the model.

Cylinder tube

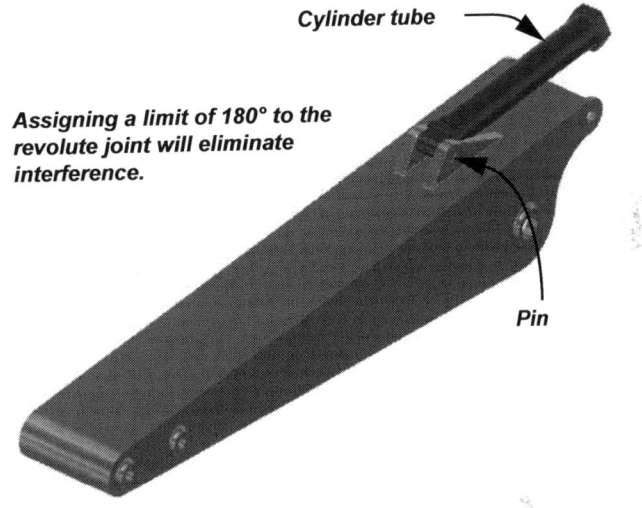

Assigning a limit of 180° to the revolute joint will eliminate interference.

Pin

Figure 15–3

To assign limits, in the **Joints** folder in the BROWSER or in the Timeline, right-click on a joint's name or icon and select **Edit Joint Limits**. Alternatively, in the BROWSER, hover the cursor over the joint name and select (Edit Joint Limits). The EDIT JOINT LIMITS palette opens as shown in Figure 15–4.

You can also locate a joint in the BROWSER and Timeline by hovering the cursor over the joint icon in the graphics window until it highlights.

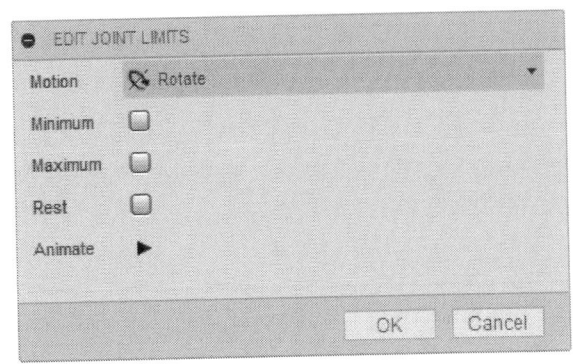

Figure 15–4

- Depending on the permitted range of motion for the joint that is being edited, the options available in the Motion drop-down list varies. For joints that have two or more degrees of freedom (DOF), select the joint that is to have limits set.

- To limit the motion in both directions for the set DOF, enable the **Minimum** and **Maximum** options. The Autodesk® Fusion 360™ software estimates these values based on when the components will come in contact. If these values are not satisfactory, enter new values.

- The values for the *Minimum* and *Maximum* fields can be entered manually, or you can drag the joint glyph in its range of motion to define the limits.

- The **Rest** option can be used to define a home position for the components referenced during the joint's reference assignment. Its values must be between the maximum and minimum values.

- Once the limits are set, click ▶ in the *Animate* area to play the animation and verify the limits.

Drive Joints

When testing the joint motion for a component, you can drag the component through its range of motion. To stop the motion at a specific point in its range, in the ASSEMBLY panel, use the **Drive Joints** tool. This tool enables you to enter a specific value for a selected joint, and moves the component to this position. This tool is ideal for positioning components for interference checking.

Video Lesson Available

Driving Joints

Video Length: 1:46

Contact Sets

One way to define the range of motion for a component is to assign joint limits. Another is to use the **Contact Sets** tool. When active, this tool analyzes for interference as you drag a component through its range of motion. Once contact is determined, motion is stopped. This method can be efficient as you do not have to manually calculate the required values used to set a joint limit, but can require significant computer processing power.

- You can use the Contact Sets tool to automatically analyze the interference between all of the components, or you can select specific components to define contact sets for analysis.

- It is recommended that contact analysis should be disabled unless you are testing movement.

Video Lesson Available

Understanding Contact Sets

Video Length: 4:48

Motion Linking

On the ASSEMBLE panel, the **Motion Link** tool enables you to set a relationship between the movement of two components. You can do this by relating the degrees of freedom of the joints that were used to constrain the components. When dragged, the components that have motion links established move based on the defined relationship. This can be used to simulate and study the motion in a design.

Video Lesson Available

Enabling Motion Linking

Video Length: 3:13

Motion Studies

In the Autodesk Fusion 360 software, you can create a motion study that enables you to simulate the motion in a design without dragging the components. A motion study runs over 100 steps where you can set values for the joints being studied to show how the design should move. Multiple joints can be added into a study and the position of each joint can be customized. When the motion study is played, the entire design is displayed in motion at once, enabling you to ensure that it has been set up correctly and is working as expected.

Video Lesson Available

Creating and Understanding Motion Studies

Video Length: 5:53

Practice 15a

Incorporating Motion Between Components in a Design

Practice Objectives

- Insert components in an design.
- Select and assign joints that capture the motion of the component in the overall design.
- Assign joint limits and contact sets to set the range of motion for components in the design.
- Conduct a motion study on the joints in the design.
- Add a motion link condition to joints in the design.

In this practice you will create a new design and insert components, as shown in Figure 15–5. To complete this design, you will create a rigid group, add joints, assign limits to a joint, and create a contact set to accurately define how the design moves. You will then create and conduct a motion study analysis to study the movement and add a motion link that relates the slider to the revolute joints.

Figure 15–5

Task 1 - Upload the components that will be used in the new design.

In this task you will prepare to create a design by loading all of the models that will be used into your Autodesk Fusion 360 project. All of the models are imported geometry from the Autodesk Inventor software.

1. In the Application Bar at the top of the interface, click ▦ (Show Data Panel). Verify that the active project is **Autodesk Fusion 360 Practice Files**. If it is not, return to the top-level folder for this project before continuing by selecting ⟁ in the Data Panel.

2. At the top of the Data Panel, click 📁 (New Folder). Type **Vise_Assembly** as the name of the new folder.

3. Double-click on the *Vise_Assembly* folder to open it.

4. At the top of the Data Panel, click ☁ (Upload).

5. In the Select files to upload dialog box, click **Select Files**. Navigate to the practice files folder on your computer and select the four files in the *Vise_Assembly* folder. Click **Open**.

6. Click **Upload** to begin the upload. The Upload progress window shows the progress of the upload.

7. Once the files have been uploaded, click **Close** in the Upload progress window. The files should display as shown in Figure 15–6.

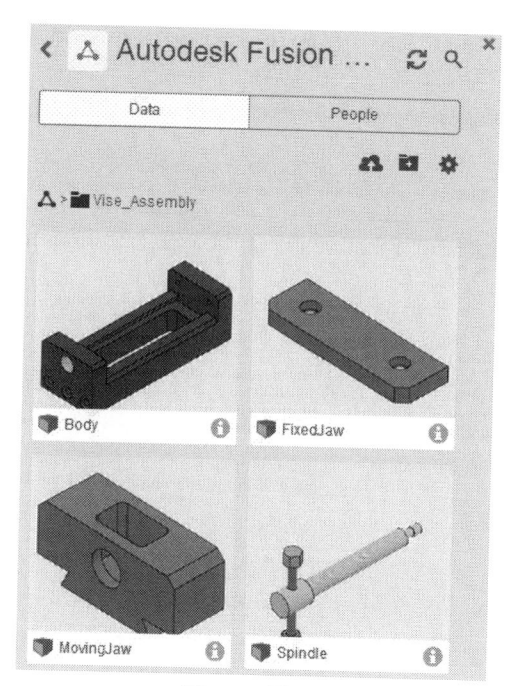

Figure 15–6

Task 2 - Create a new design and insert the first grounded component into the design.

In this task you will insert the first component into a new design and then ground the component.

1. In the **File** menu, create a new design using the **New Design** option.

2. Save the new design as **Vise_Assembly**. The components cannot be inserted into this design until it is saved. Ensure that the Save to a project in the cloud drop-down list is set to **Autodesk Fusion 360 Practice Files > Vise_Assembly**. If not, expand the drop-down list and double-click on the project and folder to select them. Click **Save**.

3. In the Data Panel, right-click on **Body** and select **Insert into Current Design**, as shown in Figure 15–7.

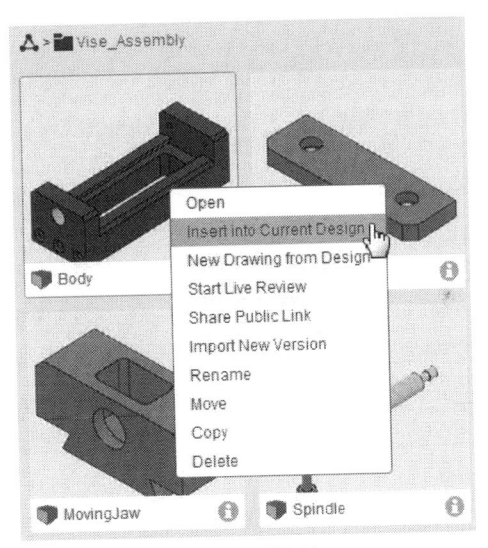

Figure 15–7

4. The component is inserted and the Move tool is activated. As the default location for this component is correct, close the MOVE palette by clicking **Cancel**.

A grounded part is fixed to a location in the assembly and is not dependent on other parts.

5. In the BROWSER, right-click on the **Body v1:1** component and select **Ground**, as shown in Figure 15–8. This sets the component as the grounded component in the assembly. This component should be grounded because it forms the foundation of the design and does not physically move relative to the other components in the design.

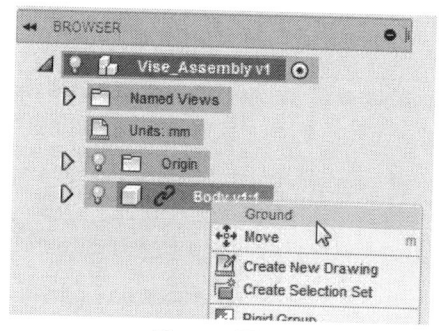

Figure 15–8

6. In the BROWSER, note that the Body component has been added with the 🔒 and 🔗 next to it. The 🔒 indicates that the component is grounded, and 🔗 indicates that the component has been inserted from a source file and a cross-reference has been created. The model displays as shown in Figure 15–9.

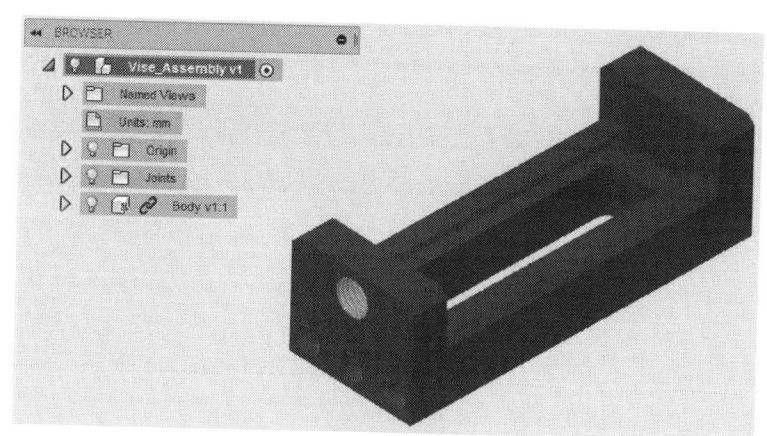

*Components that are inserted into a design maintain the link to the original component. The link can be broken in the BROWSER by right-clicking on the filename and selecting **Break Link**.*

Figure 15–9

Task 3 - Add and join the FixedJaw component.

In this task, you will add and join the FixedJaw component into the design. The final placement of the component is shown in Figure 15–10.

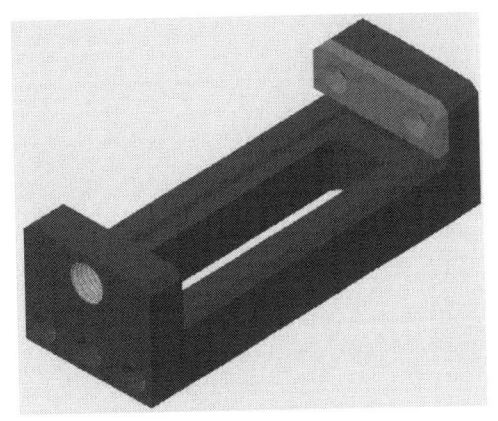

Figure 15–10

1. In the Data Panel, right-click on **FixedJaw** and select **Insert into Current Design**.

2. Using the Move triad, position the component similar to that shown in Figure 15–11. This places the component in a better location for assigning references during joint assignment. Click **OK**.

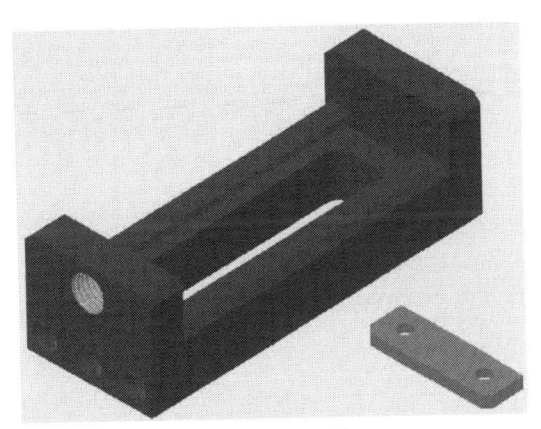

Figure 15–11

3. In the ASSEMBLE panel, click (Joint). The JOINT palette opens.

4. In the Type drop-down list, select **Rigid** (if not already selected by default). The FixedJaw component cannot move in the assembly, so the Rigid joint type is assigned.

5. The *Component1* field is active by default. Hover the cursor over the circular edge of the hole in the FixedJaw component, as shown in Figure 15–12. Once the centerpoint of the edge is active, click on the centerpoint to select it as the joint origin.

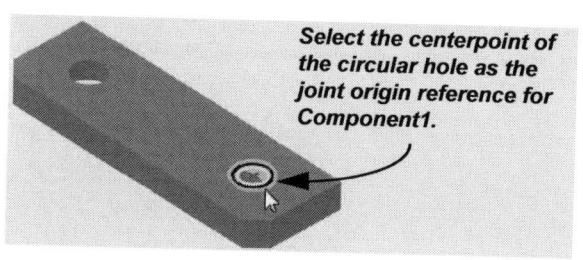

Select the centerpoint of the circular hole as the joint origin reference for Component1.

Figure 15–12

6. Hover the cursor over the circular edge of the hole in the Body component, as shown in Figure 15–13. Once the centerpoint of the edge is active, click on the centerpoint to select it as the joint origin.

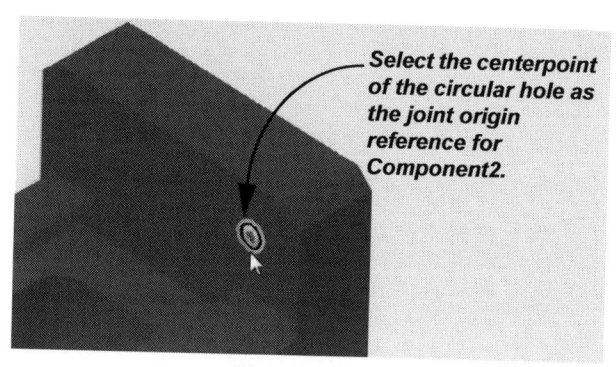

Select the centerpoint of the circular hole as the joint origin reference for Component2.

Figure 15–13

7. The FixedJaw component moves into position and a short animation of its motion is played. Because this is a rigid connection, the animated motion only shakes slightly, indicating that it has no degrees of freedom remaining.

8. Click **OK** in the JOINT palette to complete the creation of the rigid joint.

Task 4 - Add another component and add a joint to locate it in the design.

In this task, you will insert the MovingJaw component in the design and assign the Slider joint type. Once inserted and placed, the design should display as shown in Figure 15–14.

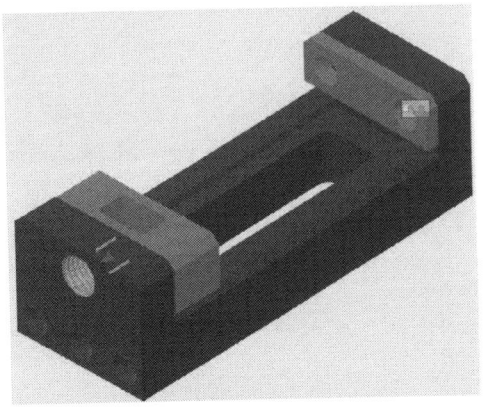

Figure 15–14

1. In the Data Panel, right-click on **MovingJaw** and select **Insert into Current Design**.

2. Using the Move triad, position the component similar to that shown in Figure 15–15. Click **OK**.

Moving components during an Insert operation can be useful to locate the component and enable easy selection of references during joint creation.

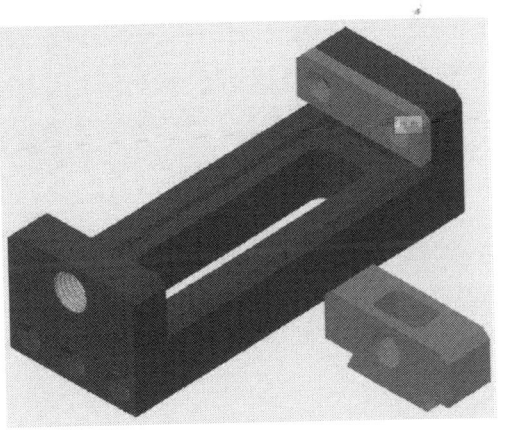

Figure 15–15

3. In the ASSEMBLE panel, click (Joint). The JOINT palette opens.

4. In the *Type* drop-down list, select **Slider**. This joint permits sliding so that the holes in the two components remain aligned.

5. The *Component1* field is active by default. Hover the cursor over the circular edge of the hole in the MovingJaw component, as shown in Figure 15–16. Once the centerpoint of the edge is active, click on centerpoint to select it as the joint origin.

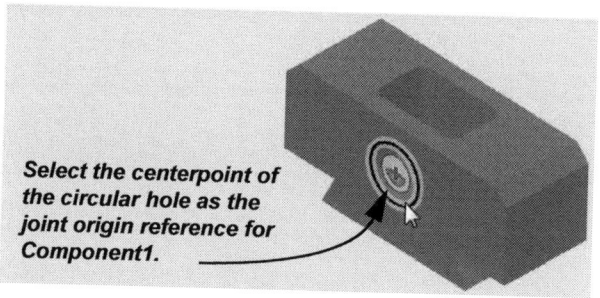

Select the centerpoint of the circular hole as the joint origin reference for Component1.

Figure 15–16

6. Rotate the design and hover the cursor over the circular edge of the hole in the Body component, as shown in Figure 15–17. Once the centerpoint of the edge is active, click on the centerpoint to select it as the joint origin.

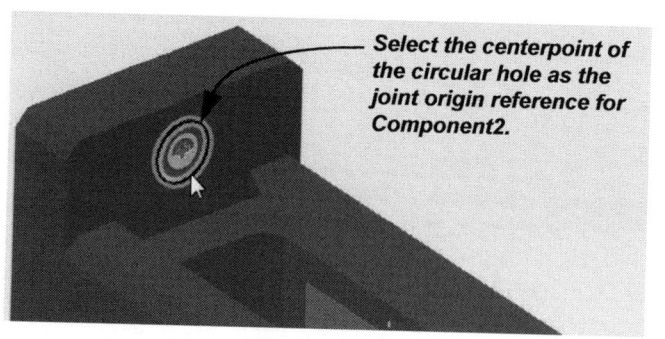

Select the centerpoint of the circular hole as the joint origin reference for Component2.

Figure 15–17

7. The MovingJaw component moves into position and a short animation of its motion is played. In the *Motion* area, ensure that the *Slide* option is set to **Z Axis** (if not, select it from the drop-down list). This ensures that sliding is permitted along the Z axis.

8. To replay the animation, in the *Motion* area, click ▶. Click ■ to stop the animated motion.

9. In the JOINT palette, click **OK** to complete the creation of the slider joint.

10. Select and drag the MovingJaw component. Note that you can drag the component through the Body component. In the next task you will learn how to constrain the movement.

11. In the POSITION panel, click (Revert) to return the MovingJaw component to the original location it was placed when it was inserted.

Note that the Rigid and Slider joint icons display on the model, helping to identify how the components are joined.

Task 5 - Define the range of motion for the MovingJaw component.

In this task you will learn how to assign limits to the motion of a component.

1. In the Timeline, right-click on the Slider joint that was added between the MovingJaw and Body components. Select **Edit Joint Limits**. Alternatively, in the BROWSER, you can expand the **Joints** folder, right-click on **Slider1**, and then select **Edit Joint Limits** or click (Edit Joint Limits) that displays adjacent to the joint name.

2. The EDIT JOINTS LIMITS palette opens. Note that the only permitted motion of this joint is sliding, as shown in the Motion drop-down list in Figure 15–18.

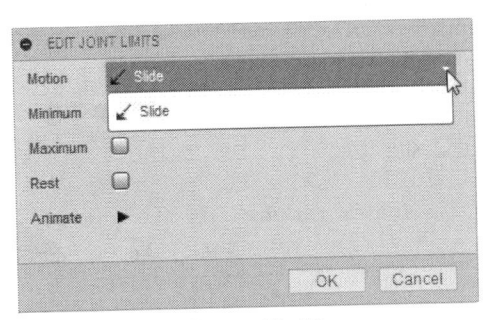

Figure 15–18

3. Select the **Minimum** and **Maximum** checkboxes to enable you to set limits on the range of motion.

---

*To toggle off the display of the Joint icons, in the BROWSER, select the ♀ associated with each joint in the **Joints** folder.*

Hovering over a joint name in the BROWSER highlights the joint in the Timeline.

4. In the Minimum drop-down list, select **Measure**. Measure the distance between the FixedJaw and MovingJaw components, as shown in Figure 15–19:
   1. Select the face of the FixedJaw component that will touch the MovingJaw component.
   2. On the MovingJaw component, select a reference on the face that the FixedJaw will touch.

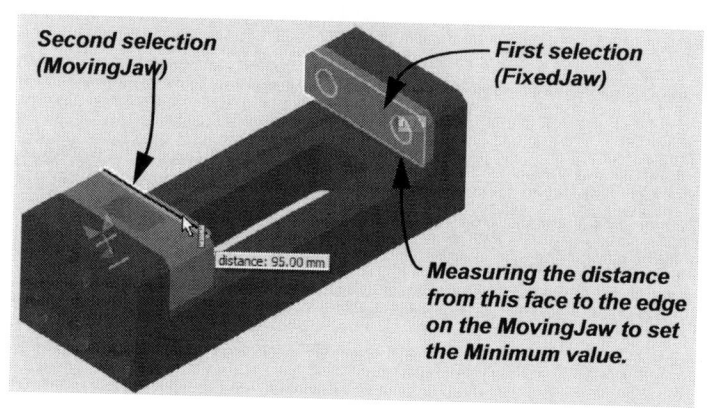

Figure 15–19

5. The *Minimum* field displays a value of **95.00 mm**. Change the value to **-95.00 mm**.

6. Enter **0.00 mm** in the *Maximum* value field.

7. In the *Animate* area, click ▶ to play the range of sliding motion. Click ■ to stop the animated motion.

8. Click **OK** to complete the limits.

9. Drag the MovingJaw component and note that it no longer moves through the Body component.

Task 6 - Insert the Spindle component and create a rigid group.

In this task, you will add the Spindle component and consider its design intent in the overall design. The Spindle component contains four design models and would be considered a subassembly in CAD terms. This was imported from Autodesk Inventor as a single model. Its design intent is that it moves as one. To accomplish this, you will define a Rigid Body.

When the Spindle was imported from the Autodesk Inventor software, the Autodesk Fusion 360 software retained the structure of the file. This is true for any imported CAD file (e.g. Inventor, SOLIDWORKS).

1. In the Data Panel, right-click on **Spindle** and select **Insert into Current Design**.

2. Move the component into a convenient location. Click **OK**.

3. Note that [icon] displays in the BROWSER, indicating that this component contains sub-components. Expand Spindle in the BROWSER to view the sub-components.

4. Select a component in the Spindle and note that it moves independently of the other components.

5. Click [icon] (Undo) in the Quick Access toolbar to undo the move.

To constrain all of the components to move together, either three rigid joints could be added, or the components could be created as a rigid group. In this practice you will use a rigid group.

6. In the ASSEMBLE panel, click [icon] (Rigid Group). The RIGID GROUP palette opens as shown in Figure 15–20.

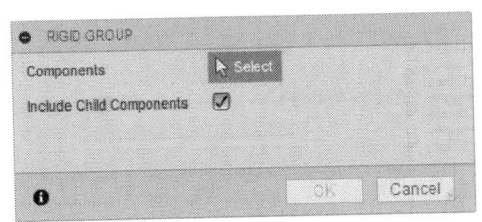

Figure 15–20

7. In the graphics window, select the four components that are in the Spindle design. The components highlight in blue, as shown in Figure 15–21.

Select all four components in the Spindle design.

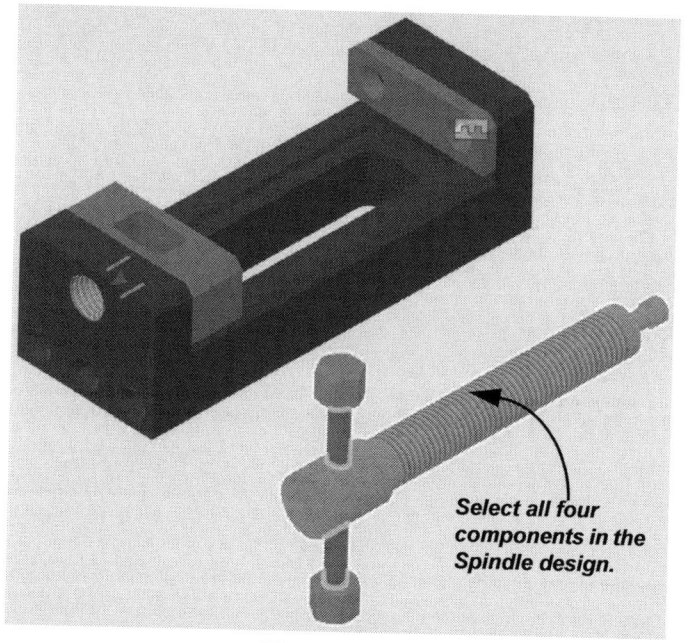

Figure 15–21

8. Click **OK** to create the rigid group. **RigidGroup1** is added to the **Joints** folder in the BROWSER, as shown in Figure 15–22.

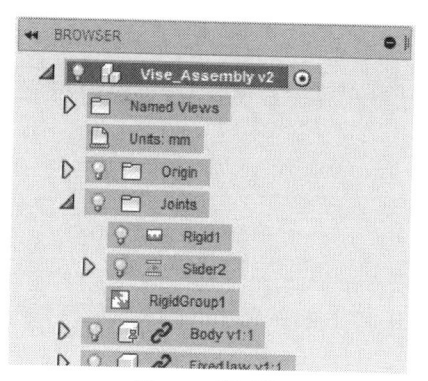

Figure 15–22

9. Rename the new group to **Spindle Rigid Group** to help you easily identify it in the BROWSER.

10. In the graphics window, try to select and drag any of the components in the Spindle. Note how the designs all move as one. At this point, only a single joint is needed to constrain the component to the rest of the design.

11. Return the components to their original position.

Task 7 - Add a joint between the Spindle and MovingJaw.

1. Drag the MovingJaw component into the middle of the Body component. This will help you to select the joint references for the Spindle.

2. In the ASSEMBLE panel, click (Joint).

3. When you are prompted that some of the components have been moved, click **Capture Position.** This ensures that the component remains where it is for component reference selection, and adds a (Component Move) action to the Timeline.

4. In the *Type* drop-down list, select **Revolute**. The Spindle component must rotate to move the MovingJaw component.

5. The *Component1* field is active by default. Hover the cursor over the circular edge at the end of the Spindle component, as shown in Figure 15–23. Once the centerpoint of the edge is active, click on the centerpoint to select it as the joint origin.

Select the centerpoint of the circular edge as the joint origin.

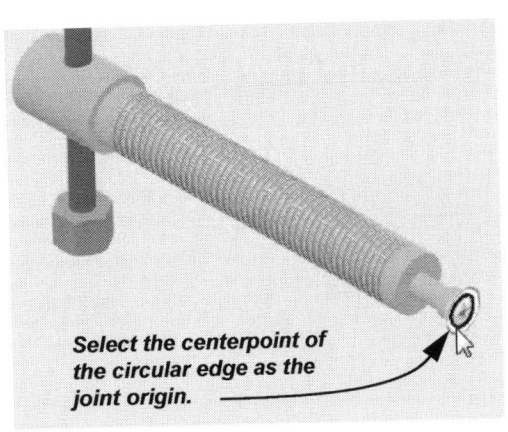

Figure 15–23

6. Hover the cursor over the face of the MovingJaw component that is shown in Figure 15–24. Once the centerpoint of the face is active, click on the centerpoint to select it as the joint origin.

Select the centerpoint of this face as the joint origin.

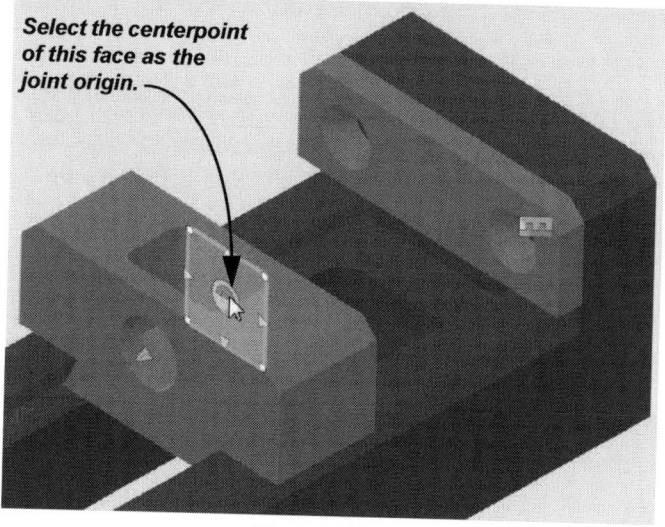

Figure 15–24

7. The spindle moves into position and a short animation of it rotating is displayed.

8. In the JOINT palette, click **OK** to complete the creation of the revolute joint. Note that all of the remaining components in the Spindle rigid group move into position to maintain the group.

9. Review the components. Note that there seems to be possible interference between the Spindle and MovingJaw components, as well as between the Spindle and the Body.

10. In the INSPECT panel, click (Interference). The INTERFERENCE palette opens.

11. Select the Spindle, MovingJaw, and Body components in the graphics window.

12. In the *Compute* area, click ▢ to run the analysis. The Interference Results dialog box and the model display as shown in Figure 15–25, indicating that there is interference. The interference occurs because the centerpoint on the face of the MovingJaw was not in line with the axis of the hole. A new joint origin must be created to place this component.

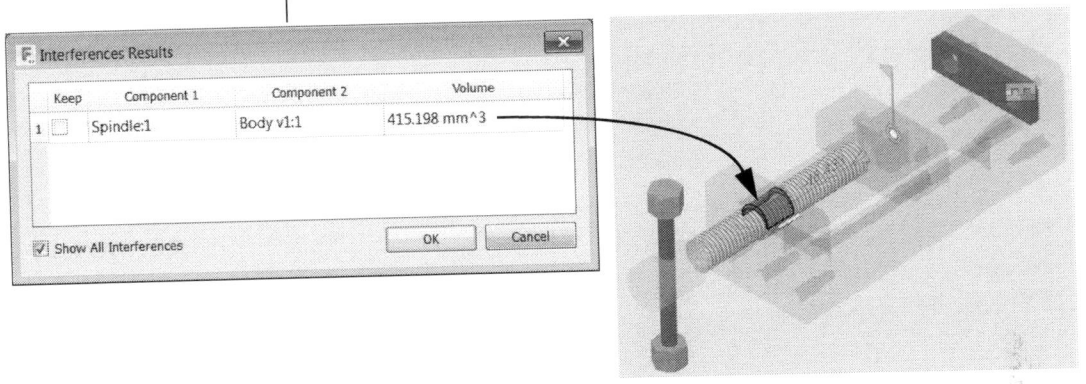

Figure 15–25

13. Click **OK** to close the Interference Results dialog box.

14. Right-click on the **Rev4** revolute joint that was created and select **Delete** to remove it.

Task 8 - Create a joint origin in the MovingJaw component.

In this task you will create a new joint origin. Since the design was created using the Distributed Design method, joint origins must be created in each individual design file so that it can be saved with the file. Once created, you will use this joint origin to create the joint.

1. In the BROWSER, right-click on **MovingJaw** and select **Open**. This opens this design in its own window.

2. Switch to the Model Workspace, if it is not already active. Rotate the design so that it displays similar to that shown in Figure 15–26. This helps to ensure that the construction entities are easily created and selectable.

3. In the CONSTRUCT panel, click **Axis Through Cylinder/Cone/Torus** and select the cylindrical face at the front of the component, as shown in Figure 15–26.

4. In the CONSTRUCT panel, click **Point at Edge and Plane**. Select the axis that you just created and then select the planar face. The references are shown in Figure 15–26.

Select this planar face to locate the Point at Edge and Plane point.

Create the axis through the center of this cylindrical face.

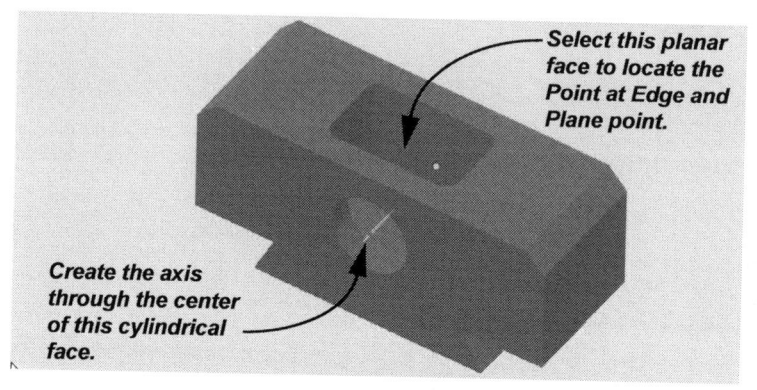

Figure 15–26

5. In the ASSEMBLE panel, click (Joint Origin).

6. In the JOINT ORIGIN palette, in the *Type* field, ensure that **Simple** is selected.

7. Rotate the model so that you can clearly see the point. Select the point that was just created on the face of the MovingJaw component.

8. Ensure that the new joint origin was created on the point and not on another vertex. Once confirmed, click **OK**.

9. In the BROWSER, clear the display of the construction features by clicking so that it displays as white.

10. Save the component.

11. Return to the *Vise_Assembly* tab. Note that the BROWSER indicates that a component and the top-level assembly are out-of-date ().

12. Right-click on **MovingJaw v1** and select **Get Latest**. The assembly updates to show the new joint origin.

13. Using the steps previously listed in Task 7, recreate the revolute joint between the Spindle and the MovingJaw components. Use the new joint origin as the *Component2* reference.

14. In the INSPECT panel, click ⬚ (Interference). Select the Spindle, MovingJaw, and Body components to test for interference again. Click ⬚ to run the analysis. No interference is detected.

15. Drag and rotate the Spindle to verify the motion is correctly defined. Note how when the vise is closed, the Spindle interferes with the Body component.

Task 9 - Define a contact set between components.

As a alternative to explicitly calculating and setting up joint limits to define the full range of permitted motion for a component, you can also define the range of motion based on the physical contact of components in the design. This is done using contact sets.

1. Drag the Spindle to a position where there is no contact between it and the Body component.

> Enabling ⬚ (Enable All Contact) verifies contact between all of the components in a design. This can be intensive on your computer's resources. In situations where there are only a few possible locations for interference, consider using the **Contact Sets** option and explicitly defining the components to be analyzed.

2. In the ASSEMBLE panel, click ⬚ (Enable Contact Sets). In the BROWSER, the **Contact: sets** node is added, as shown in Figure 15–27. This indicates that contact sets are being analyzed in the model.

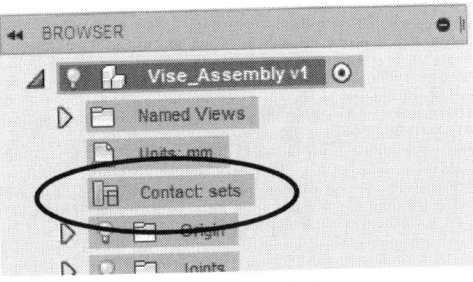

Figure 15–27

3. Currently there are no sets actually created in the model. In the ASSEMBLE panel, click ⬚ (New Contact Set). The NEW CONTACT SET palette opens, enabling you to define a new set.

4. In the graphics window, select the Body and Spindle components, as shown in Figure 15–28.

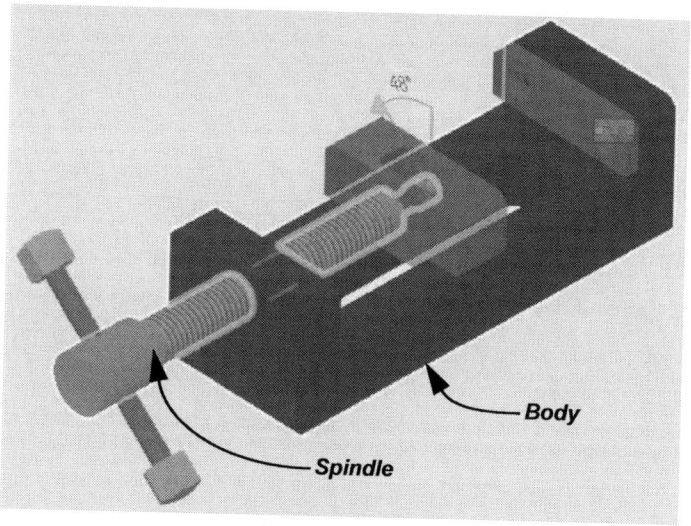

Figure 15–28

5. Click **OK** to create the contact set. It is added to the **Contact: sets** node in the BROWSER, as shown in Figure 15–29.

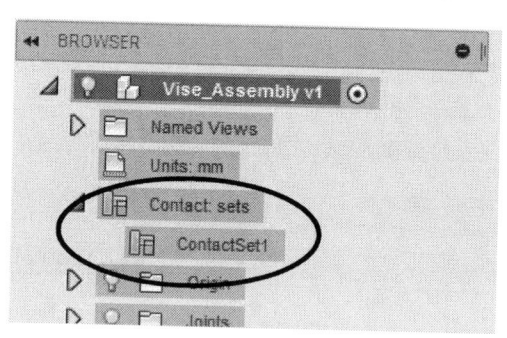

Figure 15–29

6. Rename the newly created contact set as **ContactSet: Body_Spindle** to easily identify it.

7. Drag and rotate the Spindle again and note how the vise does not fully close. When the Spindle interferes with the Body component, movement stops because contact and interference has been identified.

You can suppress a contact set to improve performance in the design when you are not concerned about testing motion.

8. Hover the cursor over the **ContactSet: Body_Spindle** set and click ▣ (Suppress contact set). Once suppressed, you can once again close the vice, even though there is interference.

9. Hover the cursor over the **ContactSet: Body_Spindle** set and click ▣ (Unsuppress contact set). The Spindle's movement now ends once it comes in contact with the Body component.

10. As an alternative to individually suppressing contact sets, you can also temporarily disable all contact analysis. Hover the cursor over the **Contact: sets** node. Note the icons that display, as shown in Figure 15–30.

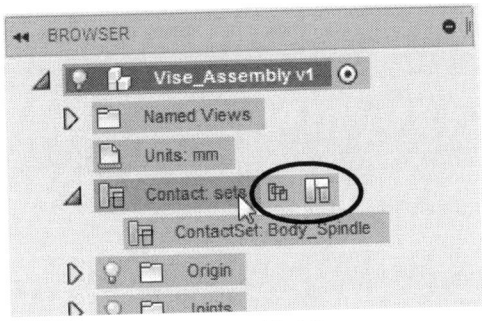

Figure 15–30

*When hovering over the **Contact: sets** node in the BROWSER, you can switch from analyzing contact sets to analyzing all contact between components by selecting ▣ (All Contact).*

11. Click ▣ (No Contact) to disable the use of all contact sets in the model. Note that the **Contact: sets** node is completely removed from the BROWSER.

12. To enable contact sets again, it must be selected in the ASSEMBLE panel. Click ▣ (Enable Contact Sets). Once enabled, all previous contact sets are displayed.

Task 10 - Define a specific rotation value for a joint.

When dragging a component through its range of motion, you are unable to enter a specific value to stop the component at a specific point in its permitted range of motion. In this task, you will learn how to use the **Drive Joints** tool to enter a value and move the design to a specific location within its permitted range of motion.

1. Drag the MovingJaw along the Body component. Note that there is no entry field to set a specific location for the component.

2. In the ASSEMBLE panel, click (Drive Joints). The DRIVE JOINTS palette opens.

3. In the BROWSER, expand the **Joints** folder and select the **Rev** joint.

4. The *Rotation* field is added to the DRIVE JOINTS palette. The default value is based on the current angular value in the model. Enter **45 deg** and note how the revolute joint angle automatically updates. This enables you to define a specific location for the handle.
    - You can also set a specific rotation value for the Slider2 joint to set the position the MovingJaw component.

5. Save the design.

Task 11 - Conduct a motion study.

Depending on the design, you might not be able to drag multiple components at one time to test their range of motion. Using the Motion Study tool, you can add specific joints to the study, assign values, and play the study to review its motion. In this task you will create a motion study that includes the Slider and Revolute joints.

1. In the BROWSER, expand the **Joints** folder. Rename the **Slider2** joint as **MovingJaw/Sliding**.

2. Rename the **Rev5** joint as **Spindle Rotation**. Renaming the joints makes it easier to identify them when using them in the motion study.

3. In the ASSEMBLE panel, click (Motion Study). The Motion Study dialog box opens.

4. In the BROWSER, select the **MovingJaw/Sliding** joint and then the **Spindle Rotation** joint.

Consider the order of selection if the motion you are simulating is sequential. In this case, add the joints that move first, then second, etc.

5. Note how each joint is assigned a color in the panel on the right of the dialog box, as shown in Figure 15–31.

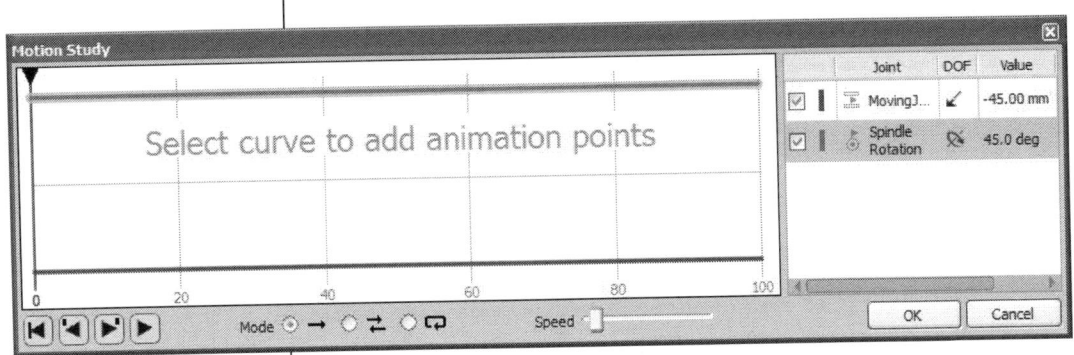

Figure 15–31

6. Hover the cursor on the blue curve (Spindle Rotation joint) and select a location near the beginning (Step 1) of the line to define its first position in the study.

7. Ensure that **1** is displayed in the *Step* field, entering it manually if required, as shown in Figure 15–32.

8. In the *Angle* field, enter **0.0 deg**, as shown in Figure 15–32.

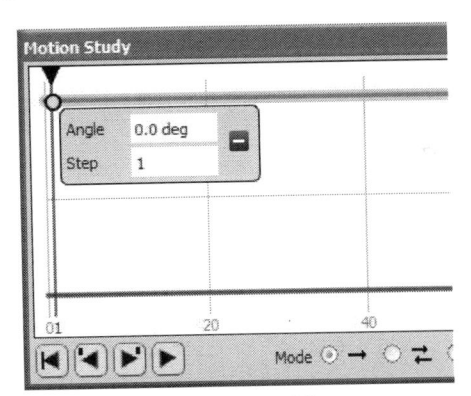

Figure 15–32

9. Move further along the blue line and select near Step 20. Ensure that **20** is displayed in the *Step* field, entering it manually if required. In the *Angle* field, enter **360.0 deg**, as shown in Figure 15–33.

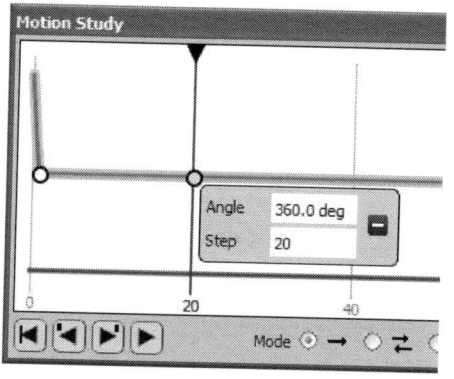

Figure 15–33

To delete a motion study point, click ▬ in the window that displays to define a point.

10. Continue to move along the blue line that defines the motion for the revolute joint and enter the following values.:

Step	Angle
40	720 deg
60	1080 deg
80	1440 deg
100	1800 deg

Once you have entered all of the points for the motion study, the dialog box should display as shown in Figure 15–34.

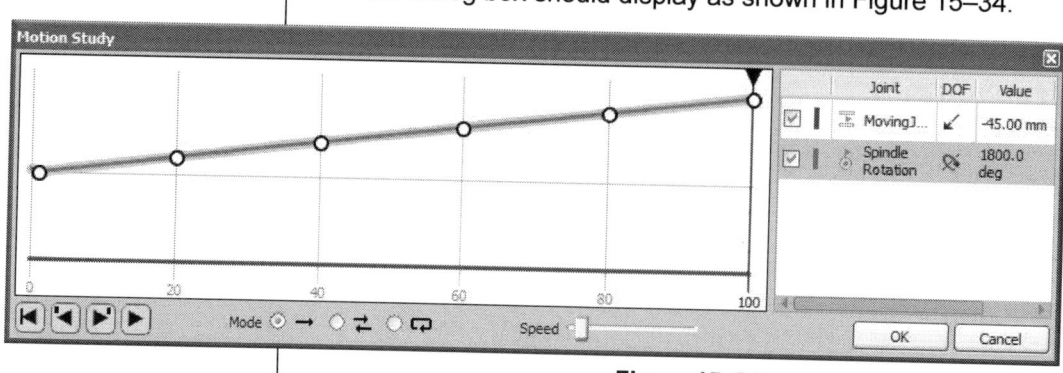

Figure 15–34

11. Hover the cursor on the red curve (MovingJaw/Sliding joint) and select a location near the beginning (Step 1) of the line to define its first position in the study.

12. Ensure that **1** is displayed in the *Step* field, entering it manually if required, as shown in Figure 15–35.

13. In the *Distance* field, enter **-55 mm**, as shown in Figure 15–35.

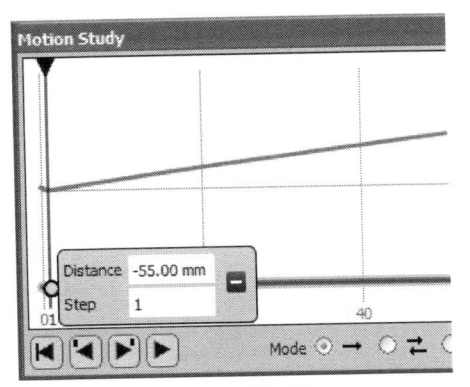

Figure 15–35

14. Move further along the red line and select near Step 20. Ensure that **20** is displayed in the *Step* field, entering it manually if required. In the *Angle* field, enter **-45 mm**, as shown in Figure 15–36.

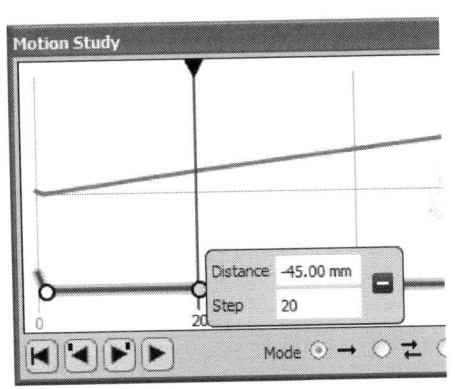

Figure 15–36

To delete a motion study point, click ▬ in the window that displays to define a point.

15. Continue to move along the red line that defines the motion for the slider joint and enter the following values.

Step	Angle
40	-35 mm
60	-25 mm
80	-15 mm
100	-5 mm

Once you have entered all of the points for the motion study, the dialog box should display as shown in Figure 15–37.

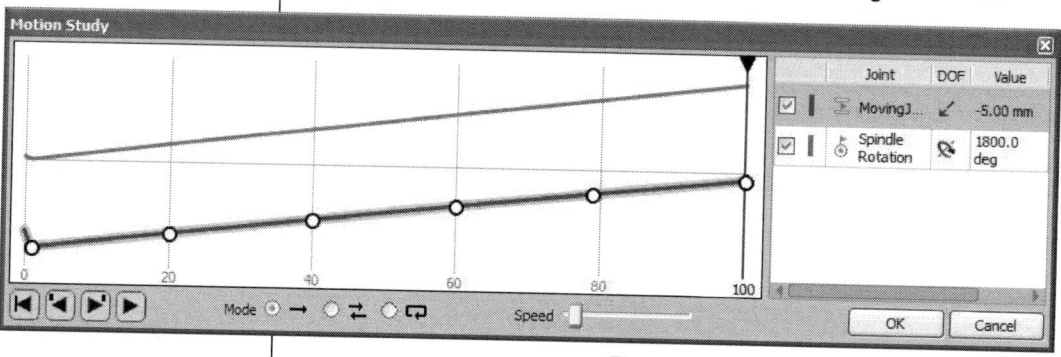

Figure 15–37

16. To play the motion study, you can do either of the following:
    - Drag the scrub line that displays in the pane on the left along the 100 step line.
    - Use the playback controls at the bottom of the Motion Study dialog box. Click ⏮ to rewind to the beginning of the study and click ▶ to play the study.

Consider using the Mode options at the bottom of the Motion Study dialog box to control the playback mode. It can be set to play forward, play forward and then backward, or loop.

17. Drag the *Speed slider* to the left to slow the motion as much as possible.

18. Click **OK** to close the study.

19. Studies are added to the BROWSER in the **Motion Studies** folder, as shown in Figure 15–38.
    - To edit an existing study, in the BROWSER, right-click on the study and select **Edit**.
    - To create a new study, in the ASSEMBLE panel, click (Motion Study).

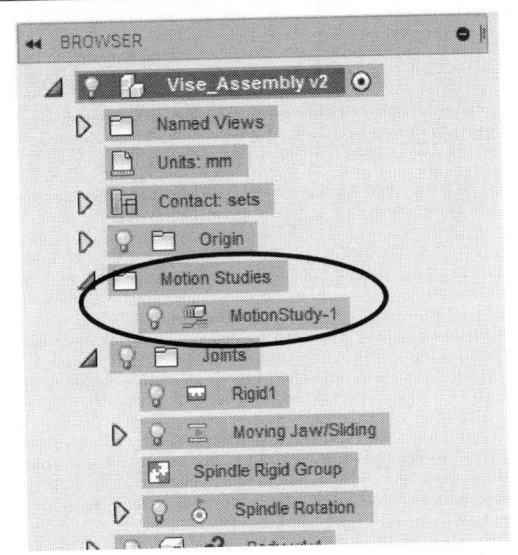

Figure 15–38

20. Save the design.

Task 12 - Create a motion link between the slider and revolute joints to simulate motion.

As an alternative to using the Motion Study tool to simulate motion, you can also use the Motion Link tool. In this task you will create a relationship between the slider and the revolute joints that defines how far the MovingJaw will slide for every 360 degree rotation of the Spindle.

1. In the ASSEMBLE panel, click (Motion Link). The Motion Link palette opens.

2. In the BROWSER, select the slider (**MovingJaw/Sliding**) joint first and then select the revolute (**Spindle Rotation**) joint.

3. In the Motion Link palette, in the *Distance* field, enter **20.00 mm**, and in the *Angle* field, enter **360.0 deg**, as shown in Figure 15–39. This sets the motion so that for every 360° rotation, the MovingJaw moves 20 mm.

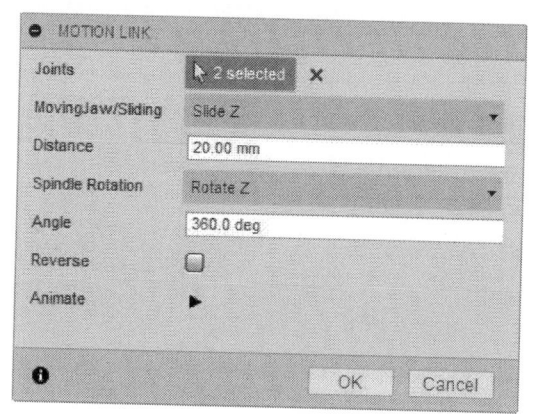

Figure 15–39

4. Click ▶ in the *Animate* area to play the range of sliding motion. Click ■ to stop the animated motion.

5. Click **OK**. Note that the new motion link is added in the BROWSER to the **Joints** folder.

6. Drag the MovingJaw and note how the motion link controls the movement of the design.

7. Save the design to the *Autodesk Fusion 360 Practice Files* project.

8. Close the file.

Chapter Review Questions

1. Which of the following best describes when you should use a rigid group in your design? (Select all that apply.)
   a. When no mechanical movement exists between components.
   b. To avoid adding multiple rigid joints between components to remove all degrees of freedom.
   c. When an applicable joint origin does not exist in the model.
   d. To define how two components that have degrees of freedom are able to move relative to one another.

2. Which of the following tools can be used to control the range of motion that exists once a joint has been added? (Select all that apply.)
   a. **Rigid Groups**
   b. **Joint Limits**
   c. **Drive Joints**
   d. **Contact Sets**
   e. **Motion Link**

3. An interference analysis can only be conducted between two selected components at one time.
   a. True
   b. False

4. Which of the following tools can be used to set a revolute joint to exactly 45 degrees after it has been created? (Select all that apply.)
   a. **Joint**
   b. **Joint Limits**
   c. **Drive Joints**
   d. **Joint Origin**

5. Which of the following statements are true regarding the BROWSER shown in Figure 15–40. (Select all that apply.)

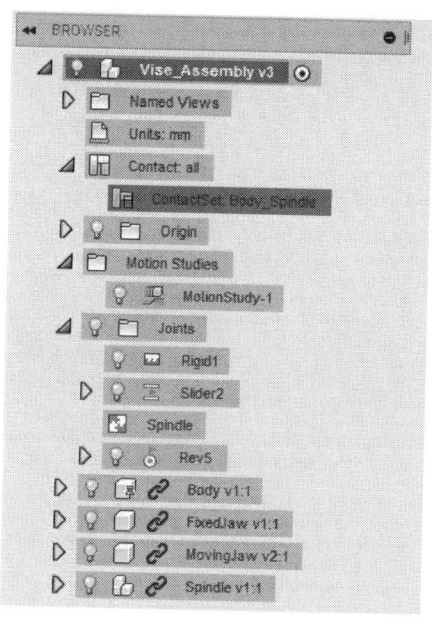

Figure 15–40

a. A contact set has been created in the design.

b. In the design, contact is only being analyzed between the Body and Spindle components, as specified in the **ContactSet: Body_Spindle** set.

c. There is one rigid group in the design.

d. A motion study has been created in the design.

e. A motion link has been created in the design.

Answers: 1.(a,b), 2.(b,d), 3.b, 4.(b,c), 5.(a,c,d)

Command Summary

Button	Command	Location
	Disable Contact	• **Ribbon:** *Model* Workspace>ASSEMBLE panel • **Context Menu:** Right-click in the graphics window and select **Assemble**. • **BROWSER:** Right-click the *Contact* node
	Drive Joints	• **Ribbon:** *Model* Workspace>ASSEMBLE panel • **Context Menu:** Right-click in the graphics window and select **Assemble**. • **BROWSER:** Right-click the Joint name or hover over the Joint name
	Edit Joint Limits	• **BROWSER:** Right-click the *Joint name* or hover over the *Joint name* and select the icon • **Timeline:** Right-click the *Joint* icon
NA	Edit Rigid Group	• **BROWSER:** Right-click the *Rigid Group name* • **Timeline:** Right-click the *Rigid Group* icon
	Enable All Contact	• **Ribbon:** *Model* Workspace>ASSEMBLE panel • **Context Menu:** Right-click in the graphics window and select **Assemble**. • **BROWSER:** Right-click the Contact node and select icon when Enable Contact Sets is active
	Enable Contact Sets	• **Ribbon:** *Model* Workspace>ASSEMBLE panel • **Context Menu:** Right-click in the graphics window and select **Assemble**. • **BROWSER:** Right-click the Contact node and select icon when Enable All Contact is active
	Interference	• **Ribbon:** *Model* Workspace>INSPECT panel • **Context Menu:** Right-click in the graphics window and select **Inspect**.
	Motion Link	• **Ribbon:** *Model* Workspace>ASSEMBLE panel • **Context Menu:** Right-click in the graphics window and select **Assemble**.
	Motion Study	• **Ribbon:** *Model* Workspace>ASSEMBLE panel • **Context Menu:** Right-click in the graphics window and select **Assemble**.

	New Contact Set	• **Ribbon:** *Model* Workspace>ASSEMBLE panel • **Context Menu:** Right-click in the graphics window and select **Assemble**. • **BROWSER:** Right-click the *Contact node*
	Rigid Group	• **Ribbon:** *Model* Workspace>ASSEMBLE panel • **Context Menu:** Right-click in the graphics window and select **Assemble**.
	Suppress Contact Set	• **BROWSER:** Right-click the *Contact set node*

Chapter 16

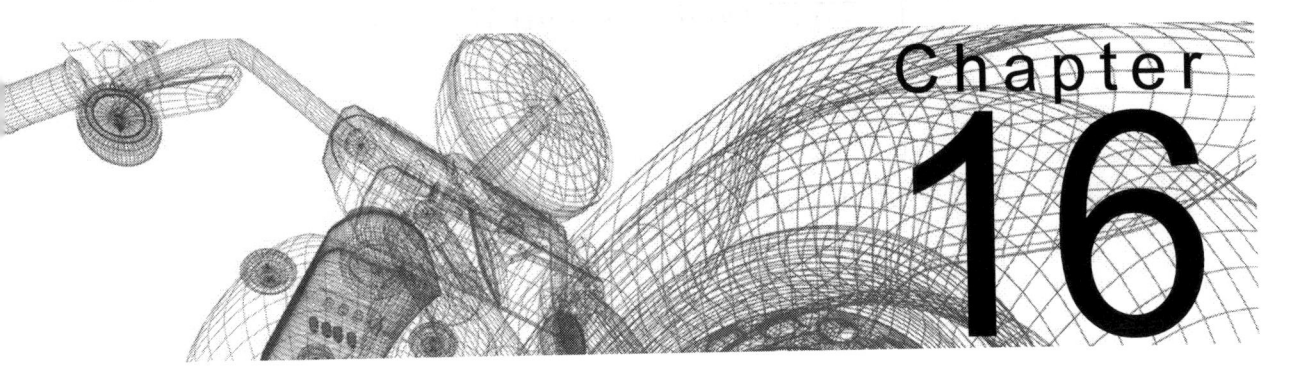

Multi-Body Design

The multi-body design method enables you to create components that form an assembled product in one design file. A multi-body design starts with a single body and additional bodies are added to represent the overall design. To complete the design, these bodies are ultimately converted to components to which joint connections can be added to constrain them. This chapter discusses the multi-body design method and outlines the tools that can be used to improve your efficiency in creating designs.

Learning Objectives in this Chapter

- Design multiple bodies in a single design file.
- Create components in a single design file.
- Duplicate components in a design file.
- Add as-built joints between components in a design.

16.1 Multi-Body Design

The process of creating multiple bodies in the context of a single design file is known as multi-body design. This is one of the methods that is available in the Autodesk® Fusion 360™ software to create a product that is comprised of multiple assembled models. This design approach enables you to create all or some of your assembled design as separate bodies within one design file. The bodies are then converted to components while still remaining within the one design file.

The advantages of creating a design using multi-bodies include the following:

- The entire design resides in a single file, and bodies are later extracted into components that remain in the same design. No top-level or subassembly design files are required.

- A complex part file can be better organized using separate bodies with respect to their function or position in the model.

- You can set up relationships between bodies. You can control the visibility of bodies as a group, rather than at the individual feature level.

All design files contain a **Bodies** folder in the BROWSER. This folder lists all of the bodies in the design. The design shown in Figure 16–1 is a folding easel. It was designed using a combination of the multi-body and distributed design methods. All of the wooden components in the easel were created in the context of the single design using bodies, and all of the hardware were inserted. Joints can be added to assign the required degrees of freedom that enable the easel to collapse and expand.

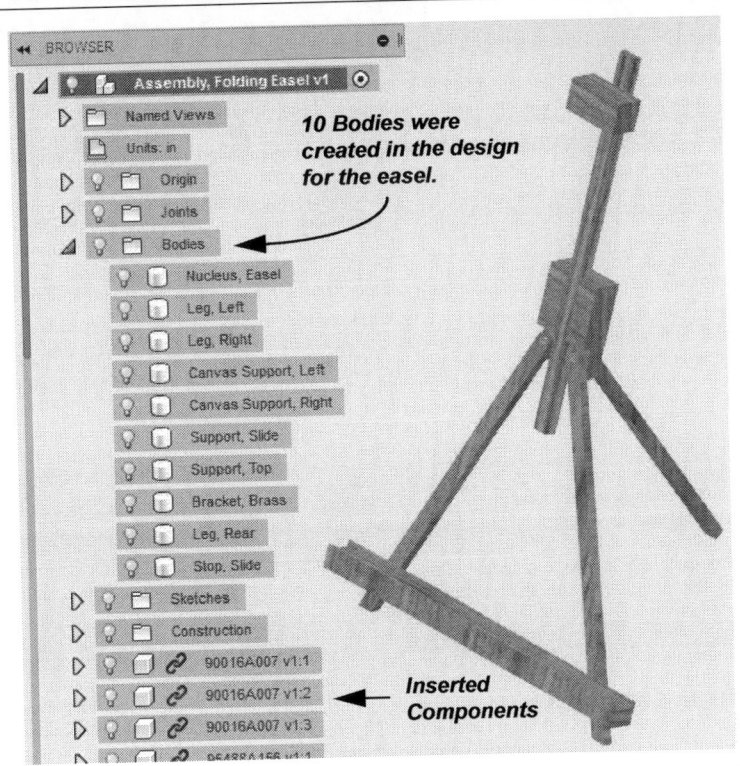

Figure 16–1

16.2 Multi-Body Design Tools

In single body design, the first solid feature in the design is added as Body1, and additional features are joined or cut away from this body as the geometry is created. You create a new body using the standard modeling tools (e.g., Extrude, Revolve, Loft, etc.).

When using a multi-body design method, you must use the Operation drop-down list to explicitly create a new feature as a separate body. Figure 16–2 shows a new extruded feature being added with the **New Body** Operation selected to create the feature as a new body.

Figure 16–2

Video Lesson Available

Understanding the Operation Drop-Down

Video Length: 3:01

In addition to defining a new body based on the Operation definition in a feature, you can also create and manipulate bodies using the following tools found on the MODIFY panel:

- Use the (Split Body) tool to split an existing body into two bodies. This is done by selecting a existing body to split (*Body to Split*) and a reference that will be used to split the selected body (*Splitting Tool*). The splitting tool can be a profile, face, or plane that divides the body.

- The (Combine) tool enables you to merge existing bodies in the design. This is done by selecting the body to which another body will be added (*Target Body*) and then selecting the body that will be added to the target (*Tool Bodies*). Multiple bodies can be combined at one time using this tool. Once combined, the bodies can be joined, cut, or result in the intersection of overlaying geometry using the *Operation* drop-down list.

The feature used to create a body still controls the geometry's size, even if the geometry is split in two.

16.3 Components

Components are used in a design to represent the parts used to form the assembled design. A component can consist of a single body or multiple bodies of features that define the required geometry. Components are either inserted from existing designs, or are created within the context of a multi-body design. Components that are created in the context of the design and that reference other components update when changes are made, enabling you to build design intent into your design.

Video Lesson Available

Understanding Components in Fusion

Video Length: 2:58

Creating Components

Components can be created in a design in a number of different ways:

- During geometry creation, in the *Operation* drop-down list, select **New Component**. The component is added to the BROWSER.

- In an existing design file, in the **Bodies** folder, right-click on an existing body and select **Create Components from Bodies**.

Timeline icon:

- In the CREATE panel, click (New Component). Using the NEW COMPONENT palette, you can either create a new empty component, or convert an existing body into a new component. Both options are available when you select the tool in the CREATE panel.

Renaming components in the BROWSER can help you to identify them in the design.

- In the BROWSER, right-click on the top-level design file's name and select **New Component**. This creates an empty component in the design. To create a subassembly type structure in a component, right-click on a component name and select **New Component**. Alternatively, you can drag and drop components to create a subassembly structure.

Any new geometry or components that are added to a design are added to the active level. By default, the top-level of the design is active. To activate another component, in the BROWSER, hover the cursor over the component and select the circle shown in Figure 16–3. The active component is displayed and all other components are faded (disabled). Any new geometry or components are added to the active component.

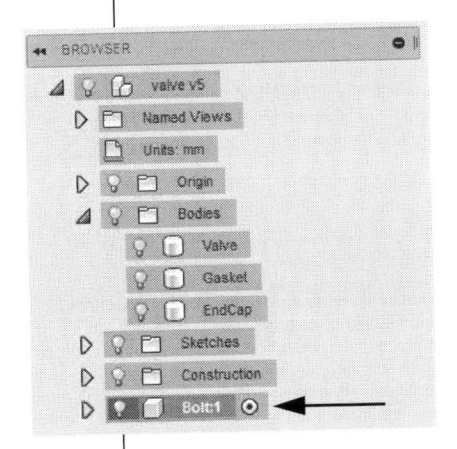

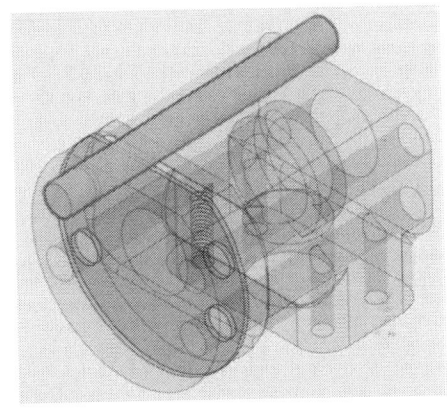

Figure 16–3

To reactivate the top-level design, in the BROWSER, hover the cursor over the design's name and select the circle adjacent to it, as shown in Figure 16–4.

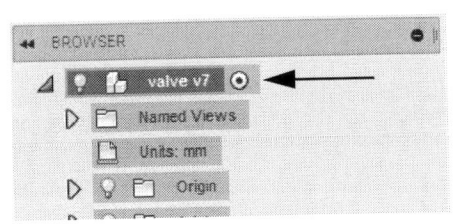

Figure 16–4

Video Lesson Available

Creating Components

Video Length: 4:53

Using the BROWSER

Understanding how to use the BROWSER and its options can help you when working with components in a top-level design. There are several tools that can improve selection and visibility in a design.

- The **Show/Hide** and **Selectable** tools enable you to control the visibility and selectability of components. This can make component selection much easier in a complex design.

- Selection sets can be created in the BROWSER to further help with efficient component selection.

- The **Isolate** tool clears the display of all except the selected component.

- Opacity can be set for components to enable you to see through the component. Note that this is only a visual setting: components that have an opacity value assigned to them function as a normal component.

The component's properties are accessed in the BROWSER by right-clicking on the component and selecting **Properties**. This provides you with details on the area, density, and mass of the design based on its assigned material.

Video Lesson Available

Working with Components in the Browser

Video Length: 3:53

Reusing Components

Components can be easily reused in a design to prevent you from needing to create the same geometry multiple times. Reusing components ensures that changes made to the source component is reflected in all of the copies. To reuse components, consider using either a pattern or the copy and paste functionality.

*While the **Mirror** and **Save Copy As** tools can be used to reuse geometry, they create new components that do not maintain associativity with the original design.*

- On the CREATE panel, the Pattern tool enables you to pattern selected components in a rectangular or circular shape or along a path. This tool functions similar to those used for geometry patterns.

- Components can be copied and pasted in a design. To copy, in the BROWSER, right-click on the component name and select **Copy**. To paste, right-click in the graphics window and select **Paste**. Once pasted, the component displays and the MOVE palette opens. Use the triad to locate the new component in the design.

Any duplicated component is added to the BROWSER as a new component. It uses the same name as its parent with an instance number added to make it unique. Joints must be added to each duplicated instance to constrain them in the design.

Video Lesson Available

Reusing Components

Video Length: 4:35

Positioning Components

Using the multi-body design method, components are generally created in their required locations. Even though the components are created relative to one another, they are not automatically constrained in the design. Consider the following:

- Use the **Ground** tool to lock a component in space. The grounded component in the design should be the component that forms the foundation of the design and does not move.

- Components can be moved by selecting and dragging them in the graphics window.
    - To move components using exact translation and rotation values, use the **Move** tool.
    - Moving does not establish a relationship between components, it only helps to locate them relative to one another.
    - In the POSITION panel, click (Capture Position) to lock a component in position as a Timeline item.

- Use the **Align** tool to align components relative to one another to help position them in the design. Similar to moving components, aligning does not establish a relationship between components, it only helps to locate them relative to one another.

To fully constrain components in the design you must add joints. Once aligned, you can also use as-built joints.

Video Lesson Available

Positioning Components

Video Length: 3:10

16.4 As-Built Joints

When the **Joint** tool is used to constrain two components relative to one another, a joint origin must be selected on both components to fully define it. In a multi-body design, the bodies that are converted to components are already in position based on how they were created. Using the **As-built Joint** tool, joint origin selection is not required, and these references are assumed based on how the selected components are positioned. The only references that are required include the selection of the joint type, and a position reference if the joint permits motion.

Video Lesson Available

Creating As-Built Joints

Video Length: 2:04

Timeline icon:

The design shown in Figure 16–5 was created using the multi-body design method. The valve was created first as a single body. The gasket was created as a second body in the design using the face of the valve as its sketch plane and projected edges. Based on its construction, the Rigid as-built joint can be easily assigned by selecting the two components.

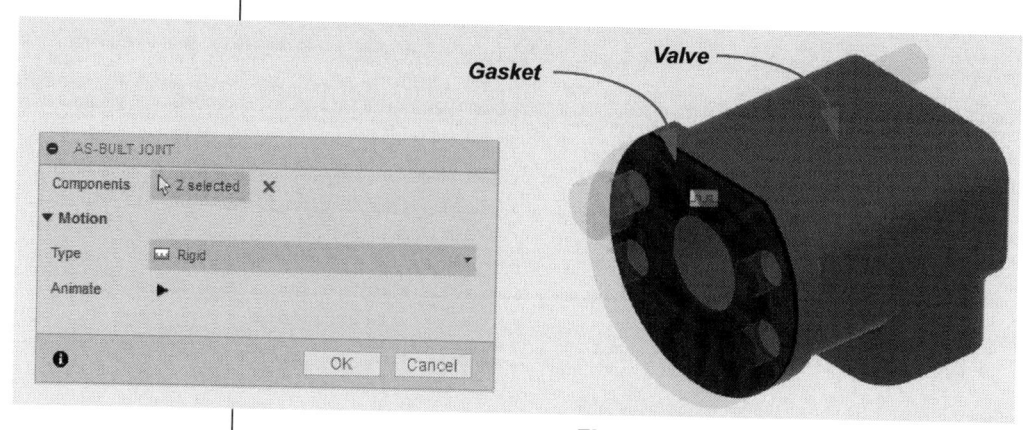

Figure 16–5

In Figure 16–6, the End Cap and Bolt are being constrained using the Revolute as-built joint. The connected faces were defined based on how the two components are positioned to one another. The revolution axis is defined by selecting the centerpoint on the bolt.

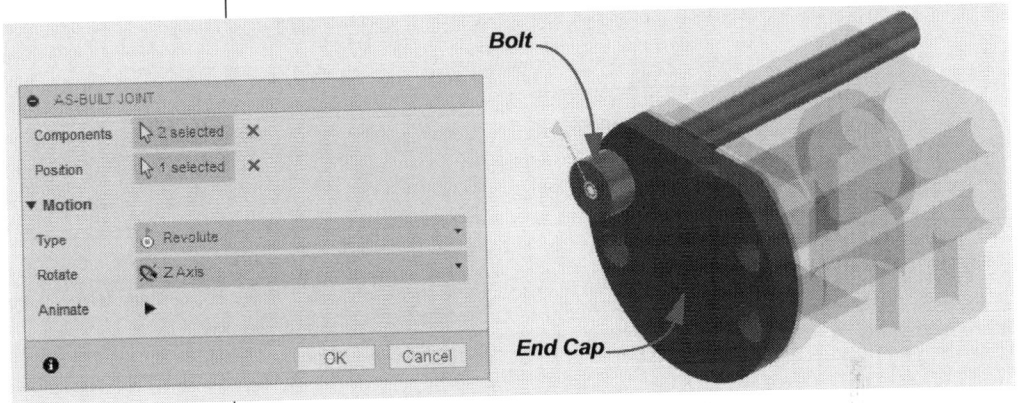

Figure 16–6

Hint: Using As-built Joints for Inserted Components

As-built joints typically work with components that are created directly in the design using the multi-body method. However, you can also use the **As-built Joint** option with inserted components. This is especially helpful if the component was inserted and moved into its exact position using the Move triad when it was placed.

Practice 16a Multi-Body Design

Practice Objectives

- Use the multi-body design method to create multiple bodies in a design to represent the components of an assembly.
- Convert bodies to components in the design.
- Create as-built joints.

In this practice, you will begin by opening a design that contains a single body that was imported from another CAD software tool. Using references on this body, you will create subsequent bodies that will each represent components in an overall assembly design. To complete the practice, you will convert each body to components and add as-built joints to constrain the design. The completed design is shown in Figure 16–7.

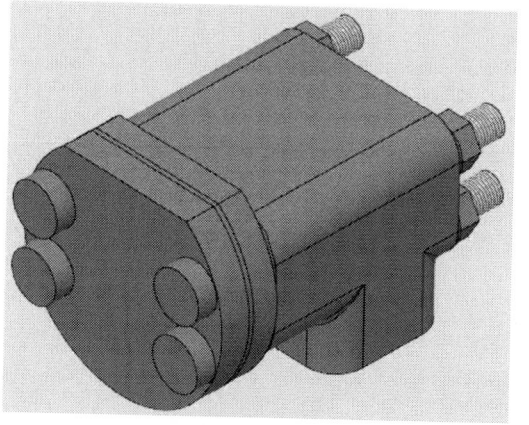

Figure 16–7

Task 1 - Open a design file.

1. Click **> New Design from File**.

2. In the Open dialog box, navigate to the *C:\Autodesk Fusion 360 Practice Files\Multi-Body Design* folder, select **valve.f3d**, and click **Open**.

3. Save the design as **Valve**.

Task 2 - Create additional bodies in the design.

In this task you will create a new body in the design using references on the existing geometry.

1. Ensure that the Timeline is displayed at the bottom of the graphics window. If it is not, at the top of the BROWSER, right-click on the valve name and click **Capture Design History**.

2. In the BROWSER, expand the **Bodies** folder and note that there is currently a single body in the design called **Body1**.

3. Rename the **Body1** body to **Valve**.

4. If not already set, change the *Visual Style* display to **Shaded with Visible Edges Only**. This helps you distinguish the bodies in the design.

5. Create a new sketch on the face shown in Figure 16–8.

Create a new sketch on this face.

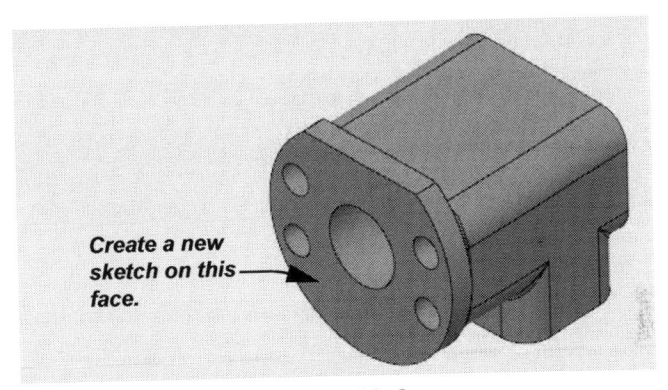

Figure 16–8

6. Complete the sketch. All of the edges that lie on the sketch plane are automatically projected.

7. Begin the creation of a new Extrude feature. Select profiles from the sketch so that the section being extruded is as shown in Figure 16–9.

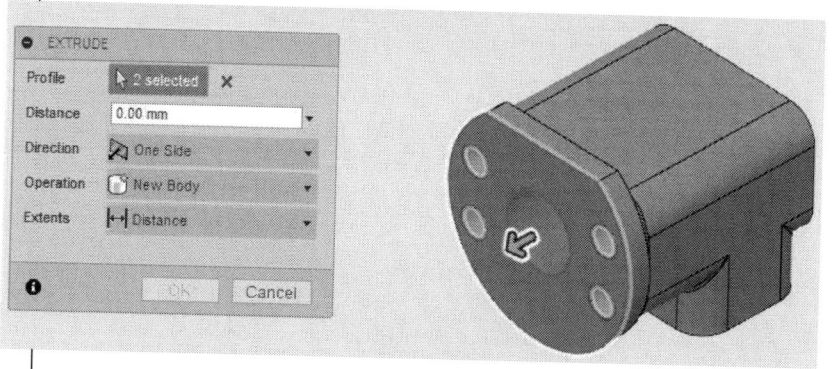

Figure 16–9

8. Drag the depth value to **20 mm**, or enter this value in the *Distance* field.

9. In the *Operation* drop-down list, note how **Join** is automatically set as the default value. Using this option would add the feature to the Valve body.

You can edit features to change the Operation if you do not select it correctly initially.

10. In the *Operation* drop-down list, select **New Body**. This creates the new feature as its own body.

11. Click **OK**.

12. Rename the newly created body to **EndCap**. The BROWSER and design display as shown in Figure 16–10.

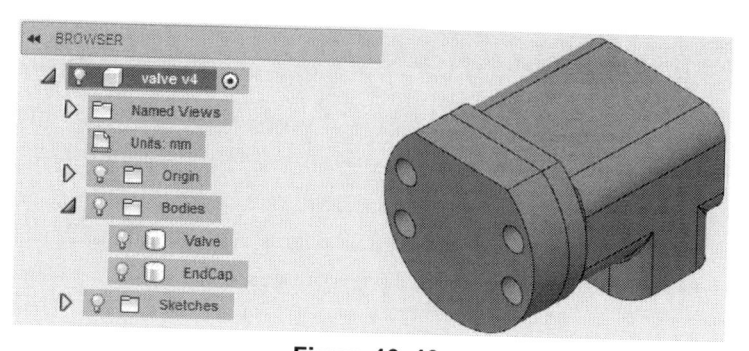

Figure 16–10

Task 3 - Split an existing body.

Prior to creating the EndCap, a gasket should have been created. This can be done using a number of different techniques. In this task you will split the EndCap body to create a new body that represents the gasket.

1. Toggle off the display of the EndCap body by selecting 💡 adjacent to its name.

2. Create a construction plane that is offset 2 mm from the face shown in Figure 16–11.

Create the construction plane offset 2mm from this face.

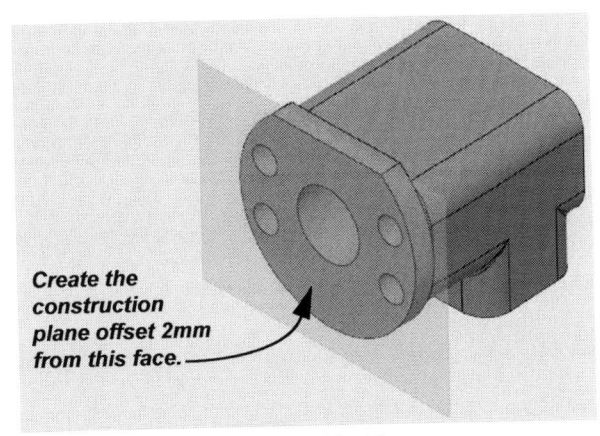

Figure 16–11

3. In the Timeline, drag the newly created construction plane's icon so that it is listed before the extruded feature that was created to form the EndCap body.

4. Toggle on the display of the EndCap body.

5. In the MODIFY panel, click (Split Body). The SPLIT BODY palette displays as shown in Figure 16–12.

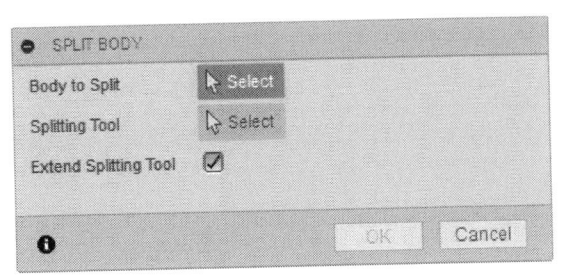

Figure 16–12

6. By default, the *Body to Split* field is active. Select **EndCap** as the body to be split.

7. Select the *Splitting Tool* field to activate it and then select the construction plane that was just created.

8. Click **OK** to split the body.

9. In the BROWSER, rename the bodies so that the body between the Valve and End Cap bodies is called **Gasket**, as shown in Figure 16–13.

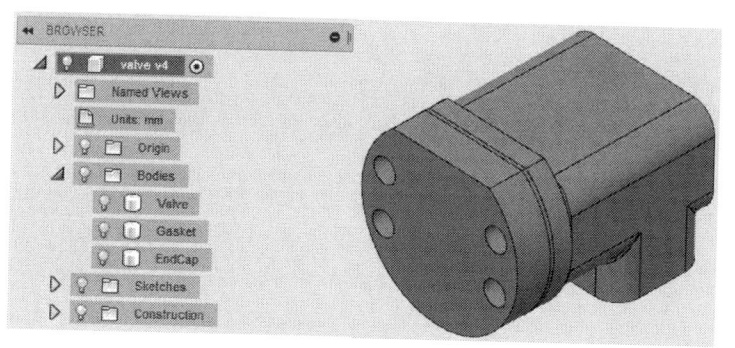

Figure 16–13

10. In the Timeline, edit the Extrude feature. Note that this feature is still 20mm. Change this to **14 mm**. This value defines the combined depth of the EndCap and Gasket bodies. Because the split plane's location does not change, the Gasket's depth stays at 2mm, while the EndCap's depth changes to 12mm.

Task 4 - Create a fastener for the EndCap.

In this task you will create a bolt for the design. The bolt could be created as a separate body (similar to how the EndCap and Gasket were created), but, in this task you will create the bolt as its own component. This is an alternate approach that you can use if you know that each body is its own component and means that you do not have to convert the body to a component later.

1. Create a new sketch on the face shown in Figure 16–14.

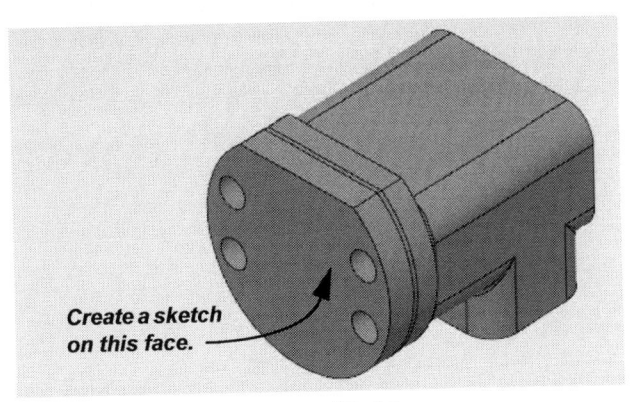

Create a sketch on this face.

Figure 16–14

2. Complete the sketch.

3. Create the extruded geometry shown in Figure 16–15.

4. In the *Operation* drop-down list, select **New Component**, as shown in Figure 16–15. This is an alternative to creating the body and then converting it to a component.

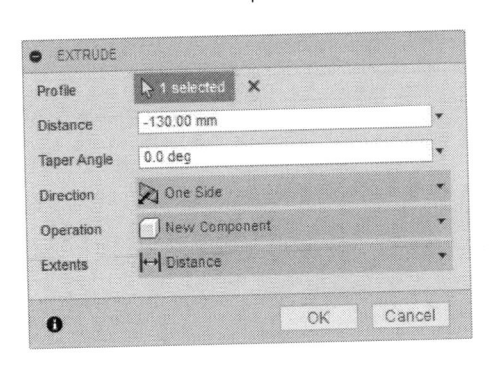

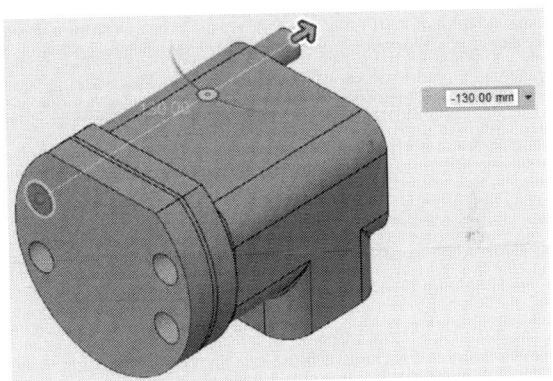

Figure 16–15

5. Click **OK** to create the new component.

6. The new component is added to the bottom of the BROWSER as **Component1**. Rename the new component to **Bolt**.

7. In the BROWSER, hover the cursor over the **Bolt:1** component and select the circle, as shown in Figure 16–16. All other components are disabled and the shaft of the Bolt is activated.

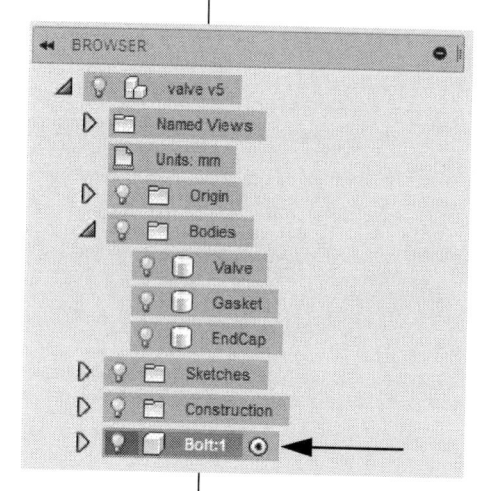

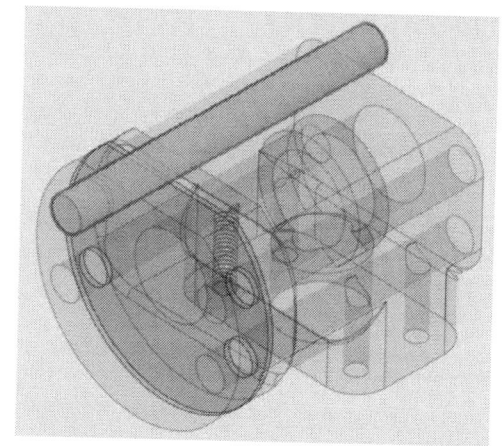

Figure 16–16

8. Using standard geometry creation tools, create the head of the bolt, similar to that shown in Figure 16–17.

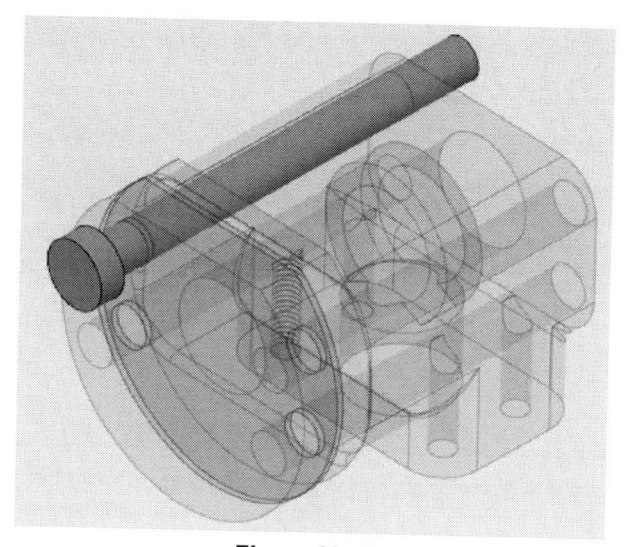

Figure 16–17

9. At the top of the BROWSER, hover the cursor over the top node in the design (**valve**). Select the circle adjacent to its name to reactivate the top-level of the design, as shown in Figure 16–18.

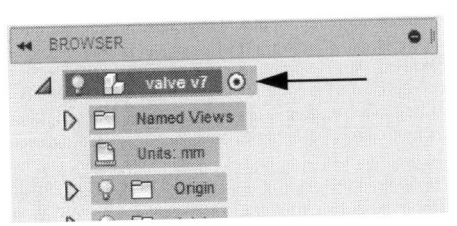

Figure 16–18

10. Save the design.

Task 5 - Convert the bodies to components.

In this task you will convert each of the three bodies that remain in the design into components. Once converted, you will rename these components.

1. In the **Bodies** folder at the top-level of the design, select **Valve**. Note the geometry that is highlighted in the design.

2. In the **Bodies** folder at the top-level of the design, right-click on **Valve** and select **Create Component from Bodies**, as shown in Figure 16–19.

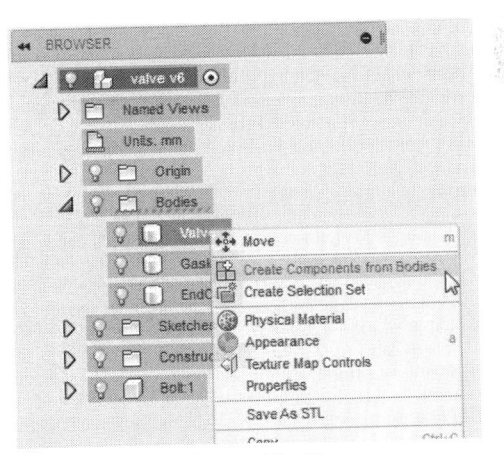

Figure 16–19

3. The **Valve** body is removed from the **Bodies** folder and is listed as a new component named **Valve**. It is identified in the BROWSER using ▢.

4. Select the component and note how it is the same geometry as the Valve body.

5. In the **Bodies** folder at the top-level of the design, right-click on **Gasket** and select **Create Component from Bodies** again.

6. Repeat Step 5 for the **EndCap** body. Once completed, the BROWSER should display as shown in Figure 16–20.

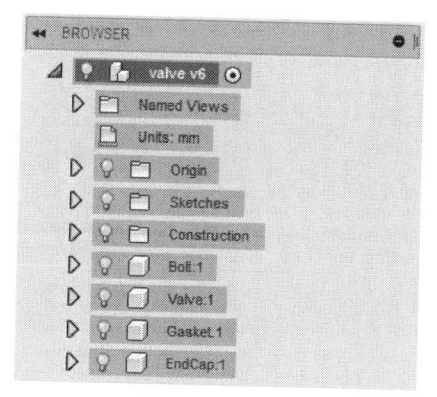

Figure 16–20

7. At the top of the BROWSER, note that is displayed adjacent to the valve design's name. This indicates that it consists of multiple components (representing an assembly).

8. Save the design.

Task 6 - Define the as-built joints in the design.

The bodies that were used to create the components in this design were created by referencing existing faces. Because of this design approach, the components are all in their required locations. Using the **As-built Joint** option enables you to define the joint based on their current location, eliminating the need to select joint origins.

1. In the BROWSER, right-click on the **Valve** component and select **Ground**. This sets the valve as the grounded component in the design.

2. In the ASSEMBLE panel, click (As-built Joint). The AS-BUILT JOINT palette opens, as shown in Figure 16–21.

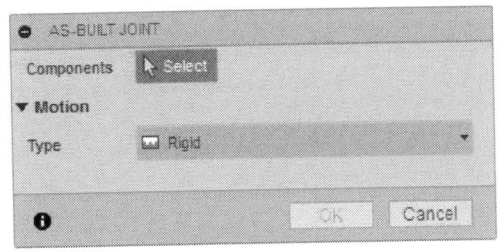

Figure 16–21

3. In the AS-BUILT JOINT palette, in the Type drop-down list, select **Rigid**.

4. In the BROWSER or in the graphics window, select the Valve and Gasket components, as shown in Figure 16–22. A shaking animation displays indicating that the two components are now rigidly connected.

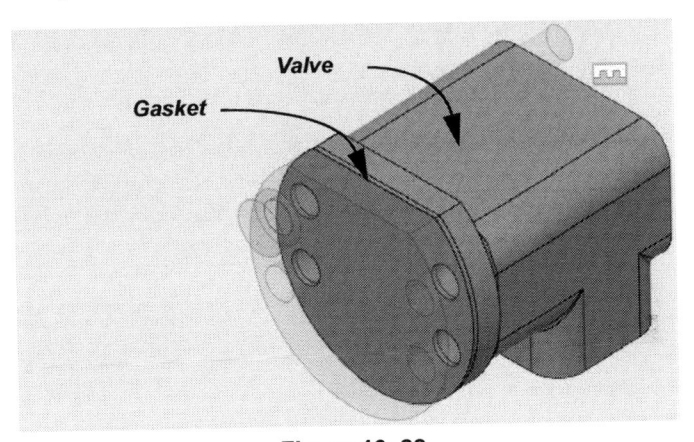

Figure 16–22

5. Click **OK**. Note that the joint is now listed in the BROWSER in the **Joints** folder.

6. Rename the joint as **Valve/Gasket**. This enables you to easily identify the joint.

7. In the ASSEMBLE panel, click (As-built Joint) again.

8. In the AS-BUILT JOINT palette, in the Type drop-down list, ensure that **Rigid** is still selected.

9. Select the Gasket and EndCap components, as shown in Figure 16–23. A shaking animation is displayed, indicating that the two components are now rigidly connected.

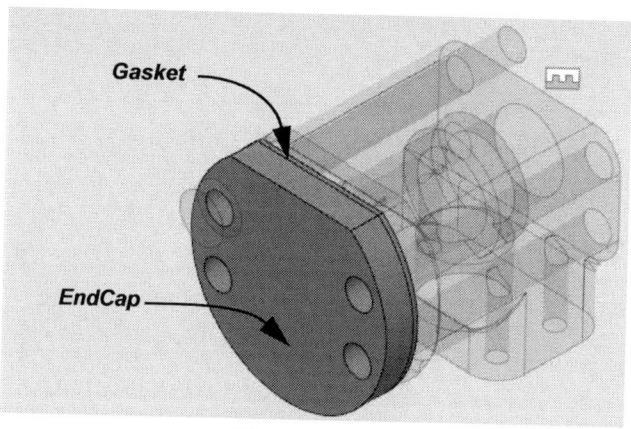

Figure 16–23

10. Click **OK**.

11. Rename the joint as **Gasket/EndCap**.

12. Drag the Bolt component and note that it can still move in the design. Undo the move.

13. Using the **As-built Joint** command, connect the Bolt and the EndCap components using a rigid joint. Rename the joint to **Bolt/EndCap**.

In general, fasteners are joined using rigid joints to represent its final assembled DOF.

Task 7 - Copy the Bolt component in the design.

In this task you will duplicate the Bolt to the three other holes. As in most designs, this can be accomplished a number of ways. You can copy and paste the component and use joints to move them into position, or you can pattern the components. In this task, you will use both methods.

1. In the BROWSER, right-click on **Bolt** and select **Copy**.

2. In the Graphics Window, right-click and select **Paste**. Drag the new component away from the design and click **OK**.

3. Use the **Joint** command to constrain the new Bolt component to the hole shown in Figure 16–24 using appropriate joint origin references.

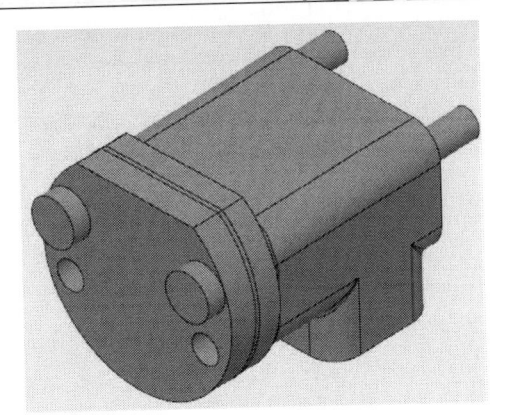

Figure 16–24

As an alternative to copying and pasting the bolt again, you will now use the Pattern tool.

Hint: Consider turning off the display of the existing Bolt components when measuring to ensure that you select the center of the holes.

4. Using the **Measure** tool, measure the distance between the top row of holes and the bottom. Ensure that this distance is 25.4mm. This distance is required for patterning the bolts.

5. In the CREATE panel, click **Pattern**> (Rectangular Pattern).

6. In the RECTANGULAR PATTERN palette, select (Pattern Component) and select the two Bolt components in the design, as shown in Figure 16–25.

7. Select the *Directions* field to activate it. Select the top linear edge on the EndCap to define the direction reference for the pattern, as shown in Figure 16–25.

8. Select the patterning direction arrow that is perpendicular to the selected edge, as shown in Figure 16–25.

Direction Reference

Activate this pattern direction

Select these components to be patterned

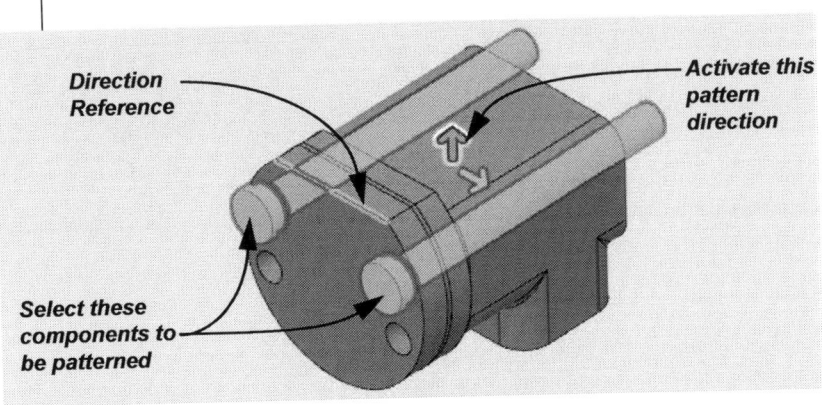

Figure 16–25

9. For the number of instances to pattern, enter **2** in the entry field that displays.

10. For the *Distance* value, enter **-25.4 mm** in the entry field that displays.

11. Click **OK** to complete the pattern.

12. Use the **As-built Joint** tool to rigidly constrain the remaining bolts.

13. Save the design to your *Autodesk Fusion 360 Practice Files* project.

14. Close the file.

> As an alternative, you could also use the pattern tool to create the bolt that was initially copied. You would do this by patterning in two directions.

Task 8 - (Optional) Complete the design.

If time permits, complete the design as follows:

- Use the multi-body design approach to create the washer and nut components shown in Figure 16–26.

- Fully constrain any newly created components in the design to remove all degrees of freedom.

- Add a thread to the Bolt component, as shown in Figure 16–26.

> To help identify the components in the design, the system can assign default colors to each component. In the INSPECT panel, click (Component Color Cycling Toggle). This temporarily assigns colors to the design until the option is cleared.

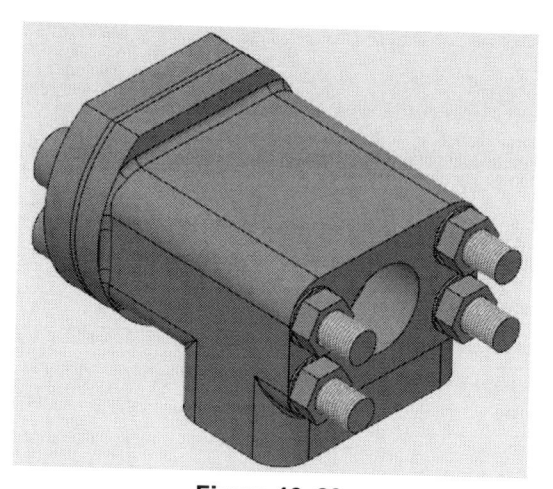

Figure 16–26

Practice 16b

Working with Multi-Bodies to Create an Assembled Design

Practice Objectives

- Upload a .F3Z file to your A360 account.
- Convert bodies to components in the design.
- Create as-built joints.
- Enable contact analysis and create contact sets between components.
- Add a motion link condition to joints in the design.

In this practice, you will work in a design that has been created for you. To complete this design you will convert bodies to components and set up as-built joints between the components to create a folding easel design. Using the tools that are available on the ASSEMBLE panel, you will also set up a motion link and contact sets to test the easel's range of motion. The completed design is shown in Figure 16–27 in its expanded and collapsed state.

Fasteners have been added into the design and rigid joints have already been set up for you.

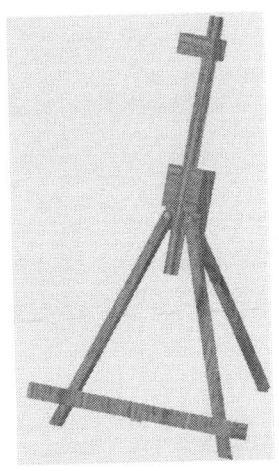

Figure 16–27

Task 1 - Upload a design file to your A360 project.

In this task you will upload a design into your Autodesk Fusion 360 project. The design file that is provided was designed using the multi-body design method. Additionally, fasteners pulled from the McMaster-Carr Content Library have been inserted.

1. Open the Data Panel and ensure that the active project is *Autodesk Fusion 360 Practice Files*.

A *.F3Z file is a compressed, archived file. It enables you to export a design file and any referenced components to share with other users. Once imported into A360, the files are automatically extracted.

2. Create a new folder in the project called **Folding Easel**, and then open the folder.

3. At the top of the Data Panel, click (Upload).

4. In the Select files to upload dialog box, click **Select Files**. Navigate to the practice files folder on your local drive and in *Folding_Easel* folder, select **Folding Easel.f3z**. Click **Open**.

5. Click **Upload** to begin the upload. The Upload progress window shows the progress of the upload. All of the components that are in the .F3Z file are shown in the list.

6. Once the files have been uploaded, click **Close** in the Upload progress window. The files should display as shown in Figure 16–28. Note that you might need to refresh the display.

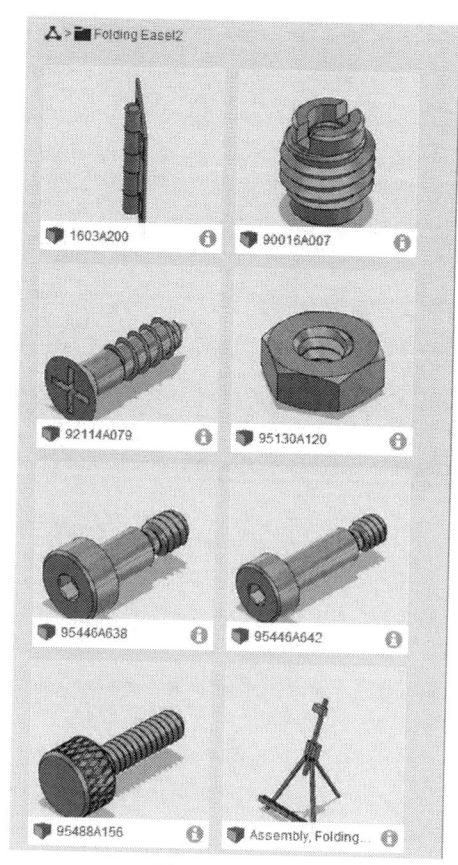

Figure 16–28

7. Open the **Assembly, Folding Easel** design. The BROWSER and design display as shown in Figure 16–29.

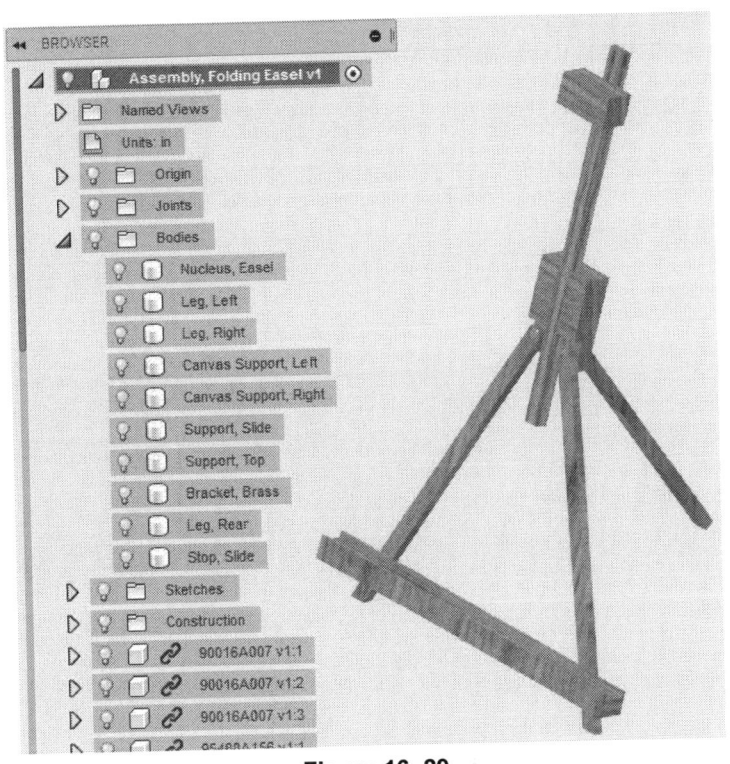

Figure 16–29

8. Complete the following in the BROWSER:
   - Select some of the components. Note how these all represent the fasteners that join the wooden pieces. None of the inserted components represent the geometry of the easel.
   - Clear the visibility of all of the fasteners from the display. By clearing them from the display, it will ease reference selection during joint definition.
   - Expand the **Bodies** folder. Note that there are 10 bodies in the folder. Select some of the bodies. They were all created in the context of this design and represent each component in the folding easel assembly.

By default, the naming convention for bodies in a design is Body1, Body2, etc. Each body was renamed in this design for clarity.

Task 2 - Convert the bodies to components.

In this task you will convert each of the bodies that have been created into components.

1. In the **Bodies** folder, right-click on **Nucleus, Easel** and select **Create Component from Bodies**, as shown in Figure 16–30.

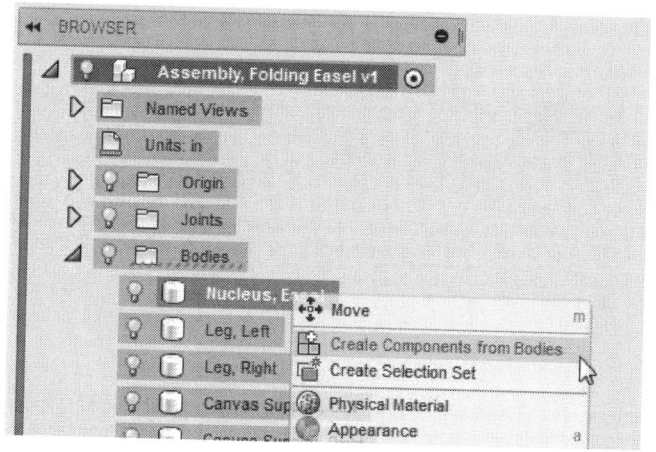

Figure 16–30

2. The **Nucleus, Easel** node is removed from the **Bodies** folder. Scroll to the bottom of the BROWSER. A new component named **Nucleus, Easel** has been added. It is identified with a ▢ in the BROWSER.

Hint: Prior to creating the new component slowly click twice on the Body's name and copy it. It can be pasted when renaming the component.

3. In the **Bodies** folder, right-click on **Leg, Left** and select **Create Component from Bodies**.

4. Create components from each of the remaining eight bodies in the Browser. Once completed, the bottom of the BROWSER should display as shown in Figure 16–31. The 10 bodies are now 10 separate components in the design.

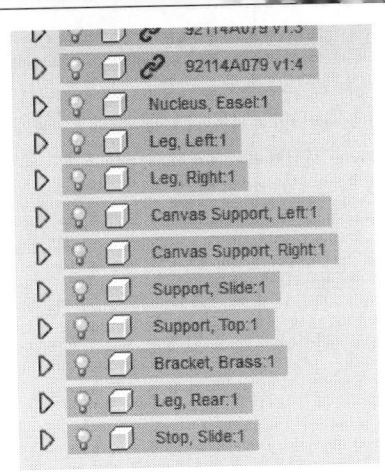

```
        ▷  ᵠ  □  ⌀    92114A079 v1:3
        ▷  ᵠ  □  ⌀    92114A079 v1:4
        ▷  ᵠ  □       Nucleus, Easel:1
        ▷  ᵠ  □       Leg, Left:1
        ▷  ᵠ  □       Leg, Right:1
        ▷  ᵠ  □       Canvas Support, Left:1
        ▷  ᵠ  □       Canvas Support, Right:1
        ▷  ᵠ  □       Support, Slide:1
        ▷  ᵠ  □       Support, Top:1
        ▷  ᵠ  □       Bracket, Brass:1
        ▷  ᵠ  □       Leg, Rear:1
        ▷  ᵠ  □       Stop, Slide:1
```

Figure 16–31

Task 3 - Define rigid as-built joints in the design.

In this task you will ground the Nucleus, Easel component, and then add a joint between the Nucleus, Easel and Bracket, Brass and the Support, Slide and Support, Top components. Both of these will be assigned using the Rigid joint type, as no motion is required between these sets of components.

1. In the BROWSER, right-click on **Nucleus, Easel:1** and select **Ground** to ground this component.

2. In the BROWSER, expand the **Joints** folder. The rigid joints that are listed were added to constrain the fasteners in the assembly.

A grounded part is fixed to a location in the assembly and is not dependent on other parts.

Note: In the upcoming images for joint creation, components that are not needed in the image have been suppressed. This was done to help you to easily identify what is being selected.

3. In the ASSEMBLE panel, click 🖉 (As-built Joint). The AS-BUILT JOINT palette opens.

4. In the AS-BUILT JOINT palette, in the Type drop-down list, ensure that **Rigid** is selected.

5. In the BROWSER or in the graphics window, select the Nucleus, Easel and Bracket, Brass components, as shown in Figure 16–32. A shaking animation is displayed indicating that the two components are now rigidly connected.

Nucleus, Easel

Bracket, Brass

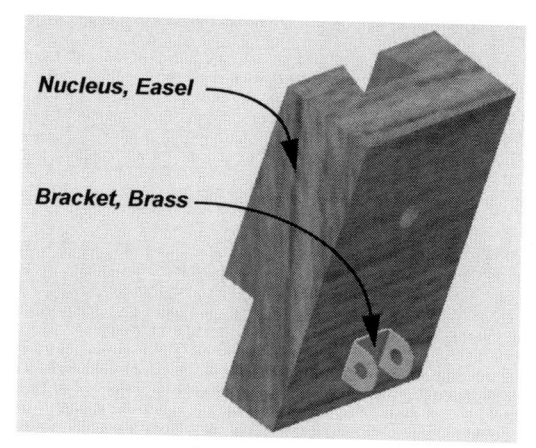

Figure 16–32

6. Click **OK**. Note that the joint is now listed in the BROWSER in the **Joints** folder.

7. Rename the last joint that was created as **Easel Nucleus/Brass Bracket**. This enables you to easily identify the joint.

8. Create an as-built Rigid joint between the Support, Slide and Support, Top components, as shown in Figure 16–33. Rename the joint as **Slide/Top Supports**.

Support, Top

Support, Slide

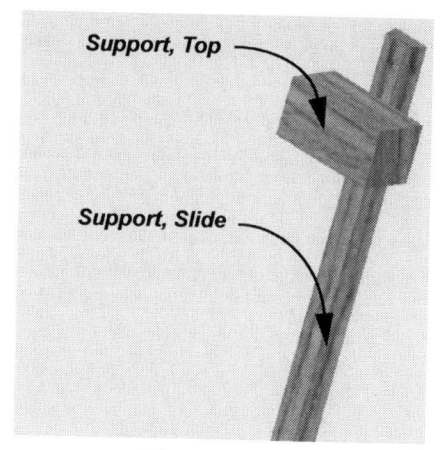

Figure 16–33

Task 4 - Define a Slider as-built joint in the design.

In this task you will add a joint between the Support, Slide and Nucleus, Easel components that permits sliding motion. You will also assign limits on the range of motion for the Support, Slide relative to the grounded Nucleus, Easel component.

1. Create a Slider as-built joint between the Support, Slide and Nucleus, Easel components, as shown in Figure 16–34.

2. For the *Position* reference, select the face shown in blue in Figure 16–34. This defines the sliding direction. Once the *Position* reference is selected, a sliding animation is displayed.

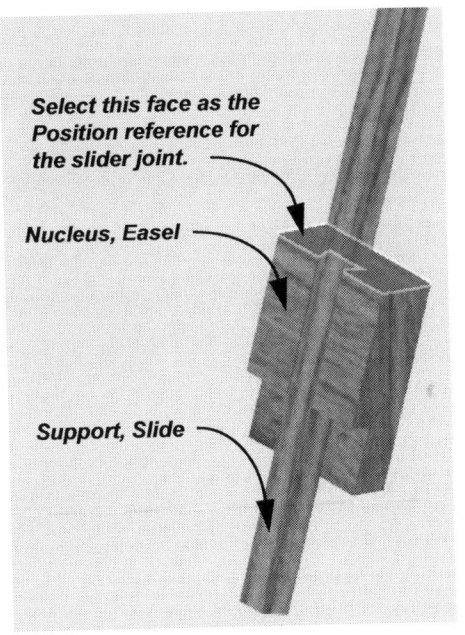

Figure 16–34

3. Click **OK**.

4. Rename the joint as **Easel/Support Slide**.

5. Drag the Support, Slide component and note how you can drag it through each end of the grounded Nucleus, Easel component.

6. Revert the component back to its initial location by selecting (Revert).

7. In the BROWSER, hover over the Easel/Support Slide joint and select (Edit Joint Limits), which displays adjacent to the joint name.

8. The EDIT JOINTS LIMITS palette opens. It identifies that the only permitted motion of this joint is sliding, as shown in the Motion drop-down list in Figure 16–35.

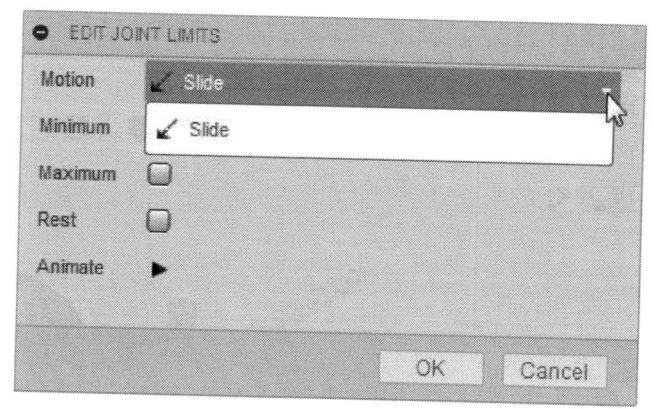

Figure 16–35

9. Select the **Minimum** and **Maximum** checkboxes to enable setting limits on the range of motion.

10. For the *Minimum* value, enter **-3.00 in**.

11. For the *Maximum* value, enter **4.00 in**.

12. Click in the *Animate* area to play the range of sliding motion. Click to stop the animated motion.

13. Click **OK** to complete the limits.

14. Revert the component's position back to where it was initially located.

15. Drag the Support, Slide component and note how the limits are assigned.

Task 5 - Complete the remaining as-built joints.

In this task you will create the remaining joints in the design to constrain the design for its required motion.

1. Create a new Revolute as-built joint between the Bracket, Brass and Leg, Rear components, as shown in Figure 16–36. For now you will permit a full 360° rotation, even though there is interference. This will be controlled later in the practice.

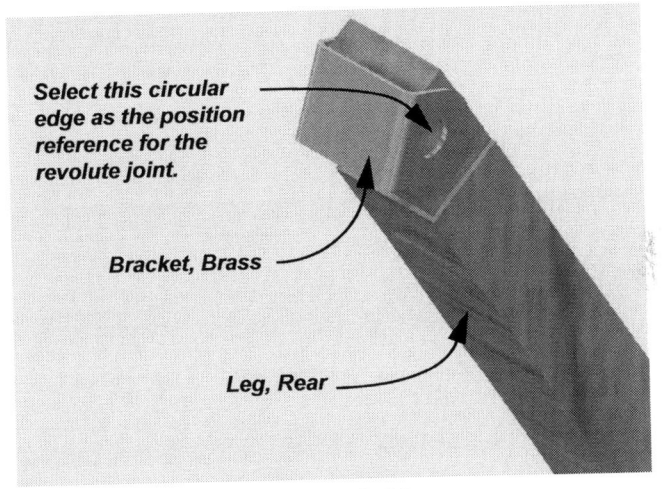

Figure 16–36

2. Rename the Revolute joint as **Bracket/Rear Leg**.

3. Create additional Revolute as-built joints between the following components and rename the created joint as shown below and in Figure 16–37. Ensure that a circular reference that defines the axis of rotation is selected as the *Position* reference.
   - Leg, Left and Nucleus, Easel components (rename the joint as **Left Leg**)
   - Leg, Right and Nucleus, Easel components (rename the joint as **Right Leg**)
   - Canvas Support, Left and Leg, Left components (rename the joint as **Left Canvas Support**)
   - Canvas Support, Right and Leg, Right components (rename the joint as **Right Canvas Support**)

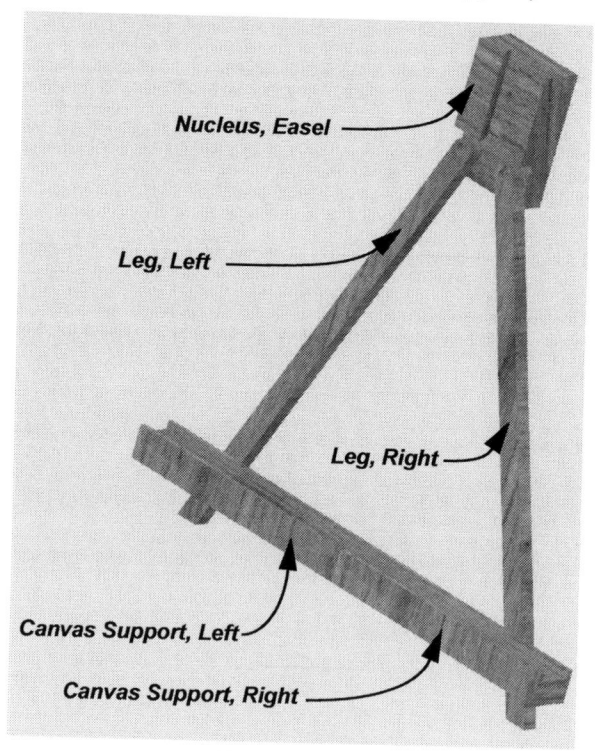

Figure 16–37

4. In the BROWSER, expand the **1603A200** node. This component contains sub-components that have been renamed for you. If the component is not displayed, toggle on its visibility.

Joints were created for you in the hinge component that permit the rotational motion of a hinge model.

5. Create additional Rigid as-built joints between the following components and rename the created joint as shown in brackets.
   - Leaf, Right and Canvas Support, Left (rename the joint as **Left Canvas Support Hinge**)
   - Leaf, Left and Canvas Support, Right (rename the joint as **Right Canvas Support Hinge**)

6. Save the design

Task 6 - Limit the motion of the easel using contact sets.

In this task, you will create a contact set to limit the motion of the design.

1. If you cleared any of the components from the display, toggle their display back on so that all components are being displayed.

2. Drag the left or right Canvas Support components to test the motion of the design. Note that the Leg, Left and Leg, Right can swing and interfere with the Support, Slide component. The Leg, Rear can also rotate through 360°.

3. On the POSITION panel, click ⌂ to return the design to its default position.

4. In the ASSEMBLE panel, click (Enable Contact Sets).

5. There are no sets currently set up in the model. In the ASSEMBLE panel, click (New Contact Set). The NEW CONTACT SET palette opens, enabling you to define a new set.

6. In the graphics window, select the Leg, Rear and Nucleus, Easel components. Click **OK**. Test that the range of motion is now as expected.

7. Create a second contact set that consists of the Leg, Left, Leg, Right, and Support, Slide components.

8. Save the design.

Task 7 - Create a relationship between the joints on the right and left legs.

1. In the ASSEMBLE panel, click (Motion Link). The Motion Link palette opens.

2. In the BROWSER, select the Left Leg and Right Leg joints.

3. For the *Left Leg*, enter **90 deg**. For the *Right Leg*, enter **-90 deg**.

Note the animated preview of the Motion Link might not display exactly as expected.

4. Click **OK** and test the motion by dragging the components to their expanded and collapsed positions, as shown in Figure 16–38.
   - Collapse the Support, Slide and the Leg, Rear components.
   - Collapse the Canvas Support, Right and the Canvas Support, Left components.

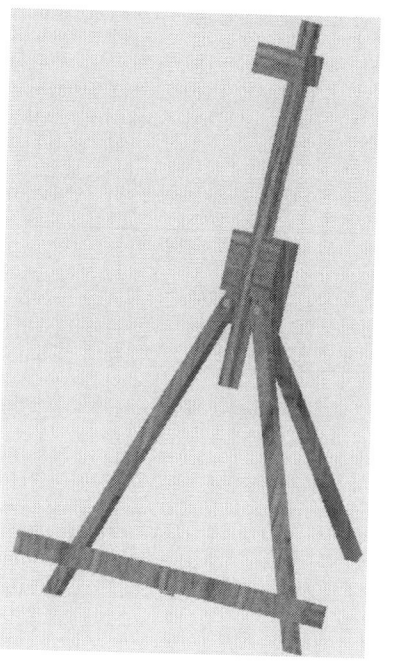

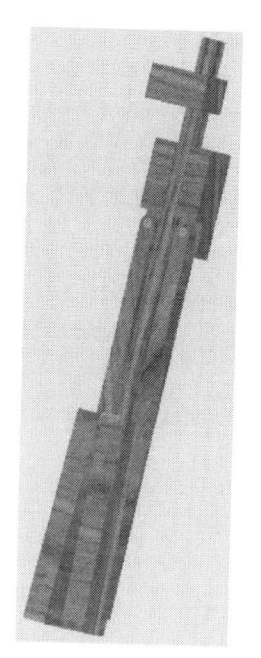

Figure 16–38

5. Save the design and close the file.

To review a completed version of this design, upload the **Folding Easel Final.f3z** file from the *Folding_Easel* folder of your practice files and open **Folding Easel Final** in the Autodesk Fusion 360 software.

Tip: 3D Printing

Designs created in the Autodesk Fusion 360 software can be prepared for 3D Printing using the tools on the MAKE panel. Individual components created in a multi-body design can be copied separately into new designs when required for printing. These copies are not associative with the original design, so new copies should be created and used for printing after changes have been made to the original design. For more information on 3D Printing, refer to Appendix A: Outputting for 3D Printing.

Chapter Review Questions

1. Which of the following feature creation tools enables you to create a new feature as a new body in the design? (Select all that apply.)

    a. **Extrude**
    b. **Shell**
    c. **Loft**
    d. **Box**
    e. **Fillet**

2. Which of the following tools should be used to split a single body into two bodies? (Select all that apply.)

    a. **Extrude**
    b. **Split Face**
    c. **Split Body**
    d. **Combine**

3. Which of the following is NOT a valid method of creating a new, empty component in a design.

    a. During geometry creation, in the *Operation* drop-down list, click **New Component**.
    b. In the CREATE panel, click (New Component).
    c. In the BROWSER, right-click on the top-level design file's name and select **New Component**.
    d. In an existing design file, right-click an existing body in the **Bodies** folder and select **Create Components from Bodies**.

4. Which of the following best describes how to create **Component3** shown in Figure 16–39? (Select all that apply.)

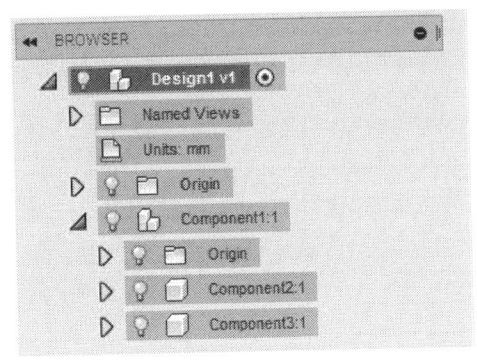

Figure 16–39

a. With the top-level design active, right-click on **Design1** and select **New Component**.

b. With Component1 active, right-click on **Component1** and select **New Component**.

c. With the top-level design active, right-click on **Component2** and select **New Component**.

5. Which of the following tools enables you to duplicate a component in the design and ensures that the duplicated version maintains associativity with the parent (i.e., if changes are made to the parent component, that change will be reflected in all duplicated versions of the component)?

a. **Mirror**
b. **Copy/Paste**
c. **Pattern**
d. **Save Copy As**

6. Which of the following tools can be used to prevent components from displaying in the graphics window. (Select all that apply.)

a. **Show/Hide**
b. **Selectable/Unselectable**
c. **Opacity Control**
d. **Isolate**

7. The **As-built Joint** tool can be used to reposition two components that are offset from one another so that two faces are touching and all degrees of freedom are removed between them (Rigid).

   a. True
   b. False

Answers: 1.(a,c,d), 2.c, 3.d, 4.(a,b), 5.(b,c), 6.(a,d), 7.b

Command Summary

Button	Command	Location
	Align	• **Ribbon:** *Model* Workspace>MODIFY panel • **Context Menu:** Right-click in the graphics window and select **Modify**.
	As-built Joint	• **Ribbon:** *Model* Workspace>ASSEMBLE panel • **Context Menu:** Right-click in the graphics window and select **Assemble**.
	Circular Pattern (feature)	• **Ribbon:** *Model* Workspace>CREATE panel • **Context Menu:** Right-click in the graphics window and select **Create**.
	Combine	• **Ribbon:** *Model* Workspace>MODIFY panel • **Context Menu:** Right-click in the graphics window and select **Modify**.
NA	Copy	• **Context Menu:** With one or more bodies or components selected in the BROWSER
NA	Create Components from Bodies	• **Context Menu:** With a body selected in the **Bodies** folder of the BROWSER
NA	Ground	• **Context Menu:** With one or more components selected in the BROWSER
NA	Isolate	• **Context Menu:** With one or more components selected in the BROWSER
	Move	• **Ribbon:** *Model* Workspace>MODIFY panel • **Context Menu:** Right-click in the graphics window and select **Modify**.
	New Component	• **Ribbon:** *Model* Workspace>CREATE panel • **Context Menu:** Right-click in the graphics window and select **Create**. • **Context Menu:** With the design's name selected or a component selected in the BROWSER
NA	Opacity Control	• **Context Menu:** With one or more components selected in the BROWSER
NA	Paste	• **Context Menu:** In the graphics window
	Pattern on Path (feature)	• **Ribbon:** *Model* Workspace>CREATE panel • **Context Menu:** Right-click in the graphics window and select **Create**.
NA	Properties	• **Context Menu:** With one or more components selected in the BROWSER
	Rectangular Pattern (feature)	• **Ribbon:** *Model* Workspace>CREATE panel • **Context Menu:** Right-click in the graphics window and select **Create**.

	NA	Selectable/ Unselectable	• **Context Menu:** With one or more components selected in the BROWSER
	NA	Show All Components	• **Context Menu:** With one or more components selected in the BROWSER
	NA	Show/Hide	• **Context Menu:** With one or more components selected in the BROWSER
		Split Body	• **Ribbon:** *Model* Workspace>MODIFY panel • **Context Menu:** Right-click in the graphics window and select **Modify**.

Chapter 17

Sculpting Geometry

A sculpt workflow enables you to create complex, visually appealing shapes using sculpted Autodesk® T-Splines® geometry. Using T-Splines enables you to create complex geometry without the complex work that would be required if using a parametric or direct modeling workflow.

Learning Objectives in this Chapter

- Enable the sculpt environment and understand how T-Spline surface geometry can be displayed in a model.
- Create sculpted T-Splines using the Box, Plane, Cylinder, Sphere, Torus, and Quadball quick shape modeling tools.
- Create T-Spline surfaces by referencing 2D sketch geometry that will define the shape of the surface.
- Fill the gaps in T-Spline surfaces using the Face and Fill Hole options.

17.1 Introduction to the Sculpt Environment

It is often difficult and time-consuming to create organic, highly shaped, and visually appealing models using conventional modeling techniques. T-Spline surface modeling is an alternate modeling approach for these types of surfaces. It enables you to create shapes that can be manipulated directly, without needing to use parametric constraints. T-Spline tools can be combined with parametric tools, where required.

Video Lesson Available

Understanding Surface Modeling

Video Length: 2:43

In the Autodesk® Fusion 360™ software, all T-Spline surface modeling is done in the Sculpt environment. To access the Sculpt environment, in the CREATE panel, click (Create Form), as shown in Figure 17–1.

> The Sculpt environment can also be activated by clicking CREATE> Create Form.

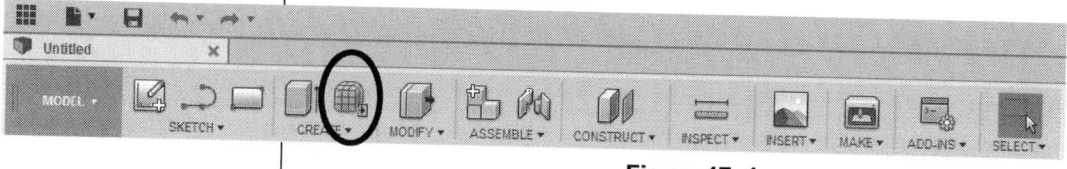

Figure 17–1

Once the Sculpt environment has been activated, you are prompted to confirm entry into this environment. Click **OK** to activate the environment, as shown in Figure 17–2. The sculpting tools display with purple icons (as compared to blue icons for solid modeling).

Figure 17–2

Control Mesh

A simple box model is shown in Figure 17–3. The mesh that overlays the T-Spline geometry is used for editing and further manipulating the shape of the geometry. This is called the control frame. The control frame consists of points that are connected by edges, and the enclosed edges are called *faces*. While editing you can select points, edges, faces, loops, or bodies for editing.

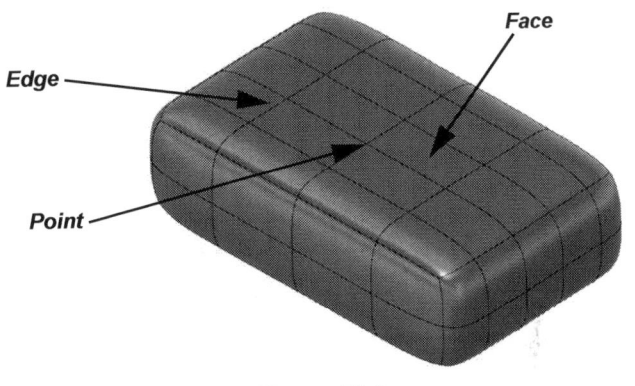

Figure 17–3

Hint: T-points vs. Star Points

- Star points exist when 3, 5, or more edges come together, as shown in Figure 17–3.

- T-points are a t-junction of edges, as shown in Figure 17–3. They enable you to add complexity only where it is needed. T-points are generally created using the modify tools.

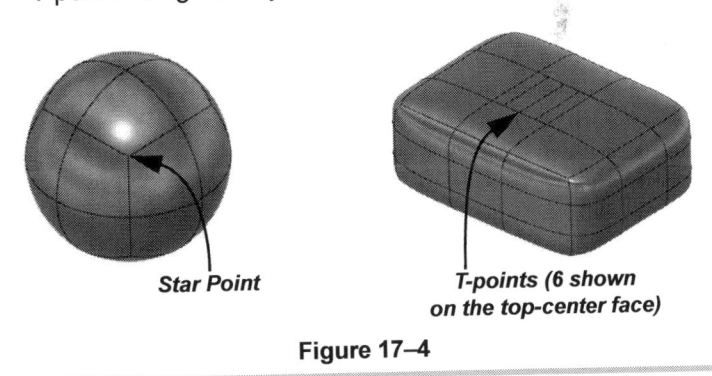

Star Point   T-points (6 shown on the top-center face)

Figure 17–4

As multiple shapes are added, combined, and edited, the sculpted shape creates more complex geometry. Note that only one sculpted shape is listed in the Timeline (⬚), regardless of the complexity of that shape.

Display Modes

When working in the sculpt environment, you can use the six standard visual styles to control how the model is displayed. These styles control the shaded and wireframe displays, and sets whether hidden edges or visible edges are displayed. In general, the **Shaded with Visible Edges Only** option is the most commonly used. This setting enables you to view and select the control mesh for easy manipulation.

As a sculpted T-Spline model becomes more complex with multiple shapes interacting, you might notice a drop in computer performance, due to the significant number of calculations that are required the vertices when you make edits. To improve performance, consider changing the Display Mode option.

To change the Display Mode option, in the UTILITIES panel, click (Display Mode). The DISPLAY MODE palette opens, as shown in Figure 17–5.

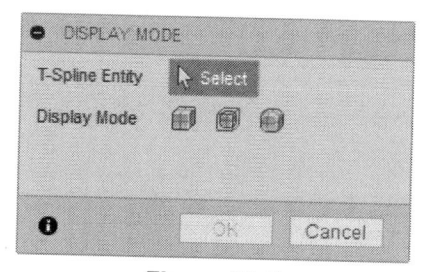

Figure 17–5

The Display Mode options include **Box** (), **Control Frame** (), and **Smooth** (), as shown in Figure 17–6. There are keyboard shortcuts available for each Display Mode option. To assign a mode to a T-Spline body, select one of its entities (face, edge, or point). Each body in a design can have different display model settings.

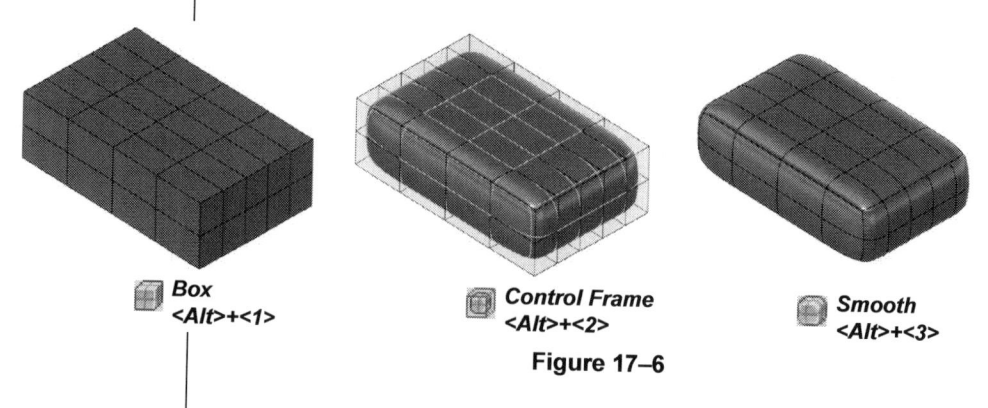

Box
<Alt>+<1>

Control Frame
<Alt>+<2>

Smooth
<Alt>+<3>

Figure 17–6

Performance Options

The Smooth and Control Frame display modes require the same processing power. The Box display mode provides the best performance, but sacrifices the ability to display the true shape of the model. When editing the shape of the model, consider using the Control Frame mode to learn the relationship between the box and smooth results.

In the UTILITIES panel, the **Enable Better Display** and **Enable Better Performance** options can further help with system performance when in the Sculpt environment. These options toggle between a better display or better performance, respectively.

- **Enable Better Display** - Displays bodies at the highest quality display (applies G1 conditions).

- **Enable Better Performance** - Displays bodies at a lower quality to improve computer performance (applies G0 conditions).

17.2 Surface Quick Shapes

Similar to solid quick shapes, the Autodesk Fusion 360 software includes quick shape tools that enable you to create surface geometry using T-Splines. Using these tools, you can draw the sketch and 3D surface geometry at the same time.

Sculpt Timeline icon:

The T-Spline quick shapes that can be created are: **Box**, **Plane**, **Cylinder**, **Sphere**, **Torus**, and **Quadball**, as shown in Figure 17–7.

Surface geometry represents only the outer shell of the design, and does not have a solid volume. Once surfaces are modeled, they can be converted to a solid if its boundary is completely enclosed.

Box
Plane
Cylinder
Sphere
Torus
Quadball

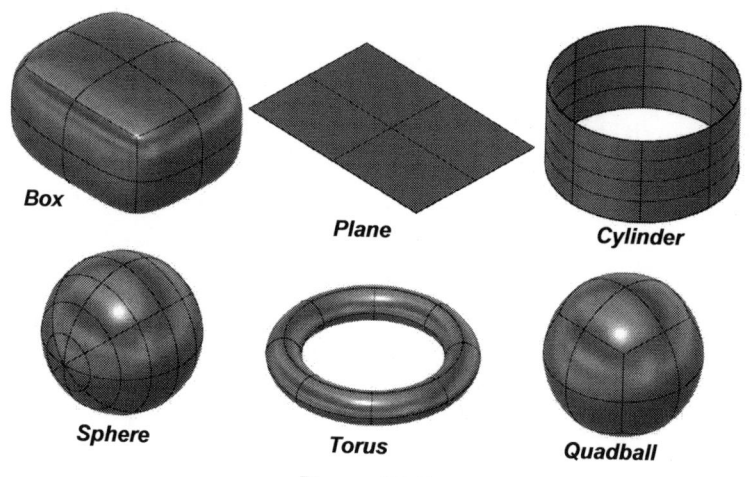

Figure 17–7

The quick shape creation options are located in the ribbon in the CREATE panel, as shown in Figure 17–8.

Pipe is also considered a Quick Shape, but is not covered in this student guide.

The options in this portion of the CREATE panel are quick shape creation options

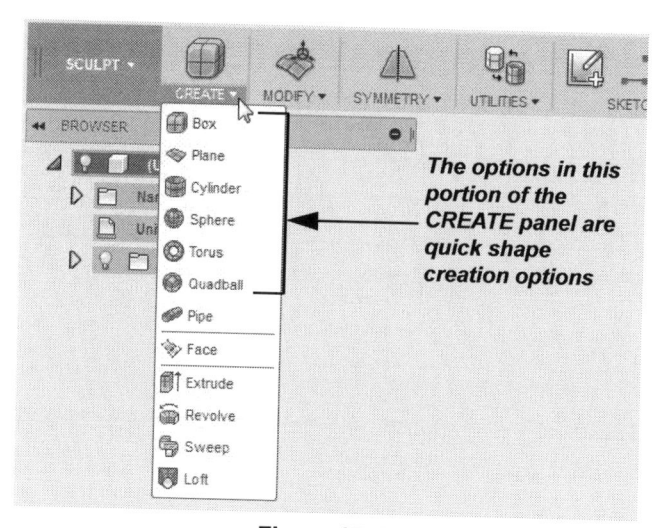

Figure 17–8

In general, the procedure for creating a sculpted T-Spline surface using the quick shapes is similar to creating the shapes as solids. You must select a placement plane, sketch a profile to create the shape, and enter the number of Faces that are to be included in the shape. The number of faces assigned in each direction defines the overall control mesh, as shown for the Box shape shown in Figure 17–9. In this example, the number of faces are: *Length*: **4**, *Width*: **3**, and *Height*: **2**.

For a sphere, a Longitude and Latitude entry field are used to define the number of faces in the complete surface.

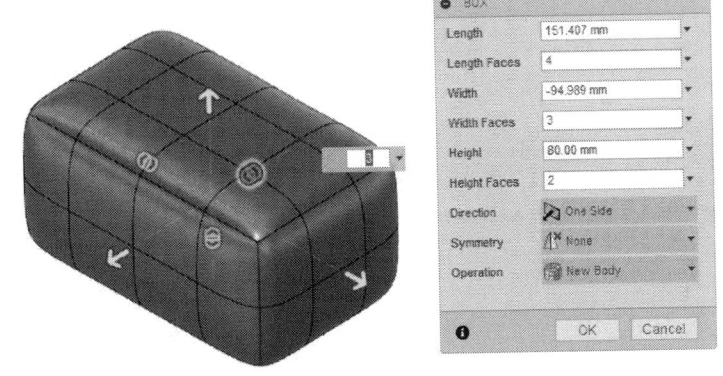

Figure 17–9

Once you complete the shape definition, click **OK**. You will remain in the Sculpt environment and you can continue to add more shapes, as needed.

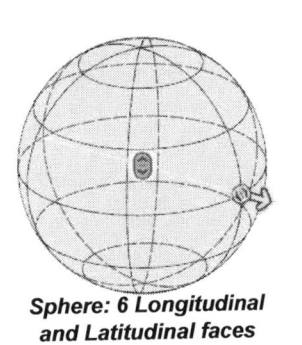

> **Hint: Quadball**
>
> The **Quadball** quick shape tool is only available in the Sculpt environment, and cannot be created as a solid feature. The creation of this shape is similar to a sphere in terms of the placement options, but the faces are defined differently. Instead of a Longitude and Latitude entry for the faces of a sphere, a quadball requires a single entry for Span Faces, as shown in Figure 17–10. 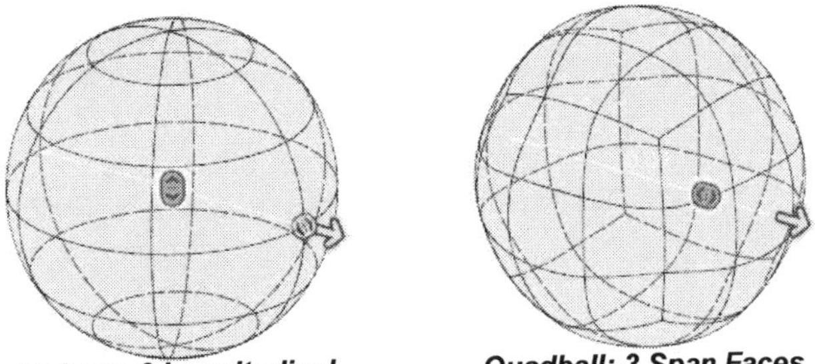
>
> **Sphere: 6 Longitudinal and Latitudinal faces** **Quadball: 3 Span Faces**
>
> Figure 17–10

Exiting the Sculpt Environment

To exit the Sculpt environment, in the FINISH FORM panel, click ![icon]. You are returned to the Model environment with access to the parametric modeling tools. If the form that was created is completely enclosed, a solid is automatically created to fill the volume of the T-Spline surface, as shown for the Box in Figure 17–11. A single sculpt form always (![icon]) displays in the Timeline, while the **Bodies** folder in the BROWSER displays as ![icon] for surface geometry and as ![icon] for solid geometry that was created in the Form feature.

A Box, Sphere, Torus, and Quadball can all be used to create solid geometry once the Finish Form option is selected.

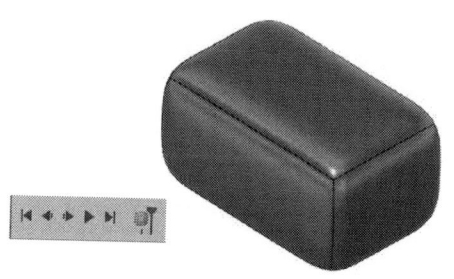

Figure 17–11

- To add additional T-Spline surface geometry to an existing form, right-click on ![icon] in the Timeline and select **Edit**.

- To add a second form, enter the Sculpt environment again. A second Form feature is added to the Timeline, as shown in Figure 17–12. All existing Form features display as transparent.

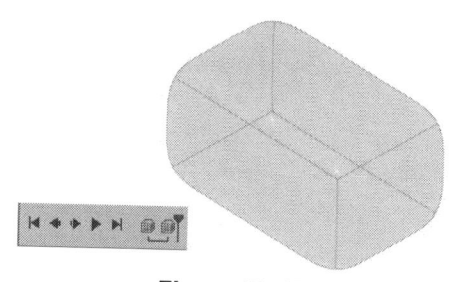

Figure 17–12

Video Lesson Available

Creating Primitive Shapes

Video Length: 9:10

17.3 Creating Sketched T-Spline Surfaces

In addition to using quick shape primitives to create T-Spline surface geometry, you can also create shapes that reference a sketch. Using the Extrude, Revolve, Sweep, and Loft options, you can create surface geometry that is extruded normal to a sketch plane, that revolves a sketch about a centerline, that sweeps a sketch profile along a path, or that joins multiple sketched profiles. When created in the Sculpt environment, the resulting geometry remains open on both ends of the geometry.

The process of creating these feature types is the same as when creating a solid. Similar to the quick shape primitives, you must define the number of faces required to define the feature's control frame.

> **Hint: Setting the Number of Faces**
>
> When using a sketched profile, the number of faces used to define the feature affects how closely a highly curved profile is matched, as shown in Figure 17–13.
>
> *Sketched Profile*
>
> *Extruded profile with 8 Faces.*
>
> *Extruded profile with 20 Faces.*
>
> Figure 17–13
>
> The Uniform and Curvature spacing options can be used to customize the resulting shape:
>
> - **Uniform:** Spaces the number of faces evenly along a profile.
>
> - **Curvature:** Spaces the number of faces based on a profile's curvature. The higher the amount of curvature, the more faces that will be generated. This option (in addition to the number of faces) affects how closely an extruded surface matches a sketch.

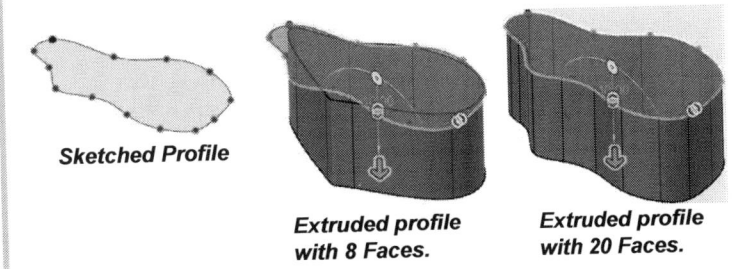

Video Lesson Available

Creating a T-Spline Surface from a Sketch with Extrude

Video Length: 5:29

Video Lesson Available

Creating a T-Spline Surface from a Sketch with Revolve

Video Length: 3:22

Video Lesson Available

Creating a T-Spline Swept Surface from a Sketch

Video Length: 4:29

Video Lesson Available

Creating a Lofted T-Spline Surface from a Sketch

Video Length: 6:23

17.4 Creating Faces & Filling Holes

Creating a Face

The Face option enables you to create a face by referencing existing vertices in a design file to fill gaps. You can also create a simple planar face between points placed on a construction plane. Examples of faces are shown in Figure 17–14.

Extruded sketched profile → **Face option used to close the top area.**

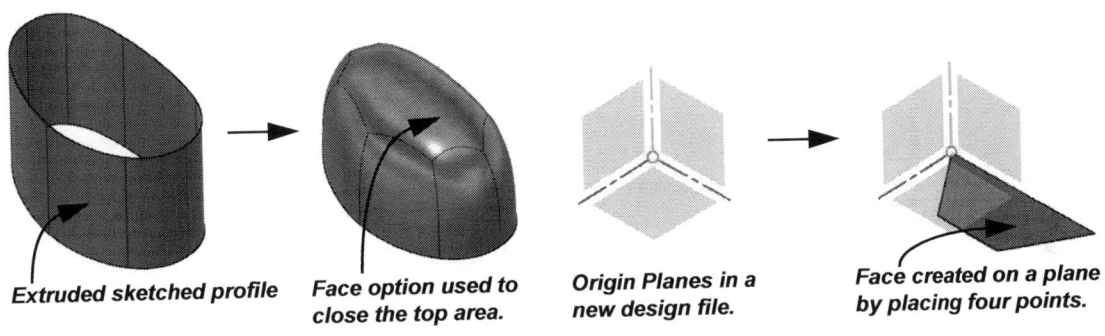

Origin Planes in a new design file. → **Face created on a plane by placing four points.**

Figure 17–14

Use the following steps to create a face in a design file:

1. In the CREATE panel, click (Face). The FACE palette opens, as shown in Figure 17–15.

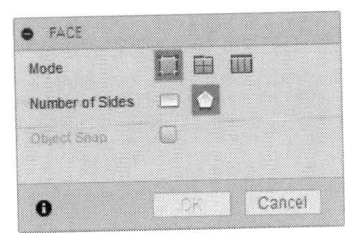

Figure 17–15

2. Set how the face is to be created using the options in the Mode area:

   - (Simple): Select individual points to define the face. The points can be vertices on existing, active, T-Spline surface geometry.

   - (Edge): Select an edge to define the first two vertices, and then select two additional points to define the face.

   - (Chain): Create a face along a series of edges by selecting an edge and then adjacent vertices to define the face.

Using (Simple), points can be selected without referencing existing entities. You can do this by first selecting a construction plane to locate the points, and then selecting the points.

3. If defining a simple face, define the number of sides in the face. The options are not available for edge or chain faces.
   - ☐ (Four): Create a face with four boundary points.
   - ⬠ (Multiple): Create a face with any number of boundary points. Once the points are selected, complete the face by selecting the first selected point a second time.
4. Select points and edges to define the face, as required.
   - Consider using the **Object Snap** and **Offset** options to locate a vertex to the closest point of other objects in the scene. Vertices can be snapped to other solid, surface, and mesh bodies that exist in the design file.
5. Click **OK** to complete the face.

Filling a Hole

Using many of the T-Spline creation options, geometry is often open at the top and bottom when it is created. In addition to using the **Face** option to close the gap, you can also use the **Fill Hole** option. This option enables you to select an edge in a chain to close a hole. The hole can be of any shape, as long as all of the edges are connected to one another. Examples of surfaces that have been created using the Fill Hole option are shown in Figure 17–16. In each example, the three fill hole mode options are displayed to show how the resulting geometry can vary.

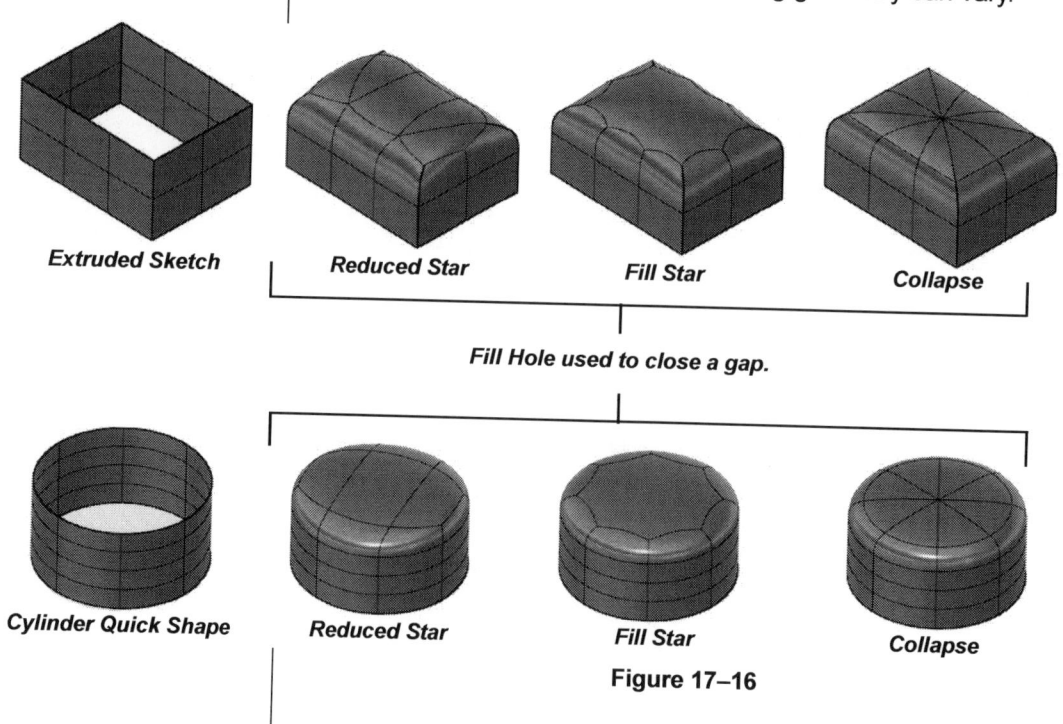

Extruded Sketch   Reduced Star   Fill Star   Collapse

Fill Hole used to close a gap.

Cylinder Quick Shape   Reduced Star   Fill Star   Collapse

Figure 17–16

Consider the following tips when filling a hole:

- Use **Fill Star** mode if minimal distortion of the shape is required. Note that it is good practice to use as few star points as possible. **Reduced Star** mode is recommended if you need to maintain symmetry.

- If **Collapse** mode is selected, enable the **Weld Center Vertices** option to weld the vertices at the center.

- Enable the **Maintain Crease Edges** option to keep any creased edges when filling the hole. A filled hole with this option both enabled and disabled is shown in Figure 17–17.

Maintain Crease Edges

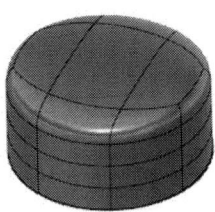

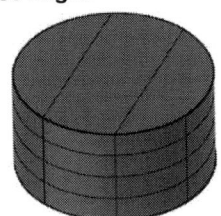

Disabled   Enabled

Figure 17–17

Video Lesson Available

Modifying T-Spline Forms
(Fill Hole topic begins at 3:20)

Video Length: 6:31

Practice 17a T-Spline Surface Modeling I

Practice Objectives

- Create T-Spline surface geometry using the quick shape primitives.
- Add T-Spline surfaces to fill gaps in the geometry.
- Change the visual display and display mode for T-Spline surface geometry.

In this practice, you will learn how to access the Sculpt environment and use several quick shape primitives to create a T-Spline surface in the design file. You will then use multiple options to close gaps in the design. Once the T-Spine surface geometry is created, you will return to the Model environment and review how it displays in the design.

Task 1 - Create a T-Spline Box design.

1. Create a new design.

2. To access the Sculpt environment, in the CREATE panel, click (Create Form). When a prompted that you are entering the Sculpt environment, click **OK**.

3. In the CREATE panel, click (Box).

4. When prompted to choose a plane, in the BROWSER, in the **Origin** folder, select the XZ plane. Alternatively, you can select the XZ plane directly in the graphics window.

5. Click on the Origin to select it as the center point and then drag the profile to approximately 75mm x 75mm, similar to that shown in Figure 17–18. Click again to define the box profile.

The ground plane lies on the XZ plane.

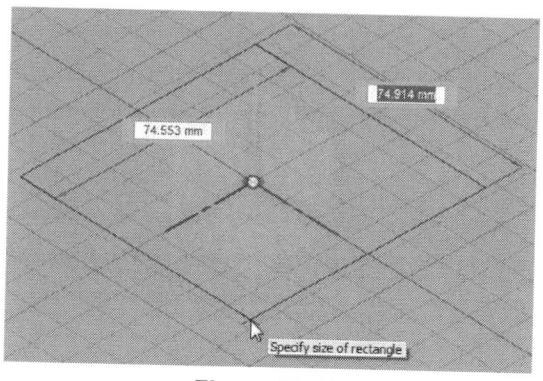

Figure 17–18

6. The shape is automatically given a third dimension, similar to that shown in Figure 17–19. Manipulators on the box enable you to manipulate it size and number of faces. The BOX palette also opens.

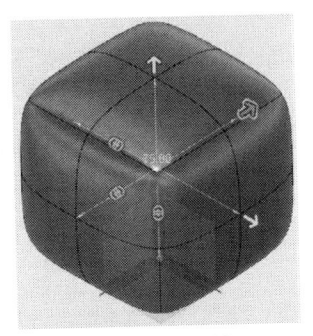

Figure 17–19

7. Select and drag any of the manipulator arrows to free-form adjust the length, width, or height of the box.

8. In the BOX palette, for the *Length*, *Width*, and *Height* fields, enter **75mm**.

9. In the three *Faces* fields, enter **3**. This divides each side of the box into 9 faces, as shown in Figure 17–20. As an alternative, you can also drag the sliders in the model to change the number of faces.

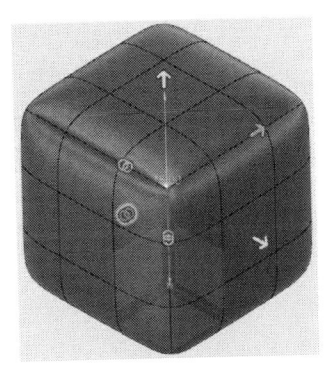

Figure 17–20

10. In the Symmetry drop-down list, select **Mirror** to assign symmetry. Select **Width Symmetry** to ensure that symmetry is maintained in the width direction when faces are modified. The edges along the mirror line in the width direction change to green to indicate that symmetry has been assigned.

11. In the BOX palette, click **OK** to create the box.

12. In the lower left corner of the Autodesk Fusion 360 window, in the Timeline, hover the cursor over , as shown in Figure 17–21. The icon is identified as **Form1** in the tooltip.

Figure 17–21

13. In the BROWSER, note that **Body1** has been added to the **Bodies** folder and that you are still in the Sculpt environment. Additional T-Spline surface geometry can be added to this form. Note that the icon associated with **Body1** indicates that it is a T-Spline surface ( ).

14. To exit the Sculpt environment, in the FINISH FORM panel, click   (Finish Form). The design file is returned to the Model environment and the geometry displays as shown in Figure 17–22. Note how the control edges and points are no longer visible. Additionally, in the BROWSER, note that the icon associated with **Body1** now indicates that it is a solid ( ). This is because the surface was completely enclosed and could form a solid.

Figure 17–22

Task 2 - Create a T-Spline Cylinder design.

1. In the CREATE panel, click   (Create Form). When prompted that you are entering the Sculpt environment, click **OK**. This will create a second independent form in the design file. Note how the first form is now grayed-out, indicating that it is not active and cannot be selected as a reference.

2. In the CREATE panel, click ▬ (Cylinder).

3. Select a centerpoint for the cylinder that is adjacent to the box, similar to that shown in Figure 17–23. Define the diameter of the cylinder.

4. Using the drag handles or entry fields, define the cylinder size and number of faces as shown in Figure 17–23.

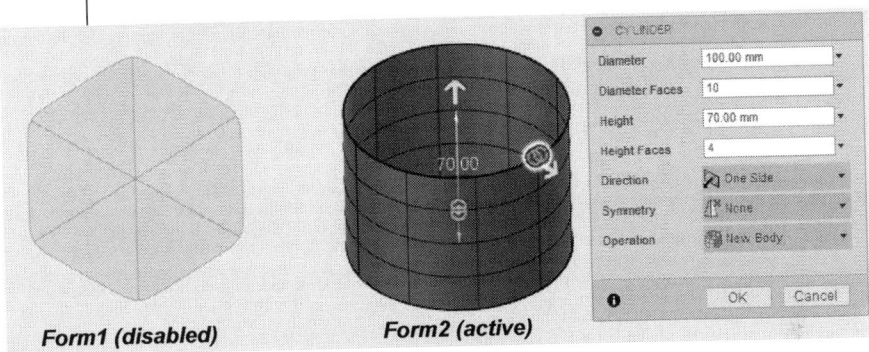

Form1 (disabled)   *Form2 (active)*

Figure 17–23

5. In the CYLINDER palette, click **OK** to create the cylinder.

6. In the FINISH FORM panel, click ▬ (Finish Form)

7. In the Timeline, note that there are two forms listed in the design file, as shown in Figure 17–24. Because the cylinder is not completely enclosed, the geometry is identified as surface geometry (▬) when you are in the Model environment.

Figure 17–24

Task 3 - Fill gaps in the cylinder form.

In this task you will use two different T-Spline surface creation options: **Face** and **Fill Hole**. You will use both options so that you can compare the resulting shapes.

1. You will add additional surface geometry to Form2 to cap its top. Start by right-clicking on **Form2** and selecting **Edit**.

2. In the MODIFY panel, click ▬ (Fill Hole).

3. Select any one of the edges along the top chain of edges of the cylinder. A preview of the geometry displays, similar to that shown in Figure 17–25. By default, **Reduced Star** is the assigned *Fill Hole Mode* option. Note that the selected edge is highlighted in blue.

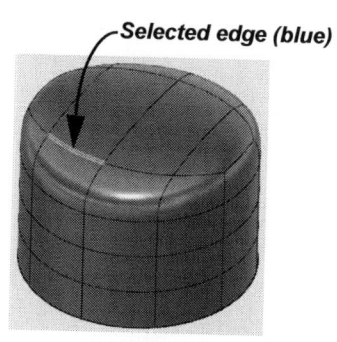

Figure 17–25

4. Change the *Fill Hole Mode* option to vary the shape of the new surface. The resulting geometry is displayed as shown in Figure 17–26.

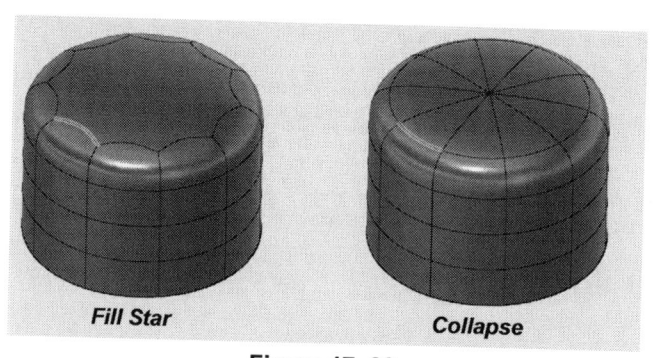

Figure 17–26

5. Click **OK** to complete the geometry. Note that a new form is not created, and instead the geometry is combined with the cylinder in Form2. The geometry acts as one T-Spline.

When working in the Sculpt environment, all geometry is additive and no feature history is stored. For this reason, the Undo command is the only way to remove individual features in the design. Note that features can only be removed in the reverse order to how they were initially created.

6. Click (Undo) in the Quick Access Toolbar to remove the geometry created by the **Fill Hole** option.

7. In the CREATE panel, click (Face).

8. In the *Mode* area, ensure that (Simple) is selected.

9. In the *Number of Sides* area, select (Multiple Sides).

10. Click to select the first point to start the face, as shown in Figure 17–27.

11. Click to select the second point, as shown in Figure 17–27.

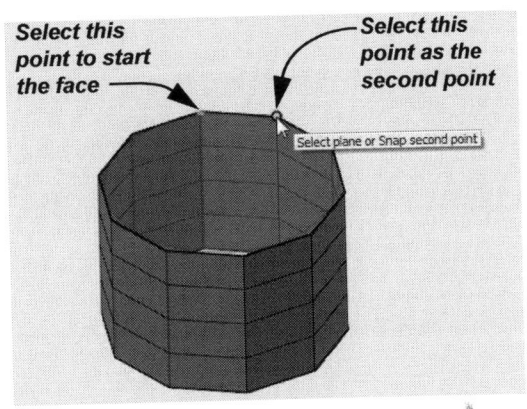

Figure 17–27

12. Continue to select each point around the edge in a clockwise direction. To complete the face, click to select the start point a second time (shown in Figure 17–28).

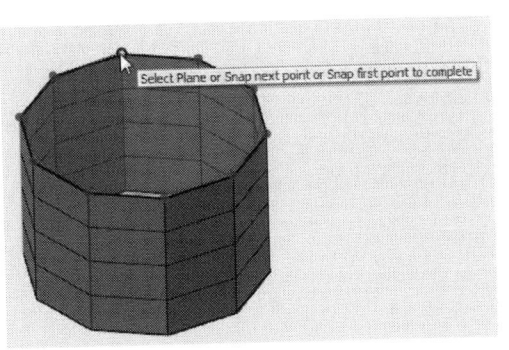

Figure 17–28

13. In the FACE palette, click **OK** to finish the face. The geometry displays as shown in Figure 17–29. This is similar to the geometry that was created using the filled hole using the **Fill Star** option.

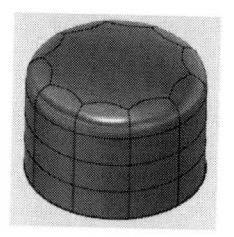

Figure 17–29

14. Click ⬅ (Undo) in the Quick Access Toolbar.

15. Restart the **Face** option.

16. In the *Mode* area, ensure that ▫ (Simple) is selected.

17. In the *Number of Sides* area, select ▫ (Four Sides).

18. Select the first point to start the face, and then select the second point as shown in Figure 17–30.

Select this point to start the face

Select this point as the second point

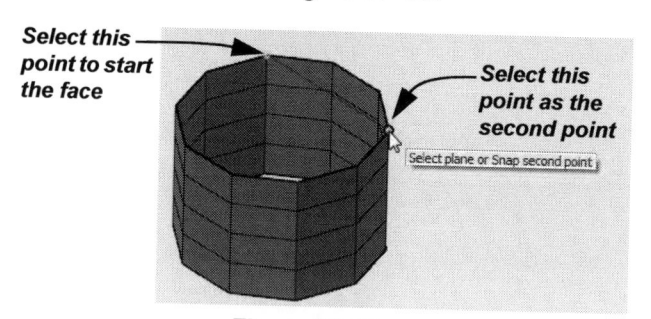

Figure 17–30

19. Select the third and fourth points as shown in Figure 17–31. **Note:** Do not click **OK** to create the face yet.

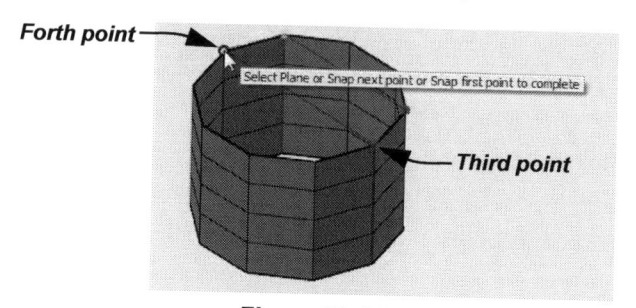

Forth point

Third point

Figure 17–31

Tip: You can also create 3 sided faces by selecting the same point as the 3rd and 4th selection.

20. With the FACE palette open, create three additional faces using the **Simple** and **Four Side** options so that the geometry is created as shown in Figure 17–32.

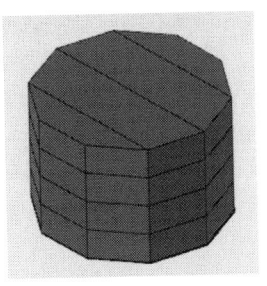

Figure 17–32

21. Click **OK** to complete the face creation. The new faces create the geometry as shown in Figure 17–33.

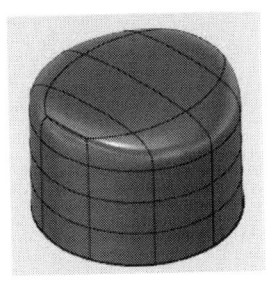

Figure 17–33

22. Undo the creation of the last face. Note how only one of the four faces was removed. Each selection of four entities created four unique faces.
    - Note how the geometry displays similar to that shown in Figure 17–34. Depending on the order of face creation, the last face undone might vary. To create a face to fill the gap (if required) you can use any of the previously discussed techniques.

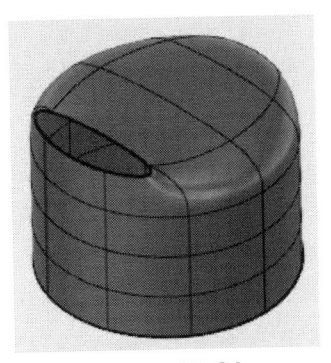

Figure 17–34

When choosing whether to use the **Face** or **Fill Hole** options, consider the resulting control frame of edges, faces, and edges that get created. In the next chapter you will learn about the editing tools and how the control frame affects the edits.

23. In the Quick Access Toolbar, click ➡ (Redo) to return the face to the display.

24. Using the ViewCube, rotate the model so that it displays similar to that shown in Figure 17–35 . This displays the open bottom edge of the cylinder.

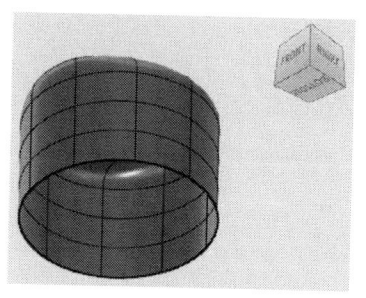

Figure 17–35

25. Using the best option, create a flat bottom face that has no control point, as shown in Figure 17–36. Hint: You will have to enable the **Maintain Crease Edges** option to achieve this face.

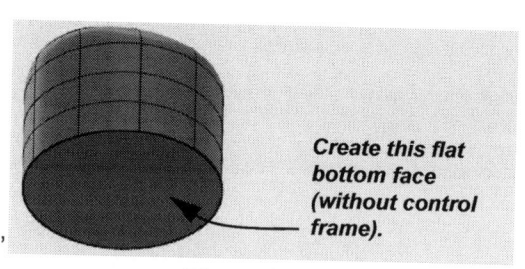

Create this flat bottom face (without control frame).

Figure 17–36

26. Finish the form feature.

- Note that both **Body1** and **Body2** are solids, as shown in the BROWSER in Figure 17–37.

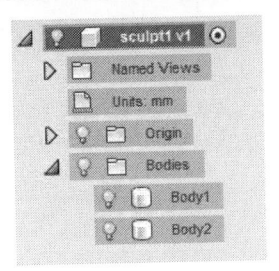

Figure 17–37

Task 4 - Review the Display Styles.

1. The Display Modes can only be controlled when working in a form feature. In the Timeline, right-click on **Form2** and select **Edit**.

2. In the UTILITIES panel, click (Display Mode). The DISPLAY MODE palette opens, as shown in Figure 17–38.

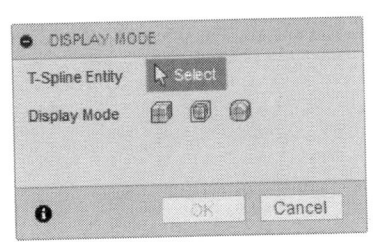

Figure 17–38

3. In the Display Mode area, select (Box). The model displays as it does when creating T-Spline geometry.

4. Click **OK**. Note that the display setting remains active. Working in this mode can help improve system performance when you are working on complex form features.

5. In the UTILITIES panel, click (Display Mode) a second time.

6. In the Display Mode area, select (Control Frame). The model displays showing both the smooth and box forms. This can help you see the relationship between the lines and smooth geometry.

7. Return to the **Box** display mode and finish the form.

8. Save the file as **Sculpt1**.

Task 5 - (Optional) Create additional quick shapes.

Continue working in the current design file and create additional form features using the other quick shape primitive options.

- Create a Plane form feature that lies on one of the construction planes.

- Create a Quadball. Like the Plane quick shape, this is a unique command in the Sculpt environment that does not exist in the Model environment.

Save the file. Click ✖ in the *New Design* document tab to close the file.

Practice 17b T-Spline Surface Modeling II

Practice Objectives

- Create T-Spline surface geometry using sketched geometry.

In this practice, you will work in the Sculpt environment to create the initial shape of a plastic bottle using T-Spline surfaces. You will use provided sketches to create a loft that will form the body of the bottle, and then you will use a torus to create the initial design of the handle. Once you have created these shapes in the design file, you will save the file. You will continue the design in the next chapter where you will learn how to edit a T-Spline's control mesh.

Task 1 - Create a T-Spline surface loft.

1. Click ▼ > **New Design from File**.

2. In the Open dialog box, navigate to the *C:\Autodesk Fusion 360 Practice Files* folder. Select **Sculpted_Loft.f3d** and then click **Open**. The design displays as shown in Figure 17–39.
   - The design file consists of 3 circular sketches on parallel planes. A spline entity connects the circles.
   - The circular sections have been broken up to consist of fours entities (quarters) so that when the T-Spline surface is created the entities blend to help create a better control mesh.

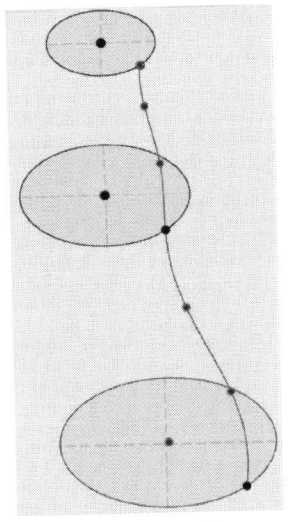

Figure 17–39

3. Open the Sculpt environment to create a new form feature in the file. This shape will form the basis of a plastic container design model.

4. In the CREATE panel, click (Loft). The LOFT palette opens, as shown in Figure 17–40. This palette is similar to that used to create solid lofted geometry, but contains additional options to control how the faces are created.

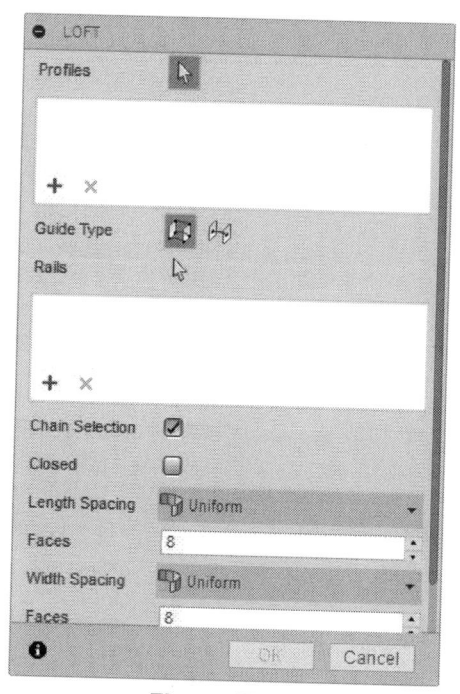

Figure 17–40

The order in which you select the profiles defines how they are lofted together.

5. By default, the *Profiles* area is active. In the graphics window, select the three profiles from top to bottom (**Profile1**, **Profile2**, and **Profile3**). You can also select the profiles in the BROWSER in the **Sketches** folder.

6. In the *Guide Type* area, ensure that (Rails) is selected and then select to enable rail reference selection.

7. In the Graphics Window or in the BROWSER, select the rail that connects each profile. The T-Spline surface is previewed as shown in Figure 17–41.

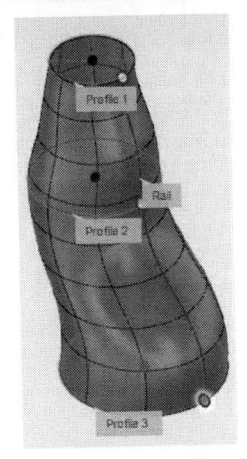

Figure 17–41

8. In the Length Spacing drop-down list, select **Curvature**. This option can create a smoother loft that closely matches reference sketches, but will generate a substantial number of faces. This isn't required in this model as we will be editing the shape further. Having too many faces would make this process more difficult.

9. In the Length Spacing drop-down list, select **Uniform**.

10. In the *Faces* field for the length direction, enter **12**.

11. In the Width Spacing drop-down list, ensure that **Uniform** is selected.

12. In the *Faces* field for the width direction, enter **10**.

13. Click **OK** to create the Loft. The geometry displays as shown in Figure 17–42.

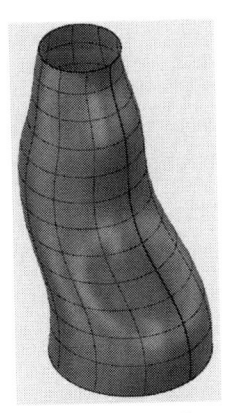

Figure 17–42

Task 2 - Create a handle for the bottle.

In this task you will create additional geometry in the existing Form1 feature to begin the creation of a handle for the bottle. This will be done using the **Torus** option.

An alternative to using ◎ (Torus) to create the handle is to sketch a path to represent the handle and use the Pipe quick shape to define it.

1. In the CREATE panel, click ◎ (Torus).

2. In the BROWSER, expand the **Origin** folder and select the XY plane. This is the same plane that was used as the sketching plane for the rail.

3. Using the ViewCube, reorient the model to the **FRONT** view.

4. Begin the creation of the torus by selecting the center-point in the approximate location shown in Figure 17–43. For the diameter, enter **6.5**.

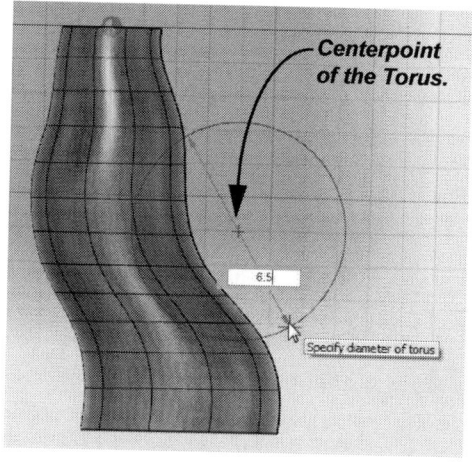

Figure 17–43

5. In the TORUS palette, set the following:
   - In the *Diameter 1 Faces* field, enter **16**.
   - In the *Diameter 2 Faces* field, enter **6**.

   The geometry displays similar to that shown in Figure 17–44.

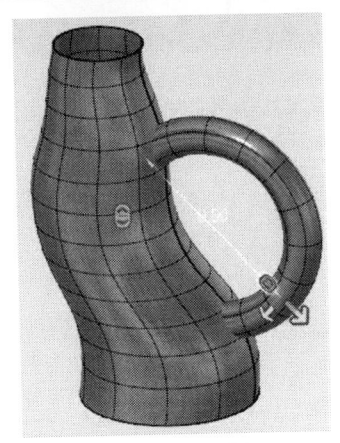

Figure 17–44

6. In the Symmetry drop-down list, select **Mirror**. Once active, select **Height Symmetry**. Enabling symmetry in this way helps to maintain the shape on both sides of the torus when you make changes to the faces.

7. Using either the manipulator handles or the entry fields in the palette, change *Diameter 1* to **5.0 in** and *Diameter 2* to **1.5 in**.

8. Click **OK**. The T-Spline surfaces update similar to that shown in Figure 17–45.

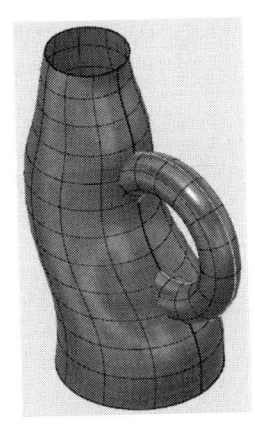

Figure 17–45

9. Save the design with the name **Sculpt_Rail_Loft** to your *Autodesk Fusion 360 Practice Files* project.
    - In the next chapter you will learn how to modify the faces in the geometry to define the final shape.

10. Close the file.

Chapter Review Questions

1. Which of the following quick shape primitives can be created in both the Model and Sculpt environments? (Select all that apply.)

    a. Box

    b. Plane

    c. Cylinder

    d. Sphere

    e. Torus

    f. Quadball

2. When creating a Quadball T-Spline shape, how many different face entry fields can be modified to define the resulting control frame of the geometry?

    a. 1

    b. 2

    c. 4

    d. None

3. Symmetry can only be assigned during the creation of the Box, Cylinder, Sphere, and Quadball quick shape primitives. The remaining quick shape primitives cannot have symmetry assigned during creation.

    a. True

    b. False

4. Which of the following statements are true based on the Cylinder T-Spline form shown in Figure 17–46? (Select all that apply.)

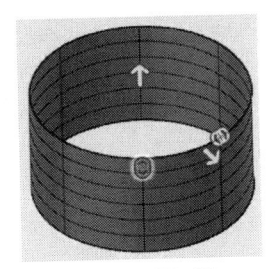

Figure 17–46

   a. The ⊜ manipulator can be used to change the diameter of the cylinder.

   b. The ⇧ manipulator can be used to change the height of the cylinder.

   c. The *Height Faces* value is 6.

   d. The *Height Faces* value is 8.

   e. Symmetry has been set for the height direction.

5. Which of the following display modes provides the best computer performance, but means that you cannot display the true shape of the model during editing.

   a. **Box**

   b. **Smooth**

   c. **Control Frame**

6. In the UTILITIES panel, which option shows the form bodies at the highest display?

   a. **Enable Better Display**

   b. **Enable Better Performance**

7. When in the Model environment, you can create a second T-Spline surface within a previous form feature (i.e. Form1) by using the CREATE panel, clicking (Create Form) and then selecting the required type.

   a. True

   b. False

8. Which of the following T-Spline Surface creation options enable you to reference an existing sketch to create new form geometry? (Select all that apply.)

    a. Box

    b. Extrude

    c. Plane

    d. Sweep

    e. Loft

    f. Face

9. T-Spline creation options that reference a sketch (such as Revolve) do not require you to define the number of faces during feature creation.

    a. True

    b. False

10. When using commands to fill gaps in a T-Spline Surface design file, which of the following are true? (Select all that apply.)

    a. The **Face** option enables you to create a face by referencing existing vertices in the design file to fill gaps.

    b. The **Face** option can be used to create a simple planar face between points placed on a construction plane.

    c. The **Fill Hole** option enables you to select a mode that defines the shape (control frame) of the new surface.

    d. The **Fill Hole** option enables you to define the area to fill by selecting points on the edges.

Answers: 1.(a,c,d,e), 2.a, 3.b, 4.(b,c), 5.a, 6.a, 7.b, 8.(b,d,e), 9.b, 10.(a,b,c)

Command Summary

Button	Command	Location
	Box	• **Ribbon:** Sculpt Workspace>CREATE panel • **Context Menu:** Right-click in the graphics window and select Create.
	Create Form (Sculpt environment)	• **Ribbon:** Model Workspace>CREATE panel • **Context Menu:** Right-click in the graphics window and select Workspace.
	Cylinder	• **Ribbon:** Sculpt Workspace>CREATE panel • **Context Menu:** Right-click in the graphics window and select Create.
	Display Mode	• **Ribbon:** Sculpt Workspace>UTILITIES panel • **Context Menu:** Right-click in the graphics window and select Create.
	Extrude	• **Ribbon:** Sculpt Workspace>CREATE panel • **Context Menu:** Right-click in the graphics window and select Create.
	Face	• **Ribbon:** Sculpt Workspace>CREATE panel • **Context Menu:** Face. • **Context Menu:** Right-click in the graphics window and select Utilities.
	Fill Hole	• **Ribbon:** Sculpt Workspace>MODIFY panel • **Context Menu:** Right-click in the graphics window and select Modify.
	Finish Form	• **Ribbon:** Sculpt Workspace>FINISH FORM panel • **Context Menu:** Right-click in the graphics window and select Finish Form.
	Loft	• **Ribbon:** Sculpt Workspace>CREATE panel • **Context Menu:** Right-click in the graphics window and select Create.
	Plane	• **Ribbon:** Sculpt Workspace>CREATE panel • **Context Menu:** Right-click in the graphics window and select Create.

	Quadball	• **Ribbon:** Sculpt Workspace>CREATE panel • **Context Menu:** Right-click in the graphics window and select Create.
	Revolve	• **Ribbon:** Sculpt Workspace>CREATE panel • **Context Menu:** Right-click in the graphics window and select Create.
	Sphere	• **Ribbon:** Sculpt Workspace>CREATE panel • **Context Menu:** Right-click in the graphics window and select Create.
	Sweep	• **Ribbon:** Sculpt Workspace>CREATE panel • **Context Menu:** Right-click in the graphics window and select Create.
	Torus	• **Ribbon:** Sculpt Workspace>CREATE panel • **Context Menu:** Right-click in the graphics window and select Create.

Chapter 18

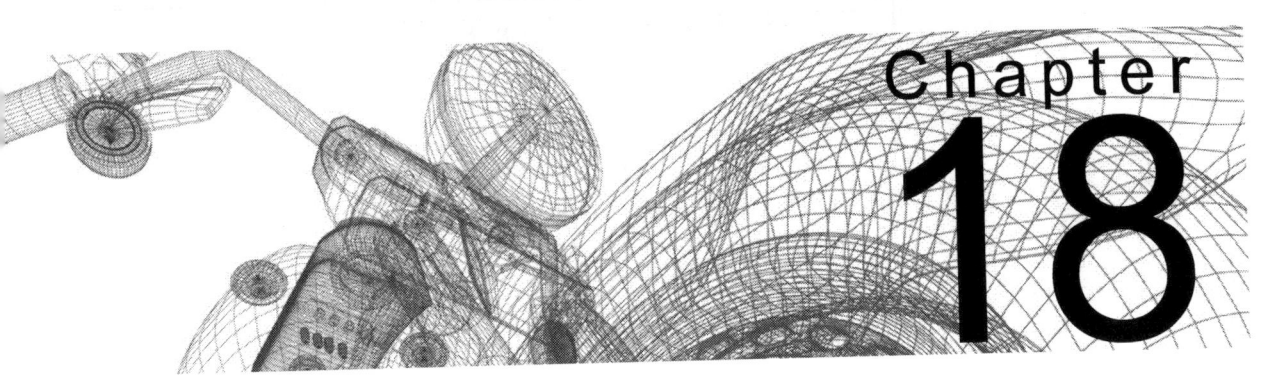

Editing Sculpted Geometry

The Sculpt environment includes a number of editing tools that enable you to refine sculpted geometry by manipulating the faces, edges, and points that make up the geometry's control frame. If the control frame does not provide you with the faces, edges, and points that are required, additional tools are available to create and change these entities.

Learning Objectives in this Chapter

- Manipulate points, edges, and faces in a T-Spline model to define its shape using the Edit Form command.
- Delete points, edges, and faces from a T-Spline body.
- Use specific edge, point, and face commands to manipulate the control frame of a T-Spline body.
- Assign symmetry to a T-Spline body.
- Use the Thicken command to offset a duplicate of the body.

18.1 Editing Form Geometry

The primary command that is used to manipulate geometry is the **Edit Form** option, which is found in the MODIFY panel. This option enables you to select points, edges, faces, bodies, or loops on a control frame to enable a manipulator triad which you can drag to change the shape of a T-Spline Surface. In the example shown in Figure 18–1, a Box was used to create the geometry shown on the left, and then manipulated using the **Edit Form** option to create the geometry on the right.

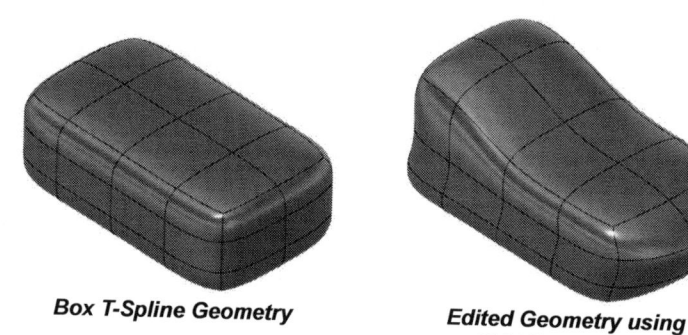

Box T-Spline Geometry   **Edited Geometry using Edit Form option**

Figure 18–1

> Feature history is not recorded to account for each of the edits. While you can undo actions during an individual session, the creation history is lost once the model is closed.

To edit a T-Spline control frame using the Edit Form option, complete the following steps.

1. In the MODIFY panel, click (Edit Form). The EDIT FORM palette opens, as shown in Figure 18–2.

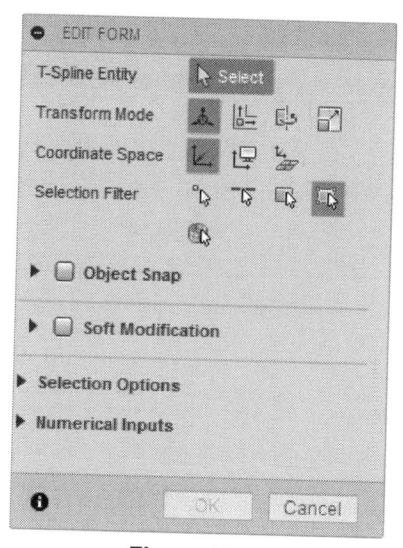

Figure 18–2

2. Select an element to edit. Points, edges, faces, bodies, or a loop of edges can be selected. The triad center is placed on the selected reference entity that is displayed in blue.
   - To select multiple entities, hold <Shift> while selecting them, or drag a selection window over the entities.
   - To select a loop of edges, double-click on an edge.
   - To select a body, double-click on a face.

   Figure 18–3 shows the manipulator triads that display when each element type is selected.

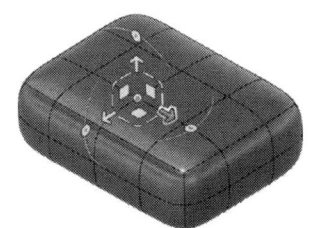

   Manipulator triad on a point 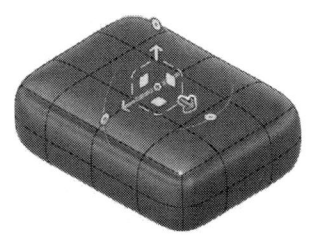   **Manipulator triad on an edge** 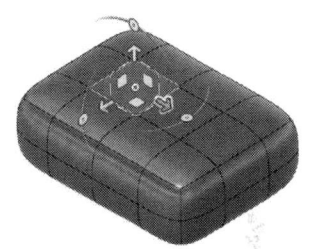   **Manipulator triad on a face**

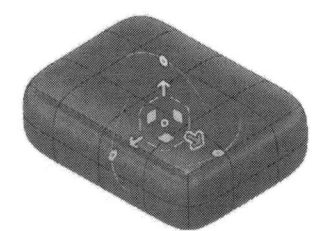

   Manipulator triad on a body 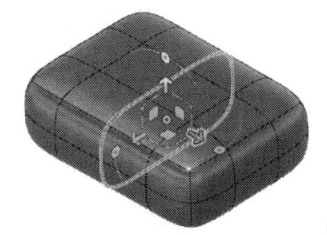   **Manipulator triad on a loop**

   Figure 18–3

3. (Optional) Filter and control the selected entities.
   - In the *Selection Filter* area, select the element type that is to be selectable. The options include the following:

Icon	Description
	When selected, only points are available for selection.
	When selected, only edges are available for selection.
	When selected, only faces are available for selection.
	When selected, points, edges, and faces are all available.
	When selected, a body is available for selection.

   - Expand the *Selection Options* area to further control the entities that are being selected. For example, commands enable you to select next references, invert selections, or select a range of entities.

To change the Display Mode while editing, select the required mode in the Selection Options area.

4. (Optional) Filter the manipulator types that are displayed on the entity's triad using the options in the *Transform Mode* area. The available options enable you to determine whether it displays controls for ( ) Translation, (Rotation), (Scaling) or all of the controls at the same time ( ), as shown in Figure 18–4. The default setting is to show all of the manipulator types.

All types | **Translation** | **Rotation** | **Scale**

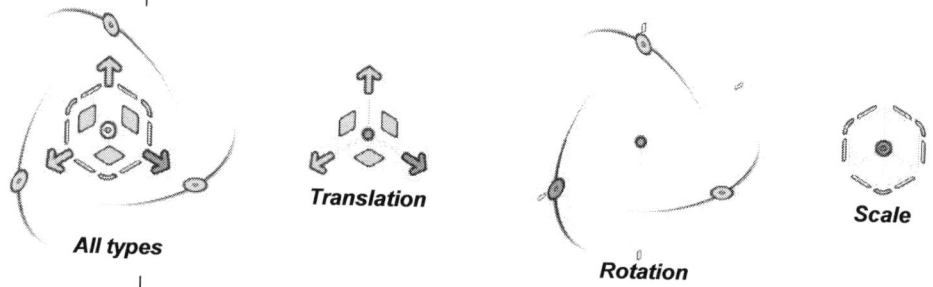

Figure 18–4

5. (Optional) In the *Coordinate Space* area, define the coordinate space that is to be used. This enables you to control the orientation of the manipulator triad.

   - (World): Sets the orientation with the model origin orientation. This is the default setting.

   - (View): Sets the orientation relative to the current view of the model.

   - (Local): Sets the orientation relative to the selected object.

6. (Optional) Use the remaining options as required:

   - Click **Object Snap** to move selected vertices to the closest point on objects in the scene. Vertices can snap to a solid, surface, or mesh body. The Snap Direction setting sets the coordinate space for snapping. Enter an offset value, as required.

   - **Soft Modification** causes the edit actions to have a more gradual impact on adjacent surfaces. When enabled, you are provided additional controls to define the *Selection Type* and *Falloff Type* for the modification.

7. Reposition the geometry using any of the following techniques to manipulate the shape of the control frame.
    - Select the triad controls to reposition the geometry. Each control on the triad enables you to manipulate the geometry in a different way. Figure 18–5 shows the controls and describes their uses. You can only manipulate one triad at a time.

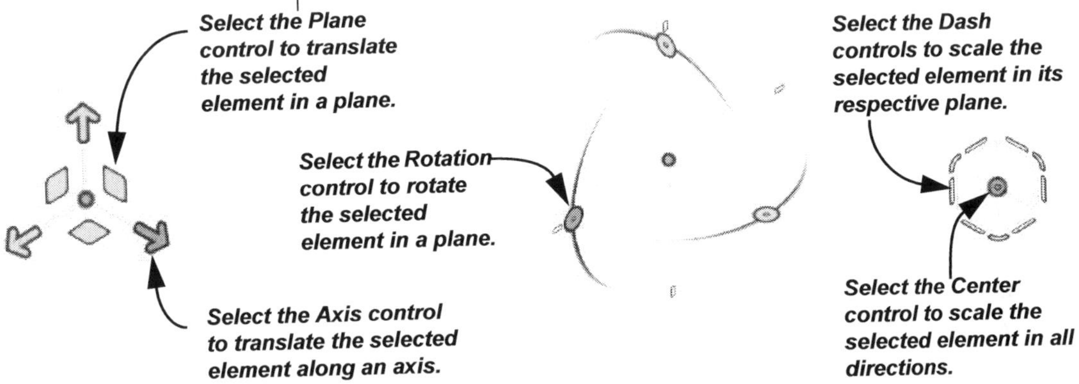

Select the Plane control to translate the selected element in a plane.

Select the Rotation control to rotate the selected element in a plane.

Select the Axis control to translate the selected element along an axis.

Select the Dash controls to scale the selected element in its respective plane.

Select the Center control to scale the selected element in all directions.

Figure 18–5

- Enter values in the mini-toolbar entry field. The available field depends on the active triad control. This value is not parametric and is not tied to the model.
- Expand the *Numerical Inputs* area to enter values.

8. Continue to select elements on the T-Spline's control frame and make changes, as required.
9. Click **OK** to complete the edit.

Figure 18–6 shows the original and final geometry after multiple edits were made to a Cylinder T-Spline shape.

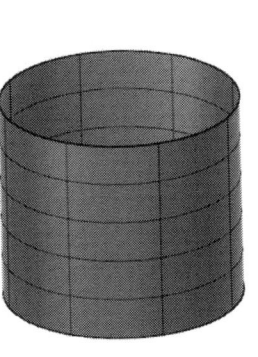

Original Cylinder T-Spline   *Edited Cylinder T-Spline*

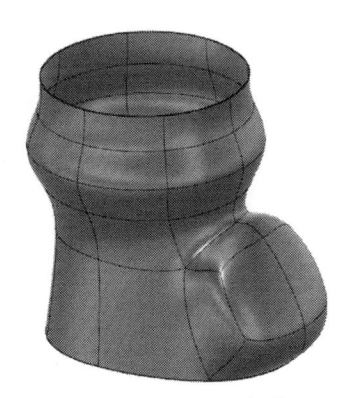

Figure 18–6

Hint: Extruding Faces

To extrude a selected face (as opposed to translating it), hold <Alt> when dragging the translation manipulator. Figure 18–7 shows the difference in a translated face manipulation with and without using <Alt>. Note that Soft Modification is not available if the Extrude option is being used.

Translated Face

Translated Face with <Alt> selected

Figure 18–7

Hint: Freezing Geometry

Located on the MODIFY panel, the **Freeze** option enables you to select and lock a face or edge so that it remains in its current position and locks it to prevents movement.

Once frozen, a selected face or edge's color changes to white and a light-blue control frame color displays on its adjacent edges to identify the entities that cannot be edited.

Video Lesson Available

Editing Forms

Video Length: 6.26

18.2 Deleting Entities

The control frame layout of a T-Spline shape defines the resulting geometry. You can further modify the shape by deleting points, edges, or faces in the control frame. Once deleted, the control frame is recalculated and changes the geometry. For example, deleting faces can create holes, and deleting points and edges can change the size of the face which might be required for better control when using the **Edit Form** option.

*The **Delete** option can also be used to delete an entire body.*

To delete entities, in the MODIFY panel, click (Delete) and then select an entity or entities to be deleted. To select multiple entities, hold <Ctrl> as you are selecting the entities. Alternatively, you can select the entities and press <Delete> or right-click and select **Delete**. Figure 18–8 shows the changes caused by using the **Delete** option to delete points, edges, and faces on a T-Spline control frame.

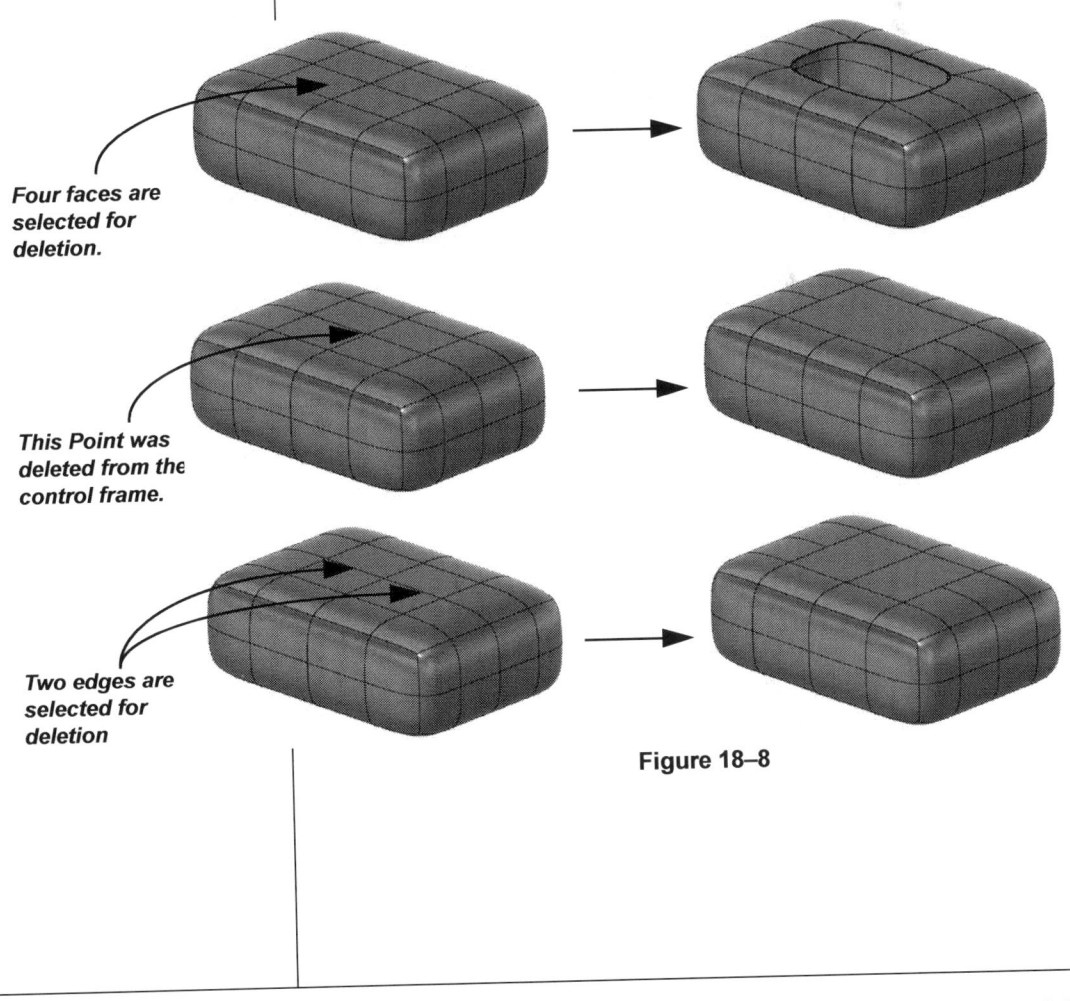

As the feature history is not recorded, consider using undo if an entity is deleted in error.

Four faces are selected for deletion.

This Point was deleted from the control frame.

Two edges are selected for deletion

Figure 18–8

© 2016, ASCENT - Center for Technical Knowledge®

18.3 Working with Edges

There are a number of different editing tools that can be used to modify the edges of T-Spline geometry. These tools are located on the MODIFY panel and include the following:

- Insert Edge
- Slide Edge
- Bevel Edge
- Merge Edges
- Unweld Edges
- Crease Edges
- Uncrease Edges
- Match Edge

Insert Edge

You can add additional edges to a T-Spline using the **Insert Edge** option. Adding edges enables you to provide additional references (edges and the points at the end of edges) that can be edited to refine the shape of the model. When inserting edges, there are two modes that can be used:

- **Simple:** Adds a new edge exactly as specified. The shape might change to add the edge.

- **Exact:** Adds edges and maintains the existing shape. Additional edges might be required to ensure that the model retains its current shape.

The images shown in Figure 18–9 show how two edges are inserted and compares how the overall shape changes when the edges are added using the Simple and Exact modes.

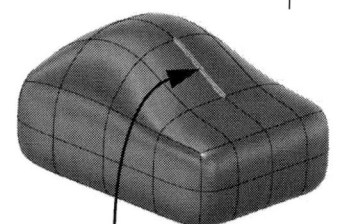

This edge is selected as a reference for the Insert Edge option

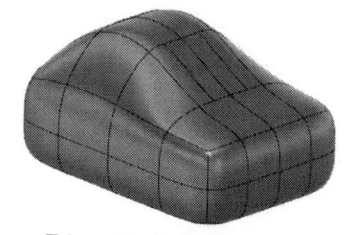

Edges (Both Sides) added using Simple Mode

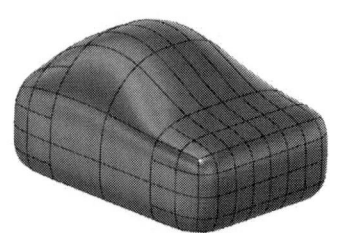

Edges (Both Sides) added using Exact Mode

Figure 18–9

Slide Edge

The **Slide Edge** option slides a selected edge normal to its existing position, as shown in Figure 18–10. Its final location can be defined by either dragging the edge manually, or by entering a value in the entry field. The entry value is entered as a percentage of the distance to the next adjacent edge in the control frame.

These two edges have been selected to be used with the Slide Edge option.

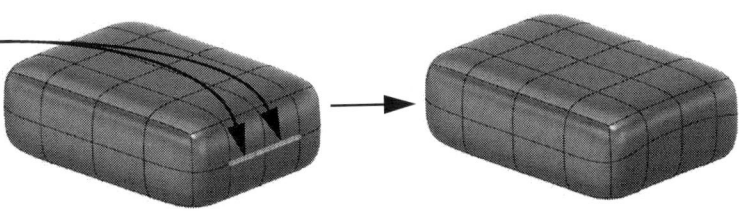

Figure 18–10

Bevel Edge

The **Bevel Edge** option adds a bevel (chamfer) to an existing edge or edges. When you create the bevel, you are prompted to enter its size (*Bevel Location*) as well as define the number of faces (*Segments*) to be created across the beveled edge. Similar to inserting a new edge, the size of the bevel is defined as a normalized value. Figure 18–11 shows existing edges being selected for beveling and the resulting T-Spline geometry after the **Bevel Edge** option is used.

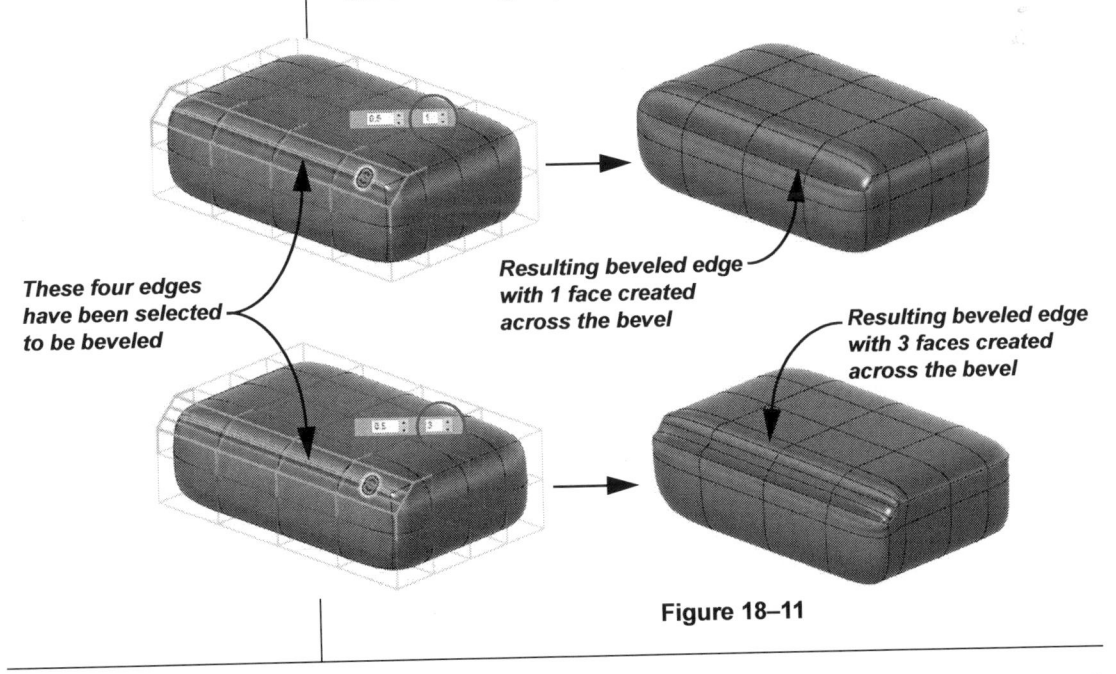

These four edges have been selected to be beveled

Resulting beveled edge with 1 face created across the bevel

Resulting beveled edge with 3 faces created across the bevel

Figure 18–11

> **Video Lesson Available**
>
> Editing an Edge
>
> **Video Length:** 5.33

Merge Edges

Use the **Merge Edges** option to merge two open T-Spline edges. This can be used to blend between two T-Spline bodies or two edges in a single body, if the geometry permits. To merge edges, use the MERGE EDGE palette and select the two sets or edges. You can select whether to maintain or ignore crease edges in the generated geometry. The order in which you select the edges affects the resulting geometry.

Figure 18–12 shows two sets of selected open edges and the resulting T-Spline geometry after the edges are merged.

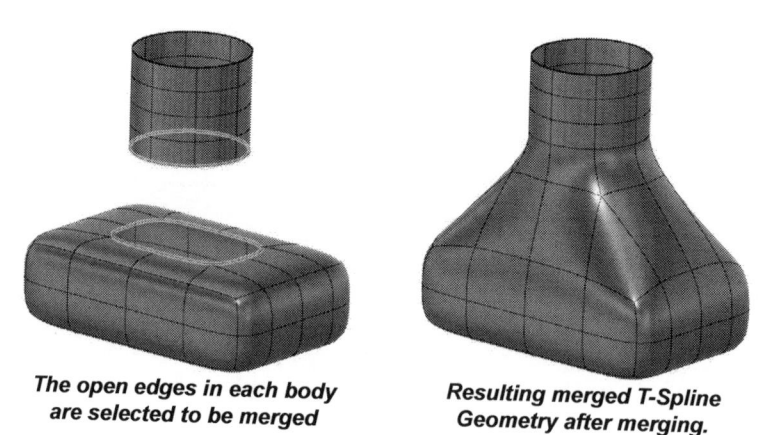

The open edges in each body are selected to be merged *Resulting merged T-Spline Geometry after merging.*

Figure 18–12

Unweld Edges

The (Unweld Edges) option enables you to select edges to separate them from a T-Spline body. To unweld, simply select the edge or loop of edges and click **OK**. Once unwelded, multiple bodies are created that can be moved independently.
Figure 18–13 shows an example of how the **Unweld Edges** option was used on a box.

Box created as a single
body (Body1)

Loop of edges selected to
be unwelded

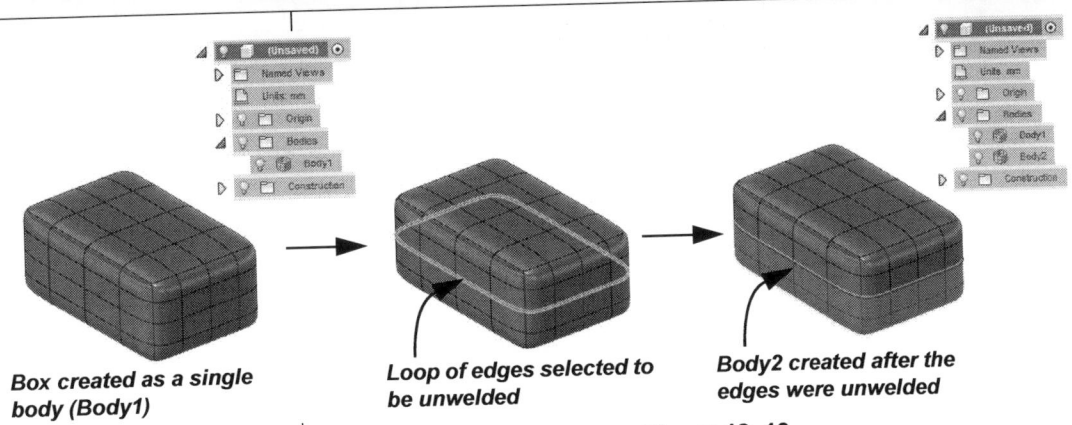

Body2 created after the
edges were unwelded

Figure 18–13

Crease/Uncrease Edges

The **Crease** option enables you to create non-curvature continuous (sharp) edges on a T-Spline body by selecting and moving an edge. In Figure 18–14, four edges were set to permit creasing. Once set, the edges display as darker black. The right-hand image shows how the T-Spline shape reacts to the crease if the edges are moved. Note how the edge is creased after it is moved.

These four edges were
selected to be creased

Resulting geometry after Edit
Form was used to move the
four creased edges

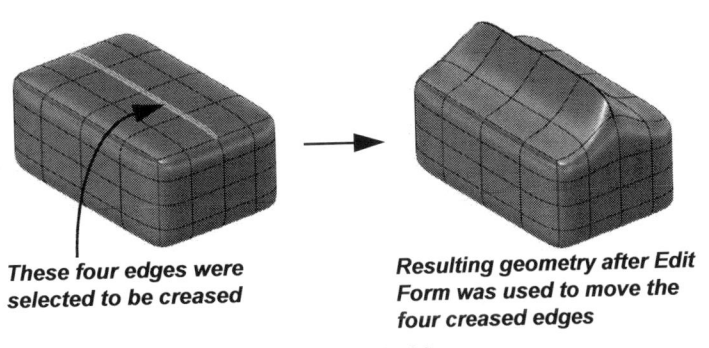

Figure 18–14

To clear the crease setting, click **Uncrease** and select the edges to be cleared. The crease is removed and the geometry updates.

Video Lesson Available

Subdividing and Creases
(Crease Topic begins at 2:10)

Video Length: 2.55

Match Edge

When designing a T-Spline shape, you might have a design requirement that the shape must match an existing edge reference. The existing edge reference (target) can be an edge, a solid edge, or a sketch. The edge can be created in the Model environment, in the same T-Spline form, or in another T-Spline form. To match the edges you can use the **Match** command. The number of vertices in each reference should be similar.

The image on the left in Figure 18–15 shows two T-Spline bodies. In the image on the right, the open edge on the box was merged with the edge of the cylinder.

If you are matching a fully enclosed entity, the references must also be fully enclosed.

Two T-Spline Bodies

Match used to match the edge in the Box to the edge on the Cylinder.

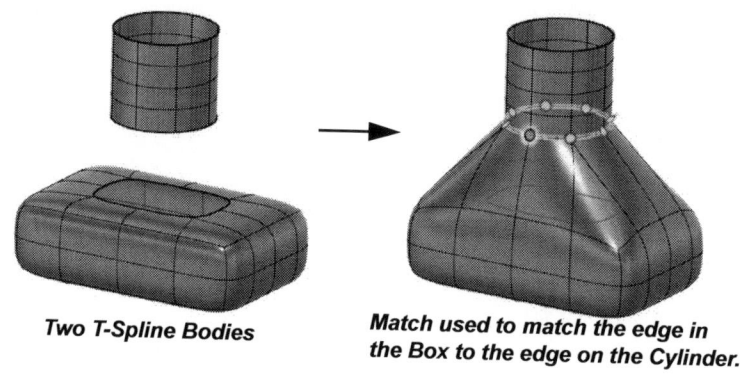

Figure 18–15

The edges are only temporarily matched and the edge is not fully constrained to the target. For instance, in the example shown above, there are still 2 bodies in the design file and the bodies separate if you edit any of the merged edges.

To prevent movement during editing, you can use the MODIFY panel> Freeze option to freeze entities after matching.

Video Lesson Available

Modifying T-Spline Forms

Video Length: 6:31

18.4 Working with Faces

You can manipulate the faces that form a T-Spline control frame to change the shape of geometry. The **Subdivide** and **Bridge** commands enable you to manipulate a face.

Subdivide

The **Subdivide** command enables you to break up a selected face into smaller faces, as shown in Figure 18–16. In general, adding faces helps you to refine the shape of the model and permits more precise editing. When subdividing, you can select one of the following *Insert Mode* options to determine the resulting T-Spline shape:

- **Simple:** Subdivides exactly as specified. The shape might change to add faces.

- **Exact:** Maintains the same existing shape. Additional faces might be required to enable the T-Spline to retain its current shape.

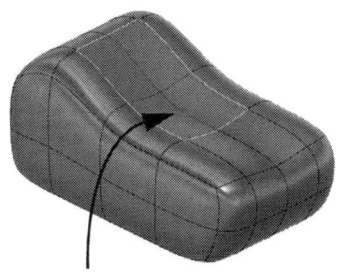

Four faces on a modified Box are selected for subdivision

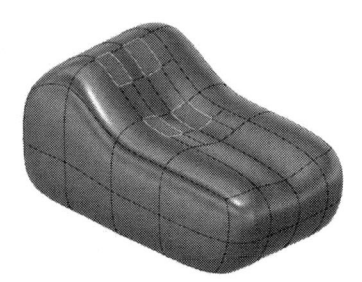

Resulting faces when using the Simple Insert Mode option

Resulting faces when using the Exact Insert Mode option

Figure 18–16

Video Lesson Available

Subdividing and Creases

Video Length: 2:55

Bridge

When using multiple T-Spline bodies in a design, you can use the **Bridge** command to connect the space between the two bodies to create a single body. The Bridge command can also join multiple gaps in a single body. When creating bridged geometry, you can define a curve to follow and assign twists and the number of faces to be generated.

The images in Figure 18–17 show how two separate cylindrical bodies are bridged by new geometry and how it can be used in a single body to create a hole.

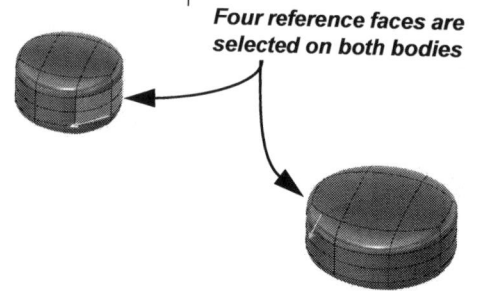

Four reference faces are selected on both bodies

Two bodies in a single Form feature

Resulting geometry after the Bridge command was added between the bodies

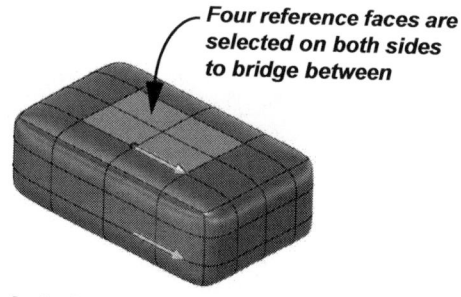

Four reference faces are selected on both sides to bridge between

A single Box T-Spline Body

Resulting geometry after the Bridge command was added

Figure 18–17

Video Lesson Available

Modifying T-Spline Forms
(Bridge Topic begins at 3:20)

Video Length: 6:31

18.5 Working with Points

The points that define edges and faces can also be modified using tools on the MODIFY panel. These tools include **Insert Point**, **Weld Vertices**, **Flatten**, and **Pull**.

Insert Point

Similar to inserting edges, points can be inserted using a similar workflow. An edge is defined when multiple points are inserted, which also defines a new face.

To insert points, complete the following steps:

1. In the MODIFY panel, click (Insert Point).
2. Select points on edges to place new points. Snap points display for endpoint or midpoints of edges, and intermediate points on an edge can also be selected.
3. Select the *Insertion Mode* type to define the shape of the new points and subsequent edges. The **Simple** and **Exact** options are the same as for inserting edges.
4. (Optional) Enable **Object Snap** to move the new point to the closest point on other objects (solid, surface, and mesh bodies) in the scene.
5. Click **OK**.

The new point breaks the edge and creates multiple edges to fully define any adjacent faces. If subsequent points are selected while the palette is open, an edge is created between the points.

Weld Vertices

Once edges are merged, you can use this option to combine vertices to help refine the faces that are generated.

The **Weld Vertices** option enables you to combine two selected vertices. To weld the vertices, select the *Weld Mode* option and select two points on the control frame. The *Weld Mode* options include the following:

- (Vertex to Vertex): Merges two selected vertices. The first vertex is moved to the position of the second vertex.

- (Vertex to Midpoint): Moves two selected vertices to the midpoint between the selections.

- (Weld to Tolerance): Combines multiple vertices within a specified tolerance.

Flatten

The **Flatten** option enables you to select multiple vertices and force them to flatten to a single plane. Once you have selected the points, you must select the *Direction* type. The options include the following:

- (Fit): Moves points to a single plane that passes through the vertices.

- (Plane): Moves points through a specified plane.

- (Parallel Plane): Moves points parallel to a selected plane.

If unable to flatten, consider selecting additional vertices as references.

Figure 18–18 shows how the **Flatten** option was used to flatten multiple vertices so that they are parallel with a selected plane.

Four points are selected along this top edge for flattening

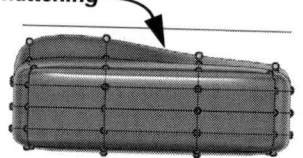

The four points are flattened and remain parallel to the selected plane

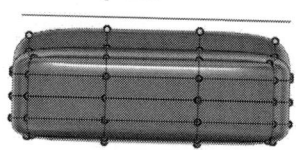

Figure 18–18

Pull

The **Pull** option enables you to select multiple vertices to a target body. The target body must be a separate form feature or solid. You can manually select the target body, or the system can auto-select based on the closest geometry.

*The MODIFY panel> **Interpolate** option can also be used to improve the control frame of a body to smooth out a bodies control points.*

Video Lesson Available

Working with Vertices

Video Length: 3:47

18.6 Controlling Symmetry

The ability to assign symmetry in a T-Spline body can be valuable when using the **Edit Form** command to push and pull a control frame to manipulate its shape. Without the use of parametric dimensions during editing, it is impossible to make the same change on two different sides. By assigning symmetry, you ensure that any edits are copied across symmetric faces.

For example, Figure 18–19 shows the difference between changes made to a Box quick shape without symmetry, and the same change after symmetry has been assigned in the Box quick shape.

Box T-Spline (no symmetry) | Face edited using Edit Form | Box T-Spline (symmetry) | Face edited using Edit Form

Figure 18–19

You can assign symmetry in a T-Spline in several ways:

- Assign symmetry during quick shape creation. For example, for a Box, symmetry can be assigned in length, width, or height, as shown in Figure 18–20.

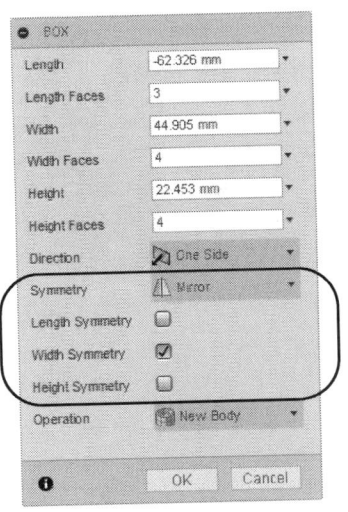

Figure 18–20

If symmetry cannot be assigned based on the references that you have selected, you are prompted to retry making selections.

- Assign symmetry by selecting faces on the control frame. This is valuable to assign symmetry after form creation. In the SYMMETRY panel, click ▲ (Mirror - Internal) and select two faces on the geometry. The Autodesk® Fusion 360™ software locates the symmetry plane and it displays as a green line, as shown in Figure 18–21.

Figure 18–21

- Circular symmetry can be assigned using the SYMMETRY panel> (Circular - Internal) option. This enables you assign radial symmetry to geometry, as shown in Figure 18–22. If multiple symmetries can be set when you are assigning circular symmetry, the possible symmetries are listed. Figure 18–22 shows 2-, 4-, and 8-sided symmetries, and the result when the 8-sided symmetry is selected.

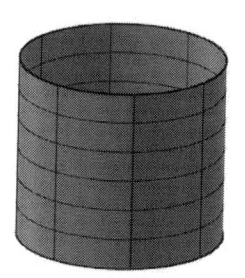

The Circular symmetry option is available when assigning symmetry during the creation of a Cylinder quick shape.

Cylinder T-Spline (no symmetry set)   **Face edited using Edit Form**   **Cylinder T-Spline (symmetry assigned)**   **Face edited using Edit Form**

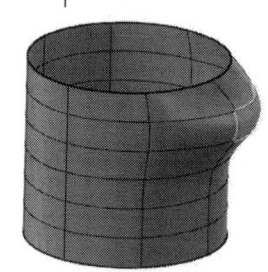

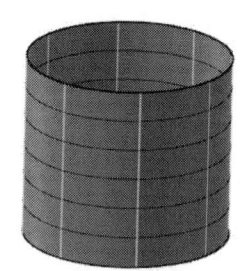

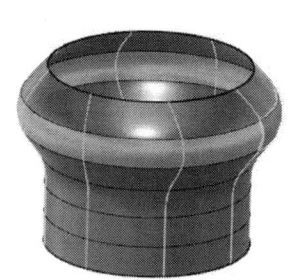

Figure 18–22

- Symmetry that has been explicitly assigned between faces can be cleared by clicking SYMMETRY panel> (Clear Symmetry).

18–18

© 2016, ASCENT - Center for Technical Knowledge®

- Use **Isolate Symmetry** to individually isolate symmetry on faces of symmetry geometry. Isolated faces display in the design as red. Note that isolated faces can still be affected by modifications made to points, edges, and faces on adjacent geometry.

> **Hint: Duplicating Bodies**
>
> The SYMMETRY panel>**Mirror - Duplicate** and **Circular - Duplicate** options enable you to mirror an entry body about a plane and pattern a body respectively.

Video Lesson Available

Assigning Symmetry

Video Length: 7:52

18.7 Thickening Geometry

You can use the **Thicken** command with T-Spline geometry to duplicate and offset an existing body by a specific value. The selected body can have open edges, or it can be a closed body. For open bodies, you can select a *Thicken Type* option to connect the resulting edges and cap the opening. The **No Edge** thicken option leaves the T-Splines as separate bodies.

Figure 18–23 shows some examples of geometry that has been thickened when the selected body is open.

Original Geometry

Thickened using Sharp edges

Thickened using Soft edges

Thickened using No Edges

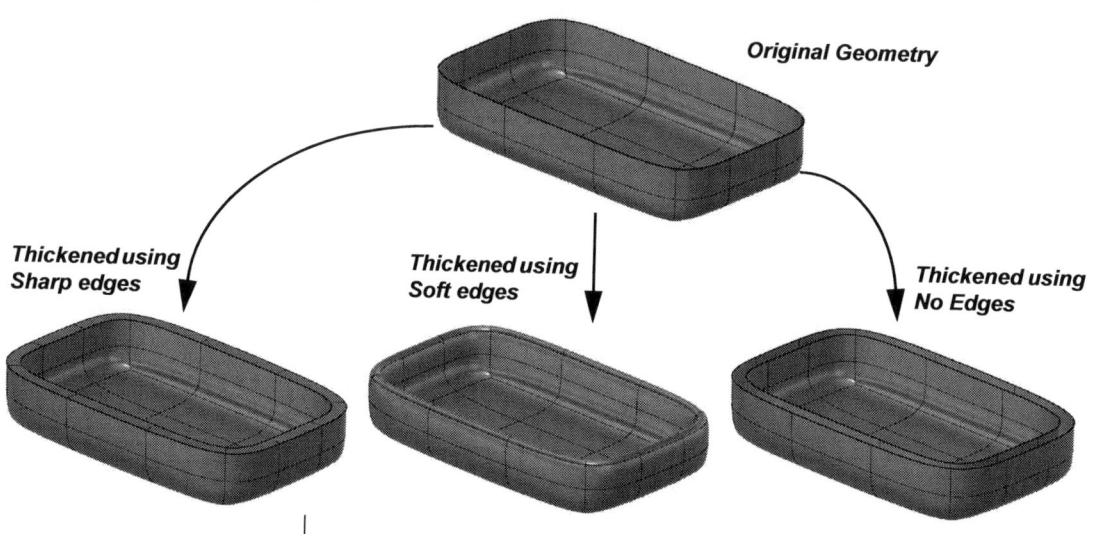

Figure 18–23

To thicken a T-Spline body, complete the following steps:

1. In the MODIFY panel, click (Thicken).
2. Select a T-Spline body to be thickened.
3. In the *Thicken Type* area, select how the thickened geometry is to be capped. Note that these options only affect the geometry results when thickening an open body. The options include:

    - (Sharp): Creates a flat face to bridge the offset.

    - (Soft): Creates a new face that is rounded to bridge the offset.

    - (No Edges): Leaves an open gap between the thickened geometry.

4. Define the offset direction using the options in the Direction drop-down list. The options include:

   - (Normal): Offsets the body normal to the selected body.
   - (Axis): Offsets perpendicular to a selected directional reference.

5. Enter a thickness value.
6. Click **OK** to thicken the selected body.

Practice 18a — Box T-Spline Modeling

Practice Objectives

- Create T-Spline geometry using the **Box** command.
- Edit T-Spline geometry so that points, edges, and faces are translated and rotated.
- Subdivide, delete, and insert elements on the T-Spline geometry to change its shape.

In this practice, you will edit a T-Spline's control frame. You will begin by creating a Box and then use the tools available on the MODIFY panel to make changes to its shape.

Task 1 - Create a Box T-Spline shape.

1. Create a new design and click (Create Form) in the Model environment to activate the Sculpt environment.

2. In the CREATE panel, click (Box). Create the box on the XZ plane and centered on the Origin point.
    - Set the dimensions to *Length*: **120mm**, *Width*: **60mm**, and *Height*: **25mm**.
    - Enable **Width Symmetry** to maintain symmetry on both sides of the XY plane.
    - Set the number of faces to *Length*: **4**, *Width*: **4**, and *Height*: **3**.

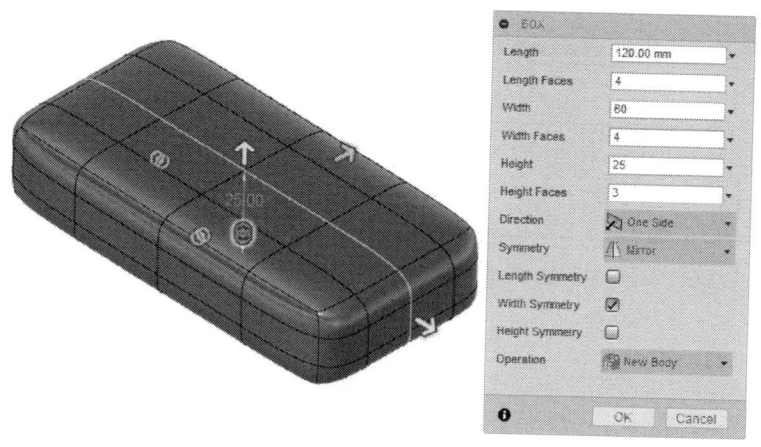

Figure 18–24

3. Click **OK** to complete the Box.

Task 2 - Edit the T-Spline geometry.

1. In the MODIFY panel, click (Edit Form). The EDIT FORM palette displays, as shown in Figure 18–25.

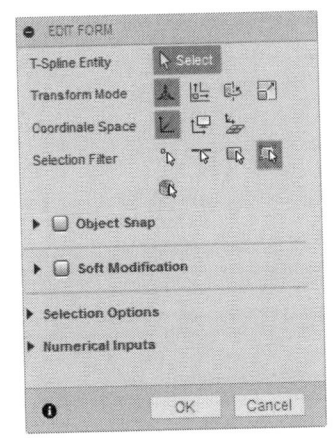

Figure 18–25

2. In the *Selection Filter* area, ensure that (All) is selected as the default option. This enables you to select points, edges, or faces. Hover the cursor over points, edges, and faces. Note that you can select any of them. Selecting the other options filters the selection to points only, edges only, or faces only, which can be useful in complex T-Spline geometry with large control frame layouts.

3. Select the vertex shown in Figure 18–26 to be translated.

4. Select the y-axis manipulator arrowhead (as shown in Figure 18–26) and drag upwards similar to that shown.

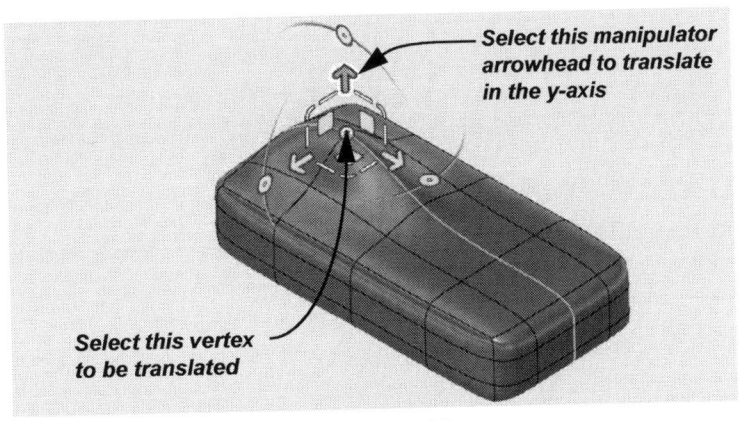

Figure 18–26

5. Select the face shown in Figure 18–27 to be translated.

6. Select the y-axis manipulator arrowhead (as shown in Figure 18–27), and drag upwards similar to that shown. Note that both sides update together. This is because the **Width Symmetry** option was selected when the box was created.

Select this manipulator arrowhead to translate in the y-axis

Select this face to be translated

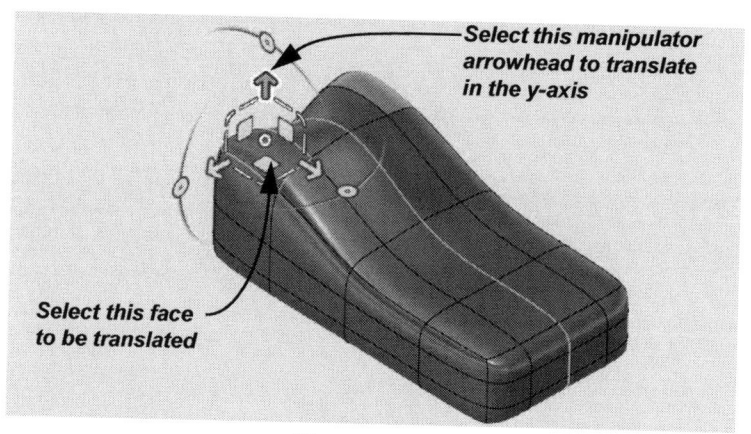

Figure 18–27

7. Select the face shown in Figure 18–28 to be translated.

8. Select the manipulator wheel shown in Figure 18–28, and drag it to rotate the face in the XY plane. Note that both sides update together.

Select this manipulator wheel to rotate in the XY plane

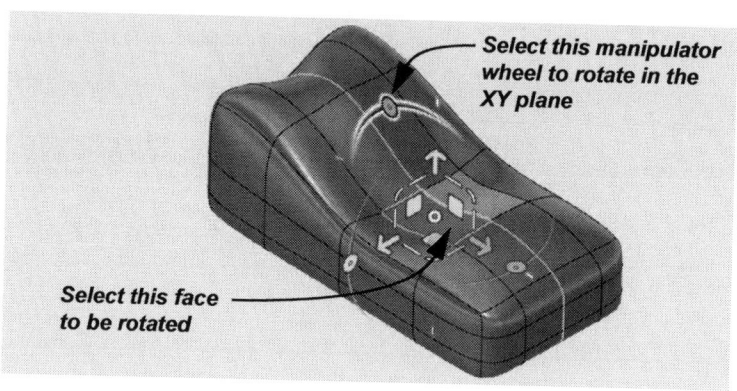

Select this face to be rotated

Figure 18–28

9. Select the front edge shown in Figure 18–29 to be translated.

10. Select the x-axis manipulator shown in Figure 18–29, and drag outward in the x-axis. Note that both sides update together.

Select this manipulator to translate in the x-axis

Select this edge to be translate

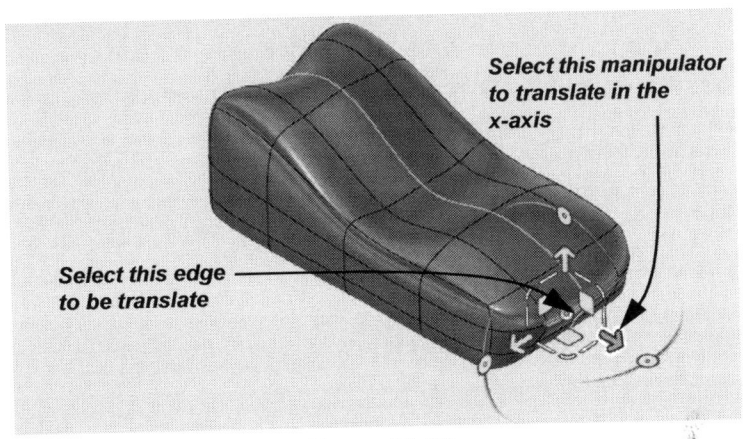

Figure 18–29

11. In the Quick Access Toolbar, click ⤺ to undo the last change to the model.

12. Select the same edge again, if it is not still selected. In the EDIT FORM palette, expand the *Selection Options* area and click 🗊 (Loop Selection). Alternatively, double-click on the edge to select the entire loop. The loop in which the edge exists highlights. Drag the x-axis manipulator handle. The model displays similar to that shown in Figure 18–30. The entire loop of edges translate forward.

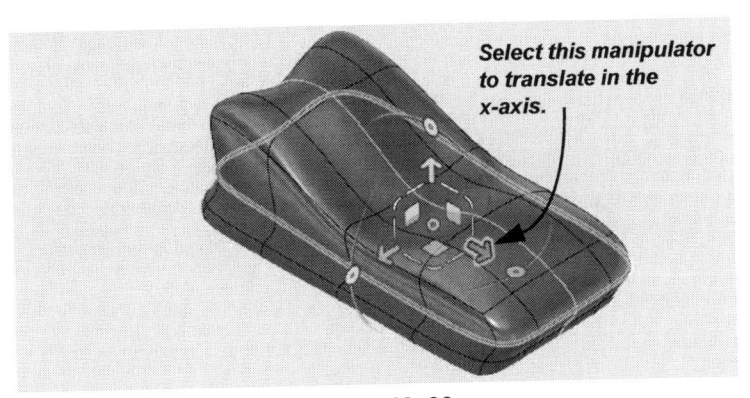

Select this manipulator to translate in the x-axis.

Figure 18–30

13. Click **OK** to complete the edit.

14. In the FINISH FORM panel, click ▦ (Finish Form). Alternatively, right-click in the graphics window and select **Finish Form**. Note that the model displays as solid geometry, as shown in Figure 18–31.

The default visual display for new models is Shaded with Edges. To clear the display of the edges, you can change to the Shaded display style.

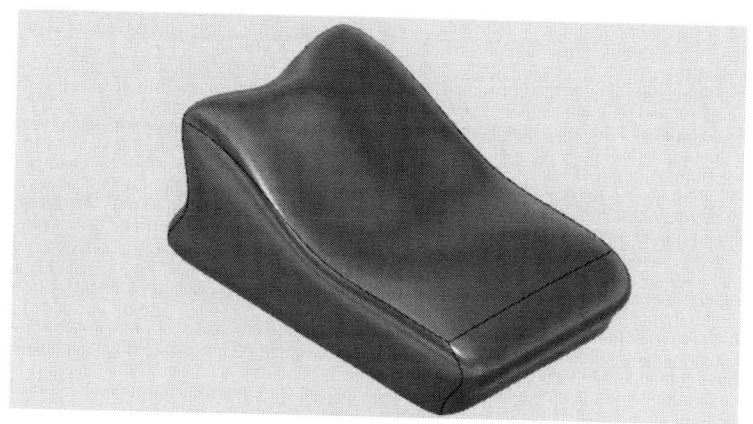

Figure 18–31

15. Save the file as **Sculpt_Box.ipt**.

Task 3 - Use the Edit tools to customize the meshed structure of the T-Spline.

1. In the Ribbon, note that the MODEL environment and all of the parametric model commands are now available. You can continue to design the model using the familiar parametric commands. To edit the T-Spline geometry, right-click on the **Form1** feature in the Timeline and select **Edit**. Click **OK** to enter the Sculpt environment.

2. The middle portion of the T-Spline needs to be subdivided to include more faces. In the MODIFY panel, click ⬥ (Subdivide) to open the SUBDIVIDE palette.

3. Select the required face to create the subdivision shown in Figure 18–32. Note that the symmetry setting that was assigned during Box creation still persists. For the *Insert Mode* setting, select the **Simple** option.

Note: The surface subdivides as soon as it is selected.

Select in this area to subdivide

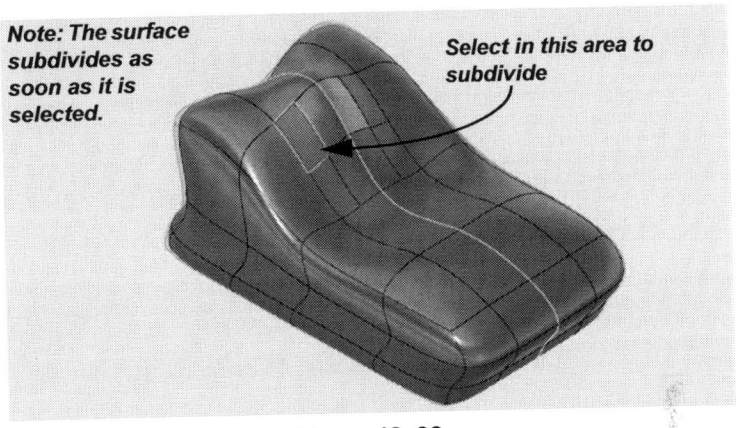

Figure 18–32

*If the change is not what you want, select **Exact** as the Insert Mode setting. The geometry shape will stay the same but additional faces are added to maintain the shape.*

4. Click **OK** to insert the face(s). Note that the geometry changed slightly to permit the subdivision. This was acceptable.

5. In the MODIFY panel, click (Edit Form).

6. Double-click on one of the edges generated by the subdivide action (as shown in Figure 18–33) to automatically select all of the adjacent edges.

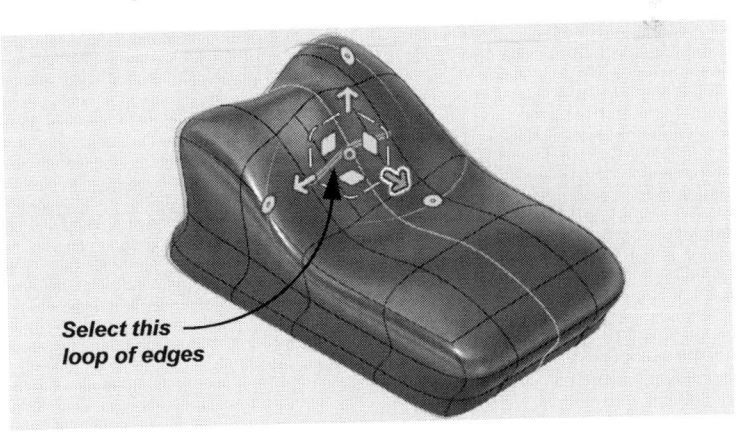

Select this loop of edges

Figure 18–33

© 2016, ASCENT - Center for Technical Knowledge®

7. In the Edit Form palette, in the *Coordinate Space* area, click (View Space). The triad changes to only display two axis manipulators, as shown in Figure 18–34.

Figure 18–34

8. In the ViewCube, select the **Front** view. Note that the triad updates to display the manipulators in the new orientation, while retaining the x- and y-directions for the view. The orientation of the model is important when using this coordinate space setting.

9. Using the ViewCube return to the Home orientation, as shown in Figure 18–35.

Figure 18–35

10. In the *Coordinate Space* area, click (Local) to change the triad location to the Local orientation. Drag the manipulators to create the geometry shown in Figure 18–36.

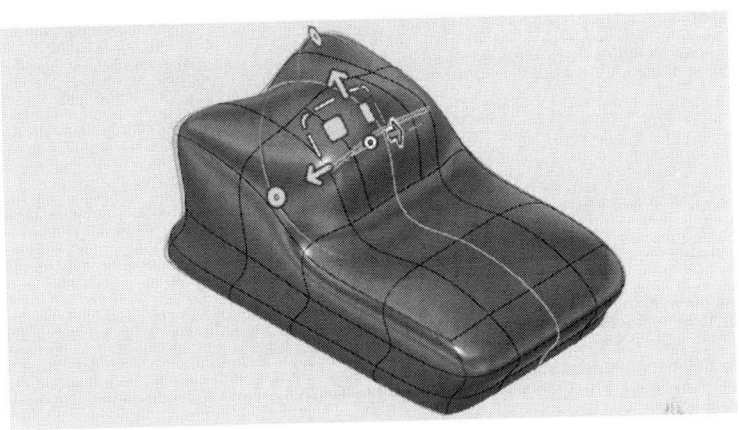

Figure 18–36

11. Click **OK** to complete the edit.

Task 4 - Delete edges from the T-Spline geometry.

1. Clear the selection of edges in the model by clicking in a blank area of the graphics window.

2. Now that the reshaping is complete, you can delete edges in the area that was subdivided. In the MODIFY panel, click (Delete).

3. Select the two edges shown in Figure 18–37. Note that their symmetric edges are also selected.

Based on the freeform nature of the Sculpt environment, your model might vary from those shown in the images.

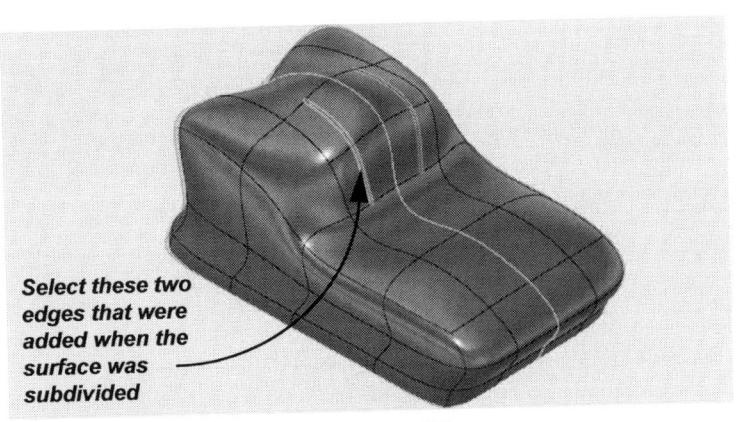

Select these two edges that were added when the surface was subdivided

Figure 18–37

4. Click **OK** to delete the edges. The T-Spline geometry updates as shown in Figure 18–38.

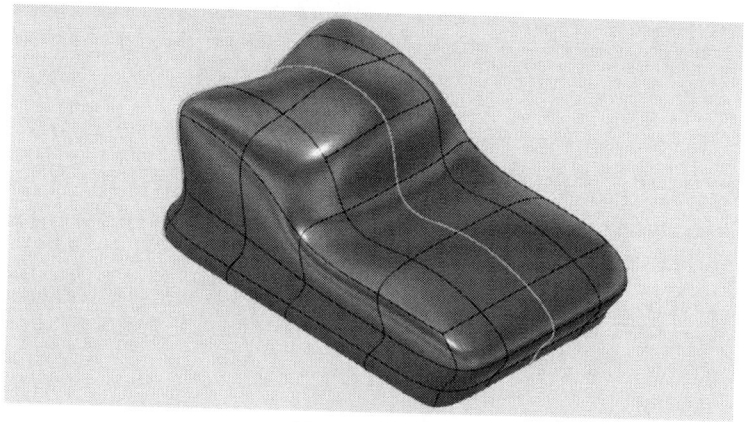

Figure 18–38

Task 5 - Insert edges on T-Spline geometry.

1. In the MODIFY panel, click (Insert Edge). The INSERT EDGE palette opens.

2. Select the edge shown in Figure 18–39. A preview of the new edge displays.

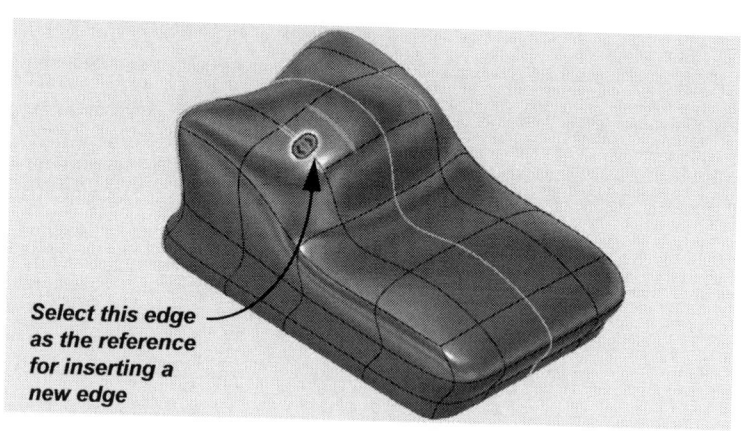

Select this edge as the reference for inserting a new edge

Figure 18–39

3. In the *Insert Location* area, set the offset value to **0.2**. The edge moves closer to the reference edge.

4. Return the value to **0.5** to create the new edge midway between the reference edge and the next edge.

5. In the *Insertion Mode* area, select **Exact**. If Simple mode had been used, the geometry would change to create the edge. In this situation, Exact mode is used because the exact shape must be retained.

6. Click **OK** to insert the edit. The new edge is created, but note that additional edges have been added to keep both symmetry and the existing shape, as shown in Figure 18–40.

Figure 18–40

7. In the FINISH FORM panel, click (Finish Form). Note that the T-Spline geometry generates a solid in the MODEL environment because it is completely enclosed geometry.

8. Save the file and close the window.

Practice 18b

Cylinder T-Spline Modeling

Practice Objectives

- Create T-Spline geometry using the Cylinder command.
- Match edges on the geometry to that of parametric sketched geometry.
- Assign and cancel symmetry to faces on T-Spline geometry.
- Freeze and unfreeze edges to control edits on T-Spline geometry.
- Use the Edit Form command to translate and scale elements on T-Spline geometry.
- Thicken T-Spline geometry.

In this practice, you will edit a T-Spline's control frame when symmetry and frozen edges have been assigned. You will begin by creating a Cylinder and then use tools on the MODIFY panel to make changes to its shape. To complete the geometry, you will use the Thicken command to create closed T-Spline geometry that will form a solid in the Model environment.

Task 1 - Create a sketch that will be referenced by a T-Spline cylinder.

1. Create a new design.

2. In the *Model environment*, start the creation of a new sketch on the XZ Plane.

3. Create a circle that is centered on the Origin Center Point with a diameter of **70mm**.

4. Complete the sketch.

Task 2 - Create a T-Spline cylinder.

1. Click (Create Form) in the CREATE panel to activate the Sculpt environment. Click **OK**.

2. In the CREATE panel, click (Cylinder). Create the cylinder on the XZ plane and centered on the Origin point.
   - In the *Direction* area, select **Symmetric** to ensure that the T-Spline is centered on both sides of the sketch plane.
   - Set the dimensions to *Diameter:* **80mm** and *Height:* **200mm**.
   - Ensure that no symmetry is assigned (**None**).
   - Set the number of faces to *Diameter:* **4** and *Height:* **8**, as shown in Figure 18–41.

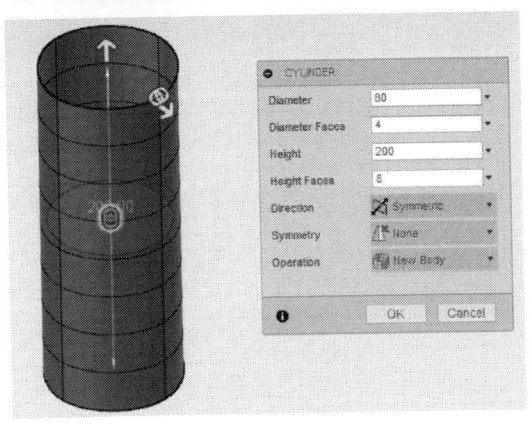

Figure 18–41

3. Click **OK** to complete the Cylinder.

Task 3 - Match and freeze an edge on the T-Spline geometry with the sketch.

1. In the MODIFY panel click (Match). The MATCH palette opens.

If you are matching a fully enclosed entity, the freeform references must also be a fully enclosed loop.

2. With the *T-Spline Edges* area active, double-click on the edge that lies on the sketch plane to be matched, as shown in Figure 18–42.

3. Select the *Target Edges* area to activate it. Select the circular sketch that was created in the first task.

4. Maintain the remaining defaults in the MATCH palette, as shown in Figure 18–42.

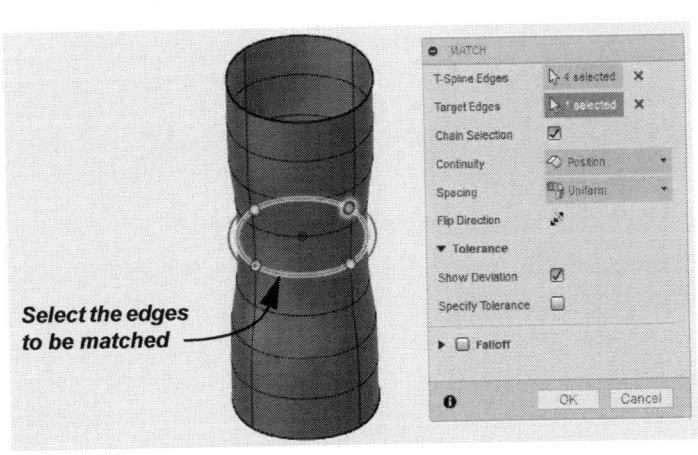

Figure 18–42

5. Click **OK** to match the edges. The T-Spline geometry updates as shown in Figure 18–43.

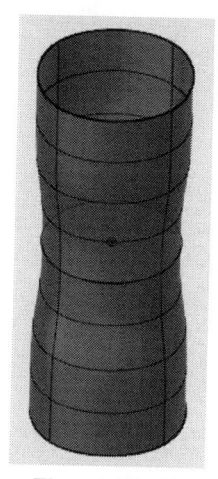

Figure 18–43

6. Use the **Edit Form** command and move one of the faces close to the matched edge. Note how the edge does not remain matched when the control frame is moved. Match is temporary.

7. Undo the change.

8. On the MODIFY panel, click **Freeze>** (Freeze). Double-click on one of the matched edges, as shown in Figure 18–44.

Select the matched edges to be frozen

Figure 18–44

9. Click **OK** to freeze the loop of edges. Note how the color changes on the control frame. This indicates that the loop of edges are frozen.

10. Use the **Edit Form** option and note how you can no longer select an edge in the loop because it is frozen.

Task 4 - Assign symmetry to the T-Spline geometry and edit the symmetric faces.

1. Start the **Edit Form** option. In the EDIT FORM palette set the following options:

    - In the *Selection Filter* area, ensure that either ▣ (All) or ▣ (Face) is selected, and then select the face shown in Figure 18–45 to be translated.

    - In the *Coordinate Space* area, click ▣ (View Space). The triad changes to only display two axis manipulators, as shown in Figure 18–45.

    Select this face to be translated

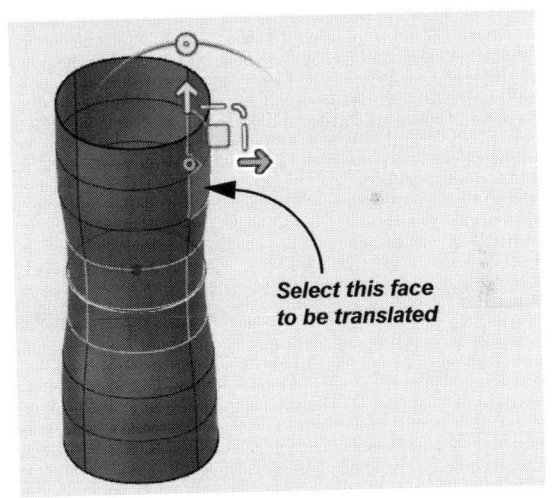

    Figure 18–45

2. In the ViewCube, select the edge between the **FRONT** and **RIGHT** sides, as shown in Figure 18–46. The model reorients.

Select this edge in the ViewCube

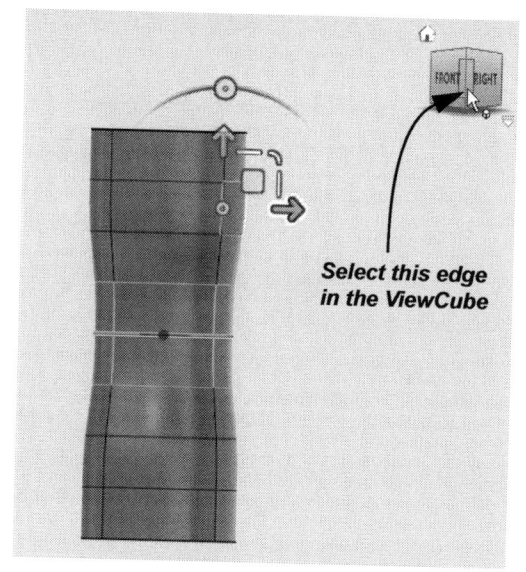

Figure 18–46

3. Select the x-axis manipulator arrowhead and drag it to the right, similar to that shown in Figure 18–47.

Select and drag this manipulator

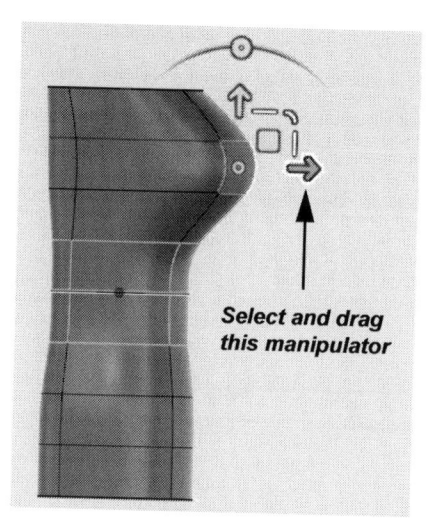

Figure 18–47

4. Note how the edit only affects one face. The intent of the change is to move opposing surfaces on each side of the circumference at the same time. Click **Cancel** to close the EDIT FORM palette and cancel the change.

5. Symmetry cannot be assigned if there is a frozen edge that prevents symmetry. On the MODIFY panel, click **Freeze** > (UnFreeze). Double-click on one of the matched edges to select the loop. Click **OK** to unfreeze the edges. The edges display in black again.

6. In the SYMMETRY panel, click (Mirror - Internal). The MIRROR - INTERNAL palette opens.

7. Select the same face that was previously selected for editing as the first reference. The reference displays in blue. Select the face opposite as the second symmetric face. The references are shown in Figure 18–47.

Select this surface as the second reference

Select this surface as the first reference

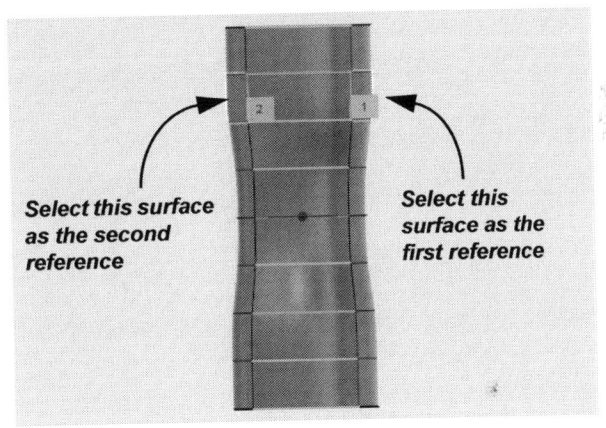

Figure 18–48

8. Click **OK** to assign the symmetry.

9. Use the **Freeze** option a second time to freeze the loop of edges that were matched to the sketch.

10. Use the **Edit Form** command to translate the face that was just translated in the x-axis direction. Now that symmetry has been assigned with this surface, its symmetric face is also selected. Ensure that (View Space) is set and that the ViewCube is oriented as was previously set in Step 2.

11. Drag the x-axis manipulator to translate the face outward, as shown on the left in Figure 18–49. The symmetric faces update.

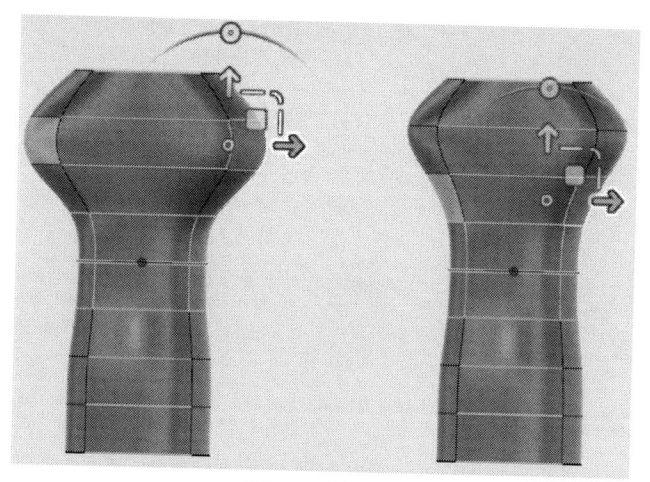

Figure 18–49

12. Select the surface shown on the right in Figure 18–49 and translate it inwards. Note that it also reacts as symmetric, but the frozen edge remains unchanged.

13. Complete the edit.

Task 5 - Complete the design and create a solid.

1. Using the **Edit Form** command, scale the two loops of edges shown in Figure 18–50 so that they increase evenly in diameter on all four edges. Consider the following Hints:

    - Remove symmetry. This can be done in the SYMMETRY panel by clicking (Clear Symmetry), and selecting the body to clear its symmetry.
    - Select a world space coordinate system.
    - Use the scale triad manipulator to change the diameter.

Select this face to scale

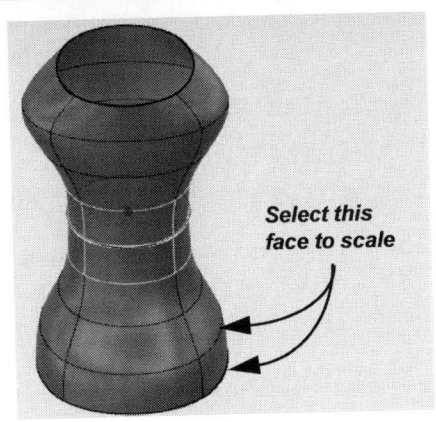

Figure 18–50

2. Complete the edit.

3. Use one of the T-Spline geometry creation options to cap the bottom of the cylinder to create a flat bottom, as shown in Figure 18–51. Hint: To create a flat bottom on this geometry, you must use the **Maintain Crease Edges** option.

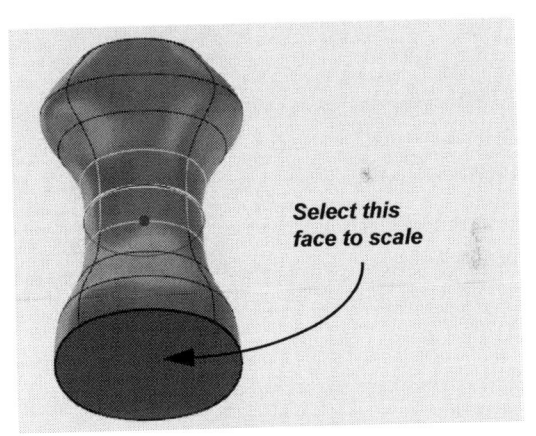

Select this face to scale

Figure 18–51

4. In the FINISH FORM panel, click (Finish Form). Note that the body does not get created as a solid because it has an open top.

5. Edit **Form1** to return to the Sculpt environment.

6. In the MODIFY panel, click (Thicken). The THICKEN palette displays.

7. Select the T-Spline body in the graphics window. Set the *Thickness* to **10mm**.

8. Ensure that the *Direction* option is set to **Normal**, and set the *Thicken Type* as **Sharp**. Click **OK**.

9. When prompted that the operation affects one or more frozen regions, clear the frozen edges by clicking **Unfreeze**. Thickening cannot be done with frozen edges in the geometry. The geometry displays as shown on the left in Figure 18–52.

10. Review the T-Spline edge at the top of the cylinder. Undo the Thicken operation and recreate it, setting the *Thicken Type* to **Soft**. The geometry displays as shown on the right in Figure 18–52.

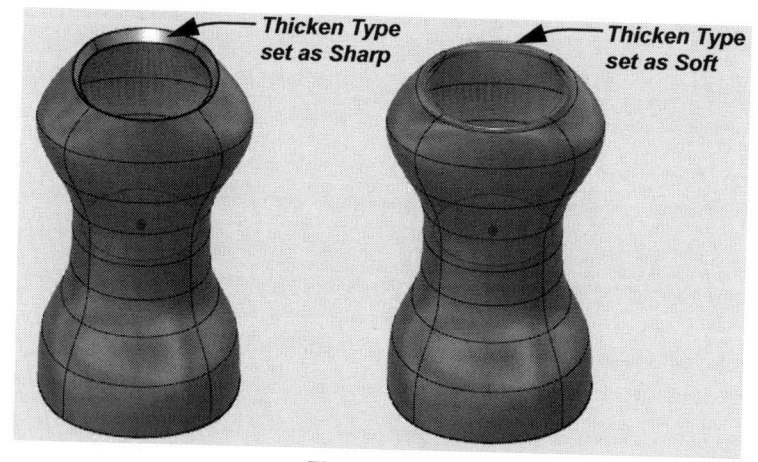

Figure 18–52

11. Finish the form. The T-Spline geometry is created as a solid.

12. Save the file as **Sculpt_Cylinder.ipt**.

Practice 18c

Working with Multiple T-Spline Bodies

Practice Objectives

- Delete faces that form a T-Spline body.
- Merge edges to create T-Spline geometry between open edges.
- Use Edit Form to manipulate the T-Spline geometry.
- Use solid modeling tools to create a solid model from the T-Spline geometry.

In this practice, you will begin by opening a model that provides the basic shape of a bottle and handle. You will merge the two bodies and use the modification tools to create the required shape. To complete the practice you will return to the Model environment and complete the solid.

Task 1 - Open an existing model and edit its Form feature.

1. Click ▬ ▾ > **New Design from File**.

2. In the Open dialog box, navigate to the *C:\Autodesk Fusion 360 Practice Files* folder, select **Sculpted_Loft_Final.f3d**, and click **Open**. The design displays as shown in Figure 18–53. This is the design that was created in the previous chapter.

The model has been created for you so that you can begin the freeform modeling with the same geometry as was used for the images in this practice.

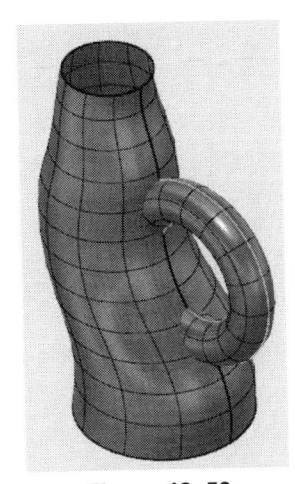

Figure 18–53

3. If the design does not open in the Sculpt environment, activate it.

Task 2 - Delete faces in the design to connect the handle to the body of the bottle.

1. Using the ViewCube, orient the model to the **FRONT** view.

2. In the BROWSER, expand the **Bodies** folder and clear **Body1** from the display by clicking adjacent to its name.

3. In the MODIFY panel, click (Delete). Select the faces and edges shown in blue in Figure 18–54 for deletion. The references can be selected using a selection window along with manually selecting faces.

Select these faces (blue) to delete

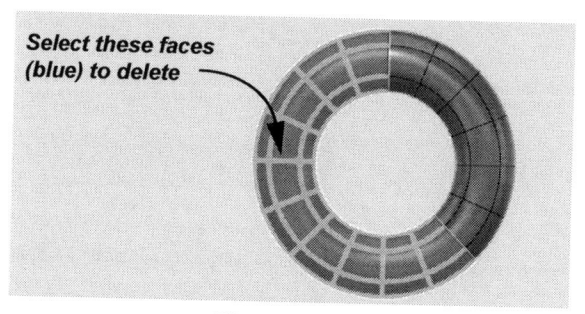

Figure 18–54

4. Toggle on the display of **Body1**.

5. Click **OK**. The T-Spline geometry should display as shown in Figure 18–55.

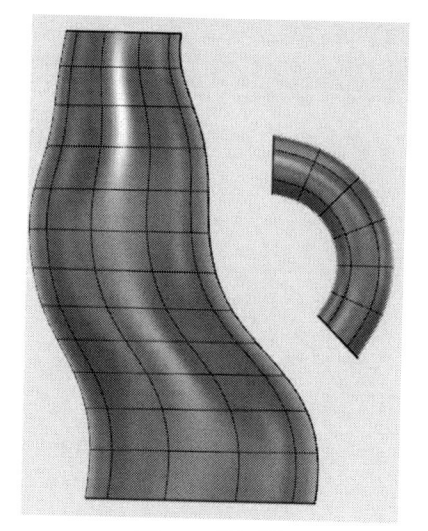

Figure 18–55

Task 3 - Edit the T-Spline geometry to merge the handle.

1. Using the ViewCube, orient the model into the **RIGHT** view.

2. Select the 8 faces shown on the left in Figure 18–56. Ensure that the correct faces are selected (3rd and 4th rows from the top and bottom), and then right-click on a selected face and select **Delete**. Alternatively, with the faces selected, in the MODIFY panel, click **Delete**. The model displays as shown on the right of Figure 18–56.

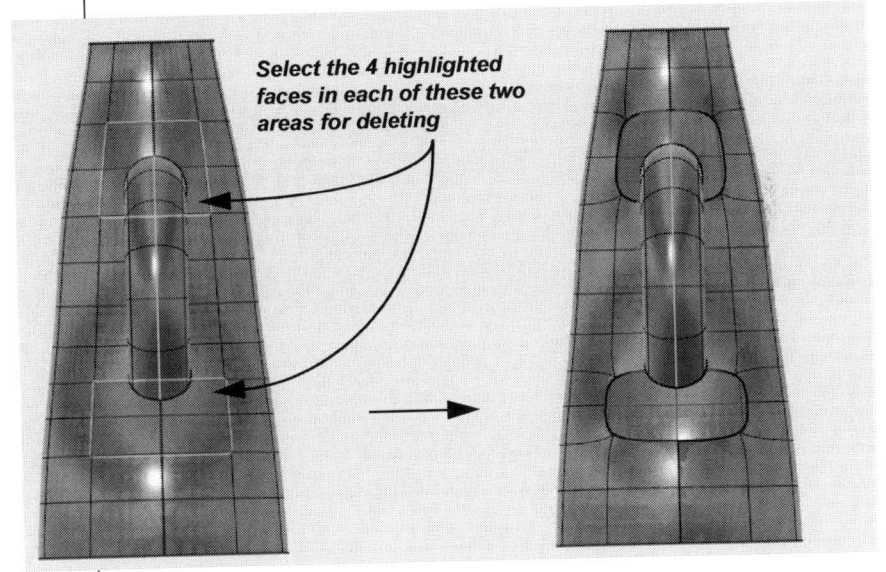

Select the 4 highlighted faces in each of these two areas for deleting

Figure 18–56

3. Using the ViewCube, orient the model to the **Home** view.

4. In the MODIFY panel, click (Merge Edge) and select the two sets of edges at the bottom of the handle shown in Figure 18–57:
   - To define *Group One*, on Body1 select the group of 8.
   - To define *Group Two*, on Body2 select the 6 edges at the bottom of the handle.
   - Click **OK** to complete the feature.

   Note that merging cannot be done while there is symmetry assigned to the handle. Undo the Merge Edge operation.

   Select the 2 sets of edges at the bottom of the bottle to be merged

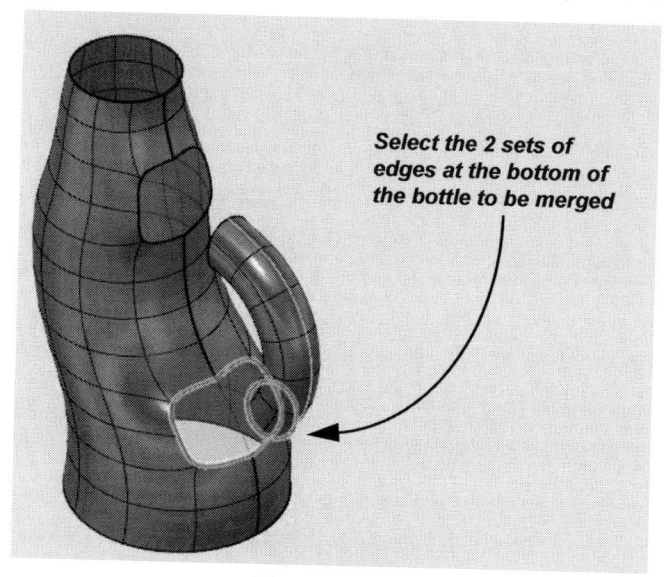

   Figure 18–57

5. In the SYMMETRY panel, click (Clear Symmetry) and select the handle (Body2) to clear its symmetry. Click **OK**.

6. Use the **Merge Edge** command a second time as described in Step 4 to merge the edges. The resulting T-Spline geometry displays as shown in Figure 18–58.

Merged T-Spline geometry

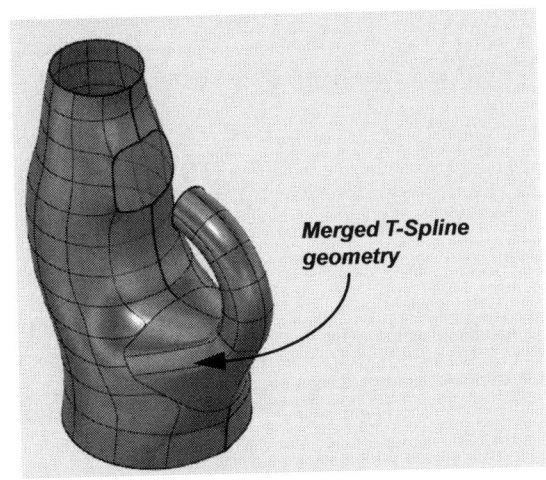

Figure 18–58

7. In the MODIFY panel, click (Merge Edge) and select the two sets of edges at the top of the handle as shown in Figure 18–59.
   - To define *Group One,* on Body1 select the group of 8.
   - To define *Group Two,* on Body2 select the 6 edges at the top of the handle.

Select the 2 sets of edges at the top of the bottle to be merged

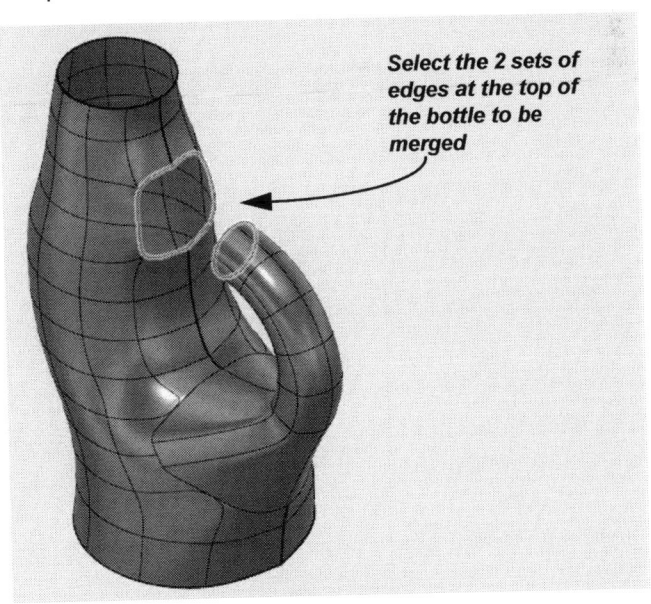

Figure 18–59

8. Click **OK** to complete the feature. The model displays as shown in Figure 18–60.

Merged T-Spline geometry

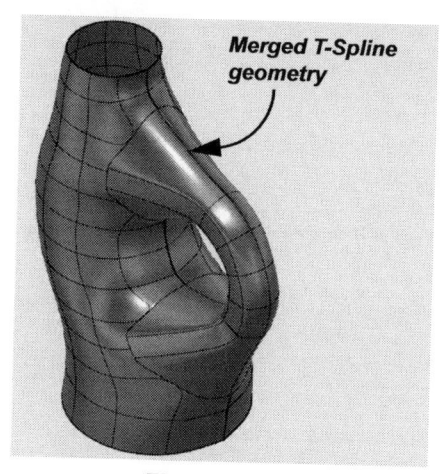

Figure 18–60

The **Make Uniform** command can be used to attempt to smooth a model by removing pinches near star points and changing non-uniform faces to uniform.

9. In the UTILITIES panel, click (Make Uniform). The model attempts to smooth the model similar to that shown in Figure 18–61.

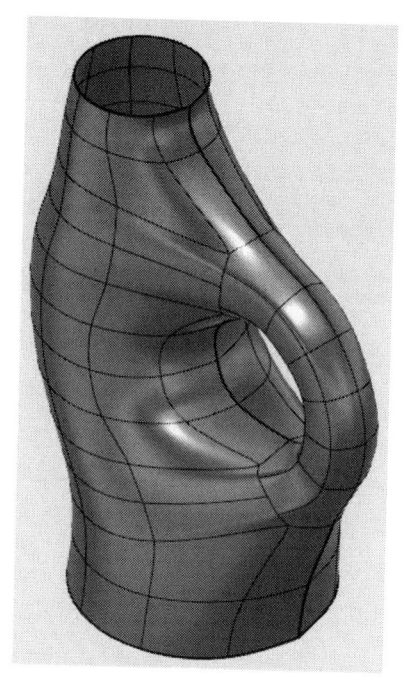

Figure 18–61

18–46

© 2016, ASCENT - Center for Technical Knowledge®

Task 4 - Assign symmetry to the bottle.

1. In the SYMMETRY panel, click ⚐ (Mirror - Internal). The MIRROR - INTERNAL palette opens.

2. Select the faces shown in Figure 18–62 and click **OK** to assign symmetry.

Select these two faces to be symmetric

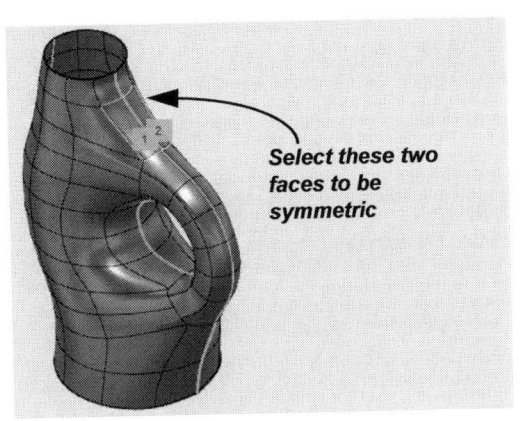

Figure 18–62

Task 5 - Refine the shape of the handle.

1. Using the **Edit Form** command, edit the location of the points, edges, and faces near the handle to create geometry similar to that shown in Figure 18–63.

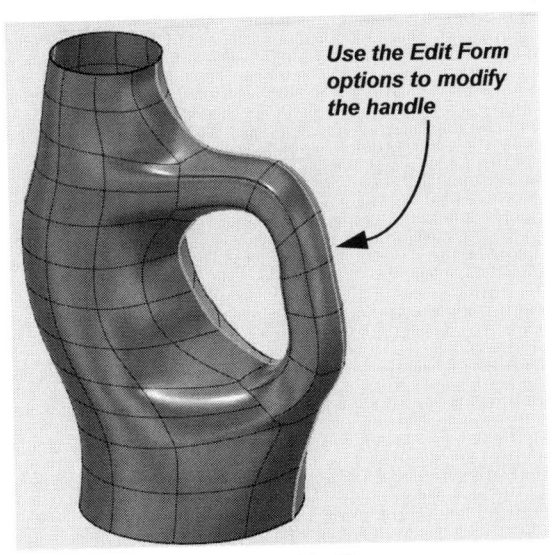

Use the Edit Form options to modify the handle

Figure 18–63

The manipulation of faces, edges, and vertices to create sculpted geometry takes practice. As you become more familiar with the tools available, you will become more proficient in creating great models.

Depending on the T-Spline geometry that is created, you might be unable to finish the form and convert the T-Spline geometry. For example, based on this geometry, if you use Fill Hole to add a flat bottom to the geometry, edges or faces will overlap and prevent the form from being able to convert.

2. Finish the Form.

Task 6 - (Optional) Complete the design.

1. Create a solid from the surfaces.
   - Use the edge at the bottom of the bottle to create a sketch and extrude downwards to create solid geometry.
   - Thicken the bottle to a thickness of **0.2 in** to create the solid.

2. Save the design as **Bottle_Complete**.

Practice 18d — Bridging T-Spline Geometry

Practice Objective

- Create two T-Spline bodies and use the **Bridge** command to generate additional geometry between them.

In this practice, you will create two cylinder freeform base shapes in a design and use the Bridge command to join them.

Task 1 - Create two T-Spline Cylinder bodies.

1. Create a new design.

2. In the CREATE panel, click (Create Form) to activate the Sculpt environment. Click **OK**.

3. Use the Cylinder quick shape feature to create a T-Spline similar to that shown in Figure 18–64. Locate the cylinder on the XY Plane and use the projected Origin Center Point as the base point for the Cylinder.

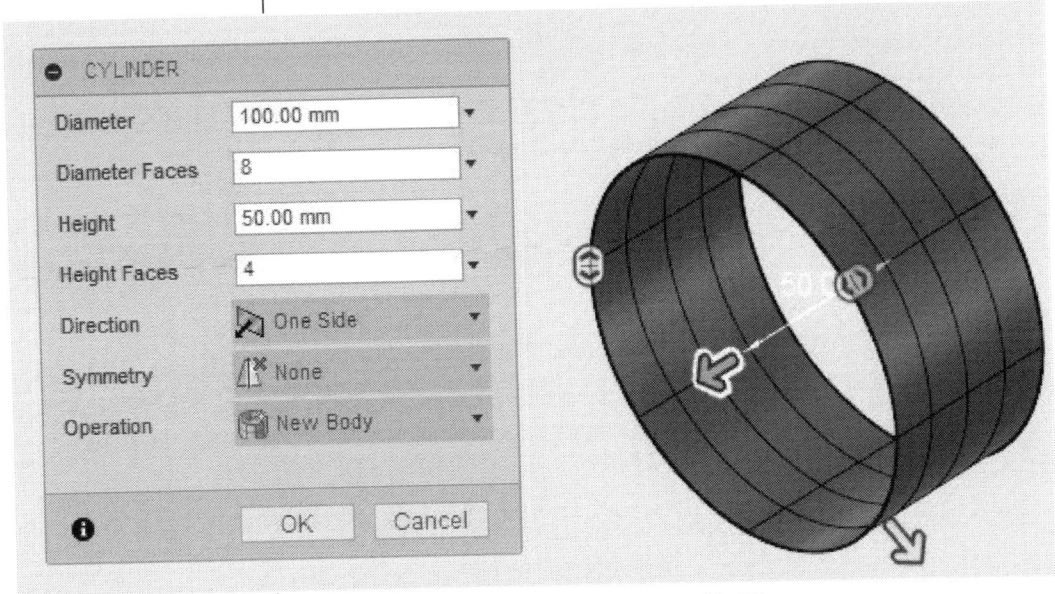

Figure 18–64

4. Use the Cylinder quick shape feature to create a second T-Spline body similar to that shown in Figure 18–65. Select the same plane, but use an origin point that is offset from the initial cylinder.

Figure 18–65

5. If the cylinders are too close to one another, use the MODIFY panel>**Move** command to reposition one of them.

Task 2 - Create geometry between the two cylinders.

1. In the MODIFY panel, click (Bridge).

2. Ensure that the *Side One* area is active. If it is not, select it to activate the area. Select the four faces on the smaller cylinder, as shown in Figure 18–66.

3. Select the *Side Two* field to activate it.

4. Select the four faces on the larger cylinder, as shown in Figure 18–66.

Select the four faces on this side of the smaller cylinder as the Side One references

Select the four faces on this side of the larger cylinder as the Side Two references

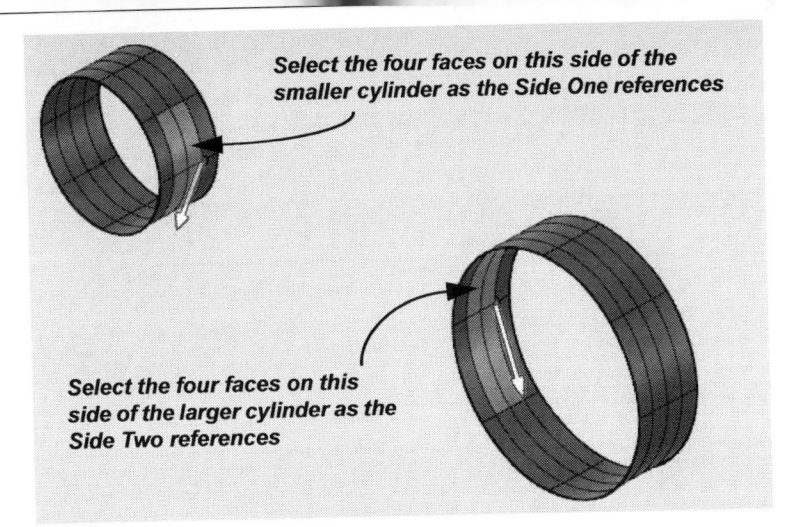

Figure 18–66

5. Maintain the default faces for the number of faces and the twist.

6. Click **OK** to create the bridge geometry. The geometry displays as shown in Figure 18–67.

Figure 18–67

7. Use the **Fill Hole** command with the Reduced Star Fill hole mode to close the four holes.

8. Finish the form to return to the Model environment. The model should display as shown in Figure 18–68 in the Shaded display style.

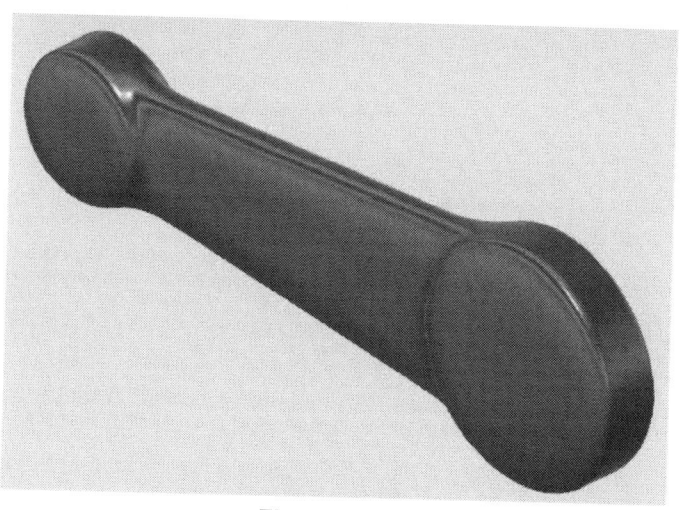

Figure 18–68

9. Save the file as **Bridge.ipt** and close the window.

Chapter Review Questions

1. When modeling in the Sculpt environment, you can use the **Match** command to match parametric sketches from the Model environment.

    a. True
    b. False

2. When using the **Edit Form** command, which of the following describe the triad manipulator controls that are available when displayed as shown in Figure 18–69? (Select all that apply.)

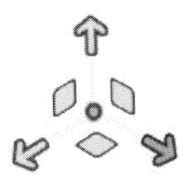

    Figure 18–69

    a. Translate in X, Y, or Z axis
    b. Translate in plane
    c. Rotate in plane
    d. Scale in X, Y, or Z axis
    e. Scale in plane

3. Which of the *Coordinate Space* settings provides you with two manipulators that can be used to manipulate the freeform geometry?

    a. (World)
    b. (View)
    c. (Local)

4. Which of the following editing commands enables you to add additional elements (points, edges, or faces) to existing freeform geometry? (Select all that apply.)

    a. **Insert Edge**
    b. **Insert Point**
    c. **Subdivide**
    d. **Crease**
    e. **Bridge**
    f. **Match**

5. The **Flatten** command enables you to select multiple points and make them parallel to a selected plane.

    a. True
    b. False

6. When subdividing a face, ▦ (Simple mode) forces the freeform geometry to remain exactly the same once the faces have been subdivided.

    a. True
    b. False

7. Which of the following commands can be used to create geometry between two freeform shapes? (Select all that apply.)

    a. **Insert Edge**
    b. **Subdivide**
    c. **Merge Edge**
    d. **Bridge**
    e. **Match**

8. For symmetry in T-Spline geometry, which of the following are true?

    a. Symmetry can only be assigned when the base T-Spline geometry is created using quick shapes.
    b. Symmetry can only be assigned using the **Symmetry** command by selecting faces on the T-Spline geometry.
    c. All of the symmetry assigned during quick shape creation can be removed using the **Clear Symmetry** command.
    d. Faces that are adjacent to a face that is a symmetry reference also update to reflect the symmetry.

Answers: 1.a, 2.(a,b), 3.b, 4.(a,b,c), 5.a, 6.b, 7.(c,d), 8.d

Command Summary

Button	Command	Location
	Bevel Edge	• **Ribbon:** Sculpt Workspace>MODIFY panel • **Context Menu:** Right-click in the graphics window and select **Modify**. • **Context Menu:** (with edge selected)
	Bridge	• **Ribbon:** Sculpt Workspace>MODIFY panel • **Context Menu:** Right-click in the graphics window and select **Modify**.
	Circular - Internal (Symmetry)	• **Ribbon:** Sculpt Workspace>SYMMETRY panel • **Context Menu:** Right-click in the graphics window and select **Symmetry**.
	Clear Symmetry	• **Ribbon:** Sculpt Workspace>SYMMETRY panel • **Context Menu:** Right-click in the graphics window and select **Modify**.
	Crease Edges	• **Ribbon:** Sculpt Workspace>MODIFY panel • **Context Menu:** Right-click in the graphics window and select **Modify**. • **Context Menu:** (with edge, point, or face selected)
	Delete	• **Ribbon:** Sculpt Workspace>MODIFY panel • **Context Menu:** Right-click in the graphics window • **Context Menu:** (with edge, point, or face selected) • **Keyboard:** Press <Delete> key
	Edit Form	• **Ribbon:** Sculpt Workspace>MODIFY panel • **Context Menu:** Right-click in the graphics window • **Context Menu:** (with edge, point, or face selected)
	Flatten	• **Ribbon:** Sculpt Workspace>MODIFY panel • **Context Menu:** Right-click in the graphics window • **Context Menu:** (with edge, point, or face selected)

	Freeze	• **Ribbon:** Sculpt Workspace>MODIFY panel
		• **Context Menu:** Right-click in the graphics window and select **Modify**.
		• **Context Menu:** (with edge or face selected)
	Insert Edge	• **Ribbon:** Sculpt Workspace>MODIFY panel
		• **Context Menu:** Right-click in the graphics window
		• **Context Menu:** (with edge selected)
	Insert Point	• **Ribbon:** Sculpt Workspace>MODIFY panel
		• **Context Menu:** Right-click in the graphics window
	Match	• **Ribbon:** Sculpt Workspace>MODIFY panel
		• **Context Menu:** Right-click in the graphics window
		• **Context Menu:** (with edge selected)
	Merge Edges	• **Ribbon:** Sculpt Workspace>MODIFY panel
		• **Context Menu:** Right-click in the graphics window
	Mirror - Internal (Symmetry)	• **Ribbon:** Sculpt Workspace> SYMMETRY panel
		• **Context Menu:** Right-click in the graphics window and select **Symmetry**.
	Pull	• **Ribbon:** Sculpt Workspace>MODIFY panel
		• **Context Menu:** Right-click in the graphics window and select **Modify**.
	Slide Edge	• **Ribbon:** Sculpt Workspace>MODIFY panel
		• **Context Menu:** Right-click in the graphics window and select **Modify**.
		• **Context Menu:** (with edge selected)
	Subdivide	• **Ribbon:** Sculpt Workspace>MODIFY panel
		• **Context Menu:** Right-click in the graphics window and select **Modify**.
		• **Context Menu:** (with face selected)
	Thicken	• **Ribbon:** Sculpt Workspace>MODIFY panel
		• **Context Menu:** Right-click in the graphics window and select **Modify**.

	Uncrease Edges	• **Ribbon:** Sculpt Workspace>MODIFY panel • **Context Menu:** Right-click in the graphics window and select **Modify**. • **Context Menu:** (with edge, point, or face selected)
	UnFreeze	• **Ribbon:** Sculpt Workspace>MODIFY panel • **Context Menu:** Right-click in the graphics window and select **Modify**. • **Context Menu:** (with edge or face selected)
	Unweld Edges	• **Ribbon:** Sculpt Workspace>MODIFY panel • **Context Menu:** Right-click in the graphics window and select **Modify**. • **Context Menu:** (with edge selected)
	Weld Vertices	• **Ribbon:** Sculpt Workspace>MODIFY panel • **Context Menu:** Right-click in the graphics window and select **Modify**. • **Context Menu:** (with point selected)

Chapter 19

Drawing Basics

A drawing is used to document 3D geometry in a 2D format. To begin creating a drawing, you must select and add drawing views that best communicate the structure of the 3D geometry. Learning how to create different view types enables you to efficiently create accurate drawings of your models.

Learning Objectives in this Chapter

- Create a new drawing based on a drawing template.
- Identify and place view types on a drawing file to appropriately document model geometry.
- Create exploded views of multi-component models.
- Delete and suppress drawing views.
- Edit drawing views to change the properties that were defined during view creation.
- Include views of multiple independent components in a single drawing.
- Modify the title block and border of a drawing.

19.1 Creating a New Drawing

Once the shape, dimensions, and orientation of a design have been defined in the modeling workspaces, the design can be documented using views in a drawing, similar to that shown in Figure 19–1. The design components are not actually contained in a drawing; instead, you create a link between the drawing and the design. If changes are made to the design, those changes can be propagated to the drawing views that reference it.

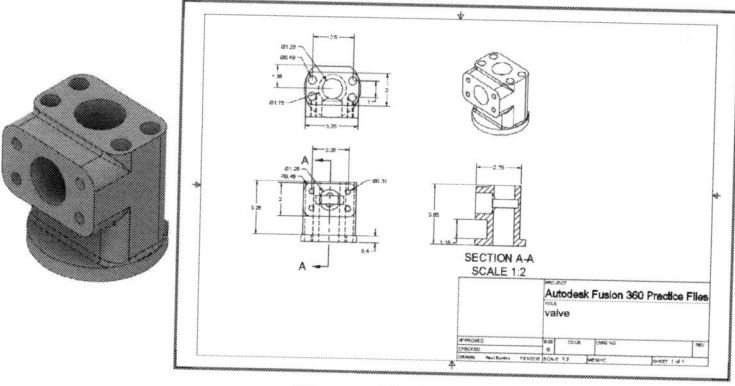

Figure 19–1

Video Lesson Available

Generating 2D Drawings from Fusion 360 Models

Video Length: 2:00

Once the drawing is created, you cannot change the standard or units, but you can change the sheet size.

You can derive a drawing from a design by selecting ▼ > **New Drawing > From Design**. The CREATE DRAWING palette displays (as shown in Figure 19–2), enabling you to specify the drawing standard (ISO / ASME), units (mm / in), and sheet size.

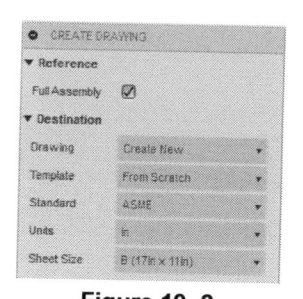

Figure 19–2

Base Views

If a drawing is being derived from a multi-component design, you can select the **Full Assembly** option to show views of the entire assembly, or clear the **Full Assembly** option to show views of just one or more components in the design.

The first view in a drawing is called the *base* view. It is used as the reference view when placing any additional views that are used to document the drawing model.

The model that was active when the drawing was created is automatically set as the drawing model. To return to the base view, in the DRAWING VIEWS panel, click ▢ (Base View). The DRAWING VIEWS palette opens as shown in Figure 19–3.

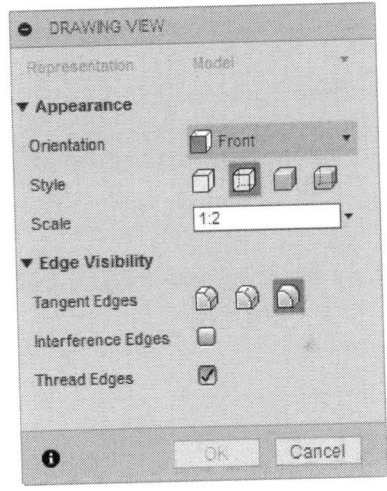

Figure 19–3

- The orientation of the base view defaults to the Front view of the design. You can select any of the named views or standard orientations from the design in the *Orientation* menu.

- You can select the desired scale from the Scale menu.

- The style options available on the *Style* menu enable you to set the view display as ▢ (Visible Edges), ▢ (Visible and Hidden Edges), ▢ (Shaded), and ▢ (Shaded with Hidden Edges).

- Edge visibility options enable you to control the display of tangent edges, interference edges, and thread edges.

Video Lesson Available

Specifying Settings for a Model Drawing

Video Length: 5:46

Projected Views

A projected view is a view that is created by projecting from a parent view. To create a projected view, the parent view must already exist. You can create eight possible views from one view: four orthographic and four isometric, as shown in Figure 19–4.

- The orthographic views are the top, bottom, and side views. These views align with the parent Base view by default. and are dependent on that view. You can break the alignment when placing or moving an orthographic projected view by pressing <Shift>.

- The isometric views are the diagonal views. These views are not dependent on the location of the parent view and can be relocated anywhere on the sheet.

- Projected views are not deleted if the parent view is deleted.

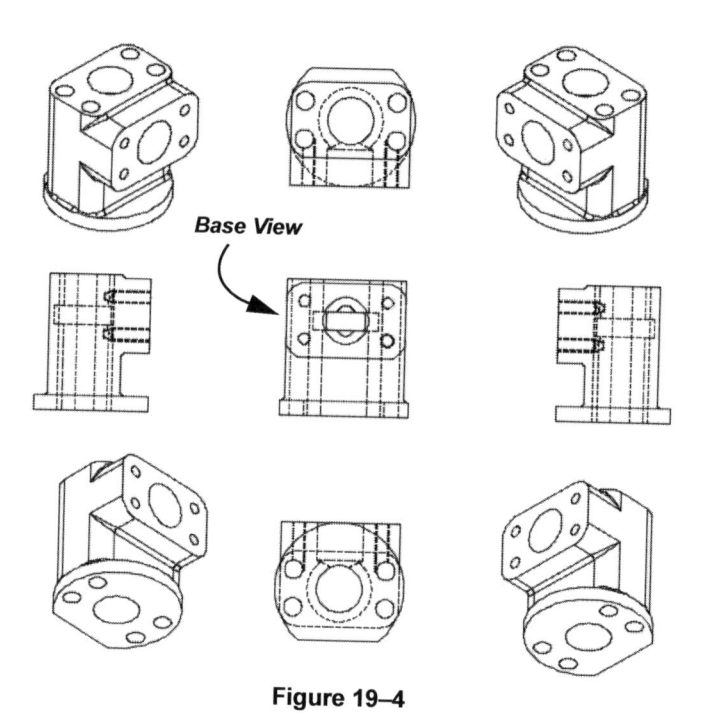

Base View

Figure 19–4

In the Drawing environment, you can press <P> to create a projected view.

To create a projected view, in the DRAWING VIEWS panel, click ▦ (Projected View). Select the view to project from, and then select the location to place the projection. With the command still active, you can continue to place multiple projected views until you either press <Enter> to complete the action, or right-click and select **OK**.

Video Lesson Available

Generating and Editing Projected Views

Video Length: 6:45

19.2 Additional Drawing Views

Additional view types are available in the DRAWING VIEWS panel, as shown in Figure 19–5.

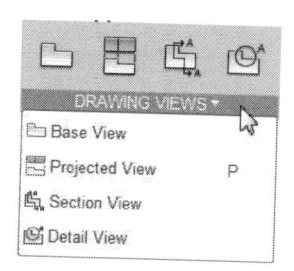

Figure 19–5

Section Views

A section view displays a component with a cutaway, as shown in Figure 19–6. A projection view line (also known as a section line) is drawn on the parent view to locate the cut. The section view shown in Figure 19–6 is referred to as a Full section view.

You can double-click on a component's hatch to modify its Pattern, Scale Factor, and Angle properties.

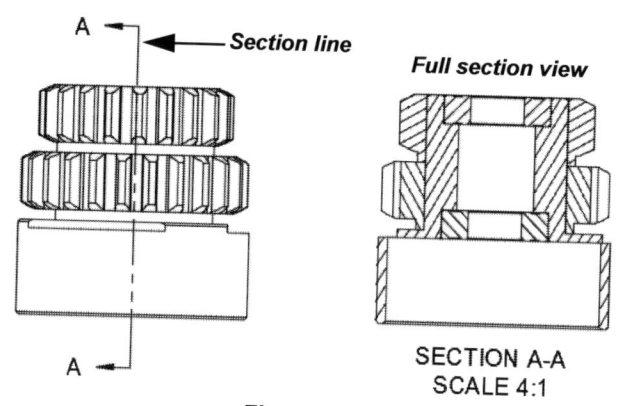

Figure 19–6

If a parent view is deleted, the section views are also deleted.

To create a section view, in the DRAWING VIEWS panel, click (Section View).

Video Lesson Available

Generating and Editing Full Section Views

Video Length: 4:28

Other types of section views can be created depending on how the section line is sketched, as shown in Figure 19–7 to Figure 19–9:

- Half section view

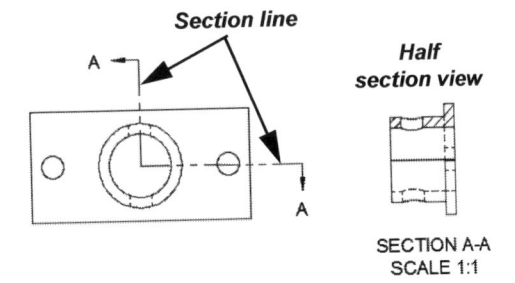

Figure 19–7

- Offset section view

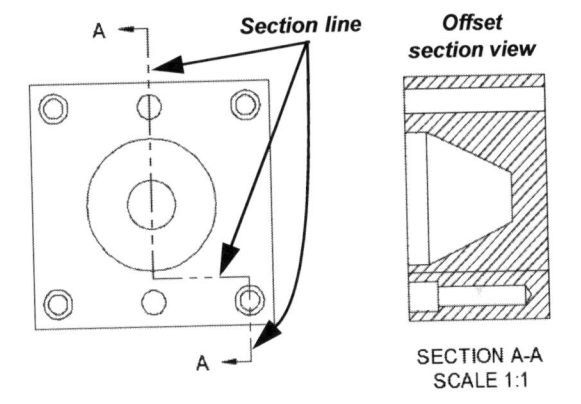

Figure 19–8

- Aligned section view

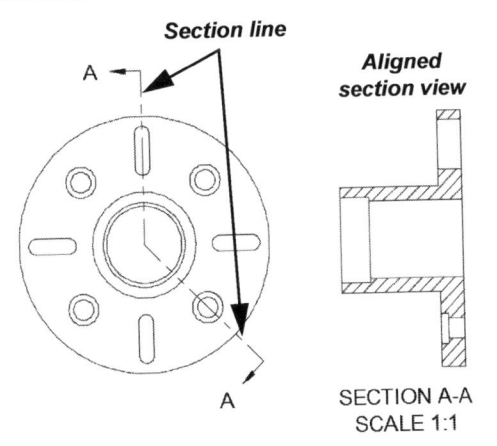

Figure 19–9

Video Lesson Available

Generating and Editing Half Section Views

Video Length: 3:46

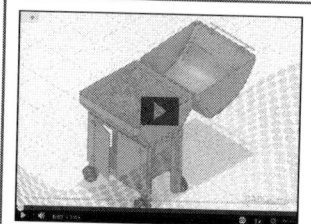

Video Lesson Available

Generating and Editing Offset Section Views

Video Length: 4:23

Video Lesson Available

Generating and Editing Aligned Section Views

Video Length: 4:50

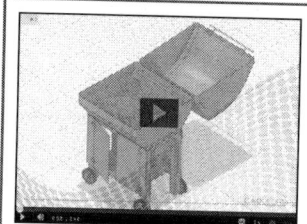

Video Lesson Available

Generating and Editing Assembly Section Views

Video Length: 8:47

Detail Views

Detail views typically enlarge an area of a parent view to display information more clearly, as shown in Figure 19–10.

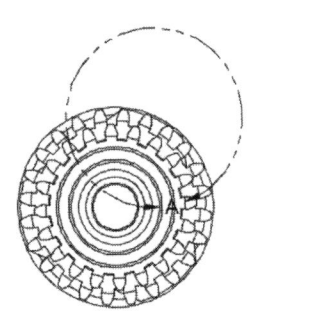

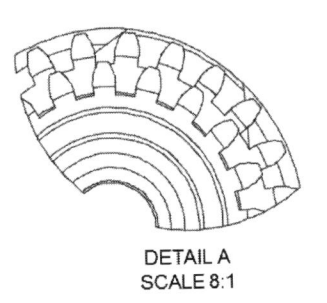

DETAIL A
SCALE 8:1

Figure 19–10

To create a detail view, in the DRAWING VIEWS panel, click ▢ (Detail View). Note that detail views are deleted if the parent view is deleted.

Video Lesson Available

Generating and Editing Detail Views

Video Length: 3:34

19.3 Exploded Views

To create an exploded view of a multi-component assembly design, you must create a storyboard in the ANIMATION workspace. In an animation storyboard, you can move or rotate the components relative to one another and add trails to indicate how they relate in the assembly. An exploded view of an assembled design is shown in Figure 19–11.

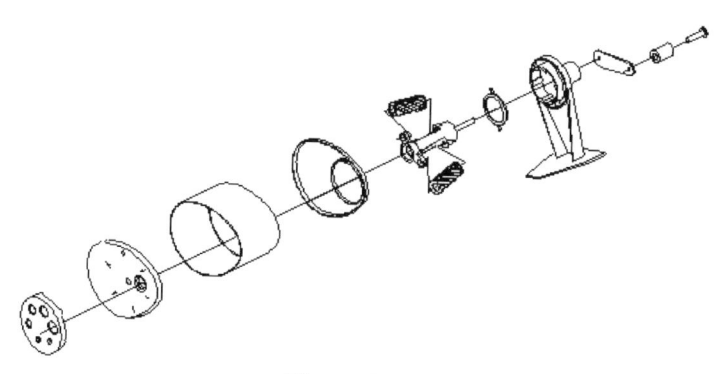

Figure 19–11

The first step in creating an exploded view of an assembly design is to open a multi-component assembly design in the ANIMATION workspace. You can enter the ANIMATION workspace by expanding the Change Workspace menu and selecting **ANIMATION**, as shown in Figure 19–12.

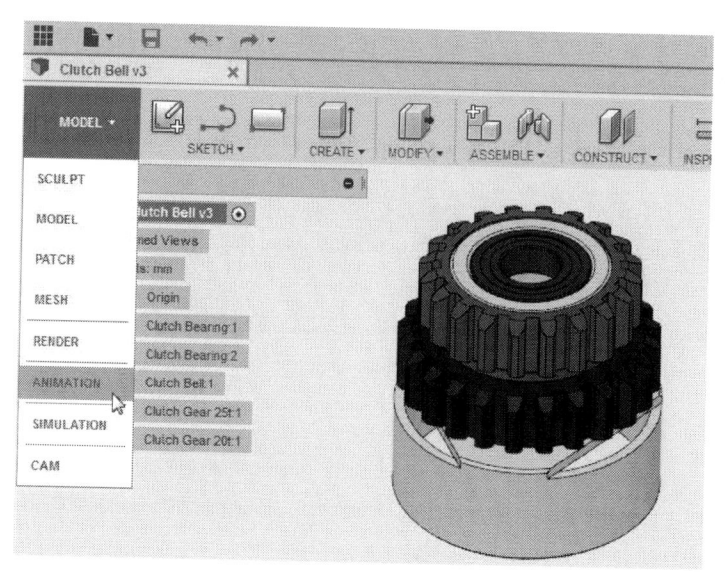

Figure 19–12

Once the ANIMATION workspace environment is active, the Animation ribbon, ANIMATION TIMELINE panel, and Storyboard tabs display, as shown in Figure 19–13.

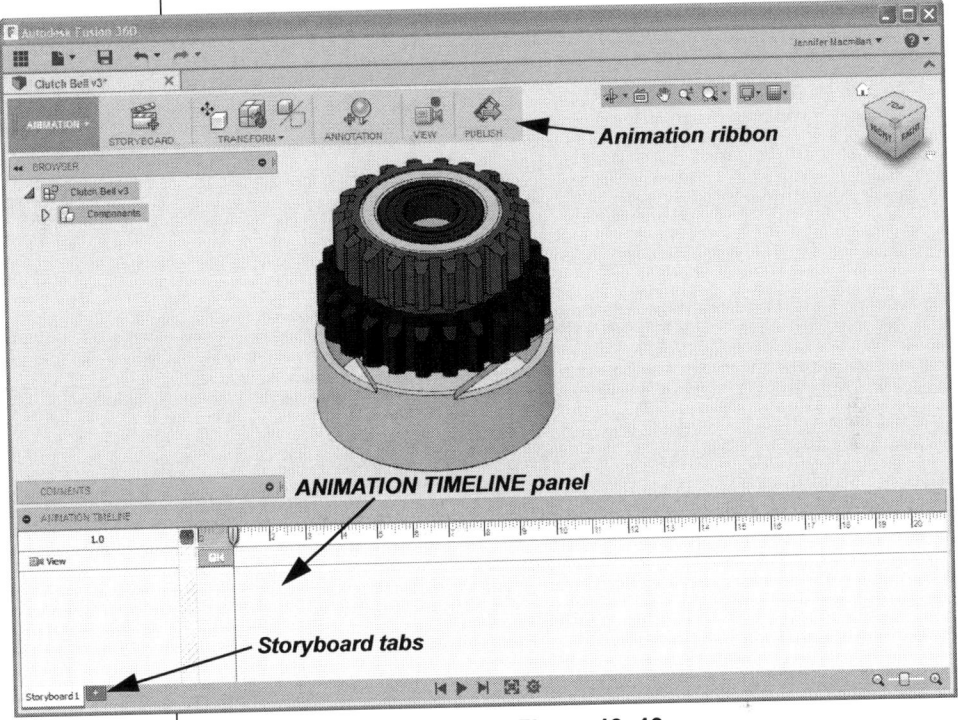

Figure 19–13

The ANIMATION TIMELINE panel, located at the bottom of the graphics window, contains the list of storyboards that exist in the animation. Each storyboard is listed on its own tab. You can use a storyboard for the following:

- Creating an exploded view of an assembly design.

- Creating an animation of the design that records component movements (i.e., assembly or disassembly).

- Creating actions to represent changes in component visibility and opacity at specific times in an animation.

- Capturing changes in camera position at specific times in an animation.

When a animation is created, a single storyboard is included. Additional storyboards can be added as required. Storyboards can be independent of one another, or they can work in combination with one another.

To create a storyboard containing an exploded view, complete the following steps:

1. With the multi-component assembly design open and active, expand the Change Workspace menu and select **ANIMATION**. In the ANIMATION TIMELINE, note that *Storyboard1* is the active storyboard.
2. In the BROWSER, expand the **Components** folder and select the top-level assembly component.
3. In the TRANSFORM panel, select **Auto Explode: All Levels**. The exploded assembly design displays with a toolbar, as shown in Figure 19–14.

Figure 19–14

4. Adjust the explode distance between components by moving the slider in the toolbar.
5. Click ✓ to complete the exploded view.

6. In the TRANSFORM panel, click **Transform Components**. This option enables you to select individual components to move in the exploded view. An example of a final exploded view is shown in Figure 19–15.

Figure 19–15

The animation containing the exploded view can now be added to a drawing.

Video Lesson Available

Generating and Editing Exploded Views

Video Length: 2:56

19.4 Manipulating Drawings

Once you have added views to a drawing, you might need to make changes to the views. There are many different types of changes and modifications that you can make to the views in a drawing.

Delete Views

Views can be deleted from a drawing using any of the following methods:

- In the graphics window, right-click on a view and select **Delete**.

- Select a view and press <Delete>.

Note that if you delete the parent view of a section or detail view, the section or detail view will also be deleted. However, if you delete the parent view of a projection view, the projection view is not deleted.

Move Views

To move a view to a different location in a drawing, select it and then click and drag the square gray handle grip at its center. You can also use the (Move) tool to move a view and align it with other geometry on the drawing.

View Alignment

Dependent views (e.g., projected views, auxiliary views, etc.) are aligned to parent views and update their position if you move the parent view.

To add or remove a view alignment, select the dependent view, and then click and hold the square gray handle grip at its center. A tooltip displays near the cursor, as shown in Figure 19–16. While still holding the mouse button, press <Shift> to toggle the alignment on or off.

- When you toggle the view alignment off, you can move the dependent view anywhere on the drawing sheet.
- When you toggle the view alignment on, the dependent view restores its alignment with the parent view.

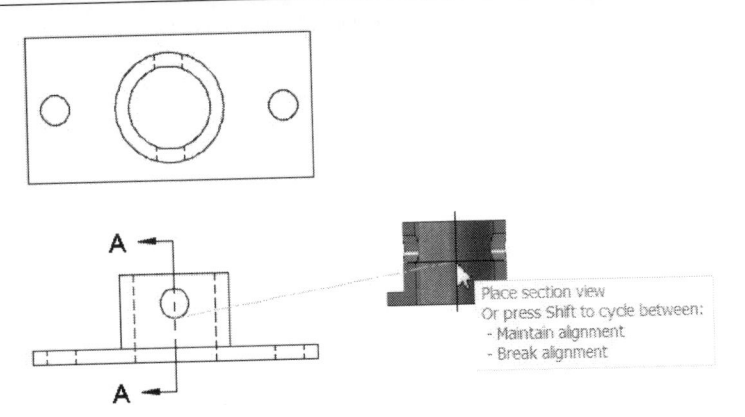

Figure 19–16

View Orientation

You can only change the view orientation of a base view when the view is being created. To change the view orientation, in the DRAWING VIEW palette, use the *Orientation* menu. Dependent views automatically inherit the orientation of their parent view.

Change View Scale

To modify a view scale, either right-click on the view and select **Edit View**, or double-click on the view. The DRAWING VIEW palette opens. In the *Scale* field, enter or select a new scale and click **OK**. Changing this value affects the scale of all child views that have not been independently scaled.

You can set the view scale of a child view (e.g., Projected view) to be independent of the parent. Right-click on the child view and select **Edit View** or double-click on the child view. The inherited scale value will be appended with (from parent) as shown in Figure 19–17. Enter or select a scale value to make it independent from the parent view.

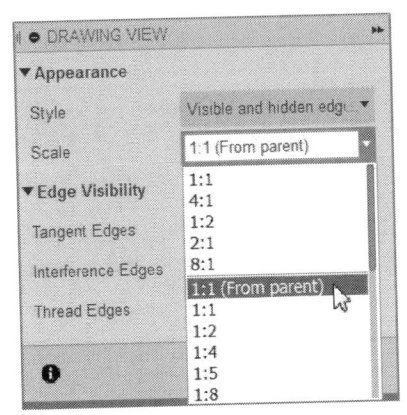

Figure 19–17

Editing View Labels

You can move labels for section and detail views by clicking on them and using the grip handles.

To add extra lines of text in a view label, or control the formatting of the text, double-click on a view label. The TEXT palette and text editor open, as shown in Figure 19–18.

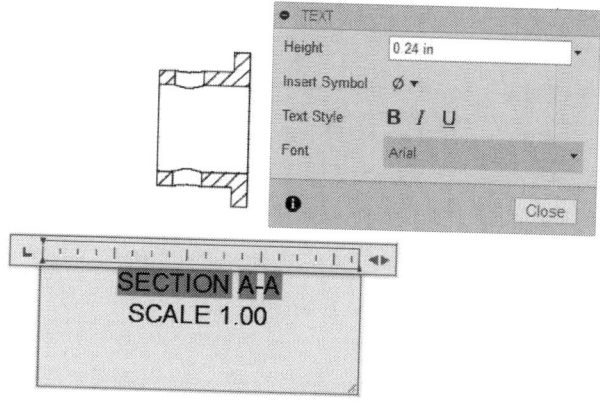

Figure 19–18

- The TEXT palette offers standard options for text formatting, such as height, font, and style. To change the font or style of existing text, highlight the text to be changed in the edit box and then apply the changes.

- In the editor, you can add or delete text, add additional lines, and change the width of the text box.

Add Component or Exploded Views to an Assembly Drawing

You can add a view of individual components to a drawing of a multi-component assembly design, as follows:

1. With the associated drawing open in a separate tab, activate the tab containing the assembled design and then click > **New Drawing** > **From Design**.
2. In the CREATE DRAWING palette, clear the **Full Assembly** checkbox.
3. In the BROWSER or in the graphics window, select one or more components in the design to include in the drawing.
4. In the CREATE DRAWING palette, in the *Destination* area, expand the Drawing drop-down list and select the name of the associate drawing, as shown in Figure 19–19.

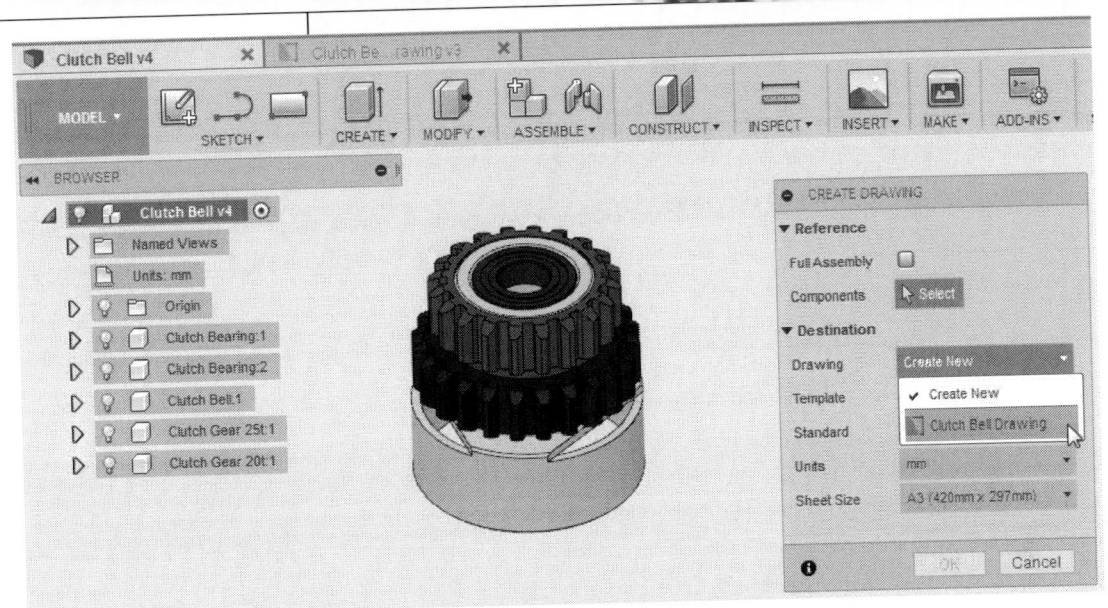

Figure 19–19

5. Place a view of the selected components on the drawing containing the full design, as shown in Figure 19–20.

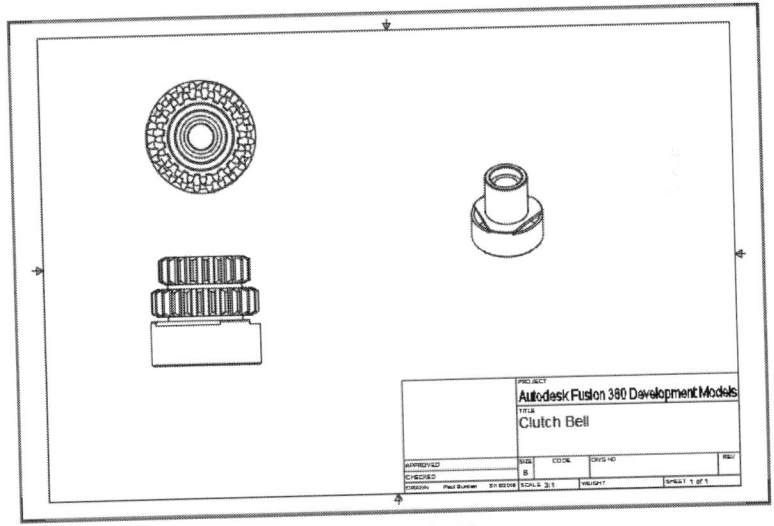

Figure 19–20

Similarly, you can add an exploded view to the existing drawing of an assembly design, as follows:

1. With the associated drawing open in a separate tab, activate the tab containing the assembled design and then click ![icon] > **New Drawing** > **From Animation**.
2. In the CREATE DRAWING palette, select the storyboard containing the exploded view.
3. In the CREATE DRAWING palette, in the *Destination* area, expand the Drawing drop-down list and select the name of the associate drawing.
4. Place the exploded view on the drawing containing the full assembly, as shown in Figure 19–21.

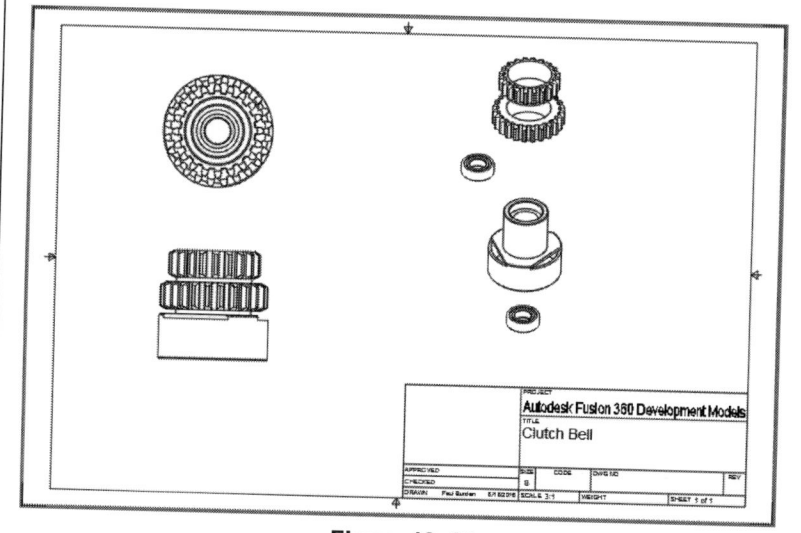

Figure 19–21

Modifying the Title Block and Border

Some of the information that is displayed in the title block is automatically populated when the drawing is created. You can edit these fields by double-clicking on the title block to open the TITLE BLOCK palette, shown in Figure 19–22. The TITLE BLOCK palette enables you to add or edit information, and upload an image which you can then scale and position in the title block.

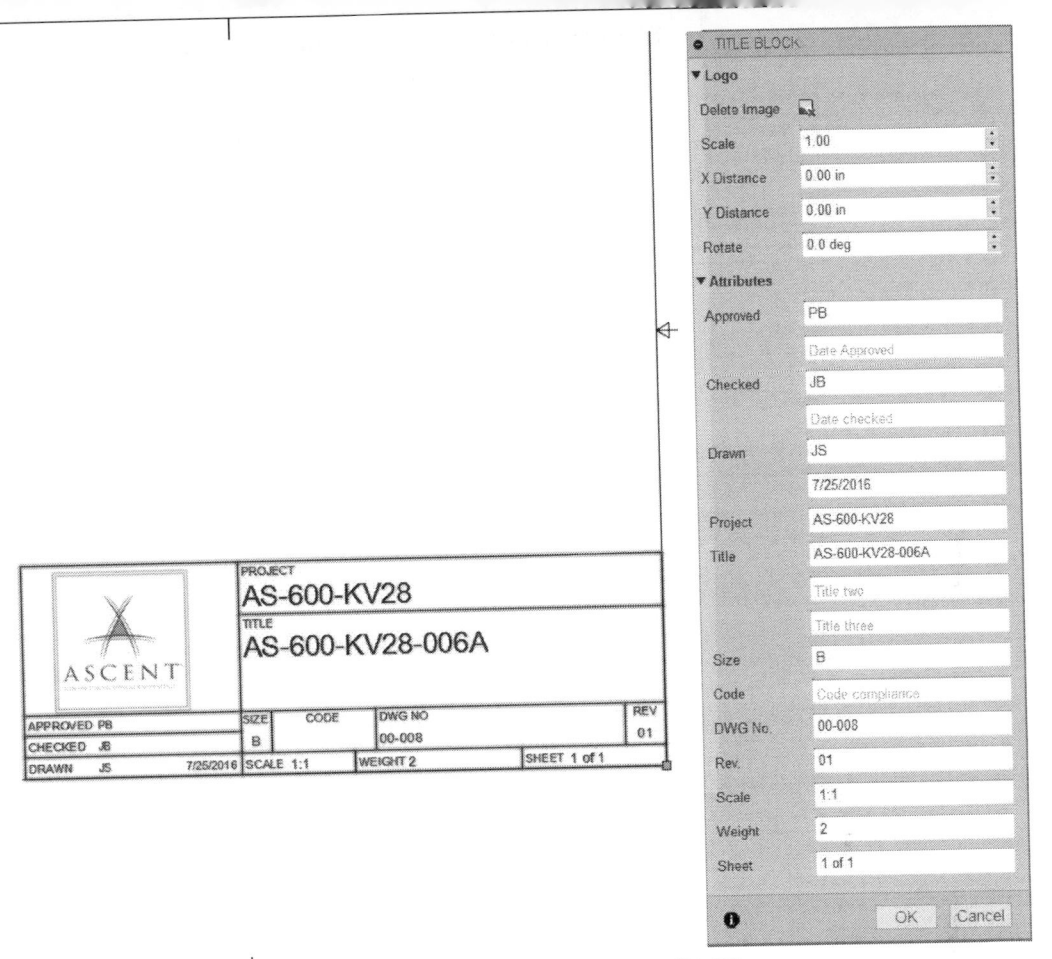

Figure 19–22

You can toggle the title block or border on and off using the

 (Sheet Settings) options at the bottom of the graphics window. This menu provides options for changing the sheet size, toggling the display of the title block, and importing a title block from a .DWG file.

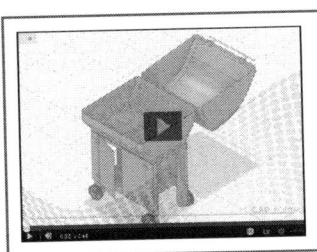

Video Lesson Available

Editing the Title Block

Video Length: 00:50

Drawing Templates

The settings you select for a drawing (e.g., standard, size, units sheet settings, etc.) can be output to a drawing template. To do this, in the ribbon, select **Output > Output Drawing Template**. To create a new drawing based on a template, in the CREATE DRAWING palette, expand the Template drop-down list and select the name of your saved drawing template, as shown in Figure 19–23. When using a template, the options for Standard, Units, and Sheet Size are grayed out in the palette as they have been defined in the drawing template.

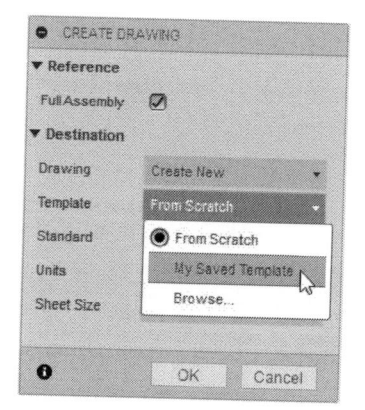

Figure 19–23

Sheets

Currently, drawings created in the Autodesk® Fusion 360™ software can have only one sheet. You can create multiple drawings from the same design and specify the sheet number in the title block.

Practice 19a Creating a Drawing I

Practice Objectives

- Create a new drawing.
- Add Base, Projected, and Section views to a drawing.
- Edit a drawing view to change its display style and scale.

In this practice, you will create a base view, projected views, and section views. You will also edit a view. The completed drawing is shown in Figure 19–24.

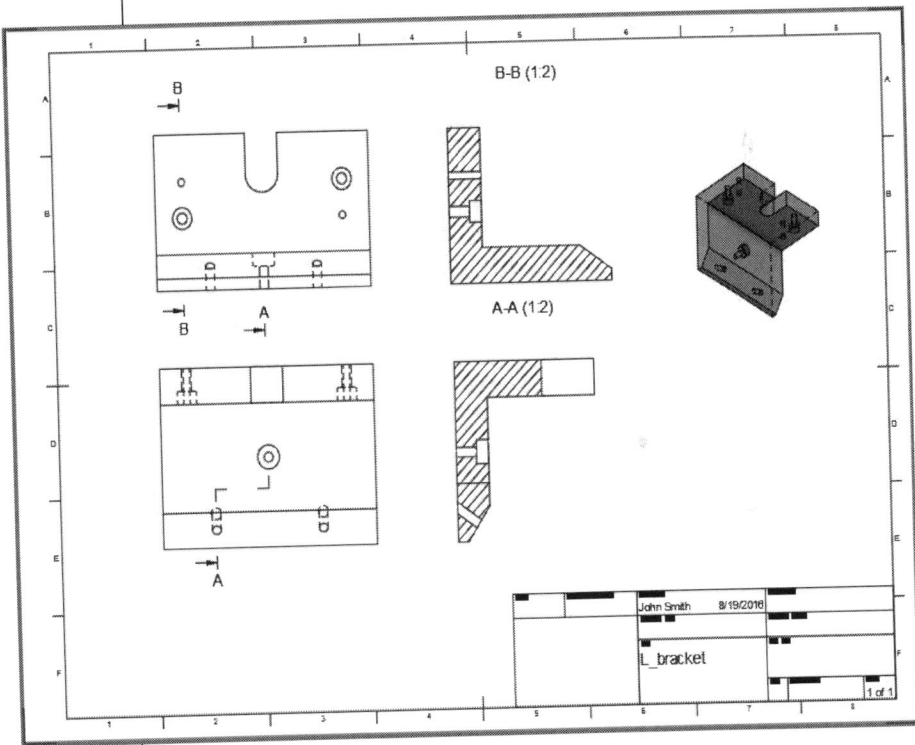

Figure 19–24

Task 1 - Create a new design from file.

1. Click ▼ > **New Design from File**.

2. In the Open dialog box, navigate to the *C:\Autodesk Fusion 360 Practice Files* folder, select **L_bracket.f3d**, and click **Open**. The design displays as shown in Figure 19–25.

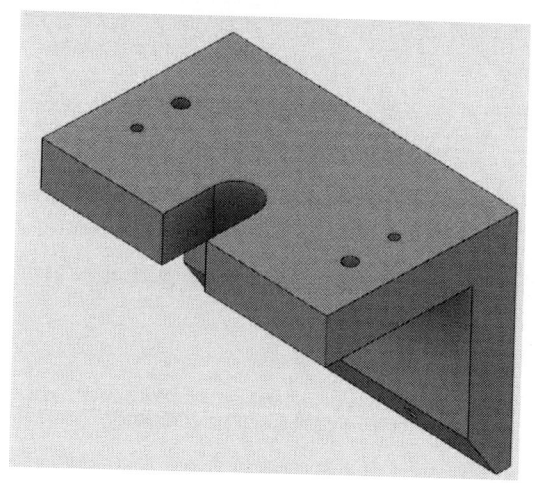

Figure 19–25

3. Save the design with the name **L_bracket** to your *Autodesk Fusion 360 Practice Files* project.

Task 2 - Create a drawing and create the base view.

1. Click > **New Drawing** > **From Design**. The CREATE DRAWING palette displays.

2. Click **OK** to accept the default settings that create a drawing based on the ISO standard of A3 sheet size. The drawing sheet displays and you are prompted to place the base view.

3. Select a location on the drawing sheet (as shown in Figure 19–26) to locate the base view.

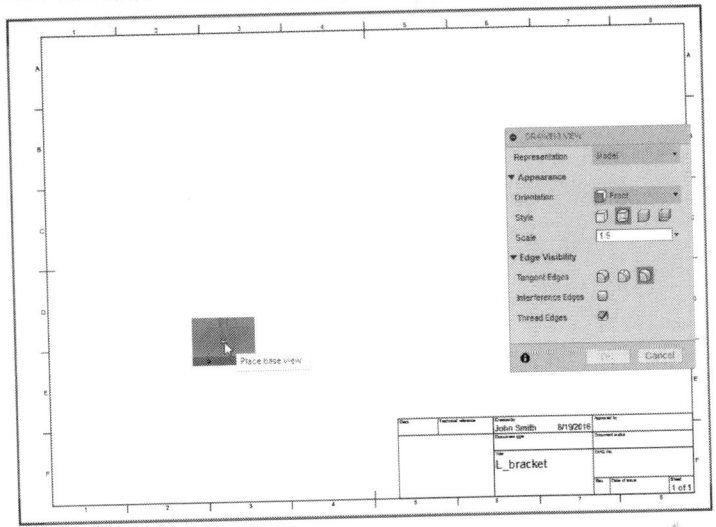

Figure 19–26

4. In the DRAWING VIEW palette, set the following:
   - *Scale:* **1:2**
   - *Orientation:* **Front**
   - *Style:* ▣ (Visible and Hidden Edges)

5. Click **OK** to complete the view. The view should display as shown in Figure 19–27.

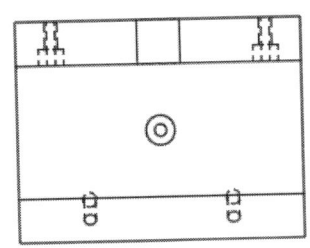

Figure 19–27

Task 3 - Create projected views.

1. In the DRAWING VIEWS panel, click ▦ (Projected View).

2. For the parent reference of the projected view, select the base reference view.

3. Hover the cursor above the base view. A preview of the projected view displays. Select a location above the base view to place the projected view.

4. Drag the mouse to the top right corner and click to create a second projected view, as shown in Figure 19–28.

5. Right-click and select **OK** to create the views that were placed. The drawing displays as shown in Figure 19–28. The visual style of the projected views (Visible and Hidden Edges) is derived from the parent view.

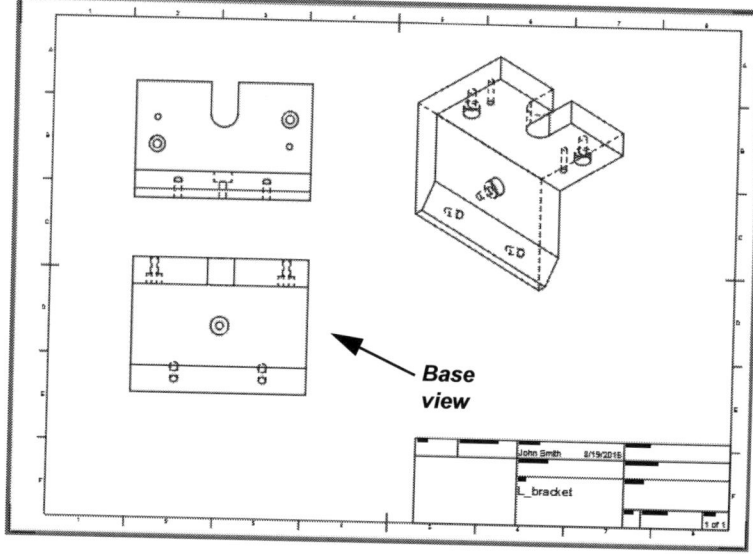

Figure 19–28

Task 4 - Edit the isometric view.

1. Right-click on the isometric view and select **Edit View**.

2. In the DRAWING VIEW palette, set the *Scale* to **1:4**. For the *Style*, click (Shaded with Hidden Edges). Click **Close**.

Task 5 - Create section views.

1. In the DRAWING VIEWS panel, click (Section View) and select the base view as the parent.

2. Draw the section line shown in Figure 19–29. To align to the center of the holes, hover the cursor over a hole and move the cursor.

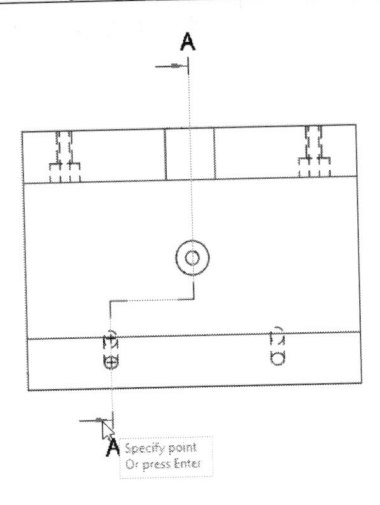

Figure 19–29

3. Right-click and select **Continue**.
4. Place the section view to the right of the reference view.
5. The DRAWING VIEW palette, click **OK**.
6. In the DRAWING VIEWS panel, click (Section View) and select the top projected view as the parent.
7. Draw the section line shown in Figure 19–30.

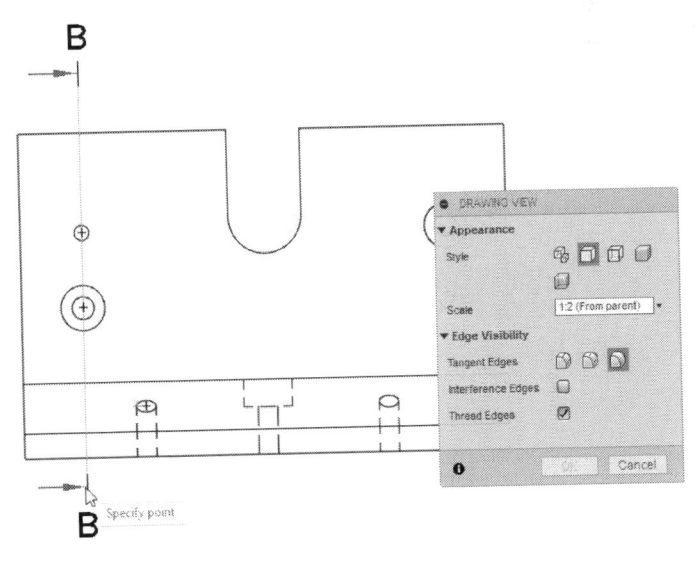

Figure 19–30

8. Right-click and select **Continue**.
9. Place the view to the right of the reference view.
10. In the DRAWING VIEW palette, click **OK**. The drawing displays as shown in Figure 19–31.

Depending on where your initial views were placed, the sections views and labels might overlap. To move a view, select it and drag the square handle at the center of the view.

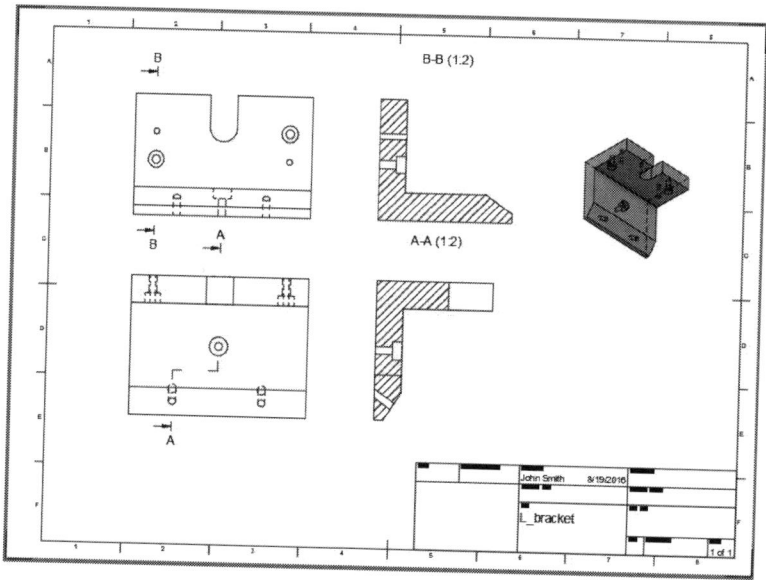

Figure 19–31

11. Save the drawing to your *Autodesk Fusion 360 Practice Files* project.

Practice 19b Creating a Drawing II

Practice Objectives

- Create a new drawing based on a drawing template.
- Add Base, Projected, Section, and Detail views to create a drawing.

In this practice, you will create a drawing with a base view, projected views, a section view, and a detail view. The completed drawing is shown in Figure 19–32.

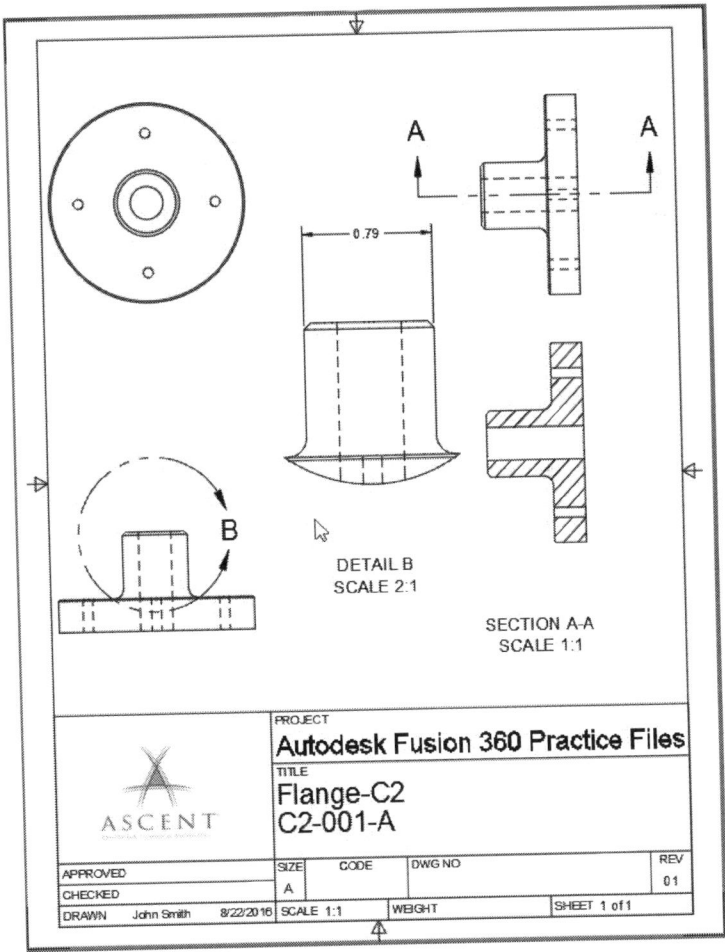

Figure 19–32

Task 1 - Create a new design from file.

1. Click ![icon] > **New Design from File**.
2. In the Open dialog box, navigate to the *C:\Autodesk Fusion 360 Practice Files* folder, select **flange.f3d**, and then click **Open**. The design displays as shown in Figure 19–33.

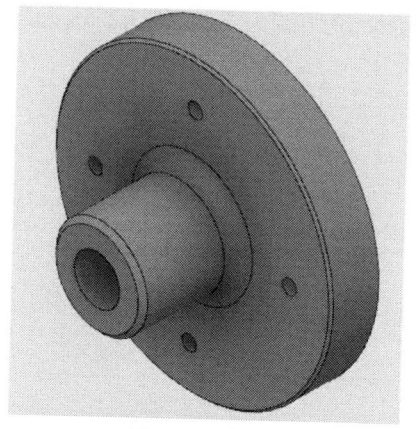

Figure 19–33

3. Save the design with the name **flange** to your *Autodesk Fusion 360 Practice Files* project.

Task 2 - Create a drawing and create the base and projected views.

1. Click ![icon] > **New Drawing > From Design**. The CREATE DRAWING palette displays.
2. In the CREATE DRAWING palette, set *Standard* to **ASME** and *Units* to **in**.
3. Click **OK** to create the drawing. The drawing sheet displays and you are prompted to place the base view.
4. Locate the view in the upper left corner of the drawing, as shown in Figure 19–34.
5. In the DRAWING VIEW palette, set the *Scale* to **1:1** and click **OK**.
6. Create the projected views shown in Figure 19–34.
7. Right-click in the graphics window and select **OK**.

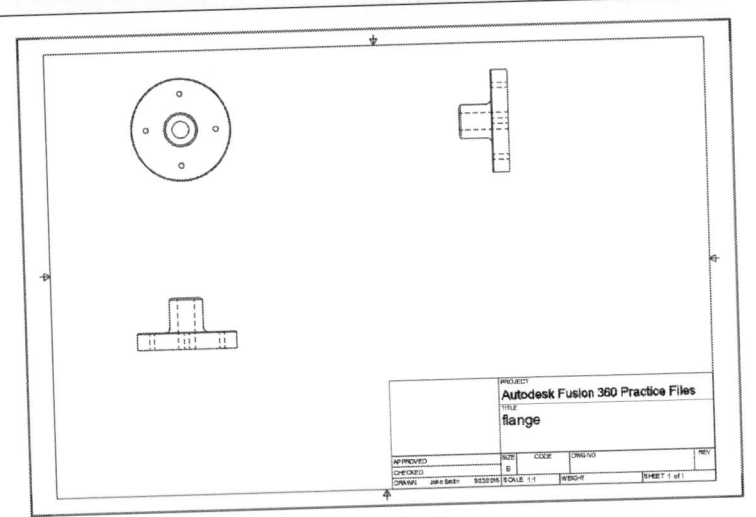

Figure 19–34

Task 3 - Create a section view.

1. Create the section view shown in Figure 19–35. Ensure that the section line cuts through the center of the part.

To move a section view label, select the label and drag the square handle that displays.

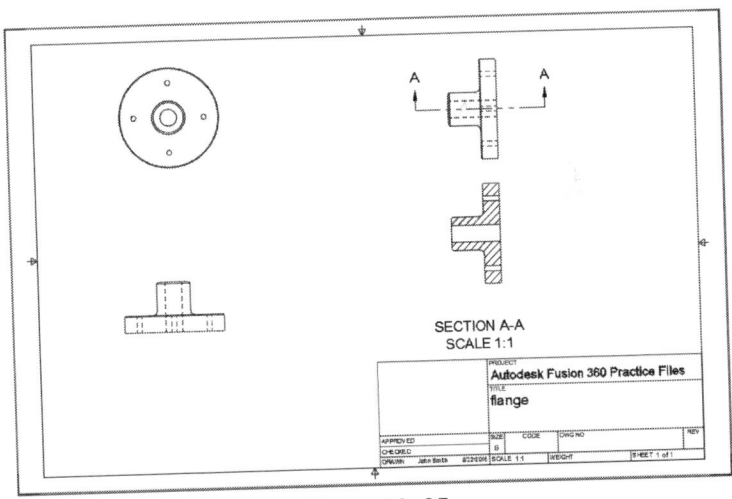

Figure 19–35

Task 4 - Create a detail view.

1. In the DRAWING VIEWS panel, click (Detail View) to create a detail view.

2. Select the bottom projected view as the parent view.

3. For the centerpoint of the detail boundary, select the midpoint of the edge shown in Figure 19–36.

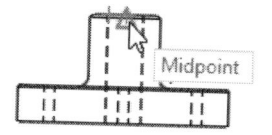

Figure 19–36

4. Drag the boundary circle to define its size. Click on the drawing sheet to create the boundary.

5. Locate the detail view in the location shown in Figure 19–37 with a scale of **2:1**. Click **OK**.

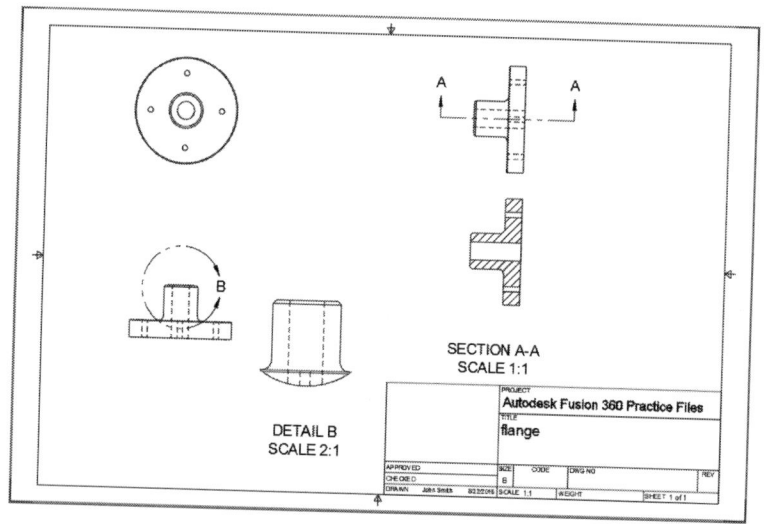

Figure 19–37

6. Save the drawing to your *Autodesk Fusion 360 Practice Files* project using the default name.

Task 5 - Modify the titleblock and change the sheet size.

1. Double-click on any of the table borders in the title block. The TITLE BLOCK palette opens. Note that some of the fields in the *Attributes* section have been auto-populated.

2. In the *Title* field, enter **Flange-C2** .

3. In the *Title two* field, enter **C2-001-A**.

4. In the *Rev.* field, enter **01**.

5. Click **OK**. The title block should display as shown in Figure 19–38.

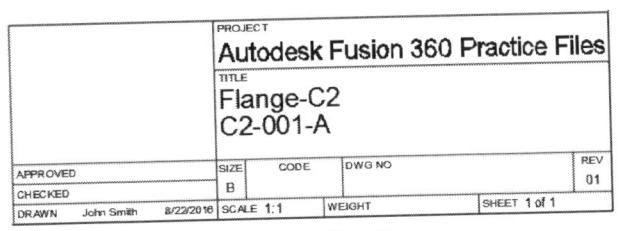

Figure 19–38

6. At the bottom of the graphics window, turn off the title block by selecting ▼ (**Sheet Settings**) > **Display Title Block**.

7. Select the option a second time to restore the title block.

8. Select ▼ (**Sheet Settings**) > **Sheet Size** > **A (8.5in x 11in)**. Note that the sheet is now in a portrait orientation, and some of the views are off the sheet.

9. Select the top, left view, select the square handle in the center of the view, and drag it near the border on the left side of the sheet, as shown in Figure 19–39. The projected view below is aligned and follows its parent view.

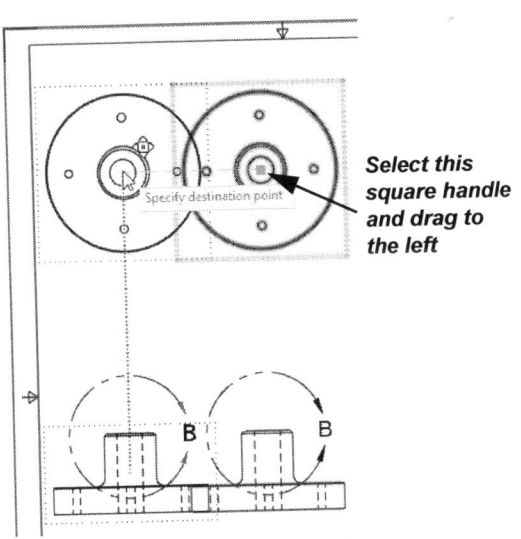

Select this square handle and drag to the left

Figure 19–39

10. Reposition the other views so that the drawing displays as shown in Figure 19–40.

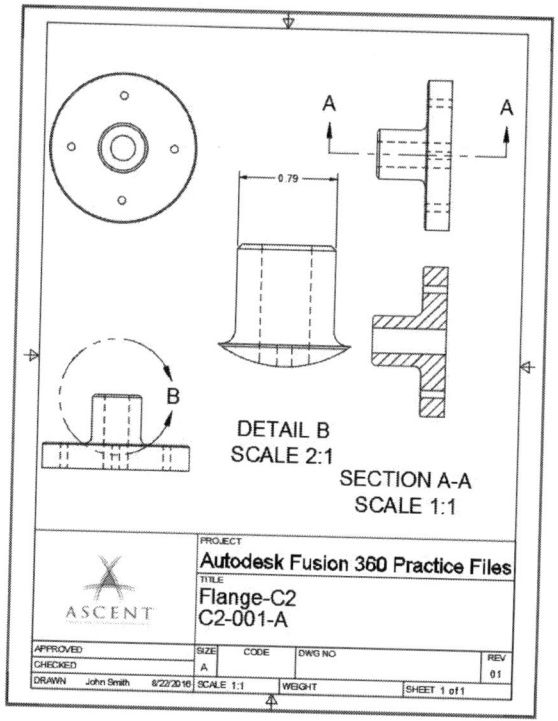

Figure 19–40

11. Double click on the label for **Section A-A**. The TEXT palette and a text editor open.

12. Select all of the text in the editor, as shown in Figure 19–41.

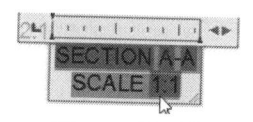

Figure 19–41

13. In the TEXT palette, for the *Height*, enter **0.15 in**.

14. Click **Close**.

15. Repeat Step 13 for the label for Detail B.

16. Move the labels closer to the views.

17. Double-click on any of the table borders in the title block. The TITLE BLOCK palette opens.

18. In the *Logo* area, click (Insert Image).

19. In the Open dialog box, navigate to the *C:\Autodesk Fusion 360 Practice Files* folder, select **ASCENT.png**, and click **Open**.

20. You are prompted to locate the lower left corner of a box representing the outline of the logo image. Place it in the square table cell shown in Figure 19–42.

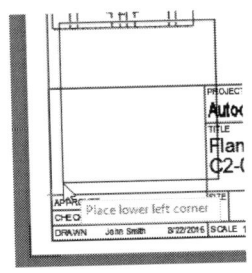

Figure 19–42

21. In the TITLE BLOCK palette>*Logo* area, set the *Scale* to **0.6**.

22. Center the logo in the table cell by adjusting the *X Distance* and *Y Distance* values.

23. Click **OK**. The drawing should display as shown in Figure 19–43.

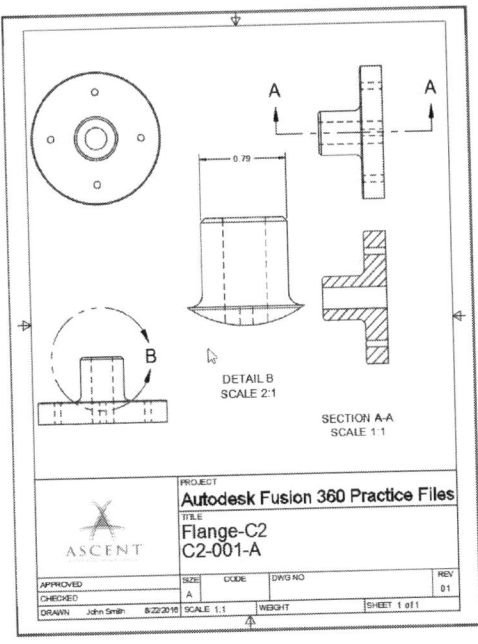

Figure 19–43

24. Save the drawing.

Practice 19c

Creating a Drawing III

Practice Objectives

- Create a new drawing based on a drawing template.
- Add Base, Projected, Section, Detail, and Break Out views to create a drawing.
- Edit a drawing view to change the location, display style, and scale.

In this practice, you will create the drawing shown in Figure 19–44. You will use the drawing commands to complete the drawing, add all the required views, and manipulate them as required.

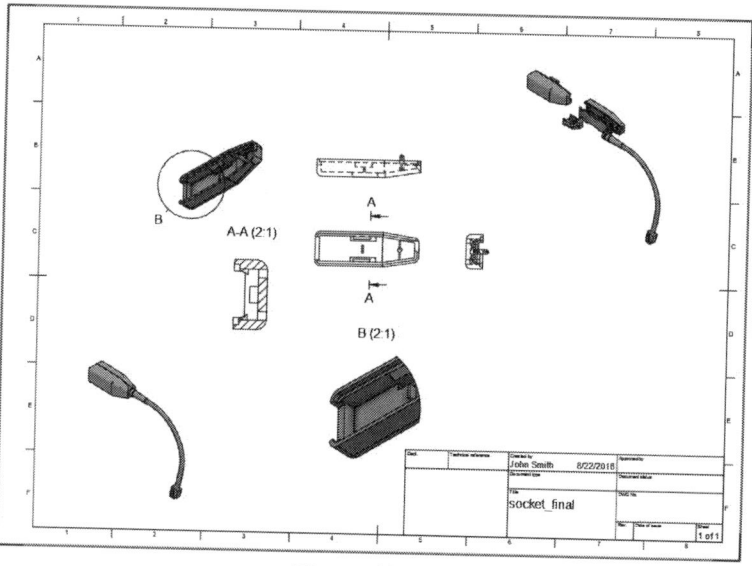

Figure 19–44

Task 1 - Create a new assembly design from file.

1. Click ▼ > **New Design > From File**.

2. In the Open dialog box, navigate to the *C:\Autodesk Fusion 360 Practice Files* folder, select **socket_final.f3d**, and click **Open**. The design displays as shown in Figure 19–45.

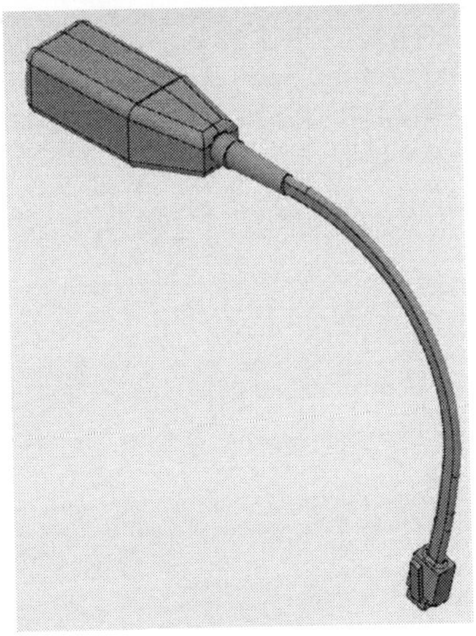

Figure 19–45

3. Save the design with the name **socket_final** to your *Autodesk Fusion 360 Practice Files* project.

Task 2 - Create a drawing and create the base view.

1. Click  > **New Drawing > From Design**. The CREATE DRAWING palette displays.
2. In the CREATE DRAWING palette, clear the **Full Assembly** option.
3. In the BROWSER, select the encbase component to include in the drawing.
4. Click **OK** to accept the default settings to create a drawing that is based on the ISO standard of A3 sheet size.The drawing sheet displays and you are prompted to place the base view.

5. To locate the base view, select a location on the drawing sheet as shown in Figure 19–46.

6. Accept the scale of **1:1** and click **OK**.

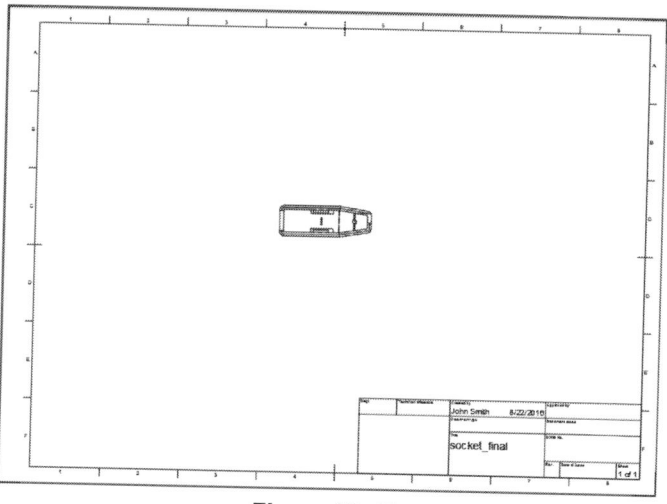

Figure 19–46

Task 3 - Add projected, section, and detail views.

1. Create the two projected views shown in Figure 19–47.

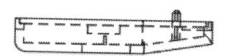

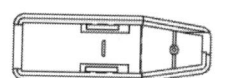

Figure 19–47

2. Add a third projected view and edit the view so that it displays with the shaded style shown in Figure 19–48.

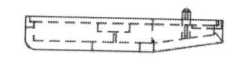

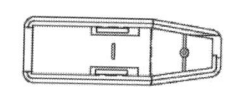

Figure 19–48

To reposition the detail view label, click on a section of the label to display its handles, and then click and drag the center square handle.

3. Create the section view shown in Figure 19–49. When placing the section view, press <SHIFT> to break the alignment with the parent view. Use a scale of **2:1**.

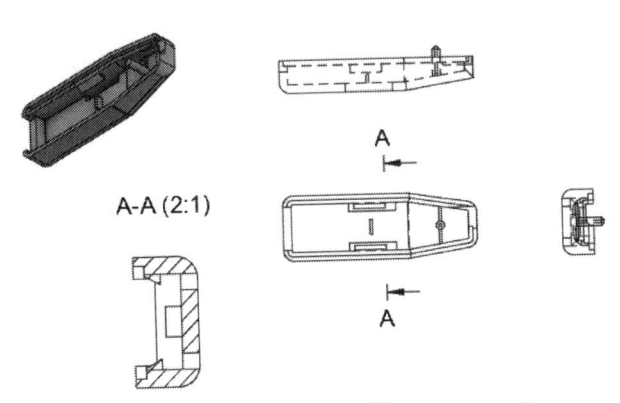

Figure 19–49

4. Create a detail view from the isometric view with a scale of **2:1**. Locate it as shown in Figure 19–50.

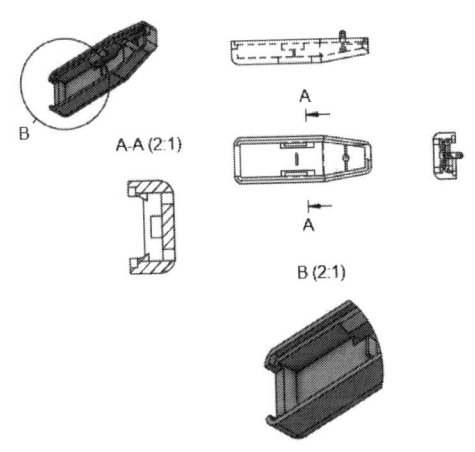

Figure 19–50

5. Save the drawing to your *Autodesk Fusion 360 Practice Files* project.

Task 4 - Add a base view of the full assembly to the drawing.

1. Without closing the tab that contains the drawing, select the tab containing the socket_final model to make it active.

2. Click ▼ **> New Drawing > From Design**.

3. In the CREATE DRAWING palette, expand the Drawing drop-down list and select the **socket_final** drawing you just created, as shown in Figure 19–51.

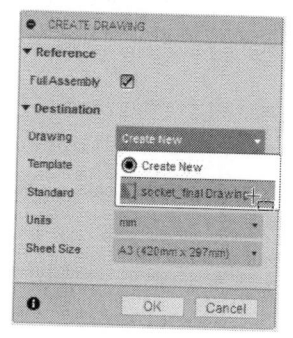

Figure 19–51

4. Note that all of the other *Destination* options are now grayed out. Click **OK**. Your previous drawing is now active, and you are prompted to place the base view of the full assembly.

5. Locate the view as shown in Figure 19–52 and using the following settings:
   - *Orientation*: **Home**
   - *Scale:* **1:2**
   - *Style:* **Shaded**

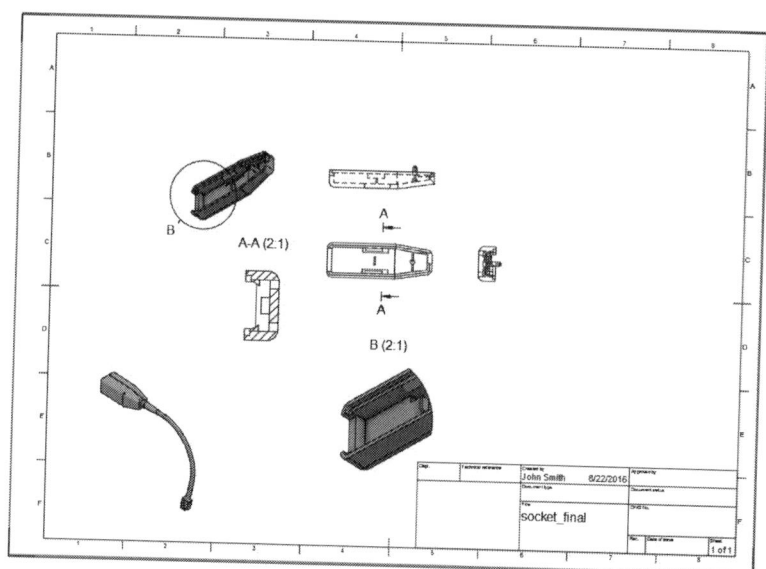

Figure 19–52

6. Save the drawing.

Task 5 - Add an exploded view of the full assembly to the drawing.

1. Without closing the tab that contains the drawing, select the tab containing the **socket_final** model to make it active.

2. With the assembly design open and active, enter the Animation workspace by expanding the Change Workspace menu and selecting **ANIMATION**. At the bottom of the screen, in the ANIMATION TIMELINE, note that *Storyboard1* is the active storyboard tab.

3. In the BROWSER, expand the **Components** node and select the **socket_final** component.

4. In the TRANSFORM panel, click **Auto Explode: All Levels**. The assembly design components explode, as shown in Figure 19–53.

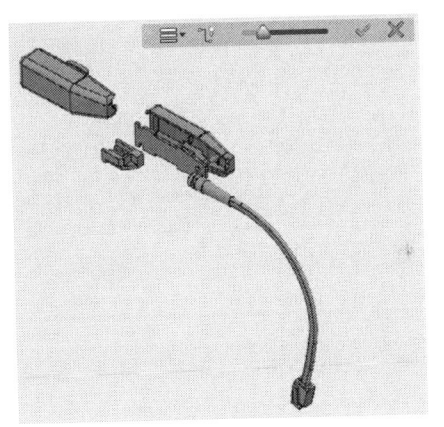

Figure 19–53

5. Click ![icon] to complete the exploded view.

6. Return to the Model workspace by expanding the Change Workspace menu and selecting **MODEL**. The design returns to the unexploded state.

7. Save the design.

8. Click ![icon] > **New Drawing** > **From Animation**. The Autodesk Fusion 360 software temporarily returns you to the Animation workspace and the CREATE DRAWING palette displays.

9. In the CREATE DRAWING palette, expand the *Drawing* drop-down list and select the name of the drawing you just created previously. Note that all of the other *Destination* options are now grayed out. Click **OK**.

10. Because you saved the design after the exploded view was created, you are warned that there is a version mismatch between the design and the drawing. Click **OK** to get the latest version of the design for the drawing.

11. Your previous drawing is now active and you are prompted to place the base view of the exploded assembly. Locate the view as shown in Figure 19–54 with the *Orientation* set to **Home**, *Style* set to **Shaded**, and *Scale* set to **1:2**.

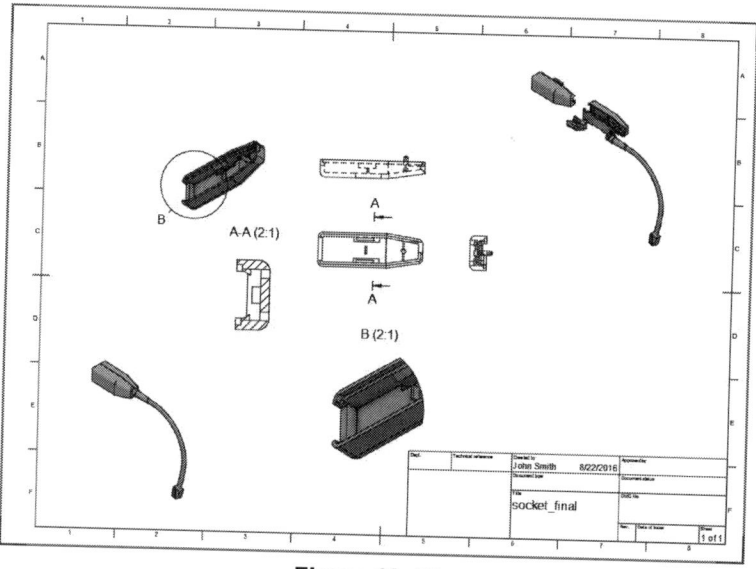

Figure 19–54

12. Save the drawing.

Chapter Review Questions

1. Which of the following view types must be the first view in a drawing?

    a. Base

    b. Projected

    c. Section

    d. Detail

2. If you have already placed the front view of a part in a drawing, which view-type most easily creates a side view that is aligned with the front view, as shown in Figure 19–55?

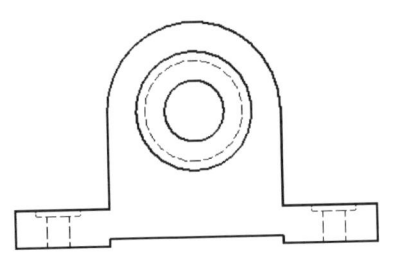

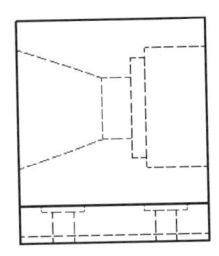

    Figure 19–55

    a. Base

    b. Projected

    c. Section

    d. Detail

3. You can break the alignment dependency between a parent and a child view.

    a. True

    b. False

4. If you change a part or assembly design, drawing views that show it update automatically by default.

    a. True

    b. False

5. To create an exploded view of an assembly design in a drawing (as shown in Figure 19–56), which workspace must you use?

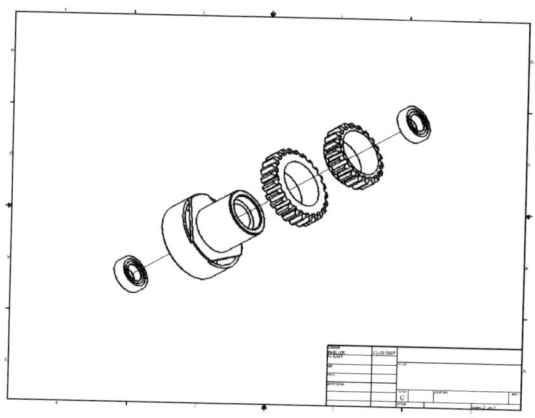

Figure 19–56

   a. Model
   b. Render
   c. Animation
   d. Simulation

6. Which types of views are deleted if their parent views are deleted? (Select all that apply.)

   a. Base
   b. Projected
   c. Section
   d. Detail

7. A shaded Base view exists in a drawing. This base view is automatically displayed as shaded and it cannot be modified to remove the shaded display.

   a. True
   b. False

8. What key do you press to remove the alignment between a parent view and its projected view?

   a. <Alt>
   b. <Ctrl>
   c. <Shift>
   d. <Tab>

9. Which of the following can be changed when you edit a view? (Select all that apply.)

   a. Scale
   b. Drawing Template
   c. Units
   d. Style

10. You can change the scale of the projected views independent of the parent view scale.

    a. True
    b. False

Answers: 1.a, 2.b, 3.a, 4.b, 5.c, 6.(c,d), 7.b, 8.c, 9.(a,d), 10.a

Command Summary

Button	Command	Location
	Base View	- **Ribbon:** DRAWING VIEWS panel - **Context Menu:** Drawing views > Base View
	Detail View	- **Ribbon:** DRAWING VIEWS panel - **Context Menu:** Drawing views > Detail View
	Projected View	- **Ribbon:** DRAWING VIEWS panel - **Context Menu:** Drawing views > Projected View
	Section View	- **Ribbon:** DRAWING VIEWS panel - **Context Menu:** Drawing views > Section View

Chapter 20

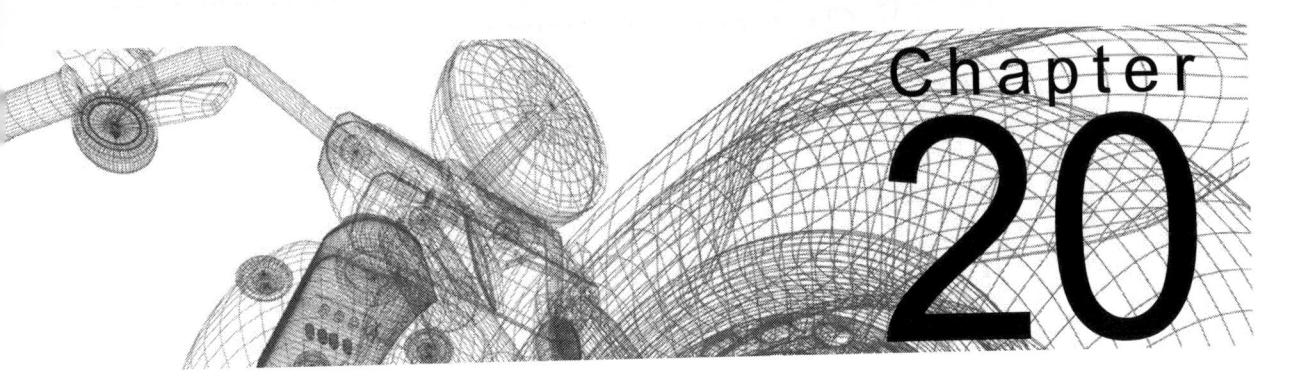

Detailing Drawings

Adding details to your drawings enables you to communicate additional design information an the 2D drawings sheet. Details can include dimensions, text annotations, symbols, parts lists, and other information. You can also apply styles to control the appearance of the drawing's details.

Learning Objectives in this Chapter

- Create dimensions to detail a drawing view.
- Create annotations to detail a drawing, such as notes, centerlines, center marks, and symbols.
- Add a parts list to a drawing.
- Create balloons that identify the components in a drawing's parts list.
- Review and edit the style options for drawing annotations.
- Output a drawing to a .PDF or a .DWG file format.

20.1 Dimensions

You can create dimensions directly on a drawing. Drawing dimensions are dependent on the design geometry and their values cannot be changed. However, if the design size changes, you can update the drawing to reflect the correct values.

Basic Dimensions

The (Dimension) tool adds basic dimensions in the same way that model dimensions are added in the part file. The type of dimension placed (e.g., linear, diameter, angular, etc.) depends on the entity or entities you select. Basic drawing dimensions that you create with this tool can be placed on orthogonal views, but not on projected isometric views.

You can create specific types of basic dimensions using the DIMENSIONS panel. Figure 20–1 shows an example of some basic dimensions.

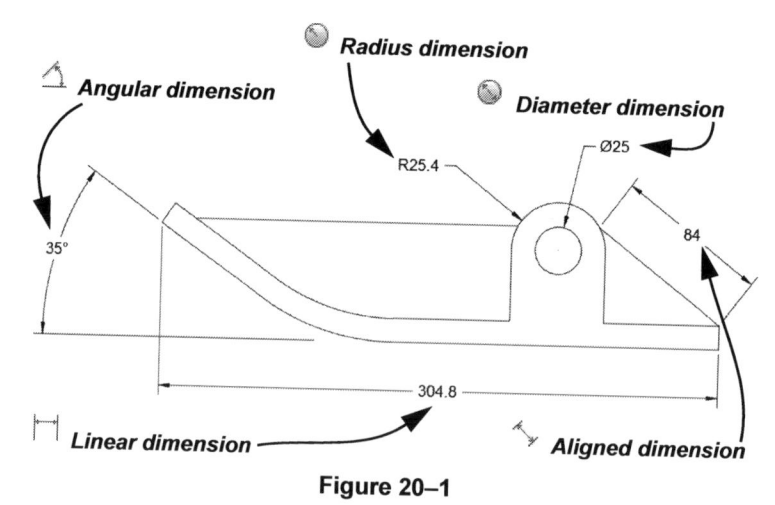

Figure 20–1

Basic dimensions that are created with these options can be placed on projected isometric views, in some cases.

Video Lesson Available

Adding Basic Dimensions

Video Length: 4:21

Baseline Dimensions

A Baseline dimension enables you to reference an existing linear dimension to create dimensions that share a common extension line. An example of baseline dimensions is shown in Figure 20–2. To create a Baseline dimension, in the DIMENSIONS panel, click ⊢⊣ (Baseline Dimension).

Common extension line

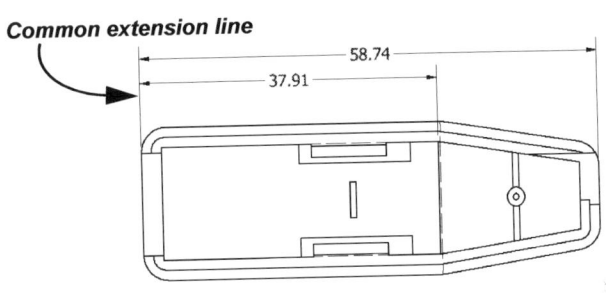

58.74
37.91

Figure 20–2

Chain Dimensions

A chain dimension enables you to reference an existing linear dimension to create multiple dimensions that are chained to one another. An example of chain dimensions is shown in Figure 20–3. To create a chain dimension, in the DIMENSIONS panel, click ⊢⊢⊢ (Chain Dimension).

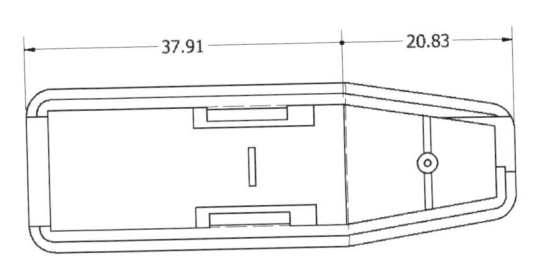

37.91   20.83

Figure 20–3

Video Lesson Available

Adding Baseline and Chain Dimensions

Video Length: 2:41

20.2 Other Annotations

Text Notes

Text is used to communicate information that cannot be communicated through just views and dimensions. You can create text with or without a leader, as shown in Figure 20–4.

To create leader text, use the [A] (Leader) option. To create nonleader text, use the [A] (Text) option.

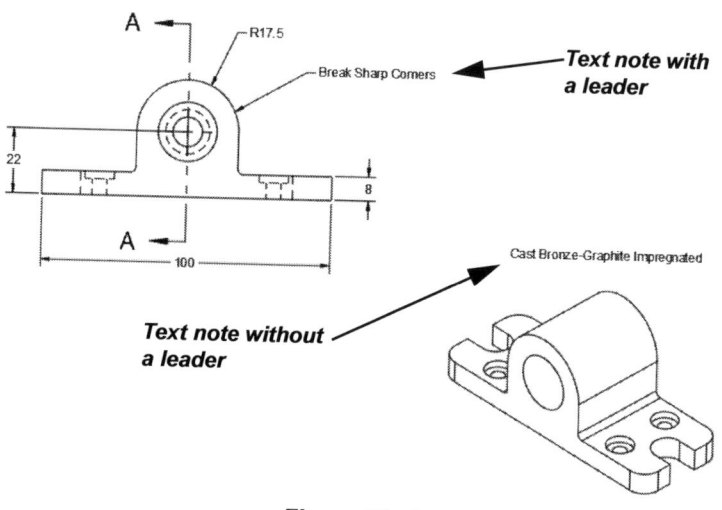

Figure 20–4

You can add text notes to dimensions to convey additional information, as shown in Figure 20–5. This is done by couple-clicking on the dimension and adding text to the dimension value.

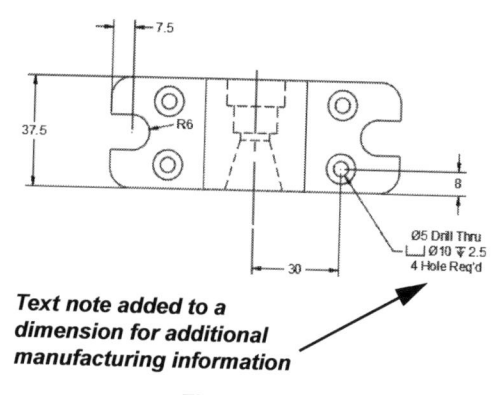

Figure 20–5

> **Video Lesson Available**
>
> Creating and Editing Text Annotations
>
> *Video Length: 8:13*

> **Video Lesson Available**
>
> Creating and Editing Leader Annotations
>
> *Video Length: 3:25*

Centerlines and Center Marks

Centerlines and center marks act as visual indicators on a drawing view, as shown in Figure 20–6. Centerlines represent the midline between two edges, while center marks show the centerpoint of circular edges. To add a centerline or center mark to a drawing, click (Centerline) or (Center Mark).

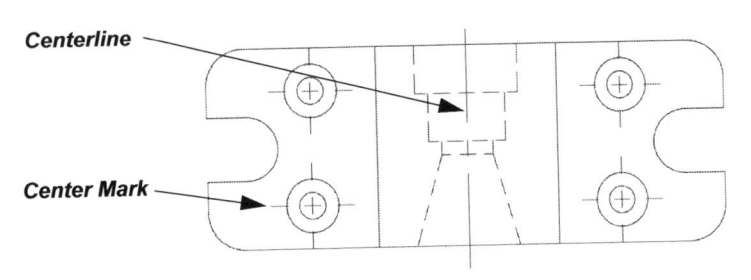

Figure 20–6

> **Video Lesson Available**
>
> Adding Center Marks and Centerlines
>
> *Video Length: 2:40*

Symbols

You can add symbols to drawings using the options available in the SYMBOLS panel. The symbols options are as follows:

- ✓ (Surface Texture)

- ⌖1 (Feature Control Frame)

- 𝔸 (Datum Identifier)

Figure 20–7 shows an example of the three symbol types.

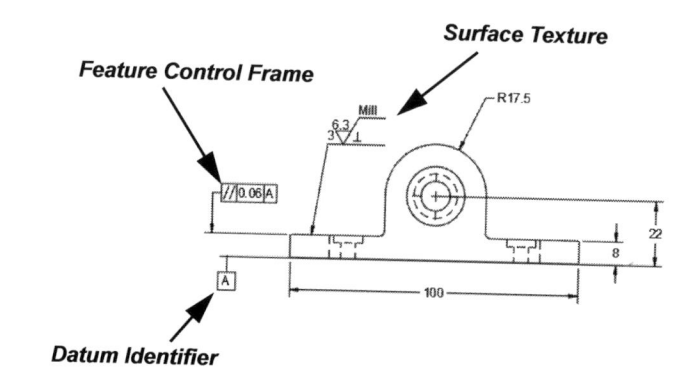

Figure 20–7

Video Lesson Available

Creating and Editing Symbols

Video Length: 3:58

20.3 Parts List and Balloons

A parts list is a list of the components in an assembly, as shown in Figure 20–8. You can add a parts list to a drawing and then use balloons to identify the components by item number.

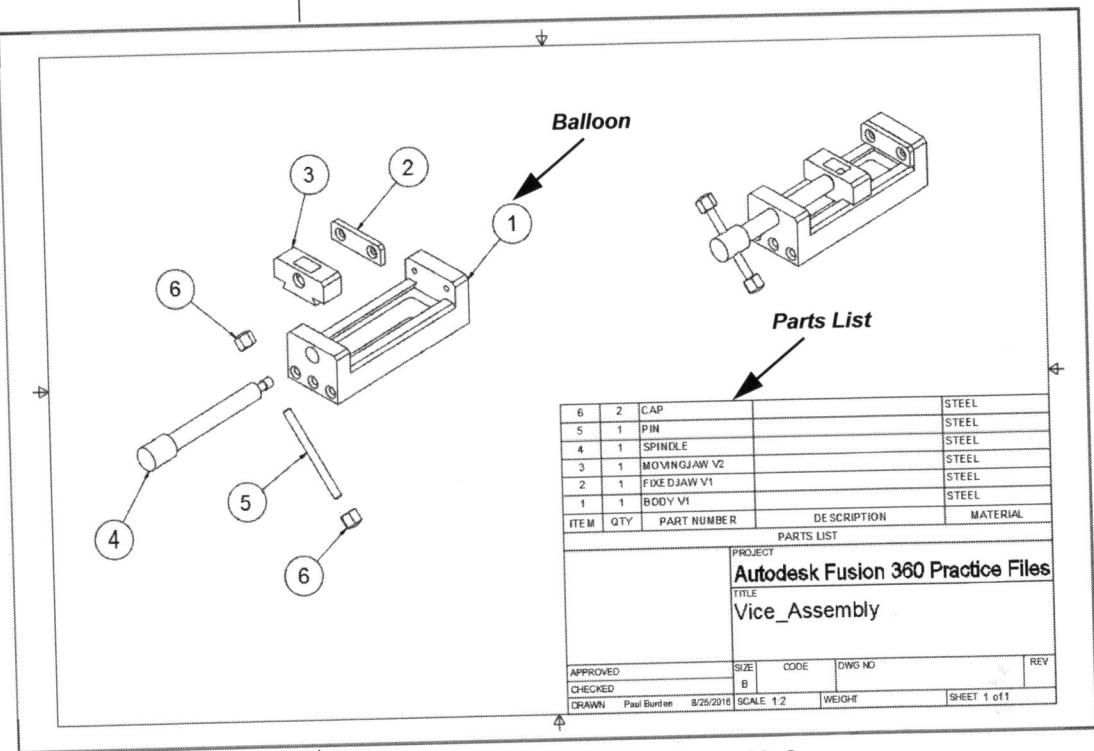

Figure 20–8

ITEM	QTY	PART NUMBER	DESCRIPTION	MATERIAL
6	2	CAP		STEEL
5	1	PIN		STEEL
4	1	SPINDLE		STEEL
3	1	MOVINGJAW V2		STEEL
2	1	FIXEDJAW V1		STEEL
1	1	BODY V1		STEEL

PARTS LIST

PROJECT: Autodesk Fusion 360 Practice Files
TITLE: Vice_Assembly

To add a parts list to a drawing, in the ribbon, click (Parts List). Once the parts list has been added, you can add balloons to identify the components in the drawing by clicking (Balloon).

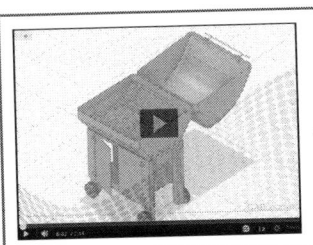

Video Lesson Available

Adding and Editing the Parts List

Video Length: 3:39

Video Lesson Available

Adding and Editing Balloons

Video Length: 3:13

20.4 Annotation and Dimension Settings

At the bottom of the graphics window, the ![icon] (Annotation Settings) menu contains options that control the appearance of annotations in your drawings.

The following options apply to all of the dimensions, text notes, and parts list text on your drawing:

- **Annotation Font:** A list of standard fonts to use.

- **Annotation Text Height:** Changes the font size.

The following options only apply to dimensions:

- **Linear Dimension Precision:** Controls the number of digits following the decimal point to which linear dimensions will be rounded (if applicable).

- **Angular Dimension Precision:** Controls the number of digits following the decimal point to which angular dimensions will be rounded (if applicable).

- **Display Annotation Unit:** Toggles the display of units (e.g., in, mm, etc.) in the dimension text.

- **Display Trailing Zeros:** Displays zeros following the decimal point up to the Linear and Angular Dimension Precision numbers. For example, a dimension that has a value of exactly 9.5 will display as 9.500 when the dimension precision is set to **0.123**.

These settings will affect all dimensions in the drawing. You can override these global settings for individual dimensions by double-clicking on the dimension and using the options in the TEXT palette, shown in Figure 20–9.

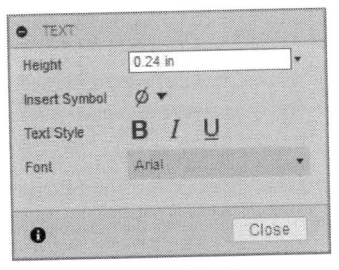

Figure 20–9

The DIMENSION palette provides additional options for Alternate Units, Tolerance, Representation, and Inspection settings, as shown in Figure 20–10.

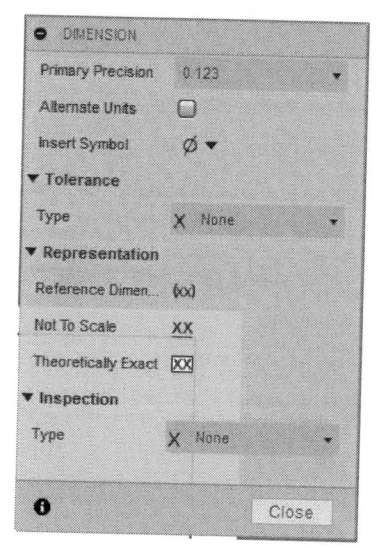

Figure 20–10

Video Lesson Available

Editing Dimension Properties

Video Length: 3:20

20.5 Drawing Output

Drawings in the Autodesk® Fusion 360™ software can be exported in two different formats: PDF ( ) and DWG ( ). To export drawings, in the ribbon, use the OUTPUT panel.

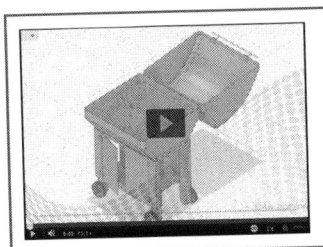

Video Lesson Available

Outputting Drawings to Other Formats

Video Length: 1:05

Practice 20a | Annotations and Dimensions

Practice Objectives

- Add centerlines and centermarks to views of a drawing.
- Add linear, radius, and diameter dimensions to a drawing.
- Add text and symbols to dimensions in a drawing.
- Add notes with and without leaders to a drawing.

In this practice, you will create a drawing and add annotations and dimensions. The completed drawing is shown in Figure 20–11.

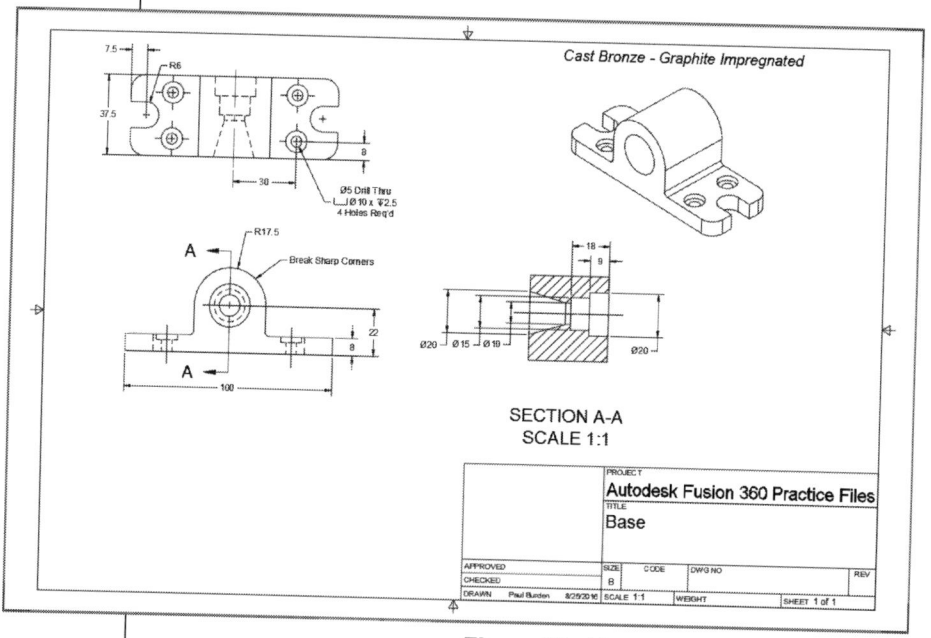

Figure 20–11

Task 1 - Create a new design from file.

1. Click ▼ > **New Design from File**.

2. In the Open dialog box, navigate to the *C:\Autodesk Fusion 360 Practice Files* folder, select **Base.f3d**, and then click **Open**. The design displays as shown in Figure 20–12.

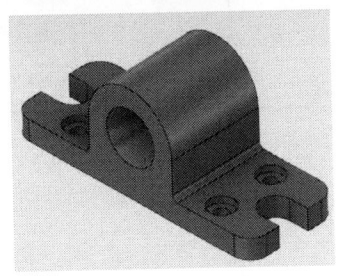

Figure 20–12

3. Save the design with the name **Base** to your *Autodesk Fusion 360 Practice Files* project.

Task 2 - Create a drawing with four views.

1. Click ▤▾ **> New Drawing > From Design**. The CREATE DRAWING palette opens.

2. Set the *Standard* to **ASME**. Accept the other default settings by clicking **OK** to create a drawing of B sheet size. The drawing sheet displays and you are prompted to place the base view.

3. Create the four views shown in Figure 20–13, using a scale of **1:1**.

4. Independently set the style of the isometric view to ▢ (Visible Edges).

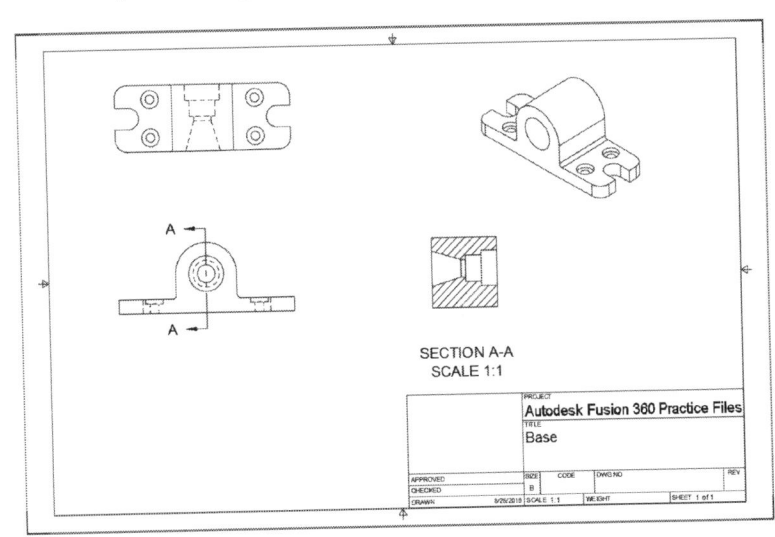

Figure 20–13

Task 3 - Create centerlines and center marks.

1. Zoom in on the top view.

2. In the ribbon, click (Center Mark) and then select the two semi-circular edges indicated in Figure 20–14. Center marks are created at the centers of these edges.

Select these two edges

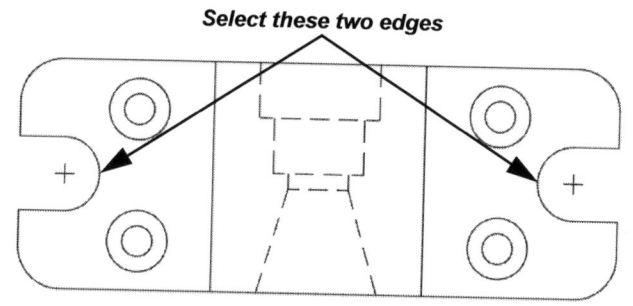

Figure 20–14

3. With the Center Mark command still running, select the outer circular edges of the four countersunk holes, as shown in Figure 20–15.

Select these four edges

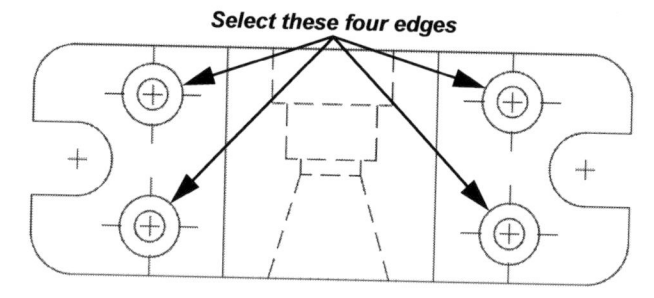

Figure 20–15

4. In the ribbon, click (Centerline). Select the two lines indicated in Figure 20–16. A centerline is created midway between these two lines.

5. Press <Esc> to deactivate the Centerline tool, and then select the centerline you just created. Gray grips should display.

6. Select the bottom endpoint grip and drag it below the bottom edge of the view so the centerline spans across the entire view, as shown in Figure 20–16.

Select these two lines

Figure 20–16

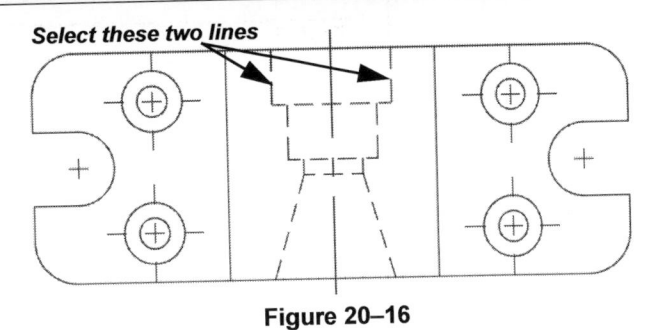

7. Click in an empty area of the drawing window to clear the selection of the centerline.

8. In the front view, create the centerlines and center mark shown in Figure 20–17.

Center mark

Centerlines

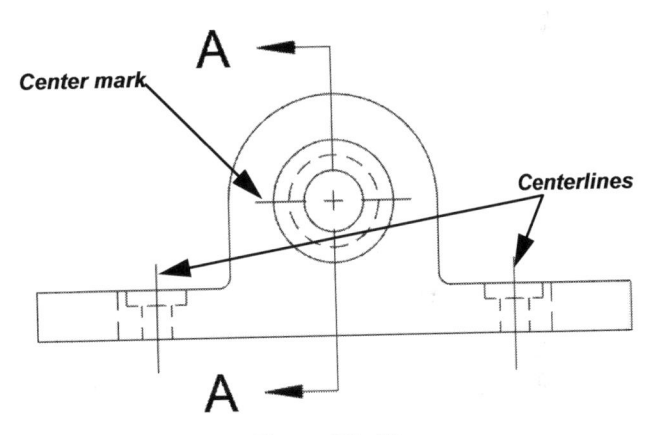

Figure 20–17

9. In the section view, create the centerline shown in Figure 20–18.

Centerline

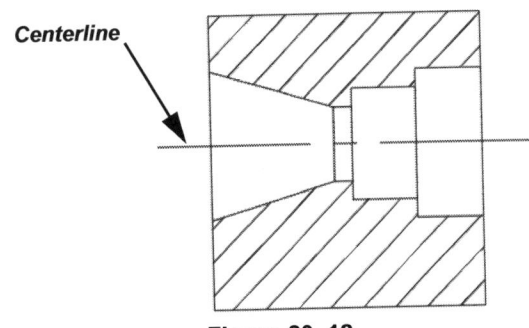

Figure 20–18

Task 4 - Add drawing dimensions.

You can place drawing dimensions similar to how you place model dimensions in a design file. However, dimensions in a drawing are dependent on the geometry, and you cannot change their value.

1. Zoom in on the top orthographic view.

2. In the ribbon, click  (Dimension). Note that you can expand this button to help you select specific dimension types (e.g., linear, angular, etc.).

3. Add the dimensions shown in Figure 20–19 by selecting the required edges, endpoints, centerlines, and center marks.

When placing dimensions, you might need to move the cursor to get the correct alignment.

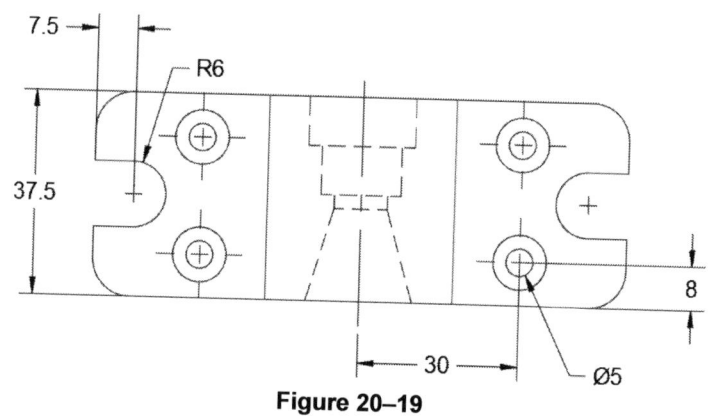

Figure 20–19

4. Zoom in on the front view and add the dimensions shown in Figure 20–20.

*If a dimension is disassociated () from the view, right-click on it, select **Reassociate**, and reselect the references.*

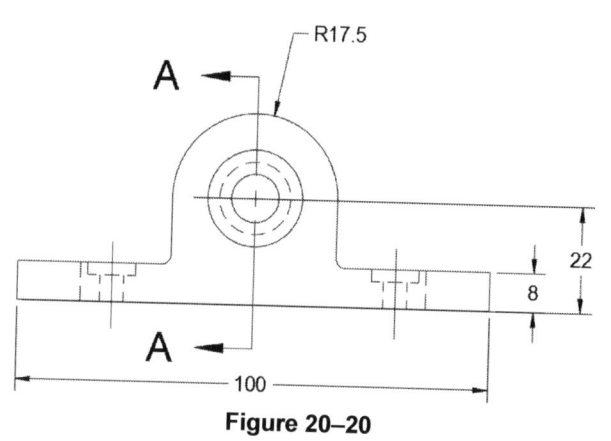

Figure 20–20

5. Zoom in on the section view and add the dimensions shown in Figure 20–21.

6. After placing the dimensions, deactivate the Dimension tool. Click on a dimension and use the grips that display to reposition the dimensions as shown in Figure 20–21.

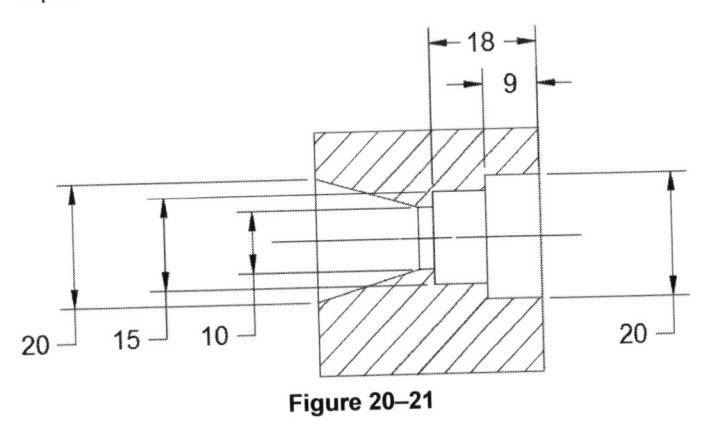

Figure 20–21

Task 5 - Add symbols to dimensions to indicate diameters.

Four of the dimensions added in the section views represent diameters. To indicate this, you will insert the ø symbol.

1. In the section view, double-click on the 10 dimension. The DIMENSION palette displays.

2. A text entry field displays on top of the dimension with a flashing text insert cursor. Move the text insert cursor to the start of the text entry field.

3. In the DIMENSION palette, click ø▼ and select the ø symbol to insert it into the text, as shown in Figure 20–22.

The cursor should be here

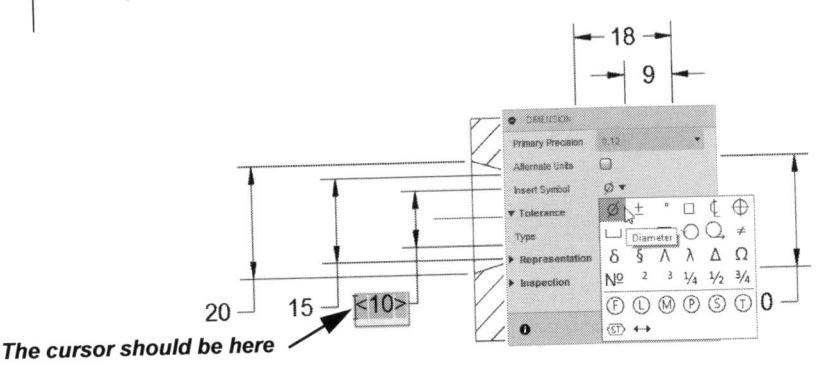

Figure 20–22

© 2016, ASCENT - Center for Technical Knowledge®

4. Close the palette. Add the ø symbol to the remaining three diameter dimensions in the section view. The dimensions should display as shown in Figure 20–23.

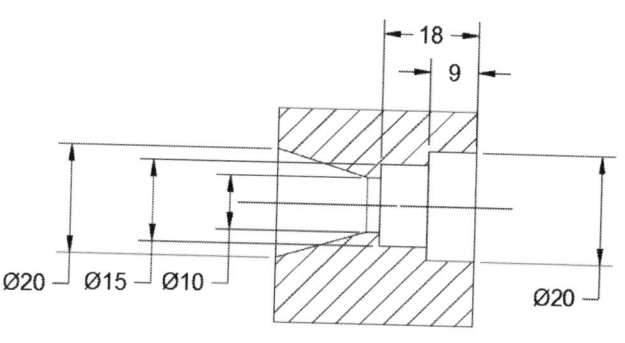

Figure 20–23

Task 6 - Add fabrication instructions to a dimension.

One of the four countersunk holes has a dimension attached in the top view. Next, you will add fabrication instructions to that dimension.

1. Zoom in on the top view and double-click on the ø5 dimension. The DIMENSION palette opens.

2. In the text entry filed that displays on top of the dimension, enter the text shown in Figure 20–24.

<Ø5> Drill Thru

Figure 20–24

3. Press <Alt>+<Enter> to add a second line in the text entry field.

4. Use text and symbols from the DIMENSION palette to add information about the countersink diameter, depth, and quantity of holes, as shown in Figure 20–25.

<Ø5> Drill Thru
⌴ Ø10 x ↓2.5
4 Holes Req'd

Figure 20–25

5. Close the palette. The view should display as shown in Figure 20–26.

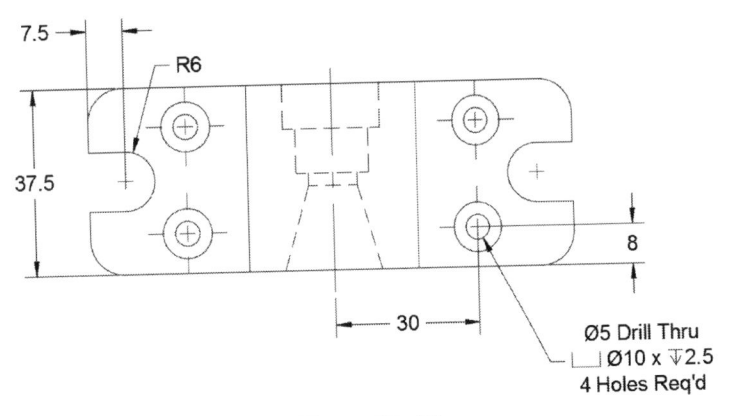

Figure 20–26

Task 7 - Add text notes.

1. Zoom in on the isometric view.

2. In the ribbon, click **A** (Text).

3. Click above the view to select a location and then drag to define the size of the text box. Click to locate the bottom right corner of the text box.

4. Enter the text shown in Figure 20–27.

Figure 20–27

5. Highlight the text you just entered and change the *Height* to **0.20 in**.

6. In the TEXT palette, click *I* to display the text in italics.

7. Close the palette. The text note should display as shown in Figure 20–28. If the text spans two lines, select the text and then drag the handles of the text box so that the text is on a single line.

Cast Bronze - Graphite Impregnated

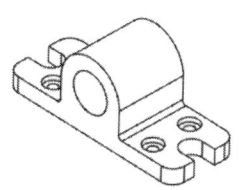

Figure 20–28

8. Zoom in on the front view.

9. In the ribbon, click (Leader).

10. Select a location on the circular edge to attach the leader, and then select a location to position the text. Enter the note **Break Sharp Corners**, as shown in Figure 20–29.

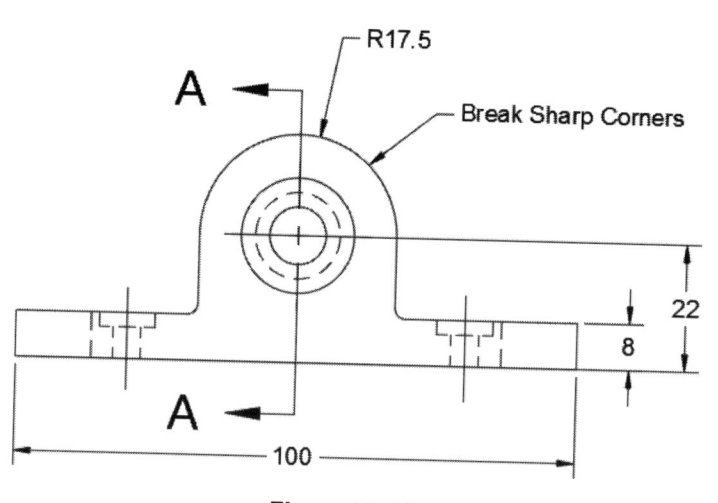

R17.5
Break Sharp Corners
A
A
22
8
100

Figure 20–29

11. Save the drawing. The completed drawing displays as shown in Figure 20–30.

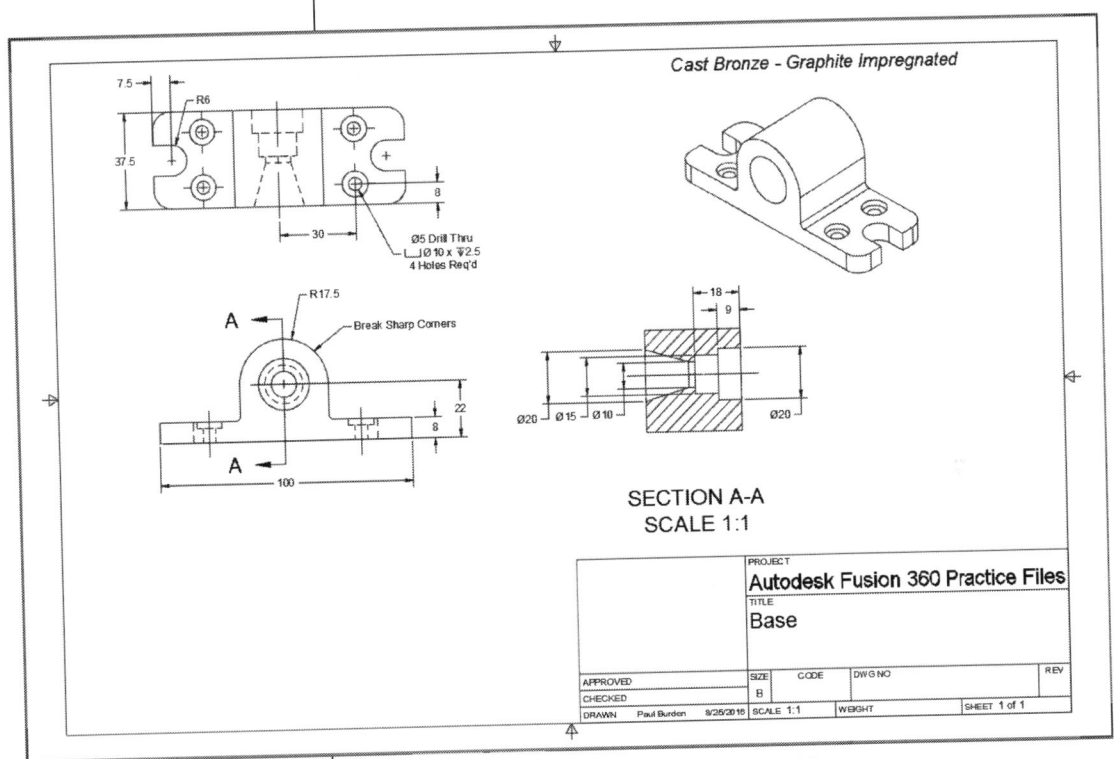

Figure 20–30

Task 8 - (Optional) Modify the annotation settings.

At the bottom of the graphics window, click (Annotation Settings) and experiment with the settings.

Practice 20b | Parts List and Balloons

Practice Objectives

- Place a parts list on a drawing.
- Place balloon annotations to identify components in a drawing.

In this practice, you add a parts list to an existing drawing, and then add balloon annotations to an exploded view to help identify the components.

Task 1 - Open the drawing file.

If you completed Practice 19c:

- Open the drawing that you created for the **socket_final** design. The drawing should display as shown in Figure 20–31. Skip to Task 2 - Create a parts list.

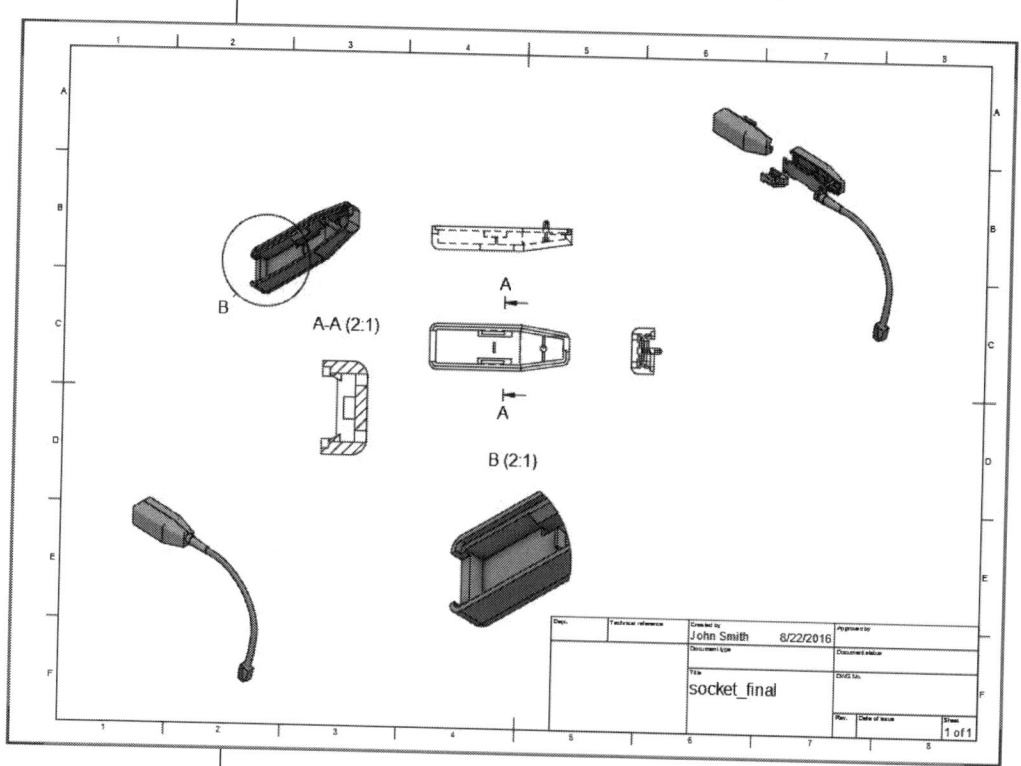

Figure 20–31

If you **DID NOT** complete Practice 19c, complete the following steps to access the required drawing:

1. Create a new folder in the project called **Detailed Drawing**, and then open the folder.

2. At the top of the DATA panel, click (Upload).

3. In the Select files to upload dialog box, click **Select Files**. Navigate to the practice files folder on your local drive and select **Socket_Final_Drawing.f3z**. Click **Open**.

4. Click **Upload** to begin the upload. The Upload progress window shows the progress of the upload. All of the components in the .F3Z file are shown in the list.

5. Once the files have been uploaded, click **Close** in the Upload progress window. Refresh the DATA panel, if required, to display the uploaded files.

6. Open **Socket_Final_Drawing**, and then continue with Task 2 - Create a parts list.

> A *.F3Z file was previously used in Chapter 16 when importing the design files for a multi-component design.

Task 2 - Create a parts list.

1. In the ribbon, click (Parts List).

2. Select the exploded view as the view that the parts list will be associated with.

3. The parts list table is attached to your cursor, enabling you to select a location to place it. Select the top right-hand corner of the drawing border, as shown in Figure 20–32.

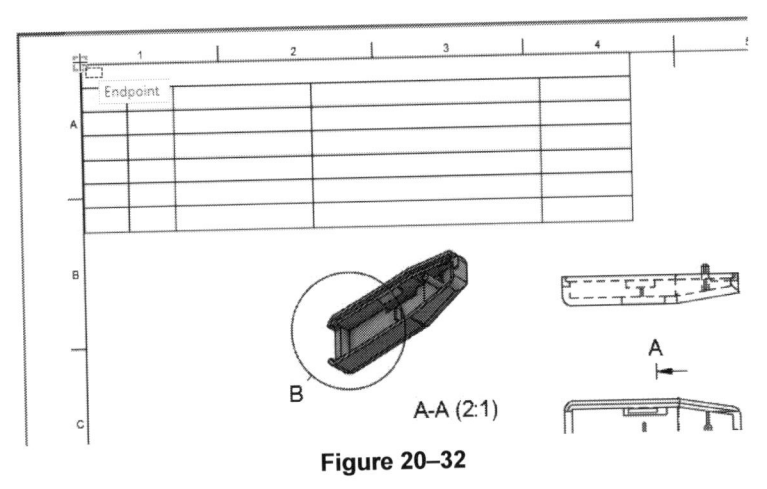

> Depending on where you place the table, the header row might display at the bottom of the table with the rows populating upward, or at the top with the rows populating downward.

Figure 20–32

4. Note that the parts list automatically displays in the table, as shown in Figure 20–33.

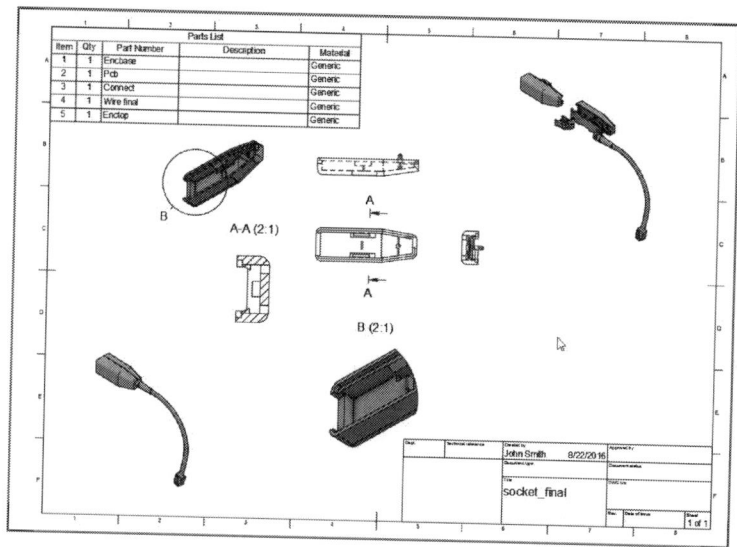

Figure 20–33

Task 3 - Add balloons.

1. In the ribbon, click (Balloon).

2. Select each of the five components in the exploded isometric view and place each balloon individually. After you select each component, click in the location where you want to place the leader. When you are finished, the view should display similar to that shown in Figure 20–34.

To move a leader, select the balloon, select the grip at the arrowhead and drag the balloon to a new location. If the balloon becomes disassociated,

right-click on ( ), select **Reassociate***, and then select a new point on any edge.*

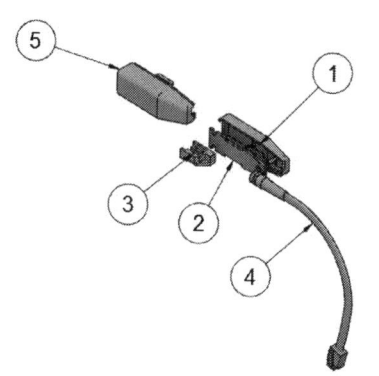

Figure 20–34

3. Save the drawing.

Chapter Review Questions

1. You can modify the value of dimensions on a drawing to update the design.

    a. True
    b. False

2. Which types of dimensions can you add to a drawing view? (Select all that apply.)

    a. Basic dimensions
    b. Baseline dimensions
    c. Chain dimensions
    d. Ordinate dimensions

3. When ⚠ displays on a detail item in a drawing, it means that...

    a. The detail item cannot be created.
    b. The detail item is out of date and must be updated.
    c. The detail has become disassociated from the view.
    d. All of the above.

4. For text on a drawing, which of the following are true? (Select all that apply.)

    a. A text note can be placed anywhere on a drawing.
    b. Text can be added to a dimension.
    c. Each text note has a leader to attach it to a view.
    d. Individual text notes can have different text fonts.

5. Which of the following entities can you select in a drawing view to place a Center Mark? (Select all that apply.)

    a. Holes
    b. Rounded edges
    c. Linear edges
    d. Vertices

6. Put the following steps in the order that best describes how a text note with a leader is added to a drawing view.

   1. Select outside the text box to complete the note.
   2. Type the text.
   3. Select to locate the leader's arrow start location.
   4. Select to locate the leader's arrow end location.

   a. 2, 3, 4, 1
   b. 2, 4, 3, 1
   c. 4, 3, 2, 1
   d. 3, 4, 2, 1

7. When modifying a body of text in a drawing, which of the following can be modified using the grips that display? (Select all that apply.)

   a. Number of columns
   b. Width of the text
   c. Text size
   d. Location of the text

8. Which of the following symbol types can be created using the Autodesk Fusion 360 software? (Select all that apply.)

   a. Surface Texture
   b. Feature Control Frame
   c. Welding
   d. Datum Identifier
   e. End Fill

9. When creating a parts list, how do you select the assembly design that is used as the source?

   a. You set the source design in the CREATE DRAWING palette.
   b. The first view created in the drawing is used as the source.
   c. You set the source design in the Preferences.
   d. You select a view in the drawing.

10. All first-level components are included in the parts list.

    a. True
    b. False

Answers: 1. b, 2.(a,b,c), 3. c, 4.(a,b,d), 5.(a,b), 6. d, 7.(a,b,d), 8.(a,b,d), 9. d, 10. a

Command Summary

Button	Command	Location
	Aligned Dimension	• **Ribbon:** DIMENSIONS panel • **Context Menu:** Right-click in the graphics window and select **Dimensions**. • **Context Menu:** Right-click in the graphics window and expand **Annotations**.
	Angular Dimension	• **Ribbon:** DIMENSIONS panel • **Context Menu:** Right-click in the graphics window and select **Dimensions**. • **Context Menu:** Right-click in the graphics window and expand **Annotations**.
	Annotation Settings	• Display Controls
	Balloon	• **Ribbon:** BOM panel • **Context Menu:** Right-click in the graphics window and select **Bom**.
	Baseline Dimension	• **Ribbon:** DIMENSIONS panel • **Context Menu:** Right-click in the graphics window and select **Dimensions**.
	Center Mark	• **Ribbon:** CENTERLINES panel • **Context Menu:** Right-click in the graphics window and select **Centerlines**.
	Centerline	• **Ribbon:** CENTERLINES panel • **Context Menu:** Right-click in the graphics window and select **Centerlines**.
	Chain Dimension	• **Ribbon:** DIMENSIONS panel • **Context Menu:** Right-click in the graphics window and select **Dimensions**.
	Datum Identifier	• **Ribbon:** SYMBOLS panel • **Context Menu:** Right-click in the graphics window and select **Symbols**.
	Diameter Dimension	• **Ribbon:** DIMENSIONS panel • **Context Menu:** Right-click in the graphics window and select **Dimensions**. • **Context Menu:** Right-click in the graphics window and expand **Annotations**.
	Dimension	• **Ribbon:** DIMENSIONS panel • **Context Menu:** Right-click in the graphics window and select **Dimensions**.
	Feature Control Frame	• **Ribbon:** SYMBOLS panel • **Context Menu:** Right-click in the graphics window and select **Symbols**.

	Leader	• **Ribbon:** TEXT panel
		• **Context Menu**: Right-click in the graphics window and select **Text**.
		• **Context Menu**: Right-click in the graphics window and expand **Annotations**.
	Linear Dimension	• **Ribbon:** DIMENSIONS panel
		• **Context Menu**: Right-click in the graphics window and select **Dimensions**.
		• **Context Menu**: Right-click in the graphics window and expand **Annotations**.
	Output DWG	• **Ribbon:** OUTPUT panel
		• **Context Menu**: Right-click in the graphics window and select **Output**.
	Output PDF	• **Ribbon:** OUTPUT panel
		• **Context Menu**: Right-click in the graphics window and select **Output**.
	Parts List	• **Ribbon:** BOM panel
		• **Context Menu**: Right-click in the graphics window and select **Bom**.
	Radius Dimension	• **Ribbon:** DIMENSIONS panel
		• **Context Menu**: Right-click in the graphics window and select **Dimensions**.
		• **Context Menu**: Right-click in the graphics window and expand **Annotations**.
	Surface Texture	• **Ribbon:** SYMBOLS panel
		• **Context Menu**: Right-click in the graphics window and select **Symbols**.
	Text	• **Ribbon:** TEXT panel
		• **Context Menu**: Right-click in the graphics window and select **Text**.
		• **Context Menu**: Right-click in the graphics window and expand **Annotations**.

Chapter 21

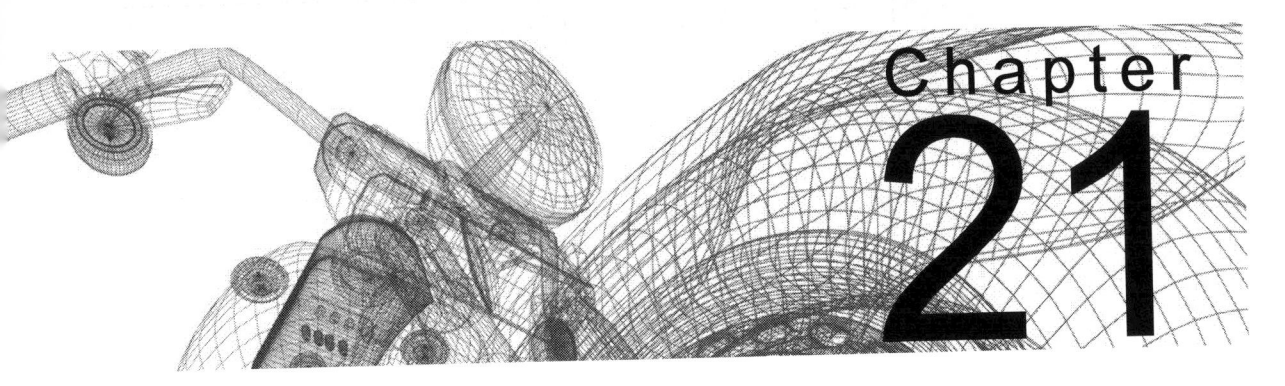

Static Analysis Using the Simulation Environment

The Simulation environment in the Autodesk® Fusion 360™ software provides access to Finite Element Analysis (FEA) tools. These tools can predict a CAD model's reaction once it is manufactured and working in a real-world environment. The inclusion of FEA in the design workflow enables designers to anticipate how the model will react and make informed decisions on whether this anticipated reaction meets design requirements. Using the Simulation environment for your designs enables you to seamlessly design, analyze, and re-design a model, all while working in the same software product. In this chapter, you will focus on how a Static analysis is created, set up, solved, and visualized, all while remaining in the Autodesk Fusion 360 software.

Learning Objectives in this Chapter

- Activate the Simulation environment and set up a static analysis.
- Accurately assign the material, constraints, loads, and contacts required to conduct a static analysis.
- Mesh a design using the default mesh settings.
- Solve a static analysis.
- Visualize the results of a static analysis.

21.1 Introduction to the Simulation Environment

The Simulation environment in the Autodesk Fusion 360 software enables you to use Finite Element Analysis (FEA) methods to predict how a design will react to the forces, vibrations, and heat that the model would experience in a real-world situation. This is done by assigning constraints, loads, and contacts, and breaking the design down into finite elements (mesh). The design can be a single body, multiple bodies, or multiple components, while the mesh can consist of thousands to hundreds of thousands tetrahedron elements. The results of the analysis enable you to predict whether a product's material will react as required (i.e, yield, deform, etc).

To launch the Simulation environment, expand the Change Workspace menu and select **Simulation**, as shown in Figure 21–1.

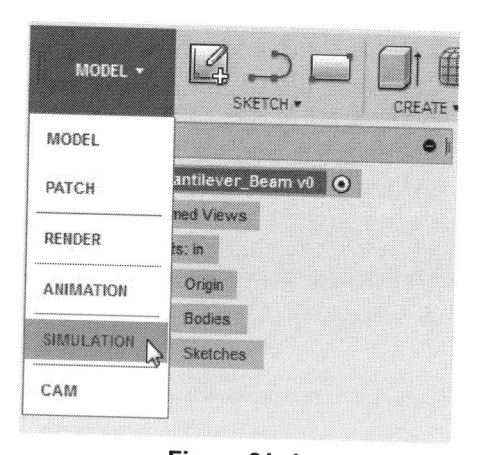

Figure 21–1

The ribbon for the Simulation environment displays as shown in Figure 21–2.

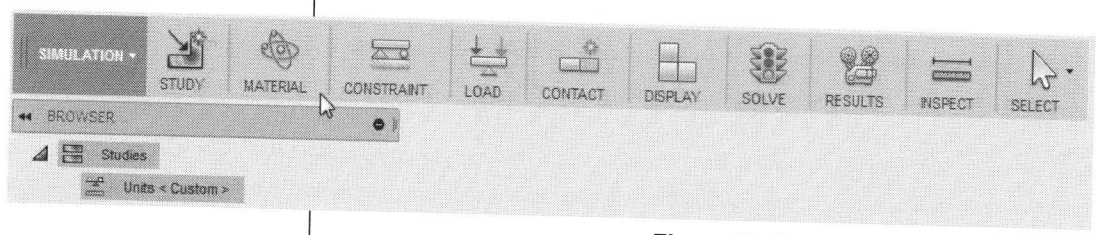

Figure 21–2

Creating a Design Study

When a model is brought into the Simulation environment for the first time, the BROWSER is empty because there are no studies available in the design. To conduct an analysis, a new design study must be created.

In the STUDY panel, click (New Simulation Study). The Studies dialog box displays as shown in Figure 21–3.

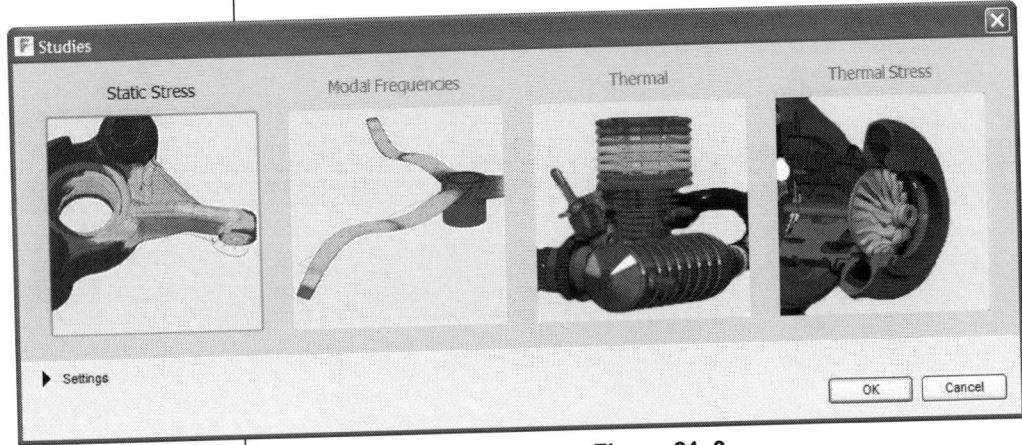

Figure 21–3

The Studies dialog box lists all of the analysis types that can be conducted in the Autodesk Fusion 360 software.

This chapter only discusses static stress simulations.

- **Static Stress:** Simulates the deformation and stress in a design caused by structural loads and constraints. A static stress analysis assumes a linear response to stress.

- **Modal Frequencies:** Simulates the natural mode shapes and frequencies of the design during free vibration.

- **Thermal:** Simulates steady-state temperature distribution and resultant heat flow through a design.

- **Thermal Stress:** Simulates temperature-induced stresses in a design.

> **Hint: Default Analysis Settings**
>
> In the Studies dialog box, you can expand the *Settings* area to review and change the default settings for each of the analysis types. The settings include the study name, the default automatic contact types, and the tolerance. You can also change these settings when you set up the analysis.

You can create multiple studies using alternate setup criteria to compare the results.

With the analysis type and settings confirmed, click **OK** to create the new study. The BROWSER displays as shown in Figure 21–4.

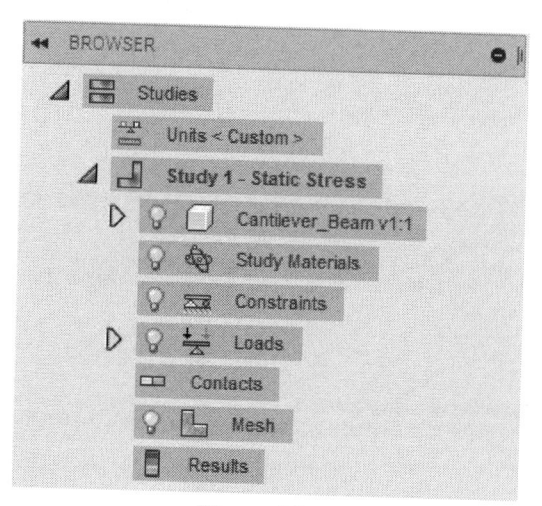

Figure 21–4

In the example shown in Figure 21–4, note the following:

- The analysis type is included in the study name by default. To rename a study, select it twice in the BROWSER and enter a new name.

- The first node in the study (**Cantilever_Beam v1:1**) describes the model that is being analyzed. In the case of a multi-component model, you can choose which components to include in this node.

- Six nodes are listed below the model name. These nodes define the setup (i.e., Study Materials, Constraints, Loads, Contacts), mesh settings, and the results of the analysis. As each node is populated with data, ▷ displays adjacent to the node, which indicates that data has been assigned. You can click on ▷ to expand the node to review and edit the settings.

Typical FEA Workflow

Assigning contacts in a multi-component design is not discussed in this student guide.

Analyzing designs using the Autodesk Fusion 360 Simulation environment follows a typical FEA workflow:

1. Create the design that is to be analyzed.
2. Activate the Simulation environment.
3. Create a new design study by selecting the analysis type. Verify the default settings for the analysis and change as required.
4. Set up the simulation inputs and the mesh that are to be assigned to the design during the analysis. These include:
   - Material to be analyzed
   - Constraints that simulate the boundary conditions (supports) in the design
   - Loads to simulate the magnitude of the load that will be applied to the design
   - Contacts to define the component contact in a multi-component design
   - Mesh layout of the design
5. Solve the analysis.
6. Visualize the results of the analysis.
7. Make changes to the design geometry or the analysis setup, as required, and rerun the analysis.

The panels in the ribbon generally progress left to right through the steps that are required to complete an analysis. You can also access the necessary tools during the analysis setup by right-clicking on the BROWSER nodes.

21.2 Setting up a Structural Static Analysis

The accurate assignment of material, constraints, and loads, directly affects the results of a structural static analysis. To predict a design's reaction once it is manufactured, the setup should mimic the design working in a real-world environment.

Assigning Study Materials

The material type that you use in a design study should be the same material that you will use to manufacture the design. By assigning it for use in an analysis, you ensure that the material's structural characteristics (properties) are considered during analysis. To assign the study material, use one of the following options:

- In the MATERIAL panel, click (Study Materials).

- Expand the MATERIAL panel and select **Study Materials**.

- In the BROWSER, right-click on the **Study Materials** node and select **Study Materials**.

The Apply Material dialog box opens, enabling you to verify and change the material as required.

- If the design being studied has multiple components, each component is listed in the dialog box.

- The *Original Material* column lists the material that was assigned in the Model environment. You can use this material in the simulation study by keeping the default **(As Original)** option selected in the *Study Material* column.

- To change the study material for a component, select a new material type from its Study Material drop-down list, as shown in Figure 21–5.

- The Safety Factor drop-down list enables you to specify whether the material's **Yield Strength** or **Ultimate Tensile Strength** values are used for safety factor calculations.

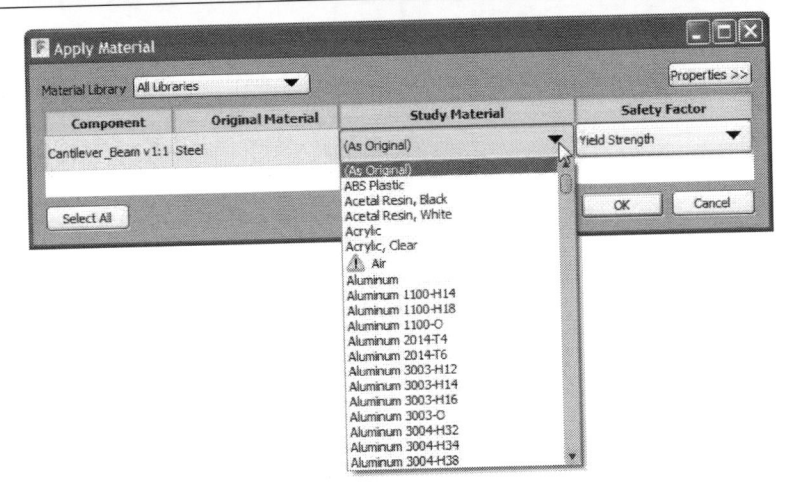

Figure 21–5

Once the material is confirmed or changed, click **OK**. The BROWSER updates, identifying the material that is used.

Hint: Default Analysis Settings

Additional options are available for reviewing and manipulating the material associated with a design study. You can access these options by right-clicking on the BROWSER node (as shown in Figure 21–6), or from the MATERIAL panel.

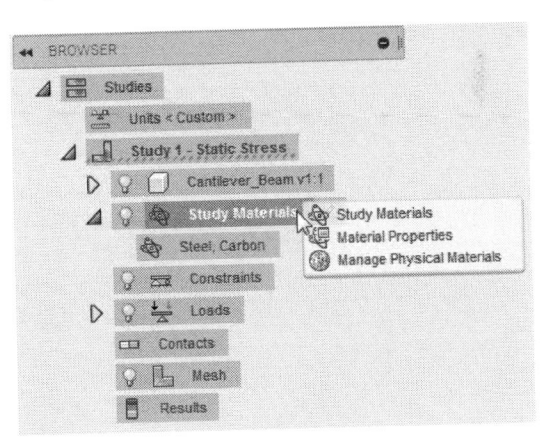

Figure 21–6

- **Material Properties:** Enables you to review the material property values of all of the materials in the Autodesk library.

- **Manage Physical Materials:** Enables you to create a custom material and assign its properties.

Assigning Constraints

Constraints are used in a simulation to represent the boundary conditions (i.e., supports) that exist in the design and should be tested. Constraints limit the displacement of the design by removing degrees of freedom. Adding constraints that incorrectly represent a boundary condition can negatively affect the accuracy of the results. You can apply constraints to the design's faces, edges, or vertices.

The constraint types for structural static stress analyzes are as follows:

- (🔒) **Fixed:** Prevents the selected face, edge, or vertex from translating or rotating in all directions (by default). When using this constraint, you can disable any of the axis buttons to permit additional movement. Once applied, the constraint icon displays as shown in Figure 21–7.

- (✎) **Pinned:** Prevents movement on selected cylindrical faces. Movement can be removed radially, axially, or tangentially by enabling the respective buttons. By default, radial and axial movement is disabled when a face is selected. Once applied, the constraint icon displays as shown in Figure 21–7.

- (🛒) **Frictionless:** Prevents the face(s) from moving or deforming in the normal direction. The face can rotate or translate in a tangential direction. Once applied, the constraint icon displays as shown in Figure 21–7.

- (🔒) **Prescribed Displacement:** Applies a fixed constraint on selected faces, edges, or vertices. Similar to a Fixed constraint, you can disable any of the axis buttons to permit movement. Additionally, you can enter prescribed displacement values for the x, y, and z directions. Once applied, the constraint icon displays as shown in Figure 21–7.

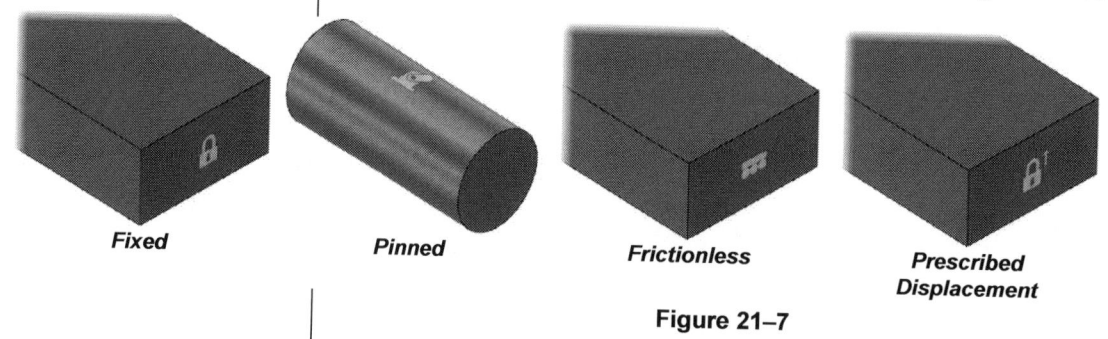

Fixed *Pinned* *Frictionless* *Prescribed Displacement*

Figure 21–7

To add a constraint, complete the following steps:

1. Initiate the creation of the constraint using one of the following two methods:
   - Expand the CONSTRAINT panel and select the constraint type.
   - In the BROWSER, right-click on the **Constraints** node and select **Structural Constraint**. In the STRUCTURAL LOADS palette, select the type of load.
2. Based on the constraint type, select the required faces, edges, or vertices to place the constraint. Once the reference is selected, the STRUCTURAL CONSTRAINT palette updates, indicating that the reference was selected. The constraint icon displays on the design.
   - For Fixed, Prescribed Displacement constraints, you can select faces, edges, or vertices.
   - For Pinned constraints, you can select cylindrical faces.
   - For Frictionless constraints, you can select faces.
3. (Optional) Customize the constraint as required. The available options vary depending on the type of constraint being added.
   - Fixed constraints: To enable movement in the x, y, or z axis, in the *Axis* area of the palette, clear the axis icons. .
   - Pinned constraints: To vary the constrained movement, toggle the Radial, Axial, and Tangential options. By default, radial and axial movement is constrained.
   - Prescribed Displacement constraints: To enable movement in the x, y, or z axis, in the *Axis* area of the palette, clear the axis icons and enter vector displacement values, as required.
4. Click **OK** to assign the constraint.

Assigning Loads

Loads are used in a simulation to represent the loading conditions that exist in the design and should be tested.

The load types for structural static stress analyzes are as follows:

- ( ) **Force:** Applies a force of the specified magnitude to selected faces, edges, or vertices. A force is applied normal to a selected face and parallel with a selected edge. Forces display on the model as a blue arrow, as shown in Figure 21–8. A surface force applies an equivalent pressure to the entire selected face by default, but you can set a target area for the force (defined by a radius value), if required.

- (↓↓) **Pressure:** Applies a pressure of the specified magnitude to selected faces. The pressure value is uniform and is applied normal to the face. Pressure loads display on the model as shown in Figure 21–8.

- (↻) **Moment:** Applies a load of the specified magnitude around a selected axis and perpendicular to the selected face. Moment loads are displayed on a face as shown in Figure 21–8.

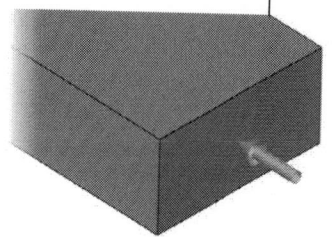

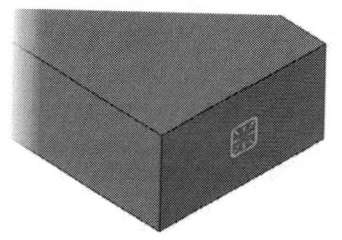

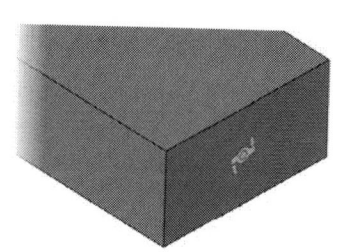

Force Load   *Pressure Load*   *Moment Load*

Figure 21–8

- (▭) **Remote Force:** Applies a nodal load to a point in space (i.e., not on the design) that is relative to a face. This enables you to properly describe a load to include a moment contribution.

- (◐) **Gravity:** Applies gravity in the negative Y-axis direction. Unlike the other structural load types, Gravity is preassigned in a model and is initially turned off.

To add a structural load, complete the following steps:

1. Initiate the creation of the load using one of the following two methods:
   - Expand the LOAD panel and select the load type.
   - In the BROWSER, right-click on the **Loads** node and select **Structural Load**. In the STRUCTURAL LOADS palette, select the type of load.
2. Based on the selected load type, select the required faces, edges, or vertices to place the load. Once the reference is selected, the STRUCTURAL LOAD palette updates to display additional settings, enabling you to define the load.
   - For force loads, you can select faces, edges, or vertices.
   - For pressure, moment, and remote force loads, you can only select faces. To define the remote force load, enter offset values in the x, y, and z-axis.

3. In the *Magnitude* field, specify the magnitude of the load.
   - By default, force loads apply to the entire area of the selected face. To reduce the force affect to a specific area, in the *Limit Target* field, assign a limit target. Then, either rag the radius handle (as shown in Figure 21–9) or enter a value in the *Radius* field.

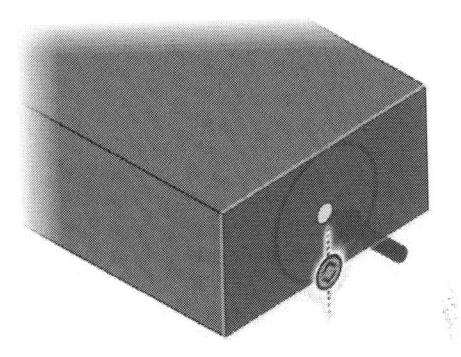

Figure 21–9

4. Specify the direction of the load. You can assign a direction for all but a pressure load.
   - Click to flip the direction of the load by 180°.
   - By default, the load is applied normal to the selected face. To select an alternate orientation for the load, expand the Direction Type drop-down list as shown in Figure 21–10. The Direction Type options enable you to define the direction of the load relative to the reference.

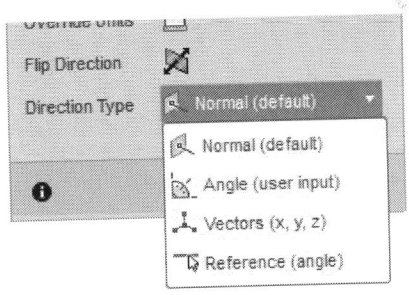

Figure 21–10

5. (Optional) Override the units of the load using the *Override Units* field. This enables you to assign a load value using non-default units.
6. Click **OK** to assign the load.

> **Gravity Loads**
>
> A gravity load is automatically created in an analysis, but is disabled by default. You can enable gravity, using either of the following methods:
>
> - Right-click on the **Loads** node, select **Toggle Gravity On**, and then select its checkbox.
>
> - In the ribbon, in the LOAD panel, toggle on Gravity.
>
> To edit gravity, you must enable it first. Then, in the BROWSER, right-click on the **Gravity** load and select **Edit Gravity**, or use the LOAD panel in the ribbon.

Assigning Contacts

Contacts can be used in the simulation setup to describe the real-world interactions in a design file. This can include interactions between faces in a single component, or between components in a multi-component design. For example, a contact can be used to define welded faces in a single design, or to define the connection made between components due to a fastener.

The contact types for structural static stress analyzes are as follows:

- (■) **Bonded**: Bonds touching faces.

- (■) **Separation (No Sliding):** Enables the contact faces to act as if they are separated in tension and compression, but does not permit sliding in-plane.

- (■) **Sliding (No Separation)**: Acts similar to a bonded contact in tension and compression, but permits sliding in-plane.

- (■) **Separation + Sliding:** Enables the contact faces to act as if they are separated in tension and compression, and permits in-plane sliding.

A contact can be assigned automatically or manually. Using the automatic creation, contact pairings are recognized by the Autodesk Fusion 360 software and are automatically assigned. With the manual method, you are able to select the target bodies and contacting faces.

To use the **Automatic Contacts** option, select it in the CONTACT panel or from the BROWSER node. Contacts are only automatically assigned if they are recognized. If contacts are automatically assigned, review them to ensure that the correct contact type was used. If a contact is not recognized, add the contact manually.

To add a manual contact, complete the following steps:
1. Initiate the creation of the contact using one of the following two methods:
    - Expand the CONTACT panel and select the contact type.
    - In the BROWSER, right-click on the **Loads** node and select **Manual Contact**. In the CONTACT palette, select the type of contact.
2. Select the components or bodies that are in contact.
3. Click in the *Targets* field to activate it, and then select the faces or edges that are in contact.
4. Click **OK** to assign the contact.

Reviewing the Setup in the BROWSER

Nodes exist for each of the setup steps. Once the material, constraints, and loads are assigned, they are added to the BROWSER and ▷ displays adjacent to the node to indicate that the node has been populated.

In the example shown in Figure 21–11, the material is set as **Steel, Carbon**, and a fixed constraint and a force load have been assigned. Additionally, the Gravity load remains inactive for this study. There are no contacts assigned in this study.

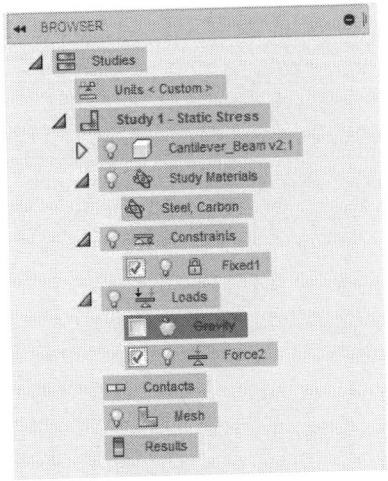

Figure 21–11

Consider the following when working with nodes and setup data in the BROWSER.

- To delete a load, constraint, contact, or material, in the BROWSER, right-click on its name and select **Delete**. In the case of loads and constraints, you can also select the load symbol and press <Delete>.

- To disable a load, constraint, or contact without deleting it from the model, in the BROWSER, clear the checkbox adjacent to its name. This temporarily removes it from the study. Alternatively, you can right-click on its name and select **Suppress**.

- To clear the load, constraint, or contact symbol from the display, in the BROWSER, select the light-bulb icon to toggle it off.

- To edit a setup item, in the BROWSER, right-click on its name and select **Edit <*item*>** to access the original palette used to create it.

- To edit the material, in the BROWSER, right-click on the material name and select **Study Materials**.

- Consider renaming setup items to accurately describe them.

21.3 Setting up the Mesh

When a study is set up, the default mesh settings are assigned to the study for use on the model. You can make changes to these global settings and assign local settings to customize the mesh size and distribution. The goal in meshing a design should be to balance precision and computation time to achieve a quality mesh that converges quickly with accurate results.

To mesh a design with the current settings, expand the SOLVE panel and select **Generate Mesh**, as shown in Figure 21–12. Alternatively, in the BROWSER, right-click on the **Mesh** node and select **Generate Mesh**.

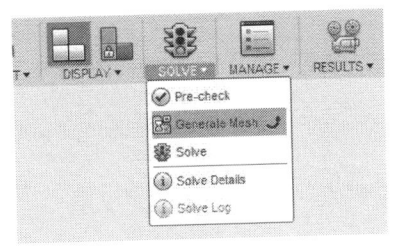

Figure 21–12

> This chapter only covers meshing the model using the default study settings.

Once the mesh is generated, it is automatically displayed on the model, similar to the mesh shown on the cantilever beam in Figure 21–13.

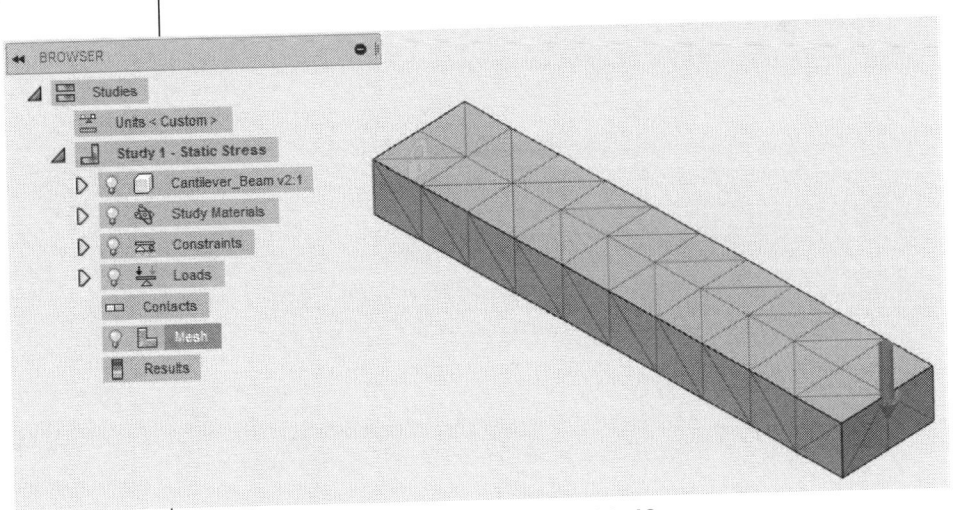

Figure 21–13

To control the display of the mesh, use one of the following options:

- Expand the DISPLAY panel and select **Toggle Mesh Visibility**.

- In the BROWSER, right-click on the **Mesh** node and select **Toggle Mesh Visibility**.

- In the BROWSER, select 💡 adjacent to the **Mesh** node to toggle the mesh on and off.

> **Mesh Settings**
>
> To review the mesh settings that were assigned to the design when the study was created, in the BROWSER, right-click on the **Mesh** node and select **Mesh Settings**. The values can be modified as needed. If changes are made after a mesh has been generated, you must regenerate the mesh to apply the new settings.

21.4 Solving a Design Study

Once the setup is complete (including the material, constraint, load, and any contact assignments), the design study can be solved.

To solve an analysis, meshing must be done on the model. If the meshing was not done as a separate step, it is done while solving.

To solve a design, expand the SOLVE panel and select **Solve**, as shown in Figure 21–14. Alternatively, in the BROWSER, right-click on the **Results** node and select **Solve**.

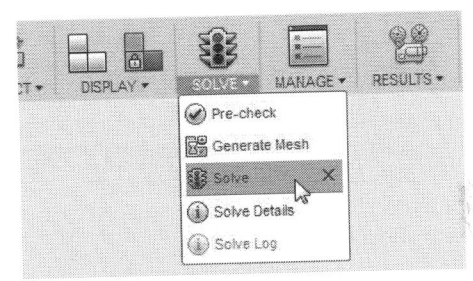

Figure 21–14

Once solved, the results are immediately displayed in the graphics window, similar to that shown in Figure 21–15. The model colors and result legend indicate that the results are being displayed. Result visualization will be discussed further in the next topic.

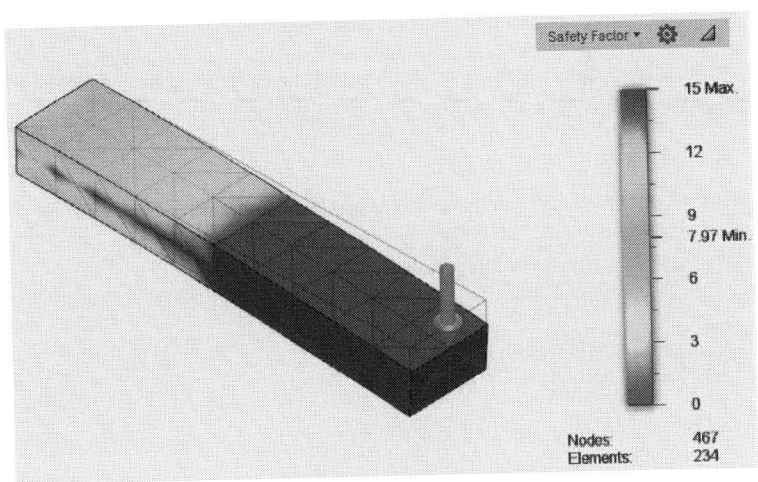

Figure 21–15

To review details on the solution, right-click on the **Results** node and select **Solve Log**.

If changes are made to the setup after the design study is solved or if the model geometry has changed, ⚠ displays in the **Results** node of the BROWSER and the node displays yellow. This indicates that the results are out of date and that the solution must be rerun to incorporate any changes. Once rerun, the solution results update and display in the graphics window.

> **Solve Button Colors**
>
> The button on the SOLVE panel displays information about the state of the design study and whether it is ready for solving.
>
> - Prior to the assignment of the material, loads, and constraints, the button displays as 🚦 (red light), indicating that you cannot proceed with the analysis.
>
> - The button displays as 🚦 (green light) when the setup is complete and the design can be solved.
>
> - The button displays as 🚦 (yellow light) to indicate a potential error. The study can be solved, but errors might be reported.

21.5 Visualizing the Results

Once a design study is solved, the results are loaded in the Results view and are immediately displayed. The Results view contains the following:

- A shaded model indicating the distribution of values for the active result type.

- A color bar (Legend) indicating the range of values for the active result type.

- Mesh information, including the number of nodes and elements.

- Unit information for the active result type (when applicable).

- Legend options for customizing the results.

For a Static analysis, the Safety Factor result type is displayed.

These tools help you to visualize the magnitude of the safety factor, stresses, displacement, and strain in the design. To inspect the results, review the Legend values and where they exist on the model. To change between results, in the Legend, expand the drop-down list shown in Figure 21–16 and select a new result type.

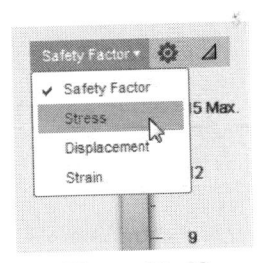

Figure 21–16

As the result type changes, the Legend header updates to display the result type. Depending on the result type being displayed, the Legend header provides different options for visualizing the results.

For example, in Figure 21–17 a Von Mises Stress result is being displayed using the MPa units. Alternate units can be selected in the units drop-down list, while an alternate stress result can be selected in the Von Mises list.

In the Legend header, ⚙ enables you to change the settings for the legend, such as color transition, legend size, etc. The ◢ enables you to toggle the display of the legend on and off. If toggled off, the threshold, min, and max are displayed by default.

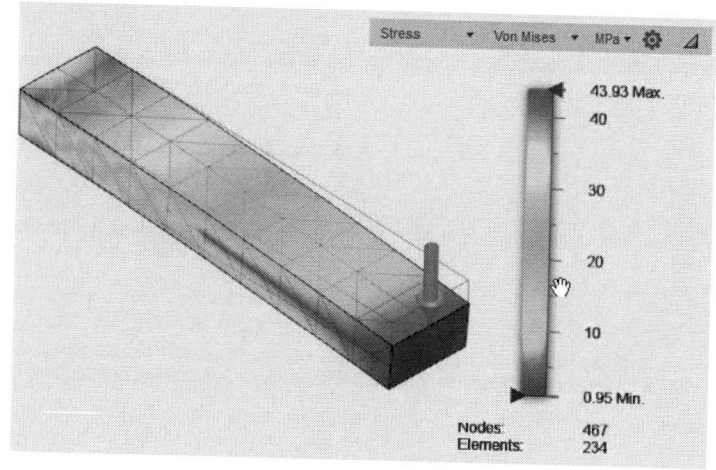

Figure 21–17

Consider the following tips when reviewing results:

- To toggle the display of the min and max result values directly in the model, expand the RESULTS panel and select 🔲 (Show Min/Max).

- To manually probe for results on the model, expand the RESULTS panel and select 🖲 (Surface Probes) or 🖲 (Create Point Probe). When surface probing, the result value displays as a tooltip when you hover the mouse over the model. When point probing, the point location displays in addition to the result value.

- To view an animation of a result, expand the RESULTS panel and select **Animate**. Use the ANIMATE panel to play, stop, record, and customize the speed and steps in the animation.

- Geometry deformation is often very small in comparison to the overall design. Consider using the RESULTS panel> **Deformation Scale** option to adjust the scaling for better viewing.

- To return to the original model display, expand the DISPLAY panel and select **Model View** (or press <Ctrl>+<M>). To return to the Results view, select **Results View** (or press <Ctrl>+<R>).

Practice 21a Cantilever Beam Analysis

Practice Objectives

- Activate the Simulate environment in the Autodesk Fusion 360 software.
- Create a Linear Static Stress design study.
- Assign constraints and loads to simulate the working conditions.
- Generate a Mesh using the default Autodesk Fusion 360 settings.
- Solve the design study.
- Review and interpret the results.

In this practice, you will simulate a simple cantilevered beam with a fixed end and a load applied to the other end. A linear response to the stress will be assumed and the applied load does not change in magnitude, orientation, or distribution. Additionally, the effects of gravity are negligible.

Task 1 - Open a design file and switch to the Simulation environment.

1. Click ▾ > **New Design from File**.

2. In the Open dialog box, navigate to the *C:\Autodesk Fusion 360 Practice Files* folder, select **Centilever_Beam.f3d**, and click **Open**. The design displays as shown in Figure 21–18.

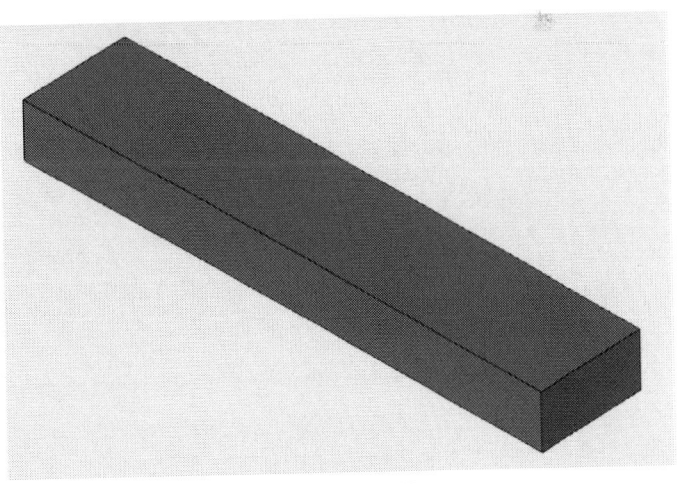

Figure 21–18

3. Save the design as **Cantilever_Beam** in the active Fusion Project.

4. Expand the Change Workspace menu and select **SIMULATION** (as shown in Figure 21–19) to launch the Simulation environment and its ribbon.

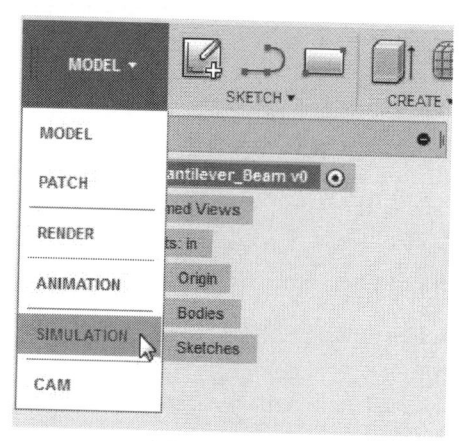

Figure 21–19

Task 2 - Create a new study and review the BROWSER.

1. By default, no studies exist unless they are explicitly created. Click ![icon] (New Simulation Study). The Studies dialog box displays as shown in Figure 21–20.

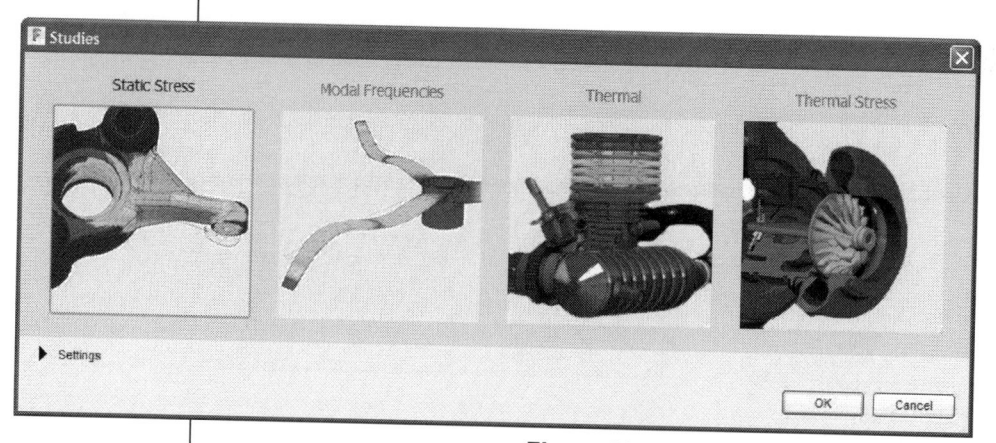

Figure 21–20

2. The Studies dialog box lists the types of studies that can be performed. Select **Static Stress**.
    - A static stress analysis assumes a linear response to the stress and enables you to analyze the deformation and stress into the model from structural loads and constraints.
    - The *Settings* area of the dialog box sets the defaults for the analysis. This analysis will be conducted using these defaults.
3. To create the new study, click **OK**.
4. The BROWSER displays as shown in Figure 21–21. In the **Study 1 - Static Stress** node, note the following.
    - The analysis type is included in the study name. To rename a study, select it twice in the BROWSER and enter a a new name.
    - The first node in the study describes the model that is being analyzed. In the case of a multi-component model, you can control which of the components are included in this node.
    - Six nodes are listed below the model name. These nodes define the setup, mesh settings, and the results of the analysis.

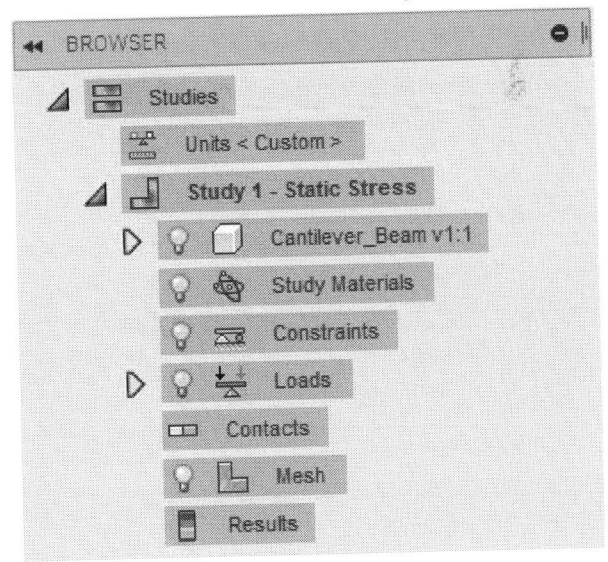

Figure 21–21

Task 3 - Define the material to be used in the analysis.

1. In the Ribbon, expand the MATERIAL panel and select **Study Materials**. Alternatively, you can access the same dialog box using the BROWSER by right-clicking on the **Study Materials** node and selecting **Study Materials**.

2. In the Apply Material dialog box, note that the *Original Material* is set as **Steel** and the *Study Material* is set to (As Original), as shown in Figure 21–22.

*To review the properties for a material, in the MATERIAL panel, select the **Material Properties** option, or in the BROWSER, right-click on the material and select **Material Properties**.*

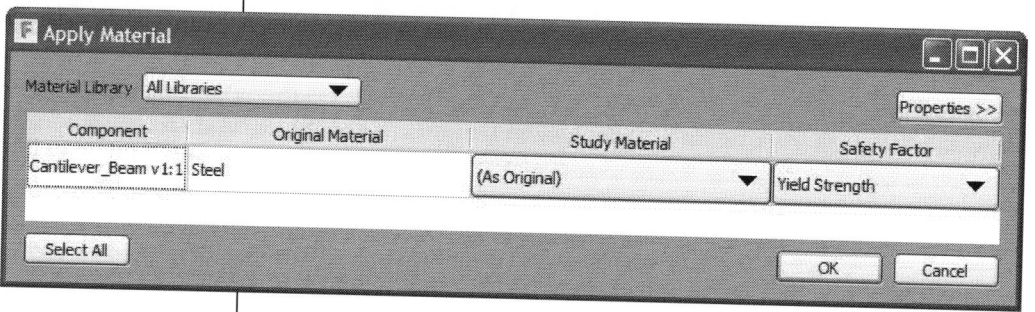

Figure 21–22

3. In the Study Material drop-down list, select **Steel, Carbon**. The Apply Material dialog box updates as shown in Figure 21–23.

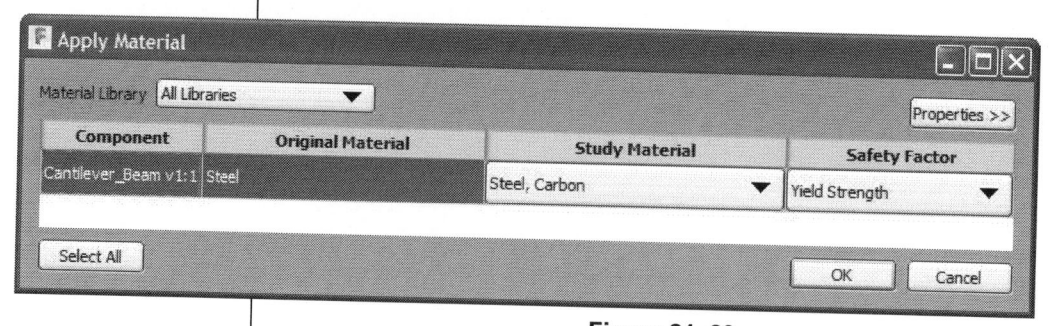

Figure 21–23

4. Ensure that the *Safety Factor* default of **Yield Strength** is selected, and then click **OK**.

5. In the BROWSER, adjacent to the **Study Materials** node, click ▷. Note that **Steel, Carbon** is now listed as the material being used.

Task 4 - Constrain the beam.

In this task, you will assign a constraint to fix the beam on one end, preventing movement in any direction.

1. In the Ribbon, expand the CONSTRAINT panel and select **Fixed**. The fixed constraint removes all degrees of freedom (no translation or rotation in any direction).

2. The STRUCTURAL CONSTRAINT palette displays as shown in Figure 21–24. Note how the Type drop-down list is set to **Fixed**. By default, the constraint is set to be constrained along all Axis (Ux, Uy, and Uz). Any of the axis can be cleared, if required. For this constraint, leave all of the axis selected.

*Alternatively, in the BROWSER, you can right-click on the **Constraints** node and select **Structural Constraint** to access the palette and assign the type.*

3. Hover the mouse over the end face of the Beam and click and hold the left mouse button to access the Select Other tool, as shown in Figure 21–24.

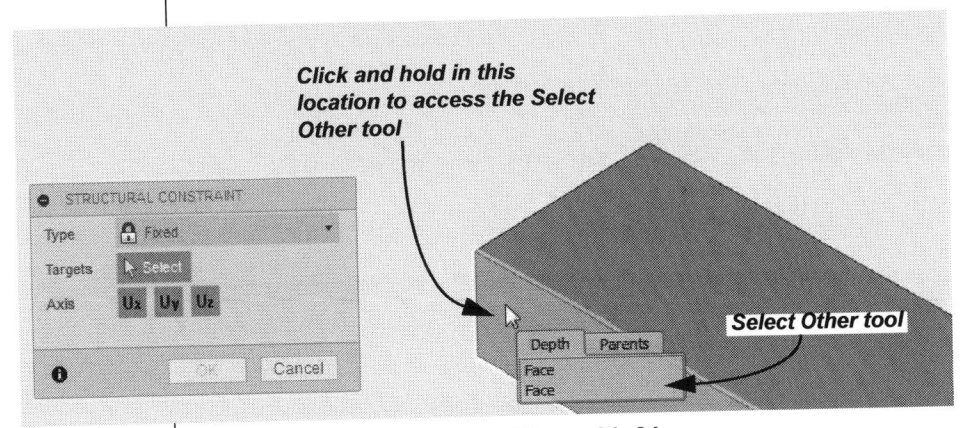

Figure 21–24

4. Scroll down in the Select Other tool to find the face at the end of the beam. Select the applicable **Face** option. The Fixed icon displays on the end face, as shown in Figure 21–25.

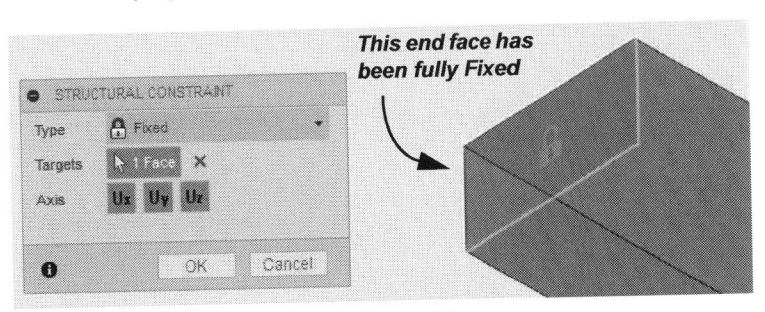

Figure 21–25

To deactivate a constraint in the model, in the BROWSER, clear the checkbox adjacent to the constraint name.

5. In the STRUCTURAL CONSTRAINT palette, click **OK** to complete the constraint.

6. In the BROWSER, adjacent to the **Constraints** node, click ▷. Note that **Fixed1** is now listed as an active constraint.

Task 5 - Load the beam.

In this task, you will assign a force load to other end of the fixed beam to simulate it being loaded in the Y-direction.

*Alternatively, in the BROWSER, you can right-click on the **Loads** node and select **Structural Load** to access the palette and assign the type.*

1. In the Ribbon, expand the LOAD panel and select **Force**.

2. The STRUCTURAL LOAD palette displays. Note how the Type drop-down list is set to **Force**.

3. Select the (unfixed) end face of the Beam to assign the load, as shown in Figure 21–26. The STRUCTURAL LOAD palette updates as shown.

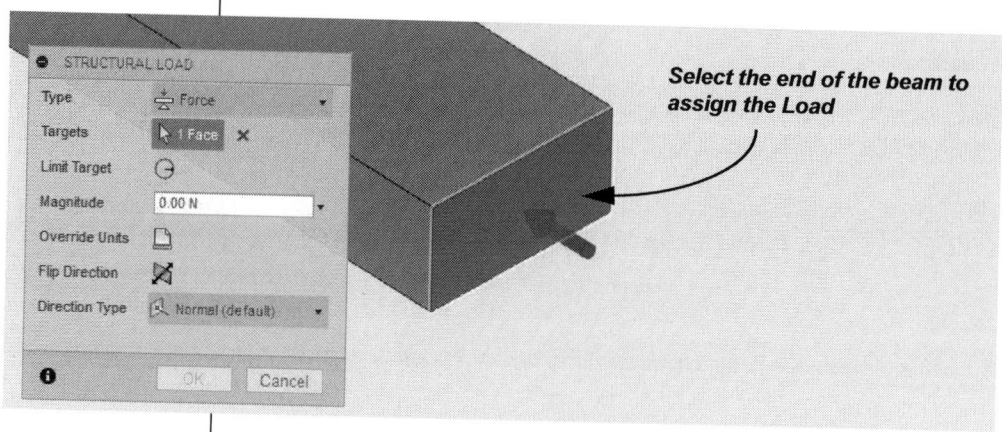

Figure 21–26

4. Note how the load is currently being assigned normal to the selected face. In the Direction Type list, select **Angle (user input)**.

5. Select the rotation manipulator (shown in Figure 21–27) and drag it to **-90 deg**. This assigns the load in the same plane as the face.

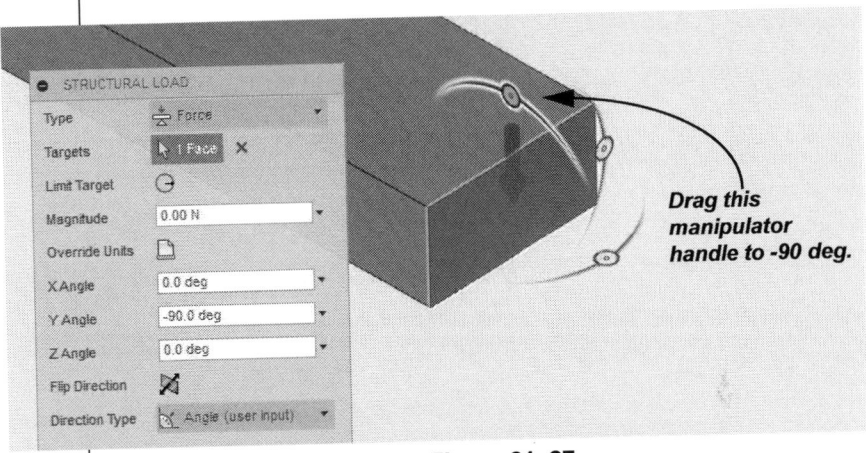

Figure 21–27

*As an alternative to entering the load in N, click ▢ to activate unit override and select **lbf** as the alternate unit.*

6. In the STRUCTURAL LOAD palette, enter **4450 N** (approximately 1000lbf). Ensure that the arrow remains pointing downwards. If the orientation of the arrow has changed, enter a negative force magnitude or flip the direction (▨).

7. In the STRUCTURAL LOAD palette, click **OK**.

To deactivate a load, in the BROWSER, clear the checkbox adjacent to the load name.

8. In the BROWSER, adjacent to the **Loads** node, click ▷. **Force1** is now listed as an active load. Additionally, a **Gravity** load is available but inactive, as shown in Figure 21–28. The Gravity load is added to all studies automatically and can be enabled as required.

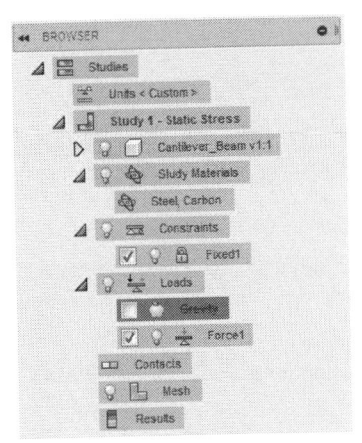

Figure 21–28

Task 6 - Mesh the beam.

In this task, you will mesh the cantilever beam to prepare it for solving. Note that the default mesh settings could have been changed when the study was created, or by right-clicking on the **Mesh** node and selecting **Mesh Settings**. In this practice you will leave the default values set.

1. In the ribbon, expand the SOLVE panel and select **Generate Mesh**. Depending on the complexity of the model and the mesh settings, the mesh generation time can vary.

2. Once generated, the mesh displays on the model, as shown in Figure 21-29.

*Alternatively, in the BROWSER, right-click on the **Mesh** node and select **Generate Mesh**.*

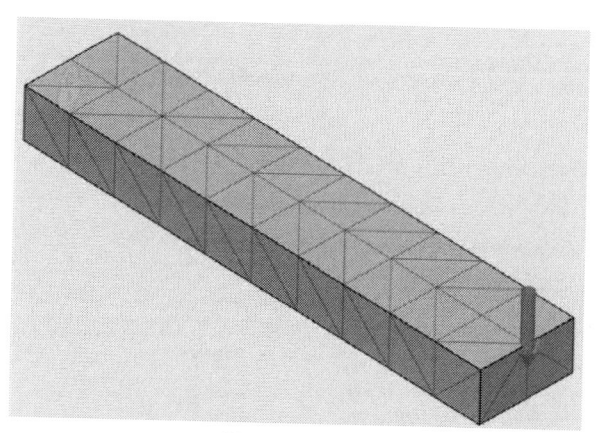

Figure 21-29

Task 7 - Solve the beam.

In this task, you will run the static stress analysis for the Cantilever Beam using the constraints and loads that have been assigned.

*Alternatively, in the BROWSER, right-click on the **Results** node and select **Solve**.*

1. In the Ribbon, expand the SOLVE panel and select **Solve**. The model and an analysis legend displays as shown in Figure 21-30.
   - In the legend, note that the minimum safety factor is **1.79** and the max value is **15**. Factor of safety results help to identify areas of potential yield. A factor of safety of 1 means that the material is essentially at yield. For this design, with the current constraints and loads, the model is not expected to yield.

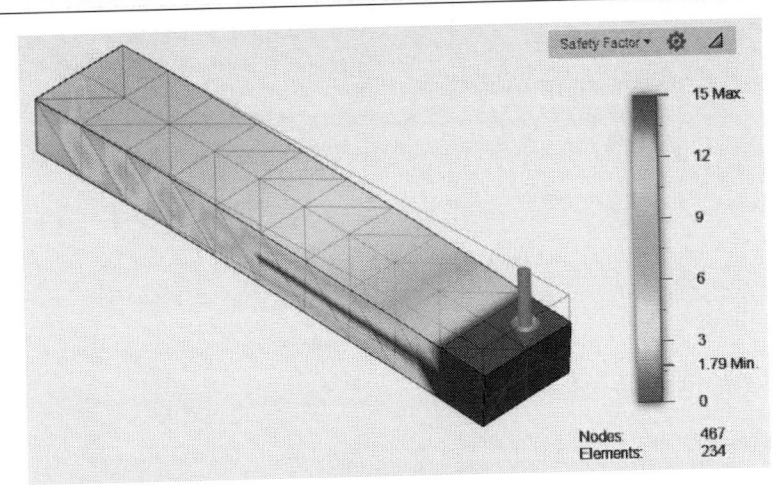

Figure 21–30

2. In the legend's heading, expand the result type and select **Displacement**, as shown in Figure 21–31.

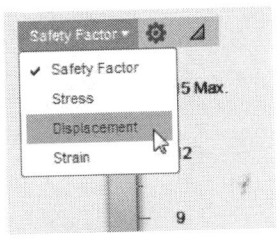

Figure 21–31

3. In the legend's heading, expand the unit type and select **in**. The results display as shown in Figure 21–32. The maximum displacement (at the loaded end of the beam) is **0.0687in**.

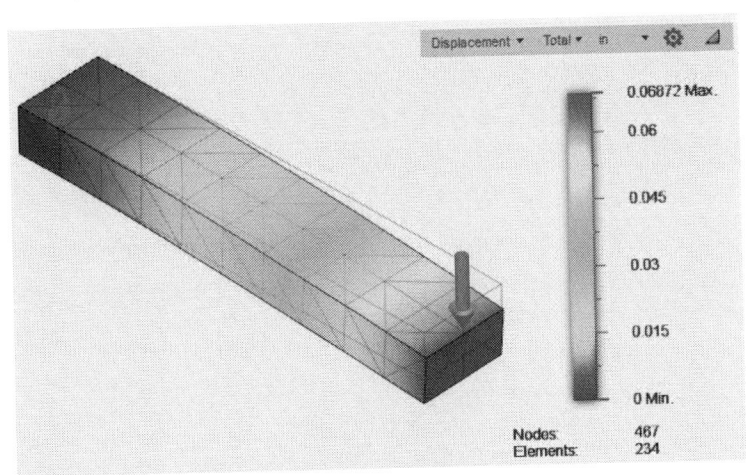

Figure 21–32

4. In the legend's heading, expand the result type and select **Stress**. Ensure that the **Von Mises** stress is displayed and that the values are displayed in **psi**, as shown in Figure 21–33. Note that the maximum Von Mises stress in the cantilever beam is 28353 psi.

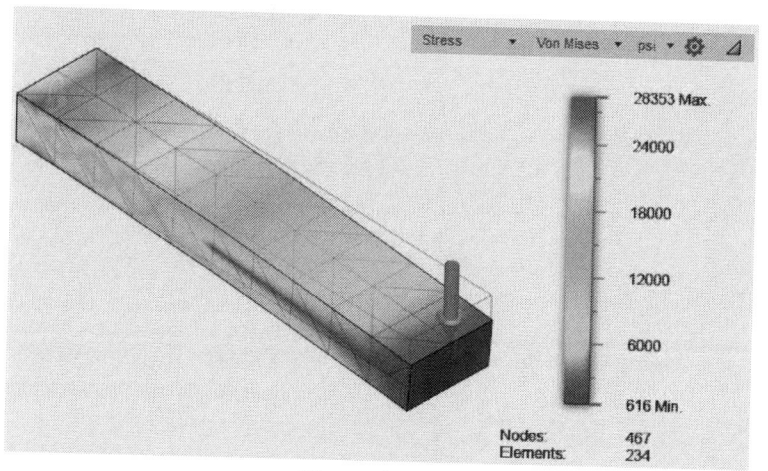

Figure 21–33

5. Expand the RESULTS panel and select (Toggle Mesh Visibility).

6. To display the minimum and maximum values on the model, expand the RESULTS panel and select (Show Min/Max).

7. Rotate the model and select and drag the callout boxes to more easily locate the locations of the maximum and minimum stress values, as shown in Figure 21–34.

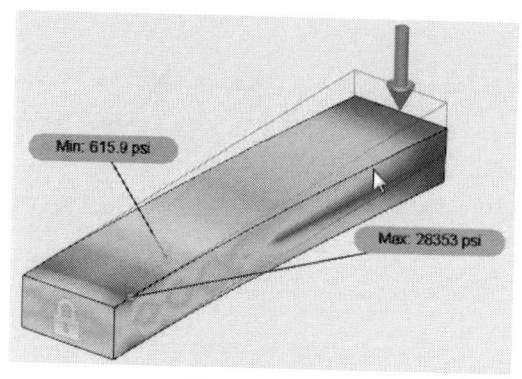

Figure 21–34

8. Save the design and close the file.

Task 8 - (Optional) Make a design change and verify the results.

Changes to either the study settings or the model will require you to rerun the results. In this optional task, you are challenged to return to the Model environment and modify the length of the beam. Once modified, return to the analysis, note that the mesh and the results are out of date, and update the results.

Practice 21b: Plant Hanger Analysis

Practice Objectives

- Activate the Simulate environment in the Autodesk Fusion 360 software.
- Create a Linear Static Stress design study.
- Assign constraints, loads, and contacts to simulate working conditions.
- Generate the Mesh using the default settings.
- Solve the design study.
- Review and interpret the results.

In this practice, you will simulate a plant hanger with two fixed locations where it connects to a wall, and a load applied to represent the hanging plant. Additionally, a contact will be assigned to represent where the hanger geometry is welded to itself. A linear response to the stress will be assumed and the applied load does not change in magnitude, orientation, or distribution. Additionally, the effects of gravity are included.

Task 1 - Open a design file and switch to the Simulation environment.

1. Click ▭▾ > **New Design from File**.

2. In the Open dialog box, navigate to the *C:\Autodesk Fusion 360 Practice Files* folder, select **Plant_Hanger.f3d**, and click **Open**. The design displays as shown in Figure 21–35.

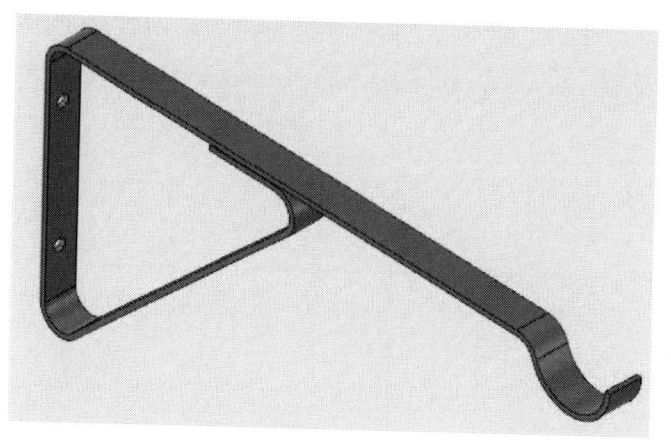

Figure 21–35

3. Save the design as **Plant_Hanger** in the active Fusion Project.

4. At the top of the BROWSER, right-click on the component name and select **Properties**. In the PROPERTIES palette, note that the *Physical Material* that is assigned to the model is **Steel**. This is the material that will be analyzed, so once it is in the Simulation environment, the study material does not need to be defined. Steel will automatically be used. Click **OK** to close the palette.

5. Launch the Simulation environment.

Task 2 - Create a new study.

1. Click (New Simulation Study). The Studies dialog box lists the types of studies that can be performed. Select **Static Stress**.

2. Click **OK** to create the new study.

3. Review the study nodes that have been added to the BROWSER.

Task 3 - Constrain the plant hanger.

In this task, you will assign two constraints to simulate where the plant hanger will be secured to a wall.

1. In the Ribbon, expand the CONSTRAINT panel and select **Fixed**.

2. The STRUCTURAL CONSTRAINT palette displays as shown in Figure 21–36. Note how the Type drop-down list is set to **Fixed**. By default, the constraint is set to be constrained along all Axis (Ux, Uy, and Uz). Select the edge of the hole to be fixed, as shown in Figure 21–36.

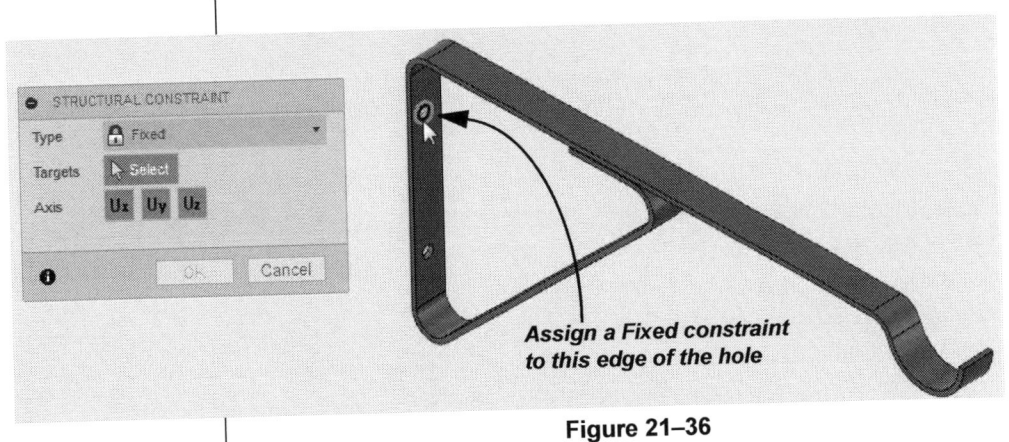

*Alternatively, in the BROWSER, right-click on the **Constraints** node and select **Structural Constraint** to access the palette and assign the type.*

Assign a Fixed constraint to this edge of the hole

Figure 21–36

3. In the STRUCTURAL CONSTRAINT palette, click **OK** to complete the constraint.

4. Repeat Steps 1 to 3 to assign a second Fixed constraint to the other hole.

5. In the BROWSER, review the **Constraints** node and ensure that both of the constraints have been assigned.

Task 4 - Assign a load to the plant hanger.

In this task, you will assign a force load to end of the plant hanger to simulate it being loaded in the Y direction. Additionally, you will enable gravity.

Alternatively, in the BROWSER, right-click on the Loads node and select Structural Load to access the palette and assign the type.

1. In the Ribbon, expand the LOAD panel and select **Force**.

2. The STRUCTURAL LOAD palette displays. Select the face of hanger (as shown in Figure 21–37) to assign the load. The STRUCTURAL LOAD palette updates as shown.

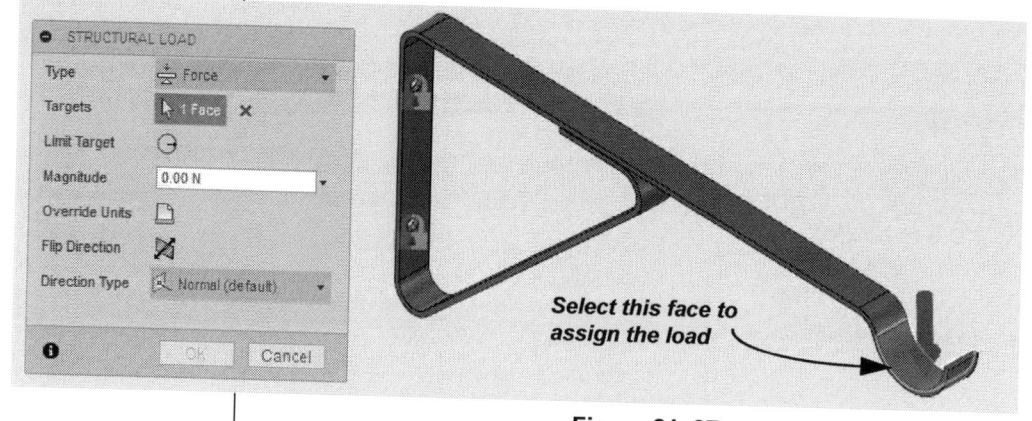

Figure 21–37

3. Select ▢ to activate unit override and select **lbforce**.

4. In the *Magnitude* field, enter **10** to define the load.

5. In the STRUCTURAL LOAD palette, click **OK**.

To deactivate a load, in the BROWSER, clear the checkbox adjacent to the load name.

6. In the BROWSER, adjacent to the **Loads** node, click ▷. Note that **Force1** is now listed as an active load.

7. Select the checkbox adjacent to the **Gravity** load to enable it. A yellow arrows displays in the graphics window in the Y-direction, indicating that gravity has been enabled. The BROWSER should display as shown in Figure 21–38.

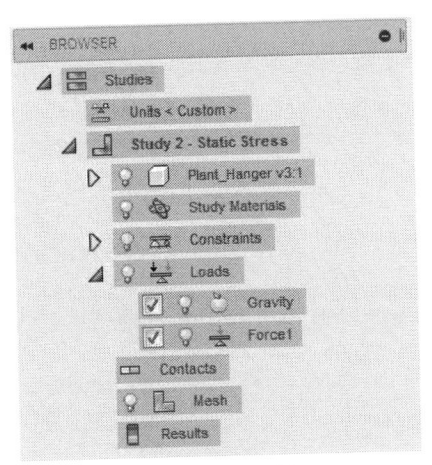

Figure 21–38

Task 5 - Mesh the plant hanger.

In this task, you will mesh the design to prepare it for solving using the default mesh settings.

1. In the ribbon, expand the SOLVE panel and select **Generate Mesh**.

   *Alternatively, in the BROWSER, right-click on the **Mesh** node and select **Generate Mesh**.*

2. The mesh displays on the model, as shown in Figure 21–39.

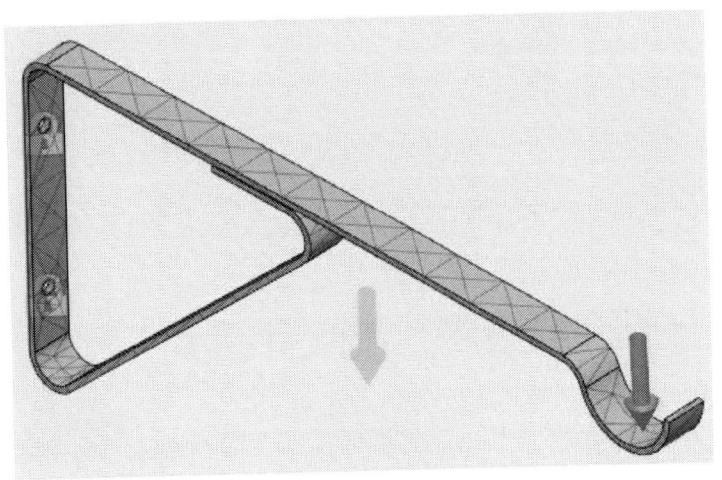

Figure 21–39

Task 6 - Solve the beam.

In this task, you will run the static stress analysis for the plant hanger using the constraints and loads that have been assigned.

1. In the Ribbon, expand the SOLVE panel and select **Solve**. The model and an analysis legend display as shown in Figure 21–40. Consider the following when deciding if there is an issue with the design or with the setup:

   - The Solve Details dialog box displays indicating that the deformation is large compared to the model size.
   - Note that the Safety Factor for most of the upper portion of the frame is very close to (if not less) than 1, indicating possible yield.
   - The bottom portion of the frame does not seem to be deformed, which is not simulating how the geometry should react. In this case, a contact between the two faces is required to properly set up the design for simulation.

*Alternatively, in the BROWSER, right-click on the **Results** node and select **Solve**.*

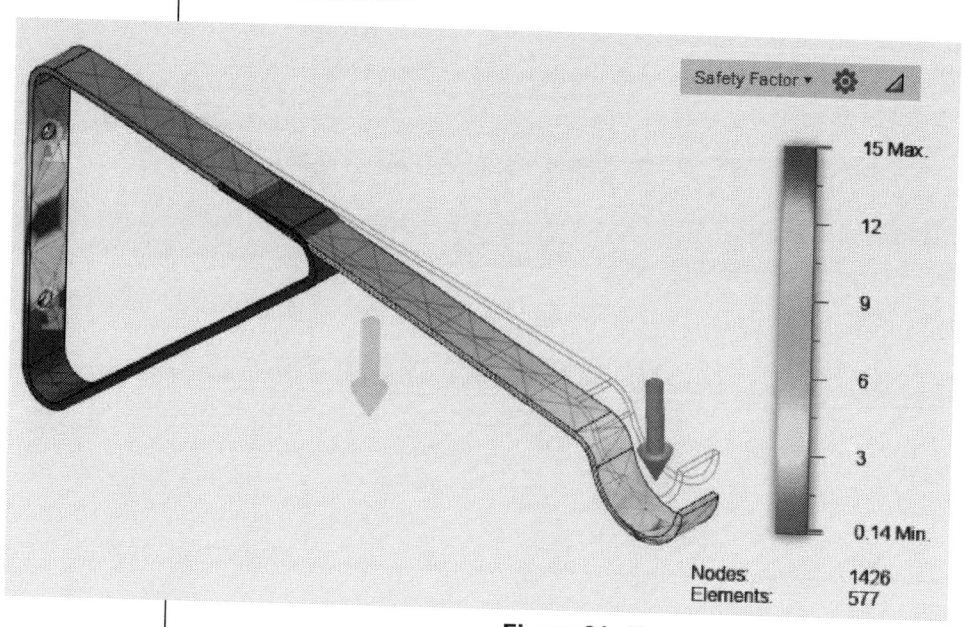

Figure 21–40

2. Close the Solve Details dialog box.

Task 7 - Add a contact to the plant hanger's setup.

In this task, you will assign a contact where the lower portion of the plant hanger is welded to the top portion.

1. In the ribbon, expand the CONTACT panel and select **Bonded**. This contact type enables you to describe the weld between the two faces for the purposes of the simulation.

2. In the CONTACT palette, ensure that the *Parts/Bodies* field is active, and then select the plant hanger design as the body.

*Alternatively, in the BROWSER, right-click on the **Results** node and select **Manual Contact**.*

3. Click in the *Targets* field to activate it. Using the Select Other tool, select the two faces that come in contact with one another, as shown in Figure 21–41.

    Hint: To use the Select Other tool, click and hold the left mouse button over a face and then select the required face from the list that displays.

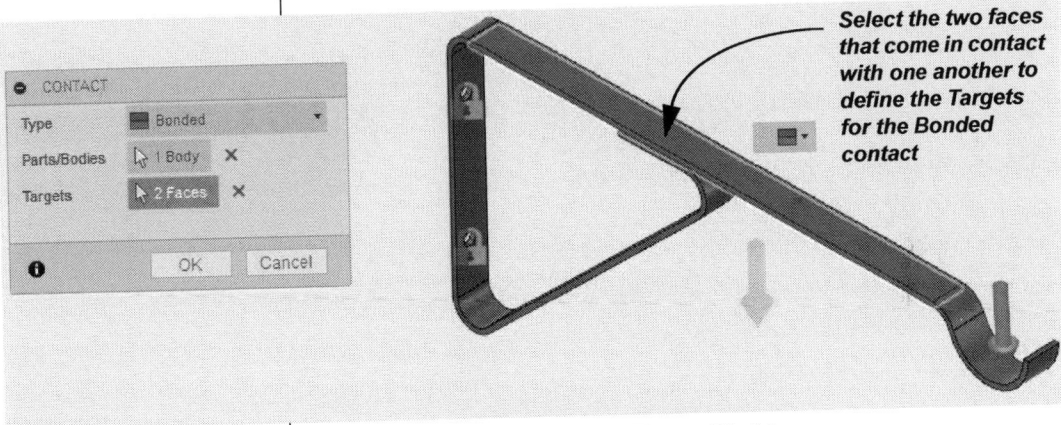

Figure 21–41

4. In the CONTACT palette, click **OK**.

5. Now that the contact has been added, note that the results display as out of date (⚠). In the BROWSER, right-click on the **Results** node and select **Solve** to rerun the analysis.

Task 8 - Visualize the results.

1. In the Results View (shown in Figure 21–42), consider the following when deciding if there is an issue with the design:
   - The contact definition now accurately represents how the model will react when loaded.
   - The Safety Factor for the end of the design that extends from the welded connection is still very close to, if not less than 1, indicating possible yield.

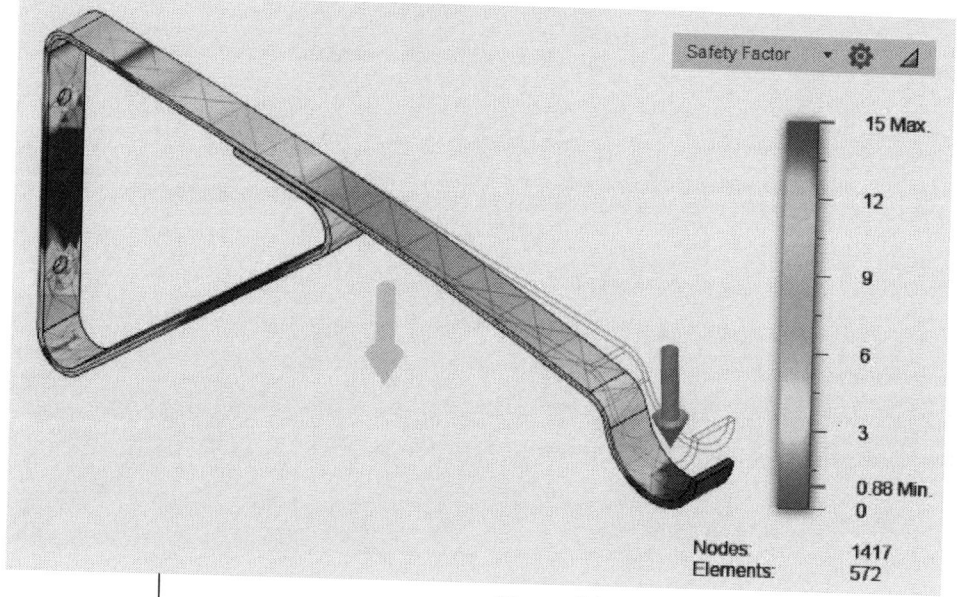

Figure 21–42

2. In the legend's heading, expand the result type and select **Displacement**. The result displays as shown in Figure 21–43.

Figure 21–43

3. Note that the maximum displacement is over 14mm at the end of the plant hanger. This value is too high for this design.

Task 9 - Make a design change and verify the results.

The geometry for the design must be changed to provide more support for the load.

1. Expand the Change Workspace menu and select **Model** to change to the modeling environment.

2. Edit **Sketch1** and modify the dimension shown in Figure 21–44 to **200.00**. Complete the sketch.

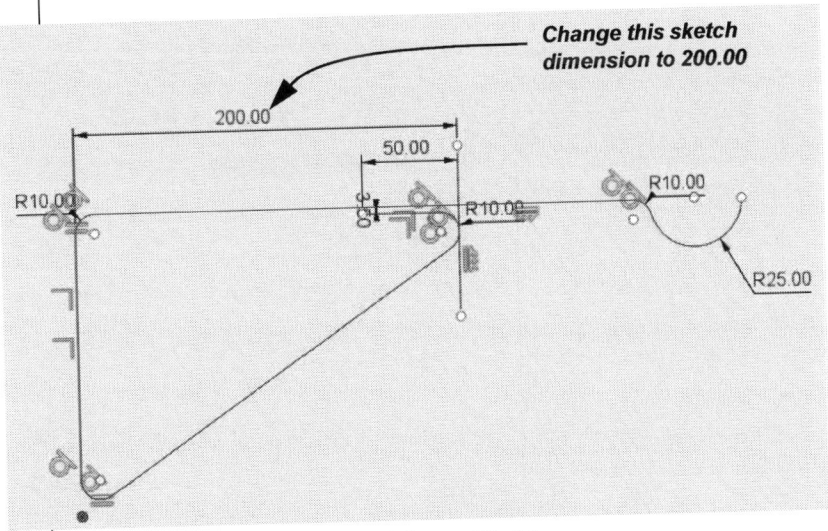

Figure 21–44

3. The geometry updates to reflect the change. Launch the Simulation environment to verify that the change in geometry provides a better solution.

4. In the BROWSER, right-click on the **Results** node and select **Solve** to rerun the analysis. Note that the mesh was also out of date after the design change, but by solving the design, the mesh automatically updates in the one step. The Displacement results display as shown in Figure 21–45.

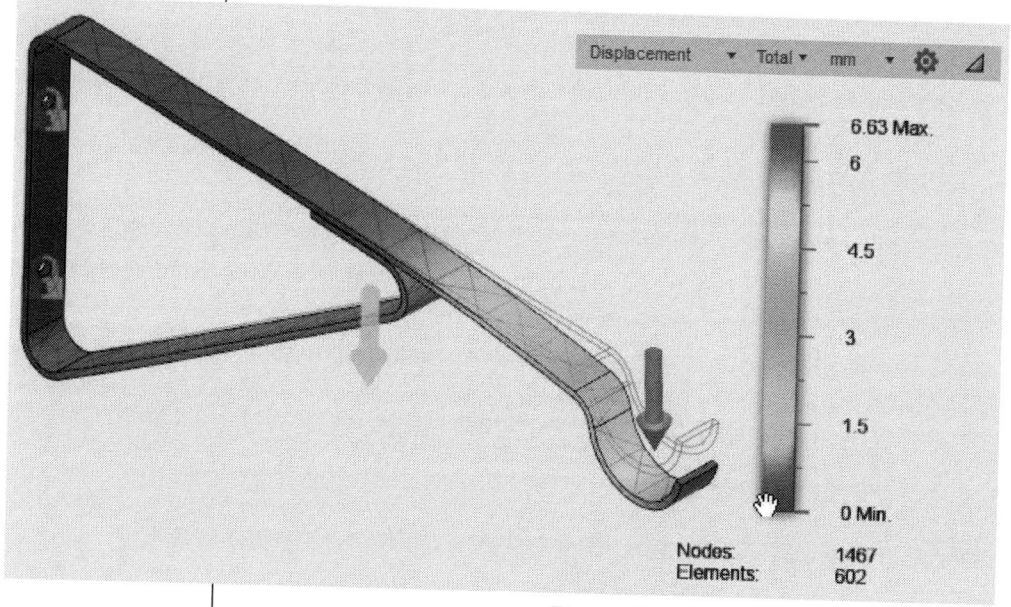

Figure 21–45

5. The max displacement value of 6.63 mm is more acceptable. Change to the **Safety Factor** view and note that the geometry has an acceptable range and material yielding is not likely to occur.

6. Save the design and close the file.

Chapter Review Questions

1. When working in the Simulation environment, you can set up multiple analyses to compare results using different criteria.

    a. True
    b. False

2. When setting up the design material for a Static analysis, which of the following is true?

    a. The Material that is required in an analysis must be defined in the Model environment.
    b. Material properties must be entered for the material being analyzed.
    c. The yield strength or the ultimate tensile strength can be assigned to define how the safety factor is calculated.
    d. Once a material is defined for an analysis, a new analysis must be created to change the material being used.

3. Which of the following constraint types enables you to prevent movement on cylindrical faces radially, axially, or tangentially?

    a. Fixed
    b. Pinned
    c. Frictionless
    d. Prescribed Displacement

4. Which of the following constraint type icons indicates that a Prescribed Displacement constraint was added?

    a.
    b.
    c.
    d.

5. Identify the load type icons in the table below.
   a. Force
   b. Pressure
   c. Moment
   d. Remote Force
   e. Gravity

Icon	Answer
↓▫	
↻	
↓⊥	
🍎	
↓↑	

6. Which of the following load types enable you to assign a limit target area to define the radius of load application.
   a. Force
   b. Pressure
   c. Moment
   d. Remote Force
   e. Gravity

7. Contacts must be used in the simulation setup to run an analysis.
   a. True
   b. False

8. A study cannot be solved unless the mesh has been generated as part of the simulation setup.
   a. True
   b. False

9. For the Results view, which of the following are true? (Select all that apply.)

   a. Safety Factor is the default results view for an analysis that has just been solved.

   b. To toggle the display of the min and max result values directly in the model, expand the RESULTS panel and select (Surface Probes).

   c. Animations can be created to display the stress results while the model is deforming.

   d. The Color Bar in the legend can be toggled off to simplify the display.

   e. The **Deformation Scale** option enables you to display the maximum deformation value on the model.

Answers: 1.a, 2.c, 3.b, 4.b, 5.(d,c,a,e,b), 6.a, 7.b, 8.b, 9.(a,c,d)

Command Summary

Button	Command	Location
🎥	Animate	• **Ribbon:** Simulation Workspace> RESULTS panel • **BROWSER:** Right-click on the **Results** node.
N/A	Contact	• **Ribbon:** Simulation Workspace> CONTACT panel • **Context Menu:** Right-click in the graphics window. • **BROWSER:** Right-click on the **Contact** node.
👤	Create Point Probe	• **Ribbon:** Simulation Workspace> RESULTS panel
N/A	Deformation Scale	• **Ribbon:** Simulation Workspace> RESULTS panel
⌛	Generate Mesh	• **Ribbon:** Simulation Workspace> SOLVE panel • **BROWSER:** Right-click on the **Mesh** node.
N/A	Model View	• **Ribbon:** Simulation Workspace>DISPLAY panel
📐	New Simulation Study	• **Ribbon:** Simulation Workspace> STUDY panel • **BROWSER:** Right-click on the **Studies** node. • **Context Menu:** Right-click in the graphics window.
N/A	Results View	• **Ribbon:** Simulation Workspace>DISPLAY panel
🔲	Show Min/Max	• **Ribbon:** Simulation Workspace> RESULTS panel
🧊	Simulation Environment	• **Ribbon:** Change Workspace menu
🚦	Solve	• **Ribbon:** Simulation Workspace> SOLVE panel • **BROWSER:** Right-click on the **Results** node.
N/A	Structural Constraints	• **Ribbon:** Simulation Workspace> CONSTRAINT panel • **Context Menu:** Right-click in the graphics window. • **BROWSER:** Right-click on the **Constraints** node.

N/A		Structural Loads	• **Ribbon:** Simulation Workspace> LOAD panel • **Context Menu:** Right-click in the graphics window. • **BROWSER:** Right-click on the **Loads** node.
		Study Materials	• **Ribbon:** Simulation Workspace> MATERIAL panel • **Context Menu:** Right-click in the graphics window. • **BROWSER:** Right-click on the **Study Materials** node.
		Surface Probes	• **Ribbon:** Simulation Workspace> RESULTS panel
		Toggle Mesh Visibility	• **Ribbon:** Simulation Workspace> DISPLAY panel • **BROWSER:** Right-click on the **Mesh** node. • **BROWSER:** Toggle the lightbulb icon

Appendix A

Outputting for 3D Printing

The Autodesk® Fusion 360™ software provides an easy way to out put a design for 3D printing.

Learning Objective in this Chapter

- Generate .STL files for 3D printing.

A.1 Generating a .STL File

An .STL file is a file that is generated by the Autodesk Fusion 360 software to print a design and passed directly to a 3D print utility, such as the Autodesk Print Studio or Autodesk Meshmixer software.

To create an .STL file, complete the following steps:

1. With a design open, click [icon] > **3D Print**, or in the MAKE panel, click [icon]. The 3D PRINT palette displays.
2. Select the component or body to be printed.
3. Ensure that the **Preview Mesh** checkbox is selected to display the mesh on the design, as shown in Figure A–1.
4. Select the level of refinement and adjust the refinement settings. A higher level of refinement means a smoother output, but also more data to process.
5. Choose the output method. You can output directly to the Autodesk Print Studio or Autodesk Meshmixer software, or clear the **Send to 3D Print Utility** checkbox to save a .STL file that can be opened in other 3D print software.

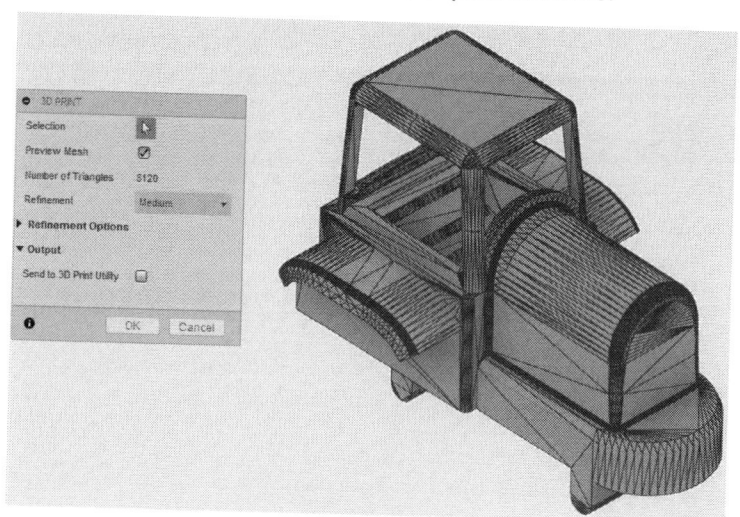

Figure A–1

Video Lesson Available

Printing Your Design

Video Length: 3:57

Printed in Poland
by Amazon Fulfillment
Poland Sp. z o.o., Wrocław